Born along the Color Line

Born along the Color Line

*The 1933 Amenia Conference and the Rise
of a National Civil Rights Movement*

EBEN MILLER

OXFORD
UNIVERSITY PRESS

OXFORD
UNIVERSITY PRESS

Oxford University Press, Inc., publishes works that further
Oxford University's objective of excellence
in research, scholarship, and education.

Oxford   New York
Auckland   Cape Town   Dar es Salaam   Hong Kong   Karachi
Kuala Lumpur   Madrid   Melbourne   Mexico City   Nairobi
New Delhi   Shanghai   Taipei   Toronto

With offices in
Argentina   Austria   Brazil   Chile   Czech Republic   France   Greece
Guatemala   Hungary   Italy   Japan   Poland   Portugal   Singapore
South Korea   Switzerland   Thailand   Turkey   Ukraine   Vietnam

Published by Oxford University Press, Inc.
198 Madison Avenue, New York, NY 10016

www.oup.com

Oxford is a registered trademark of Oxford University Press

Eben Miller wishes to thank the Crisis Publishing Co., Inc., the publisher of *The Crisis*,
the magazine of the National Association for the Advancement of Colored People,
for the use of the images first published in the December 1930,
September 1935, March 1936, and April 1937 issues.

Library of Congress Cataloging-in-Publication Data
Miller, Eben.
Born along the color line : the 1933 Amenia Conference and the rise
of a national civil rights movement / Eben Miller.
p.   cm.
Includes bibliographical references and index.
ISBN 978-0-19-517455-7
1. Amenia Conference (1933) 2. National Association for the Advancement of
Colored People—History—20th century. 3. Civil rights movements—United States—
History—20th century. 4. African Americans—Civil rights—History—20th century.
5. African Americans—Economic conditions—20th century. 6. Redding, Louis L.
7. Harris, Abram Lincoln, 1899–1963. 8. Jackson, Juanita C. 9. Weston, M. Moran, 1910–2002.
10. Bunche, Ralph J. (Ralph Johnson), 1904–1971. I. Title.
E185.61.M626   2011
323.1196′073—c22   2011010832

1 3 5 7 9 8 6 4 2

Printed in the United States of America
on acid-free paper

For Tracey

CONTENTS

ACKNOWLEDGMENTS

It is humbling to contemplate the sources of inspiration, encouragement, and support that have sustained this project. *Born along the Color Line* began as a dissertation at Brandeis University, where I had the great fortune of holding a Rose and Irving Crown Fellowship in American History among a talented and generous cohort. A writing group including Benjamin Irvin, Molly McCarthy, Hilary Moss, Paul Ringel, Greg Renoff, and Jeff Wiltse commented thoughtfully on the earliest versions of this work. Ben read multiple chapters, and Molly was kind enough to open her home to me during several research trips to New York. I relied, too, on the perspectives and camaraderie of Jason Opal, Anthony Smith, and Jacob Weir-Gertzog. I am especially beholden to Anthony for the many lunches and coffees along the Red Line, for putting me up in Cambridge when I needed to complete just one more day of research, and for his assistance years later when I could no longer easily access the troves of documents housed at Harvard University. I began this project in early 2000 while taking Jane Kamensky's course on narrative strategies. It was a privilege to learn from Jane, who embraces the challenge of writing about the past with unparalleled care and grace. My dissertation committee included James Campbell, who offered concrete advice for revising the dissertation for publication. I still have the notes David Engerman kept during my dissertation defense, as well his many insightful prescriptions for improvement. I returned to these repeatedly for guidance during the revision process and I remain appreciative of his steadfast support of my research and for his eagerness to introduce me into the academic profession.

The Gilder Lehrman Institute of American History, the Rockefeller Archives Center, the Sophia Smith Collection at Smith College, and the Louis, Frances, and Jeffrey Sachar research fund at Brandeis University helped underwrite early research. A Dissertation Year Fellowship from the Brandeis University Graduate School of Arts and Sciences allowed me to complete the dissertation. The professionals staffing the archives and special collections I depended upon provided expertise and assistance, including at Atlanta University; the Beinecke Rare Books and Manuscripts Library at Yale University; Brown University; Columbia University; the Delaware Historical Society; the Library of Congress; the Moorland-Spingarn Research Center at Howard University; the Schomburg Center for Research in Black Culture; Smith College; the Rockefeller Archives Center; the University of California, Los Angeles; the University of Delaware; the University of Massachusetts Amherst; and the University of Pennsylvania. Undertaking this project would have been far less feasible had I not enjoyed access to the miles of microfilm held in the libraries of Harvard University. Hopefully the reading room at the W. E. B. Du Bois Institute will continue to be open for browsing. The proprietors of the Troutbeck Inn and Conference Center allowed me to tour Joel and Amy Spingarn's former estate and shared a few fascinating examples of ephemera that remain there. Teaching courses on the African American freedom struggle at Brandeis University and Southern Maine Community College (SMCC) forced me to clarify my understanding of the long civil rights movement. At SMCC, my academic dean, Janet Sortor, and my department chair, Bill Sutton, supported my course development, for which I remain thankful. I wish to express my appreciation, too, to the students who made the experience of teaching some of the contents of this book so rewarding.

Jason Opal invited me to participate in the Southern Maine American Historians Research Group at the perfect moment during late rounds of revision. The feedback offered by him and by Chuck Dorn, Joe Hall, David Hecht, Matt Klingle, Jennifer Scanlon, David Scobey, and Jeff Selinger was especially useful during the last stages of revising. Beneficial responses to my work also came from fellow conference participants, including Beth Tompkins Bates, Martha Biondi, Prudence Cumberbatch, Crystal Feimster, Rea Ferguson, Erik Gellman, and Patricia Sullivan. Jonathan Holloway and Kenneth Janken read the original manuscript for Oxford University Press, each offering helpful commentary. I thank Jonathan especially for the kind encouragements. Colleagues at George Mason University, including Joan Bristol, the late Roy Rosenzweig, Randolph Scully, and Lauren Sklaroff offered warm and welcome support. Leslie Schwalm expressed an enthusiasm about an earlier chapter on Juanita Jackson that I thought of often while revising the manuscript. Rick and Sherri Salvatore provided hospitality during a trip to Philadelphia. Joe Hummer generously helped make my research in Los Angeles so enjoyable. Molly McCarthy and Melissa Sundell devoted time and attention to improving the penultimate version of the manuscript. I remain appreciative of the opportunity to have met the late Moran Weston during the earliest stages of my research. He and his wife, Mrs. Miriam Weston, graciously invited me to Florida, where I spent portions of two days asking about, among other things, his youth in North Carolina, what he recalled of the 1933 Amenia Conference, and his life in New York City.

This book simply would not exist without the patience and perceptive suggestions of my editor, Susan Ferber, who guided the project through publication. I cannot thank Jacqueline Jones, my mentor at Brandeis, enough for connecting me with such an effective champion. Jackie encouraged my work from inchoate idea to completed dissertation, coaxing me always to consider the big picture, and modeled how to write with both empathy and objectivity about the social and economic conditions people endured in the past. I am grateful to have been her student. I am likewise thankful to have been a student and, for a number of years now, a friend and neighbor of Hilmar Jensen. His Bates College seminar "Prelude to the Civil Rights Movement" first inspired me to explore the civil rights struggles of the early twentieth century. Since then, I have come to rely on his perspective and willingness to share his near photographic recollection of original sources. It is hard to imagine writing this book without his influence.

It is impossible to contemplate ever completing this work without the sustenance of my family in Maine. The Guilleraults—Roger, Robbi, Tim, and Andy— have been in my corner since the beginning, as have my four siblings and their families—Andy, Ocea, Brey, and Wyeth; Kaitlyn and Cory; Lisbeth; and Alec. I will always be appreciative of the place Andy made for me at Copper Tops. My parents, Garry and Martha, provided support that is impossible to catalogue; I trust I can reciprocate by loving my own children, Cecilia and Calvin, with equal devotion.

I dedicate this book to Tracey, my most important collaborator, with profound gratitude for her generosity, partnership, and love.

Born along the Color Line

Introduction

At 5:45 on the evening of Friday, August 18, 1933, the New York Central Railroad sounded its arrival at the hamlet of Amenia. The train had departed Grand Central Terminal nearly two hours earlier, then followed the Harlem Valley line north out of Manhattan toward rolling, rural Dutchess County, passing through the towns of Wingdale, Dover, and Wassaic before braking, slowing, and hissing into Amenia, New York, at the southern reach of the Berkshires. Just two and a half miles east of the town center rose Oblong Mountain, a thousand-foot forested foothill sheltering Joel and Amy Spingarn's eight-hundred-acre estate, Troutbeck.

If the train whistle echoed as far as Troutbeck, it reached ready ears. That day the Spingarn manor had buzzed with preparations for the Amenia Conference, a three-day civil rights retreat held by the National Association for the Advancement of Colored People (NAACP), of which Joel Springarn was president of the board of directors. The Spingarns had hosted an earlier NAACP conference at Amenia in 1916, one that had helped the Association to achieve national prominence. By reprising the event in 1933, the NAACP hoped to reestablish its standing at a moment of economic crisis, floundering membership, and challenges from the radical left.

In anticipation of the conference, seven large canvas tents had been delivered and pitched on a flat field, having been trucked up from Manhattan along with several dozen sleeping cots, blankets, and sundry supplies—enough to host over thirty visitors for the weekend. Joel Spingarn planned to greet at least eleven of his guests who were arriving on the 5:45, then escort them in his limousine back down Leedsville Road to Troutbeck. Guests who drove themselves—from New York City; from Montclair, New Jersey; from Philadelphia; from Wilmington, Delaware; from Washington, DC; from Hampton, Virginia—followed Route 22 north to Amenia, turned right at the village center, then watched for the signs the Spingarns had placed all along the road: "This way to the Amenia Conference: Amenia Conference 1 Mile!"

Tracing the wooded curve off Leedsville Road toward Troutbeck, the Spingarns' guests crossed an arched stone bridge over the Webatuck, a picturesque spring-fed brook, then rounded a cul-de-sac lined with tall, graceful sycamores first planted in 1830s. From the drive, a long front lawn ("not a lawn," as one visitor described it, "but a grass grown cathedral") rose gently toward the main house. Gathered before its stone terraces, gardens of exotic flora bloomed, and, all about, more than two hundred varieties of clematis—Joel Spingarn's passion—draped from trellises, climbed porches, and shone from greenhouse walls in an array of hues, shapes, and shades.

Amid the gardens stood the Spingarn home, a twenty-eight-room, slate-roofed, gray stone mansion. Through its heavy casement windows, opened invitingly onto the grounds, were exposed-beam ceilings and a library befitting the former Columbia University professor of comparative literature turned gentleman gardener. Lining the shelves were volumes from the Italian Renaissance, works of the American transcendentalists, local histories tracing the origins of Troutbeck to the 1760s, botanical treatises, and Joel Spingarn's own published poetry, among them the verses:

> In the grace of twilight, what outer fate
> Can pass this portal, this garden gate?
> All the world is rent with doom,
> But here these furies find no room.

By the time daylight began to wane beyond Sun Set Rock, just to the west of the Oblong, activity filled the Spingarns' home, gardens, and great lawn. Beneath the biggest tent was served a camp dinner of gumbo, roast lamb, and fresh peas and potatoes—"glorious food," one guest remarked. For August, the evening air was pleasant—warm, slightly humid—and guests were invited to swim and canoe in Troutbeck Lake, walk the charming quarter-mile circuit around the immediate orchards, gardens, and woods, or remain beneath the big tent and enjoy the company.

After nightfall, the gathering included the Spingarns, a handful of NAACP officials and friends, and twenty-six African American conference delegates, each in their twenties or thirties, and each deemed, as Joel Spingarn had written that spring, "coming leaders of Negro thought." That evening the Spingarns' guests were to get acquainted, establish formal conference committees, then sleep well. Over the next several days, in this secluded setting, away from the "furies" of a fourth summer of economic depression, it was hoped the Amenia conferees would achieve significant progress in solving several unpleasant problems facing the nation's inchoate civil rights movement, including—indeed, especially—the perceptible erosion of support for the NAACP.[1]

A modest body of sources documents what took place that weekend in Amenia. In the papers of the NAACP are preserved files recording the meals to be served, how many cots the Spingarns' guests would need, and tentative outlines for group discussion. A photograph Amy Spingarn snapped captured the camaraderie evident among the conferees: they are standing and sitting in three rows in front of one of the conference tents, smiling and jousting, their enjoyment that Saturday afternoon undiminished despite a good dousing of rain. In the October 1933 issue of the *Crisis*, the Association's monthly magazine, editor W. E. B. Du Bois published a brief review of the gathering. Du Bois, the sixty-five-year-old exemplar of elite black leadership, had helped organize the conference, had helped handpick the attendees, and had even stopped in Pennsylvania and New Jersey on his drive north to personally deliver three of the invitees—a college professor, a physician, and a librarian—to Troutbeck. Once arrived, their commitment to solving "the Negro problem," as Du Bois put it, was palpable. He counted nineteen young delegates who, at one point or another, spurred on the days' discussions. "When anyone got the floor," Du Bois noted, "they really took hold of the thought and did something with it."

While there is no verbatim record of these contributions, the conferees did endorse a summary "Findings Report," which Du Bois duly reprinted in the *Crisis*. Witnessing "a period in which economic, political, and social values are rapidly shifting, and the very structure of organized society is being revamped," the conferees surmised that the primary problem facing African Americans in the summer of 1933 was not civic or political but economic. Concluding that "the welfare of white and black labor are one and inseparable," the conferees encouraged a radical transformation of the NAACP. They suggested the quarter-century-old civil rights organization transform its traditional efforts to secure African Americans' civil and political equality and, rather, foster an interracial workers' alliance pledged to achieving economic justice.[2]

Such discussion struck writer and critic Lewis Mumford, a neighbor of the Spingarns' invited to make his acquaintances, as familiar Depression-era discourse. "They were all," he wrote in a letter the next day, "these young doctors, professors, lawyers, librarians, tussling with the eternal dilemma of all intellectuals today: how to be a communist without wilfully swallowing the fierce ignorances, the blind hatreds, the wilful dogmatisms of the orthodox revolutionists who are preparing for a final pitched battle between communism and capitalism." Correspondence collected within the respective papers of the NAACP, Joel Spingarn, and W. E. B. Du Bois confirms this tussle. There are a number of letters (thank-you notes, mainly) that the conference participants themselves wrote about the three days they spent at Troutbeck. Of these, an especially detailed note the Delaware lawyer Louis Redding wrote just after the conference underscores the radical tinge of the discussions. In the coming years, it was this characteristic that Ralph Bunche recollected of the Amenia Conference while writing a research memorandum, that W. E. B. Du Bois thought to record in his autobiography, and

THE 1933 AMENIA CONFERENCE. Langston Hughes, *Fight for Freedom: The Story of the NAACP.* Special Collections and University Archives, W. E. B. Du Bois Library, University of Massachusetts Amherst.

that Moran Weston remembered, in a conversation with me, sixty-seven summers later.[3]

From these sources, it is possible to narrate an account of the 1933 Amenia Conference. It is possible to picture the proceedings at Troutbeck that weekend: the introductions, the conversations, the declarations, the spats, the singing (off key, according to Du Bois), and the resolutions. It is possible to explain why the NAACP called the conference, a distinct event that took place at a critical moment for the Association—and in the history of the civil rights movement. It is possible to gauge the impact the conference had, compelling the NAACP to balance the pursuit of economic opportunity its younger supporters demanded

with its longstanding efforts to ensure that African Americans be treated as full and equal citizens. But it is also possible to look again at the photograph Amy Spingarn took and to consider what it might reveal about the figures gathered there in Amenia. That snapshot conveys more than the jovial mood among the conferees that Saturday afternoon in August 1933. It is also a portrait in miniature of a remarkable cohort of African American intellectuals and activists who contributed to the struggle for black equality during the first half of the twentieth century.

The pages that follow knit a narrative of this signal moment in the history of the NAACP with discrete biographies of five of the conferees whose lives portray their generation's role in the fight for African American equality: Louis Redding, Abram Harris, Juanita Jackson, Moran Weston, and Ralph Bunche.

They were born at the turn of the twentieth century, when the legalization of segregation drew color lines across the nation. Born along the color line, they came of age during the 1910s and 1920s, after the politically conscious black elite (whom Du Bois named the Talented Tenth) had firmly eschewed any acceptance of the Jim Crow racial order. Inheriting the mantle of African American leadership between the 1920s and 1940s, their generation acknowledged the insistence of civil rights organizations, such as the NAACP, that they reject, confront, and actively undermine segregation. Adopting the Talented Tenth protest tradition, they also strove to adapt the contemporary movement for racial equality during an era when millions of African Americans were migrating to the industrial cities of the North and West, when economic depression was fostering pivotal transformations in American life, and when the fight against international fascism was prompting the nation to reconsider its own fundamental democratic creed. During this period, the generation of elite black leadership represented at Amenia sought to expand the civil rights struggle to include an interracial movement for economic rights. They attempted to bring national unity to an emergent network of local movements and employed a range of strategies—literary and legal, grassroots and intellectual, legislative and cultural—to demand the full works of civic equality for African Americans. Collectively, such endeavors eroded the foundations of segregation and propelled the ongoing movement for African American civil rights, linking the turn-of-the-century era of W. E. B. Du Bois, Ida B. Wells, and Booker T. Washington with the watershed years of Martin Luther King, Jr., Fannie Lou Hamer, and Malcolm X. Together, their experiences depict a distinct era in the twentieth-century black freedom struggle, demonstrating how the impulse to defy the Jim Crow order that germinated in such modest settings as Louis Redding's Wilmington, Delaware, during the 1910s came to reshape the nation by midcentury.[4]

Invited to Amenia in 1933, Louis Redding embodied the Talented Tenth tradition of elite black leadership the NAACP hoped would advance the movement to undo the prevailing racial order. The son of a Wilmington, Delaware, postman, Redding was born at a moment when some black leaders argued that African Americans ought to accommodate themselves to racial segregation. There appeared little alternative when white dominance enjoyed Supreme Court precedent, was sanctioned by state laws, and was enforced through violence and intimidation. Redding's relatively privileged, educated, and middle-class black community on Tenth Street Hill in Wilmington, however, refused to accept a circumscribed status and continually challenged manifestations of inequality. Expressions of white supremacy (the screening of *The Birth of a Nation*, public rallies of the Ku Klux Klan, discriminatory public accommodations) met with consistent rebuttals, often from the local branch of the NAACP, founded by Redding's father and fellow neighbors on Tenth Street Hill. Considering the color bar in the courtroom a particular affront, during the 1920s the Wilmington NAACP strategized to arrange for Louis Redding—a graduate of Harvard University Law School—to become the state's first African American lawyer. After being admitted to the bar in 1928, Redding set up a general practice in Wilmington, served as counsel for the local NAACP, and earned the notice of the national Association, which, in 1933, invited him to join a unique gathering of "coming leaders of Negro thought" at the Spingarns' home in Amenia.

Among them, Abram Harris voiced a generational concern with a tradition-bound civil rights movement. Harris arrived at Troutbeck as the best known intellectual of his generation grappling with how best to shift a civil rights agenda then devoted to ending discriminatory practices to a program dedicated to securing economic equality. Hailing from Richmond, Virginia, Harris had a middle-class background, like Louis Redding, but disdained the black bourgeoisie's blithe embrace of capitalism. While the Reddings of Wilmington read the *Crisis*, Harris tended toward the *Messenger*, a black socialist monthly. Drawn to its radical critique of the political economy, and especially attuned to the plight of black laborers, he aspired to a role that would help foster an interracial workers' movement. This aspiration led Harris to serve two stints (in Manhattan and in Minneapolis) with the Urban League, a civil rights organization oriented toward economic uplift. With this experience, Harris entered Columbia University and commenced a pathbreaking scholarly career, becoming one of the first African Americans to earn a doctorate in economics. As much a public intellectual as an academic, during the 1920s and early 1930s, Harris published a series of essays and reviews, as well as a much heralded book (*The Black Worker*) that challenged prevailing assumptions about race. Widely understood as static and immutable, race, Harris argued, was only given significance in particular social and economic contexts. If underlying economic factors separated the races, his work contended, then economic transformations could diminish such divisions. This insight had natural implications for the civil rights struggle: it would be necessary to consider economic rights as important as civic and political liberties. His work, to his regret, did not win him wide acclaim during the heyday of the Harlem Renaissance, which celebrated the cultural ferment of the African race, but it did earn him a respected position in the Howard University economics department and an influential place amid both progressive labor and civil rights circles. Having formed a friendly bond with W. E. B. Du Bois, NAACP officials were intent on the Howard professor's participation in the Amenia Conference.

At Troutbeck, Abram Harris was among the first to speak. Amid his peers in August 1933, he offered his NAACP hosts an ardent explanation of why an interracial movement dedicated to economic justice was absolutely critical to the future of the Association—and to the black freedom struggle. Du Bois may have counted nineteen voices wrangling with "the Negro problem" at Amenia, but it was Harris who most vociferously insisted that the economic problem was paramount. The weekend conference actually featured a wide range of discussions that bespoke a generation's pragmatic, not dogmatic, view of the civil rights movement. There, talk ranged from economic radicalism to racial nationalism, but because so little remains to document the whirling discussions that took place that weekend, in retrospect Harris's influence over the proceedings seems all the more profound. After all, the "Findings Report" the conferees endorsed as their summary statement was, effectively, the handiwork of Harris, chair of the conference Findings Committee.

If Abram Harris had an outsized influence at the 1933 Amenia Conference, it was also his suggested transformation of the NAACP that contributed to the tensions the Association experienced as it reached its quarter-century mark.[5] While Harris embodied the new generation of leadership on the brink of changing the "plan and program" of the NAACP, an internecine dispute at its uppermost echelon kept the organization from implementing his vision. In the aftermath of the meeting, W. E. B. Du Bois left his position as editor of the *Crisis* and executive secretary Walter White assumed undisputed charge of the NAACP. Cognizant of Harris's criticisms, and wary of upstart rival organizations (such as the National Negro Congress), White nonetheless adamantly opposed putting Harris's proposals into practice, maneuvering to sustain the Association's traditional legal and legislative programs. Under White's stewardship, Abram Harris would not represent a new guard at the NAACP. The bright young face of the organization, instead, would be that of his fellow Amenia delegate: Juanita Jackson.

Only in her early twenties when Walter White courted her to become his special assistant, Juanita Jackson was already recognized as a star youth organizer within the Methodist Episcopal Church's youth movement and within the Baltimore civil rights movement. Born in Arkansas, Jackson had a devoutly Methodist and determinedly Talented Tenth upbringing in Baltimore. As in Wilmington, in Baltimore there was a wellspring of black protest that nourished a spirited, elite-led civil rights struggle. After an auspicious rise, however, the formidable Baltimore NAACP was embarrassingly diminished at the outset of the 1930s, when the Jackson family initiated the City-Wide Young People's Forum, a Methodist youth group that quickly evolved into a dynamic vehicle of civil rights agitation. When White offered her a position, Jackson accepted, endeavoring to translate her success in Baltimore into a vibrant national network of NAACP youth councils. Nominally based at the Association's office in New York, Jackson spent much of her three years as NAACP special assistant traveling across the eastern half of the United States, coordinating a campaign to challenge discrimination, eradicate the scourge of lynching, and abolish segregation in the nation's schools. During the mid-1930s, Jackson's efforts to found a youth movement suggest a collection of NAACP councils coming to comprise a nascent, national civil rights struggle.

Harlem, where Moran Weston lived, was at the hub of that national movement. Weston left the Amenia Conference in August 1933 intending to soon join the clergy. From a line of North Carolina Episcopalians, he took a divinity degree in New York, at Union Theological Seminary. When discrimination in the North kept him from donning the cloth, Weston instead vowed to pursue a gospel of social justice. While the NAACP muted its commitment to workers' rights, Weston grew dedicated to a radical economic agenda, joining civil rights and labor organizations (such as the National Negro Congress and the International Workers Order) committed to galvanizing an interracial workers' alliance. With the coming of the Second World War, Moran Weston served on the staff of the Negro Labor Victory Committee and wrote "Labor Forum," a column appearing each Saturday in the New York *Amsterdam News*, one of the city's African American weeklies. With the Victory Committee, and within his weekly columns, Weston was devoted to defeating "Hitlerism" on the warfront and at home. In Harlem, the Victory Committee leveraged resonant wartime rhetoric in support of an interracial coalition of workers, civil rights advocates, and left-leaning politicians. In its more than three-year campaign to end domestic fascism (discrimination at the polls, in industries, amid the troops), the Victory Committee collaborated with unions, found employment for thousands of workers, lobbied local and national governments, and engaged in vigorous electioneering. As field secretary, Moran Weston involved himself in the entirety of this program, even as he helped organize the Victory Committee's most memorable contribution to wartime New York: the Negro Freedom Rallies held each June, between 1943 and 1945, at Madison Square Garden. The annual extravaganzas, drawing inspiration from the Popular Front and official wartime propaganda, showcased the participation of leading black celebrities. The rallies employed patriotism and pageantry to strike resounding blows against Hitler and Jim Crow. The spectacle of the civil rights movement in wartime New York suggested a new apex of the black freedom struggle, but the Negro Labor Victory Committee—and those in its radical orbit—also provoked a conservative backlash.

It was unsafe to remember a radical past in May 1954, the month Ralph Bunche was impelled to testify to his loyalty to the nation. In the postwar years, antiradicalism crippled the progressive coalitions formed during World War II and, as the experience of Bunche demonstrated, even came to muffle the legacy of a generation of African American leaders in pursuit of a fundamental transformation of Jim Crow society. In 1954, few Americans enjoyed the stature of Ralph Bunche. The former Howard University political scientist had served in the Office of Strategic Services and the State Department; he had won a Nobel Peace Prize and was a top representative of the United Nations, a beacon of a new international order devoted to democratic freedoms. Misplaced anti-Communist fervor, however, imperiled his position. When informants characterized Bunche as a clandestine Communist, the nation's leading diplomat was compelled to submit to a hearing with a federal loyalty board. During that hearing, Bunche offered a nuanced explanation of his intellectual trajectory, his formal written response filling more than one hundred pages. The impromptu autobiography he related took care to parse his political beliefs, beginning with his Depression-era qualms about American capitalism. The argument that such skepticism was commonplace at the time proved less significant than a friend's act of self-sacrifice. When a former collaborator admitted to consorting with Communists during the 1930s, he sated the loyalty board's interest in identifying traitors and safely distanced Ralph Bunche from an ostensibly vast conspiracy to undermine the nation.

The Supreme Court announced its *Brown v. Board of Education* decision voiding the "separate but equal" doctrine as applied to the nation's schools in May 1954, the very month Ralph Bunche found it dangerous to discuss his radical past. The culmination of a decades-long challenge to the legality of racial segregation, the ruling was hailed by contemporaries as a second Emancipation Proclamation. Soon, the decision was also perceived as an inspiration for the boycotts and sit-ins, protest marches and voter registration campaigns that effloresced throughout the nation, comprising a new phase in the ongoing African American freedom struggle. It was a movement of many origins, but the era of anti-Communism partially silenced one that had seemed so meaningful to the delegates who arrived at the Troutbeck estate in Amenia, New York, in August 1933: the effort to achieve social, political, and economic justice through an interracial workers' movement.

The pursuit of such a progressive alliance, a central concern of the Depression and World War II years, and the object of scrutiny by the early 1950s, remained a prized purpose during the height of the modern civil rights movement. When a quarter million Americans assembled together at the National Mall in Washington, DC, in August 1963, it was in the name of jobs and freedom—a pair of goals that would have been familiar to participants in the first Negro Freedom Rally in 1943, and to the conferees who met at Troutbeck a decade earlier. The persistence of such a radical set of objectives speaks to the perseverance of the generation of African American intellectuals and activists who met at Amenia. Born at the nadir of the Jim Crow period, they came of age during an era when a select upper echelon of African Americans was expected to uplift the race. The cohort who embodied the Talented Tenth ideal between the 1920s and the early 1950s, though, did not blindly hew to how their predecessors' conceived of the role of the black elite. Pragmatic about fostering a national civil rights movement, they were willing to consider such strategies as mass organizing and interracial labor-based alliances, hopes borne not out of a dogma but out of a dogged commitment to crippling the legal, political, and social sources of segregation.

Their insistence on economic justice was only one strand linking generations in the long struggle to secure civil rights during the twentieth century. To trace the experiences of the generation born along the color line is to chart an arc toward African American freedom. Abject at the turn of the century, by midcentury African Americans were gaining fundamental civil equality. No simple outcome of social beneficence or political munificence, in great part this was the legacy of African Americans like Redding and Harris, Jackson and Weston, and Ralph Bunche, who strove to eradicate the baleful vestiges of segregation. As their lives demonstrate, it was likewise a legacy of the communities they hailed from and worked in. In dozens of settings across the nation, grassroots defiance of the Jim Crow order grew enormously in scope and intensity from the 1910s through midcentury. Wilmington, Baltimore, and Harlem—as well as cities like Atlanta and Washington, DC, Boston and Minneapolis, Gary and New Orleans—shone amid a wide constellation of communities, as local organizing came to coalesce into a national civil rights movement. Interest in aligning civil rights and labor rights in a progressive front for social, political, and economic equality certainly animated much activism and organization during this period. But so did agitation for equal education, for antilynching legislation, and for open access to employment and the ballot. Forging such local efforts into a broader black freedom struggle was the lifework of a remarkable generation of African American leaders represented at the 1933 Amenia Conference. Helping foster the rise of a national civil rights movement, the group who posed for Amy Spingarn's photograph at Troutbeck fundamentally altered the nature of American democracy.

PART ONE

"Those who prefer to motor . . . should take Route 22, the main route to the Berkshires."

—Joel E. Spingarn, *summer 1933*

1

Louis Redding's Invitation

On August 18, 1933, Louis Redding stepped from the one-room, second-floor law office he kept at 1002 French Street in Wilmington, Delaware, an unlit English Oval between his lips, filter end out. Seldom was he without a cigarette, and he had taken his tobacco this way ever since his undergraduate years at Brown University during the early 1920s. Redding never smoked; he chewed. Dressed in Brooks Brothers, a sartorial preference cultivated on College Hill, Redding rounded the corner for his home.

Redding lived up the hill at 203 East Tenth Street, a two-story red brick house, with his father, several siblings, and a cousin or two. His mother had died a decade earlier. His father, Lewis Redding (or Papa, as the family called him, putting the accent on the second syllable), was a postman and had purchased the home in 1907, making the Reddings the first black family on the block. Within a few years, white residents moved away, and a number of black dentists, teachers, and physicians came to make their homes on the Hill. There, the residents on Tenth Street Hill—the Sykes on East Tenth, the Americas on Tatnall, the Hoxters on Walnut—fostered a black middle class enclave away from the city's poorer Eastside neighborhoods, where most African Americans in Wilmington lived. It was a "good segregated block," Redding remembered many decades later, with no little irony. As the color line was etched through American society at the turn of the twentieth century, neighborhoods like the Reddings' on the Hill survived the entrenchment of the Jim Crow order and preserved a legacy of elite black protest that undermined racial segregation. To come of age on Tenth Street Hill during the 1910s and 1920s, as the thirty-two-year-old Louis Redding had, was to inherit a tradition of demanding dignity and unfettered access to civic life for African Americans. The diplomas—Brown, class of '23, and Harvard University Law School, '28—that hung in Redding's office offered the briefest testimony of that tradition. The invitation he had received to attend the Amenia Conference offered more.

As many of his neighbors were aware as he collected his car at 203 East Tenth, that afternoon Louis Redding was driving to the Spingarns' home in picturesque

LOUIS REDDING, 1930s. Special Collections and University Archives, W. E. B. Du Bois Library, University of Massachusetts Amherst, reprinted with the permission of the Crisis Publishing Company.

Dutchess County, New York. Joel Spingarn and the NAACP were well known on the Hill. Two decades earlier, Spingarn had visited Wilmington to arouse interest in the newly founded Association, advocating a "New Abolitionism" meant to topple the emerging Jim Crow order. At the time, Lewis Redding had been among the first to organize the local branch of the NAACP, which initially met among neighbors on Tenth Street Hill. In the years since, the Wilmington NAACP spearheaded civil rights agitation in Delaware, and the Reddings became an NAACP family, devotedly reading the Association's monthly magazine, the *Crisis,* and well involved in the branch's leadership. By the early 1920s, when Lewis Redding assumed the presidency of the branch, the Wilmington NAACP and the Redding family were decidedly entwined. As the branch turned its attention to the segregation of the state court system, it launched a campaign of political suasion that led Louis Redding, in 1929, to become the first black lawyer in the state—an achievement of national note, for Redding, for the family, and for the Wilmington branch of the NAACP. By 1933, the postman's son served as legal counsel for the Wilmington NAACP and had been selected to participate in the Amenia Conference, as his invitation put it, as one of the "coming leaders of Negro thought." It was an honor for Redding and the Wilmington community in which he was reared.

All packed, Redding exchanged goodbyes and then steered his car from Tenth Street Hill down to Market Street, over the Brandywine, and onto the Pennsylvania Pike, the route north out of Delaware. He had planned to arrive at Joel Spingarn's Troutbeck estate by six but would be late. While the Amenia Conference opened with a dinner and introductions, Redding was still en route that humid August evening, nearing the New York state line and watching for Motor Route 22, the main road to Amenia.[1]

The call to Amenia had arrived with the rest of Redding's office mail three months earlier, during the second week of April 1933. If the unfamiliar New York postmark on the envelope had not immediately distinguished this piece of correspondence, the two sheets of paper inside certainly did. On the first, an invitation was typed on Joel Spingarn's personal letterhead—an unadorned page with simply "Troutbeck," "Amenia," and "New York" in three staggered lines toward the upper right-hand corner. Should he accept, the short note read, he could expect to join some "thirty or forty" of his contemporaries, "young representatives of the colored race" each "to discuss the present and future situation of the Negro." Enclosed, Spingarn explained, was "a brief account of the conference and what it hope[d] to accomplish."[2]

Redding studied the accompanying page closely. To begin with, the retreat was called, appropriately if plainly, "The Amenia Conference." It would be held, without publicity, at Spingarn's home later that summer, from Friday, August 18th, through Monday the 21st. A train departing regularly from Grand Central Terminal could carry conferees on the two-and-a-half-hour trip to Amenia Center; from there, a member of the Spingarn family could ferry them to Troutbeck. Those preferring to drive could take Route 22 directly to Amenia, following that "main route to the Berkshires." Indeed, simply glancing at a map revealed Amenia to be near the southwestern edge of those mountains. Several peaks along the Housatonic River, across the Connecticut line, bordered to the east; the Hudson Valley lay just to the west. Redding needed little more than intuition, then, to predict that the "simple and intimate spirit of the out-of-doors" would pervade the weekend. But his invitation confirmed it: life at the conference would be decidedly rustic. He and the other conferees would spend the weekend "housed in tents pitched on the shore of Troutbeck Lake." Inside the largest they would convene for meals and meetings. But the "serious business of the conference" would also be "interspersed with the simple recreations of the countryside," including "rowing, canoeing, fishing, swimming, woodland walks, and the like." Still, as the invitation made clear, while this informal setting would surely promote a certain "sense of leisure" that no "mere discussion in a public hall or urban center" ever could, conferees were not to allow their relaxed surroundings to translate into indifferent conversation nor into lax planning of

what was to be a "new programme suited to these times." The conference organizers intended to foster just the opposite, actually. They hoped the pastoral surroundings at Troutbeck would underscore the delegates' freedom that weekend
to openly and seriously confer on how to best meet the challenges African
Americans faced in 1933.[3]

Clearly, openness was intended to be a hallmark of the Amenia Conference.
During the group's discussions that weekend, Redding's invitation assured
him, he and his fellow "young leaders or potential leaders of the race" could
expect to enjoy "perfect freedom" of "opinion and expression." Despite the "assistance in the mechanics of organization" that the NAACP had provided, this
meeting was not to be explicitly "an NAACP conference." Neither host Spingarn nor his associates on the conference committee (Walter White, the
NAACP's recently appointed executive secretary, and W. E. B. Du Bois, a
founding member of the NAACP and editor of the *Crisis*) would brook any
"attempt to limit discussion to the ideals or programme of that Association." Of
course, the work of the NAACP would necessarily enter the conversation at
some point—after all, the Association had been the nation's preeminent civil
rights organization since its inception in 1909. Still, Redding's invitation was
clear on this note. He had been chosen to attend the Amenia Conference not
because of any supposed predisposition to the NAACP but rather for his independent character. Indeed, he had been invited because his ideas, Redding may
have been pleased to read in his invitation, had not yet "hardened into conventional modes."[4]

That this was a critical point, Redding could agree. The very success of a conference on issues of current importance to black America depended on participants' constructive and clear thinking, on thought unfettered by association
with any particular program or organization. Only independent minds could be
asked to make innovative suggestions for bolstering current civil rights efforts.
And this was exactly what 1933 seemed to call for: new approaches in fighting
for the full works of citizenship rights for African Americans. Occupying the
thoughts of the civil rights–minded, even those from Wilmington, Delaware,
was nothing less than the effects of the Depression on black America. Predictably, in Wilmington the poor economy weighed particularly heavily on its
unskilled black laborers, most of whom lived down the Hill from Redding, near
the Brandywine Creek, in one of the city's oldest and shabbiest neighborhoods.
Economic hard times, of course, did not end at the Delaware border, nor did the
effects of the Depression end with unemployment. Even in Wilmington, Louis
Redding could see its impact on civil rights efforts. And what he did not himself
witness he read about in the morning newspaper, the black weeklies, and the
copies of the *Crisis* and *Opportunity* magazines that arrived monthly at 203 East
Tenth Street.[5]

Above all, these sources alerted Redding to the increasing volume and militancy with which the political left (and the Communist Party, in particular) had taken up civil rights—a cause that had previously been the concern, principally, of such betterment organizations as the NAACP or the even more moderate National Urban League. Since late March of 1931, for instance, stories had appeared regularly out of Alabama concerning the Scottsboro trials. The case, involving the purported rape of two white women by nine black teenagers on a train outside Scottsboro, had inspired agitation in seemingly every major northern city. The case had sparked particular concern among NAACP members when the Association, normally at the forefront in the courtroom, backed away from the case, allowing the International Labor Defense (a legal affiliate of the Communist Party) to handle the trials. In Wilmington, Louis Redding shared this concern. Elsewhere, from Chicago to Boston, the case provoked activism that meshed with local boycott movements and other civil rights militancy. The result threw into relief the differences between the demands made by the radical left and the more moderate programs of established civil rights organizations, leaving many a local NAACP branch member, if nothing else, confused. In New York, at the Association's national offices at 69 Fifth Avenue, the matter appeared a good deal worse. The Association, already hobbled by dwindling membership nationwide and atrophying local branches, now faced the added challenge of a serious competitor for African Americans' grassroots support.[6]

While Wilmington lacked an organized left on par with larger cities like Chicago and New York, over the past several years membership woes had affected the city's local branch of the NAACP. With Redding's father its immediate past president, and he its current legal counsel, Louis Redding was witness to the group's recent struggle to stir local passions. Just a few years earlier his neighbor and branch secretary, Alice Baldwin, had written the New York office "of the very discouraging condition of the affairs of the Branch." Not once, in a year of meeting on the first Tuesday of each month, had attendance constituted a quorum of a dozen members. After trying "Public meetings, Baby Shows, Rummage Sales, Card Parties, even serving refreshments after meetings," each an Association-prescribed tonic for the dormant branch's ills, she despaired when "none of those seemed to offer inducement to people to attend." Despite an active place in the city since 1912, by 1930 the local branch had obviously diminished in its appeal. Similarly vanishing was the desire of the incumbent branch officers, who had been "*forced* to remain in office" because "for several years it has not been possible to have an election," to continue efforts to revive the branch. "Both Mr. Redding and I," wrote Baldwin, by now certain that the final vestige of her local branch was the very Wilmington NAACP letterhead on which she typed, "feel that it is useless for *us* to try to keep the Branch alive under the circumstances." Only in the past two years, since 1931, had the branch begun to come back to life, due mainly to the diligence of several younger leaders in Wilmington, including Pauline Young, the librarian at Howard High School; George Johnson, the school's principal; and Louis Redding.[7]

Even from his vantage in Wilmington, then, Redding could understand the emphasis the national NAACP organizers placed on the 1933 conference in Amenia. According to his invitation, he and his fellow Amenia delegates faced a significant, collective task. Each would be expected to ensure "that a new vision of the Negro's future, and a new programme, will arise out of this independent discussion." Pausing to consider the NAACP's own history, as well as his understanding of the past generation of civil rights efforts, Redding probably thought this was an appropriate expectation. The NAACP itself had resulted from a conference (the 1909 National Negro Conference in New York City), and the early twentieth century had been peppered with similar attempts to convene leading African Americans and civil rights–minded white folk to confront the bedeviling, persistent implications of segregation, often euphemistically described as the "Negro Problem." Just in the past several years the Laura Spellman Rockefeller Memorial (a philanthropic arm of the Rockefeller Foundation) had launched an annual Negro Problem Conference in New Haven, lasting through the late 1920s. In 1927, middle-class black North Carolinians in Durham had established an annual Stock-Taking and Fact-Finding Conference on the American Negro, continuing until the early 1930s. And the NAACP, of course, had for the past twenty-four years met each summer in cities across the country for its annual conference. The previous summer, in fact, Louis Redding had attended the Association's conference in Washington, DC, joining a panel devoted to black lawyers, but also serving on a Committee on Resolutions that insisted on developing "a definite economic program" as a "chief plank in a platform for future reform" of the NAACP.[8]

Yet the Amenia Conference stood apart from past endeavors. Far smaller than the NAACP's annual conference, which normally convened hundreds of Association members, its exclusiveness smacked of the New Haven confabs, which drew handfuls of strictly the most established civil rights figures. And yet, while the Amenia delegates would be few in number, they would also be young, African American, and generally unattached to any specific program or organization. The proposal interested Redding. The conference imperative was stated clearly enough, its ambition palpable. Though, remarkably, the conference would be held out of doors rather than in a university auditorium, church, or public hall, the NAACP intended the tenor of the meeting, and indeed its ultimate importance, to be no less profound than any recent civil rights conference. Furthermore, in Amenia Redding would have the opportunity to engage the elite of his generation, considering issues broadly and learning about others' perspectives on the future of the civil rights struggle.

While undoubtedly skeptical that the NAACP's imprint would be as light on the weekend's proceedings as the invitation claimed, his eagerness for such a conference outweighed any reservations.

Redding marked his calendar, then placed a page of his own letterhead into the typewriter he kept in his office. He scrolled the page until "Louis Lorenzo Redding, Attorney at Law" appeared, then typed his acceptance. Most of the others Joel Spingarn invited that spring did the same. As the update Redding received from Troutbeck in late May reported with some satisfaction, the Amenia Conference, though still two and a half months away, was "already assured of success" because of the "number, distinction, and representative character" of those who had committed to making the trip that August. No fewer than twenty-seven young black men and women of promise had pledged to attend, each keen on making new acquaintances and eager to forge a new civil rights agenda.[9]

Some of these, as Redding might have guessed, had attended that month's Washington, DC, summit on the Negro and the New Deal. The economic conference, sponsored by the Julius Rosenwald Foundation, had dominated the headlines of the black weeklies during the third week in May. Although hundreds had attended, and dozens of prominent speakers had addressed the significance of both the Depression and the New Deal, the prevailing message was hard to miss. The struggle for citizenship rights needed to incorporate the fight for blacks' economic rights. For the NAACP, which had long concentrated its efforts in the legal and political spheres, this would necessitate significant changes in its current program. Indeed, as those scanning news articles on the Rosenwald conference would note, the Depression had already begun reshaping the Association, starting with its upcoming annual convention in Chicago. The economic situation had forced the shortening of what had been a six-day program to just four days. Anticipated social entertainments, the highlights of past sessions, would be put off. "For the first time in many years," the *Baltimore Afro-American* reported, even the Saturday evening session would be devoted to a conference meeting. When the *Crisis* arrived at the Reddings' in June, it noted that a significant portion of the proceedings would cover "the subject of employment and the part young people play in the Association's work." An echo, certainly, of the themes in his Amenia invitation, the message was made clearer the next month.[10]

Though the conference had been shortened and trimmed of added expense, and was the product of only five weeks' preparation, the August *Crisis* deemed the just-ended Chicago meeting "one of the most successful in the Association's history." Many panelists had arrived prepared to criticize the current program of the NAACP, and, with "complete freedom of discussion and expression of opinion," they had produced "one of the liveliest sessions of the Conference." Also contributing to the vibrancy of the convention "was the presence of many alert, intelligent, trained younger delegates." Rayford Logan, representing Carter Woodson's Association for the Study of Negro Life and History, had delivered an "impressive paper" charting the growth of radicalism among black leaders. Charles Houston, currently engaged in "brilliant" legal work for the NAACP, had addressed the "great closing mass meeting" on Sunday afternoon, stressing the need for moderate, but deliberate, transformation of the NAACP's program to secure civil liberties for African Americans.[11]

The conversation such younger leaders had begun in Chicago would continue at Amenia. Confirmation came when the next update on the conference arrived shortly after the August *Crisis*. In this, the third envelope Redding had received from Spingarn since April, he found a postcard on which to return word on his plans to travel to Troutbeck. In response, he took up his pen and thinly, evenly inked his answers: he would arrive by car, in the "early evening." But the next page called for closer scrutiny. Here, the conference committee had mapped out an agenda to lend definition to that weekend's discussion. After a Friday evening of introductions, the election of officers, and adjournment into smaller committees, the conferees would devote Saturday and Sunday to critical discussion of topics ranging from the "Weaknesses and Accomplishments of the older programmes" to "voluntary and involuntary segregation with group loyalty and nationalism." In between, during afternoons spent paddling the lake, strolling the gardens, or following local Civilian Conservation Corps boys on a snake hunt, Redding could plan to dedicate a few hours on the tennis court to his overhand serve. But by Sunday evening, he would have to trade his tennis shorts for trousers and repair once again to the big tent for a final convocation. Collaborative articulation of the conference findings would complete the Amenia delegates' work. He and his fellow conferees would be free to return home that night, or the following morning, where they would then work to fulfill their collective obligation: to lead the civil rights struggle they had inherited.[12]

Indeed, beyond detailing logistics, the correspondence regarding the Amenia conference encouraged the invitees to consider their responsibility to forward the civil rights legacy of their predecessors. As Louis Redding's invitation indicated, several older leaders would "attend from day to day," some of whom had in fact convened at the Spingarn estate seventeen years earlier. To Spingarn, the 1916 gathering at Troutbeck had "produced results which were of real importance to the destiny of the American Negro." He asked that Redding and his fellow invitees familiarize themselves with the commemoratory pamphlet he had commissioned W. E. B. Du Bois to write about the meeting. The pamphlet— *Troutbeck Leaflet No. 8*—underscored the significance of the first conference held in Amenia; Spingarn's request that it be read suggested his aspirations for the second. In 1916, Du Bois wrote, the Dutchess County estate, with "its slow rocky uplift of land, the nestle of the lake and the steady murmur of brooks and brown rivers," had lent the perfect backdrop to foster unity among disparate supporters of racial uplift. A year earlier the powerful and divisive Booker T. Washington had died, and with him had passed broad acceptance of accommodation, the notion that African Americans ought to cast aside political aspirations for the present and instead cultivate the economic skills and moral virtue necessary to amicably integrate into American society. More than fifty of the nation's most distinguished advocates of racial advancement ventured to Amenia. Never before, Du Bois observed, had "so small a conference of American Negroes had so many colored men of distinction who represented at the same time so complete a picture of all phases of Negro thought." Remarkably, even former rivals experienced rapprochement there, the diminishing of old enmities resulting in significant new backing for the NAACP, then in just its seventh year. "On account of our meeting," Du Bois concluded, contemporary civil rights leadership "was more united and more ready to meet the problems of the world than it could possibly have been without these beautiful days of understanding." To Du Bois, this affirmation of the NAACP's program during the Amenia conference was a seminal moment in civil rights history, an August 1916 eclipse of accommodation.[13]

Asking Louis Redding and his fellow invitees to read this leaflet was meant to suggest they recognize their place within the tradition of black protest that had led to, and subsequently benefitted from, the gains made in 1916. Arranging for the Amenia delegates to mingle with their predecessors beneath the tents at Troutbeck only strengthened this suggestion. There they would represent two generations of the caste of elite Negro leadership that W. E. B. Du Bois, thirty years earlier, had named the Talented Tenth. Redding, for one, would be quick to acknowledge that the legacy of Talented Tenth activism and the emergence of the NAACP had entwined to shape his own coming of age in Wilmington during the first decades of the twentieth century.

In homes like the Reddings' on Tenth Street Hill were found the writings of W. E. B. Du Bois, the most cogent articulator of the Talented Tenth tradition. *The Souls of Black Folk*, published in 1903, was the touchstone text; commencing in the fall of 1910, the *Crisis* offered monthly expression. But Du Bois most clearly explicated his thoughts on the Talented Tenth in a piece appearing in *The Negro Problem*, a turn-of-the-century collection of essays voicing the contemporary African American perspective. In "The Talented Tenth" Du Bois portrayed the long struggle for black freedom in a heroic key: from the outset of New World bondage, a black vanguard arose with each successive generation to lead America's African descendants one step closer to freedom. "From the very first," Du Bois observed, "it has been the educated and intelligent of the Negro people that have led and elevated the mass, and the sole obstacles that nullified and re-tarded their efforts were slavery and race prejudice." In the Revolutionary era, during the founding of the United States as a slave republic, the very existence of such learned blacks as the poet Phillis Wheatley and Benjamin Banneker, the famed almanac maker, discredited late-eighteenth-century explanations of in-equality between the races. Du Bois also enshrined figures like Wheatley, Ban-neker, and the Boston merchant Paul Cuffe as early avatars of the Talented Tenth, dedicated to destroying that "awful incubus": slavery. Banneker spoke for more than even his own generation when he urged the United States to abide by its own founding creed—"that all men are created equal." Revolutionary rhe-toric remained a convincing device through the 1820s, when the black aboli-tionist David Walker—"that Voice crying in the Wilderness"—appealed to the inalienable rights of American liberty to justify severing the ties of bondage, a call that culminated in the National Negro Convention of 1831. Such voices, Du Bois held, were a prelude to "the work which the Talented Tenth among Negroes took in the great abolition crusade" through the 1860s. "There was Purvis and Remond, Pennington and Highland Garnett, Sojourner Truth and Alexander Crummel, and above, Frederick Douglass," Du Bois recounted, plucking names from the pantheon of antebellum black leaders. "They were the men who made American slavery impossible," who ensured the abolition of black bondage in 1865. Between the American Revolution and the Civil War, Du Bois traced a discernable arc toward freedom; the role of the black elite remained just as crit-ical during the era of emancipation that followed the Civil War. With the pas-sage of the Thirteenth, Fourteenth, and Fifteenth Amendments—ending slavery, affording African Americans the rights of citizenship, and extending the franchise to black men, respectively—Du Bois noted the "new group of edu-cated and gifted leaders" who rose to the task of representing the race in elected office during Reconstruction. The late nineteenth century saw an impressive roster of leaders—"Langston, Bruce and Elliot, Greener, Williams and Payne"—who collectively strove "to uplift their people" through political agitation, through moral comportment, and especially through the establishment of edu-cational institutions.[14]

Looking back from the turn of the twentieth century, it seemed such leaders had laid a foundation for African Americans' future freedom. Yet at the moment Du Bois was writing this piece, the promise of Reconstruction remained unful-filled. By the early 1900s the rise of the Jim Crow order, a denigrating system of racial segregation asserted through a combination of white supremacist vigilan-tism and legal mandate, imperiled the legacy of Talented Tenth protest. Du Bois's own generation of the Talented Tenth, born during the Civil War and Re-construction, responded by drawing from the vital tradition of black protest that had compelled the nation to abolish slavery and grant citizenship to African

Americans. To quote Du Bois's evocation of an era only offers the briefest regis-
ter of race leaders who rose to confront the Jim Crow order—there was Church
Terrell and Weldon Johnson, Wells, Chesnutt and Dunbar, Hawkins Brown,
Burroughs and Pickney Hill, and above, W. E. B. Du Bois.

As Du Bois wrote in "The Amenia Conference," his cohort disdained accommodation as being responsible for "the consummation of Negro disenfranchisement, the decline of the Negro college and public school, and the firmer
establishment of color caste in this land." The Niagara Movement, a short-lived
effort he and two of his former Harvard University classmates had organized in
1905 especially for the men of the Talented Tenth, offered an alternative. "We
believe," announced the Niagara pledge, that African Americans "should protest
emphatically and continually against the curtailment of their political rights."
The right to vote, indeed, was irreplaceable; the erosion of black political power
had led directly to the debasements of the Jim Crow order. "To ignore, overlook, or apologize for these wrongs," the Niagarites contended, "is to prove
ourselves unworthy for freedom." Rejecting the rhetoric of acquiescence, the
Niagara Movement evinced a fervent spirit of protest that harkened back to
the previous century's struggle to overturn slavery. Over the next four years the
Niagara Movement grew from twenty-seven dentists and teachers, scholars and
editors, to a membership numbering in the several hundreds (including many
women), representing dozens of local councils. Regrettably, their method of agitation consisted of little more than annual statements, and their consistently
empty coffers and failed attempts at sustaining a monthly magazine testified to
their limited appeal beyond the politically conscious black middle class. Nevertheless, as the Niagara Movement faded, it provided a national network—and,
in some respects, a model—for the most significant civil rights organization of
the era, the NAACP.[15]

The NAACP was formed in outrage, inaugurated during the 1909 National
Negro Conference, a meeting in New York City of white progressives and black
leaders incensed by the previous year's Springfield, Illinois, race riots. Commemorating the centennial of Abraham Lincoln's birth, the NAACP's founders
imagined that the author of the Emancipation Proclamation would be dismayed
by the debasement, discrimination, and disenfranchisement African Americans
endured more than four decades after freedom. Assessing the scope of segregation at the turn of the twentieth century, the NAACP's founders posited that
"the problem" was a national one, as white supremacist wrath culminated in
"lawless attacks upon the negro . . . even in the Springfield made famous by Lincoln." Acknowledging that "silence under these conditions means tacit approval,"
the NAACP intended to voice its protest. At the outset, the Association was
quite small, composed of fewer than two hundred prominent white progressives
and members of the fading Niagara Movement. Yet modest membership rolls

belied the NAACP's resolve. The NAACP's first year of activity ranged from an opening mass meeting at Cooper Union in New York City—where experts presented evidence negating scientific racism; where W. E. B. Du Bois maintained that the suppression of the black vote was the manifest issue of the day; where Progressives argued for the mutuality of civil rights, the rights of the worker, the settlement movement, and feminism—to private meetings in the tony parlors of sympathetic benefactors, where discussion of the "new slavery" facing African Americans was meant to loosen purse strings and arouse a "New Abolitionism." And for those who missed the lectures, news of the Association arrived monthly in the W. E. B. Du Bois–edited "Journal of the Darker Races," the Crisis.[16]

First published in November 1910, the Crisis was a staple in the households on Tenth Street Hill—not only read but "studied." In the earliest issues, Du Bois fulfilled the Talented Tenth's commitment to execrate the Jim Crow order and memorialized even the race's most modest advances. But the Crisis was no blithe paean to Negro progress. News of the construction of a colored hospital in Nashville, of the enthusiastic reception of a young Negro pianist at Yale, and of the celebration of Emancipation Day throughout the South was imbued with political resonance. Descriptions of Negro thrift, artistic achievement, civic ambition, commitment to education, and social engagement appeared month after month in the first issues of the Crisis, underscoring an ongoing confrontation of the color line. The November 1910 issue reported that "New York is becoming an art center for colored people"; the December number noted that blacks in Richmond, Virginia, owned property valued at more than two million dollars. The January 1911 issue heralded the curricula at Howard, Lincoln, Wilberforce, Virginia Union, Atlanta, and Shaw Universities, as well as the local fundraising efforts for the construction of a new school in humble Plateau, Alabama. A portrait of newly elected Henry Bass, "First Colored Member of the Pennsylvania Legislature," was showcased on the February cover. The March issue reported that "the colored citizens of Memphis" had condemned the segregation of the city's parks and that "a mass meeting of colored citizens of New Orleans" had called for equality in education and on the city's street cars. In April, the poetry of William Stanley Braithwaite graced the center spread of the magazine. From political participation to poetic expression, throughout the nation the darker race was refusing to submit.[17]

As the first issues of the Crisis detailed, there was much to confront. "The function of this Association," wrote Du Bois in the inaugural number, "is to tell this nation the crying evil of race prejudice." Indeed, within the first year of its publication, the Crisis reported a range of iniquities, from the introduction of legislation prohibiting interracial marriage in the Massachusetts, Nevada, Michigan, and Washington state legislatures to the disenfranchisement of black men in Arkansas, Kentucky, and Oklahoma, where prospective voters in the former Indian Territory were handed selections of the state constitution to read aloud, with legal terms—in Latin—and county names (Cimarron and Obage; Kiowa and Muskogee; Okmulgee and Okfuskee; Pottawatomie and Howata) awaiting tripping tongues. A prominent minister and the principal of a local high school, Du Bois reported, were among those who failed this literacy requirement. White vigilantism, the *Crisis* also made clear, posed a constant terror—and it was not isolated to southern communities like Turner County, Georgia, or Baxterville, Mississippi. Each month, readers on Tenth Street Hill learned of new outrages. In Oklahoma City, updates published during the spring of 1911 detailed how a number of black farmers were seeking refuge from a conflict over the purchase of land to cultivate cotton; terrorized and disenfranchised, many black Oklahomans were in fact migrating as far away as Nova Scotia. In Kansas City, the handsome new home of a prominent colored man (constructed at the expense of $5,000) was dynamited just before completion. Less fortunate were the men lynched in Shelby County, Kentucky, and Montezuma, Georgia. Or the six colored prisoners taken from unprotected cells in Lake City, Florida, shot and left to moulder in a nearby swamp. Or the black man assailed in Livermore, Kentucky, where a mob paid admission to shoot him to death onstage at a local theater. Beginning in December 1910, such horrors were tallied in a table entitled "Colored Men Lynched Without Trial," enumerating sixty-five victims in the previous year. In the center spread of the January 1911 issue was a sketch titled "The National Pastime," of a bereft woman swooning across a table after reading the newspaper headline: "Negro Lynched—Brute Struck White Man—Made Confession—Mob was quiet and orderly." Her head lying on her arm, her gaze points toward a small framed portrait of a man as well dressed as any member of the Talented Tenth. Reading the caption ("Seventy-five percent of the Negroes lynched have not even been accused of rape") was enough to remind that claims of Negro brutality thinly veiled the sport—the *pastime*—that white terror had become.[18]

Remembering the mob murder of a young man outside Wilmington some years earlier, readers of the *Crisis* on Tenth Street Hill knew all too well that lynching was a national menace, even as Coatesville, Pennsylvania, became bywords for brutality during the summer of 1911. "The mob spirit is far from dead," wrote Du Bois in the August issue of the *Crisis*, scoffing at the notion that African Americans enjoyed constitutional protections of rights. "Every schoolboy knows that Negro Americans are disfranchised in large areas of the South for no other reason than race and color." The consequence: "mob and murder." From Indian Springs, Georgia, to Pineville, Louisiana; from Purcell, Oklahoma, to Augusta, Arkansas; from Farmersville, Texas, to Granville, South Carolina, the blood spilled in 1911 offered awful proof of Du Bois's maxim of

THE NATIONAL PASTIME.
Seventy-five per cent. of the Negroes
lynched have not even been accused of
rape.

"THE NATIONAL PASTIME." This illustration by John Henry Adams was published in
the *Crisis* in 1911. Special Collections and University Archives, W. E. B. Du Bois Library,
University of Massachusetts Amherst.

the mob spirit. "Come, Americans who love America," Du Bois urged in the
wake of the Coatesville lynching, "is it not time to rub our eyes and awake and
act?" It was not enough to decry such atrocities; it was necessary to respond in
a movement to secure African Americans' safety, dignity, and civil liberties.
Paging through the *Crisis*, the Lewis Reddings learned of the response the
NAACP took in defense of two southern sharecroppers facing execution, dramatic action that hearkened to abolitionist protection of fugitive slaves during
the decade before the Civil War.[19]

In South Carolina, Pink Franklin had been set upon before dawn, assaulted
for leaving his landlord's farmstead before settling his debts. Awakening to a
home invasion and wounded in the shoulder, Franklin met revolver fire with
gunshot, killing the warrant officer who had attacked him. Defended by two
African American lawyers, Franklin was convicted of murder, then sentenced to
death, a decision that was upheld despite appeal to the Supreme Court. Only a
governor's commutation would save Franklin. At this juncture, the NAACP interceded. Lacking a formal legal program, the Association's well-connected
leaders prodded powerful acquaintances, friends, and family members to heed
their consciences and assist NAACP efforts. Letters were written on behalf of
Franklin. Southern white lawyers were convinced to speak with the governor.
President Taft was persuaded to mediate, arguing with some diplomacy that
South Carolina should not be stained by gross injustice. Remarkably, moral

suasion succeeded in saving Franklin's life. As a principled gesture, Franklin's sentence was commuted to life imprisonment as the governor left office. While the NAACP declared life in prison too harsh a penalty, at least one northern newspaper suggested the Association deserved admiration for a defense reminiscent of the famous Dred Scott case of the 1850s.[20]

In Arkansas, Steve Green likewise committed an unforgivable act of self-defense. After leaving his tenancy Green had hired himself out for a day at a neighboring farm, ignoring his former landlord's warning never to work again in Crittenden County. Green bolted when the man confronted him, revolver drawn; bullet wounds to the neck, left arm, and right leg did not keep him from reaching his cabin—and his Winchester. Now armed, he returned fire, then fled via creek and treetop. A weeks-long chase ensued, reminiscent of antebellum flights from bondage, replete with a manhunt and bloodhounds, nights spent following the North Star, and assistance from anonymous "colored friends" who supplied sanctuary, sundry supplies, and $32. On a secluded island in the Mississippi River, Green enjoyed three weeks' respite from the chase, then again journeyed north. He arrived footsore in Chicago, only to have a confidante betray him to the police. Green had murdered his assailant; Arkansas demanded extradition. Like a runaway slave awaiting his return to shackles and chains, Green was held on false charges for four days. Provided no food, offered no drink, Green sought peace: he swallowed two boxes of matches, was hospitalized, but did not die. When his former landlord's nephew arrived in Chicago to identify him, Green was promised another end, this time by the strike of a match: the rope and faggot awaited him in Arkansas, he was told, where the whites of Crittenden County were eager to watch him burn. News of Steve Green's plight provoked swift response. In New York, Joel Spingarn read of the case in his newspaper and made a decision: "I don't care what happens, Steve Green will never be extradited to Arkansas." His donation of $100 for Green's defense marked Spingarn's entry into the NAACP; in a month he would be invited to join the Association's Executive Committee. In Chicago, Ida Wells-Barnett, the anti-lynching crusader who had attended the founding of the NAACP, coordinated the effort to save Green. While the NAACP remained on the alert, her Negro Fellowship League arranged for lawyers and a court order that returned Green to Chicago. Before a formal hearing on his extradition took place, Chicago's Talented Tenth borrowed a final strategy from the abolitionists, guiding Green to Canada.[21]

The Pink Franklin and Steve Green cases demonstrated the NAACP's willingness to intervene on behalf of imperiled African Americans. Indeed, the two cases prompted the NAACP to establish a formal legal department and organize permanent local vigilance committees to defend the darker race. The *Crisis* recounted the organization's many endeavors to challenge the legality of segregation, including confrontations over Jim Crow municipal zoning laws, discrimination in education and professional organizations, segregation in transportation, and suppression of the black vote. The local committees, founded first in New York and Chicago, Baltimore and Boston, Philadelphia and Washington, DC, quickly became independent branches of the NAACP, and accounts of their vigilance along the color line revealed the existence of a vibrant network of Talented Tenth agitation—in which the neighbors on the Hill eagerly wished to participate.

Colored Wilmington observed the emergence of the NAACP with admiration. "I am impressed by the splendid work you are doing in putting forth a paper that is worth while in the highest sense of the word," Alice Dunbar-Nelson wrote with approbation in a letter sent to W. E. B. Du Bois at the *Crisis*, not five months after the "Record of the Darker Races" was first published. The former Mrs. Paul Dunbar, herself an author, English instructor at Wilmington's Howard High School, and avowed member of the Talented Tenth, professed her approval of the strident tone of the NAACP's new periodical.

> It is bromidic to say that it "fills a long-felt want," but that is just what it does. Definite facts presented without exaggeration and shrieking comment; a square and honest way of looking at the situation, without hysterical unbalance, and above all the *truth*, be it pleasant or unpleasant, is what Negro journalism has wanted for many years. . . . May THE CRISIS live long and accomplish its mission.

As news of the NAACP's endeavors arrived each month in the *Crisis*, the Talented Tenth in Wilmington was ready to mobilize.[22]

The branch began, informally at least, in 1912, with Alice Dunbar-Nelson and Lewis Redding among the founding members. That year, they and a small group of ministers and homemakers, teachers and physicians, and at least one hairdresser, began meeting regularly on the Hill. They gathered in one another's parlors for social conversation but also to discuss how best to support the NAACP. Alice Dunbar-Nelson wrote directly to W. E. B. Du Bois late that year explaining her group's interest in raising funds for the NAACP locally. Yet even while she appreciated the urgency of supporting the national office in New York, she knew that her own city, too, deserved attention. To begin with, she estimated, "We have about 8000 Negroes here and only about 100 of them buy the *Crisis*, and about one hundred and twenty-five read their friends' copies." To improve this ratio, she suggested "a campaign of education here." By March 1913, when the *Crisis* began publishing regular reports of local branch news, there was monthly proof of a movement among the Talented Tenth. With eleven branches chartered at the end of 1912, the NAACP's membership, though a modest 1,100, remained unswervingly committed to confronting the Jim Crow order. A local branch in Wilmington, too, could surely check segregation in Delaware.[23]

The founding members of the Wilmington NAACP understood the critical nature of such a fight in Delaware. Though never a part of the Confederacy, Delaware had been a slave state through the Civil War and revealed "its strange attitude," as Alice Dunbar-Nelson described it, of supporting the Union while rebuffing legislation designed to protect African American citizenship. Following the war, as the nation struggled to define the terms of black freedom, the state voted to reject the Thirteenth, Fourteenth, and Fifteenth Amendments. Though each amendment was eventually ratified, through the late nineteenth century Delaware witnessed vigorous and continuous attempts to deny its black minority the rights of citizenship. The state's powerful Democratic bloc, in control of the state legislature during the decades following the Civil War, sequestered African Americans to the margins of civic life. Between 1873 and 1897 a poll tax requirement (known as the Assessment and Collections Law of 1873) effectively disenfranchised the state's black voters, thus guaranteeing the dominance of the Democratic Party, the party of white supremacy during the origins of the Jim Crow era. Wincing at the prospect of funding black education, in 1875 the state's Democrats created a separate tax on colored citizens for their own segregated schools. Refusing the possibility of integrated public education, in 1875 the state went a step further by passing legislation that permitted the segregation of public accommodations and transportation. "That is not to say that there are separate street or railway cars or waiting rooms," Alice Dunbar-Nelson explained nearly fifty years after the bill's passage, "but restaurants and soda fountains, except in rare instances, will not serve Negroes, nor will theatres admit them, save in one or two instances, and then only to the gallery." Beyond public accommodations, de facto segregation drew color lines through the neighborhoods of Wilmington, and discriminatory hiring practices constrained black Delawareans overwhelmingly to unskilled labor and domestic service. During the first decades of the twentieth century, restricted educational opportunities for black Delawareans did little to erase the color line in employment.[24]

Even in Delaware, to violate the mores of Jim Crow was to risk death. The 1903 lynching of George White underscored the reach of racial violence beyond the old Confederacy and affirmed the strength of white supremacy. By the early twentieth century, as a glance at the solemn tally recorded in the first issues of the *Crisis* revealed, a black man or woman was lynched every two or three days. When white Americans took note of lynching, it was mainly with the grim understanding that its victims deserved the rough justice they received. That was true, as the anti-lynching crusader Ida B. Wells contended, because most believed in the "old threadbare lie" that black men posed a ubiquitous threat to white women. Gruesome extralegal retribution was the only means to prevent the bestial black fiend from ravishing white ladies of the South. More likely, as Wells's 1890s investigations clarified, the victims of lynching had somehow defied the etiquette of the prevailing racial order. A misstep on the sidewalk. Eye contact on a streetcar. A prideful countenance. Or, most damning, willingness to confront the constraints of segregation. Any perceived breach of the color line sufficed to justify the lynch mob.

It was not evidence that damned George White; it was that "old threadbare lie." When Helen Bishop, a white eighteen-year-old, was discovered near death along the road to Price's Corner in June 1903, about a mile outside of Wilmington, Delaware, she was alone. No one had seen her attack, though several witnesses claimed to have seen George White, a twenty-four-year-old black laborer, in the vicinity several hours earlier. White's landlord said she recognized a knife found near Bishop; a search of White's workplace turned up a cap said to be the murdered girl's. That was enough. White was quickly detained. When the municipal court schedule delayed his trial until September, however, frustration simmered among white Delawareans. Within a week, and after at least two attempts to kidnap White from the county workhouse, hundreds of men thronged the jail, succeeded in extracting him, and then manhandled White to a bonfire at Price's Corner, the scene of the assault on Helen Bishop. A crowd of thousands waited. White reportedly screamed "mercy" as he was bludgeoned; one blow severed his right foot. After he collapsed into the flames, his life extinguished, revolver shots were fired into the corpse. Once it cooled, White's body was dismembered, ransacked for grisly trophies, his skull and right foot spirited back to Wilmington to be displayed in the window of a downtown tavern, a macabre token of white supremacy.

This chilling showcase on Market Street did not mark an end to the violence. Though only one man was held for the murder of George White, a white crowd numbering in the thousands gathered at the Wilmington city hall to demand his release. Once he was freed, some members of the mob then turned on black spectators and passersby, a number of whom had assembled to protest the authorities' lack of vigor in responding to White's lynching. "Every Negro that chanced to get in their way was forced to fly to escape a possible beating," one reporter observed. Though one black man was killed in the lawless scene, and dozens of others sustained wounds, as the *Wilmington Evening Journal* reported, the only "rioters" to receive "heavy sentences" were African Americans. Like the lynching of George White, the riotous aftermath would close without a trace of justice.

In Delaware, the white press reacted with a pretense of horror when known members of the lynch mob avoided prosecution. In fact, Wilmington's papers had in part incited and then tacitly accepted the terrible miasma that poisoned the city in June 1903. Public indignation came instead from Wilmington's Talented Tenth. From the pulpit of the city's Bethel African Methodist Episcopal Church, Reverend Montrose Thornton denounced White's lynching as a consequence of white barbarity. Thornton even endorsed armed self-defense in the face of such terror. Yet the city's black leaders did not reach for Winchesters. Reasonably, some feared retribution for decrying the violence too avidly. Rather, they saw the lynching of George White and the ensuing attacks on blacks in Wilmington as enclosed within a wider scramble to assert control over the state's African Americans. For instance, during city elections held that June, just weeks before White's murder, the Democratic Party had called for a formal end to black suffrage. In the face of this challenge, Rev. Thornton, for one, decided that protecting African Americans' right to vote, not brandishing rifles, would best ensure black liberty. The following spring Thornton therefore helped organize a statewide Negro Convention, held in Dover, determined to protect even the limited civic freedoms extended to black Delawareans. Representing Delaware's Talented Tenth, members of the March 1904 meeting issued a collective protest "against any effort to degrade and humiliate our race by the deprivation of any of our rights and privileges."

Though some among his French Street congregation recoiled at Thornton's militancy—and after the violence of June 1903, endorsing such a statement assuredly was militant—the state would never officially strip black men of the franchise. It is not certain that the stance of the 1904 Negro Convention alone stilled talk of the outright disfranchisement of black voters. That the black electorate offered the Republican Party the chance for majority power in the state was certainly a significant factor. Regardless, no statement issued from the Talented Tenth entirely thwarted white supremacy. Even if no lynching occurred again in the state, colored Delaware lacked full equality before the law, leaving the possibility of a legal lynching. When two black teenagers from Georgetown, in southernmost Sussex County, who were falsely accused of murdering a white boy were sentenced to death in 1911, an all-white judge and jury might have had the equivalent result as mob law, but with the façade of fairness. In this instance, as in the cases of Pink Franklin and Steve Green, legal counsel from the national office of the NAACP arrived and fought to reduce the teenagers' sentences to life in prison. This was not justice, precisely, but the two boys lived.[25]

The Talented Tenth in Wilmington wished to improve this fragile state of freedom. Shortly after a visit by Joel Spingarn, then on a speaking touring to promote the "New Abolitionism," eight neighbors from Tenth Street Hill signed the application that turned their parlor meetings into official musters of the Wilmington branch of the NAACP. On the last day of November 1914, the Wilmington NAACP was formed, pledging "To uplift the colored men and women of this country by securing to them the full enjoyment of their rights as citizens, justice in all courts, and equality of opportunity everywhere." Alice Dunbar-Nelson and several other African American women initially led the branch, serving in all four executive positions. Elizabeth Williams America, a hairdresser, took the helm as the first branch president. Howard High School teachers Anna Broadnax and Alice Baldwin were vice president and secretary, respectively. Their principal, Edwina Kruse, was the branch's first treasurer. Together the women of the Wilmington NAACP, in the words of Edwina Kruse, "had the matter of our association at heart" and understood the imperative to react to "the growth of prejudice against our race." Wilmington's new branch members intended to accomplish more than just sending dues to the New York office. The Wilmington NAACP would be a model of determined action, and it took little time to identify a target for their inaugural campaign.[26]

In the spring of 1915 the theatrical release of D. W. Griffith's film *The Birth of a Nation* provided the branch with an instant rallying point. Based on Thomas Dixon's 1905 novel *The Clansman*, an ode to white supremacy set during Reconstruction, the film vividly illustrated the rationale behind the American racial order. *The Birth of a Nation* portrayed black political participation during Reconstruction as a dismal mockery of American democracy, a travesty from which the Ku Klux Klan heroically saved the republic. Most likely to stir filmgoers' passions was Griffith's exploitation of the sexual fears at the crux of American racism. The film brought to leering, dramatic life the violent threat black men ostensibly posed to southern white women, a threat long used to justify both segregation and lynch law. While critics denounced Griffith's picture as deliberate race baiting, President Wilson (a former classmate of Thomas Dixon's at Johns Hopkins University) expressed visceral awe at the film's visual narrative: "It is like writing history with lightning. And my only regret is that it is all so terribly true." Understandably, the film's romantic retelling of the rise of the Ku Klux Klan and its vicious portrayal of African Americans raised the ire of the national NAACP. The cogency of this new medium was especially worrisome, to the point that Association leaders such as W. E. B. Du Bois and Joel Spingarn advocated censorship of the film. This position was not taken lightly. But with white Houston theatergoers hollering "lynch him" at black characters; with the murder of a black fifteen-year-old following a screening in Lafayette, Indiana; and with the film inspiring the 1915 rebirth of the Ku Klux Klan in Stone Mountain, Georgia, banning *The Birth of a Nation* appeared to be an issue of public safety.[27]

Wilmington NAACP members were likewise troubled and joined the wider Association campaign to ban *The Birth of a Nation* from local theaters. The May issue of the *Crisis* arrived on Tenth Street Hill with an inspiring account of the Association's efforts to censor the film. The Los Angeles NAACP, the first chapter to learn of the film, had begun the protests, followed quickly by New York and Brooklyn. In between, branches from Des Moines to Cleveland were moved to join the fight. But "the center of the fight," the *Crisis* reported, "has been Boston," where, as the accompanying photograph illustrated, one afternoon rally had not only filled Tremont Temple, a seat of nineteenth-century abolitionism but had flooded into the Boston Common as well. By the time the June *Crisis* appeared, recounting even more branch news, the Wilmington NAACP had been similarly impelled. Like its counterparts nationwide, the Wilmington chapter did not want something so alarmingly racist screened in their city. To keep the film out of theaters they could not even themselves enter, members quickly turned to Wilmington's sole black city councilor, John O. Hopkins. Between them, Hopkins and the Wilmington NAACP drafted a city ordinance "to prohibit the exhibition of any moving picture likely to cause ill feeling between the white and black races." When the Wilmington City Council passed the measure in May 1915, the branch had demonstrated its commitment to taking concerted action in the local civil rights movement. No small victory, the effort prevented the showing of *The Birth of a Nation* and spurred support for the local branch of the NAACP.[28]

By the end of the Wilmington NAACP's first full year, no parlor on Tenth Street Hill, however large, was spacious enough anymore for branch meetings. Without a permanent home, during 1915 the branch rotated its "well attended" events among several public spaces and churches downtown, including a mass meeting that reportedly "taxed the standing capacity of the Odd Fellow[s]' Hall." Throughout the year, growing audiences enjoyed an encore appearance by Joel Spingarn, as well as renowned speakers such as Mrs. Butler R. Wilson, wife of Boston's distinguished Negro attorney and a driving force in the Boston branch of the NAACP, and William Pickens, then dean of Morgan State College in Baltimore and himself a leader in that city's own powerful local branch. By 1916, the appeal of such lectures, in addition to its successful *Birth of a Nation* campaign, had helped the Wilmington NAACP attract enough support that membership leaped from the original eight to 240.[29]

That December, the *Wilmington Morning News* took special note of the growing local chapter. A reporter on hand for the branch's "first public mass meeting of the season" held at the National Theatre on French Street near the Hill (owned by councilman Hopkins, it was the only city theater open to blacks) found the venue "crowded to its doors," its hall overflowing with an audience who "represented the best element in the city among the colored people." Inside, the keynote speaker, Leslie Pinkney Hill, a Pennsylvania educator and charter member of the national NAACP, engaged the teeming theater with a lecture based in part on his reading of W. E. B. Du Bois's recently published book, *The Negro*. Many in the audience, presumably, had noticed the full-page advertisement the *Crisis* had been running each month for the past year describing the work as an "authentic romance of the black man," a history "at once scholarly, earnest and eloquent." Hill appended this history with verve, attempting to match his fellow Harvard alum's erudite flair, and borrowing liberally from Du Bois's synthetic revision of the history of the darker race across both civilizations and continents. Hill felt "proud," he announced to Wilmington that afternoon, "not only to be a member of the association, but to be member of the colored race." He was filled with "the pride which every self-respecting man ought to have in the race and what it means to be a member of a race, which has its historic beginning back in the earliest age of the history of the world." But with such pride came duty. Though a minority appreciated the "modern problems" facing the Negro, Hill announced that it was his own responsibility, and indeed that of all black Americans, to "help themselves" by confronting the challenges "forced upon [them] by the past three hundred years." If the effect of his reading may not have quite equaled the sight of the goateed, aristocratic Du Bois, whose very carriage gave reason for such "pride in the race," even Hill's paraphrase met appreciative ears and nodding heads.[30]

The message reverberated beyond the walls of National Theater. As if taking Hill's gospel of racial pride public, that month the Wilmington NAACP expressed "indignation on account of the Wilmington press in writing the word Negro with a small letter [n]." Several members joined in a committee to challenge the spelling. Though it may have seemed an innocuous practice to local editors, the demeaning small "n" spelling chafed against African American readers' self-respect, just as the simian depictions of blacks in *The Birth of a Nation* had. No doubt each member found inspiration for this endeavor when the February *Crisis* arrived. In it, Du Bois himself explained the necessity of printing "Negro" properly. "Not to capitalize Negro," he stormed, "is a direct, and in these days a more and more conscious, insult to at least 15,000,000 human beings and no person or institution will persist in this insult if these people regard the usage as such." In other words, it was critical that such groups as the Wilmington NAACP make the insult plain. Over the next several weeks, branch members met with a group of editors and succeeded in convincing much of "the press of the city to capitalize the word Negro."[31]

Here the branch publicly matched private, ongoing efforts among blacks in Wilmington, such as the training Edwina Kruse's Howard High School offered the younger generation in becoming capital-N Negroes. The previous summer, in fact, the audience at the Howard commencement had applauded declamations on "The Negro's Civil, Political and Social Rights" and "The Negro in American History," each addressing the culmination of lessons in both scholarship and self-respect. But instilling youth with a sense of dignity began, too, within individual households, an effort that had not missed at the two-story, red-brick edifice at 203 East Tenth Street where the Lewis Reddings lived. They were "an upper-class Negro family," the Reddings' youngest son later wrote, with parents "deeply sensitive to the tradition of ridicule and inferiority to color." Both mother and father were determined that no color line would restrict their children's future. Each, beginning with Louis, was "trained at home in the declining art of oratory," and, as a rule, were "regularly contestants for prizes at school." Such preparation both Redding's mother, raised among the black middle class of Alexandria, Virginia, and his rural-Maryland-reared and Howard University–trained father deemed essential if their two sons and two daughters were ever to surmount the dual obstacles of race prejudice and segregation. Papa was reminded of the alternative to capital-N success whenever his mail route took him to his less fortunate neighbors down near the eastern bend of the Brandywine Creek. No, Lewis Redding's children would live on the Hill.[32]

Louis, the eldest, took the first steps, walking each school day from his house to the corner of Tenth and Orange, where he passed the city's lily-white YMCA, and then walking two blocks on Orange to Howard High School. Howard High, among the nation's finer colored high schools, trained the sons and daughters of the Wilmington Talented Tenth, but was also a reminder of the segregation manifest in the state's educational system. The majority of black Delawareans paid high tax rates for chronically underfunded, dilapidated, segregated schools. During the 1910s, as Louis Redding advanced through his school years, the typical single-room rural school in Delaware offered only the most rudimentary training during an abbreviated academic year. To white Delaware that was enough. But as the *Crisis* noted in 1915, "the wretched condition of the colored schools" had aroused "the colored people of Delaware" to demand reform. In 1917, when Pierre S. du Pont, a leading white philanthropist and vice president of the State Board of Education, first proposed reforming the state education system, the prospect of improving black education instigated bitter political debate. For several years local elections hinged on the "School Code Fight," as white voters wavered over whether or not to accept Pierre du Pont's personal pledge of five million dollars to improve the state's schools on the condition of ending discriminatory funding based on segregated taxes and improving black teachers' salaries. The state legislature's rejection of the plan recalled the long-held sentiment that, as the governor of Delaware had expressed it in 1866, "all attempts to elevate the negro to the social or political equality is the result either of wicked fanaticism or a blind and perverse infidelity, subversive of the ends for which this government was established, and contrary to the doctrines and teachings of our fathers."[33]

While Delawareans debated the merits of separate schools, Redding met his parents' expectations, becoming an honor student in Howard High School's Fiftieth Anniversary class. His success in school depended upon more than his parents' influence, on more even than his own hard work. The resident of the house across the street from the Reddings, at 206 East Tenth, Edwina Kruse, as principal of Howard since 1876, had pushed for excellence from her student body and faculty alike. Kruse knew well one of the unintended ironies of segregation, and used it to her advantage. Because segregation blocked even the most talented African Americans from teaching positions in any but segregated school systems, Kruse was able to recruit particularly gifted instructors to lead the small high school classes at Howard. The staff she compiled held degrees from Oberlin, Radcliffe, Pembroke, Cornell, and the University of Pennsylvania. To Redding the "well prepared teachers" Kruse hired were important not just because of the knowledge they imparted but also because they "were highly conscious that they had an obligation to do their best for the pupils." Under Kruse the faculty worked with a "curriculum," one of Louis Redding's Howard classmates remembered, "that consisted solely of an academic course which was extensive and compulsory and that the smallness of the classes permitted almost individual attention." (Redding would remark in retrospect, "We had some damned good teachers," each "a real source of inspiration for anyone who wanted to be inspired" and keen on preparing their students for "colleges everywhere.") By his sophomore year, Redding's courses included Latin, mathematics, English, and foreign languages, and his math teacher, a Pembroke graduate, was already encouraging him to attend Brown University.[34]

By the late 1910s such advancements in the Redding household became interwoven with the progress of the civil rights struggle, nationally and locally. After the nationwide *Birth of a Nation* campaign and the success of the 1916 Amenia Conference, the NAACP welcomed the establishment of scores of new branches, maintained its staunch commitment to ending lynching, and even scored seminal Supreme Court victories in *Guinn v. US*, which struck down the Oklahoma "grandfather clause" that had prevented thousands of African Americans in that state from voting, and *Buchanan v. Worley*, which overturned residential segregation statues in Baltimore, Louisville, and New Orleans, among other southern cities. The Wilmington branch broadened its own programs, agitating for greater equality in the state's education system, and instituting new campaigns to address poor blacks' housing conditions and to add a black police officer to the city's force. Legal efforts proved more difficult to undertake. While the national office had at its disposal a cadre of prominent attorneys competent enough to address the Supreme Court, the Wilmington branch had few legal allies within the state and stood on decidedly unequal footing inside local courthouses. Delaware had no black lawyers and, as yet, no prospective candidates. No African Americans served on juries, and judges and bailiffs alike even kept seating in local courtrooms strictly segregated. But as the news of the Association's national legal campaigns arrived each month in the *Crisis*, Wilmington's branch members knew that the success of their own local movement depended on developing a legal program.[35]

"It matters not what our cases may be," wrote Rev. H. Y. Arnett, a branch member who opened his church to Association functions; "we feel that we have not a fair show when we cannot engage a colored lawyer." The issue weighed heavy on his fellow branch members. "We are studying now how best to get even handed justice in the courts," Arnett reported to the national office in 1918, "in regard to the seating" and concerning the desegregation of the bar. The effort to erase the color line in the courts would certainly follow the precedent set during earlier campaigns. Then, as with this new endeavor, the Wilmington NAACP insisted on citywide recognition of black dignity. But opening the bar to black lawyers would require greater concessions than earlier efforts to ban *The Birth of a Nation* and to capitalize "Negro" had won. Still, coming off earlier successes, the Wilmington NAACP was hopeful of achieving this admittedly less symbolic advance.[36]

With no proper candidates for the bar available, the branch began in the Wilmington courts. Conveniently, challenging "the segregation of Negroes in the Court Rooms" did not confront any statutes preventing integration. No such law existed. The branch was thus saved the hurdle of striking down a law upholding segregation, a task beyond its means. Yet it would prove just as difficult to alter a presiding judge's habit of seating blacks off to the right side of the gallery. The effort to desegregate Wilmington courts squarely faced the decades-long denial of full citizenship to the state's African Americans. Adding to the difficulty, black Wilmington's influence as a voting bloc appeared worthless. The bench did not need black votes the way the city's ward Republicans did; nor did Wilmington Republicans seem to have much fear that African Americans would defect to the Democrats. Without a legal argument or political bounty to offer, then, the branch was left with attempts at moral suasion—personal appeals to individual judges to repeal segregation in their courtrooms. Such petitions, apparently, could be easily ignored. No matter the degree of the Wilmington NAACP's diligence, frustration followed. "Not much has been accomplished as yet," explained an update sent to the national office in New York in 1918. Even so, it remained committed to the campaign its members thought so essential to black advancement. Despite disappointment, the branch was determined to persist in the coming year, "to stick to it if it 'takes all summer.'" Fortitude alone, though, was not enough. The Wilmington NAACP could claim no progress on this front by 1919, when Louis Redding, to the satisfaction of his community on Tenth Street Hill, left for college.[37]

After graduating with honors from Howard High School, Louis Redding left a group of his cheering neighbors at Wilmington's downtown depot, stepping up into the train he would ride to Providence, Rhode Island. He departed from Wilmington with more than upcoming academic challenges to consider. Papa

likely reminded him of his greater responsibility to his race. "Son," as Lewis
Redding would say to his youngest son a few years later, "remember you're a
Negro. You'll have to do twice as much twice as better than your classmates.
Before you act, think how what you do may reflect on other Negroes. Those
white people will be judging the race by you. Don't let the race down, Son." The
care with which Louis needed to frame his actions, both parents believed, began
with choosing his course of study. "There were just two professions," Redding
later recalled, that were acceptable to his parents, "the law or medicine." Either
career might give their son the opportunity to live a little less bound by the color
line, offering the trappings of respectability and the potential to earn a living not
afforded most African Americans. When Redding arrived at Brown he pursued
medicine and for the next two years intended to become a doctor. But by his
junior year he switched his major from biology to English.[38]

That decision reflected developments within the Wilmington branch of the
NAACP. Back home, on Tenth Street Hill, Lewis Redding had accepted the
branch presidency and with it the five-year-old campaign to integrate the Delaware bar. Black Delawareans could practice medicine, the new branch president
knew, but they were still waiting for their first lawyer. Who better to cross the
color line than his talented oldest son? Significantly, that same year the Wilmington NAACP gained new leverage in its assault on Jim Crow during the fallout
following the national fight to pass federal anti-lynching legislation. In 1922 the
national NAACP watched a federal anti-lynching bill sponsored by Representative Leonidas Dyer, a St. Louis Republican, pass through the House of Representatives, only to slowly perish in the Senate. The Dyer Anti-Lynching Bill had
wide approval—from the American Bar Association and from leading jurists,
who assured the Senate of the bill's constitutionality. Yet between January and
July the bill labored even to get out of the Senate Judiciary Committee. Writing
in the Crisis, W. E. B. Du Bois declared it a "great victory achieved" when the
Dyer bill was at last placed on the Senate's late-summer legislative agenda, and
he urged his readers to demand the support of their elected representatives. The
legislation would be a landmark, offering reparations of up to $10,000 and fed-
eral recognition of the violent scourge that had taken the life of thousands since
the 1860s, including George White in 1903. "Every voter, and especially colored
voters, must keep these facts clearly in mind!" Du Bois declared. "And, more
importantly, we must keep them clearly in the minds of our senators!" NAACP
branches from Colorado to West Virginia composed resolutions for their states'
Republican Conventions, but to no avail. When the Dyer bill at last reached the
floor of the Senate in September, many Republicans simply walked out of the
chamber. The bill's challengers quickly called for a quorum. When only twenty-
seven answered, discussion of the legislation was postponed until after the
November elections—that is, the bill was left for dead. The NAACP knew the

Dyer bill had the greatest chance of gaining the Senate's approval before the elections, when, assuredly, Republican candidates needed the support of African American voters. NAACP executives James Weldon Johnson and Walter White had tactfully impressed upon the party the importance of the bill to the black electorate, but the bargain was plain: pass the Dyer bill and expect African American voters to support the party in November. If Republicans "laughed at" the Association's tactics, the *Crisis* was satisfied to note that "some of those who laughed have found that the threat was not an idle one." After the bill's failure, the *Crisis* identified those congressmen who deserved to lose their seats in Washington, including Delaware representative Caleb Layton, who opposed the Dyer bill, and Senator T. Coleman du Pont, who refused to answer the crucial September roll call. On the matter of voting the traitors out, Du Bois, for one, was adamant. "In the next two years," he wrote, "the Republican Party expects us to forget that they have failed and deceived us; but if we Black voters, male and female, forget what the Republican party did to the Dyer Bill, we deserve disfranchisement now and forever."[39]

On Tenth Street Hill, colored Wilmington concurred. In Delaware, the Wilmington NAACP was one of several groups (along with the Anti-Lynching Crusaders of Delaware, the Independent Citizens' Voters League, and the Anti-Layton League, to name a few) dedicated to electoral justice. The recent enfranchisement of women voters only gave branch members like Alice Dunbar-Nelson added incentive to pursue a leading role in the campaign. Black voters could tilt the balance of power in Delaware, and, like Du Bois, Dunbar-Nelson, the first African American woman on the State Republican Committee of Delaware, advocated stern retribution. During the August 1922 Delaware State Republican Convention, black Republicans insisted that the party jettison Layton for his refusal to support the Dyer bill. Instead, Layton was renominated and three black members of the Republican Committee were forced out. Infuriated by this betrayal, Dunbar-Nelson helped coordinate a statewide campaign to dump Layton. Election meetings were held throughout the state, including public rallies featuring national NAACP officers James Weldon Johnson, Walter White, and Robert Bagnall, as well as the National Association of Colored Women's Mary B. Talbert, founder of the Anti-Lynching Crusaders, which represented roughly one million women nationwide. At such rallies, over 20,000 anti-Layton leaflets, pamphlets, and flyers demanding the congressman's ouster were distributed to black voters. The November results reflected the influence of Delaware's infuriated African American voters. Representative Layton, as the *Crisis* recounted with evident satisfaction, "was defeated by a vote of between six and seven thousand, a difference which is just about equal to the loss of colored votes." Senator du Pont likewise suffered a humiliating, albeit less decisive, defeat. For the first time in a quarter century, political sway statewide shifted toward the Democrats.

Similar scenarios played out in New Jersey, Michigan, and Wisconsin, where black voters swept out elected officials either indifferent or hostile to the Dyer bill. To Alice Dunbar-Nelson, the lesson for black Delawareans was obvious: "Organize, organize and again organize. Then vote for men who are friends to the race, irrespective of party or political superstition. And let the organization of our own race be so strong and compact that it will be felt as a force wherever the Negro has the vote."[40]

Thus organized, and with Lewis Redding at the helm, the Wilmington NAACP turned to the desegregation of the Delaware bar.

On College Hill, Louis Redding seemed a promising candidate. Compiling a record Brown University would call "enviable," by 1922 he was among the university's more distinguished students—and not simply for his newfound appreciation for Brooks Brothers tailoring and the taste of a fine cigarette. In October of his senior year he was cited during the school's first University Honor Day. The careful preparation his Oberlin- and Radcliffe-trained instructors offered at Howard High School had proved indispensable. His early successes in Delaware speaking contests had evidently provided useful preparation, as well, for he had also earned a reputation as one of the most gifted orators on campus. During the spring term of his junior year he won honors for elocution, collecting the Second Carpenter Prize. Among the flush of accolades he received at Brown, Redding's capping triumph came during his final semester, when he won the Gaston Medal, "one of the most coveted prizes on the Hill," as the student newspaper buzzed. Before a Manning Hall auditorium brimming with students and faculty (including an admiring class in public speaking) Redding delivered an original paper on "The Significance of Booker T. Washington." According to the discerning ears of one student reporter, he "spoke with a mellowness of tone and enunciated perfectly." More importantly, the judges concurred; they announced his victory after a performance by the Varsity Quartet. Redding had trumped two of the university's most accomplished students, including its star debater and the school's next Rhodes scholar, becoming the first African American to take the Gaston medal. His prize came not just with a one-hundred-dollar honorarium but also with a spot on the Commencement Day program.[41]

In June, with his Gaston essay in hand, Louis Redding took the podium in the Meeting Hall before the Brown University Class of '23. In the crowd that day, Lewis Redding was overcome by the honor his son had earned and by recollections of his own commencement speech at Howard University nearly thirty years earlier. While his father "cried for joy," the younger Redding spoke on the foremost Negro leader of his father's generation. Although his was an NAACP family, Redding appreciated the "demonstration of personal greatness" that Booker T. Washington, the ex-slave who founded the Tuskegee Institute, had embodied. "This man, born without patrimony or name," Redding marveled, had nonetheless left "a vast heritage," a legacy much "magnified by being shared among the thousands." Redding's words showed his fealty to both self-improvement and to social uplift, lessons that Papa and his instructors at Howard High had also hoped to impart. They served, too, as an homage not just to Washington but to an entire generation of African Americans who had made the most of freedom—and to his father in particular, who had raised himself from Maryland-shore farmhand to middle-class postman. In these words, Redding recognized at once his debt and his duty; like his predecessors, he hoped to also bequeath a legacy of his own to be "shared among the thousands."[42]

He decided (and Papa agreed) to begin back home, in Wilmington, where the Talented Tenth continued to combat the threat of Jim Crow. During the summer of 1923, in the face of just one such menace, Lewis Redding addressed the Wilmington City Council on behalf of the NAACP, insisting that the Ku Klux Klan be denied permission to rally on the steps of the Wilmington Municipal Building. Revived in 1915, by the early 1920s the KKK declared itself an "Invisible Empire," claiming a national membership above three million, dominating state politics in Oregon and Indiana, and marching in Maine and Michigan, states disturbingly distant from the Klan's 1866 origins in the former Confederacy. The Wilmington NAACP was rightfully wary of the growth of the Klan in Delaware. The hooded knights were especially active in the rural, Democratic counties downstate. Redding warned the City Council "that riotous acts might be provoked" by a Klan rally downtown. Council members perhaps recalled the mayhem following the lynching of George White twenty summers earlier; the Talented Tenth certainly had not forgotten. Permitting the Klan on the steps of the Municipal Building would be an unconscionable endorsement of white supremacy, not to mention an affront to the city's black electorate. The latter point, it seems, helped keep the Klan at bay. As Alice Dunbar-Nelson remarked to the national NAACP, she "had it on good information" that city leaders, including the mayor, were Klan members but were "afraid to show themselves for fear of losing Negro and Jewish votes."[43]

Louis Redding returned home that summer with plans of studying law. The only hindrance to such a plan was financing it. With two of his siblings already attending college, he knew his father could little afford the added expense of tuition for law school. Redding would have to defray much of the cost on his own. But he found himself in the same position as had his highly trained instructors at Howard High School. Even someone with his impressive credentials, whose graduation from a prestigious Northeastern university had earned him an appearance in the pages of the annual "Education number" of the *Crisis*, had relatively few prospects to choose from. In the face of this circumstance, but also with that sense of racial responsibility Papa was always ready to remind him of, Redding accepted an offer from the American Missionary Association, taking a position as assistant principal and instructor of English at the Fessenden Academy, a black secondary school eight miles outside the town of Ocala, Florida.[44]

Nothing like the leafy quads of College Hill greeted him in Ocala. Instead, Redding stepped from his segregated train car into flat, oppressively hot central Florida in midsummer. Fessenden Academy, a former freedman's school devoted to industrial training, had since 1900 been run by the American Missionary Association. "Aunt Mary Ann," as Redding called the group, had overseen the modernization of the school's facilities and the inclusion of academic courses, but even by 1923 the academy continued agricultural courses that contrasted with Redding's classical training at Howard. This was not the only contrast Ocala offered. He had known humidity in Delaware, but in Florida, Redding wrote, any morning might bring "a veritable dog day," and with it, a "tenuous heat-haze" that "drifted in the vaguely quiet air."[45]

Yet rural Florida was a new climate in other ways as well. Redding learned there, as he would tersely describe it, "something of Negro life there where Negroes abound." No genteel enclave like his own "good" block back on the Hill, here Redding was thrust into proximity with a rural black culture he knew little of—and one that at home had disconcerted him. Back in Delaware he had dismissed the Big Quarterly, a traditional African American festival held each August in downtown Wilmington just blocks from his home, as an embarrassment. Like some others from his neighborhood, he resented the chance it gave white Wilmington to mock a black culture they perceived as primitive. In Florida that culture pervaded black life. Even church seemed strange to him in Ocala, leaving him an uneasy witness of rural, "uncivilized" congregations. Ultimately, he condemned not the congregants but the circumstances in which they worshipped for the church's character—Floridian segregation was just as oppressive as its heat. Avoiding specifics, segregation, he later recollected, "was followed to the hilt," far eclipsing what was found in Wilmington. In central Florida, the color line eased but once a year, during the annual county fair. Ironically, the discomfort he may have felt at such an occasion in Delaware yielded to satisfaction as he and several friends "took full advantage of this no segregation thing." Like many of his generation, Redding had journeyed south to teach, but Ocala had offered an education of its own.[46]

Hoping to leave the rural South, Redding accepted a position the next year to teach English in the high school division of Morehouse College in Atlanta. Although he found urban Georgia, like Ocala, to be "a very segregated place," he also had to admit that life in the city was "interesting." More tolerable, certainly, than rural Florida, yet, in some measure, more welcoming than even Wilmington, segregated Atlanta, with its black businesses and entertainments offered a kind of a buffer zone that had not existed back home, where only a block from his neighborhood African Americans had little to choose from among Jim Crow lunch counters and movie theaters. One of several black colleges located near downtown Atlanta, Morehouse offered Redding the new experience of a vibrant, urban black community. Not surprisingly, his new surroundings offered a better chance to keep up with his reading of the *Crisis* and the new black monthlies the *Messenger* and *Opportunity*. Though often filled with social science, *Opportunity* and the *Crisis*, in particular, offered Redding the possibility of keeping abreast, even from his dormitory room in Atlanta, of the wave in black arts and letters emanating from Harlem. Not long after he settled in at Morehouse, in fact, *Opportunity* announced a contest, conceived broadly, calling for submissions by Negro authors for Negro readers. Inspired, Redding drew from his recent experiences in Florida for an entry in the "personal experience sketch" category, and from his imagination for a short story submission.[47]

During the fall semester at Morehouse, Redding remained apprised of the continuing struggle along the color line in Delaware. In the radical black monthly the *Messenger*, his former English teacher, Alice Dunbar-Nelson, reported that while the Wilmington NAACP was "always on the alert" and continued to "see to it that The Birth of a Nation and pictures of like ilk would always be banished from the state," Jim Crow "custom and maneuver" kept blacks from practicing law and serving on juries. In the November 1924 issue of *Opportunity* Redding found Dunbar-Nelson's elaboration on the effects of this "most humiliating segregation." As she reported, "In the past several years three colored women and girls have been raped by white men." Despite rape being a capital crime in the state, "it is worthy of note that not one of the men charged with the heinous crime has been punished as the law provides. The charge is usually made a minor one, or a failure to indict remains." This, she observed with obvious understatement, "has added to the political unrest of the colored people."[48]

Indeed, in 1924 the Wilmington NAACP intervened in two such cases. In each instance the lack of adequate counsel proved a challenge. The first came in May, when the branch saw that a black woman accused of murdering a white policewoman was in danger of going undefended. When the lawyer the branch had retained from out of state did not file the paperwork necessary to represent a client in Delaware in time, this "point of law" left the accused without counsel. Stymied, Lewis Redding sought direction from the national office. But the NAACP could manage little support, offering only unhelpful advice: since "no Negro lawyers are allowed to practice in Delaware," the Wilmington chapter would do well to retain "a good lawyer" from outside the state because "local white lawyers might be prejudiced against the woman." The Wilmington NAACP was similarly hamstrung that September when local authorities had not charged a white man who had confessed to raping a black woman. Reporting the "miscarriage of justice to our people" to the national NAACP, branch president Redding again looked to the Association for guidance. Unable to send its own legal representative to Delaware, the national office urged the Wilmington branch to prevail upon the state government. "A large and representative delegation of intelligent colored people should call upon the Attorney General," was the response to Redding's appeal. They should arrive at the office with "a carefully prepared statement of the facts giving chronologically the history of the case and closing with an unequivocal demand for the punishment" of the confessed. "A spokesman" from the Wilmington NAACP "should make the demand verbally," lending personal weight to the petition. Meantime, the branch should begin a publicity campaign by sending copies of their statement "to the city editors of each local newspaper." Finally, should these acts of suasion fail, the Association offered a familiar refrain: "Engage the very best lawyer obtainable."[49]

When such efforts came to naught, the Wilmington NAACP redoubled its campaign to attain equal footing in the courts. Through the fall of 1924 and into the winter of 1925, "the Branch kept at work upon the Segregation in the Court rooms until it succeeded in getting that *abolished*," branch secretary Alice Baldwin reported. First, the branch appointed a committee to approach municipal court judge Daniel O. Hastings. Members had reason to suspect that Hastings could be persuaded. A former deputy attorney general and Delaware secretary of state, in 1911 Hastings had resigned his post as associate justice of the state Supreme Court with hopes of rising among the ranks of Delaware Republicans. Since that time he had served as special counsel for the state legislature and then as Wilmington's city solicitor, but Hastings had advanced little further. In a symbolic admission of defeat, in 1920 he accepted a place on the bench of the Wilmington municipal court. Still, his ambition had not wholly evaporated and after several meetings with branch members Hastings saw the advantages of courting Negro voters. With a mind to a future election, Hastings publicly announced the decision to desegregate his courtroom during a meeting of the Wilmington NAACP. Not entirely convinced, the branch decided to test the strength of Hastings's pledge—"to visit the courts to see what would happen," as the chapter secretary explained to the national NAACP. The first group to call at the court was chagrined to find they were gruffly directed to the right side of the gallery, where "'all your people belong.'" Hastings was not in court that day for them to confront in person, so the branch immediately posted a letter to him demanding clarification. Could the Wilmington NAACP "*know* whether or not he had abolished segregation" in his court? Attempting to allay the branch's concerns, and wishing to preserve the electoral support its members could deliver in the future, Hastings insisted that he would settle the matter to the Wilmington NAACP's satisfaction. Subsequent visitors in the following weeks found that "the officers [would] motion colored people to the right side," but none were "molested" when they refused.[50]

This partial victory for the Wilmington NAACP accompanied clearer tokens of personal success for Louis Redding. That May, he took two honorable mentions in the *Opportunity*-sponsored literary contest. By the time his two submissions appeared in October and December 1925, Redding had needed to put any writing career he may have privately coveted on hold. After nine months in Atlanta (and a summer working in the Chicago post office, no doubt arranged by Papa), Redding began his first year at Harvard Law School. Between settling into his rented room north of Harvard Yard in Cambridge and enduring the rigors of the first-year law student, he would not have the time to compose subsequent submissions. At Harvard, he did not garner the same accolades he had at Brown. Nonetheless, he made an impression on his professor of criminal law, Felix Frankfurter, a future Supreme Court justice who would come to refer to Redding as one of his most brilliant students, regardless of race. Clearly, black Wilmington had its lawyer-in-training.[51]

And none too soon. Despite the progress the branch had seemed to make the previous year, during the spring of 1926 the need for a local lawyer became indisputable yet again. Downstate, another attempted rape case involving a white assailant was dismissed; outraged, the NAACP spearheaded a mass meeting at Bethel AME Church denouncing the contemptible hypocrisy. In Wilmington, a group of black children and their teacher were denied entrance to one of the city's public parks. In both instances the Wilmington branch appealed to the national NAACP but received only the insistence that the group secure adequate local counsel. Discouragingly, the desegregation of the municipal court was also in doubt. This Redding himself experienced. That December, midway through his three-year program at Harvard, and more than a full year after Judge Hastings's assurances, Redding decided to spend one day of his holiday break observing the proceedings at the municipal court. After Redding took his seat, a bailiff appeared before him insisting he move to the right side of the gallery. Redding refused, preferring to exit with dignity than to remain without it. He would not return until 1928, this time with a degree from Harvard Law ready to be framed and hung—just as soon as he could begin a practice in the state.[52]

After seven years in the northeast and two in the deep South, Redding returned to Wilmington, twenty-seven years old, highly educated, and, above all, impatient with "the kind of proscription" he found in Delaware. Wilmington, in his candid description, was "a hell hole, in many regards" for blacks. But he had returned with intentions of changing that and, in fact, joined his father's branch of the NAACP as one of his first acts. He left law school, he later reflected, just one of a "generation of lawyers," though small in number, who worked "to abolish distinctions" whenever "those distinctions were based solely on color." Of course, in order to do so, he would first have to break the color line at the state bar. He put it politely in the pages of the *Crisis*. According to the Law Examining Board, he explained, "no former Negro applicant had satisfied the technical requirements for admission." As well as meeting a residence requirement and passing both the preliminary and final examinations "on the principles of law and equity," aspiring black lawyers faced two such "technicalities," both sure to prevent African Americans from practicing law in the state. Considering the required "certification of integrity and good moral character" and a six-month apprenticeship "in the office of a lawyer who has been in practice in the courts of Delaware for at least ten years," Redding dryly noted that it was "not difficult to understand that if a settled prejudice against Negroes did exist" these points "could be readily employed as an effective barrier to their admission." Yet he would try.[53]

Redding immediately passed the preliminary examinations. With certification of his character and a term of clerkship remaining, Lewis Redding called again on Judge Hastings. After several years of negotiating, Hastings had been the first Wilmington judge to agree to the admittedly fitful integration of his courtroom. Now came the time to convince him to desegregate the bar. "Colored people," wrote Alice Dunbar-Nelson, shortly after news of the meeting, "have hammered on that 'No Lawyers in Delaware' for a number of years," and it had been "one of the best campaign slogans against the existing administration that could ever have been invented." Having "hammered at it until the powers in charge turned green at the thought of the word lawyer," the NAACP branch president thus had a good opportunity—in addition, his well qualified son, newly arrived with the nation's most prestigious law degree, was certainly the best candidate imaginable. Hastings found the political stakes too great to ignore. Current Delaware senator T. Coleman du Pont, he knew, would soon leave his seat to convalesce after a long illness. With an eye to national concerns, the state party, too, needed black votes to defeat New York Democrat Al Smith in the upcoming presidential election. Conceding to such electoral circumstances, Hastings granted black Wilmington's long standing petition: he would proctor Louis Redding.[54]

"The ice," the *Wilmington Star* announced, "has been broken in Delaware." While it was a veritable event on Tenth Street Hill, the news even carried to Providence, Rhode Island, where Redding had attended Brown. The *Providence Journal* ran the headline "First Delaware Negro Lawyer in Making," and borrowed liberally from the *Star* press clipping. "Within the next year," the Wilmington news item read, "this State and, particularly, this city, will have a full-fledged Negro lawyer." Though others had "aspired to membership in the New Castle County Bar Association" it "remained for young Mr. Redding to break through the barrier of years and years standing."[55]

Following the news, Lewis Redding received visitors at his home, welcoming their congratulations on his son's success. And, initially, the younger Redding expressed enthusiasm about the arrangement. "In a few days," he wrote to a friend in early September, "I shall begin work in the office of the judge of the municipal court. I am eager for it." Now that he was to become the first to breach the color line, he believed that "in the future every Negro who qualifies for membership in the Delaware Bar will be admitted on the basis of that qualification." This, perhaps, might have counted as the sort of legacy he had referred to during his Brown commencement speech five years earlier. Not three weeks later, though, his eagerness to pursue the proctorship with Hastings had dissolved. One evening, during the first month of his clerkship, he walked over to the 900 block of French Street to call on his longtime friend Pauline Young, living at the time with her aunt, Alice Dunbar-Nelson. "Pauline had gone to Washington," Dunbar-Nelson noted in her diary later that night, but Redding "seemed to want to come in anyhow." He sat with his former teacher for "nearly two hours" before admitting what was so obviously distracting him during their conversation. "Something seemed on his mind," she noticed. "It came out just as he was leaving." September had not yet ended and he had "already discovered what kind of man Hastings is." Troubled not only by his mentor's character, Redding despaired even of his own. He worried that "he must compromise with his own soul if he is to remain in Hastings' office and 'get on.'" He considered ending the arrangement, but, Dunbar-Nelson knew, "his father [was] very keen on his being the 'first colored lawyer' in Delaware." Redding, "already wondering if the price he must pay in compromise" merited the "renunciation of ideals" necessary to work with Hastings, was not convinced the whole affair was "worth the dubious honor" of becoming the state's first black attorney. Not wishing "old man Redding thinking I have interfered with his affairs," Dunbar-Nelson avoided giving specific advice. She replied, rather, that this "was something he would have to fight out for himself."[56]

Hastings, apparently, had agreed to the proctorship in name only. Once it began, he refused to aid Redding one iota and even suggested that his would-be protégé make himself scarce whenever the judge visited the office. Despite understandable disappointment, Redding adapted to the circumstances. His dislike of Hastings grew as the judge's "ultraconservative scary" leanings became evident and as the judge's efforts to gain political office advanced. But the less they interacted, perhaps, the fainter the stain he would bear. Throughout the fall of 1928, Redding used Hastings's office only sparingly, studying instead at home on the Hill or in the Wilmington Law Library. By early December, when Hastings was awarded du Pont's Senate seat, Redding was completely on his own, free to supplement his law reviews with articles on the rights of African Americans.[57]

Then, seeking to rub off the tarnish from his proctor completely, Redding instituted the Open Door Forum. In part, he later confided in an interview, this was a "way of getting back" at Hastings, by having "this forum where there were not such conservative people." But the forum also filled the void left by the NAACP branch, whose membership had dwindled by the late 1920s. Assuming the presidency of the organization, he convinced the principal of Howard High School to join as vice president and to allow them to use the school's auditorium. Redding's friend Pauline Young, a school librarian, served as secretary. Meeting on Sunday afternoons between the fall and spring, the group hoped to give Wilmington's citizens an opportunity to bridge the interests between the Talented Tenth and, in Redding's words, members of the "great Negro mass." To do so, they invited speakers ranging from such black luminaries as W. E. B. Du Bois and Howard University professor Alain Locke to other notables like William Jones, managing editor of the *Baltimore Afro-American*, who addressed the group in March 1929 to discuss the "Present Trend of Negro Journalism."[58]

When William Jones visited the Howard High auditorium, he arrived to a Wilmington buzzing about the Open Door Forum president. That week, the city's papers reported Redding's success before the New Castle County bar. Intrigued, Jones rewrote the item for his own Maryland weekly. "Redding," he reported upon his return to Baltimore, "has just passed his law examinations with high honors." After taking "the test with other candidates for the bar about two weeks ago," he awaited only the formality of appearing before the Delaware Supreme Court. Redding himself told Jones that he expected "no difficulty" and would indeed, as his father had long hoped, become the state's "first colored lawyer." Canvassing Redding's friends and acquaintances, Jones found that his hometown regarded him as "an outstanding type of his race." Indeed, he wrote, "his leadership in the civic and educational life of the city" had already made "a deep impression" on the city's black leaders; undoubtedly, the work he had already accomplished "assured his success" in the future.[59]

But it became apparent that he would need continued perseverance when the Delaware Supreme Court convened in April. During the oath, Justice James Pennewill singled Redding out, offering him a few solemn words on the occasion of his integrating the Delaware bar. "Young man," Pennewill said, avoiding the salutation the ever-formal Mr. Redding no doubt preferred, "I hope that by your conduct as a lawyer, you will justify your admission today." In Pennewill's words echoed unmistakable, prevailing assumptions about black inferiority that the Wilmington NAACP had longed to stamp out. "I will," Redding must have responded, either in words, or by an unsmiling nod. He kept to himself, of course, his own ideas of what sort of conduct would justify his admission to the guild of Delaware lawyers.[60]

The aspirations of Redding's white counterparts that day might have included employment in one of Wilmington's most prestigious firms, or, more likely, the remunerative careers awaiting them at the Du Pont Company. Delaware's only black lawyer opened a beginner's office in a rented room, in a house near the heart of Wilmington's black community. Thrust into what he felt was a "gratuitous prominence" because "hoary prejudice" had made "seeking to engage in [his] profession unusual," Redding made his first task eliminating once and for all such prejudice from courtroom decorum. "From the very beginning," he later remembered, attempting to explain "the kind of trauma" he felt "in the old days when the courtrooms themselves were segregated," he "encouraged people to ignore the segregation expectations of the bailiff and to sit" wherever they wished. Redding's public commitment to lifting "the burden" now extended beyond the Open Door Forum. And at 1002 French Street, colored Delaware at last had an attorney of their own race to call upon.[61]

As Redding found, though, it would require more than a law degree, no matter how prestigious, to prevent the legal lynching of Theodore Russ. A year after Louis Redding passed the bar and began his practice, an all-white jury downstate convicted the twenty-four-year-old Russ of raping the wife of a white bootlegger in Dover, the same "threadbare lie" that had doomed George White in 1903. Russ confessed to being a lifelong drinker, but, he maintained, he had harmed no woman. He admitted to scuffling over a jug of whiskey with his longtime suppliers but not to rape. During the fight Russ had found himself outnumbered two to one and, fearing murder, had stuck one of his attackers with a small knife. Then, he ran; hearing a gunshot, he ran even harder—all the way home, and into bed. When the Dover police arrived the next morning Russ must have expected an assault charge. Once in police custody, a doctor made a physical examination "particularly with regard to his sexual organs." The seriousness of his situation was suddenly plain.[62]

Forty-five miles to the north, Redding noted the happenings downstate. The Russ family had retained the only reputable attorney in Dover willing to defend black clients, not to mention one charged with raping a white woman. Still, in late April Redding drove on Dupont Boulevard south to the Kent County courthouse where he attended the first day of the trial. From his seat in the gallery he carefully observed all aspects of the trial: the attentiveness of the judge, the veracity of the witnesses, the reactions of the jury, the expressions of the defendant, and, especially, the competence of the defense attorney. The testimony, which went unchallenged, was damning. Four witnesses claimed to have seen the rape in progress. Despite this, Redding believed that the atmosphere in the court was neither "impassioned" nor "prejudiced." As for the competence of counsel, Redding would only say that a "country jury, more or less illiterate," faced with such circumstantial evidence, obviously would do nothing other than convict. Predictably, the next day the jury did just that, and "without recommendation for mercy." Russ was sentenced to hang on July 25.[63]

With the Wilmington NAACP languishing in the midst of the Depression, the Russ defense became largely a personal endeavor and, until July, a slow-moving one. With less than three weeks to go before the execution, the effort to spare Russ began in earnest among a small group of blacks in Wilmington. After several late-night strategy sessions in Alice Dunbar-Nelson's kitchen, Redding pursued a motion for a new trial. Dunbar-Nelson wired the NAACP in New York, impressing upon them the need to send along another lawyer to aid Redding with his briefs. Meanwhile, Redding exhausted all legal avenues and turned to drafting a petition to the governor for a stay of execution. At the last moment, it came—Russ's stay would last until August 22. The next afternoon, a member of the Association's counsel arrived. He and Redding motored to the Kent County workhouse to meet, for the first time, with Theodore Russ. There they found him to be "a more or less handsome country type" with a "nice phy-sique" and, despite the circumstances, making "a splendid appearance for a country boy." He wore "his hair very fastidiously" and just as meticulously claimed innocence.[64]

Other than eyewitness statements, the evidence against Russ was flimsy. But now the only option left was to convince key witnesses to recant, to reverse their testimony and to admit perjury before the Board of Pardons. Facing such impos-sibilities, the Association refrained from dedicating further resources to the case. NAACP counsel repaired to New York; Redding returned to Tenth Street Hill, where a Citizens Committee stepped into the breach, holding a mass meeting and collecting contributions for the Russ defense. Still, Redding despaired that the case was beyond resuscitation. With a week to go before the execution, Redding, Dunbar-Nelson perceived, was "a mess." Desperate, he had even approached Hastings, his old proctor and municipal judge, now a senator—to no avail. With the stay expiring, he appealed until the 21st of August, when he was denied his final motion for a new trial. Redding returned home from Dover, then walked a few doors down to Alice Dunbar-Nelson's. In her kitchen, with no further strat-egies to consider, they commiserated over cigarettes, Redding looking "pitifully tired." The next day, Russ was hanged.[65]

Ten days later, Redding was back at the Dunbar-Nelsons' for Labor Day, look-ing "like the skeleton at the feast" and spending the holiday "blackly reading and saying nothing." Two Septembers earlier he had hoped to wipe away Hasting's stain. How could he overcome the hanging of Theodore Russ?[66]

Over a year later, in mid-December of 1931, the Wilmington branch of the NAACP breathed anew, following a "revival" conference attended by Associ-ation field secretary Robert Bagnall. At the gathering, prominent African Americans such as Shiloh Baptist Church's Rev. Arthur James and Alice Dunbar-Nelson accepted the top two branch offices. After the New Year, its secretary, Pauline Young, along with its legal counsel, Louis Redding, proved among the more important revivalists, committed to reinvigorating the branch and with an eye on national concerns. The Scottsboro case, in particular, interested members—more so, the question why the Association had pulled out, leaving the case to the International Labor Defense. The move, reminiscent of the Association's decision not to commit resources to the Theodore Russ case, left the branch's executive committee, which included both the elder and younger Redding, "disgruntled" and "earnestly inquiring about the withdrawal." In February of 1932, each would have the chance to question the Association's executive secretary himself.[67]

Walter White arrived in Wilmington to address the Open Door Forum, to learn how the newly revived branch's membership campaign was proceeding, and to face some pointed questions from Louis Redding, who sought clarification regarding the legal details of the Scottsboro case. Back in New York, White's thoughts soon returned to the pensive young lawyer. In the spring of 1932, wishing to add new blood to the Association's national legal committee, White considered asking, among other leading black lawyers, Wilmington's "lawyer Redding." Robert and Alice Dunbar-Nelson, White recalled, had recently entertained him with "the dramatic story" of how Louis Redding "came to be the first Negro lawyer in Delaware." When making further inquiries of the Harvard alum, White had received the highest praise from Felix Frankfurter, a Harvard law professor and one of the most prominent members of the NAACP legal board. James Cobb, the esteemed black federal judge from Washington, DC, too, had offered his support of the Redding nomination. White's decision thus cinched, he was pleased by Redding's prompt acceptance, though perplexed at the terse note he received in response to his request for a biography, for publicity's sake. Hoping to reveal some of the drama of Redding's story in a press release, White had only been given the "bare outlines." Indeed, Redding had replied with characteristic modesty. "There isn't much in the way of biography," he wrote the NAACP's executive secretary:

> Graduated from high school in Wilmington, Delaware, and from Brown University in Providence, Rhode Island. After college, taught a year at a mission school in Florida and a second year, English, at Morehouse College, Atlanta. Entered the Harvard Law School and graduated. Admitted to the Delaware Bar in 1929 and have been practicing three years.

White, ever the publicist, fretted about how to complete the "right kind" of story about Redding with just the "irreducible minimum of information" he had in front of him. But even without the details, he felt satisfied to have brought aboard a man of Redding's "training, ability, enthusiasm, and youth," and soon came to rely on the Wilmington lawyer as one of a network of local contacts from across the country.[68]

That summer, for instance, after Redding attended the annual convention of the NAACP in Washington, White asked him to suggest a list of questions to pose to Herbert Hoover and Franklin Delano Roosevelt, both then campaigning for the presidency. In November, Redding helped White "dramatize the significance of the Negro's part" in the election. No lackey to the party of Lincoln (disgusted with local Republicans like Daniel Hastings, he had lately flirted with the idea of backing Democrats), Redding castigated his state's old-guard Negro leadership for their self-interested alliance with the Republican Party. His detailed observations of the Delaware scene impressed White with their precision, acidity, and independence of thought. The next spring White offered Redding's name as a candidate for the newly opened federal judgeship in the Virgin Islands, but he probably felt an invitation to the upcoming Amenia Conference to be more appropriate.[69]

During the first weekend in April 1933, then, as White, his new assistant, Roy Wilkins, and board members Joel and Arthur Spingarn met in one of the Association's offices at 69 Fifth Avenue in New York, White made sure they did not pass over his Delaware contact among the names of hundreds of suggested delegates. In a week, Louis Redding's invitation arrived at 1002 French Street, typed on letterhead bearing the signature of Joel Spingarn.[70]

Louis Redding reached the humid Hudson Valley near sunset, Friday, August 18, 1933, then merged onto Route 22, following "the main route to the Berkshires" north to Amenia. He spent the hazy evening driving into the hills of Dutchess County, riding beneath the shadow of deep green ridges interrupted by brief vistas of silo-studded cow pastures and rolling fields of ripe, head-high corn. With dusk, the damp and quickly cooling country air offered some late relief from the day's heat. After dark, he reached the towns of Wingdale and then Dover, the bouquet of surrounding farms hinting at a summer bounty he could no longer quite see. Just before ten o'clock, he left Wassaic, entered the hamlet of Amenia, turned east, and then descended two miles down the low road to Troutbeck. There, in a dale beneath piney Oblong Mountain, lay the Spingarn manor. From the sound of it, his destination fairly swelled with the representatives of "Youth and Age" who had already arrived.[71]

Nearly four hours late, he stepped from his car, then gingerly walked down a dew-slicked slope behind the main house. There, he found the second Amenia Conference under way among several small groups huddled in conversation beneath a tent. As he approached he could discern a few familiar faces, among them Pauline Young and her friend and fellow University of Pennsylvania alum Virginia Alexander, the Philadelphia physician whom the *Crisis* had profiled that winter. He could also pick out NAACP secretary Walter White, as light-skinned as his surname, his straight hair parted evenly on the right, and a puff of cigarette smoke hanging above his head. He recognized Roy Wilkins, the Association's tall and dark thirty-two-year-old assistant secretary, and, of course, the goateed and bow-tied W. E. B. Du Bois, the distinguished embodiment of the Talented Tenth. Joel Spingarn had just a spray of graying hair left, and sported a perfect rectangle of a mustache, one that nearly disappeared beneath his smiling cheeks when he offered the newcomer a warm hello.[72]

Accepting his host's greetings, Redding entered the light under the largest tent and was introduced around. He recognized the names, if not the faces, of several of his fellow delegates. There was Fisk University sociologist E. Franklin Frazier, and Ira Reid, director of the Urban League's research division. Five others had arrived from his father's alma mater, Howard University—Ralph Bunche, a political scientist and an acquaintance from when both attended Harvard during the late 1920s; Emmett "Sam" Dorsey, an instructor in the department of government; Charles Houston, the vice dean of the university's law school, whom Redding had met at the NAACP convention in Washington earlier that summer; Sterling Brown, the English department's acclaimed poet and author of a regular literary column in *Opportunity*; and Abram Harris, an economist whose 1925 article on West Virginia's black coal miners, Redding may have recalled, had appeared just below his own "Florida Sunday."[73]

Redding had met Washington attorney Edward "Eddie" Lovett at the NAACP convention in June; Roy Ellis, recently an assistant to the Congressional Committee on Labor, was also from Washington. Juanita Jackson was the twenty-year-old president of the City-Wide Young People's Forum of Baltimore. Truly Hayes taught carpentry at the Hampton Institute in Virginia. Thelma Louise Taylor represented the Cleveland Public Library. Arriving from Chicago was Howard Shaw, an electrical engineer employed by the Pullman Company, and Mabel Byrd, a research assistant in the department of sociology at the University of Chicago. Hazel Browne had come from Louisville, where she taught at the segregated Municipal College for Negroes. Harry Greene had traveled from Institute, West Virginia, where he headed the education department at the State College. Frank Wilson had a shorter trip, from New York City, where he served as a staff member of the national board of the YMCA. Marion Cuthbert and Frances Williams, both staff members of the national board of the YWCA, had also come from New York, as had Anna Arnold and Wenonah Bond, each employed by the YWCA on 137th Street in Harlem; Sara Reid, of the 135th Street branch of the New York Public Library; and Moran Weston, a student at the Union Theological Seminary. [74]

They were twenty-six in all, this group of African American contemporaries whose averaged age matched Redding's own thirty-two years. And the conversations Redding had heard among them when he first started toward the tents resumed. Joining in, he spent the next "couple of hours in talk with a group who increased" his "sense of a deep momentousness in the conference" as their conversation turned to the topic of how the Talented Tenth could make greater connections with the "great Negro masses." He was game to start, just not tonight. Although this company renewed his sense of excitement, he was sapped after the hours of travel from Wilmington to Amenia, having driven most of the day and much of the night. He needed rest and retired after midnight, falling asleep on an army cot in one of the smaller hip-roof tents pitched on the lawn at Troutbeck.[75]

2

Abram Harris and the "Economics of the Race Problem"

After sunrise on Saturday, August 19, 1933, Abram Harris drew back his blanket and rose. The thirty-four-year-old Howard University economics professor put on his glasses, dressed, and stepped from his tent. Troutbeck had cooled overnight, and dewy grass dampened his shoes and socks as he trod toward the big tent to enjoy a buffet of coffee and corn muffins, bacon and eggs, fruit and cereal. The spirited conversations of the previous evening continued over breakfast. Looking around, Harris knew many of those enjoying the morning meal. There was his friend W. E. B. Du Bois, with whom Harris had driven to Amenia the day before, along with Virginia Alexander (a Philadelphia physician widely known to be Du Bois's lover) and Pauline Young of Wilmington, Delaware. There were several of his Howard University colleagues—political scientists Ralph Bunche and Emmett Dorsey, the poet Sterling Brown, and Charles Houston, head of the university's law school. There was the Fisk University sociologist E. Franklin Frazier, a friend who had been Harris's houseguest in Washington, DC, the previous summer. There were Elmer Carter and Ira Reid, former colleagues at the Urban League. There was Marion Cuthbert of the YWCA; just a week before he had participated in a conference with her in Harlem. And there was Joel Spingarn. Long acquainted with the NAACP, Harris knew his host, as well as Association officials Walter White and Roy Wilkins.

Even those delegates he did not know well, or whose faces he could not immediately place over the breakfast buffet, likely knew of the bespectacled Howard professor, recognized as one of his generation's highest regarded intellectuals. Writing since the early 1920s, his work comprised a number of essays and reviews, as well as an academic monograph that charted, in Harris's words, "The Economic Foundations of the Race Problem." His work contended that race, stripped of broader economic and political contexts, mattered little as a factor shaping the African American experience; it followed, then, that economic and political concerns trumped all else when considering strategies for racial

ABRAM HARRIS, 1930s. Special Collections and University Archives, W. E. B. Du Bois Library, University of Massachusetts Amherst, reprinted with the permission of the Crisis Publishing Company.

advancement. In August 1933, during the fourth year of the Great Depression and just months after Franklin Roosevelt initiated the New Deal, this attention to the economic conditions shaping race relations might have appeared to be only good sense. Yet, for years, the theses Harris posited had seemed counterintuitive. During the early 1920s, his contention that race was insignificant contrasted with the influential pseudoscience that drew distinctions between primitive colored peoples and the superior white races (the Nordics and the Aryans) responsible for world civilization. It also departed from the defining movements of the decade that celebrated the African race: the cultural nationalism inspired by Marcus Garvey and the vogue for Negro literature, music, and art dubbed the Harlem Renaissance.

At the time, some of his contemporaries were confounded. "The thing few people can understand about me is that I am a Southern Negro," he observed in 1925. How had the Richmond, Virginia, born Abram Lincoln Harris, Jr., whose very name bespoke the significance of race, reached this conclusion? "My friends who are black and others (white) can't understand how a Negro or in fact why a Negro should have such a leaning as I have." It was, as Harris put it, a "medley of experiences" that had turned him from a would-be radical in Richmond to Howard University professor of economics who wished to guide the civil rights movement toward an inclusive agenda that united advocates for workers' rights with those who pressed for African Americans' advancement. After coming of age in Virginia's capital, where the rise of the Jim Crow order had crippled a vibrant black political culture, Harris perceived the limits even the most committed members of the Talented Tenth faced when attempting to overcome racial restraints. Inspired by the socialists of the 1910s, he envisioned labor and civil rights groups joining in common cause to attain economic security and civil liberties. Not temperamentally inclined toward activism or organizing, Harris wished to serve an intellectual role. During the 1920s he pursued "the economics of the race problem" by earning a bachelor's degree at Virginia Union University, a master's at the University of Pittsburgh, and a doctorate at Columbia University. Such academic pursuits did not earn Harris the accolades enjoyed by the New Negro artists of the decade, but Harris was insistent, for he believed that African Americans could only achieve significant social progress within a movement predicated on interracial class unity. His scholarship amended Du Bois's thirty-year-old maxim that the problem of the twentieth century was the problem of the color line. But, to his chagrin, it had not won him immediate plaudits. Aspiring to intellectual stature, Harris had instead spent a portion of the 1920s bouncing between short-term academic and social work appointments and ruing his inability to place his articles in leading mainstream periodicals. By the early 1930s, however, his work had new resonance. Publication of Harris's first book, *The Black Worker* (coauthored with Sterling Spero), in 1931 coincided with early years of the Great Depression, when a growing number of civil rights advocates—W. E. B. Du Bois emphatically included—were willing to consider the economic underpinnings of the black freedom struggle. Reading the work, Du Bois lauded it in the pages of the *Nation* as "the most thought-awakening of recent publications on the Negro and points along the color line," and courted Harris to contribute to the NAACP. When Du Bois and Joel Spingarn first seriously discussed holding another Amenia conference, they thought immediately of Abram Harris.

That morning, Harris's thoughts turned toward the opening conference session. According to the schedule he had received earlier that summer, it would start at nine and introduce a "General Discussion" concerning the "Weaknesses and Accomplishments of the older programmes" the leading civil rights organizations had followed. The delegates would also be encouraged to envision what a "Possible new program" might entail, ranging from "general and liberal reform" to even "socialism [and] communism." For the past few months Harris had been convalescing, following a prescription of rest, milk, and cod-liver oil, attempting to heal an indeterminate lung ailment. He may have wondered how the three days at Troutbeck would affect his health, but no brush with tuberculosis would keep Harris from offering his expertise to the NAACP. In April, Harris had replied to his invitation with a near boast ("You can count on my presence"), implying his contribution to proceedings would befit the stature he had earned over the previous decade. He would start that morning, insisting that the civil rights struggle be envisioned anew—as part of an interracial movement for economic justice.[1]

Before the Civil War, Abram Harris's grandparents had been slaves. With emancipation, they commemorated their family's first generation of freedom in the name of their son: Abram Lincoln. During the late nineteenth century, Abram Lincoln Harris learned a skilled trade (he became a butcher), married Mary E. Lee (a normal school graduate), and made a home among the prosperous and politically engaged black community in Richmond, Virginia. By the end of the 1890s the city was home to thirty-three thousand African Americans and boasted a network of Negro fraternal orders, churches, four weekly newspapers, benefit societies, businesses, and centers of learning, including the newly founded Virginia Union University. In 1899 the Harrises named their own son Abram Lincoln Harris, Jr., marking a second generation of freedom.[2]

Yet at the turn of the century, such freedom was fragile. In January 1900, just months after Abram Lincoln Harris, Jr., was born, the *Richmond Times* called for the "color line" to be drawn "in every relation in southern life." Following the Civil War, Richmond had witnessed the emergence of a dynamic black political culture rooted in churches and with influence on the city council. During the mid-1890s, however, like other cities throughout the South, Richmond stripped African Americans of their political sway. In 1902 a new state constitution confirmed the emerging status quo. The Jim Crow order followed black disenfranchisement. With blacks effectively barred from the ballot box, the color line was drawn through streetcars and even the very streets of Richmond. During Abram Harris's youth, a separate economy of black businesses—banks, funeral parlors, groceries, newsstands, and at least one butcher shop—was restricted to the Jackson Ward and East End neighborhoods.[3]

The city's Talented Tenth did not fail to respond—yet disenfranchisement limited their ability to challenge the Jim Crow order. With perturbed indignation, such figures as John J. Mitchell, Jr., a leading Republican, city alderman, and editor of the *Richmond Planet*, refused to acquiesce. From the pages of the *Planet*, Mitchell sought to end the segregation of the city's streetcars by making segregation economically unfeasible. "The good Lord has blessed most of us with big feet," one article read, "and we see no reason why we should not start early to work and proceed to use them." If colored Richmond "would agree to make the sacrifice and walk for a year," the *Planet* contended, "the agony produced on the white man's nerve center, which is his pocket, would tend to cause an amelioration of our condition." This point was persuasive. For over a year, between 1904 and 1905, African Americans in Richmond refused to patronize Jim Crow streetcars.

That the boycott bankrupted the city's streetcars attested to a dogged commitment to resist the imposition of second-class citizenship. That the streetcars were allowed to fail rather than be integrated indicated the inflexibility of white supremacy. That concerted economic pressure could not overturn segregation even on public conveyances was a disheartening realization for a community that had so succeeded in the generation since emancipation.[4]

Despite the proscriptions of segregation, the butcher's son would be as well educated as any black Virginian. Abram Lincoln Harris, Jr., graduated from the academic course at the city's segregated Armstrong High School in 1918, earning him admittance into the state's premier Negro institution of higher education, Virginia Union University. Abram Harris and Virginia Union shared birth dates; founded in 1899 when Washington, DC's Wayland Seminary and the Richmond Theological Seminary merged, the university quickly developed one of the leading academic programs among black colleges. When Harris matriculated in the fall of 1918, he could choose among courses ranging from classical literature and languages to economics, history, and sociology. At Virginia Union, he found the classroom stimulating, if not completely satisfying—he was soon eager to apply his newly acquired tools of scholarship to life beyond the Baptist campus.[5]

A chance came in 1919, during the first semester of his sophomore year, when William Monroe Trotter, the fiery editor of the *Boston Guardian* and former Niagara Movement cofounder, visited Richmond's City Auditorium on a lecture tour. Trotter spoke of nothing that evening befitting his reputation as an agitator for black civil rights, because before he began, Richmond's chief of police had warned him that he would "close the house" at the first mention of anything he believed was "calculated to cause any friction." Among "the throng of fifteen hundred" in the audience was a contingent of officers ready to see that no "strife among the races" was stirred up, ostensibly placed there to thwart the sort of racial violence that had afflicted so much of the nation during the bloody summer months of 1919.[6]

Afterward, twenty-year-old Abram Harris seethed. He mailed an "open letter" to Richmond's "white dailies" in "protest of the uncivil and brutish treatment accorded" Trotter (a copy of which he forwarded to W. E. B. Du Bois for potential use in the *Crisis*), revealing two hindrances to black freedom—white power and black acquiescence—and his own New Negro militancy. The excuse used by Trotter's censor—to prevent a riot—obscured the true causes of racial violence that had recently torn through such cities as distant as Omaha and Chicago, and closer by in Washington, DC. A "matrix of hatred, prejudice and antagonism" had led to the "Red Summer" of 1919, and Harris identified that inauspicious trinity, too, in white Richmond. "It is you," Harris wrote, reviling his white readers, "who by your sheer advantage of political power, discriminate, muzzle and trample the rights of the people." Had black Richmond not been cowed, had they "acted rightly" in response to Trotter's humbling, "they would not have sat in their seats and passively submitted to this new form of Autocratic tyranny." Silencing Trotter was reason "enough to start any riot," Harris averred, "and if it had been anywhere else but Richmond where Big-Little Bankers walk in a public audience," he believed the black citizenry "would have arisen due to resentment." And the blame would have been white Richmond's. Condemning colored Richmond for failing to rise to Trotter's defense, Harris likewise challenged what he perceived as the capitulation of the leaders of the local black community. Black resolve had regrettably deteriorated in the previous decade and a half, since John J. Mitchell, Jr., had helped coordinate the boycott of Richmond's streetcars. By 1920, Mitchell—the "Big-Little Banker" himself—instead stood for a brand of conservatism that honored individual success over collective social progress. To Harris, it was telling that Mitchell, now the prosperous director of the Mechanics Savings Bank, toured the city streets comfortably in his Stanley Steamer automobile while most of his bank's depositors were forced to ride segregated streetcars.[7]

Harris, like his New Negro contemporaries militantly denouncing segregation in such publications as the *Messenger*, was loath to so accommodate the Jim Crow order. Harris also adhered to the radical outlook of the *Messenger* crowd by supporting the Socialist Party as an alternative to the Democrats, the party of white supremacy, and the Republicans, who in 1920 had segregated the party's state convention. With Mitchell representing black Republicans in Richmond, Harris had little interest in aligning with the party of Lincoln, even when local party members formed their own "lily black" ticket. Rather, Harris and several friends from Virginia Union sought to establish a black local of the Socialist Party. One evening that fall, despite the fact that the Ku Klux Klan had just launched a campaign to organize in the city, Harris crossed into white Richmond to locate the small cadre of southern Socialists whom he hoped to convince to act on their acknowledged mission to "obliterate class and race lines." Harris returned to campus "assured that the colored brothers would be organized." As promised, a new branch was inaugurated, but swaying even ostensibly "progressive Negroes" to the cause proved difficult. Harris found that "almost to a man" the African Americans he spoke with "expressed contempt for an association of respectable colored folk with 'po' white workers—the Negro's traditional enemy." Harris and his fellow black militants were also scolded for impracticality, for "throwing their vote away" on a radical left that stood no chance in the elections, and for perhaps undermining an otherwise strong voting bloc to elect a black Republican. At the prospect of an electoral challenge, though, the likes of John Mitchell were unworried. They "scoffed" at the notion, wagering, as Harris put it, "that this freak movement launched by two eccentric college students and a professor would finally resolve itself into a debating society, preaching parlor socialism."[8] It was not an unwarranted prediction. The party local seemingly reached its peak when an audience of about "one hundred Negroes and twenty-five whites" appeared "in an auditorium in the colored section" of Richmond to hear Harris and others speak about the Socialist platform and the party's candidate, Eugene V. Debs, then imprisoned for criticizing the United States' participation in World War I. It was a modest apex. Despite "frequent applause and nodding heads of approval," Harris was chagrined when none of the blacks in the audience "enlisted." By winter, even the hint of a groundswell of interest dissipated. Membership dwindled from twenty enthusiasts to a mere five comrades. But rather than disband, Harris's cohort committed "to studying the labor problem and different phases of Socialism," sponsored talks by "leading socialists," and presented lectures on "the class struggle, the Open and Closed Shop, Syndicalism and Marxian Socialism." As feared, they had become parlor socialists. When, by spring, none of these efforts had galvanized either black Richmond or their Baptist campus (despite, as Harris wrote, "faculty claims of radicalizing the students") the five remaining members of the local wondered whether the Richmond party might "eliminate the colored branch" and welcome them into the fold. "Such a measure," Harris observed, however, "was too 'red' for the reddist Red in Dixie." When Harris took umbrage at the segregation of blacks in their own gallery during a railway strike meeting, the party summarily revoked his membership, ironically, for agitation.[9]

Harris's foray into the left was equal parts disenchanting and demonstrative. Neither black nor white Richmond was interested in radical, interracial unity. At Virginia Union during the fall of 1921, and as an Urban League fellow in New York the following year, Harris turned from political organizing to the study of political economy to better understand why. In his senior year he signed up for coursework in sociology and history with the new professor Gordon Blain Hancock, a Colgate University alum who had recently completed a master's thesis at Harvard on Irish and black immigrants in Boston. Harris studied economics and history, too, with Clarence Maloney, and a perhaps less cutting-edge brand of sociology with professor Joshua Simpson, an original Virginia Union faculty member who was likely responsible for the position waiting for him after graduation at the National Urban League in New York City. If Virginia Union fostered his academic ambitions, Harris's New York experience broadened his intellectual aspirations. Following Virginia Union's June 1922 commencement, Harris began serving as an assistant to Charles Johnson, the Urban League's director of research and author of the seminal sociological study *The Negro in Chicago*.[10]

In 1922 Abram Harris arrived in a New York transformed by black migration. Although the Urban League maintained its office in downtown Manhattan, Harris found a flat in Harlem. Each morning as he went to work he experienced the emergence of this Negro mecca. Leaving his apartment on West 139th Street, he could walk east toward the subway on Lenox Avenue, to stroll along tree-lined

Strivers' Row. Harris would not have missed the appeal of the Row to the Negro professionals who in the past four years had made the block one of black Manhattan's most fashionable. Its elegant three-story brownstones came complete with a distinguished provenance (they had been designed in the 1890s by esteemed architect Stanford White) and only Sugar Hill, the new neighborhood of choice taking shape a few blocks up Edgecombe Avenue, rivaled the Row in resplendent exclusivity. A few steps further along the Row, Harris could see the construction on the corner of the next block. He had missed the cornerstone-laying ceremony on the site of the new Abyssinian Baptist Church by just a few months. In early April 1922, several hundred colored celebrants had lined Seventh Avenue in their Sunday best to commemorate the occasion. Now each day he witnessed the progress on the church, stone by stone, the latest confirmation of how radically the city's racial geography had changed since the turn of the century.[11]

Had Abram Harris stood at the corner of Seventh Avenue and 138th Street in 1900, he might not have seen a single black face. Walking past the same spot in 1922, he might have lost count. In two decades black Manhattan had effectively relocated from farther south, out of the Tenderloin and San Juan Hill sections between the West Twenties and West Sixties, to the blocks between roughly Eighth and Fifth Avenues and between 110th and 140th Streets. At first, the move uptown had begun with just a few hundred African American families who chose to pay higher rents in order to live in the safer, less crowded neighborhood north of Central Park. The appearance of even a small number of colored neighbors, though, precipitated a quick exodus of whites from Harlem. Given the choice of renting to blacks or letting their buildings sit empty, landlords allowed black realtors to recruit more and more Negro tenants. The arrival of black churches in Harlem only confirmed the trend. In 1910 St. Philip's Protestant Episcopal Church, black Manhattan's most elite congregation, followed its parishioners, moving almost eighty blocks north, relocating to West 134th Street; in 1914, St. James Presbyterian moved from West 51st to West 137th Street.[12]

The transformation of Harlem had also corresponded with a wave of tens of thousands of southern blacks moving to the urban North—including Abram Harris. And as Harris strode past the new Abyssinian Baptist Church and turned south on Lenox Avenue, out of the small enclave of elite blacks and toward the subway, the result of this migration was clear, in the faces he saw and in the southern—and Caribbean—accents he heard. Harris could not help being struck by the movement one Caribbean migrant, Marcus Garvey, had inspired. A galvanic orator, Garvey arrived in 1916 in Harlem, where his street-corner exhortations proceeded to conjure a following numbering in the hundreds of thousands under the banner of the Universal Negro Improvement Association. The UNIA commenced publication of the *Negro World* in 1918, enunciating an unabashed racial pride celebrating African heritage. When Harris walked the streets of Harlem four years later, the UNIA's capacious Liberty Hall was the headquarters of the most significant race movement of the era. Yet, though the UNIA's mass meetings, mammoth parades, and unflinching expressions of Negro unity impressed him, Harris grimaced at the group's unwise investments (such as the doomed Black Star Line, a shipping venture), its martial regalia (Garvey himself was chauffeured during parades decorated in the manner of a general), and its unblinking devotion to the African race. While Garvey was a figure of great controversy, particularly among the light-hued Negro elite who considered the ebony Jamaican transplant a crass and impolitic upstart, Harris disapproved of the UNIA leader's adherence to racial nationalism. Then formulating his own critique of race and insistent upon interracial unity, Harris preferred the radical New Negro message that could be heard at the corner of 135th and Lenox, where the soapbox orations of black socialists competed with the stepladder proselytizers of the UNIA. Here at "the Campus," near vital black institutions like the Harlem YMCA and the 135th Street branch of the New York Public Library, the cacophony of voices on the street joined those in print on the newsstands. The *Crisis*, the *Messenger*, *Voice*, *Negro World*, the *New York Amsterdam News*, the *Brooklyn Eagle*, and the *New York Age* each beckoned to black readers. Harris was disinclined to join the speakers on 135th Street, but he certainly hoped to be read. *Opportunity*, the Urban League's monthly magazine, would first appear in print in January 1923, and with it, so would Abram Harris.[13]

The subway ride from Lenox Avenue deposited Harris over one hundred blocks south at Twenty-Third Street, but the concern in the offices of the Urban League was for 125th Street—Harlem—and similar settings in cities around the nation. Since its founding in 1910, the League stressed a mission of helping rural black migrants adjust to urban environments, particularly by assisting them in locating employment. The League also funded sociological studies, such as Charles Johnson's work on Chicago, illuminating the scope of the challenges confronting African Americans in the urban North. Harris's role was to help coordinate such surveys, but he was also soon involved in Charles Johnson's new foray in publishing, *Opportunity* magazine. Harris had enrolled at the New York School of Social Work and had matriculated at New York University, where he studied economics and journalism; his work for *Opportunity* fused each of these interests. Although he was listed on the masthead as business editor, Harris also appeared in the debut issue of *Opportunity* as a contributor. His review of H. P. Fry's *The Modern Ku Klux Klan* not only began his career in print but, as he debunked Fry's key thesis on the basis of the author's "almost total unfamiliarity with social movements within Negro groups," also was the first of a string of reviews and short articles that showcased his sharp prose and confident analysis. In May, the *Messenger*, the black Socialist monthly he had read since college, published a review revealing his emerging facility in describing the intertwined, even symbiotic, relationship of labor and capital. In June, *Current History* published his essay on recent black political and intellectual currents.[14]

When "The Negro Problem as Viewed by Negro Leaders" appeared in *Current History*, a mainstream magazine published by the New York Times Company, it was not only a financial coup (Harris had sold the article for no less than fifty dollars, he would later brag) but an intellectual accomplishment as well. In the essay, Harris summarized the past thirty years of African American intellectual and political leadership with a clarity and assurance exceptional for such a young author. Indeed, the piece reputedly "evoked considerable comment" as a "brilliant article," marking Harris as one of the rising black writers. Harris's article undertook a wide survey of black thought and politics, from Booker T. Washington to Marcus Garvey, but made essentially two points. First, he argued that W. E. B. Du Bois had been the most important African American intellectual leader since the turn of the century. His influence, Harris argued, stemmed from his editorship of the *Crisis*. "Scathing, yet admittedly brilliant and scholarly in his attacks upon the race situation in this country," Du Bois had provided "the genesis of the militant Negro," who had been raised reading his magazine. Harris believed that he and his contemporary inheritors of the "passionate ardor for civil rights" were specifically indebted to Du Bois. Recognition of such debt led to his second conclusion. A "new group of militants" led by *Messenger* editors A. Philip Randolph and Chandler Owen, who not only "champion[ed] the doctrine of unlimited equality" but who also fought to realize such equality "by urging the unionization of white and black workers in trade unions on an equal basis of admission," had in the past several years "eclipsed" Du Bois. Though their base of appeal may have been small (and was in fact dwarfed by Marcus Garvey's following), what the *Messenger* editors lacked in mass following they made up for in quality of supporters. "Randolph and Owen," Harris explained, "have a following which comprises some of the best trained minds in the race"— including Harris himself.[15]

In such writing, the Virginia Union–trained Harris evinced a precocious sense of authority, as did the broader ambitions he was pursuing. A year out of college, he began to unveil in his publications the economic underpinnings of race. This outlook compared with the materialism of the *Messenger* radicals and the social science of the Urban League, but ran counter to widely accepted explanations of the essential nature of race. Of significant influence during the early 1920s, works published by the racialists Madison Grant (a eugenicist and avowed opponent of the Nordic race's immutable foes—immigration and miscegenation) and Lothrop Stoddard (whose Ph.D. in history from Harvard lent decided legitimacy to his screeds) advanced histories of civilization as being rife with racial triumph and cataclysm, pitting the numerically few white peoples against a "rising tide" of colored primitivism. Such a vision dovetailed with the contemporary nativism apparent in the revival of the Ku Klux Klan and congressional curtailment of immigration. In an essay on the Ethiopian Art Players, a Harlem theater troupe, Harris instead underscored the elasticity of culture—that it is defined over time by history, not by biology—to argue that race is but pigmentation given significance by underlying economic factors. Similarly, in a book review appearing in the September *Crisis* he refuted the notion that any essential differences between races exist, positing that searching beneath the "white man's civilizational coating and the externalities of crude African culture" would reveal "the 'world ground' of humanity." In each of his publications, then, whether describing "the Negro Problem," assessing black leadership, or reviewing the Harlem stage, Harris contended that race itself was an inadequate analytical concept. He insisted, rather, on identifying the economic causes of racial inequality. That fall, when he accepted an Urban League fellowship to pursue master's work at the University of Pittsburgh, Harris committed to making a more systematic investigation using the migration of black workers to the city as a case study to better understand the causes and consequences of the Great Migration.[16]

It was with reluctance that Harris left New York, the city he considered his adopted home. Along Wylie Avenue, in the Hill district just east of downtown Pittsburgh, he found the heart of the city's black community, which in the past several years had grown to over thirty thousand. But Wylie Avenue did not match Lenox Avenue. In 1923, about all Pittsburgh and Harlem appeared to share was the recent influx of thousands of southern blacks. While migration may have seemed to contribute to Harlem's vibrancy, in Pittsburgh Abram Harris found less to cheer. He came, in his perspective, to a city troublingly crowded with African American laborers who had been drawn by the prospect of industrial work in one of the steel and coal mills east of the city between the Allegheny and Monongahela Rivers. The Urban League fellowship would fund a year of master's work, and Harris devoted that year to studying the experiences of the black workers who had resettled in Pittsburgh. Though he continued to publish, and even sent the *Crisis* an autobiographical account of his experiences with the Socialist and Workers' Parties in Richmond, completing his master's thesis demanded most of his time and effort.[17]

The Pittsburgh study represented his most sustained foray yet into the economics of the race problem. Balancing statistical analysis, his own observations, and other social workers' investigations, Harris's case study on recent black migration to Pittsburgh depicted "a cross-section of the industrial, civic and social problems of the colored workers." The work honed his understanding of the specific challenges African Americans faced in the industrial North and underscored the fundamental difficulty of radicalizing the black proletariat. The latter point demonstrated his limited belief in economic determinism, a position that differentiated him from the more dogmatic Marxists. Harris was deeply skeptical that class consciousness among African Americans could be easily awakened, with black workers' "individualism" and rampant discrimination among traditional unionists hedging the possibility of an interracial labor movement. He was skeptical but not despairing. Harris hoped his work—like that of his Urban League mentor, Charles Johnson, on Chicago, and the academic oeuvre of W. E. B. Du Bois—could point toward progress. "We seldom study the condition of the Negro to-day honestly and carefully," Du Bois had written in 1903. "It is so much easier to assume that we know it all. Or perhaps, having already reached conclusions in our minds, we are loth to have them disturbed by facts." Seeking to portray the experiences of African Americans at the turn of the century, Du Bois had journeyed through rural Georgia and walked the streets of Philadelphia, in a pioneering effort to prove the illuminating utility of sociological research. A generation later, Harris surveyed the lives of Pittsburgh's newly arrived black migrants to offer "in microcosm," he wrote, "the social problems of these newcomers to the industrial North."[18]

Conditions in industrial Pittsburgh closely resembled those throughout the urban North during the early 1920s. In the past decade hundreds of thousands of African Americans had left the rural South in what became known as the Great Migration to cities such as Pittsburgh, Los Angeles, Chicago, Gary, Seattle, Minneapolis, Cleveland, and Detroit. During World War I the surge in production compelled industries to employ black laborers, and for wages that far surpassed the meager earnings of southern tenant farmers and domestic servants. Black newspapers such as the *Chicago Defender* heralded the prospect of advancement in the North and cast the many migrants leaving the "benighted South" as part of a broader movement of African Americans seeking opportunity, dignity, and civil liberty. In response, black migrants from throughout the South wrote hundreds of letters to the *Defender* appealing for aid in the journey north, expressing their aspirations for better employment, and attesting to "the menace of mob rule" they wished to escape. The *Journal of Negro History* published many such documents in 1919, and Harris could surmise how such motivations also helped to explain the migration of African Americans to western Pennsylvania.[19]

If migrants arrived in Pittsburgh with grandiose expectations of a northern promised land, they were mistaken. As Harris found in his Pittsburgh survey, the conditions newly arrived African Americans found in the North posed particular "social problems." Following the "mushroom-like" population increase of the 1910s and early 1920s, the possibility of securing proper housing and employment were dismal. As on the South Side of Chicago and in the Black Bottom ghetto in Detroit, the "deserted hovels and dilapidated shacks" that served "as shelter for the new-comers" in Pittsburgh made for living conditions that Harris judged "unwholesome to say the least." Beyond the "gambling and trafficking in bootleg liquor with resultant brawls, shootings, cuttings and murders" that marked the worst sections of the city, migrants crowded into dwellings lacking water and sewage connections—and yet they still paid exorbitant rents. When the jobs most took were as low paying, unskilled laborers, migrants became locked in miserable circumstances that mocked the notion that untold opportunity awaited in the North.[20]

Lacking organization, Harris believed, such workers faced dim prospects. Advocates of the labor movement may have perceived a silver lining amid such grim conditions, predicting that the introduction of black workers to the industrial North could initiate an interracial labor movement in the spirit of the Knights of Labor, the integrated national union that had its heyday in the 1880s. Harris was not so sanguine. With most blacks denied skilled employment, it did not seem likely, Harris observed, "as is being prophesied by a number of economic determinists that the Negro's introduction to machine production will awaken in him a spontaneous outburst of economic class consciousness." The rampant discrimination and hostility among white workers that left African Americans leery of unions was but one hurdle. Harris also perceived an inherent individualism (a result, he thought, of the "experience as an agricultural peasant") in "the great masses of southern black folk" arriving in Pittsburgh that left them less inclined to organize. Those who believed "the stupid exclusion policy of white-unionism" and blacks' inexperience in the industrial arena could be quickly overcome and allow for "an immediate future participation in the class struggle by these new Negro workers" were, as Harris put it bluntly, "suffering illusions."[21]

Harris found the basis for interracial understanding in Pittsburgh similarly illusory. Writing in *The Souls of Black Folk*, W. E. B. Du Bois contended that the color line segregating the nation, among other ills, prevented the development of a sense of empathy between the races. When "the best of the whites and the best of the Negroes almost never live in anything like close proximity," it was a prescription for racial friction. In this respect, the outlook for Pittsburgh was troubling. "Possibly in no large Northern city," Harris observed, "is there as great a lack of acquaintance between white and colored as in Pittsburgh." Harris realized the baleful consequences of failing to foster empathy across the color line: white mobs had rampaged through the streets of Chicago in 1919 and had left the African American section of Tulsa, Oklahoma, in charred ruins in 1921. He was perhaps not too surprised to count only one white church sponsoring "interracial forums where members of both races may meet to thrash out problems highly significant for inter-racial under-standing and good will." But the "apathy of the educated and intelligent colored people of the city" in the wake of recent horrors was confounding. Echoing his earlier castigation of conservative black Richmond, Harris urged the black leaders of Pittsburgh to sponsor a brand of public discourse endorsing "a program for local economic and social uplift."

They needed to reveal "the problems of industrial community life" and reverse "the complacency and laissez-faire which characterize Negro Pittsburgh" concerning "its own problems." Admittedly, this was no elixir. Rather, it was an incremental step toward necessary progress—the sort Harris wished his scholarship would inspire.[22]

With a body of work that rejected the very concept of race as a meaningful analytical category, insisted that racial inequality had economic roots, and demonstrated the overwhelming challenges facing black workers in the industrial North, Harris wished to offer intellectual guidance to advocates of workers' and African Americans' rights that would advance a broader struggle for social justice. Harris did not mistake his master's thesis for one of W. E. B. Du Bois's Atlanta University studies or for Charles Johnson's *The Negro in Chicago*, which enjoyed both wide readership and influence. But by 1924, the author of "The Negro Problem as Viewed by Negro Leaders" considered himself among the more militant agitators for black freedom, whose work fused the investigative, academic approach of Du Bois and Johnson with the economic radicalism of the New Negro cohort. He was not a socialist labor organizer, like his *Messenger* colleague A. Philip Randolph, nor was he a mere compiler of statistics. As he published his essays in various periodicals and worked for the Urban League during the early 1920s, Abram Harris was still defining his role as a politically conscious intellectual.

After finishing the Pittsburgh study, Harris no doubt preferred to return to New York, the cultural and political hub of the urbane intelligentsia to which he wished to belong. His best offer of employment, though, came from the West Virginia Collegiate Institute in Institute, West Virginia, in an Appalachian hollow just six miles west of the state capitol at Charleston, along the Kanawha River.[23]

Harris joined the faculty of the West Virginia Collegiate Institute in June 1924, at the beginning of the summer session, with an appointment as professor of social economy. Before the school's founding in 1891, the town of Institute had been named, with equal banality, Farm. With the construction of Fleming Hall, the main academic building and focal point of the ten-acre campus, and particularly since the arrival of its energetic young president, John W. Davis, in 1919, the Collegiate Institute had become a reputable regional black college with particular connections to the small but politically active middle-class African American community in Charleston.[24]

If the position was humble, his ambition was not. From his position, Harris planned to initiate a broader study of "The Economic Foundations of the Negro Problem" that would transform African Americans' collective struggle for social justice—an aspiration that would define the early years of his academic career. But from the start, he had difficulty adapting to the stifling environs of the college. Harris's reputation had apparently preceded him to Institute, leading to a measure of friction. "Some folk here knew my name before I got here," Harris wrote a friend that autumn, "and had linked me with all the 'isms' they thought detestable and despicable. So you see my liberalism must proceed cautiously." No doubt these conclusions were based on Harris's published work, which likely rankled the more conservative members of the community. He was cautious, perhaps, but not entirely inhibited from envisioning the launch of a significant academic career. He planned "to build a real department of social economy" at Institute, "or somewhere," he wrote. "To that end," in the coming year he intended to "write and engage" himself "with research" that bucked the tedium of traditional economics. In the classroom, he was interested in teaching a seminar "in the Cultural Consequences of Economic Development" that would certainly delve into the issues his Pittsburgh survey had plumbed. Meantime, he offered "Economic Interpretation," with its radical resonance, in the guise of a technical survey of "Banking, Money, Credit, Commerce and Foreign Exchange." Similarly, Harris treated the blandly titled "Economic Theory I and II, Economics III, [and] Industrial Society" as vehicles for "a critical analysis of the evolution of modern industrialism its antecedents and cultural consequences." He called the latter course his "baby"; he could "get across a whole bunch of radical thought without calling it such."[25]

Though Harris was able to guilefully pursue his agenda in the classroom, he worried that his scholarly turn was adversely affecting the articles he was writing. They were "not as controversial as might justly be," he admitted, since his topics were usually "scholarly but unoffensive." The academic tone he fretted over showed in his piece on "Negro Migration," an article that appeared in the September 1924 issue of *Current History*. The essay, Harris's second to appear in that periodical, drew from his recent work in Pittsburgh to provide an overview "of the exodus of negroes from the rural South." The piece, which evinced a keen assurance comparable to his impressive portrait of black leadership, took issue with the argument that recent black migration was "exclusively racial." Harris stressed that race itself had little impact on the character of the migration, except that southern segregation had compelled many migrants to abandon the region. Rather, he found "normal social forces at work in the negro migrations," including an "urbanization of the negro population" that he ascribed to "the growth of machine industry, and of the lack of economic freedom and the non-assurance of a margin of subsistence under the one-crop share system of the agricultural South." In fact, Harris argued, blacks would have migrated earlier but for "the slave regime, which prevented their free and early movement and their consignment to the scarcely mitigated serfdom of the rural South upon the dissolution of the slave system." When considering black migration, Harris concluded, "it must at all times be remembered that the underlying causes are economic." Race only mattered within this context; it was not itself a causal factor.[26]

Eager to write and conduct more research, Harris invested the modest windfall from his publication of "Negro Migration" in books and magazine subscriptions. Harris endeavored to sustain connections with intellectual currents beyond Kanawha County. As he wrote a new friend in Baltimore, he hoped his growing personal collection would enrich his planned study demonstrating the "Economic Foundations of the Race Problem in America." Harris's confidant was George Goetz, a white twenty-four-year-old Johns Hopkins graduate and public high school English instructor who had taken the pseudonym V. F. Calverton in order to publish his fledgling radical *Modern Quarterly* in anonymity. Corresponding from Baltimore, Calverton provided Harris, who often felt isolated while in Institute, with more intellectual sustenance than any acquaintances or colleagues in West Virginia. Unlike those in Fleming Hall who were wary of Abram Harris's "isms," Calverton, then engaged in sociological and economic interpretations of literature, encouraged the Institute professor to continue revealing similar factors behind the race problem.[27]

When Harris saw the October number of *Opportunity*, he decided to devote immediate attention to this inchoate idea. Editor Charles Johnson, he read, was sponsoring a nationwide literary contest. The notice inspired hundreds of submissions (including the Florida reminiscences of Louis Redding, then a first-year English instructor at Morehouse College). For his part, Harris intended to compose an entry titled "The Sociological Basis of Negro Emancipation" and began soliciting the necessary texts in order to begin. He considered using "Economic" rather than "Sociological," but opted for the latter; the former he decided he would instead use in Calverton's *Modern Quarterly* in an essay on "The Negro and Organized Labor." If only the research "material which has been promised me" would soon arrive, he griped to Calverton, he could begin right away. It would be a first step, just one of "a short group of essays" devoted to "The Economic Foundations of the American Race Problem." By the end of October Harris's submission to *Modern Quarterly* was late but written, despite "some of the crudities and literary inelegances" Harris thought marred the piece. His hopes of entering the *Opportunity* contest, though, were rapidly dwindling, a casualty of the institute's minimal resources. "I have given up entering that prize essay contest," he wrote Calverton in a fit of spleen. "I tried to get source material," he explained, "but to no avail. So the project had to be abandoned." Harris had planned to consult A. M. Simons' *Social Forces in American History* as well as "two or three references on the Frontier in American history," but none of these, "to say nothing about authoritative material on Negro Slavery and African freemen in the Slave Regime," were available along the Kanawha River. "This damned little library at Charleston," Harris swore, "with its (3) five foot book shelves and its supercilious but vacuous brained attendants could give scant material." The institute could not offer any help either, he explained, because, he wrote, "I have requisitioned so many books that I knew it would be useless to ask the administration for a further increase in its allowance to my department." His salary did not permit the purchase, but without access to such sources his essay, and indeed his visions for a larger interpretive project, would languish. "Sometimes I think if I am to do creative work, I must get out of this ossifying environment," he told Calverton. "One is constricted from the best intellectual contact by a life pocketed amid these Appalachian slopes."[28]

As for nearby Charleston, Harris was similarly pessimistic about developing connections with like-minded members of the community. He was impressed with Mordecai Johnson, the thirty-four-year-old pastor of the First Baptist Church and one of colored Charleston's leading citizens. Johnson, whose congregation included many of the city's black professionals, most of whom belonged to the local branch of the NAACP he had helped found several years earlier, struck Harris as "a peach of a fellow. Brainy but unassuming—a scholar and a gentleman." Not only that, but "for a preacher gentleman," Johnson evinced a surprising "knowledge of sociology and appreciation of revolutionary economic and social doctrine." But Harris was less enthusiastic about most of his other acquaintances, including those he joined in an informal "political Economy club." Among them, Harris found himself in the unwelcome position of instructing his peers. During one meeting he addressed the forum for forty-five minutes on "Past and Present Tendencies in Radical Economic Thought," but because his was "an audience comprised of folk who know nothing of Economic doctrine, to say nothing about a knowledge of the foundations of radical economic philosophy," what may have otherwise been a stimulating discussion devolved into a "ponderous" lecture. Harris already had students; he needed friends.[29]

When Harris left Institute for Baltimore during the Christmas holiday, he sought out the company of two of his closest friends. In Baltimore lived California Starks—Callie, to Abe—the daughter of a black Baptist preacher who, as he intimated in letters to Calverton, had thoroughly charmed him. And so had Calverton, whose brick townhouse at 2110 East Pratt Street had become the hub of Baltimore's young and well-educated bohemia, serving as both the editorial office of the *Modern Quarterly* and the home of a regular Saturday night salon. Among the company of twenty-something Johns Hopkins graduates and young white progressives, Harris partook of some good (and illicit during Prohibition) schnapps and spoke about "black and liberal thought." In contrast to the dull reading group at Institute, he was so invigorated after this discussion that nearly a month later he was still mulling how "to expand and develop more logically and cogently" his talk that night into an article surveying "The World of Black and Liberal Thought."[30]

Such a project would build on the work he had produced that fall. The pieces included a book review that appeared in the January 1925 issue of *Opportunity*, in which he rejected the presumption that race is biological, and "The Negro and Economic Radicalism," which Calverton published in the *Modern Quarterly* that February. Harris devoted the *Modern Quarterly* article to explaining why African Americans' ambivalence to socialism and affinity for capitalism was not unique to blacks, a thesis he had proposed in his last *Current History* contribution and which grew out of his Pittsburgh study. Harris believed individualism to be ingrained in the national culture, citing a general lack of class consciousness among American workers of both races. In a nation pledged to free-market capitalism, and which recently elected business-friendly Republican Calvin Coolidge as president, this thesis made considerable sense. Harris wished to demonstrate that race was not an immutable biological factor preventing African Americans from being affected by such currents in the national culture. Like many whites, African Americans' "hostility or apathy to organized labor" was "as much attributable to his inheritance of bourgeois temper and training in American institutions as to the racial discrimination practiced by trade unions." Their antipathy to economic radicalism, as he similarly concluded of black migration, could be traced to social, not racial, causes.[31]

Soon after Harris returned to Institute in early 1925, his desk was piled with partially drafted essays, class lectures, and book notes. He had plans for articles and new ideas for courses, and he had even brainstormed about founding a new discussion movement based on a network of interracial clubs "formed in all of the big cities." But the circumstances in Institute, including an "extreme race psychology" that he felt was emerging on campus, left him shaking his head: "Damn the Negro intellectual is in a hell-u-va-way." Harris began searching for another "position not as much isolated as here" and hoped that New York would be his "next place of abode," as he wrote his friend back in Baltimore. "It is my home of adoption, anyway." While letters from Calverton that winter and spring were "a balm to a wounded and rebellious disposition," Harris was unsure if his friend could truly contemplate his position. Not long before, Calverton had urged Harris to expand his scope beyond the race problem. Harris, in fact, was planning "to undertake a piece of work having little to do with the Negro. If the Negro comes in he will be only incidentally considered," he explained. Yet, while Harris appreciated the limits of race as an analytical category, he could not ignore the consequences race had in his life—implications that went beyond the conceptual. This he was not sure his friend understood. "It is strange," he wrote Calverton, "that you have never known the world behind the veil as W. E. B. Du Bois calls it. That's the damned thing I hate so implacably about race separation; it makes strangers of people who by nature and education ought to associate with each other."[32]

The difficulty Harris had publishing in leading white magazines only heightened his frustration. That spring he asked Du Bois to return "Black Communists in Dixie," an autobiographical article he had sent the *Crisis* editor from Pittsburgh the year before. When the manuscript arrived, Harris immediately posted it to the *Nation*, where Calverton was a periodic contributor. Harris envisioned himself, too, as a regular among the liberal monthlies, only he had had a difficult time finding willing publishers. Though he had scored twice with *Current History*, he had not been successful since. When three weeks passed without word from the *Nation*, he was wounded. "For the life of me," he scribbled in a note to East Pratt Street, "I can't see why the articles I think best won't sell. My second raters find an easy market." He would keep trying, though, and was considering sending *Dial* an essay on "Race Psychology, Intellectual Freedom and Liberalism."[33]

If he could not publish in *Dial*, an opportunity seemed to open at Howard University when the philosophy department's Alain Locke wrote with a "congratulatory remark" on Harris's recent contribution to *Modern Quarterly*. Locke also forwarded along copies of the March 1925 issue of *Survey Graphic* that he had edited—it was a "Harlem number," devoted to the vibrant literary and cultural critical mass that had developed north of Central Park. Harris responded to the praise gratefully. His article, he explained to Locke, "has caused some adverse criticism; and little favorable comment." Harris supposed it was "the price of trying to be objective in one's analysis!" but he wondered, given Locke's enthusiasm, if as associate editor of the *Howard Review* he might be interested in a piece on social sciences in the college curriculum. As for the stack of *Graphics*, he had "distributed about half to 'children of the Age'" among his Institute and Charleston acquaintances. "I must say," he wrote, complimenting Locke, "that this number of the Survey is a tribute to your insight into such things and an example of what this generation of Negroes may do under a favoring environment." If only Harris had been included in the volume.[34]

Despite his sunny response, Harris could not be blamed for any frustrated second-guessing, wondering whether he might have found himself represented in the pages of the Harlem issue had he not left the city two years earlier. A year spent in Pittsburgh and another in West Virginia had kept him from the zenith of the New Negro Renaissance that the *Survey Graphic* announced and that *Opportunity* and the *Crisis* commemorated, throwing lavish award ceremonies in New York for the winners of their respective literary contests. Even though Harris had been productive since leaving New York, he regretted the lack of attention his work was receiving. He had struck up correspondence with Locke, Du Bois, and others, but while teaching in the Appalachians he was not able to join in the cultural life flowering in Harlem. That his own work downplaying the meaning of race sounded a different chord than the current poetry and literature celebrating the descendants of Africa in America seemed far less significant to Harris at the moment than his physical remove from the happenings in New York. He wanted to leave West Virginia, but, he asked Calverton, "Where in the hell may one go?" He urged his friend to see about openings "in the New Negro high

school in Baltimore," and asked similar favors of his New York contacts. Charles
Johnson and the Urban League soon came through on two fronts. Johnson commissioned a review of Calverton's new book, and the League invited him to be
the first executive secretary of the new Minneapolis branch which was to be
founded that summer.[35]

This latest correspondence, however, likely reached an empty office. By May,
Harris was engaged in a study of coal miners on strike across West Virginia. At
the request of T. E. Hill, a prominent black member of the state Republican
Party and director of the three-year-old West Virginia Bureau of Negro Welfare
and Statistics, Harris had taken a train to the northern end of the state and was
in the middle of a survey that would investigate the situation of black workers in
thirty mines. Speaking with black miners, white mine operators, and members
of the United Mine Workers of America in such outposts as Fairmont, West Virginia, may have been "a ticklish proposition, and a little dangerous," but Harris
hoped that the work would help launch his "long planned labor union study involving the Negro miner." In fact, when Johnson learned of his activity he asked
to publish Harris's report on the strikes.[36]

When Harris returned to Institute later that month, he found himself "damned
busy with classes, examinations" and preparing the mining study. In the coming
weeks he would need to settle his affairs at the institute and ready himself for a
new life in Minnesota—one that would include a June bride, the former Callie
Starks. Their marriage, however, would begin unceremoniously: Callie remained
in Baltimore while he made a final trip to "the hectic arena of industrial confusion," where he met for a "week with coal operators and officials of the United
Mine Workers." He returned to "the somnolent environment that Institute may
bestow," completed his review of Calverton's book for *Opportunity*, finished a
bottle of schnapps, then left for Minneapolis.[37]

On the train to Minnesota, Harris had disavowed "the cap and gown life" but
still hoped "to assist in emancipating the Negro's mind." Reaching Chicago, he
wrote Alain Locke, "The new birth which intellectual America is about to experience is a thing of which the old Negro college professor knows nothing."
Indeed, he surmised, most "Negroes know little of the big social issues that
engage the attention of white liberals and some few of the most intellectually
advanced Negroes." Though just twenty-six, Harris believed himself among the
few such elite black thinkers and writers; released from the isolation of his Appalachian hollow, he intended to prove it.[38]

Harris had a room waiting for him in a home on Fourth Avenue, among a
neighborhood of well-to-do blacks in south Minneapolis. And as soon as he arrived, he was off to St. James African Methodist Episcopal Church for the inauguration of the new Urban League branch. Eugene Kinckle Jones, the League's
national secretary, was on hand for the evening celebration, as were T. Arnold

Hill, the League's industrial secretary; Elmer Carter, executive secretary of the neighboring branch in St. Paul; and Gertrude Brown, head resident of the city's Phyllis Wheatley settlement house. Each spoke before an audience that included the League's local benefactors and several professors from the University of Minnesota. Hill and Jones approached "The Industrial Situation" and "The Problems of the Urban League," respectively, from a national perspective, while Brown and Carter steered the dialogue to local interests, discussing "What the Community Needs." Carter had helped secure over 450 jobs for blacks in the Twin Cities since the St. Paul Urban League was founded two years earlier, and Harris's prediction of similarly impressive accomplishments across the river in Minneapolis drew applause.[39]

Initially, after the constraints he felt at Institute, both the new position and novel environment charmed Harris. "I have much work to do here," he wrote Calverton the day after the branch inaugural. He suspected that he might not be able to devote as much time to his "more or less theoretical work" as he would like, but he believed himself "to be in a lovely place in which to work. Race prejudice is less keen here than in the last—even including New York the most cosmopolitan center of civilized urban life. Frankly I like it here, perhaps this will be the end of the track for me. I do not know just yet but I do like the general impression the whites and blacks have already given me." In fact, Harris was not in Minneapolis two days and he had already received speaking invitations. He so enjoyed the attention that he had immediately begun "preparing talks and literature on the whole subject of race relations in this country" with which to enlighten concerned Minneapolitans.[40]

In short time, though, his esteem for his new life in the Midwest diminished, his dejection coinciding with professional disappointment. Within weeks he was disillusioned with the insular black community he found in the Twin Cities and disappointed that his writing career seemed to be in the doldrums. Despite his initial impression, he found that he had been "thrown in the midst of rampant individualism" after all, he wrote to Calverton in a note equally redolent of loneliness and alcohol. "The Negro group, despite homes and other physical accomplishments of great wealth, are as backward spiritually as the earliest frontiersmen," he fumed, likely after an early lecture appearance met with a tepid reception among the more conservative members of the Negro bourgeoisie. "Ye Gods and such insolent ignorance buttressed by a splendid isolation which none but the imponderably mighty can penetrate. Poor lil Abe Harris—a damned social worker and erstwhile professor in a backward nth class college has the effrontery to attempt to speak authoritatively on something." That Callie had not yet joined him in Minnesota no doubt exacerbated his frustration. Moreover, he found he far preferred the life of the mind to the administrative business that accompanied running an Urban League branch. When Harris's Minneapolis office officially opened downtown in late July, the *Chicago Defender* reporter who visited observed that "Mr. Harris possesses a pleasing personality and keen executive ability and is thoroughly capable of handling the problems of the branch." Despite this unsolicited vote of confidence, Harris was privately struggling with the seeming permanence of the move to Minneapolis. That month, one of his few remaining connections to New York was severed. In August, Abram Harris appeared for the final time on the masthead of the *Messenger*; the Minneapolis Urban League executive was a contributing editor to the radical monthly no longer. Meantime, the results of what effort he was able to devote to his writing continued to disappoint in their reception. Both the *Forum* and *Current History* had rejected articles; *Current History* considered the submission "too dialectical," confirming his fear that an overly scholarly tone would keep his words from print. His name continued to appear in *Opportunity*, however; "Black Communists in Dixie," which told of his brief turn as a radical in Richmond, was finally published in the July issue, but the journal had been at best his third choice, and it had already appeared on his résumé many times. That *Opportunity* continued to be the only outlet for his work certainly hindered his goal of becoming an important intellectual voice in America.[41]

When Harris's review of Calverton's *Sociological Criticism of Literature* ran in the August *Opportunity*, it seemed he had even failed to be recognized as an important African American intellectual. Harris lauded his friend's interpretation that "social environment determines culture" and that "social forces are themselves the result of certain economic antecedents"; the result, he wrote, advanced literary scholarship in a measure equal to the recent innovations of historians Charles Beard and E. R. A. Seligman. But of as much interest to both Calverton and Harris was the note appearing just after the review. "A New Book," the column read, "under the title of 'The New Negro: An Interpretation,' edited by Alain Locke, a volume of stories, articles, poems and discussions will appear this fall with the imprint of A&C Boni." That Harris was not listed as a contributor to this collection, drawn from the *Survey Graphic* Harlem number, baffled Calverton. In his Minneapolis office, Harris was again reminded of his distance from the pulse of the African American intellectual elite. When Calverton broached the topic, he provoked a spirited exchange of correspondence that lasted through the end of the year. "No," Harris responded in scrawled, excited longhand, "I suppose, my work, has not been of sufficient weight to merit my being asked to participate in such a symposium." That his work challenged the very meaning of race at a moment devoted to celebrating black culture made him distinctly out of style. Moreover, while he had attempted to establish himself professionally by corresponding with such intellectual elites as Du Bois and Locke, he was experiencing the height of the New Negro Renaissance on the outside looking in. While *Opportunity* and the *Crisis* passed out literary awards, and while the illuminati of Harlem and Washington made being "Negro" fashionable, Harris had spent his time on fronts where blackness was decidedly not in vogue—among Pittsburgh's unemployed, among West Virginia coal strikers, and among migrants lately arrived in Minneapolis. Clearly dejected, he unconvincingly claimed ambivalence about Calverton's offer to write Locke on his behalf. "I leave it to you," he wrote, but "surely Locke and the rest will want to know what in the hell I've done to merit such gratuitous mentioning."[42]

And yet perhaps his work in Minneapolis would help establish his profile after all. Though a refined doctor of philosophy such as Alain Locke might not be inclined toward hands-on sociological work, Harris was convinced of the public worth of a comprehensive survey of black Minneapolis. Professionally, the work might also be profitably combined with his thesis on Pittsburgh, the two projects in tandem yielding enough primary evidence to support a broader study of the economics of the Negro problem, such as he had described to Calverton the previous fall. In early September the Urban League convened a mass meeting at the 13th Ward Branch Library to discuss the survey. Harris would not labor on the project alone. A ladies' auxiliary formed in conjunction with Gertrude Brown's Phyllis Wheatley House would assist in conducting the survey, each canvasser assigned her own district to cover. Harris would then compile and interpret the findings in a substantive report to be jointly published by the League and the Phyllis Wheatley House and made available to enhance the public's knowledge of the African American experience in the Twin Cities.[43]

Harris would not pin his professional future solely on the Minneapolis study. And he would not allow disappointment at recent publishing rejections and his exclusion from *The New Negro* to wholly hobble him. While directing the survey from his Urban League office, he arranged to have his paper "on typical conditions of Negroes" in Pittsburgh read at the tenth anniversary conference of the Association for the Study of Negro Life and History in Washington, DC. He mailed a typescript of his first article on the West Virginia coal strike to Charles Johnson in New York. "Race Psychology, Class Consciousness and Liberalism" was already in Chapel Hill, "in the hands" of University of North Carolina sociologist Howard Odum, who seemed inclined to publish it in *Social Forces*, a new interdisciplinary journal that published academic essays in the social sciences. As the canvassing of Minneapolis's black neighborhoods began, he submitted a dissertation proposal on the history of black labor in the United States to Columbia University, revealing a lofty goal: a doctorate. While awaiting word from Columbia, Harris opened the 1925–26 Twin Cities lecture season with a talk before the Minneapolis Sunday Forum at the Phyllis Wheatley House and began a series of speaking engagements sponsored by the Urban League ladies' auxiliary.[44]

With the publication of his article on the West Virginia coal strikes in the October *Opportunity*, Harris had the advantage of compelling his audiences not only with his comportment and nuanced vision of the material factors under-lying the race problem but also with plain old good storytelling. His article, "The Plight of Negro Miners," was a fitting example, given its impressionistic form, drawn from the notes he made during his investigations across much of West Virginia, and based on his interviews of black miners and of white union leaders and mine superintendents. His luncheon audiences may have been startled at the examples of discrimination black miners working on the Ohio border endured, with friction coming from white miners and superintendents contributing to "the growing Ku Klux spirit in many of the northern counties" of West Virginia.[45]

With his frequent public addresses and his visibility as an Urban League officer, Abram Harris quickly became a fixture in Minneapolis. And Callie was finally able to join him at the end of the October. Harris traveled to Chicago late that month to meet her and then ride the train together back to their new home in south Minneapolis. In an auspicious bit of the timing, his trip to Chicago co-incided with a singular event in the recent history of the black radical left: the convening of the American Negro Labor Congress. While in Chicago, Harris observed the proceedings and sketched notes for an article he planned to write about the significance of the convention. What he witnessed during the sessions refuted the belief that the Soviet Union was attempting to try to radicalize Afri-can Americans and foment mass rebellion in the United States. The "Workers' (Communist) Party of America," Harris explained, not the Soviets, had spon-sored the convention; regardless, the result was not "a very revolutionary assem-blage" no matter who had backed it. Harris approved of the group's assertion that "race prejudice" traces its roots to "modern capitalism," but he rejected the Par-ty's dogmatic insistence that the "barriers of race" were about to disappear under the banner of workers' solidarity. "Proselytizing for the class struggle" just might inspire the next social movement among African Americans, but Harris repeated his belief that "color psychology in the labor movement" first needed reckoning with. As he had found in his Pittsburgh study, discrimination against black workers and blacks' longstanding reluctance to align with labor would be diffi-cult hurdles to clear.[46]

Believing that he might help cure this myopia on the left, though, did not en-tirely overcome the slight he continued to feel at having been left out of *The New Negro*. When they arrived back from Chicago, Harris returned to a mischievous note from Calverton bringing up again his absence from Locke's New Negro an-thology and chiding him for preferring to make observations about black leader-ship rather than actually joining its ranks. Annoyed with both points, Harris scrawled a half-angry, half-anguished response: "I wish I could get on the Wool-worth Building and say God-damn the Negro and his problems so loud that the pronunciation would ring in the years of a universal audience." Later, he wrote Calverton, "You are damned correct when you say that I'll never lead my people.

I have no desire to do it, either. Damn *my* people, if I must confess to having a people." To his young white friend, Harris was comfortable articulating his resentment that he was somehow held responsible for his race, even if, he repeatedly argued, race held no actual significance. To the Negro intelligentsia— including W. E. B. Du Bois, who had famously (and just as melodramatically) pledged himself to uplifting his race after a heady celebration of his twenty-fifth birthday—Harris was not as frank. Despite undeniable frustration with life "behind the veil," he would continue to write about the African American experience. In late November, when Howard Odum at last accepted "Race Psychology" for publication in *Social Forces*, he had finally placed another article outside the few respected black periodicals. Invigorated, Harris then pitched to Du Bois an idea for a New School for Social Research that he had mentioned to Calverton in the spring and to Locke over the summer. This, as he explained his idea to "the father of the Negro intelligentsia," was Harris's idea of leading his race.[47]

While Harris envisioned a national forum, he did his best to create an intellectual atmosphere among his fellow Minneapolitans. But, just as in Institute, he most often found himself in the position of instructor rather than peer. Harris spoke at the "Modern Book store" on the "Radical School Movements and Theories before a group of Negroes who [were] trying to become intellectual." He walked a YMCA audience through the intricacies of understanding the "Sources of Racial Myth," during which he demonstrated "the economic foundation of American race psychology" and described "public opinion on the race problem." He led discussions on "social equality" with the proper white "'Y' ladies" who met at the Radisson Hotel's Cosmopolitan Club, and lectured on "The Negro in the American Labor Movement" for a University of Minnesota economics seminar. In December Harris was asked to speak at a holiday social at the home of Minneapolis Urban League president and former United States senator Lowell Jepson. After the New Year he was privy to plans to organize St. Paul's black sleeping car porters—though an exciting development, any involvement would be at the expense of his writing and Urban League duties.[48]

In six months Harris had become one of Minneapolis's most recognized young black figures, but "these talks," he confided to Calverton, "combined with a promised article" to Charles Johnson "on the Negro in the Coal Mining Industry" due in January, were testing his capacity for work. That December he was also "bound hand and foot by this Survey of the Negro population." Overwhelmed, Harris simply did not have the energy to develop the study into a sterling work of social science. It would simply be "a little book called the Negro in Minneapolis—nothing great however. Just a social text for the agencies that deal with the Negro's social problems." If he could just complete the survey, he told himself, he could begin his long-planned book on "the Economic Foundations of the American Negro Problem." Even that project, however, was, he wrote

Calverton, "giving me hell right now," as he attempted to wade through the survey results and place several of his shorter pieces. As another string of rejections arrived, he could not decide if "the best thing to do [was] to stop trying to write short essays and get to work on a more elaborate work." Adding to his discontent, Calverton wrote with comments on *The New Negro*, in case it had not yet appeared on the shelves at the Modern Bookstore. The article on the American Negro Labor Congress he offered to *Scribner's* in November had been returned to him "post haste"; he forwarded it along to the *Nation*, but had little confidence that "Lenin Casts his Shadow upon Africa" would appear in print anytime soon. When his prediction proved prescient, and the *Nation* rejected his latest submission, he could not help exclaim: "God-damn—I am getting *sick* of so many refusals." *Atlantic Monthly* had returned another essay on the "Foundations of Racial Myth" on vague grounds, and Harris's expectations for the piece had diminished to indifference about its placement, as long as it appeared "in the immediate future." At home, Callie tried to redirect his attention from the disappointments of the literary marketplace to his book, but he was unable to even conceive of a title, and he had a good "six months of reading" to finish before even "beginning to write."[49]

With the new year came consolation. Harris's spirits lifted a bit when the December *Social Forces* containing his essay "A White and Black World in American Labor and Politics" arrived. Upon rereading it, he thought it needed revision before appearing in book form, but he still considered the article his best yet. The essay echoed his *Modern Quarterly* contribution but elaborated on why most blacks balked at aligning with liberals. "The Negro's apathy toward economic reform and progressive political action," he argued, "must be considered in the light of" the historical context of "general racial friction," especially between black and white workers, and the "sentimental" relationship African Americans had had with the Republican Party since emancipation. "Uttering a few Marxian epigrams," Harris wrote, would not be enough to overcome this history and awaken "economic class consciousness" among black workers. Broad social forces such as African Americans' recent northward migration and urbanization might, he suggested, spur organized labor to admit black workers by necessity and thus introduce blacks to radicalism. More likely, though, Harris thought such a shift among African American laborers would only follow an effort among black community and political leaders to encourage participation in the labor movement. Of course, complicating such "a revolution of opinion" was "a growing race consciousness," most apparent in the Harlem Renaissance and Garvey movement. Black leaders also evinced this in their "demands for Negro business enterprises," such as John J. Mitchell's successful bank in Richmond, and "efforts to create in the Negro a deeper appreciation for his cultural contributions to Western Civilization," such as Du Bois's work *The Negro*. While he was attuned to reasons for racial pride, it vexed Harris to exacerbate already deep chasms of cultural separation. He feared that "if the Negro's ever-increasing self-assertion is not guided by Negro intellectuals possessed of catholic vision," the result would be a separate "black world oblivious to things white." Such Harlem Renaissance sponsors as Alain Locke, W. E. B. Du Bois, Charles Johnson, and Walter White considered the celebration of black arts and letters a strategy to achieve indirect cultural advances. To Harris, though, this attention to race left African Americans unable to grapple with the broader trends shaping the national experience. Indeed, at the moment, Harris wrote, "So absorbed is the Negro intellectual with the race problem that problems of labor, housing, taxation, judicial reform and war, all of which affect him, must needs be relegated to the limbo of minor significance."[50]

To achieve any semblance of social progress, Harris maintained, the "Negro problem" had to be considered integrated with greater economic, not strictly racial, afflictions of American society. Enunciating this perspective may have put Abram Harris at odds with the most significant racial movements of the day, but following the publication of his *Social Forces* essay, he persevered with this intellectual charge, placing several articles, completing the Urban League survey, and speaking throughout the Twin Cities. "The Negro in the Coal Mining Industry," appearing in *Opportunity* in February, compared the mining industry in several states, demonstrated the similarity in the experiences of both black and white miners, and repeated his thesis that race alone could not be a powerful category of social analysis. "Lenin Casts his Shadow upon Africa" appeared in the April number of the *Crisis*, along with a brief biography and portrait, hinting of Harris's rising stature. In the photograph, the bespectacled, round-faced author looked younger than his twenty-seven years; in print, he seemed older. Beneath his picture was Harris's best-crafted article to date. He had penned his account of the October 1925 American Negro Labor Congress in Chicago with flair, erudition, and a sense of humor. Harris's careful scholarship, if not his wit, also marked "The Negro Population in Minneapolis: A Study of Race Relations." Integrating statistics compiled through extensive questionnaires and social workers' reports, Harris provided a useful depiction of the challenges facing blacks in Minneapolis, from decrepit housing conditions to the dearth of employment opportunities. He lectured on such issues in sociology and economics classrooms at the University of Minnesota, and even spent several days with his old acquaintance and former *Messenger* comrade A. Philip Randolph helping organize a Brotherhood of Sleeping Car Porters local in Minneapolis-St. Paul, a fitting fusion of his academic and activist interests. Indeed, early 1926 found Harris in a position he had longed for: playing the part of the politically engaged public intellectual, speaking with a group of black porters "on the purpose and significance of organized labor" (in a talk he titled "New Day for the Negro Worker"), addressing a forum convened by the St. Paul NAACP, and selling an article on the challenges of radicalizing black laborers to *Current History*.[51]

By spring's end, Harris had done much to burnish his professional bona fides, ensuring that he would continue in this role after leaving the Twin Cities. During an earlier funk, when he was feeling most "damned sick of the Mwst.," Harris had remarked that he might have to "pack my trunk, sojourn east and demand a position somewhere." Now it was he who was in demand. With offers to teach at Fisk University in Nashville and Morehouse College in Atlanta—each among the best opportunities for black scholars during the 1920s—Harris chose to return to New York City, where he would begin his doctorate at Columbia University. Long hoping to live again in New York, Harris intended to fulfill his aspiration of explaining the economic foundations of the American race problem in a manner that redirected the movement for African American rights. Harris arrived at Columbia in the fall of 1926 with academic ambitions and a scholarly activism that earned him a place among the most regarded young African American intellectuals of the day, including a position at Howard University and rising influence among progressive labor and civil rights circles.[52]

If Abram Harris had veiled his "isms" in such outposts as Institute, West Virginia, and Minneapolis, Minnesota, in New York he felt no such compunction. Determined to pursue a rigorous scholarly agenda, his doctoral work, covered, as he described it, the elements of "straight Political Economy," including "economic theory, economic history, statistics, Marxist Socialism, labor problems and labor movements, banking and credit theory, trusts and corporations, and finance." He was just as resolute about having an influence beyond the academy. When not hunkered down in Low Library on the Columbia campus, he maintained a home just four blocks north of his first New York apartment, at the bottom of Sugar Hill. Employment in the Columbia anthropology department helped support his life near the tony neighborhood, but he was not satisfied with mere proximity to Harlem's intellectual elite—he wished to join them. He inquired of Du Bois about opportunities at the *Crisis* (there were none), renewed his ties to the *Messenger* (he became assistant editor), and cultivated new speaking engagements (such as his March 1927 address on the "Economic Prospects of the American Negro" before an "Inter-racial Workers Forum") that continued the engaged intellectualism he had developed in Minneapolis. While each bespoke the interest Harris had in fusing the civil rights and labor movements, his participation in a spring 1927 symposium on black labor suggested his new public stature.[53]

That May, Harris traveled some forty-five miles north of Manhattan to Brookwood Labor College, in Katonah, New York, to partake in an interracial conference bringing together a host of labor and civil rights advocates. Inaugurated in

1921 to challenge the discriminatory practices of the American Federation of Labor, the most powerful labor organization in the nation, Brookwood attempted to lend the labor movement intellectual—and generally socialist—guidance. An invitation to join validated Harris's rising profile, offered an additional credential, and put him in contact with a network of liberal lights. He found himself "sequestered away in the dales of Westchester County," as he reported in the pages of the *Crisis*, with both white and black Socialist leaders, including Norman Thomas, Benjamin Stolberg, W. H. DesVerney, Frank Crosswaith, and A. Philip Randolph. Brookwood founder A. J. Muste presided over the proceedings, which included discussion of papers read by NAACP field organizer Robert Bagnall, *Opportunity* editor Charles Johnson, and E. Franklin Frazier, former director of the Atlanta School of Social Work and current doctoral candidate in sociology at the University of Chicago. Also among the presenters, Harris was able to draw from his most recently published article, "Economic Foundations of American Race Division," which had appeared in the March number of *Social Forces*. His second essay published by Howard Odum reaffirmed his contention that economic forces shaped racial experiences, demonstrating that "the economic and social subjugation of" African Americans had determined interactions between blacks and whites. African Americans, he argued, had come "to adopt the culture of the dominant" white society; the recent "surging of race consciousness among Negroes" was a case in point. Some had "mistaken it as the Negro's attempt to establish a Negro culture within the United States." But the rise of Garveyism, the flourishing of black businesses and institutions, and the celebration of Negro arts and letters so evident during the decade ought not to be considered examples of separatism. Rather, African Americans were attempting to compensate for their "thwarted ambition for full participation in American institutions" by creating their own. Tracing this dynamic to "economic foundations," Harris enjoyed a sympathetic audience at Brookwood, a gathering that offered an important showcase, as he put it, of "the nature of intellectual guidance on labor economics fused with racial issues." After being an isolated academic at the West Virginia Collegiate Institute for Negroes and a dispirited administrator at the Minneapolis Urban League, Harris could not help but be heartened by the recognition the Brookwood symposium bestowed.[54]

That spring, his old West Virginia acquaintance Mordecai Johnson, the Baptist clergyman, also recognized Harris's importance, offering him a position as assistant professor of economics at Howard University. Johnson, who had become the University's first African American president in September 1926, himself had been hired with a mandate to offer Howard more stable leadership. During the previous several years the University had suffered student strikes and deteriorating relations between the faculty and administration. The school's board of trustees hired their new president to steady the campus, but Johnson also had ambitions of modernizing Howard. He hoped to make the University a "power in the life of the Negro people and the nation," he wrote less than a month into his tenure, planning to both upgrade the campus's outdated facilities (in 1926, the newest addition was the football team's University Stadium) and attract a core of talented, young black faculty members. Abram Harris was one of his first hires.[55]

His thrall to New York would not keep Harris from accepting such a prestigious offer. Before leaving for Washington, Harris continued his assistant editor duties with the *Messenger*, compiled trade statistics for Columbia's banking department, and attended summer lecture courses in the economics department. He had forged two important relationships that year in New York. He had befriended his thirty-year-old white classmate Sterling Spero, with whom he would collaborate on a dissertation on "Economic Forces in Negro History." At Columbia, too, he worked with Wesley Clair Mitchell, an economics professor who urged him to focus on the work of Karl Marx and Thorstein Veblen. Harris's reading of these scholars inspired him to pursue serious theoretical work that had nothing explicitly to do with the African American experience, even as he moved into a Second Street apartment at the southeastern corner of the Howard campus, near the heart of black Washington, referred to colloquially as "the Secret City." Mordecai Johnson may have had plans for developing an intellectual center at Howard, but what Harris noted during his first month on campus was not A. Philip Randolph's mass meeting for black sleeping car porters at the Florida Avenue Baptist Church, nor Talented Tenth bandleader Duke Ellington's appearance at the Murray Palace Casino, a popular black dance hall, but rather the uproar over the Howard University football team's strike. Harris quickly decided, with typical dismay, that community reaction to the strike signified that "these black folk of the middle class are more determined to have football games and the inane display which accompanies them than they are to have serious academic life." The display was enough, after only one month, to make him search for the strength to persevere: "God help the Negro who would be an intellectual in a clime like Washington." Considering the uproar over the football team, he conceived of writing an article on "The Prospects of Black Bourgeoisie." But with whom could he discuss his idea? In his first two months in Washington, Harris had found it difficult to make meaningful connections on campus, and beyond. "These people are quite sequestered you know!" he wrote a friend from Columbia. "Washington intellectuals I am beginning to believe are much different from my New York friends. The former lead lives of contemplation and have no time to talk inconsequential pish-posh."[56]

Over the next two years, as teaching, research, and writing competed for his attention, and as Howard University increasingly became a dynamic intellectual center, Harris could devote only so much time to "pish-posh" himself. That fall, he finished "The Prospects of Black Bourgeoisie," which he agreed to contribute to Charles Johnson's forthcoming anthology *Ebony and Topaz*, and which located the origins of black sympathy for capitalism in the banks and other institutions the "Negro aristocracy" founded during the late nineteenth century. Harris hoped to follow this with other articles on "Negro middle-class strivings," but he had a degree to complete. When Sterling Spero visited Washington in December, they began to map out a plan for cowriting their dissertation. For both, financial concerns were paramount, and Columbia kept them waiting on word about funding until late spring of 1928. With grant money at last secured, Harris happily decamped to Harlem for the summer. He took an apartment at 405 Edgecombe Avenue, just off West 155th Street on Sugar Hill, in one of the five-story buildings that stood in the shadow of the fourteen-story 409 Edgecombe, home to many of Harlem's elite. The advantages of this location were more than social. In New York he had access to the library stacks at Columbia as well as to primary sources in the offices of the NAACP and the *Crisis*—each of which, with Du Bois's permission, had opened their files to him. He had a similarly generous contact in the Urban League's Ira Reid, a friendly fellow Virginian who had been a League scholar at the University of Pittsburgh the year after Harris. Returning to "prosaic" Howard for the fall semester, where the arrival of a number of young faculty members (including Ralph Bunche, a twenty-five-year-old Harvard University M.A. hired by Mordecai Johnson to create a political science department) promised enlivened collegiality, Harris devoted much attention to his doctoral work. Between readying for exams at Columbia and arranging for funding to complete his dissertation (not to mention teaching his own courses), his time was so restricted as to exclude placing new articles or penning reviews. Uncharacteristically, his words were not in print again until 1929, when "The Negro and the New Economic Life" appeared in V. F. Calverton's *Anthology of American Negro Literature*—and even this was very nearly a reprint of his *Ebony and Topaz* essay. It was a necessary pause. In July 1929, Harris was back at 405 Edgecombe, on sabbatical, combing the office files at the *Crisis* for his dissertation research, corresponding with labor officials, and busy writing on "Economic Forces in Negro History." In the fall, Harris split his time between New York, where he passed the language exam required for his doctorate, and Howard, where Sterling Brown, another young Harvard-trained faculty member, and Emmett Dorsey, a 1927 Oberlin College graduate, had arrived on campus to teach English and political science, respectively. Along with Bunche, Harris, Brown, and Dorsey formed a cohort of young black faculty members who began to meet regularly. And now that he had completed most of his portion of the dissertation manuscript, Harris could share with them his new plans for embarking on a "study of the Theories of the Evolution of Capitalism," with a focus on Thorstein Veblen, an economist who had wryly skewered the excesses of the Gilded Age and articulated an intriguing alternative to conventional Marxism.[57]

Harris entertained hopes of penning similar challenges to orthodoxy as the nation fell into an economic depression during the final months of 1929. With his dissertation nearly completed, he was quick to oblige when his Brookwood acquaintance A. J. Muste had asked him to contribute a "comprehensive statement" on "the Negro Worker and the labor movement." The article was to appear in January 1930 in *Labor Age*, representing Muste's new political venture, the Conference for Progressive Labor Action. The essay, like his nearly finished dissertation, grew from a decade of observation and writing, concluding that "the two great obstacles to labor solidarity are the psychology of craft unionism and the psychology of race prejudice." While "a rapprochement between white and black labor" was no easy accomplishment, Harris pointed out that leaders of organized labor deserved criticism "not for its failure to effect greater harmony" but for its refusal to even begin the process. *Labor Age* readers might agree with this assessment, but Harris warned that progressives who hoped to step into the breach, by attempting to bring "Negro and white workers into closer alignment for economic and political action," ought at least to "understand the difficulties" both trade unionists and intellectuals had failed to overcome. Not only, he suggested, did progressives have to win over white workers, but they must convince black workers to the merits of organizing as well. While he hoped leaders would act soon, Harris wrote, "progressives must realize that Negro economic and political leadership"—such as he had observed from Richmond to Minneapolis—"is opportunistic and petty bourgeoisie" and not easily moved to the side of labor.[58]

When the article caught the attention of the *New York Times*, Harris no doubt hoped it would whet the reading public's appetite for his forthcoming book, *The Black Worker*. Meantime, the reading audience his *Labor Age* article reached grew significantly when W. E. B. Du Bois, with whom Harris had become increasingly friendly, reprinted it in the March 1930 issue of the *Crisis*. Harris had corresponded with Du Bois for some years, writing him as early as 1919, during the flap over William Monroe Trotter's visit to Richmond. In the following several years he had kept Du Bois apprised of his career, published "Lenin Casts his Shadow upon Africa" in the *Crisis*, and relied on the NAACP's office files for his dissertation research. The reprinting of his *Labor Age* essay, though, demonstrated a newly collaborative relationship between the Howard professor and the *Crisis* editor. In Du Bois's mind the younger scholar's importance among the coming generation of the black intelligentsia was crystallizing. In 1930, after all, it was clear that Harris had been prescient to devote his scholarship to "the economic foundations of the American race problem." Celebration of black culture had been a central concern during the 1920s, but the advent of the Great Depression called for new perspectives on the very issues Harris was indisputably expert. Hopeful that Harris's perspective might help invigorate the *Crisis*, Du Bois requested a confidential meeting with him and "some other of the younger liberal minded leaders concerning The Crisis and its future." Harris was willing, though impromptu confabs would be easier to arrange over the summer when he was back in New York, addressing a National Urban League Conference on "New Attitudes of Labor," putting the final touches on the book manuscript, and completing his requirements at Columbia. Receiving the good news in September 1930 that the Columbia faculty had accepted his dissertation, and that *The Black Worker* was being prepared for an early 1931 publication, Harris began to guage interest among his friends at Howard. "I have talked with several of the younger men at the University, since my return, about the things you and I are concerned over," he wrote Du Bois. "I think there is considerable unrest." Howard colleagues Sterling Brown and Emmett Dorsey, as well as his New York friend Ira Reid, joined Harris in believing "that there should be a re-valuation of social philosophy as it relates to Negro problems." They were, he confessed, "a little hazy on what should be done." Could Du Bois soon join them for an "informal discussion" to help them "clarify our own views"? Du Bois was only too willing. They planned to meet during the spring. In the meantime, Harris would keep Du Bois abreast of their views.[59]

With Du Bois's imprimatur, and the necessity of responding to the deepening economic depression, during the fall of 1930 Harris was all the more emboldened to make the "unrest" felt among his peers apparent to the Negro elite and their white benefactors. One chance came that November when an "American Inter-Racial Traveling Seminar, for the consideration of race relations" convened in Washington. Though the organizers had commissioned special Pullman cars to transport the members of the integrated seminar through several southern states, Harris was not satisfied with its members' commitment to confronting the economic dimensions of the race problem. Addressing the group, he let loose a castigation of the older leadership that stunned most of those present. "Man I raised a hornet's nest," he told Benjamin Stolberg, a liberal white journalist in New York and a like-minded friend. Speaking on "The Black Man and this Economic World," he condemned with equal intensity the black bourgeoisie, "the exclusive and reactionary tactics of the American Federation of Labor with respect to Negro labor and white unskilled workers, white philanthropy as the means of delaying Negro labor consciousness, the separatist tactics of Negro leadership, the otherworldly religiosity of the Negro church, and the attempt of the Negro intellectual to get away from the masses." Along the way, he clashed with George Haynes, the conservative black Christian leader who had addressed Harris's Virginia Union commencement eight years earlier, in an exchange that, Harris noticed, had made Anson Phelps-Stokes, the white philanthropist in the next seat, squirm. To some, challenging the effect white philanthropy had in shaping black intellectual life in this company marked Harris as impolitic—one colleague present even dismissed him as suffering from a "persecution complex." To characterize Harris this way was to willfully miss his point. He felt compelled to point out that his own work challenging American capitalism, for instance, had suffered from a lack of support, while he could name several well-funded studies drawing palatable conclusions about the race problem. That summer, for instance, the Julius Rosenwald Fund had granted resources to a southern white scholar to survey "The Economic Status of the Negro." The results were so egregiously ill informed, so fundamentally misguided, that the *Baltimore Afro-American* coined a new pejorative ("Woofterism," after the survey's author, Dr. T. J. Woofter, Jr.) for white social scientists' ostensibly objective findings that failed to treat its black subjects impartially. With the challenges African Americans faced at the outset of the 1930s, favoring white scholars' biased findings over a clear-sighted economic interpretation of race relations endangered any advance toward actual social justice. If his generation's scholarship was to adequately address the race problem, Harris insisted that their work be unconstrained by an outlook that dated to the accommodationist days of Booker T. Washington.[60]

Harris made a less controversial impression during two gatherings held in December 1930. Traveling to Illinois, Harris participated in a "Human Relations Parley" held at Northwestern University, and then returned east to the Brookwood Labor College for another A. J. Muste-sponsored "meeting on worker's education." At Brookwood he was reunited with his Howard colleague Emmett Dorsey and mingled with a number of other Harlemites, including Frank Crosswaith, a socialist with experience organizing for the Brotherhood of Sleeping Car Porters, as well as with the poet Langston Hughes and Louise Thompson, young, prominent figures on the Harlem left. He was also brought back together with W. E. B. Du Bois, who chaired the Brookwood sessions. While Harris flayed the conservative hindrances to social progress, Du Bois helped herald his entrance among the black intelligentsia, trumpeting the news of his Columbia Ph.D. and the publication of *The Black Worker* in the pages of the *Crisis*. The "Along the Color Line" column of the December *Crisis* captured Abram Harris in two profiles: in a photographed portrait of the tweedy young scholar, and in an applauding note quoting the head of the Columbia economics department saying that Harris had "passed successfully one of the most brilliant examinations in the history of the Department." When Columbia University Press released *The Black Worker*, Du Bois placed the book atop his list of recommended reading.[61]

In addition to impressing Du Bois, *The Black Worker* offered Harris entry into the upper echelon of contemporary black scholars, even as it reflected the culmination of a decade of experience, both inside and outside of the library. One question in particular animated his work: why were African American workers not integral to the American labor movement? To adequately explain this, in *The Black Worker* he delved into the history of slavery and the origins of racism, analyzed the structure and policies of craft unions, interpreted the implications of early twentieth-century black urban and northward migration, and evaluated the importance of the black middle-class. He had first found the problem significant as a twenty-year-old would-be Socialist Party organizer at Virginia Union University, and he had since investigated the "economics of the race problem" in the black neighborhoods of Pittsburgh and Minneapolis, and in the West Virginia coalmines, and had published his conclusions in outlets ranging from *Opportunity* to *Social Forces*. He concluded, drawing from theses he had developed during the 1920s, and based on several years of new research he had undertaken while at Columbia and Howard, that white racism and the difficulty of radicalizing blacks prevented the easy forging of an interracial labor movement. That nothing else matched his scholarship on this topic secured Harris's position at Howard. Having recently been promoted to associate professor, Harris met with university president Mordecai Johnson in early 1931 to discuss his future on campus. Even as the contracts of other teachers at the school were left to expire and as professors endured 10 percent pay cuts as the nation endured yet another year of depression, Johnson assured Harris of a permanent place on the faculty. "The sky is your limit at Howard University," he told Harris, urging him not to "pay attention to any other offers that may come" along. As an expression of this support, Johnson offered him additional research funds. This "means that my bourgeoisie study will be done," Harris was pleased to realize. "Then I shall attack Marx and Veblen."[62]

That *The Black Worker* had implications for both the civil rights and labor movements meant Mordecai Johnson had company in wanting to associate his institution with the coauthor of *The Black Worker*. W. E. B. Du Bois, who extolled the book in a review for the *Nation*, wished to arrange a transformation of the editorial board at the *Crisis* and hoped Harris would join the effort. The enfeebled *Crisis* budget meant he would be unable to remunerate Harris, but Du Bois appealed to his young friend's innate sense of social responsibility: "I need not point out how important this matter is. We have got to inject into the veins of this organization some young radical blood," wrote Du Bois, and "unless it is done, we are done for." Flattered, Harris pled poverty. He could not absorb the expense of monthly travel from Washington to New York. With *The Black Worker* completed, he was also committed to launching his long-considered project on "The Negro as Capitalist." He had explored the labor side of the equation but had yet to fully cover African Americans' faith in capitalism. A Social Science Research Council grant through Columbia would allow him to embark on a study of "the relation between Negro finance institutions and business enterprises," a dynamic he sketched in his contribution to *Ebony and Topaz* in 1927, and that had been brewing ever since his contact with the "big little bankers" of

Richmond. Although undertaking this work occupied much of Harris's effort that summer, he did not completely put off Du Bois's request. Du Bois was by now a frequent visitor, staying in Abe and Callie's guestroom when he traveled between the NAACP offices in New York and his teaching post at Atlanta University. In July Harris invited him to join one of his Howard cohort's regular discussions of "social politics," including the economist Charles Wesley, Sterling Brown, and Emmett Dorsey. Du Bois had not been able to bring Harris over to the *Crisis*, but he was moved to suggest to Joel Spingarn—recently named president of the NAACP's board of directors—that the NAACP convene representatives of Harris's younger generation. Putting the Howard circle in conversation with others from around the nation might yield results significant to them individually and to the broader civil rights struggle.[63]

While the NAACP considered this proposal, Harris pursued his new project on black capitalism. Invited back to Brookwood Labor College in August 1931, Harris was able to share new findings. One Howard colleague described his latest work as a "smashing and unanswerable article on the capitalistic ideology of American Negroes." Du Bois hoped to use it in the *Crisis*, but Harris intended to place it in a mainstream publication. He had just had a near success with both *Harper's* and *Scribner's*, his efforts frustrated only because NAACP executive secretary Walter White had an essay on the Scottsboro trials pending. With the marketplace for works by black authors apparently saturated by a single forthcoming article, Harris's piece would not be published. The *Nation*, however, came through with an offer to review Edwin Embree's *The Brown American*, and Harris was convinced that his second book, though requiring much research, was "going to be a definitive work" that would "put 'The Black Worker' to shame." Yet, just as he had difficulty placing articles on the topic in publications addressed to a broader readership, he also found himself denied adequate research funding.[64]

Without support, Harris feared his financial position would hobble his work; it already had compromised his convictions. The lure of cash, for instance, had overruled his reluctance to speak before a New York gathering of the International Labor Defense, the legal arm of the American Communist Party, an association he thought intellectually bankrupt but which had assumed a visible role defending the Scottsboro Boys. His research grant had long ago evaporated, and his Howard salary was more meager each year, the result of University-wide pay cuts and the regular allowance he provided his family in Depression-stricken Richmond. His prospects brightened somewhat when the Social Science Research Council awarded him six hundred dollars, but it was "just enough," he lamented, "for me to live on this summer." He needed at least twice that just to underwrite his primary research in Pittsburgh and Chicago. He would accept the money, of course, but he confided to a friend, "I don't know how in hell I am going to get the rest of the information that I should have to complete the study."

Continuing to receive invitations to participate in A. J. Muste's Brookwood meetings in Katonah, Harris found himself "almost crazy trying to find money to carry on" his research. He despaired over the naked politics of the funding process, writing to Benjamin Stolberg who had criticized such conservative attitudes in a recent *Crisis* piece: "I am sure that I would get a large grant from the Council, if I turned out a monograph, purely meaningless statistics about the Negro banks and insurance companies, without connecting them up with the development of black bourgeoisie." It would also be possible to exploit the new connection he had made with Edwin Embree at the Rosenwald Fund, whose largesse had subsidized no small number of anodyne studies of the Negro problem. "But," he vowed, "I'll die before doing so." He was willing to accept an honorarium from a body of radicals; he could not, however, bear to "resort to fact finding to get some of papa Julius' estate."[65]

Overlooking such woes, Harris had a busy spring of engagements that only underscored his importance to the NAACP, which, by early 1932, was serious about convening members of the Howard University cohort in a civil rights retreat. After hosting an Intercollegiate Social Science Conference on the Howard campus in April (at which he had gotten Du Bois to appear), Harris agreed to participate in the annual convention of the NAACP in May, to be held in Washington, DC. Joining, as the local newspaper put it, a "formidable list of speakers" at Shiloh Baptist Church, just south of the university campus, Harris planned to speak on "Economic Reconstruction and Negro Welfare" during a panel on the ongoing Depression that included Du Bois and an Ohio senator. Tempted to use the forum to settle a score with Carter Woodson (Harris suspected that founder of the Association for the Study of Negro Life and History had poached his idea to write about black businesses), Harris instead enunciated a broader indictment of the established Negro leadership. The thesis he spelled out that night concerning the future of the civil rights struggle—and which he continued the following morning during a session on "The Negro in the Changing Economic Order"—was familiar. "We must begin from the ground and build a new labor movement," he averred. The fate of "white and black workingmen" depended "on a leadership which will educate them into a realization of their identity of economic interests and the necessity of a united front for achieving common welfare." That Harris singled out the American Federation of Labor as inadequate to the task surely came as no surprise, particularly to those familiar with his scholarship. But the intensity of his criticisms of black leaders, who Harris said were suffering from "general confusion and sterility of ideas," even made his good friend Du Bois wince. Nevertheless, in Harris the NAACP recognized a cogent critic who could aid the Association during this third year of the Depression. After the convention, Joel Spingarn and NAACP executive secretary Walter White each met privately with Harris to discuss their plan to reprise the 1916 Amenia Conference. Harris was warm to the idea and offered to stock the proceedings with his friends and allies, including Sterling Spero, Benjamin Stolberg, Sterling Brown, Emmett Dorsey, Fisk sociologist E. Franklin Frazier, and African American journalist George Schuyler, who had pushed for black "economic power" during the May convention.[66]

The prospect of an Amenia Conference intrigued Harris, particularly the potential to shape an economic program for the NAACP. Having combed through the Association's files while writing *The Black Worker*, he knew that this was a substantial weakness of the organization. When a run on his bank resulted in his account being frozen for much of the summer of 1932, however, he had to revise his early eagerness and respond with regrets to the NAACP's invitation. (He would not miss anything, though; the planning being in a bit of a shambles, the NAACP was forced to postpone the conference until the following summer.) What attention Harris was unable to offer the NAACP he devoted to a deeply theoretical project on three economists—Karl Marx, Thorstein Veblen, and his Columbia mentor Wesley Clair Mitchell—that he hoped would establish his academic reputation as one of the most important young economists, regardless of race. If grants to support his study on black capitalism were to remain elusive, he wished to pursue other avenues. He sent the result, a long manuscript on "Types of Institutionalism," to the editors of the prestigious *Journal of Political Economy* at the University of Chicago. The experience was unusually inspiring. After writing the article he moved swiftly on to a more focused study of Marx, which resulted in an unexpected coup: a book contract from Harcourt, a New York publishing house. Harcourt's enthusiasm about publishing a short, readable volume—"a little classic on Marx," Harris beamed—motivated him throughout the fall. He delivered an address to the undergraduate History Club on "The Economic Interpretation of History," then dedicated himself to polishing his second *Journal of Political Economy* submission. He viewed this piece as a prelude to his volume on Marx, and had become so involved in it that he even rejected old friend V. F. Calverton's request for an article for his new *Modern Monthly*.[67]

The recent correspondence from Calverton, coinciding with his work on Marx, may have reminded Harris of the letters he had written his friend some years earlier, pledging to concern himself with issues that transcended the Negro problem. Now that he was ensconced in such theoretical study, though, he was drawn back to the inescapable vexations of the race question. When Abram Lincoln Harris, Sr., passed away at the end of 1932, the butcher's son returned to Richmond for the funeral. It was a misery to return to the city of his youth. "I want to tell you what a hell the South is," he wrote Benjamin Stolberg once he was back in the comparatively cosmopolitan District of Columbia. "My God, those sweet benevolent vestiges of the planter aristocracy sent me to bed with a raving headache," he wrote, and he wondered for whom he mourned more—his father or for black southerners and their cringing concessions to Jim Crow. "I suppose," he wrote, "the acceptance by my friends and relatives of this paternalism embittered me so that I thought I was grieving over my father when I was actually burning with madness because of a racial situation to which for some unknown reason I have remained oblivious." In his absence black Richmond seemed to have become even more conservative than when he had tried to organize a black Socialist local as an undergraduate at Virginia Union. Now, Harris lamented, even questioning segregation among "the Negro citizens" was enough "to raise the hell" that he had experienced during his visit. The need for transformation was all the more apparent, and it would require the commitment of an elite vanguard to effect the change: "All I have to say now," Harris wrote to Stolberg, "is that giving the Negro civil liberties means very little. He needs an internal bath. Nothing will be done with him or for him until the Negro intellectual brings about a transformation within the ghetto."[68]

As the year ended, Harris endeavored to achieve just that kind of transformative intellectual influence, and as 1933 began, he engaged in further collaboration with W. E. B. Du Bois to offer new direction for the civil rights movement. Welcome validation of his academic credibility arrived in the December issue of the *Journal of Political Economy*, which included his article "Types of Institutionalism"; he would send the second, an article titled "Economic Evolution: Darwinian and Dialectical" that he thought had useful political implications, off to Chicago as soon as he had it back from the typist. Then he would clear his desk and begin making "notes on Marx and the American Mind," his ideas for which, encouragingly, already filled several pages. There even seemed hope for his nearly orphaned study of the black bourgeoisie. At the end of December the American Academy of Political and Social Science awarded Harris the Simon N. Patten Fellowship.[69]

Learning of the recognition, which carried a $1,000 stipend, Du Bois wrote with heartfelt congratulations (the "scholarship is about one-fifth as large as it should be but I presume it is to be regarded as a great concession on the part of scientists") and a request for advice. Like Harris, Du Bois believed an invigorated black intellectual leadership was necessary to reverse the very trends Harris had recently witnessed in Richmond. "You have perhaps seen," he wrote Harris, "my tentative program for the re-examination of the Negro problem" in the January issue of the *Crisis*. In this article, Du Bois had suggested that a reconsideration of Marx was appropriate given the nation's economic woes. He was now writing to invite the Howard professor to provide him with a crash course in Marxism. Intending to print a follow-up essay in February, he asked Harris to rush his recommendation of the "four or five best books which the perfect Marxian must know." Eager to discuss Du Bois's piece during his next visit at the end of January, Harris named several works that would provide "the intellectual and social background of Marx's works," and even promised to "arrange a little gathering" for further discussion upon his arrival in Washington. Following their parley, an impressed Du Bois, who had already assigned *The Black Worker* to his Atlanta University students (and had invited Harris to address his class), commended Harris's new theoretical work to his *Crisis* readers. Not only had Harris set a benchmark for comprehending the black proletariat, he now offered guidance for understanding the new era of "technocracy" that the incoming Franklin Roosevelt administration was sure to usher in with its New Deal for Americans.[70]

The nation was awhirl in early 1933 as Roosevelt entered office amid the ruins of American capitalism, and Harris was eager to play a productive role. But as the banking system neared collapse at the end of February, and as the Roosevelt administration entered office in March initiating domestic legislation that transformed the federal state, Harris wondered what that role might be. He and others were "groping after new values in a period in which the old values seem incapable of guiding social action or of stimulating leadership," he wrote his *Journal of Political Economy* editor. "At present," Harris observed,

> no one seems to know where we are headed or for what in this country, in spite of "new deals," "brain trusts," "bonus marchers," "evangelical socialists," and "shrieking communists." I therefore think that about all a student of economics can do is to understand what is going on around him, evaluate it as critically as his faculties will permit and transmit his evaluations to those upon whom his ideas will have the greatest effect in terms of future leadership.

For his part, Harris was prepared to offer such critical evaluations in his capacities as a university professor, scholar, and advisor to social leaders like W. E. B. Du Bois. The essays Du Bois had recently composed on Karl Marx and the Negro problem already demonstrated his influence. Marx, as Harris reminded Du Bois, had long ago suggested that "labor in a white skin cannot emancipate itself without emancipating labor in a black skin." Keen to communicate this more broadly, Harris wished to tarry no longer with black capitalism. ("I will be damned glad when I am through with that N. banking study," he wrote one friend with characteristic impatience; "I am sick of it. I must do Marx and Veblen! That's real stuff which will make me. Black business wont.") Looking ahead to the next several months, Harris had ambitions of finishing his Marx project for Harcourt, of reworking his comparative study of Marx, Veblen, and Mitchell into book form, and of cowriting an entry (with Sterling Spero) on "The Negro Problem" for the *Encyclopedia of Social Sciences*. Learning that the NAACP's Amenia Conference had been rescheduled for the summer, Harris was adamant about expanding his guiding role: "You can count on my presence," he assured Joel Spingarn.[71]

He was also assuring himself. Recently plagued by symptoms of fatigue, Harris had received a medical checkup that revealed startling but thankfully small "cloudy areas" on his lungs. Naturally he feared tuberculosis—a blight in urban black communities across the nation, another morbid consequence of segregation—but was told the spots would "disappear very shortly," he wrote, "if I get plenty of sleep, drink milk regularly, take the prescribed doses of cod-liver oil and cut down on my work." Between cod-liver oil and rest, the latter was the less palatable prescription. Escaping his Washington apartment (which was "hot as blazes" in the summer) for a cooler environment, he thought, might enable him to remain productive, even if only for a few hours a day. Brookwood, where he had attended a number of conferences, was a possibility, but he supposed the cool, damp air of the Croton Reservoir at Katonah might hamper his recovery. Rather, he arranged for an apartment in Montclair, a New Jersey suburb about ten miles west of Manhattan that kept him from the stifling metropolitan air yet allowed for an easy commute to the collections of the New York libraries he would surely wish to consult. It was an uneasy compromise. He was able to make his scheduled appearance at Swarthmore College's Institute of Race Relations, but he was conspicuously absent from the Washington, DC, Rosenwald conference on the Negro and the New Deal in May, a seminal summit that addressed the African American's status in the contemporary political and economic climate. He made progress on shorter projects, such as his encyclopedia contribution and a book review commissioned by the *Nation*, but he was unable to make great strides on his Marx manuscript.[72]

All the while, the economics of the race problem beckoned. He did not "deny that you can still fight for Negro rights," he wrote his friend and Howard colleague Ralph Bunche during these weeks of convalescence, yet gaining citizenship rights would be "only half of the job." Just as the New Deal was remaking the national economy, it remained necessary for black leaders to develop a comprehensive economic program for the civil rights movement. Too unwell to attend the Rosenwald conference in May, by August Harris had regained enough vitality to broach the topic during the annual Teachers' and Students' Educational Conference at the 135th Street Branch of the YWCA in New York. Ira Reid, of the Urban League, had invited him to address the challenge black labor faced during the current economic crisis. He was back in "the Campus," the Harlem neighborhood he had walked through most days, on his way to work at the Urban League a decade earlier. At the time he had never taken a spot among the speakers on the corner of Lenox Avenue and 135th Street, but now he took the podium in the Harlem YWCA with the authority a doctorate, prestigious academic appointment, and well-regarded monograph bestowed. Harris spoke on "Our Changing Economic Status," sketching arguments he had been developing since his first contributions in *Opportunity*, the *Messenger*, and *Current History*. His talk was well practiced but no less resonant for its wear. Indeed, in the context of the Depression and New Deal, his message was all the more meaningful. He challenged both black and white laborers to consider a course of united action and excoriated the American Federation of Labor for its refusal to organize black workers, its failure to represent unskilled labor, and its focus on raising wages rather than challenging the structural inequities inherent to capitalism. "There is practically no working class solidarity in America," Harris told the YWCA audience, "without which the case of the Negro worker is almost hopeless."[73]

Harris was not without hope, but it was clear that neither the labor movement nor current civil rights leaders could be relied upon to foster such progress at the moment. It would require the steady guidance of an enlightened intellectual vanguard of the sort that he, Du Bois, and his Howard colleagues had discussed to advance an interracial movement dedicated to economic and social justice. In the days following the YWCA gathering, he looked forward to offering such guidance at the Amenia Conference.

W. E. B. Du Bois collected Harris from muggy Montclair the following Friday, August 18th, on the way to the Spingarns' Troutbeck estate. Du Bois had set out earlier that day from Philadelphia, and was joined by two other invitees, Virginia Alexander and Pauline Young. Together the editor, professor, physician, and librarian followed Route 22 north through Westchester County, passing not far from the Brookwood Labor College, where Du Bois and Harris had attended conferences the past few years, then rambled through the villages and farms of the Hudson Valley toward Amenia. When Du Bois rounded the cul-de-sac at Troutbeck, it was clear that the country estate surpassed Brookwood's spartan, if sylvan, setting in Katonah. A row of century-old sycamores stood before the slate-roofed stone manor that put Du Bois in mind of "a beautiful spacious country mansion with pools and gardens in the English style." A fire had devastated the home in 1917, but Spingarn had soon restored the grounds with a flowering splendor. The climbing vines of which he was an enthusiast—clematis—dressed the estate and filled his greenhouses with an array of hues. As Du Bois knew, the 250 species Spingarn had collected constituted the largest single collection in the world. In demand among garden clubs as a guest speaker, Spingarn routinely donated his lecture fees to the NAACP. Those arriving that afternoon would be instructed on the correct pronunciation. The emphasis, the author of *The Climbing Clematis* and *American Clematis for American Gardens* explained, falls on the first syllable—"as if one were about to say clementine." ("Stressing the second syllable was a sure way of winning a dunce cap from the NAACP's militant gardener," one conference participant noted.)[74]

Adjacent to the house were more gardens and a verdant lawn leading to the one-and-a-half-acre Troutbeck Lake, partially obscured by a stand of conifers and several tents arranged for the conference. Harris was pleased to be there. After an evening of reunions and introductions, he retired to one of the smaller tents to sleep. A few of his delegates discussed "serious matters" until dawn, yet were energetic enough to "laugh hilariously" during breakfast on Saturday morning. Harris took his buffet and listened, at nine, when Elmer Carter, elected by the older observers to chair the conference sessions, said a few words to direct breakfast chatter toward constructive conversation regarding the morning agenda: a "General Discussion" of the "Weaknesses and Accomplishments of the older programmes" of such organizations as the NAACP, and thoughts for future plans and programs. When Carter finished, Harris offered to speak. Now that his Howard cohort was finally convened as part of a larger meeting of younger black leaders, as he and Du Bois had discussed for the past several years, Abram Harris wished to make his presence known.[75]

PART TWO

"Perhaps the second Amenia conference will not be as epoch-making as the first, but on the other hand, it is just as possible that it will be more significant for the future than any conference which colored people have yet held. That depends entirely upon what reactions follow this meeting."

—W. E. B. Du Bois, *Crisis, September 1933*

|| 3 ||

At Troutbeck

Joel Spingarn found a seat among the wooden folding chairs arranged under the big tent. Breakfast had been cleared; conference chair and *Opportunity* editor Elmer Carter was yielding the floor in the opening session to Abram Harris. As the trim, bespectacled Howard University economist began to speak, Spingarn recognized the position Harris was outlining. The Association, Harris had long maintained, ought to lead an effort to unite black and white workers, in his opinion the only endeavor that could actually assure meaningful social progress. Harris, Spingarn recalled, had made such an argument the year before in a speech during the NAACP's annual conference in Washington. Several of the two dozen other Amenia delegates had also been in attendance at Shiloh Baptist Church in May 1932, as had Spingarn's NAACP colleagues now present at Troutbeck. Arthur Spingarn, Joel's brother and NAACP board member, *Crisis* editor W. E. B. Du Bois, executive secretary Walter White, and assistant secretary Roy Wilkins were each seated among the Amenia delegates this morning. From invitees such as Harris they hoped to derive a strategy to improve the existing structure and programs of the NAACP.

Du Bois, Joel Spingarn knew, was particularly keen on the young professor. Spingarn was likewise sympathetic to the suggestion that the NAACP develop a stronger economic program within its broad agenda of securing the full range of citizenship rights for African Americans. But what did other young African Americans think? The Amenia Conference was meant to be their forum, eliciting their contributions to the evolving debate concerning the NAACP's program and the future of the civil rights struggle. Spingarn and his fellow Association officers hoped that the twenty-six men and women convening in the privacy of his estate would help to elucidate exactly how the up-and-coming generation of black leadership perceived the past, present, and future of the fight for African Americans' civil rights.

Planning for the conference had begun in earnest that spring, when the NAACP had whittled the list of invitees down to those now seated under the canvas tent. But it had been more than a year since Joel Spingarn first discussed

TROUTBECK, 1930. Yale Collection of American Literature, Beinecke Rare Book and
Manuscript Library.

the idea of holding another Amenia Conference with his NAACP associates
W. E. B. Du Bois and Walter White. The idea of the conference reflected Spingarn's
concern for the future of the NAACP and constituted an effort to reconcile its program with the calls for change that younger African Americans especially were
making during the early 1930s. Bringing them together for a few days at Troutbeck
seemed to Spingarn a way to initiate a concerted response to the concerns that had
worried the NAACP over the past several years.

The year 1931 had been difficult for the NAACP. After two decades of making
the protection of African Americans' civil liberties its priority, by the early 1930s
the Association was compelled to acknowledge the significance of the economic
issues affecting black Americans. In the past, the Association had been willing to
leave this to the National Urban League, whose program specifically focused on
black employment. For its part, the NAACP took up litigation and civil liberties.
In the past decade the NAACP vigilantly, if unsuccessfully, fought for anti-
lynching protections and won the acquittal of Detroit physician Ossian Sweet,
who faced execution after using arms defending his home from a white Ku Klux
Klan–enflamed mob. The previous fall, as the Association moved its offices from
70 to 69 Fifth Avenue in New York, incoming executive secretary Walter White
pitched a successful campaign to prevent the Supreme Court confirmation of
John J. Parker, a North Carolinian notorious for having questioned African

Americans' right to suffrage during the state's 1920 gubernatorial race. Yet even after such a victory, the NAACP faced pressure to alter its program. While the Depression deepened during the early 1930s, it was apparent that the Association needed to heed the radicalism inspiring the "Don't Buy Where You Can't Work" boycott campaigns taking place in Harlem and the new attention garnered by such Communist Party–affiliated groups as the International Labor Defense and the League of Struggle for Negro Rights. When leading black intellectuals like Abram Harris insisted that civil rights organizations adopt a labor-oriented outlook, and when NAACP branches such as the Wilmington, Delaware, local wished to revitalize its mission, the Association was persuaded to consider developing a meaningful economic program. During the annual conference in Pittsburgh that July, where hundreds of delegates gathered for meetings held in Soldiers' Memorial Hall, the NAACP drew resolve from W. E. B. Du Bois's discussion of "The Negro's Economic Future." Afterward, the Association conferees agreed in a collective mandate that representing the black worker would be an essential aspect of the NAACP's future.

Still, the NAACP remained a target for criticism and was experiencing inner turmoil. With the terrible level of black unemployment, conference resolutions seemed an ineffective salve to economic hard times. Worse, the Association even appeared to have faltered in its celebrated legal efforts, despite recent gains. In May 1931, special counsel Nathan Margold (a protégé of Harvard Law constitutionalist Felix Frankfurter) delivered a report to the Association's board of directors mapping a transition from piecemeal attacks on Jim Crow to a systematic assault designed to incrementally, but no less surely, hobble the legal foundation of segregation. That summer, too, NAACP lawyers kept Jess Hollins, a black Oklahoman accused of raping a white woman, from execution. Even so, since March, the imbroglio over the Scottsboro case had tarnished the Association as opportunistic. It appeared the NAACP would only take cases that seemed both winnable and reputable. In this case, the NAACP left nine boys wrongly accused of the gang rape of two white women to face the judgment of an all-white Alabama jury. Had the International Labor Defense not mobilized on their behalf, the nine would have been among the many victims of legal lynchings. Only after the International Labor Defense took action was the NAACP roused; and then, it appeared the Association was concerned as much with protecting its turf as it was with the young defendants' fate. While criticism of its failure to act more concertedly on behalf of the Scottsboro Boys eroded support for the NAACP, attrition also had begun to have an effect. Many of the Association's original supporters had passed away by 1931, leaving once-vital local branches, in such as former hubs of the new abolitionism in Boston and Baltimore, shrinking in membership and sway. Trouble appeared in the national office, too. That fall, the Depression forced supporters of the NAACP to curtail projected gifts, further decreasing what was already a fast dwindling endowment. In the face of budget concerns, Walter White undertook a secret efficiency study suggesting the Association release two popular veteran field secretaries who had devoted a combined twenty-three years of service to the NAACP. In December 1931, when Du Bois penned a letter protesting White's actions, an old feud between the two was rekindled. At the crux this time was control of the *Crisis*. The monthly magazine had begun to bleed money under Du Bois's watch and was again ending the year in debt. Now, as Du Bois criticized the new executive secretary's leadership, White wondered aloud how much longer Du Bois ought to retain the editorship he had held for two decades.[1]

Holding another conference at Troutbeck, as Joel Spingarn and W. E. B. Du Bois discussed while tension at 69 Fifth Avenue spilled into 1932, would not solve all of the NAACP's ailments, but, the Association's board chairman thought, it might help to stem the tide. Du Bois agreed. The *Crisis* editor readily acknowledged criticism that the NAACP was too highbrow (some claimed the acronym actually stood for the National Association for the Advancement of *Certain* People) and could not deny the impecunious position of his monthly magazine. With such criticisms in mind, he had been trying for some time to arrange a conference including Abram Harris, a few of Harris's Howard University colleagues, and several other leading young minds, to discuss future strategies concerning both the Association and the *Crisis*. When at the beginning of 1932 Spingarn invited Du Bois to put his ideas concerning the scope and character of a second Amenia Conference on paper, he acted quickly. The plan Du Bois drew up called for the selection of "a list of about 30 persons, preferably 30–40 years of age, to be invited" to attend the conference. To produce such a list the *Crisis* editor conceived of a procedure aimed at comprehensiveness: they would begin with nominations from each of the Association's officers, then call upon "Friends of the NAACP and acquaintances and prominent citizens" to name from "their community one or more young men or women of education and intelligence, character and courage." Du Bois himself had hundreds of contacts in black communities from Savannah to Seattle who he knew would be only too happy to pass along the names of their brightest young people. When these responses reached New York, a Committee of Administration would then have an elite register from which to handpick "about 30 of the most promising."[2]

Du Bois gave both Spingarn and White copies of his proposal in early January. During the winter and spring of 1932, plans for another conference in Amenia remained informal, as the NAACP had dozens of substantive competing projects to consider. Between January and March the Association's board of directors oversaw an internal examination of the financial situation of the *Crisis*, prepared for the annual conference in Washington, DC, in May, and debated its ongoing participation in the Scottsboro trials. In Alabama, the state's supreme court had upheld the death penalty conviction for all but the youngest of the Scottsboro defendants. Yet while many in the Association, including W. E. B. Du Bois, regretted the International Labor Defense's unsuccessful litigation as a year-long fiasco, the attraction the Communist Party held for many African Americans was understandable, and apparent. That spring, a House of Representatives Committee on Communist Propaganda called Walter White to testify on connections between the NAACP and the Communist Party. While White disavowed even the appearances of a relationship, the Association was indeed concerned about the growing interest among blacks in the Party. The April and May issues of the *Crisis* carried statements from fourteen leading black newspaper editors to help make sense of the matter. On balance, the editors professed to understand the appeal of Communism and they supported the Party's aim of achieving racial equality, if not necessarily the foundation of a workers' state. Carl Murphy of the *Baltimore Afro-American* voiced the most searching articulation of this in the April issue of the *Crisis*, writing, "The Communists appear to be the only party going our way. They are as radical as the NAACP was twenty years ago. Since the abolitionists pushed off the scene, no white group of national prominence has openly advocated the economic, political and social equality of black folks."[3]

The Association's board of directors, among whom were several white new abolitionists, sought to address the sentiment that the NAACP was not as radical as when it was founded. In April, a committee of board members chosen to undertake a "Survey of the NAACP's Work" presented its findings at 69 Fifth Avenue. After noting troubling results, the committee advised taking significant measures to strengthen the Association: granting local NAACP branches more autonomy, for instance, and also establishing "a definite and consistent economic program." Conducting his own informal canvass, board member and Harlem physician Louis Wright reported that the Association "seems to be losing ground with the average man on the street" and "does not attract and hold the minds of the young people." Word "regarding the Association's legal work," he said, ostensibly the NAACP's chief activity, was "not reaching the masses." This main failing, Wright contended, could be traced to "inactivity on the part of our branches," which had long been relied upon to publicize the Association's work through mass meetings and special community events. If Wright's anecdotal evidence was accurate, the implications for the organization's future could be serious. He, for one, wanted a committee to "take up this whole matter."[4] As Wright concluded his remarks, Joel Spingarn sensed it was an appropriate moment to broach his own proposal. He did not want to form another committee, he told the board. He agreed that the Association should regard Wright's concerns with care, but pointed out that an existing committee devising a possible economic program would likely overlap with the one Wright proposed. Furthermore, such a topic would be appropriate to present to a wide audience of NAACP members at that month's annual conference in Washington, DC, where members could voice their own feelings. Spingarn acknowledged that the issue of the NAACP's future demanded special attention and moved that a meeting be devoted to the topic, which he was willing to host at his home later that summer—a second Amenia Conference. As his fellow board members would recall, the Amenia Conference held in 1916 had forged unity among civil rights leaders at a key moment in the early years of the NAACP. With the situation in 1932 as critical for the Association as it had been sixteen years earlier, the board agreed.[5]

Two weeks later, Spingarn announced the dual goals of improving the NAACP's present program and inaugurating an economic agenda at the Association's twenty-third annual conference. As he delivered the opening address to the Association members congregated in Shiloh Baptist Church, a venerable black institution several blocks south of Howard University, he proposed the need to conflate the struggle for African Americans' political and economic rights. During "this period of depression and economic catastrophe," Spingarn said, "our first thought should be of the economic situation of the American Negro." After over two decades of fighting for "political emancipation," the NAACP's next task was to ensure the "economic emancipation" of black workers. "We are framing an economic programme for the Association," he explained, "and we hope to carry it through side by side with our programme for civil rights. The world has learned that the political and the economic struggle must go hand in hand."[6]

The next night W. E. B. Du Bois continued the message, addressing the question "What Is Wrong with the NAACP?" on a panel with Abram Harris. The *Crisis* editor began by professing that the work of the Association he had helped found twenty-three years earlier had been "nothing short of extraordinary." Since 1909, the group had grown from several dozen progressives to a national organization that could claim hundreds of victories along the color line. Even so, he thought it "equally true that the NAACP has not only not settled the Negro problem, it has hardly begun to settle it and what it has not done is far greater in extent and importance than what it has done or has tried to do." Only by taking complaints about the NAACP seriously, he said, could the Association "hope to revise and rearrange our program and strengthen our action and face an even more critical and exacting future."[7]

Du Bois acknowledged several criticisms. First, despite its intentions, the Association had been accused "of being a high-brow organization," disinterested "in the great mass of people." As a result, there was a real need to democratize the organization, "to decentralize the power of the central office" at 69 Fifth Avenue. Officials in New York, critics charged, drew high salaries and seemed to ignore fieldwork, except for "high-profile cases" that promised to earn enough attention to bolster the Association's fundraising campaigns. One consequence seemed to be that the NAACP was "not attracting youth" and, indeed, suffered from the growing perception it had lost its relevance among civil rights organizations. Du Bois thought it not simply an issue of perception: "We are failing in our program to recognize that political and social reform depends today primarily upon economic reform and that without a thorough-going and even revolutionary change in our organization of industry, there can be no frontal attack on race prejudice." Not only did "outdated" programs demand revamping, but the Association also needed to better cultivate younger leaders. "We must realize," Du Bois affirmed,

> that we are receiving yearly a body of three or four thousand trained young people who must be used for the emancipation of the Negro race. Their use for this purpose has been unfortunately limited. Even if they step into life filled with enthusiasm, ideas and the spirit of sacrifice, the opportunities for them to work, particularly for their own people, are limited to an extent which is almost ridiculous. The NAACP has done almost nothing directly to guide and employ these young people, and has done very little to organize them and encourage them to membership and voluntary activity. It is one of our greatest failures, and it calls for the serious attention of this organization in its central office and in all its branches. It is not enough to train our young people. We must ensure them proper employment and the opportunity to forward our ideals.[8]

Abram Harris was among a handful of speakers invited to offer "the viewpoint and the aspirations of young and insurgent Negroes." While Du Bois pointed to the lack of direction the NAACP offered emerging leaders, Harris was not convinced his generation needed the Association's guidance, particularly considering, he said, "the general confusion and sterility of ideas that the depression has shown to exist among old leadership." That evening, Harris discussed "Economic Reconstruction and Negro Welfare," offering criticism of the old guard in the NAACP, which he noticed miffed several Association officers in the audience, including Walter White. But Harris also spoke as an economist, explaining underlying factors of the "present unemployment and industrial derangement." In his expert opinion, the problem of "democratic control of the industrial system" ought to be the "absorbing concern of those individuals who are most disastrously affected by depressions and unemployment." In other words, he argued, "white and black workingmen" needed to unite and assert control of their fate. Of course, strong intellectual leadership would be necessary to overcome entrenched prejudices, on the part of both white and black labor. "Whatever workers will do in facing this problem," Harris explained, "depends upon a leadership which will educate them into a realization of their identity of economic interests and the necessity of a united front for achieving common welfare." This was the future of the civil rights struggle; it would be up to the NAACP to assume a role in it, or not.[9]

Du Bois listened, but he thought Harris overestimated the ability of intellectuals to effect quick, meaningful change. The Howard professor "painted a most beautiful and scientific picture," he said, "of the economic difficulties of the present and the position of the Negro workers," but seemed to conclude "that all we have to do is paint that picture and wait for the white and black workers to get together." The "trouble," as Du Bois saw it, "is that the white and black workers just [were] not getting together," no matter how intellectuals acted. And "until they do get together," he observed, "the Negro has to make a living 'within the color line.'" But with such a status quo unacceptable, Du Bois argued it was imperative that the NAACP "go to the masses with an economic program."[10]

Debate continued the following morning, when Harris served as a discussion leader on "The Negro in the Changing Economic Order." Later that day George Schuyler, the black journalist and head of the Young Negroes Cooperative League, suggested that the NAACP help found "a consumer's co-operative society" in every city where the Association had an active branch. While Harris rejected the notion of creating a separate economy as reinforcing segregation, Schuyler envisioned an opportunity, born of necessity, to "do something economically constructive." Schuyler posited that

> there is only one thing that will save the Negro group from degradation
> in American society and that is intelligent economic organization. As
> long as the Negro's economic life is controlled by white capitalists he
> will be their political victim no matter whether his so-called legislative
> representatives are white or black. Indeed, so long as the Negro has no
> economic power it does not matter a great deal whether he has the suf-
> frage or not.[11]

On this point Harris agreed. But the question of how to take economic control remained; of course, Harris considered the solution evident. It "requires the united organization of black and white laborers," he repeated. "However much these workers may think the problem distinct no one but a fool can fail to observe the identity of economic interest between white and black proletarians." In response to Du Bois, Harris made it clear he fully realized the need to do more than describe the situation and believed the NAACP needed to take a leading role in organizing an interracial workers movement. The conference discussions seemed likewise to convince members of the Association that "what the Negro needs primarily is a definite economic program, and such a program we present as our chief plank in a platform for future reform." As the annual convention concluded, the NAACP's Committee on Resolutions resolved (as its members had the year before in Pittsburgh) to insist upon equal treatment of black and white workers, asserting that blacks cannot cooperate with the current labor movement, which had "betrayed the interests of the Negro worker." The Association needed to take an active role in helping black workers, the committee resolutions stated, in concert with its current programs demanding full suffrage and citizenship rights.[12]

Back in New York in June, Joel Spingarn could be assured that the themes of the 1932 annual conference neatly dovetailed with the plan to sponsor the upcoming Amenia Conference. To the board chairman's chagrin, however, any momentum built during May had dissipated once the NAACP's officers faced the actual administrative challenge of hastily calling such a meeting together that summer. As planning for the conference stalled, Spingarn confided to Association field secretary William Pickens, an old friend, that he wanted the Association to "assume the initiative & do the work" of organizing the conference. Enjoying semiretirement among his gardens at Troutbeck, all he would "offer this year is the idea, the site, & the hospitality." Yet no one at 69 Fifth Avenue seemed interested in taking on the task. By the time of the June board meeting Spingarn was forced to dole out the first orders; he wanted Walter White "within the next few days [to] begin actual work on arrangement for the Conference." White was to invite (as Du Bois's January memorandum had initially proposed) between "twenty to thirty young leaders of opinion."[13]

White promptly arranged to meet with Abram Harris to discuss the content and possible invitees to the conference, but the names Harris suggested troubled Roy Wilkins, the Association's thirty-one-year-old assistant secretary. In particular, Wilkins wished to omit white intellectuals Sterling Spero, Benjamin Stolberg, and Jay Lovestone from the delegate roster. The conference, he believed, ought to be reserved exclusively for young African Americans. Wilkins, a favorite son of colored St. Paul, had come to the Association during the summer of 1931, recruited from the *Kansas City Call*, a reputable black weekly, whose circulation had boomed during his eight-year tenure. Arriving in a setting where "the pall of office politics and intrigue was thicker than smog in Los Angeles," Wilkins had nonetheless decided to stand his own ground. Walter White could not have disagreed more strongly with his protégé, and he expressed as much to his colleagues. "Such a man as Benjamin Stolberg," he argued, "would have a great deal to contribute," as would John Henry Hammond, Jr., a young man he described as endowed with "the finest of instincts." Upon consideration, though, Joel Spingarn opted to heed Wilkins, the very embodiment of emerging Negro leadership. "No white people should be included" in the Amenia Conference, Spingarn decreed. Nothing would prevent white visitors from dropping by Troutbeck for a day to observe, of course, but "the purpose of the conference is to ascertain the aspirations of colored youth."[14]

Spingarn had other reasons than this dispute to be concerned about the conference. Settling the question of interracial participation had taken two weeks, and an invitation list had yet to be drawn up. With time waning, Spingarn attempted to gauge the commitment at 69 Fifth Avenue to the Troutbeck retreat. "The conference," he reminded the Association's officers, "requires a good deal of work and expense, and should not be attempted unless the staff is enthusiastic about it, and begins to master all the details." Sensing that he would bear the burden of seeing to most of these details, Roy Wilkins cautiously voiced his reservations. Should they postpone planning, he wondered in a note to Walter White, "or do you think, in view of the vacation schedules and the work necessary to get it up, that we had better abandon the idea?" Instead of either of these, they did nothing. During the July board meeting Wilkins reported on the still incomplete delegate list and the tentative agreement to hold the conference at some point in late August. Chairman Spingarn, frustrated at White and Wilkins's foot dragging, joined the board in insisting that a date be picked and invitations be sent within the week.[15]

A helpful letter from Du Bois arrived at the NAACP offices the next day. Du Bois, too, suspected that it was rather late to pull off an August gathering. Even so, he gamely suggested a list of forty-one "young college men, over thirty and under forty, who are interested in the problems which we should discuss." (The masculine cast of this roster echoed the sentiment Abram Harris had articulated in an earlier conversation with Du Bois about holding a meeting of Howard colleagues at his home. "Social politics are so confused that get-togethers of the kind I have in mind are highly desirable," Harris had written to Du Bois the previous summer. "You see I have asked no women. Their presence adds to the confusion.") Du Bois did not know all of the men he recommended personally, he explained, but they represented a register of likely conferees. The nineteen most distinguished included over a dozen Ph.D.s and educators, as well as a handful of lawyers—seemingly matching of the caliber and character of Talented Tenth men Du Bois had invited to Niagara Falls a generation earlier. Under a deadline, and at the risk of Joel Spingarn's further reproach, Wilkins immediately set about choosing invitees, relying nearly exclusively on Du Bois's list. Many of the Du Bois selections made the final list, as did Walter White's lone suggestion. In all, Wilkins mailed twenty-six invitations to a veritable who's who of young, degree-holding African American men.[16]

"Sixteen years ago next month," the invitation began, "there was held a private meeting known as the Amenia Conference, which brought together leaders of colored opinion of all schools of thought."

The purpose was to confer in an easy, informal atmosphere and agree on the minimum demands which all colored people could make to secure relief from the disabilities they were suffering.

Today the NAACP believes another such conference might well be held but with slightly different personnel and purpose. The world is in a crisis. Great changes are occurring almost over night. The problem of racial adjustment in America and the world is a constantly shifting one.

How adequate is the present program of the NAACP in this changing state? In 1910 the Association's program was regarded as radical, as being a generation ahead of its time. How is the program regarded today? How should the program be changed or enlarged or shifted or concentrated toward certain ends? The Association wishes these questions to be the theme of a second Amenia conference next month, August 25–27. It seeks frank council from a group of conferees and promises a minimum of publicity, if any. The persons invited are in the main younger men who have finished their training and begun their careers and yet are still thinking and inquiring.

The National Association for the Advancement of Colored People would be glad to have you present at this conference. President J. E. Spingarn of the Association has graciously offered his country estate "Troutbeck," at Amenia, NY, eighty-five miles north of New York City as the seat of the gathering. There will be no fees or expenses of any sort except travel to and from Amenia.[17]

The idea of such a privileged gathering met with uniformly positive response. From Philadelphia, the Harvard Law School–trained attorney Raymond Pace Alexander was among those who perceived in the invitation "many thoughts and suggestions that the younger people of vision and constructive ideas have been discussing for quite a long while." Predictably, not many invitees could attend on such short notice. Among those declining was a key potential delegate, Abram Harris. It was obvious that the significance of the Amenia Conference would be hindered by the NAACP's lack of preparation. White and Wilkins conferred with Spingarn, and all agreed to postpone until the following year. Not two weeks after sending invitations, letters of regret went back out to the twenty-six "outstanding young colored men." In August, the board would be assuaged by the fact that each invitee had "expressed keen interest in the meeting for 1933." Publicly, the Association cited "the economic depression" as the reason for postponement, but Spingarn also rued the lack of effective organizing shown at 69 Fifth Avenue.[18]

* * *

That winter, Spingarn—the Troutbeck gardener—intended to nip potential disappointment for 1933 in the bud. During the fall, Walter White had sought to maneuver the African American voting bloc into a position of advantage. After the strength black voters had demonstrated in the 1930 Judge Parker fight, White had hoped to make gains for the African American electorate during the 1932 presidential elections. The executive secretary's success in pressuring candidates Herbert Hoover and Franklin Roosevelt to enunciate a civil rights platform was at best marginal, however, and by the end of fall Joel Spingarn was eager to focus on fostering change within the Association. In late December, Spingarn directed White and Du Bois to initiate planning of the Amenia Conference. The past summer the NAACP had not followed Du Bois's suggestion that invitees be picked from a "wide correspondence" among Association members across the country. This winter, however, Spingarn wished them to follow such a procedure—and they would have to begin immediately. In order to allow potential delegates the opportunity to arrange their summers around the conference, invitations needed to be mailed by February or March. Finally, Spingarn even provided suggestions for a conference program to accompany each invitation. All the New York office had to do, then, was choose the delegates.[19]

Still, by March the board had yet to endorse the conference, conferees had yet to be chosen, invitations had yet to be mailed, and Joel Spingarn had given up. Stonewalled, he sent a letter of resignation to be read at the March board meeting. While staggered Association officers rallied to appease Spingarn, the board officially accepted the proposal of sponsoring another Amenia Conference. In a week, Du Bois could report to New York that "conference fever" was "in the air." Walter White had again argued for including "younger *white*" representatives, and was even interested in organizing an immediate, though supplemental, conference to discuss overcoming the generation gaps in local branches that seemed to "discourage initiative on the part of young people." But even the task of inviting only African American delegates "to obtain a new vision of the future of the American Negro" soon became daunting enough. Chairing the conference committee from Atlanta (where he taught at Atlanta University while continuing to edit the *Crisis*) Du Bois pressed no fewer than eighty-five well-stationed friends from Los Angeles to Cincinnati to nominate potential conferees. The nominees, he insisted, ought to be educated but also dynamic—above all, they must not be "fixed in their ideas."[20]

The volume of the response surpassed even optimistic expectations. From the YMCA's National Board, Channing Tobias sent his regards and ten suggestions. George Arthur of the Rosenwald Fund, a leading philanthropic contributor to African American causes, provided the names of twelve candidates he deemed appropriate. The principal of Baltimore's newly opened Frederick Douglass High School, himself a veteran of the first Amenia Conference, offered a handful of promising young people to consider; Indianapolis's Raymond W. Cannon overwhelmed the Association with a list of ninety-five. Noting that "the response from the letters sent out has been so cordial and so many persons have been recommended that it has been unnecessary to send the follow-up reminder," Du Bois forwarded 579 names to the New York office, no doubt happy to leave the initial selection process to his colleagues.[21]

Meeting to identify likely candidates, Joel and Arthur Spingarn, Walter White, and Roy Wilkins each confessed their amazement "at the mass of names so quickly assembled." But the unwieldy roster needed pruning down to twenty-five. The four went through the correspondence, culling candidates, then returned to Du Bois the names of forty possible invitees arranged in two lists of both "A" and "B" selections (this time including men *and* women). From these he was to choose a compromise of thirty-two delegates—the most that could fit in eight tents. Together, the names combined in a still shot of coming "leaders of Negro thought," the best and brightest of the Talented Tenth's next generation. Impressed after reviewing the results of the nationwide search, White remarked that simply compiling "this list of young key people throughout the country" validated the Association's efforts. Du Bois agreed; he suggested inviting them all.[22]

During the second week of April, Joel Spingarn typed the invitations on his Troutbeck letterhead, mailing them from Amenia, New York, to prospective delegates. In a few days they reached a room on the second floor at 1002 French Street in Wilmington, Delaware; the national office of the YWCA on Broadway in New York City; the sociology department at Fisk University in Nashville; the Cleveland Public Library; the Jackson home on Druid Hill Avenue in Baltimore; the engineering division of the Pullman Company in Chicago; and the economics, political science, and English departments at Howard University. The invitees shared the imprimatur of older leaders and a Talented Tenth pedigree of higher learning and political conscience. Beyond this, however, those receiving Joel Spingarn's invitation harbored an array of outlooks. Some, like the lawyer Louis Redding, who had crossed the color line in Delaware, exemplified the generational transition taking place in the civil rights struggle—the promising young leaders' inheritance of an elite black protest tradition that remained unswervingly defiant of the Jim Crow order. Others, like the academic Abram Harris, were no less accepting of their place within the legacy of Talented Tenth protest but wished to fundamentally redefine the race struggle by incorporating an economic agenda that would transform traditional protest organizations such as the NAACP. In the months after they received their invitations, a number of the invitees reflected the range of actions their generation was taking by arguing, writing, and litigating along the color line. Even as the NAACP wished to reassess its program, during the spring and summer of 1933 many Amenia invitees were engaged in characteristic efforts to demonstrate the precariousness of the contemporary black experience and to advance the civil rights struggle.

In May, for instance, two of the more established Amenia delegates, Ira De A. Reid, director of the National Urban League's department of research, and Fisk University sociologist E. Franklin Frazier, both figured prominently at the Rosenwald Fund's Conference on the Economic Status of the Negro held at the Department of the Interior in Washington, DC. The conference was intended to initiate breakthroughs in the integration of unions and industry, but when the American Federation of Labor and most business and government representatives snubbed their invitations, the conference instead served as a mecca of black social scientists and social workers. Amid the group the six-foot-three Ira Reid stood tall, literally and figuratively. The lanky, likeable Virginian had followed Abram Harris as an Urban League fellow at the University of Pittsburgh in 1924. Since then, as a representative of the New York Urban League and as Charles Johnson's successor in the national office, Reid had produced a score of works (largely published in *Opportunity*) that had established him as among the leading black sociologists. During the Rosenwald Conference, Reid demonstrated his expertise by cataloguing the challenges that black professionals and entrepreneurs had experienced during the recent years of depression. He also showed a pragmatic independent-mindedness, challenging the black bourgeoisie to discard its traditional embrace of capitalism by suggesting that black businesses adopt a measure of cooperative economic action in the hopes that "the Negro mass might share both the control and the profits." This position placed Reid alongside Abram Harris, with his ongoing interrogation of black capitalism, a critique E. Franklin Frazier had built upon in his own stirring evisceration of "La Bourgeoisie Noire."[23]

E. Franklin Frazier likewise attested to the deleterious impact of the Depression and even more strongly challenged black conservatism. An expert on the black family, Frazier delineated the dire circumstances African Americans endured eking out a peasant's subsistence in the South and "the severe struggle to survive in the keen competition of the urban environment" in the great Negro ghettos of the industrial North. During the proceedings, Frazier was characteristically disinclined to remain a detached observer, publicly sparring with Kelly Miller, his former sociology professor at Howard University, who had bizarrely proposed a "back-to-the-farm movement." Their squabble, which made headlines in the *Baltimore Afro-American*, reflected the same aversion to accommodation that had forced him from his directorship of the Atlanta School of Social Work in 1927; in June of that year, Frazier had published "The Pathology of Race Prejudice" in *Forum*, an essay controversially contending that racism resulted from white psychosis and—most explosively—from whites' barely suppressed sexual desire for the black body. Discovering that the author "Edward F. Frazier" was in fact the Atlanta professor, the city's daily newspapers reacted fiercely to the article; and when death threats started to arrive, Frazier began to fear for his and his wife's lives. The trustees at Atlanta University, however, declined to extend Frazier much protection. Frazier had troubled the university for some time, going back to his reputedly poor rapport with a white female colleague. Eager to leave Atlanta, Frazier appealed to W. E. B. Du Bois, for whom he had recently completed a study of Negro common schools in the South. Sympathetic, Du Bois tried but could not prevail upon his alma mater, Fisk University, to hire Frazier to head its sociology department. Gossip about Frazier's tenure in Atlanta had marked him as caustic and, more troubling to administrators in Nashville, unable to get along with southern white folk. Instead, having already earned his master's degree from Clark University, Frazier enrolled in the distinguished sociology department at the University of Chicago to begin work toward his doctorate. In five years, his dissertation appeared to acclaim as *The Negro Family in Chicago*, a case study that Frazier drew upon during the Rosenwald Conference to describe the effects of the Depression on the social dynamics of the African American family. Quarreling with Kelly Miller at the conference made for a good deal of tittle-tattle, but it also displayed a rejection of the deference so common among the members of his generation who had no intention of acceding to white supremacy or to misguided Negro elders. Frazier's temperament may have led to professional difficulties, yet it also marked him as the sort of black intellectual the NAACP wished to confer with in Amenia.[24]

Certainly, no one mistook Charles Houston for deferential. Among those called to Troutbeck, Houston was most responsible for advancing the NAACP's agenda that summer. He did not attend the Rosenwald Conference in May 1933—he was a lawyer, not a social scientist—but a week later he spoke during a mass meeting held under the auspices of the Washington Scottsboro Action Committee at Lincoln Temple Congregational Church, in the Secret City's U Street district, several blocks south of Howard University, where Houston headed the law school. Pledging commitment to the Scottsboro defense, and standing next to his slight, trim colleague (and fellow Amenia invitee) Edward "Eddie" Lovett, six-foot Charles Houston looked decidedly imposing. And when he spoke, it was clear why he was considered the most distinguished black lawyer under forty and, moreover, the black attorney arguably most firmly on the frontlines of civil rights litigation. The law office of Houston and Houston was on F Street, in the cluster of African American neighborhoods several blocks northwest of the Capitol. Houston's sixty-three-year-old father, William, had founded the practice in 1910, after earning his law degree during night classes at the Howard University Law School. The younger Houston had a more exalted education. A pupil at the esteemed M Street High School, which groomed the District's Talented Tenth, Houston was an Amherst College Phi Beta Kappa and graduate of Harvard Law, where he served as the first African American editor of the *Harvard Law Review* and took a doctorate in jurisprudence, his record earning him plaudits in the pages of the *Crisis*, as well as the enduring respect of several faculty members. Over the years he became personally close with several of the nation's most celebrated legal thinkers, including Roscoe Pound, Felix Frankfurter, and Joseph Beale. After winning Harvard's coveted Sheldon Traveling Fellowship in 1923 to study civil law for a year at the University of Madrid in Spain, Houston returned to Washington in the fall of 1924 where he joined both his father's practice and the faculty of Howard University Law School. A Washington homecoming, though, meant returning to the segregated world. Loath to accommodate, he and several other African American lawyers in the city formed the Washington Bar Association. While the group tried to persuade the lily-white DC Bar Association to open its law library to black attorneys, Houston also became involved in the modernization of the Howard University Law School, which would offer respectable training to those students denied entry elsewhere.[25]

In the fall of 1927, a conversation concerning "the problems of legal education for Negroes" with Leonard Outhwaite, executive director of the Rockefeller Foundation, led Houston to take an even more considered look at the status of his fellow African American lawyers. Offering funding, Outhwaite proposed that Houston undertake "some special inquiries regarding the status and activities of the Negro lawyer in America" and "the relation of the American Negro to legal justice." Houston was more than receptive to the idea. He initially planned to start his survey with several short field trips "within easy travel distance of Washington," including to New York, Philadelphia, Baltimore, and Richmond, but by the following spring Houston had toured most of the United States east of the Mississippi and proposed extending his research further west. The weeks spent in the South proved the most affecting. "Since I have been South," he wrote Outhwaite from Louisville in April 1928, "I have tried to expose myself to every experience within the range of Negro life. I have been in the mills, theaters, churches, courts, schools, jails, insane asylums, docks, farms, gambling houses and every place else I could get into. I have walked the field with an industrial insurance agent, and been with a doctor on his calls." Having visited fourteen cities, Houston better understood the role a committed cadre of Negro lawyers could play in solving "the race question" in the South—by securing the protection of civil rights and by embodying African American dignity and responsibility. Upon his return home to Washington in May, Houston was inspired to produce a document of significance, something far more substantial than the fifteen-page preliminary findings he had already written for Outhwaite. A devastating bout of tuberculosis (perhaps contracted while visiting a southern jail or gambling house) felled him that month, however, preventing him from completing the project he envisioned and, indeed, of even working for nearly a year. When Houston regained his strength in the spring of 1929, he accepted the deanship of Howard University Law School, which he transformed into a modern, accredited institution that trained black lawyers in both jurisprudence and social responsibility. Graduates of Howard Law were "social engineers," as he would describe the role of the black lawyer, expected to advance the status of African Americans.[26]

Beyond Howard Law, Houston established just such a role himself, becoming one of the NAACP's most valued litigators during the early 1930s. In the summer of 1933 Houston was involved in case work that he hoped would demonstrate the NAACP's dedication to protecting black defendants as well as undermine one of the central pillars that supported segregation: all-white juries. While the NAACP endured fallout from the Scottsboro trials, Houston could speak to the Association's ongoing commitment to defend African Americans' civil liberties. A month earlier, *Opportunity* carried an account Houston had written of an NAACP lawyer's defense of a black teenager in Philadelphia facing execution for rape and murder; like the Scottsboro case, which had resulted in a legal precedent assuring accused blacks of adequate legal counsel, the acquittal of this young defendant hinged on convincing the court that African Americans were entitled to a fair trial. Addressing the Washington Scottsboro Action Committee at Lincoln Temple in May 1933, Houston took up the recent, and similarly exemplary, case of George Crawford, a thirty-year-old black ex-convict who had been accused of the brutal slaying of two well-to-do white women during a botched robbery in rural Virginia during the winter of 1932. The NAACP had only become involved in the case a year later, after Crawford was discovered having fled to Boston. Initially, the Boston NAACP had protected Crawford; he claimed to have alibi witnesses placing him in Massachusetts at the time of the murder. Butler Wilson, a seventy-three-year-old black attorney and longtime president of the local branch (with whom Houston had become acquainted during his survey of Negro lawyers) had helped engineer a successful defense, blocking Massachusetts from extraditing Crawford to Virginia on the grounds that he would not receive a fair trial in a state that did not allow blacks to sit on its juries. Whether the federal court would uphold the decision was still undecided in May, but Houston had prepared remarks to discuss during mass meetings such as this, emphasizing the importance of the Crawford defense for challenging the constitutionality of segregated southern juries. As Houston could explain, dismantling all-white southern juries would in turn offer future black defendants better assurance of a fair trial. It would be one more strike at the legal foundation of Jim Crow, just the sort of social engineering Houston argued civil rights lawyers could achieve, and just the sort of precedent the NAACP was committed to securing.[27]

Involvement in the Crawford case enhanced Houston's profile, making him among the most prominent and influential of the men and women invited to Amenia. Having already placed Houston on the Association's National Legal Committee, executive secretary Walter White was considering naming him as NAACP special counsel, its lead legal strategist. Meanwhile, in July, the Association invited Houston to serve as a featured closing speaker during the NAACP's annual conference in Chicago. Stressing the need for moderate but deliberate change, Houston gave measured voice to his generation's impassioned call for greater attention to the economic issues faced by African Americans. Observing Houston's prominence during the summer of 1933, the *Washington Tribune* considered the dean of the Howard Law School a sterling example of the emerging black leadership. "Outspoken in his championship of such 'radical' movements as the work of the Scottsboro Action Committee" and an equally fervent advocate of the NAACP, Houston had proven willing to throw "himself boldly and militantly into every fight and effort for racial betterment, local and national, that his time and means would permit."[28]

When Houston stopped off at 69 Fifth Avenue later in the month to discuss the Crawford case and the upcoming Amenia Conference, it was clear that the New Deal was affecting the nature of the fight for racial advancement. In late July, the NAACP office was abuzz with reactions to recent developments in Washington. Amenia invitee Emmett Dorsey, an affable political science instructor at Howard, had just been in New York consulting with Walter White. Since March, the Roosevelt administration had overseen the passage of a host of legislative reforms creating such new federal initiatives as the Civilian Conservation Corps, the Tennessee Valley Authority, the Agricultural Adjustment Authority, the National Recovery Administration, and the Public Works Administration. Such programs promised to put thousands of Americans to work, to create new infrastructure in neglected regions of the nation, and to offer hope to a populace worn after several years of woe. Considering the impact this sweeping liberal legislation could have on African Americans, Dorsey impressed upon the executive secretary "the necessity of having an economist stationed in Washington this summer for the purpose of analyzing the new legislation and code regulations governing industry and governmental activity." While Dorsey suggested that the NAACP consider creating a position for his colleague Abram Harris, all were aware that a pair of young Harvard-trained African Americans, John P. Davis and Robert Weaver, had already launched the Negro Industrial League, an improvised watchdog group overseeing New Deal code hearings in Congress to ensure equal treatment of black workers. Even without Dorsey's insistence, it was evident that the gathering in Amenia would certainly have to address the potential impact of the New Deal.[29]

Walter White may have considered adding Davis and Weaver to the list of invitees—though, with legislative aide Roy Ellis already committed to attending, he may have felt that they already had at least one conferee with intimate knowledge of congressional machinations. Besides, the tents would be full and, along with Houston's visible ascendancy that summer, the current roster of Amenia delegates appeared impressive enough. Their endeavors that summer reflected the breadth of backgrounds and the arrangement of voices that would be heard at Troutbeck. A year after publishing his first volume of poetry, *Southern Road*, to high acclaim, Howard University poet Sterling Brown had confirmed his status not only as a premier folk poet but had also cemented his literary credentials—in both "The Literary Scene," his monthly *Opportunity* column, and "The Negro Character as Seen by White Authors," a work of careful scholarship published in the April issue of the *Journal of Negro Education*. Ralph Bunche, the handsome former basketball standout at UCLA who was pursuing his doctorate at Harvard University, had returned to Washington that spring (where he taught political science at Howard University) from a ten-month trip abroad in Paris and West Africa. Traveling by boat and automobile ("the latter being driven by natives," noted the *Washington Tribune*) Bunche had trekked through the interiors of Togoland and Dahomey, and had also toured Morocco, Sierra Leone, Senegal, and French Guinea. Over the summer, he could be found among the stacks of Harvard's grand new Widener Library, busy turning his field notes into what promised to be a formidable dissertation on the politics of colonial West Africa. Moran Weston, a twenty-two-year-old student at the Union Theological Seminary, had recently organized a national Student Conference on Negro Student Problems held at Columbia University's McMillin Theatre. Pauline Young, librarian at Howard High School in Wilmington, Delaware, had just published a bibliography of essential works on African Americans in a leading professional journal. Juanita Jackson—of the Baltimore Jacksons, the epitome of the city's Talented Tenth—was spending several weeks on tour in the South and Southwest for the Methodist Episcopal Church. And both E. Franklin Frazier and the national YWCA's Marion Cuthbert had appeared that month at the inaugural Institute of Race Relations at Swarthmore College, outside Philadelphia.[30]

Charles Houston, as the nation's black weeklies detailed that summer, was back on the road with Edward Lovett. After visiting the NAACP's New York offices at the end of July, the two traveled first to Charles County, Maryland, to consider defending a forty-two-year-old man accused of murder; then, in early August, the two were in Alabama, where the Birmingham NAACP had requested help challenging the death sentence of a wrongly convicted man, and where two teenagers had been lynched outside of Tuscaloosa. In the middle of the month, Houston and Lovett returned to Washington. Houston was to have been among a delegation of civil rights advocates to report to President Roosevelt on the

Tuscaloosa incident. Arriving for the appointment, however, Houston and his colleagues were treated brusquely by the White House staff (including the grandson of Jubal Early, a Confederate general and vocal supporter of the "Lost Cause"), were asked to wait for hours, and were ultimately dismissed with the vague excuse that Roosevelt could not spare a moment's attention away from the economic crisis. Leaving Washington for Amenia, Houston and Lovett had the opportunity to consider what this rebuff signified: a president guarded by segregationists and reliant upon key southern Democrats in the House and Senate would make for an uncertain ally in the movement to secure African American civil liberties.[31]

The delegates arriving in Amenia that afternoon and evening may have made their mark that summer—but much remained to accomplish. On Friday, August 18, the Spingarns welcomed them to Troutbeck.

As the sun cleared the treetops east of Troutbeck Lake on Saturday morning, August 19, Joel Spingarn listened to Abram Harris finish making his argument. It was a practiced refrain. But in this context, Harris's words offered a vivid transition. It was hardly midmorning and the Amenia conferees had already signaled the difference between this and Du Bois's initial assembly of men of the Talented Tenth at Fort Erie, Ontario, in 1905. Then, the Niagara Movement's talk of racial uplift and the need to secure civil liberties had resounded at the Erie Beach Hotel; a generation later, beneath the big tent at Troutbeck, Abram Harris spoke of the need for action, calling not to lift the masses but to galvanize all African Americans in pursuit of economic as well as civil rights. If the NAACP was willing to redefine its priorities, the effort could begin in Amenia.

The NAACP, Harris contended, ought to stress interracial working class unity as a primary supplement to its current focus on the struggle for blacks' political rights. Harris had expressed such thoughts as recently as the week before during an address at the Harlem YWCA, but they had appeared most fully in print as the final chapter of *The Black Worker*, his 1931 monograph. In particular, he noted significant roadblocks to true social progress for African Americans. Each grew from a debilitating "race psychology," especially among white unionists, but also among advocates of black separatism, unwilling to align with "po' whites," and each was the result of the influence of middle-class blacks, whose support of capitalism Harris could trace to the 1860s. But the Amenia Conference was a better venue for describing the failure of contemporary labor and civil rights leadership than for teaching a history lesson.

Harris had a measure of respect for the NAACP, and had even described the Association in *The Black Worker* as "the most intelligent" of any organization representing "racial leadership." Still, he argued, black leaders within the NAACP were imbued with the same characteristics as most other middle-class "educated leaders of the Negro community" who "see only the racial aspect" of blacks' condition in the United States. "Negro leadership of the past generation," he asserted, "has put its stress on the element of race. Their people's plight, they feel is the plight of a race. They turn a deaf ear to those who say that the Negro's plight is the plight of the working class in general merely aggravated by certain special features. All of the various schools of Negro thought which have had real influence upon Negro life have had one end in view, the elimination of racial discrimination," not economic equality. To Harris, the narrowness of this vision was obvious—he hoped the circumstances of the Depression might convince others, too, of the necessity of adding an economic program to ongoing attempts "to stop lynching and Jim Crowism in all its forms." Civil rights leaders might demand "that the Negro receive decent and equal treatment in all public places and that he be accorded all those constitutional rights, including full suffrage," but Harris felt that "if all these disabilities were removed," the NAACP, like most groups, would be "satisfied with the world as it is." Yet, even with full protection of citizenship rights, Harris believed, most African Americans would still face significant, structural disadvantages preventing their joining society on an equal level. Some who recognized this, he noted, had succumbed to the temptation of designing an independent black economy. He thought the folly of such an endeavor obvious; even attempting separatism would be poisonous to potential interracial unity. It would be up to such local and national black leaders as the Amenia delegates to convey these messages and begin the work of transforming the future of both black and white America.[32]

Emmett Dorsey, like his fellow Howard University colleagues Sterling Brown, Ralph Bunche, and Charles Houston, was well versed in Harris's position. But others, such as the of the YMCA National Board's Frank Wilson, Louisville instructor Hazel Browne, Cleveland librarian Thelma Taylor, and Chicago engineer Howard Shaw, likely heard Harris for the first time that morning. Whether he convinced these members of his audience or not, the conversation Harris joined during the opening session of the conference took on a radical tinge. Louis Redding spoke little that morning, but he listened carefully. He found "the pronouncements of those who opened discussions at the Conference," he wrote a short time later, to be "rather insistent" about "the imminence of basic change in the political, economic and social structure of our country." Exactly "what the change would bring no one would prophesy," but "equally insistent was the judgment that the older policies for Negro advancement had failed and were inappropriate to the changed order impending." Ralph Bunche noticed the same sentiments. "It was early apparent," he later reminisced, "that many of the members of this group had no deep reverence for the elder statesmen of the Negro race." Several of the Amenia delegates engaged in "vigorous plain talking" as "the opinions of men such as James Weldon Johnson, Du Bois, Walter White and

William Pickens, were scathingly criticized and in their presence." To Bunche, there was the whiff of youthful hubris and misplaced confidence. It seemed there were some "whose egos expanded unduly in the belief that they had suddenly blossomed into important leaders in the race because they found themselves among the select circle of choice few who had been invited to 'Troutbeck.'" While "there was much talk about 'leaders,'" some of those who spoke offered "a discouraging lack of any evidence of clear thinking and courageous approach to the Negro problem." Several delegates evinced "a striking independence of thought and a vigorous militancy," but instead of proposing new programs, "the NAACP itself came in for a good deal of criticism." Such delegates made it "abundantly clear that in the minds of many of the conferees the programs of Negro organizations such as the NAACP were considered short-sighted and in-adequate." Bunche preferred analysis to vitriol, though, and hoped that the same voices disparaging the NAACP would next offer concrete proposals for new, concerted action.[33]

Noon lunch arrived before the group considered taking specific steps. The character of the morning session was a topic of conversation over delegates' plates of melon, roast beef, and potato salad. The NAACP had convened the conference, in the words of W. E. B. Du Bois, with "a definite object." They had gathered this particular group in order to "bring together and into sympathetic understanding, Youth and Age interested in the Negro problem" and with the hope of recommending a clear future program for the Association. Yet to Ralph Bunche, to Du Bois, and to several of the delegates, Saturday had not started off well. Frank Wilson of the YMCA, for one, sensed that "the younger Negroes in attendance seemed to take this conference as their real opportunity to demon-strate a certain conversance with the literature of Marxism." He grumbled, "The more vociferous of the group seemed far more concerned about demonstrating their intellectual identity with the proletarian masses than in addressing them-selves to the peculiar problems" that, as he saw it, "were immediately affecting" most African Americans. Roy Ellis, an assistant clerk with the House of Repre-sentative's committee on labor, singled out the remarks Abram Harris made that morning as removed from the actual daily struggle most blacks faced. Assistant secretary Roy Wilkins, too, wished to dismiss Harris as "an angry young econo-mist" who did not speak for the majority.[34]

The taciturn Louis Redding, however, was less put off by the session. Indeed, he was ready for such open discussion. He had kept company, after all, with people from a range of political opinions in his home state—from conservative and moderate local politicians to even the radical perspectives of "leaders of Communist thought and activities" he had organized in the Wilmington Open Door Forums. With each group he had been willing to argue "their philosophy and its application to Negroes," and "whenever these discussions crystallized for definite action," Redding had been "active in pursuit of whatever ends were set up." But on Saturday morning, action appeared to be, at best, a ways off. After the session's call for such broad changes, Redding thought it "a logical necessity that there should be a resolute decision to junk the old policies, followed by a clear-cut outlining of basically new philosophies, or policies." Ideally, he hoped, these "would be adaptable to the Negro masses rather than considerate only of the 'talented tenth.'" Though discussion that morning had emphasized labor as an issue to bridge the black masses and elites, to Redding the absence of an actual plan was frustrating.[35]

After lunch, such frustrations were set aside for recreation. As promised, visitors arrived. NAACP stalwarts Mary White Ovington and James Weldon Johnson drove from their respective summer residences thirty miles to the north in Great Barrington, Massachusetts. William Pickens interrupted his survey of Hudson Valley NAACP branches to make an appearance; Daisy Lampkin likewise briefly broke from her branch work. Prominent Harlemites and NAACP benefactors Ernest and Lillian Alexander were welcomed, as was Lewis Mumford, a white writer and beloved neighbor of the Spingarns' who noted, with some mirth, that the Leedsville Road had been "placarded" with signs ("This way to the Amenia Conference: Amenia Conference 1 Mile!") despite his friend's insistence on "secretly entertaining a secret conference." Mingling with the assembled guests, Mumford was taken with the rustic conviviality of the occasion. "They had no mattresses on their beds, no place except the lake to wash in, and no place wherever to shave in." No matter, one guest joked: "Fortunately our race is supposed to be the least hairy of the three great divisions of mankind." Smiling at that, Mumford thought he had never seen "such a lot of jolly, hearty, strong, confident, chaffering, good-natured people anywhere."[36]

To Mumford, it was easy to ascribe such geniality to the contemplative surroundings at Troutbeck. Joel Spingarn spoke of his property in unpretentious terms, calling it simply "our place" or "the land"; Mumford thought "the Domain of Troutbeck" a romantic wellspring with a distinctive history. An eighteenth-century inhabitant of the valley (centenarian Eunice Mauwee, the "Queen of the Schaghticokes," according to the Moravians who recorded their 1859 conversation with "the last full-blooded Indian of her tribe") called the region Webutuck—"Pleasant," in her tongue, or, more expansively, "the Pleasant Hunting Grounds." For generations, the Schaghticokes had annually burned the valley, attracting deer to the abundant sweet grass that grew from the ashes. Only a few ancient elms and oaks had survived the yearly flames, and the colonists settling the open valley during the eighteenth century saw in the sheltered meadows hundreds of acres of tillable alluvial pasture. They also found iron ore. In the years before the American Revolution, Dunham Forge was founded near the base of thousand-foot-high Oblong Mountain, one of a number of furnaces that dotted the colonial

Hudson Valley. A century and a half later, they were crumbling relics. Spingarn had shown Mumford such sites—including the defunct "Yellow City" mine on the southwestern edge of his property—during amiable excursions through a Dutchess County by then devoted to farms and dairies, but whose place names (such as the hamlet of Irondale, just to the north of Amenia) bore echoes of the colonial era. Troutbeck Lake itself was formed over an old iron-ore bed, giving the springwater dammed there a yellow tint Mumford had noted while resting on the same wooden diving dock that the Amenia delegates were leaping from that afternoon.[37]

Those who preferred not to swim in the shallow, warm lake could canoe, match up on the tennis courts behind the main house, or wander across the estate, which Mumford believed had a revivifying effect on its visitors: across the meadow, where a number of guests had struck up a game of baseball, to "the rocky flanks" of the Oblong where one was "close to the same primeval wilderness the Indians found here and may rouse a covey of partridge, or hear, in the distance, the high bark of the red fox." From this vantage could be seen a pleasing vista of the countryside, from tree-lined Wardwell Peak over Withypool, a small lake cupped between the hills, toward the village of Amenia, whose name, derived from the Latin, meant, like its native counterpart, "pleasant." With rattlesnakes known to nest among the ledges there, the leery could be forgiven for wishing to hasten back downhill to the paths that wound through the estate. In all, trails traced a three-and-a-half-mile circuit around the Spingarns' intervale sanctuary. In "an hour's tramp," marveled Mumford, one passed from the limestone ridge to the cover of cedar and birch and pine, along the elecampane and primroses that edged marsh and icy brook, toward the orchards, sunken gardens, and greenhouses where Joel Spingarn's renowned clematises flourished in the lime-rich soil. The less adventurous could walk the well-trodden quarter-mile circuit surrounding the main house with its heirloom orchards and rare shrubs (some of them brought from the Arnold Arboretum in Boston), and terraces and trellises and rock walls. Fittingly, there were trout to spot in the spring near the house and towering oaks, wide willows, and a stand of sycamores to linger beneath as the rain began to fall.[38]

With the coming of rain that afternoon, Spingarn showed some of his guests into his home, an L-shaped stone manor with a steep slate roof, heavy casement windows, and south-facing main rooms that fostered "a sense of being snug, protected, inviolate." One visitor thought it "the kind of English country-house that had once brought together philosophers and poets and fostered the literary life and the development of thought." Indeed, Spingarn, himself a scholar of the Italian Renaissance, consciously carried on a literary legacy at Troutbeck that he cherished as much as his gardens. Some decades earlier, its previous owners, the Benton family, had named the environs "Troutbeck" after the English Lake

District village that had inspired the works of the Romantic poets William Wordsworth and Samuel Taylor Coleridge. Moved by the American transcendentalists as well, the Bentons had formed the Amenia Literary Society during the 1850s. After listening to Henry David Thoreau lecture at the Poughkeepsie Lyceum, Myron Benton had even penned a meditation on the Webutuck, in the manner of Thoreau's *A Week on the Concord and Merrimac*. A conscientious steward of tradition, Joel Spingarn kept artifacts of this heritage in the library, including an old copybook containing the minutes of the literary society and Charles Benton's history of Troutbeck. (The Benton history detailed his family's poetic inclinations and even speculated that, unlike so many other landholders in the Hudson Valley at the turn of the nineteenth century, they had renounced slavery from the beginning of the Republic. Certainly they paid homage to such abolitionists as Thoreau and Wendell Phillips, the latter having even once visited the Benton homestead, a history that the "new abolitionist" Spingarn treasured.) Since purchasing the estate in 1910, Spingarn had lent cottages on the property to young writers, published a series of "Troutbeck Leaflets" on a private press, and convened numerous symposia of scholars and novelists, painters and poets, which found the likes of Sinclair Lewis, Van Wyck Brooks, and Lewis Mumford happily sequestered in "the sheltered valley" of the Dutchess County gentleman gardener. In Spingarn, Mumford detected a touch of Aristotle's "*Magnificent Man*: one who uses his riches for some purpose"; Van Wyck Brooks believed his friend and mentor—indeed, his "guardian"—"the incarnation of the *genius loci*."[39]

Entering the Spingarn home that Saturday afternoon, one Amenia delegate was less reverent. The splendid setting elicited not fawning awe but a rude comment from a "young man" whose identity a mortified W. E. B. Du Bois would conceal under the name "Jones." This "well-educated and in some ways brilliant" delegate (likely Emmett Dorsey, who was planning a master's thesis on Leninism and known to be rather blunt) was to Du Bois's mind "a communist and also irresponsible and unreliable." Each of these flaws was in ample evidence as the group stepped into Spingarn's home. Jones "stood in the parlor and grinned," Du Bois remembered, "and said aloud to the visitors: 'Comes the revolution, and Commisar Jones will live here!'" The remark punctured the afternoon idyll. Spingarn, Du Bois noticed, "did not appreciate the joke." Neither did Du Bois, particularly not after the direction the conversation had taken during the Saturday morning session. The remark, even if made in jest, made an indelible impression. Some years later, Spingarn's brother Arthur, also present at the conference, scribbled out a note naming some of those he thought had participated in the "Amenia Conference 1934." The list was short and some of the names were wrong, as was the date of the conference. But he did not forget to list the "'Comes the revolution' man."[40]

For some, the remark might have seemed an appropriately facetious jab. There was a significant irony in having to rely upon the largesse of ennobled white benefactors, such as the Spingarns, no matter how dedicated to the cause of new abolitionism. While Joel Spingarn enjoyed the privileged life of the country squire, protected in his secluded seat, so many Depression-ravaged, dark-hued others bore the burdens of the current crises along the color line—and it was to them that the Communist Party appealed. Members of the Party were agitating in Harlem, making the Scottsboro Boys an international cause célèbre, and organizing Alabama sharecroppers otherwise left vulnerable to feudal oppression and white terror. In comparison, convening a handful of the Negro elite for an August retreat seemed an insultingly limpid gesture. But if anyone thought this or cheered Dorsey's comment, they did so silently, with a smirk or a glance; none were so bold as to second him, not after the chilly reception in the Spingarns' parlor.

Rather, the Amenia conferees took up an impromptu two-hour discussion ("even though it wasn't called for in the program," noted Mumford) that acknowledged the danger of blindly embracing revolutionary philosophies, an option of obvious temptation during this fourth year of the Depression. Mumford well recognized the quandary they articulated that afternoon. "They were all," observed Mumford,

> these young doctors, professors, lawyers, librarians, tussling with the eternal dilemma of all intellectuals today: how to be a communist without willfully swallowing the fierce ignorances, the blind hatreds, the willful dogmatisms of the orthodox revolutionists who are preparing for a final pitched battle between communism and capitalism—if they are not providing a rationalization for the even more ferocious hatreds and brutalities of fascism.

Mumford empathized with their "predicament of not wanting to sacrifice everything for a cause that may easily dissolve and be replaced by its opposite in the course of battle itself"—witness the recent bludgeoning of bolshevism in Italy and Germany, where the fascist dictatorships of Mussolini and Hitler now reigned. Weighing the future of democracy in the broadest of international contexts, the tone of the conversation that afternoon stepped back noticeably from the morning's call for radical change. No one was actually prepared to storm Troutbeck. It was no Summer Palace, and Spingarn no czar. At most, they wished, like many Americans at the moment, to glean the most practical lessons from such revolutionary world events as the creation of the Soviet Union. Indeed, Emmett Dorsey's faux pas may actually have enhanced the retreat as such delegates as Anna Arnold, who were "flattered" to participate in the conference, took more vocal and moderate positions. Having kept mum that morning, both Spingarn and Du Bois were also more outspoken during the conversation that afternoon, no doubt provoked by the specter of "Commisar Jones."[41]

No such dissension haunted the photographs Amy Spingarn snapped that afternoon. Arranged before the largest conference tent, delegates and visitors posed in finery that better spoke of the privileged occasion than the rustic accommodations—Sterling Brown in knickers and a collar stylishly flared over his jacket lapel, YWCA "gals" in patterned dresses and florid hats, Howard men in fedoras and neckties, Frank Wilson in an impeccable dark suit and round spectacles, Du Bois in suspenders and bowtie. The camera caught a few in a candid moment of jaunty laughter, Juanita Jackson's beaming grin, Moran Weston's insouciant slouch, and Walter White, in a white tennis sweater, making quick work of a cigarette. At the center, Joel Spingarn was smiling.[42]

By evening, having posed for photographs and having downed an "excellent camp dinner," a less critical tone marked the second formal conference session, though the central issue of how to achieve an integrated society was no less controversial. According to the program, the delegates were to discuss the merits of interracial organizations as well as the "relation of the American Negro to the Negro in Africa, the West Indies, and South America, relation of American Negroes to East Indians, other Asiatics, and other colored people," and, finally, "relation of American Negro to the white race." Ralph Bunche, recently engaged in field work in Africa for his Harvard dissertation; Mabel Byrd, who had lived abroad, in Geneva, Switzerland, while working for the League of Nations; and Frank Wilson, whose duties with the YMCA had taken him to India, each could well address such international perspectives. Yet among the most vocal on Saturday evening was Fisk sociologist E. Franklin Frazier, who took earnest interest in questions surrounding the topic of "voluntary and involuntary segregation," and especially in issues of "group loyalty and nationalism." During that session, Frazier later remarked, he "advocated the conscious development of nationalistic sentiment" that likewise drew from the example of democratic socialism he had witnessed more than a decade earlier as a visiting scholar in northern Europe. During the 1920s, Frazier had joined like-minded black intellectuals in excoriating the cultural nationalism and uncritical capitalism of Marcus Garvey, but believed it foolhardy to simply dismiss someone "who has aroused the Negroes of Georgia as much as those of New York." Taking black cultural solidarity seriously as a social movement, Frazier wondered if there was a way to infuse racial nationalism with a sufficiently radical political outlook that would nevertheless lead to integration. Calling it "radical nationalism," Frazier suggested it as a method "of developing morale, group solidarity, and efficient opposition to the walls of racial segregation and prejudice." By strengthening bonds of resolve within the black community, Frazier hoped to turn segregation upon itself as a weapon. "Racial solidarity," he said, would thus serve "as a cohesive force among a people who were exploited by the white master class in this country."[43]

THE AMENIA CONFEREES, AUGUST 19, 1933. Library of Congress, Prints and Photographs Division, Visual Materials from the NAACP Records.

Frazier's remarks were reminiscent of the comments Du Bois had made the previous May in Washington. Like it or not, as Du Bois had said during the Association's annual conference in 1932, "the Negro has to make a living 'within the color line.'" Frazier's thinking, though, stood in stark contrast to the morning's proclamations for united, class-based action among black and white workers. Instead, Frazier accepted the impossibility of eliding race in the face of Jim Crow—at least for now. If the Fisk sociologist won a few converts, his friend Abram Harris, who was intolerant of racialism in any measure, would not have been among them. But what troubled Louis Redding most that evening was the shift the conversation seemed to have taken from demands of radical transformation of the civil rights struggle, to more conciliatory efforts to revise existing programs within the broader international context, to the paradoxical pursuit of revolutionary nationalism as a path to eventual assimilation. The problem with such digressions, he thought, was that they ultimately "inhibited any real contemplation of the condition of the great Negro mass." While some of the day's talk seemed like mere banter to Redding, he was also troubled that the more genteel among them had "so subtly become infused with middle-class American 'success philosophy'" that they simply had accepted the virtues of capitalism. He could not help but wonder if this conference was to be simply a diverting palaver among a handful of black mandarins instead of a chance to address the realities of ordinary colored Americans, the "poor, ignorant, uncounseled and exploited people," like the clientele from whom he accepted payments in barter.[44]

When the Saturday evening session ended, visitors dispersed. Some of the conferees retired to their mattress-less cots, and some gabbed well into the night. Lewis Mumford returned home along Leedsville Road impressed with the "keen discussion" that had just taken place. Louis Redding returned to his cot feeling pessimistic. Later, he attributed his perhaps overserious disposition to the enthusiasm the previous evening's conversation had stirred in him. He may also have suffered from a night of imperfect rest. "Out of twenty-six" younger delegates, an annoyed Du Bois could not help but notice, "five did as they pleased with regard to noise, sleep and enjoyment with utter disregard of the perfectly evident desires of the rest." Also within earshot of the late-night ruckus, Howard colleagues Ralph Bunche and Emmett Dorsey were disturbed by a certain lack of "social discipline" among a loud minority of the conferees. If the rumpus emanated from the women's tents where the "YWCA gals" slept, as an irritated Dorsey implied, it did not bother the youngest of the group. Wenonah Bond of the Harlem YWCA was fond of her friends who "could talk of serious matters until five A.M. yet laugh hilariously at an eight o'clock breakfast" the next morning.[45]

After breakfast on Sunday, gravity soon replaced hilarity. Joel Spingarn (still smarting from Dorsey's barb) opened the morning session with an unrecorded but passionate statement that Cleveland librarian Thelma Taylor, for one, appreciated as "clear, vibrant, throbbing." With this inspiration the conferees resumed discussion. For those wondering about the implementation of their ideas, an encouraging opportunity appeared with the surprise arrival of a cabinet member: Henry Morgenthau, Jr., Spingarn's Dutchess County neighbor and Roosevelt's secretary of the treasury, who wished to choose a Negro advisor to serve as special assistant in the Farm Credit Administration. His visit, orchestrated by Spingarn, resulted first in a private meeting between Morgenthau and Du Bois. When the two addressed the body of delegates, conversation turned specifically to the plight of the Negro farmer, with Abram Harris, Ira Reid, and E. Franklin Frazier inevitably chiming in. Of this new development Louis Redding approved. "The thought given to the concrete problems of Negro farmers in the South (and these, after all, are a large sector of the Negro mass)," he felt, "was a most valuable accomplishment, made more valuable by what seemed like the promise of a Negro adviser and Negro agents under the ameliorative Farm Credit Administration." After years of presidential neglect, Redding applauded the prospect of proffering federal aid and bureaucratic positions to African Americans during the Depression. Elmer Carter was equally impressed, anticipating that hiring Negro advisors—a Black Cabinet, as the colored press soon dubbed the appointees—would help to secure important gains. A critic might claim tokenism, but the conversation aroused by Morgenthau's visit, not to mention the commitment to name a black advisor to this New Deal agency, assured Carter that the conference would "become as historically significant as the first Amenia conference." Morgenthau's visit, he wrote, "and the presentation by the conferees on the position of the Negro in the agrarian economy of the South was one of the most important incidents in the history of the Negro in the last quarter of a century." In a gesture intended to solidify the conference's connection to Morgenthau (and, hopefully, to the Roosevelt administration, despite the influence of segregationists), the group voted to add him to the "advisory committee" along with W. E. B. Du Bois and Ira Reid. Privately, the treasury secretary had at best tepid interest in offering the advisory post to an academic intellectual like Reid or Abram Harris, no matter their expertise. "Morgenthau's request for suggestions about a Negro advisor," Spingarn divulged to Du Bois "in strict confidence," insisted on a preference for "having a man who has grown up with the problem and knows it from the ground up, rather than a professor of Economics or an intellectual who only knows it from books." Harris, Spingarn said, "is exactly the type he objects to." Had he been privy to these thoughts, it would have been reasonable of Harris to understand such reservations as indicating the secretary's interest in hiring someone malleable and inoffensive. The likes of Harris, Reid, Frazier, or even Du Bois would not do. Unaware of Morgenthau's preference, though, the Amenia delegates remained buoyed by the expectation that their meeting with a cabinet member would come to enhance the fate of thousands of ordinary African Americans, the masses Redding had worried would go neglected.[46]

Lifted by the Morgenthau visit, the Amenia delegates resolved to end the conference on a forceful note. When group discussion resumed under the big tent that evening, their conversation wound from the specifics of the black agrarian South to freewheeling attempts by several delegates to shape a future civil rights program. On Sunday evening, the final formal conference session culminated in talk, as Wenonah Bond recorded it, of "opportunism," "expediency," "intermediate steps," "immediate objectives," "long run ideals and goals," "sacrifice," "pan-Africanism," "planned work," "labor solidarity," "farm relief," "destruction peonage," and "a soviet of engineers." From Bond's perspective, it seemed that each of the delegates participated in their own way that evening. "The college professors knew facts," she wrote, "the social workers had had experiences; some of the youngest people were quiet because they knew very little, some were talkative for the same reason; some were conservative and some radical in methodology; some advocated bi-racialism, and others opposed it; some insisted on inter-racialism, and others scoffed at the idea." But, in all, they expressed a "common urge toward some sort of program which would offer ever increasing opportunity for self-expression and unhampered development to the coming generations of American Negroes." Not just a blur of competing thoughts, the conference's final session produced a dynamic conversation resulting in an acknowledged consensus that, in Louis Redding's mind, "justified" the entire weekend. Likewise listening more than contributing, an unabashedly awed Union Theological Seminary student Moran Weston considered the dialogue "the pinnacle of the conference." While agreeing upon a set of conference findings, the delegates had struck on the notion of "reformed Democracy" as the most likely option for the future (after feeling compelled to officially discount both Communism and fascism), and also, as Redding recorded, agreed to a common goal of "a program designed to lead to full and undiscriminatory integration of Negroes into every phase of American life." Most participated in this exchange to define the basis of integrating American society, but four delegates in particular—E. Franklin Frazier, Roy Wilkins, Charles Houston, and Emmett Dorsey—suggested programs to unify civil rights leaders' current "patchwork efforts."[47]

Quietly listening and taking notes in fastidious longhand, twenty-two-year-old Moran Weston keenly felt his youth as E. Franklin Frazier and W. E. B. Du Bois (undoubtedly drawing from his essay "On Being Ashamed of Oneself," set to appear in the September *Crisis*) each lectured on the attraction of "the Garvey sentiment." Returning to the position he had advocated Saturday evening, Frazier reconfirmed his conviction "that black nationalism was something Negroes would have to come to terms with honestly, and that the performance of charlatans didn't discredit the idea or explain away its appeal." Indeed, Frazier argued, "a spirit of Negro nationalism is a thing which, because of external pressure applied to them, Negroes can hardly escape."[48] While Frazier had sounded a similar chord during the 1920s, Du Bois's contribution did more than echo the remarks he had made in response to Abram Harris at Shiloh Baptist Church in May 1932. Under Harris's tutelage, the *Crisis* editor had begun a recent reappraisal of Marx, yet he remained bound to depart from orthodox material interpretations of the race problem to suggest a potential program of intraracial unity. In his most recently published manifesto, for instance, Du Bois had outlined several new imperatives, including the dictate that "the leading group of Negroes must make common-cause with the masses of their own race." Calling for the "upper class of colored Americans" to dismiss their "secret shame" in being identified with the hundreds of thousands of impoverished African Americans, Du Bois understood the challenges facing the erasure of class lines among blacks. Still, "a new plan must be built up," he maintained. "It cannot be the mere rhodomontade and fatuous propaganda on which Garveyism was based. It has got to be far-sighted planning. It will involve increased segregation and perhaps migration." Du Bois, as Moran Weston and his fellow conferees must have been startled to note, was even willing to consider the potential need for some blacks to move to Africa to achieve this revolution. In the face of immovable segregation, Frazier and Du Bois argued, it was time for dramatic departures, time to turn discrimination and race prejudice upon itself. Then, the very rigidity of the American racial order would ultimately, and ironically, lead to its eventual dismantling. "Our advance in the last quarter century has been in segregated, racially integrated institutions and efforts," Du Bois contended, such as black businesses, secondary schools, and colleges, "and not in effective entrance into American political life." Because, he concluded, "there seems no hope that America in our day will yield in its color or race hatred any substantial ground and we have no physical nor economic power, nor any alliance with other social or economic classes that will force compliance with decent civilized ideals," the time had clearly come for a "new organized group action along economic lines." The effect of such action demanded italicization:

> *The next step, then, is certainly one on the part of the Negro and it involves group action. It involves the organization of intelligent and earnest people of Negro descent for their preservation and advancement in America; and no sentimental distaste for racial or national unity can be allowed to hold them back from a step which sheer necessity demands.*

To illustrate this, at Troutbeck that Sunday Du Bois produced several charts and graphs representing the trends he discussed, which Amy Spingarn, for one, observed with delight.[49]

Roy Wilkins, too, appreciated the seriousness of such observations, but he envisioned a new type of organization to harness African American reaction to segregation. The former Kansas City newspaperman advocated "the 'Negro bloc' idea." For this to work, "a fluid body of informed Negro opinion and influence is indispensable," he said. The group

> must be a directive agency—a propagandizing bureau; it must have articulate vehicles of expression. If possible, it should have a nation-wide organization. It would have to concern itself with manifold and intricate problems affecting Negroes, these problems varying with time and place. It would be frankly opportunistic because the difficulties surrounding Negro life in America would make it so.

Wilkins recalled that this idea, while drawn from observations he had made as an editor of the *Kansas City Call*, had also grown out of his trip to the Mississippi delta the previous December. While surveying the ravages of massive river flooding and reporting on a veritable "system of peonage" among black laborers there, he perceived the limits of civil rights work directed from a Fifth Avenue office. In discussion with his fellow NAACP officers, he had recently "raised the idea of forming a Negro bloc of informed, influential leaders, highly organized, national in scope, and with a franchise to tackle all the problems of Negroes— not just civil rights." His plan rebuffed within the Association's inner circle as impractical and unmanageable, he welcomed this opportunity to make a "small slap" back, and introduced his proposal to the Amenia delegation.[50]

Fresh in Charles Houston's mind was the call for tempered suggestions of transforming the civil rights struggle he had made that July during the annual NAACP conference in Chicago. At Troutbeck the head of Howard University Law School had the opportunity to impress upon his fellow delegates the need to pursue legal avenues for civil rights, but, like Wilkins, Houston also understood the need to see beyond the particular work the NAACP could engage in, and to expect African Americans themselves to take charge of their political fate. Indeed, just as his own tour of the South had revealed in 1928, the responsibility of local black lawyers went beyond efforts in the courtroom. Their work (and the work of black leadership more broadly) lay in transforming their communities with dignity and shrewd politics. "Houston's idea," Louis Redding would write in his French Street office a week later, was "that Negroes should distribute themselves among all political parties." The Wilmington lawyer himself deemed this plan particularly appropriate because of the "danger that in a given locality Negroes, in gratitude for supposed past recognition, will vitiate their political strength by mass adherence to a single party." Redding recognized that an overwhelming and uncritical alliance with the Republican Party undermined the full power the black voting bloc ought to have had, just the situation that had occurred in Delaware. Such predictability left blacks with no leverage with either major party. Republicans had little reason to act on blacks' behalf when they could count on votes, and Democrats would not act without any hope of support at the polls.[51]

Finally, Emmett Dorsey, apparently not chastened into repentant silence after his desultory attempt at humor the previous afternoon, contributed the "idea that Negroes must keep in view certain long range objectives inherent in all comprehensive social planning." As he had emphasized in his conversation with Walter White in July, Dorsey considered it imperative for Negro leadership—whether organized by the NAACP, by John Davis and Robert Weaver's Negro Industrial League, or by some other entity—to keep close watch on the New Deal administrations and reforms that had been so rapidly legislated into existence. Abram Harris backed Dorsey on this, and even suggested a federalized social insurance program for African Americans to reverse the injury of segregation, a proposal for racial reparations that stood no chance of consideration in a segregationist-controlled national legislature but which reflected an insistence on influencing the New Deal to achieve equitable redress. "The broad objective of the whole program" endorsed by the Howard professors, it seemed obvious to Louis Redding, "would be the integration of Negroes fully into every sphere of American life." Here Dorsey amplified the critique established on Saturday morning that the current "formulae and ideologies of racial adjustment and advancement were no longer adequate." He also rejected the position Frazier and Du Bois were hashing out, arguing that when social progress could only be achieved by addressing structural faults in the economy, "militant racialism becomes at a time like this dangerous conservatism."[52]

Even as Dorsey dissented, a number of those listening perceived a basic unity underlying the past days' discussions. Despite the tensions inherent between several of the Amenia delegates' propositions, as the evening sessions concluded Ira Reid believed that the weekend's "excellent job of mental ploughing" had allowed the group to arrive at a kind of concord. "Those of us who thought a program of assimilation had failed," he wrote, "saw concrete evidence of its complete acceptance by the young Negro." Redding agreed. "Diversity of opinion," he asserted, between the likes of Abram Harris and E. Franklin Frazier, between Emmett Dorsey and W. E. B. Du Bois, "was not nearly as great as on the surface appeared, for at the root, I think, of all utterances at the Conference lay the desire that the Negro become a full and equal participant in every phase of American life." Even Du Bois, who espoused the use of separatism within the civil rights struggle, also observed common ground concerning "the fight against race segregation and color discrimination in any form." Yet he also discerned a "Marxian economic determinism" shared by many of the delegates, not simply the more vociferous and obviously militant among them. "Most of the younger trained college group," he observed, "were convinced that the economic pattern of any civilization determined its development along all cultural lines." This concern for the economic underpinnings of the existing social order, he believed, had uniquely affected the conferees. "Everybody," he wrote, who "was present, old and young, was seized with a new concern for the welfare of the great mass of Negro laboring people. They felt that too much in the past we had been thinking of the exceptional folk, the Talented Tenth, the well-to-do; that we must now turn our attention toward the welfare and social uplift of the masses" through new economic programs. This was in marked contrast in "the old liberalism" he thought "resurgent in the leadership of the NAACP officials" who, rather, stubbornly "wished to reiterate and strengthen everything that we had done in the past, as the only program for the future."[53]

The preliminary Findings Report that several of the conferees drafted on Sunday gave credence to Du Bois's observations. In the security of private deliberations, the Amenia delegates had tested a number of opinions and ideas on Sunday evening, but they would make one theme available to public scrutiny. The NAACP, and indeed any civil rights organization, needed to incorporate a significant economic program to complement its efforts to protect African Americans' civil liberties. The committee responsible for summarizing the conference's discussions consisted of Charles Houston, Anna Arnold, Hazel Browne, Ira Reid, Mabel Byrd, and Abram Harris. The findings committee hoped, Reid wrote, to impress upon their readers "the utter shortcomings" they "felt those older movements have." But they also intended, as Roy Wilkins put it, "not to set out to put down in one-two-three-order what ought to be done," but rather "to analyze critically the position of the Negro in a changing world and to suggest broad lines upon which future programs ought to be built." After listening to the results that evening, West Virginia State College's Harry Greene confirmed that the findings "summarized in fine fashion the flood of ideas and suggestions which pervaded the several sessions, and gave a certain definiteness and accomplishment to the Conference as a whole." Yet, though the committee was charged with drawing up the results of the conference, the tone was remarkably similar to that of the Saturday morning session. The conference findings, as Elmer Carter understood them, "expressed the opinion that a new labor movement, cognizant of the economic and political forces of the present day, must be evolved before the Negro worker can attain fair treatment in America." Abram Harris's influence on the findings was unmistakable; he had had the first word, and seemed also to have had the last.[54]

For this, Louis Redding, for one, was thankful. Harris, after all, shared his concern about expecting an overly bourgeois black elite to uplift the Negro masses. After listening to the reading of the conference findings, Redding left Troutbeck around midnight, the exhilaration of the evening discussions giving him the adrenaline to drive straight through the night. Other delegates stayed the night, then departed the following morning by rail and auto for New York and Louisville, Chicago and Washington, Philadelphia and Baltimore. Back at 69 Fifth Avenue the next day, Roy Wilkins wrote a friend in Washington, "I wish very much you could have been with us at Amenia, because in many ways it was the most significant conference of all the racial and interracial conferences which have been held within the last thirty years." Seminary student Moran Weston was likewise aglow, voicing a feeling shared by many of his fellow conferees returning home, telling Du Bois he was "very eager to translate into concrete action some of the implications of our discussions and findings at the Second Amenia Conference." Imbued with a similar commitment to action, YWCA officer Marion Cuthbert expressed the common prediction that the events of August 1933 would no doubt have "a compounding effect" on the development of civil rights leaders over "the next ten years."[55]

That the influence of the conference would reverberate well beyond 1933, of course, was Joel Spingarn's (and the NAACP's) hope. And Spingarn believed that it might. As he mentioned to Du Bois, once the tents had been removed from the grounds at Troutbeck, he had drawn "new inspiration from association with these fine young spirits," even if the conference had not proceeded quite as he had envisioned during the months of planning. Actually, Spingarn admitted to confusion over exactly what the discussions "may or may not have accomplished." He had rather hoped the delegates might chart a specific course of action, not merely submit general suggestions for future programs. Nevertheless, he took satisfaction with the thank-you notes mailed to him in Amenia, and particularly the impressions of such conference-goers as Wenonah Bond, who was sure that the true "'Achievements' of the Conference may not be clear for ten or fifteen or twenty years." In time, Spingarn hoped, the seeds sown during the conference sessions at Troutbeck would climb and flower as prolifically as his prized clematis vines.[56]

‖ 4 ‖

69 Fifth Avenue

In September 1933 a framed autographed photograph of W. E. B. Du Bois stood on the desk in the study of Abram Harris's new airy, sunny apartment just off the Howard University campus. The portrait of Du Bois was an "old picture with the little 'go-tee,'" and when the light was right Harris could catch his own reflection on the glass pane over the image of his old friend, the "dear professor." That month, Du Bois's portrait overlooked scattered piles of work on Harris's desk—manuscript notes for what would become *The Negro as Capitalist*, pages of lecture notes, typewritten correspondence, and the Findings Report of the Amenia Conference that he had helped to draft during the last week of August.[1]

The Findings Report, an abridgment summary of the discussions at Troutbeck, was meant to reveal how the conferees envisioned shifting the struggle for African Americans' civil rights in a new, economically oriented direction. Just weeks after the conference, the NAACP was already considering how these findings might transform the organization, deliberations that coincided with many months of transition at 69 Fifth Avenue marking a turbulent end to the Association's first quarter century. A bitter scrum was escalating between W. E. B. Du Bois and Walter White, which witnessed the waning of the editor's influence and the waxing of the executive secretary's guidance of the NAACP. While his NAACP mentor's authority dimmed, Harris nonetheless pressed for the adoption of a comprehensive economic program, a position that was shared among his intellectual cohort in Washington, DC. White was all too aware of the pressure to transform the Association; it came from Harris, as well as from others within and without the NAACP. Wishing to minimize any structural reconfiguration of the NAACP, however, White was insistent that any new economic agenda dovetail with the Association's traditional legal program and branch work—especially with Amenia delegates Charles Houston in charge as special counsel and, hopefully, Juanita Jackson in place to assist in the revitalization of braches.

From his desk in Washington, Abram Harris was not fully attuned to the machinations at 69 Fifth Avenue. But he knew the ongoing disputes over the

NAACP's future reflected an evolution taking place in the civil rights struggle, with his own generation replacing the fading leadership of the age of Du Bois, James Weldon Johnson, and William Pickens.

He was also aware of, and irked by, the snippy reaction to his generation's contribution at Troutbeck. "I understand that the latest gossip in New York is that our Amenia Conference was a rank failure," Harris wrote Du Bois during the first week of September. "This seems to be the opinion of Messrs. White and Spingarn (both). It seems those gentlemen expected the conference to tell the NAACP what its next move should be." Instead, the Amenia delegates had made their reluctance to offer a "concrete program for any organization for administrative guidance" especially clear in their conference findings. Indeed, the very first paragraph of their report announced that it would only "consider underlying principles for future action." Harris likely took exception to such a whispering campaign because his imprint was clearly on Findings Report, more so than any other delegate. He had put the final touches on the report after the other members on the findings committee had returned home, and its language paraphrased parts of the last chapter of *The Black Worker*. More than a reiteration of his past work, the document served as an official announcement of his generation's commitment to harnessing economic radicalism. While the Amenia cohort may not have precisely plotted the Association's "next move," the group had nonetheless given clear voice to an emerging consensus—an imperative Harris had considered it his responsibility to put to paper. Harris's care for molding the Findings Report to his perspective was obvious to his fellow conferees. "I would call Abram Harris and ask him to come in and look over it," conference chair Elmer Carter told Roy Wilkins, who was preparing a press release including a copy of the report, "because he would be very anxious that an accurate statement is sent out." Yet, no matter Harris's imprint, the conference findings had met the delegates' approval; it would be up to the NAACP to take specific action.[2]

The Findings Report, as the Amenia delegates had specified during their final conference session, was meant to provide a philosophical backdrop for future efforts. The conferees agreed, the Findings Report explained, that of all "the special problems of the Negro within the larger issues facing the nation" at the moment, the exploitation of black workers had become the most debilitating. The "primary problem is economic," the report concluded. Yet most black leaders had done little to alter "the historic status of Negro labor," even with the "grave danger that this historic status will be perpetuated" in the New Deal. The key was to convince existing betterment organizations that "the welfare of white and black labor are one and inseparable." The work of agencies should be in educating both black and white workers of their common ground. "The traditional labor movement" is an "ineffective agency for aligning white and black labor," the Findings Report maintained, because it is "based upon craft autonomy and separatism" and is "non-political in outlook." Still, a "new labor movement" would be necessary to organize "the great mass of workers both skilled and unskilled, white and black." Interracial cooperation, of course, would be essential to achieving these ends, but the effort must be initiated by "the Negro himself." African Americans would need to challenge whatever "artificial class differences may seem to exist within the Negro group" and acknowledge "that all elements of the race must weld themselves together for the common welfare." "This point," the report suggested, "must be indoctrinated through the churches, educational institutions and other agencies working in behalf of the Negro. The first steps toward the rapprochement between the educated Negro and the Negro mass must be taken by the educated Negro himself." The conference session among select members of the black elite called to Troutbeck could be considered just such a first step.[3]

Roy Wilkins mailed copies of the Findings Report to the press at the beginning of September, and that fall it appeared widely in print. Du Bois included an annotated copy in the *Crisis*; the *Journal of Education*, published at Howard University, also included it in full. Several black weeklies ran the document, and journalists and readers alike considered it the measure of the conference's success—or failure. The *New York Amsterdam News*, not mincing words, accused the conference of blatant elitism, bordering on "black paternalism." This was "a group of Negroes advocating labor organization as the solution to the Negro's present plight," the paper's editorial read. "And yet in the entire group there is not a single representative of the industrial masses through which this salvation is to be achieved. This exclusion of representatives of the working class is the essence of paternalism." Not only that, the paper also detected hints of "faddism," suggesting the Amenia delegates had forgone careful thought and discussion and simply voiced current sentiment concerning economic radicalism. "Ten years ago such a conference would have resolved to foster the New Negro cult," the paper quipped. "Twenty years ago education and wealth would have been the answer." Writing in the *Pittsburgh Courier*, the acerbic George Schulyer, too, found much about the conference to mock, and Howard University's former professor of sociology Kelly Miller penned a column calling the Amenia delegates lackeys of the Soviet Union. The officials of the NAACP preferred cast such reactions as unsurprising examples of the *Amsterdam News's* usual "prejudiced presentation" against the Association, Schuyler's practiced sarcasm, and Miller's well-known disdain for the NAACP. Of course, the Association welcomed the positive accounts (including some hyperbolically announcing the birth of a new movement) in the pages of the *Norfolk Journal and Guide, Chicago Defender, Baltimore Afro-American,* and *Washington Tribune* as more accurate assessments of the gathering at Troutbeck.[4]

The extent to which the Amenia Conference would actually influence the NAACP's program was open to question, but Association officers hoped to draw strength from both the Findings Report and the conferees themselves. Walter White wondered about "possible ways of following up the Amenia Conference and, quite selfishly, turning it to the benefit of the Association." Roy Wilkins, too, suggested convening members of the continuation committee to see how the conference might "be followed up and how we can continue and make concrete the interest of those who were there." While White and Wilkins traded internal memoranda, that fall W. E. B. Du Bois worked to bring several of the Amenia delegates into the Association's fold. In October, Joel Spingarn appointed Lillian Alexander and Mary White Ovington (both of whom had visited the proceedings at Troutbeck) to join Du Bois on a committee to nominate new board members. Du Bois leapt at the opportunity to shake up the board, suggesting they shelve inactive members as titular "vice presidents," and offering a list of new representatives that included six Amenia conferees. Charles Houston, the Washington lawyer and vice dean of Howard Law School, had already been representing the NAACP as counsel in dozens of investigations and legal cases, and thus made perfect sense as an addition to the board, Du Bois argued. Also meriting attention were E. Franklin Frazier, "our best expert in social studies"; Virginia Alexander, "the young Philadelphia physician"; Abram Harris, "our best theoretical economist"; Mabel Byrd, "a young woman of wide experience" and a social scientist whom the NRA had just hired to investigate wage codes, thus adding to the Black Cabinet; and Sterling Brown, a celebrated poet who "represents the literary angle." The committee quibbled over exactly whom to nominate but eventually agreed upon the parameters Du Bois proposed, offering, among others, Alexander, Brown, Harris, and Marion Cuthbert (of the National YWCA, another Amenia delegate) advisory roles in the NAACP.[5]

As the Du Bois committee decided on future board members, Walter White's attention, meanwhile, had turned elsewhere. A gruesome mob lynching in Prince Anne, Maryland, that October (which followed only by a month two incidents of terrible violence in Tuscaloosa, Alabama) steeled White's resolve to recommit the NAACP's resources to efforts to usher federal anti-lynching legislation through Congress. The NAACP had fought to outlaw lynching since the inception of the organization in 1909, though the Association had not begun a new campaign since its failed lobbying to enact the Dyer Bill during the early 1920s. But White, author of the exposé *Rope and Faggot*, and whose fair complexion, blond hair, and blue eyes had allowed him unprecedented access to investigate southern lynching mobs during the early 1920s, was eager to inaugurate another anti-lynching campaign. In November, the NAACP announced that it had begun work with Colorado's Democratic senator, Edward Costigan, in drafting an anti-lynching bill; soon, New York Democrat Robert Wagner agreed to cosponsor the legislation in the Senate. While White moved to effect change in the legislature, he also sought to cultivate local contacts in support of the campaign. In the wake of the Prince Anne lynching, White visited with what was perhaps Maryland's strongest civil rights organization, the Baltimore City-Wide Young People's Forum. During a visit to the city he arranged for a meeting with the Forum's twenty-year-old president, the effervescent Amenia delegate Juanita Jackson, hoping to instill a spirit of cooperation between the group and the Baltimore NAACP. This, to White, was a welcome outcome of the Amenia conference: the ability to better project the NAACP's national program through contacts made at Troutbeck.[6]

That fall and early winter, as the NAACP's reinvigorated anti-lynching plat-form filled headlines among the leading black weeklies, Du Bois kept Abram Harris apprised of the developments concerning the Association's board of directors. The Howard professor officially learned of his election just after the start of the new year, in January 1934. Harris accepted, sending, as requested, a picture of himself to be hung at 69 Fifth Avenue. His photograph might overlook the Association's New York offices, but he was skeptical of his ability to actually effect meaningful change within the NAACP. After Amenia, Harris had polished the Findings Report for the NAACP press release; moved from Montclair, New Jersey, back to Washington; and then traveled to Pittsburgh and Chicago for, in his words, "the dope" on black banks. He had returned to Washington in late September with notes for his study of the black bourgeoisie, an African tapestry (a gift to Callie Harris from the former Columbia anthropologist Melville Hers-kovits, now teaching at Northwestern University), and a number of plans for the coming year, none of which included the NAACP. "Any movement" lacking "in-tellectual guidance based upon an understanding of present day economic ten-dencies," he wrote a friend at the time of his election to the NAACP board of directors, "would be doomed to failure." Though inspiring such a movement would be "stupendous," there would not be "much glory in it," as dubious public reaction to the Amenia Conference had made clear. Nonetheless, Harris averred, "what we must do in this generation is to give the black masses a new sense of direction and the capacity to see" that their circumstances are linked with "the economic mess the whole world is in."[7]

Between Du Bois's December 1933 and January 1934 visits to Washington, Harris posed to "My dear Dr." the question of fomenting such a movement within Walter White's NAACP, an organization avowedly dedicated to the legal struggle for African American citizenship rights, and now also clearly leaning toward a renewed anti-lynching campaign. In December, the *Crisis* had pub-lished John P. Davis's essay, "What Price National Recovery?" revealing rampant discrimination against black workers nationwide (and trumpeting the impor-tance of the Davis-led Joint Committee on National Recovery) but Harris was unconvinced that the article indicated a strong commitment to developing an economic program. While Du Bois argued, "It is that economic program that we have got to attack and we cannot wait until somebody attacks it for us," Harris was not willing to endorse the program of "racial self-help" that Du Bois had in mind, and which he had begun to spell out in "On Being Ashamed of Oneself" in the September *Crisis*. While E. Franklin Frazier may have endorsed Du Bois's stance at Troutbeck, to Harris the idea of "racial self-help" was simply anathema to any meaningful social progress. "From the standpoint of social direction and intellectual perspective," he insisted, "there should be no *Negro* movements." Harris recognized that his steadfast position concerning an interracial workers' movement had earned him a growing notoriety in some circles, but he had only become more committed to it as time passed. "I know that I am criticized for constantly demanding that the Negro intellectual think of the race problem in terms of general economic and social changes," he admitted to Du Bois. "But the more I study the economic life of this country the more I am convinced that if the Negro intellectual does not begin to think in this fashion he will effect no permanent change in the conditions of the Negro masses." Harris realized that his vision of interracial working-class harmony was, for the moment, chimerical; he was prepared, therefore, to accept as a stopgap a pragmatic compromise between the "guild socialism" he observed taking hold among laborers and the "Negro co-operative movement" that Du Bois, among others, had begun to hail. Whatever the solution entailed, Harris considered the guidance of the black intelligentsia crucial to any prospective movement's success.[8]

After assessing the need for "independent Negro intellectuals" to guide African Americans toward a new outlook ("and we have got to give the Negro masses a new set of values if anything is to be accomplished," he reminded Du Bois), Harris could think of only one Negro leader of sufficient stature, organizational prowess, and intellectual dexterity to head such a movement: W. E. B. Du Bois. But with Walter White at the NAACP's helm, he told Du Bois, in this round "you are going to have a much harder fight on your hands than you did against Booker T. Washington." With the *Crisis* editor nearing sixty-six years old, Harris acknowledged the need to share the burden, yet he was equally aware that very few blacks of influence held both these ideas. In the meantime, he rehashed an idea he had first enunciated a decade earlier during his first semester of teaching in West Virginia. Harris proposed that he and Du Bois inaugurate a nationwide network of lectures by prominent intellectuals—the most promising vehicle, he believed, for laying the groundwork for the kind of movement the NAACP would never willingly foster. He knew the process would take years, but with "these intercollegiate lectures," he explained to Du Bois, "we can at least open up a new world of ideas to the Negro student and thus lay the basis for the necessary leadership of tomorrow."[9]

Du Bois politely received Harris's proposal, even if he thought it naively academic. He found the potential of instituting a new movement among young black leaders beyond the purview of the NAACP more intriguing. "I think we have got to get together this spring or summer," he responded to Harris, "and talk sincerely over the matter of future program and organization." For now, as he considered specific planning, Du Bois asked Harris to mull over possibilities for exactly whom to include in "an inner group of people of sound learning and reliable character," as well as a supplementary, but quite larger, "general group of young persons who would be glad to co-operate in a great movement." Meanwhile, Du Bois suggested, they both ought to consider the infusion of new members to the NAACP board of directors that winter an important first step in altering the Association's particular program. Whether they worked "inside or outside the NAACP," Du Bois argued, was ultimately moot. Either way, he assured Harris, they would "start the Negro race on a proper economic program."[10]

The expense of traveling to New York (as well as commitments to serve as an advisor to the Agricultural Adjustment Administration and to finish two scholarly essays) kept Harris from the February and March meetings of the NAACP's board, though he wanted to attend. In January, a private meeting with Walter White, Mary White Ovington, and Sterling Brown on the Howard campus had begun to firm his resolve, and a visit from Du Bois had finally convinced him to actively participate on the board. Despite ongoing tensions at 69 Fifth Avenue, the *Crisis* editor felt confident the two were "going to be able to carry out . . . plans concerning the NAACP." Not one to limit his options, however, Du Bois also sought to foment a larger Negro Youth Movement, beyond the scope of the NAACP. He conceived it as an extension of the Amenia Conference, asking for the participation of the delegates as well as dozens of others who had not been invited to Troutbeck, as he explained it, "on account of limited accommodations." As soon as he had mailed out inquiries in late February, however, the situation at the NAACP diminished the possibility of a Du Bois-Harris tandem recharting the Association's future.[11]

1934, the twenty-fifth anniversary of the NAACP, was to be its year of jubilee. On Lincoln's Birthday that February, Joel Spingarn described the Association's first quarter century during a national radio broadcast. The January *Crisis* contained Walter White's announcement of the Association's victory in sparing George Crawford from the death penalty in Virginia, as well as a celebratory essay by Mary White Ovington recounting the Association's major achievements since 1909. From anti-lynching campaigns to efforts in striking down residential segregation ordinances; from branch work to the precedents set by Association lawyers from Moorfield Storey, a Bostonian of nineteenth-century abolitionist stock, to the up-and-coming, Harvard-trained black Washingtonians Charles Houston and William Hastie, the NAACP, Ovington pointed out, had been at the forefront of the civil rights struggle. But while Ovington noted, "We have accomplished much," she also acknowledged that "there is infinitely more to do." "Discrimination, discrimination and again discrimination," she repeated, "must be fought over and over again. We have just begun." Indeed, as field secretary William Pickens put it in his call for a new fundraising campaign among the local branches, "We have now passed through one generation in the first systematic effort to make American Negroes economically, politically and socially a free people. This is but the first mile." They awaited the second mile, the work of the next generation.[12]

In the same issue, W. E. B. Du Bois also looked back on the first twenty-five years of NAACP work. But to some readers the conclusion Du Bois had arrived at was a startling one. The "thinking colored people of the United States must stop being stampeded by the word segregation," Du Bois asserted. As he had remarked during the NAACP's annual conference in Washington in 1932, as he and E. Franklin Frazier had each articulated at Amenia in August 1933, and as he had begun to delineate in "On Being Ashamed of Oneself" in the September 1933 issue of the *Crisis*, there was potential strength in racial unity. Eschewing class solidarity as wishful thinking, Du Bois believed that it would be "the race-conscious black man . . . who will eventually emancipate the colored race, and the great step ahead today is for the American Negro to accomplish his economic emancipation through voluntary determined cooperative effort." Du Bois's contemplation of segregation in the terms of voluntary separatist efforts continued in February. That month, while Walter White arranged for an Association contingent (including Baltimore's Juanita Jackson) to appear during the Senate's anti-lynching hearings, Du Bois traced the attitude of the NAACP toward "separate Negro organizations" (such as banks, businesses, and labor groups) since 1909, pronouncing its viability as a strategy to better the race. "Race pride and race loyalty," Du Bois wrote, "Negro ideals and Negro unity, have a place and function today, the NAACP never has denied and never can deny." Indeed, his emphasis on economic autonomy in the black community had a strong resonance, even among NAACP supporters. Yet Du Bois's use of the word "segregation" to frame his argument provoked confused and angry responses within the Association, a few of which were printed as a symposium in the March *Crisis*, featuring contributions from Joel Spingarn and Walter White. When Du Bois continued penning his "segregation" essays through the April number (including an editorial insinuating that Walter White had not experienced the full brunt of racial oppression, given his near-white complexion), members of the Association's board of directors scrambled to delineate their position. The first order of business during the April board meeting was to agree on a "Resolution on Segregation." When debate concluded, the board decided to take two approaches. First, they would formulate a written position together during the meeting; next, Joel Spingarn would appoint a committee "to study the various aspects of segregation." The statement the Association adopted contrasted with Du Bois's recent work, asserting its "unyielding opposition" to "both the principle and practice of enforced segregation." The board argued that "by its very existence" segregation implies "a superior and inferior group and invariably results in the imposition of a lower status on the group deemed inferior." As for the Committee on Segregation, Spingarn chose Abram Harris as chair of a committee including Louis Wright, James Weldon Johnson, Sterling Brown, and, charitably, W. E. B. Du Bois.[13]

Harris accepted the chairmanship, but he did not expect to attend each upcoming meeting. Characteristically, he lacked both funds and time. Harris had attended the April meeting only after several board members personally appealed to him to make the trip to New York, but, he complained, "These devilish meetings are expensive as hell." Moreover, Harris explained, "I do not see how I am going to do all the work I have on my hands" with the additional responsibility of the NAACP committee Spingarn had created. At the moment, he was drafting an essay to be included in a festschrift for his Columbia mentor, Wesley Clair Mitchell. He also had a backlog of statistics to compile for his banking study and had recently been elected to serve on the Consumer Advisory Board, the prospect of joining Roosevelt's Black Cabinet exciting the economist, who wrote that "it affords one an opportunity to see how the whole price machinery under the NRA actually works." Beyond such professional considerations, that spring Harris's younger sister was dying of tuberculosis, the very ailment he had been fortunate to dodge the year before. At that moment, his family in Richmond depended on whatever assistance he could spare. Still, Harris was reluctant to pass up the opportunity to implement the ideas he had put forth in the Findings Report of the second Amenia Conference and had long discussed with Du Bois. The future of the NAACP, as he had argued at Troutbeck, rested in its ability to inspire a united movement among black and white workers. He had dim hopes of composing "a manifesto of the black masses and capitalism" that coming summer, but he realized he could work toward the same end from within the NAACP. In fact, he had been engaged in ongoing conversations with W. E. B. Du Bois and Rachel Davis DuBois (a white sociologist who, like Harris, had joined the NAACP board that January) on how to change the Association. And though the Committee on Segregation was narrowly conceived to consider the Du Bois imbroglio, he thought this might be his chance to act. Harris made his first decision as chairman to ask his fellow committee members for their reflections on "the practice and policy of the NAACP concerning segregation" and proposals for a future position for the Association to take.[14]

While Harris polled his committee, in May the NAACP board voted to censor Du Bois, precipitating the *Crisis* editor's noisy resignation from the Association. Du Bois had printed an editorial in that month's *Crisis* detailing, and criticizing, the Resolution on Segregation the board of directors had drafted in April. (In an adjacent editorial Du Bois had also issued a challenge to the Association's handling of the Crawford case, winning him no favor from Charles Houston, whom the NAACP officially appointed special counsel that month, replacing Nathan Margold.) The board would not abide the tone and content of "The Board of Directors on Segregation"; Du Bois would not submit to the NAACP's censorship. For his part, and beyond the fray, Harris felt impatient with Du Bois. His latest *Crisis* essays had evinced more of the myopic "racialism" Harris thought ill considered, but beyond intellectual misgivings about the editor's program for racial advancement, he also had very little interest in joining what he believed had devolved into an ugly scrum.[15] Yet, while Harris had lost one potential ally in redirecting the Association when Du Bois resigned, during the June board meeting Rachel Davis DuBois succeeded in winning approval of a new Committee on the Future Plan and Program for the NAACP. To Harris this seemed to offer a chance to continue pressing for change within the Association, with or without the support of the former *Crisis* editor.[16]

It would be difficult, however, to outflank Walter White. That spring, White was preparing for the challenge that, along with Du Bois's departure and the controversy over a proper stance on segregation, promised to polarize the twenty-fifth annual convention to be held at the end of June at Oklahoma City's Calvary Baptist Church. While Du Bois repaired to his Atlanta University post to finish *Black Reconstruction* (for the first time in twenty-five years without a connection to the NAACP), Walter White assessed the Association's future, even as his singular influence within the organization grew more secure, with his Sugar Hill friend Louis Wright succeeding Joel Spingarn as board chairman and his protégé Roy Wilkins supplanting Du Bois as editor of the *Crisis*. Yet if White wished to retrench and maintain the Association's traditional outlook and programs in the wake of the tumult at 69 Fifth Avenue, it was clear he would meet objection from others besides Abram Harris.[17]

That spring White solicited input on, as he put it to E. Franklin Frazier (who had just joined the Howard University sociology department), what should be "the paramount issues" stressed at the upcoming annual conference. He also wondered what were the "methods and objectives which should guide the NAACP, especially during the next few years." Predictably, Frazier did not mince words. "A militant organization like the NAACP," he replied,

> must be militant. My present criticism of it is that what was radical and militant twenty years ago is not radical and militant today. Militancy on

the part of an organized minority can prevent segregation and other forms of ostracism from becoming fixed in the ores of the country. Therefore, instead of sitting down, contemplating philosophically the phenomenon as Du Bois advocates, the NAACP ought to become more militant and enlist every form of strategy to break down the walls of segregation.

Broadly advocating the catholic approach to the current crises evident in the final evening discussion at the Amenia Conference—when conferees had endorsed a number of strategies, from Emmett Dorsey's insistence that the NAACP keep close watch over the New Deal to Charles Houston's encouragement of political pragmatism—Frazier ultimately aligned with Harris. "I would suggest that the economic factor" take center stage, Frazier wrote, seconding Harris's suggestion that the NAACP organize and educate black workers "whether they are taken into the unions or not."[18]

Charles Houston was similarly inclined. In May, the Association's newly appointed special counsel expounded on the position of the NAACP and the civil rights struggle during an address to the YWCA's national convention in Philadelphia, where he encouraged advocates of black freedom to avoid dogmatic adherence to past programs, to seek the full works of citizenship for African Americans with flexibility and determination. Referring to the Amenia Conference, Houston was self-deprecating, coining a turn of phrase to describe the previous summer's confab. It had "gone down in history," he joked, "as the anemic conference of Amenia," criticized in some quarters for failing to "lay down a program for the race." Nevertheless, Houston spoke for his fellow former conferees when he acknowledged that the Association needed a "certain reorientation and a measure of reorganization." On the point that economic issues needed a hearing, he concurred, citing fellow Washingtonian John P. Davis's Joint Committee on National Recovery as an effective endeavor in seeking protection for blacks under the National Recovery Administration.[19]

Walter White had further occasion to consider Houston's perspective, as well as the work of John P. Davis, weeks later at the convention in Oklahoma City. To White, the convention was an opportunity to regroup, to move beyond Du Bois's resignation and to assert the NAACP's continued prominence in the fight along the color line. Though the Association's new anti-lynching campaign, disappointingly, had stalled with the summer adjournment of Congress, during the opening night of the convention White vowed an "unending war" against segregation. This avowal was evident in the very decision to hold the convention in Oklahoma, a state whose appalling record of white terror included the 1921 devastation of black Tulsa. Significantly, his challenge to Du Bois's recent salvos was echoed in the remarks of Mary White Ovington, a white founder of the NAACP who spoke of the organization's first quarter century, and Charles Houston, who stressed the need for interracial unity in the coming struggle for Negro rights. Such commentary may have solidified White's support, but John P. Davis made for the boldest headlines of the conference, elevating economic issues to principal importance during discussion of the future of the civil rights struggle. Davis was the cofounder of the Joint Committee on National Recovery. This "committee" was really a two-man organization, consisting of Davis and his fellow black Harvard graduate Robert Weaver. It had evolved out of the previous summer's invention, the Negro Industrial League, and was devoted to protecting African Americans' interests within New Deal programs. Davis, a star on the renowned Bates College debate team during the mid-1920s, treated Oklahoma City as a national podium, enthralling his audience of NAACP conferees with vivid descriptions of the failure of the New Deal to relieve the economic inequalities pressing African Americans. During a conference delegation's visit to the state capitol, Davis became the first African American to speak from the floor of the legislature, where he irritated a number of state representatives and delighted the black press with his forceful denunciations of the "raw deal given [the] Negro farmer" under Roosevelt's reforms. Invigorating the annual conference, Davis ensured that it would be all the more difficult for Walter White to table the younger leaders' suggestion that the NAACP broaden its program to include a call for economic equality.[20]

Cognizant of the outsized impression the small-statured John P. Davis was making at the convention, White was also carefully cultivating an ally in this period of organizational transition. White fully recognized the NAACP's need to appeal to young people, the very concern his friend Louis Wright had voiced to the board of directors in 1932. To express this appeal, though, White had in mind not such ambitious challengers as Davis or Abram Harris but Juanita Jackson, the precocious Baltimore activist. Since the conference at Troutbeck, White had kept apprised of Jackson's success as a youth organizer and invited her to Oklahoma City to address the issue of attracting young members to the NAACP. Jackson arrived at the annual convention as president of the Baltimore City-Wide Young People's Forum, having also just completed a tour of Midwestern youth conferences for the Methodist Episcopal Church. Formed in 1931, the Forum, White knew, was the most active civil rights organization in Maryland, a group grounded in the churchgoing Talented Tenth. Scheduling its program of activities between October and April, the Forum met either at Baltimore's Sharp Street Methodist Episcopal Church, or a few blocks away at Bethel African Methodist Episcopal Church, taking the place of the nearly moribund local branches of the NAACP and Urban League. In the past few years, while the local NAACP foundered, the Forum had led protests against lynching, fought for jobs for black social workers, launched voter registration drives, and picketed the stores along black Baltimore's main thoroughfare that refused to employ African Americans. Few NAACP branches could match this record of activism, and the group welcomed its place in the tradition of Talented Tenth protest. Conscious of the mantle they were inheriting, the group invited such noted speakers to their meetings as W. E. B. Du Bois, Charles Houston, Ira Reid, Elmer Carter, Carter Woodson (the founder of the Association for the Study of Negro Life and History), Howard historian Charles Wesley, and Charles Thompson, professor in the Howard University School of Education and editor of the *Journal of Negro Education.* "With the success realized from our efforts," Juanita Jackson reported in the *Crisis* in early 1933, "has come self-assurance and faith in ourselves which is most necessary for Negro youth who must take over the torches of leadership in the near future." By then, the Forum boasted three hundred members and regularly drew between 750 and 1,000 audience members to its lecture series. Its success, Jackson thought, owed to the fact that it not only discussed problems but also took action. "That has been the secret of the success of our Baltimore group," she later wrote an acquaintance wishing to duplicate the Forum's success in another city. "We have acted."[21]

While the Baltimore NAACP was nearly dormant, the City-Wide Young People's Forum displayed vibrancy. This had not escaped the attention of Walter White. When her name appeared among the lists of recommended Amenia delegates (the principal of Frederick Douglass High School had nominated her), the Association invited Jackson to Amenia, and in the months after meeting with her at Troutbeck, White had kept in regular contact with the Baltimore Forum president. At the end of November 1933, he asked Jackson to convene a small gathering of Forum members whom he might address on the work of the NAACP. White left Jackson two hundred membership blanks, hoping she would be willing to help bolster the Baltimore branch of the NAACP. The following February, while Du Bois issued his call for a Negro Youth Movement, White sought Jackson's help in supporting the passage of the Costigan-Wagner anti-lynching bill, urging the Baltimore NAACP to unite with the City-Wide Young People's Forum in demonstrations, and even inviting Jackson to come to Washington to speak "for Negro youth" at a Senate hearing on the bill. Since then, Jackson had spent much of the spring helping spearhead a picketing campaign for jobs for African Americans in A&P groceries in Baltimore. While Du Bois pondered voluntary segregation, the Baltimore youth took direct action that insisted on equitable integration.[22]

Jackson undoubtedly discussed the boycott in her Oklahoma City address that June on "the task of Negro Youth in the fight for the rights of the race." Under Walter White's watch, Jackson accompanied the NAACP contingent to the Oklahoma House of Representatives, where John P. Davis made his stirring appearance, and also served on the conference's Committee on Resolutions, along with Davis, and fellow Amenia delegates Louis Redding and Charles Houston. White had the opportunity to become even better acquainted with Jackson when she accompanied the Association executive secretary, Houston, and Davis on a two-day drive from Oklahoma City to Memphis, where the quartet visited areas devastated by recent flooding. After motoring east to Tennessee, Houston and Davis were to begin a tour of southern New Deal projects, starting in the Tennessee valley and continuing south through the Mississippi delta; their findings would soon appear in the pages of the *Crisis*. White was headed back to New York for the July board meeting and to begin planning for a renewed summer and fall drive for anti-lynching legislation. Jackson needed to board a train for Philadelphia, where she was to attend the Institute on Race Relations at Swarthmore College.[23]

As they embarked from Memphis, White considered the potential contributions of each of his traveling companions. With Davis as a point man on the New Deal in Washington, with Houston as the director of the Association's legal program, and with Jackson as a youth organizer, he might just be able to maintain the NAACP's prominence on the civil rights vanguard, even as he responded selectively to the Future Plan and Program of the NAACP that Abram Harris was hastening to conceive.

The successes of the twenty-fifth annual convention and a recent attack on the Association's legal program published in the *Nation* were both fresh in Walter White's mind during the July board meeting when Abram Harris proposed that he exchange his chairmanship of the Committee on Segregation for that of the Committee on the Future Plan and Program of the NAACP. It was not an unanticipated request. Harris had arrived in New York in between seminars he was conducting at the Swarthmore Institute (where he had occasion to meet Juanita Jackson again), and with the board's approval he immediately began working to demonstrate "the necessity of the Association changing its whole ideology."[24] He proposed to spend a week in New York later that summer undertaking a survey of the NAACP's office files to better evaluate the Association's work over the past twenty-five years—it would be his own way of commemorating the NAACP's jubilee year. The endeavor, he explained to Walter White, "grows out of my expressed convictions on the necessity for changing the central purpose of the Association."

> As long as civil liberty and political rights were the main principles for which the NAACP stood, agitation and protest were naturally the best methods of operating. Today, however, the problems are different. You agree with me that they are fundamentally economic. Sheer protests and agitation about differential wages and employment of the Negro

worker do not bring out the fundamental maladies of economic society from which both the Negro and white workers suffer. If the organization is to continue its effectiveness it seems to me that it must go to the Negro workers and farmers with a program based upon knowledge of what is happening to them in the present economy. This program must show white workers that the problem of differential wages is their problem. It will seek through practical lessons to show white and black workingmen that as contradictory as it may seem they have a real identity of economic interests. This is a hard job I know. But it can be done through pamphlets, books and articles written in simple language analyzing the agricultural and industrial conditions of white and black workers in various localities and throughout the country as a whole. The Association might begin by holding a series of labor and farmer congresses to be followed by the organization of workingmen's circles in various sections of the country.

White professed enthusiasm for these "not only good, but practicable" proposals. Still, as he organized the upcoming fall campaign sponsoring another anti-lynching bill, he was also hopeful Harris would not abandon issues of citizenship when writing his report.[25]

Though the board had scheduled discussion of the forthcoming Harris report for early September, Harris also had an immediate suggestion. He suggested White offer John P. Davis—the talk of that summer's annual convention—a six-month interim editorship of the Crisis. Davis had actually served in a similar capacity several years earlier, when W. E. B. Du Bois had left him at the helm of the magazine during a trip abroad. This time, Harris expected that Davis could pen feature items "on his observations of the Negro under the AAA, TVA, NRA, and the FERA," thus expanding on his Oklahoma City performance. These articles, Harris argued, "would not only attract interest in the Crisis but would also tie in with the Association's new economic program." Davis's expertise was clear, but White deferred making a decision about the Crisis until later that summer when, he hoped, the Harris committee would convene at Joel Spingarn's Troutbeck estate, a year after the 1933 Amenia Conference.[26]

Characteristically, Harris attempted to fit his NAACP work into a summer already brimming with responsibilities. Awaiting word on when the committee would reconvene, he spent the remainder of the summer in eastern Virginia, collecting banking data, and in Washington, polishing several book reviews, essays, and his manuscript on "Mr. Black Bourgeoisie," his interpretation of "the economic basis of the black middle class" as revealed by records of black banks from Norfolk to Chicago, to be published by the University of Pennsylvania Press. By the end of August he was also mulling finally starting his long-planned "opus" comparing Karl Marx and Thorstein Veblen's "Theories of Economic Reconstruction." But Marx and Veblen, again, would have to wait. Harris devoted a two-week stay at the Hudson Valley home of a friend to composing his report on the future plan and program of the NAACP.[27] After a late-August meeting at the NAACP's New York office (the group had not been able to arrange an Amenia meeting after all), Harris was dispatched with fifty dollars to defray expenses and the suggestion that he divide his committee's focus into several areas, including "Economic Program, Political Action, Education, Publicity, Finances, and Legal Activity."[28] Harris agreed, issuing a series of missives eliciting ideas on revamping the NAACP's program to colleagues from within and without the ranks of the Association. Then, over the next nine days, he took up his own study of the NAACP's history. A year to the week after drafting the Findings Report of the second Amenia Conference, Harris delved into the files in the Association's New York office. He also received a stream of documents from Walter White, including memoranda, annual reports, and other evidence the executive secretary had dug up on the NAACP's past programs, and began drafting a preliminary report for a future plan and program for the organization.[29]

"Your Committee on Future Plan and Program of the Association has been actively at work," Harris assured the board in early September 1934. In fact, Harris had resigned from his duties with the Consumer Advisory Board to devote more time to the NAACP report. But he had not been able to finish in time for that month's board meeting. Back in Washington, Harris consulted John P. Davis and Charles Houston on what he had written, corresponded with Walter White about revisions, then mailed his preliminary report to members of the board for a special meeting in late September. "In working out the plan for the Association," Harris later wrote, "I drew upon ideas I had expressed as far back as 1927." Indeed, Harris's report reprised the central argument of several of his articles, *The Black Worker*, and the Amenia Conference Findings Report. Civil rights leaders, he had consistently argued, and insisted here as well, needed to foster interracial unity among black and white labor in order to truly forward African Americans' social progress.[30]

Appropriately, "Economic Activities of the NAACP" was the longest section of the memorandum Harris had composed, comprising nearly half of the sixteen-page report. Although the NAACP had waged a handful of important "persistent protests against discrimination and segregation of Negroes in industry," Harris deemed that "the work of the Association in the economic field has been conducted as an incidental phase of its civil liberty program." And even these efforts were problematic. The NAACP, he argued, endeavored to secure African Americans' rights of citizenship "under prevailing economic and social conditions." In this way, the Association was "the spiritual descendant of the Abolitionist Movement," which itself had roots in eighteenth-century liberalism—that is, in the belief that individual freedoms are guaranteed in the social contract. Harris acknowledged the NAACP's philosophical roots, but he also argued for a fundamental shift away from individual rights to common cause. "Instead of continuing to oppose racial discrimination on the job and in pay and various manifestations of anti-Negro feeling among white workers," he wrote, the NAACP ought to "attempt to get Negroes to view their special grievances as a natural part of the larger issues of American labor as a whole." Such a program, he suggested, would "show that the world which labor would gain is not a white world, nor a black world, and that it can only be gained through the solidarity of white and black labor."[31]

The trick was in effecting this transformation. Harris believed the NAACP had a ready-made solution in the very existence of its local branches, if the Association was willing to democratize its bureaucratic structure. Repeating the suggestion he had made to Walter White in July, Harris submitted that the NAACP organize workers' and farmers' councils "in strategic industrial and agricultural centers" across the country. These councils would serve several purposes. They would educate workers, galvanize a broad labor movement, and, importantly, "lay the intellectual basis for united action between white and black workers in local, state and national politics." Harris saw the existing network of local NAACP branches as an advantage in effectively organizing a council movement. They could be, he wrote, "transformed from centers of sporadic agitation to that of permanent centers of economic and political education and agitation conducting public lectures, forums, the dissemination of information on local conditions and aiding in the formation of cooperative societies." He also thought John P. Davis's Joint Committee on National Recovery could be profitably incorporated into the Association. Of course, significant structural reorganization within the NAACP would accompany the integration of such a comprehensive economic program. To begin with, the new NAACP would need to be decentralized. Authority would no longer emanate from 69 Fifth Avenue; rather, power in this "democratic type of organization" would be spread across several regional divisions. The Association's ongoing political and legal programs would continue, but every attempt would be made to "tie up its economic program with its political and legal activities." Harris also had specific recommendations for guidelines on awarding the annual Spingarn Medal and for revamping and enlarging its educational program, as well as general ideas about the future of the *Crisis* as an outlet for publicizing the NAACP's economic, civil rights, and political programs. He would not even attempt to estimate the cost of implementing his recommendations, but expense was a lesser concern than the vitality of the civil rights struggle.[32]

Cost was just one concern at 69 Fifth Avenue. "It seems to me that the committee has exceeded its function, exhibited bad taste, and placed the Association in an embarrassing situation," Roy Wilkins huffed to Walter White upon receipt of the report. To Wilkins, Harris made a serious faux pas in recommending John P. Davis as economic advisor by name. His plan also suffered from its inattention to the financial outlay necessary to developing the programs he described. Moreover, Wilkins remained skeptical of adopting a meaningful economic program. "I am convinced," he told White, "that the masses of Negroes in this country are concerned primarily with the injustices that beset them on every hand because of their color." While Harris sought to eliminate root causes of racial antagonism, Wilkins considered the approach unrealistic. Most African Americans, the assistant secretary had concluded since his recent tour of the Mississippi delta, were "concerned with lynching, discrimination, segregation, insult, denial of opportunities in schools, businesses, and taxation without representation. Only a small minority is at all concerned with the question of integrating the race into the economic and political pattern of the day." To appease such a minority would be to risk losing their largest bases of support, and Wilkins was "afraid that if we go off too heavily on a theoretical social and political and economic program, we will find that we shall have cut ourselves loose from the support of the bulk of our followers."[33]

When the board convened in late September, most seconded Wilkins' dim appraisal of the Harris report. Harry Davis, a Cleveland attorney, deemed the cost of implementing the Harris report prohibitive and considered the recommendations flawed. Decentralization was a recipe for uncoordinated action, he counseled, not efficient planning. From Boston, Joseph Prince Loud sounded an even more urgent alarm concerning "the proposed changes in policy from that of claiming full citizenship rights for the Negro" to what he considered "one of partisan and class appeal." This smacked of outright Communism. Harris's proposals were "based on unsound facts"; they were of the sort that "cannot appeal to right thinking people," he charged, warning that adopting the Harris report "would be suicidal both for the Association and for the Negro race." Philadelphia's Isadore Martin and Great Barrington's Mary White Ovington concurred. Martin thought little in the report merited action; Ovington opposed any structural change in the NAACP, and she had strong reservations about incorporating a comprehensive economic program that would undermine the Association's new abolitionist tradition. "We were formed," she wrote, "and have always battled to obtain for the Negro his full rights in the United States, 'civil, political, social.' I have yet to talk with any Negro who does not agree with this platform." She had sympathy for some of Harris's proposals, but, like Wilkins, she believed that "the philosophy of this program of action is held by very few Negroes." Without mass support, Ovington argued, concurring with Joseph Prince Loud's point, the consequence of transforming the purpose of the NAACP would be dire. NAACP field secretary Daisy Lampkin did not issue so extreme a response, but she nonetheless expressed her doubts about the financial efficacy of Harris's memorandum; several of the ideas seemed dubious and ill planned. Even support of the Harris report was tempered. Both William Hastie and Charles Houston were "convinced that the Association should expand and organize its work for the economic advancement of the Negro" but considered it "but one aspect of a many-sided program." Rather than revamping the entire NAACP, they advocated simply hiring John P. Davis to direct economic activities.[34]

Abram Harris mustered a dispirited defense. His committee was "purely advisory," he replied. If the consensus was that his report would be "too marked a departure from the NAACP attitude," then that was their decision. He had fulfilled his duty, he thought, simply by drafting the report. It was up to the board to approve or strike down his recommendations. The group deferred making a decision about adopting the report until October. That month, as a brutal lynching in Marianna, Florida, galvanized support for the Association's anti-lynching campaign, the board again put off their decision on Harris's plan and program. In the meantime, Charles Houston had presented the board a report of his own, detailing a future legal program for the NAACP and offering his services to the Association full-time, beginning in June 1935. Once he had fulfilled his responsibility at the Howard University Law School the following spring, Houston planned to promote the Association's legal program to help boost local interest in both the NAACP and civil rights agitation; he thought the new, systematic attack on Jim Crow (and, in particular, on segregation in education) would prove fundamental in this regard. In fact, Houston and Edward Lovett had just returned from a tour of several southern states; in South Carolina they had made a "moving picture" of rural educational conditions the Association felt was sure to have a profound impact.[35]

While he waited for the NAACP board to act, Harris could take some solace in John P. Davis's evaluation of him in an article on black Washington slated to be published later in the year in *Fortune*. In it, Davis ascribed to Harris leadership of a new movement of economic radicalism among African American intellectuals. "The Harris wing," Davis contended, had become as significant as those led by Du Bois and Booker T. Washington a generation earlier—especially considering the NAACP's potential adoption of his proposed future plan and program.[36] In the meantime, however, the only concrete action the NAACP seemed interested in taking concerning the Harris report was to absorb Davis's Joint Committee on National Recovery—an overture Davis refused to entertain.[37] Davis was only too happy to use the *Crisis* as a forum for the results of his investigations (the latest was a collaborative article he and Houston had prepared, based on their tour of federal projects outside of Memphis in July), but he was unwilling to compromise the Joint Committee's autonomy.[38] A month passed before a special meeting of the NAACP board convened in late November to amend language used in the Harris report. To Harris, though, the board's second reason for the meeting revealed the true level of resistance facing the implementation of his report.

During the November 1934 special meeting of the NAACP board of directors, Walter White announced his intention to hire Juanita Jackson to his national staff. White had first broached the idea to Charles Houston earlier that month.[39] "Personally," Houston had allowed, "she is swell." But even if Jackson promised to become a fine representative of the NAACP, as he thought she no doubt would, Houston hesitated to fully endorse her hiring, especially if it would be at the expense of other improvements of the Association. "Frankly the thing that bothers me about your own set-up" at the NAACP, he put it bluntly to White, "and your personal thinking is it is too white-collar." Houston wanted to see the Association develop "some strength on the industrial side," as recommended in the Harris report. This, he asserted, "frankly you do not get . . . in Juanita." Jackson might be valuable for "the contacts she brings with student groups and church circles," he wrote, "but I most decidedly feel that you are topheavy with white-collar interests and attitudes."[40]

Despite Houston's hesitation, White proposed to the board that Jackson, "the dynamic and personable young woman who is behind the very alive City-Wide Forum at Baltimore," serve as his special assistant. In this capacity she would function both as a fundraiser and youth organizer, for which she had earned high regard in Baltimore and beyond. In fact, after attending the Swarthmore Institute on Race Relations that summer, Jackson had toured California for the Methodist Episcopal Church—in August, she had even been elected vice president of the church's National Council of Negro Youth. That fall the twenty-one-year-old Jackson was studying for her master's in sociology at the University of Pennsylvania, where she had embarked on a thesis about, White wrote, the "exploitation of colored women in industry in Philadelphia." While in Philadelphia, Jackson had also become active in a group called the Young People's Fellowship, an arm of the local Committee on Race Relations, a Quaker organization that cosponsored the annual Swarthmore Institute. In October the Young People's Fellowship had contacted Walter White with the idea that it serve as a junior division of the Philadelphia branch of the NAACP. White was pleased, believing it an opportunity to conduct a "laboratory experiment" in getting young people interested in the NAACP's program, as well as a chance to breathe life into a local branch whose own president acknowledged it was "very much in a rut from the standpoint of enthusiasm." Based on the experience in Philadelphia, White thought the Association could better estimate the worth, and the logistics, of creating an NAACP youth movement. If Jackson agreed, on the basis of her work in Baltimore she could first oversee the creation of Philadelphia youth branch and then build a nationwide network. Jackson thought the offer tempting, as she explained when she met with several members of the board in late November. But while she was flattered by the overture, she simply could not join the NAACP staff until the following June, after graduation from Penn.[41]

Unsurprisingly, in the wake of the November board meeting, Abram Harris expanded on Houston's reluctance to hire Jackson, no matter when she was to arrive. White understood Harris's position, but he took exception to the Howard professor's curt reaction. "It is true that she is young," White wrote, "but I think you are somewhat unjust to her in your appraisal of her ability." While Harris had in mind an expensive, uncertain overhaul of the NAACP's existing program, White wished to rouse more support for its ongoing work. A master publicist who had helped stir passion for Negro rights during the sensational Sweet trials of the 1920s, White perceived a reflection of his own talents in the effervescent, intelligent Ms. Jackson. White argued that "it is necessary that there should be clear thinking and careful planning not only of an immediate program but of a long-range one as well, integrating into the whole economic, political and racial scene. But it is futile to have a program on paper unless one is able to sell that program to the masses of people." In his view, Jackson's "youth, energy and enthusiasm can be of great value in selling the NAACP's program to a greater number of people"—and particularly to the young people on whom the future of the Association rested. Moreover, White was satisfied to report, Houston, too, upon reflection, had come to agree with the idea of hiring Jackson. "The more I think of Juanita," Houston had written White later in the month, upon return from a tour of southern black colleges to recruit prospective Howard Law students, "the more I think she has the makings." Recalling their trip from Oklahoma City to Memphis that July, he concurred that Jackson had "plenty of guts and fight." With greater seasoning, Houston predicted, "she'll be a whirlwind."[42]

Harris was unwilling to concede, but he did not possess the temperament to engage in a pitched battle. Besides, it seemed possible that an alternative vehicle for his vision was coalescing among his Washington, DC, intellectual cohort that fall. There was a palpable sense of a coalition forming beyond the reach of the NAACP during the Conference on Social and Economic Aspects of the Race Problem that Harris, Ralph Bunche, and E. Franklin Frazier participated in at Shaw University in Raleigh, North Carolina. In the weeks before the Shaw conference, John P. Davis's urgency had grown with each mile he traveled through North Carolina, Virginia, and South Carolina on tour with Association lawyers Charles Houston and Edward Lovett. After documenting the ravages of impoverishment and racism, Davis stepped up to a lectern at Wilberforce University to deliver an emphatically economic interpretation of his most recent southern experiences. Back in Washington, Harris's Howard cohort, too, evinced a vigorous militancy—in December, Bunche and Houston had plans to engage in a protest against lynching just steps from the National Mall. Harris's own plan for the

NAACP shared the fundamental impulses the activists among the Washington crowd also felt; not only that, he believed it would help the Association build from the energy that had obviously invigorated the local civil rights struggle in the capital. The very idea of adding Jackson to the Association's national staff, Harris contended, therefore ran counter to the spirit of his attempt to redirect the NAACP. "I do not think that the Association should expend almost $1,000," he wrote to White, "for an executive assistant when in view of the newly adopted program other types of work necessitate more important appointments. If the Association really believes in the economic program that we have worked out," Harris argued, "it will have to use more and more of its resources for the appointment of people who will execute that program rather than for expansion of purely administrative personnel. This is a position from which I cannot recede."[43]

If Harris would not back down, he was equally unprepared to remain long in the fray. At that moment, the task of preparing his application for a research grant from the Guggenheim Foundation had come to consume much of his attention. He also had two outstanding book manuscripts to complete, which would be impossible if he had to devote energy to supporting his plan and program for the NAACP. "During the past year," he explained to White, "the work in which I am really interested has suffered tremendously because of my outside activities." Furthermore, he wrote, "I feel that I have made my contribution to the Association, however small it may be, and should, therefore, resign." Neither Walter White nor the NAACP board of directors quite believed him, but W. E. B. Du Bois could have predicted it. "The trouble with Harris," he wrote after his own resignation that summer, "is that he is primarily a scholar, and is fitted neither by temperament or desire for the kind of executive fight this thing calls for. I knew when I urged his election to the Board that his value would be in times of calm, when we were planning and wanted expert knowledge. In times of storm, he would rather be writing about Karl Marx." That Harris continually delayed his scholarship to press for change within the NAACP, even when he understood there was only a slim chance he would succeed, suggests this criticism was not entirely warranted—particularly when Du Bois had just lost his own contest of will with White. Yet it was true: when the NAACP was slow to adopt his blueprint for reform, Harris opted to leave the wrangling behind him. "Inasmuch as I cant fight journalistically or politically," Harris confided to a friend when he left the Association, acknowledging the limits of his bureaucratic acumen, "I think I had better stick to my more or less academic weapons."[44]

Even as Harris withdrew from active participation in the NAACP to finally complete *The Negro as Capitalist* (his study of "Mr. Black Bourgeoisie"), Walter White was optimistic about the Association's future. Though Harris's report on the Future Plan and Program of the NAACP had not officially been adopted,

White predicted it would be a valuable source from which to cherry-pick ideas about expanding the Association's influence. In the meantime, White could see ample evidence of the NAACP's health. Its continued fight for anti-lynching legislation, for instance, had recently proven an important rallying point. In December, White was pleased to acknowledge a picketing campaign Houston and assistant secretary Roy Wilkins had helped stage during the Attorney General's National Crime Conference at Constitution Hall, just off the National Mall in Washington. When the conference refused to endorse federal anti-lynching legislation, members of the Washington NAACP appeared outside the hall to protest. Four carried pickets—Emmett Dorsey, Edward Lovett, Roy Wilkins, and the Baltimore Afro-American's George B. Murphy, Jr.; each toted a sign denouncing lynching, and each was hauled away in a patrol wagon for "violating the sign law." Houston caught the scene on "moving picture" film; two days later, he returned outside Constitution Hall with Howard University professor Ralph Bunche and seventy others, including over fifty Howard students, standing still (to avoid the parade law) and wearing lynch ropes dangling from their necks (to elude the sign law). "Ropes Are Not Placards," the Baltimore Afro-American read in explanation of Houston's tactic the next week. The group had staged a "most gruesome demonstration," the Washington Tribune noted, but had skirted a second round of arrests. "From all I hear," White wrote Bunche, "it was a swell show."[45]

The Association's legal program also promised to remain a galvanizing influence, now that Charles Houston was at the helm. Houston explained his vision in "The Need for Negro Lawyers," which appeared in the January 1935 Journal of Negro Education. Recalling the conclusions he had reached during his 1928 southern tour for the Laura Spellman Rockefeller Memorial Fund, Houston advocated the training of a new cohort to join, since "throughout the South the young Negro lawyers are challenging the established traditional discriminations and oppression of the South." Nationally, the NAACP would continue to challenge the color line, particularly in the realm of public education, with the intention of gradually winning the Supreme Court precedent necessary to reverse the Plessy doctrine of "separate but equal." Privately, Houston also encouraged Walter White to effect a greater democratization of the NAACP—to grant local branches (and local leaders, such as the attorneys he envisioned advancing the NAACP's legal program) greater voice in direction of the Association. This, he believed, would only further invest communities' backing for the Association, ultimately allowing the NAACP to challenge Jim Crow on many fronts at once—local and national, legal and economic. Indeed, despite Harris's resignation, Houston advised White to direct the Association's development of an economic program on par with his attempts to force the passage of anti-lynching legislation. While Houston could only do so much on his own, he advised White that "there should be a three-ring fight going at all times," applying continual pressure on the social, legal, and economic edifices of the Jim Crow order.[46]

White took Houston's counsel seriously. Not only had Houston become an important confidante and collaborator, but White was also eager to rebuild the dozens of Association branches that had struggled through the past few years. He also wanted to foster appreciation for the NAACP among young people. Naturally, White thought of Juanita Jackson. Jackson would make an energetic addition to the NAACP staff in 1935, he thought, and would also help broaden her generation's interest in the Association. She had declined his offer to serve as special assistant the previous fall, but she was an obviously committed activist. Even while pursuing her graduate degree at the University of Pennsylvania, she led a successful student effort to open the university's dormitories to black students. Off campus, she addressed students as distant as New Haven, Connecticut, pressing her peers to support passage of the Costigan-Wagner anti-lynching bill. She arranged to have the renowned author and former NAACP executive secretary James Weldon Johnson (and an Amenia Conference contact) speak at the City-Wide Young People's Forum in Baltimore, and was also working to develop NAACP activity among young people Philadelphia. After a short time coordinating with members of the Philadelphia YWCA and the Young Peoples Interracial Fellowship, Jackson alerted Walter White in early 1935 that her Philadelphia group was already "quite a progressive and militant one," dedicated to "arousing public opinion against lynching and segregation." With the end of the semester mere weeks away, another job offer seemed appropriately timed.[47] Jackson accepted the opportunity to serve as special assistant to the executive secretary, beginning that September. Though her primary responsibilities would be to raise funds, Jackson would also be given the opportunity to organize youth groups nationally under the auspices of the Association. In the meantime, after her exams at Penn, Walter White wished her to become acquainted with the Future Plan and Program Abram Harris had drawn up for the NAACP the previous fall, and which would be voted upon by the delegates at the annual convention in St. Louis.[48]

In the weeks leading up to the convention, the need for the NAACP to develop a comprehensive approach to the economics of the race problem appeared all the more apparent. In March, the aftermath of a major riot in Harlem came to demand much of the NAACP executive secretary's resources and attention. Declaring that it would be a serious mistake to ignore the economic distress the city's black community endured, White maneuvered to put the Association at the forefront of examining the origins of the crisis. Treating the riot as a product of the same forces that motivated lynching, he kept in constant contact with associates in Harlem and with New York Mayor Fiorello La Guardia concerning the appointment of a task force—he worked to have the dependable and unassailably forthright E. Franklin Frazier direct the study of the outbreak of racial violence in the city.[49] Meanwhile, while the Harris report was in the possession of 69 Fifth Avenue that spring, it was not the only potential outline for expanding the economic reach of the civil rights struggle. Since winter, Howard University political scientist Ralph Bunche and the Joint Committee on National Recovery's John P. Davis had been coplanning a large meeting at Howard on "The Position of the Negro in Our National Economic Crisis." In May, 250 delegates arrived at the newly opened Frederick Douglass Memorial Hall just off Georgia Avenue for three days of discussion and deliberation. On the final day of the conference, several dozen conferees crowded into Bunche's home on the Howard campus for a private debate of Davis's suggestion to found a National Negro Congress. Although the challenge of federating labor and civil rights groups within a larger democratic organization did not seem to Bunche a pragmatic solution, Davis determined to mount a mass movement against American capital and racial hegemony. Bunche readily demurred, and not simply out of disagreement. Like Harris, he was already well ensconced in academia—the Howard professor had two major articles to produce, as well as *A World View of Race*, a short book-length promised as part of his colleague Alain Locke's adult education series.[50]

As John P. Davis set about willing such a grassroots movement into existence, the endeavor drew suspicious reaction from Walter White (not to mention the ire of Kelly Miller, the syndicated conservative black columnist and former Howard dean, and the federal scrutiny of a Congressional investigation into possible Communist influence during the spring parlay off Georgia Avenue). Realizing Davis's expertise, the NAACP executive secretary surmised that any such Congress would eventually trespass onto the Association's own economic program, which would be officially inaugurated during the annual conference that summer. That June, as Davis quickly began promoting the National Negro Congress, the Harris report became a touchstone of the NAACP's St. Louis conference, rekindling themes that had marked previous gatherings in Pittsburgh, Washington, Chicago, and the year before in Oklahoma City. As the *Crisis* put it, "The ever increasing importance of the economic plight" marked speeches by Davis, Brotherhood of Sleeping Car Porters leader A. Philip Randolph, Harlem politician Hubert Delany, and Joel Spingarn. Even though Spingarn felt that there would "still be need for the old role of the NAACP," the chairman of the Association's board of directors recalled the 1933 Amenia Conference during his address to the NAACP delegates and cited the Harris report as ample proof of why the Association "must now emphasize more the economic aspect of the Negro problem." The St. Louis delegates agreed, voting in the auditorium of the segregated Vashon High School to accept the plan to democratize the Association's structure and to further develop an economic program. This vote, though, did not fundamentally redefine the NAACP; Harris's memorandum was adopted with important qualifications that White could easily stomach. In contrast to Harris's original report, the NAACP was not compelled to convert its local branches into workers' councils, nor was the executive secretary's administrative control diminished. While the St. Louis delegates endorsed change, White remained in command of any strategy to adapt the Association's program. And despite the potential challenge of the upstart National Negro Congress and the NAACP delegates' interest in expanding the economic agenda of the organization, White recognized that the NAACP's traditional arena was strengthening under the helm of Charles Houston. He would not endanger the legal work of the Association at this crucial moment.[51]

Charles Houston might have objected to nullifying the Harris Report this way, but he did not travel to Missouri that June. Although the conference offered occasion to mark Houston's new official capacity as a full-time member of the NAACP's national staff, his remarks had to be read in absentia. The film footage he and John P. Davis had recently taken documenting discrimination under New Deal relief works, as well as *A Study of Educational Inequalities*, which depicted the gross inequality between white and colored schools in the South, was also shown in his absence. Each demonstrated the conditions the NAACP's legal team was working to challenge, and Walter White could hope they lent dramatic legitimacy to the Association's revamped legal program. Houston had already begun work and, as the delegates came together for the St. Louis convention, was in court in Washington arguing for the desegregation of the University of Maryland Law School. The trial illustrated the transition from the NAACP's habit of waiting for likely cases to appear to a more aggressive strategy of seeking out suits that, in concert (and if they succeeded), would gradually hobble Jim Crow and finally allow for a direct attack on *Plessy v. Ferguson*, the 1896 Supreme Court decision upholding segregation. Of course, to administer such an assault Houston needed not only winnable cases and an unimpeachable constitutional strategy but willing local advocates as well. In St. Louis, the NAACP conferees heard why Houston was optimistic on this score. "The most helpful sign about our legal defense," Houston had written for that audience, in a speech he planned to repeat later that summer in Nashville during the yearly meeting of the African American National Bar Association, "is the ever increasing number of young Negro lawyers, competent, conscientious, and courageous, who are anxious to pit themselves against the forces of reaction and injustice." Among those in the audience in the Vashon auditorium, in fact, St. Louis's Sidney Redmond served as a fine example, eying a similar education suit in Missouri.[52]

Yet willing lawyers would not be enough, no matter their qualifications, no matter their courage. The Association would also have to build a groundswell of support, beginning among local NAACP branches. The NAACP needed popular backing not only to fund litigation but also to muster a meaningful sense of morale—enough to sway African American communities nationwide behind a concerted, if long term, struggle to end *de jure* segregation. While Walter White had talented and experienced field secretaries in Daisy Lampkin and William Pickens, he anticipated that the addition of Juanita Jackson would propel NAACP membership and enthusiasm among a younger generation, arousing youth to support the Association's campaigns to end lynching and thwart Jim Crow.

Buoying White's expectations, Jackson, though not yet an NAACP staff member, made a promising impression in St. Louis. Between sessions at Vashon High School, Jackson affiliated herself with a number of younger delegates proposing that the NAACP offer a youth section during future conferences. The youth, she argued, wanted "an opportunity to become a more integral part of and to have more of a vital share in the functioning of that organization." Jackson expanded the proposal while serving on the resolutions committee, then gave a rousing presentation at the Pine Street YMCA during a meeting of the nomination committee. She had attended the conference, in part, she said, to promote the idea that the next annual conference be held in Baltimore. Her remark came at an opportune moment (just as the NAACP had struck against Jim Crow at the University of Maryland Law School), and Jackson's words received a passionate round of applause. Walter White endorsed the idea as well, and even made reviving the membership of the Baltimore branch, in preparation for holding the conference, Jackson's first duty upon officially joining the New York staff in September.[53]

While the NAACP emerged from the annual conference firmly under Walter White's direction, Jackson returned east from St. Louis as a scholarship student at the Swarthmore Institute of Race Relations. Now a trained sociologist, she and eleven of her classmates spent July interviewing over five hundred families for a study demonstrating the public health crisis in the city's segregated neighborhoods. When the term at the Swarthmore Institute finished at the end of July, she caught her breath, then embarked on a month-long tour of western interracial conferences for the Methodist Episcopal Church. By the time she finally arrived home to 1216 Druid Hill Avenue in Baltimore at the beginning of September, she found a stack of letters awaiting her from Walter White and field secretary Daisy Lampkin concerning the upcoming local NAACP branch membership campaign.[54]

In the mail, too, was the September 1935 issue of the *Crisis*, featuring a photograph of the twenty-two-year-old Juanita Jackson smiling in three-quarter profile from its cover. "Leader of Young People Joins NAACP Staff," read the caption beneath the newest face of the NAACP.

PART THREE

"The 'Achievements' of the Conference may not be clear for ten or fifteen or twenty years."

—Wenonah Bond, *September 1933*

Juanita Jackson, Leading Negro Youth

Juanita Jackson approached the microphone at the front of the small wooden stage erected on the corner of Etting and Dolphin Streets, beneath the stone façade of Baltimore's Sharp Street Methodist Episcopal (ME) Church. It was no misnomer; the church had relocated from Sharp Street at the turn of the century, as African Americans moved to the city's northwestern neighborhoods. Outside the church it was a brisk, early autumn evening. Against the cool night air Jackson had donned a full-length wool overcoat, with dark fur trimming the cuffs. The poised special assistant to the executive secretary encouraged the crowd gathered at the corner to join in support of the local branch of the NAACP. "You Can't Win by Yourself" read one of the posters denouncing lynching plastered on the side of the stage. Another heralded the Association's educational campaign: "To Get Equal Schools for Colored People in Md."[1]

Handpicked to restore Baltimore's former powerhouse local branch, Jackson had also been chosen to ensure the NAACP would continue to build on its established legal and legislative programs, despite the challenge of a rising African American left demanding economic justice, from Abram Harris at Howard University to the National Negro Congress that John P. Davis was then developing. White perceived in his new special assistant a young woman with a respectable Talented Tenth upbringing who possessed the ability to graciously interact with older NAACP benefactors across the country; she could serve as the bright representative of the NAACP's up-and-coming generation, even as she touted the Association's commitment to its traditional agenda. White knew that Jackson was a dynamic organizer who was maturing into a model of her generation's increasingly militant female leadership, with the myriad contacts and practical experience needed to cultivate fresh support for the NAACP.[2] While in recent years Abram Harris had insisted that the NAACP reorient its program in a synthesis of labor and civil rights advocacy, in Juanita Jackson he had an assistant who was fiercely committed to undercutting segregation and not wedded to the notion that the Association required wholesale reinvention. Hesitant to further democratize the NAACP, and certainly unwilling to transform the organization

SEPTEMBER, 1935 **THE** **FIFTEEN CENTS**

CRISIS

JUANITA E. JACKSON
(Leader of Young People Joins N.A.A.C.P. Staff—See page 272)

ETHIOPIA AWAKENS
By Reuben S. Young

JUANITA JACKSON, 1930s. Special Collections and University Archives, W. E. B. Du Bois Library, University of Massachusetts Amherst, reprinted with the permission of the Crisis Publishing Company.

into an arm of the labor movement, White placed remarkable faith in Jackson to resuscitate the Association at the grassroots, such as in this membership drive in Baltimore. He trusted that she would help the NAACP endure the doldrums of the Depression and encourage a constellation of local communities to collaborate in a national movement pressing for black freedom, mobilized to support the Association's condemnation of Jim Crow education and its dedication to secure legislative protection from lynching. That she reported directly to White was no afterthought; having the young, and perhaps impressionable, Ms. Jackson serve at his pleasure assured the secretary of the direct control he was keen to maintain over the NAACP.

Addressing the crowd gathered at Sharp ME, Juanita Jackson took warm notice of the younger faces. From a young age, since becoming active in the Methodist youth movement a decade earlier, she had enjoyed the confidence to speak (and sing) with a distinctive cogency and clarity and grace. As a leader of the Baltimore City-Wide Young People's Forum during the early 1930s she had met with, rallied with, prayed with, demonstrated with, and sung with the young people of Baltimore. Hers was a trusted voice. Speaking of the NAACP's efforts to push the Costigan-Wagner anti-lynching bill through the legislature, they listened. Recounting the courtroom fight to erase the color line at the University of Maryland Law School, they cheered. Walter White may have wished for an acolyte, but the object of Jackson's ambition was here, among the young people congregated on the corner of Etting and Dolphin. She wished to use her position with the NAACP to organize a national youth movement dedicated to the cause of African Americans' civil rights.

She would begin with a revival in Baltimore.

Not a month on the job, Juanita Jackson was already predicting success in her native city. During the first week of October 1935, local radio broadcasts publicized the ten-day membership drive, which was to feature a rousing parade through the city's northwest neighborhoods and a "monster" mass meeting to hear prominent speakers such as Walter White, *Afro-American* editor Carl Murphy, and Association field secretary Daisy Lampkin to close the campaign. Two decades earlier, the Baltimore NAACP had been an exemplary local branch—one of the first founded—and a critical Talented Tenth bulwark against the emerging Jim Crow order. But by 1935 the branch could claim hardly a hundred members. Jackson was hopeful the branch would reclaim its activist tradition. As the drive began that October, "flying squads of soap box orators" addressed crowds from street corners in northwest Baltimore. Volunteer speakers—students, clergy, journalists, educators, and activists—exhorted passersby along "the Strip" of black businesses on Pennsylvania Avenue. They strode up and down Druid Hill Avenue, home to the local NAACP, colored branches of the YMCA and YWCA,

Union Baptist Church, Bethel African Methodist Episcopal (AME) Church, and several long blocks of three-story, brick- and stone-faced row houses, including, at number 1216, the Jacksons.[3]

Black Baltimore, where Keiffer and Lillie Jackson had settled their young family more than twenty years earlier, boasted a privileged heritage shaped by both segregation and a collective insistence on dignity. At the turn of the century, the city's aristocrats of color—the Bishops and the Browns, the Masons and the Murrays—traced their lineage to families who were free before the Civil War, intermarried with the "upper tens" in Washington and Philadelphia, vacationed in Cape May, sunbathed at Highland Beach, and formed exclusive clubs with names like the Baltimore Assembly and the Baltimore Annex of the New York and Newport Ugly Fishing Club. Debutantes appeared during annual balls that were duly documented in the society pages of the *Afro-American Ledger*, along with weddings and whist tournaments and women's auxiliaries. Distinctions were drawn between the masses and the fair-skinned, the well-mannered, and the descendants of the old families. But an influx of migrants also gave the city the second largest population of African Americans in the nation: eighty thousand, behind only New Orleans. This migration precipitated a transformation of black Baltimore. In the decades following the Civil War, most blacks had resided in the city's southern and eastern neighborhoods, along narrow alleys and among blocks of decrepit housing—an area which, at the turn of the century, was being condemned for the use of the Baltimore & Ohio Railroad. Spurning dismal surroundings that were growing even more intolerable, the city's colored elite moved to the historically white neighborhood in the northwest, just a mile from downtown and renowned for its "splendid houses on wide streets, amid sanitary surroundings." Churches and schools soon followed. Sharp Street ME kept its name when it relocated to the corner of Etting and Dolphin; the Colored High School, soon to be named for Frederick Douglass, was moved to near Druid Hill Avenue. With thrift and prudence, the *Crisis* observed, black Baltimoreans had "saved their money and purchased nearly the whole length of Druid Hill avenue," establishing "one of the best colored streets in the world."[4]

White Baltimore called it a "Negro Invasion" and crafted a strategy meant to mute the impact of black migration. In 1910 the Baltimore City Council adopted a measure, named the West Segregation Law, to designate "white blocks" and "black blocks" throughout the city. Should the color line be transgressed, the ordinance called for a penalty of $100 and up to a year in city jail—with an exception carefully made for black domestic servants. While the ordinance inspired similar plans from Atlanta to Louisville, the *Crisis* condemned this development, which the black elite perceived as a purposeful affront to Negro respectability, the criminalization of genteel aspiration. In the February 1911 number, an ink-drawn diptych depicted the conundrum. In the first panel, labeled "1900," a finely dressed colored couple, the very embodiment of the respectable black middle class, sit at their secretary, conscientiously assessing their finances. The accompanying inscription iterated a reassuring homily Booker T. Washington himself could have comfortably uttered: "The colored man that saves his money and buys a brick house will be universally respected by his white neighbors." A more troubling maxim was apparent in the following panel. A decade has passed and the same formally dressed man is regarded with suspicion after making a bank deposit: "New and dangerous species of Negro criminal lately discovered in Baltimore. He will be segregated in order to avoid lynching."[5]

Not particularly beholden to Washingtonian accommodation, the black elite in Baltimore rallied a typically Talented Tenth assault. A number of black professionals who had fought to maintain the franchise and thus made it difficult for Maryland Democrats to enact a comprehensive, *de jure* suite of segregation statutes banded together in such associations as the Negro Suffrage League and an NAACP vigilance committee. In coordination with one of the earliest local branches of the NAACP, attorney W. Ashbie Hawkins, a former member of the Niagara Movement, brought suit to repeal the West Segregation Law, forcing the city council to pass four separate measures through 1913. Responding to black Baltimoreans' vigilance along the color line, the national NAACP followed with its own challenge to residential segregation in the city of Louisville, resulting in the 1917 Supreme Court decision *Buchanan* v. *Warley*, which outlawed such ordinances.[6]

The Jacksons returned to Baltimore amid the fight over residential segregation, their Maryland homecoming arriving shortly after their daughter Juanita was born in Hot Springs, Arkansas, in 1913. Lillie had been a teacher before marriage, but during the early 1910s the couple had traveled the country while Keiffer sold religious films to black churches. Back in Baltimore, the Jacksons successfully invested in real estate and became immersed in the city's Talented Tenth institutions. During the 1920s Lillie even briefly accepted the vice presidency of the local NAACP, but resigned when she recognized that the ossified branch leadership was little inclined to even call a meeting. Assuming an influential role at Sharp Street ME, Lillie encouraged her daughters Virginia and Juanita to join in church-sponsored activities, imparting a devotion to social responsibility. Juanita soon shined. She graduated from the city's colored Frederick Douglass High School with honors at fourteen years old. When the University of Maryland refused to admit even such an extraordinary Negro student, she matriculated at Morgan College, an unaccredited black institution founded by the Methodist Episcopal Church in east Baltimore. Juanita excelled at Morgan, garnering both high grades and recognition for skills in oratory, but she and her family wished for greater academic challenges. After two years at Morgan, Lillie Jackson persuaded

1900

"The colored man that saves his money and buys a brick house will be universally respected by his white neighbors."

These illustrations by John Henry Adams, published in the *Crisis* in 1911, depict the reaction to the "Negro Invasion" in Baltimore. Special Collections and University Archives, W. E. B. Du Bois Library, University of Massachusetts Amherst.

1910

"New and dangerous species of Negro criminal lately
discovered in Baltimore. He will be segregated in
order to avoid lynching."

the University of Pennsylvania to admit Juanita as a transfer student. Juanita entered Penn as a junior, with all of her Morgan credits but "Bible." In Philadelphia, she engrossed herself in both coursework and a busy social schedule that gravitated toward progressive outreach, including membership in the Social Service Club and volunteering for the university settlement house and local YWCA. Graduating from Penn in 1931 with distinction and a degree in education, Juanita returned to Baltimore, planning, at eighteen, to teach.[7]

The whirlwind of organizing, though, proved more alluring than the classroom. Eschewing a deskbound existence, Juanita instead pursued church-based activism that confronted the color line. She spent the summer of 1931 on the first of what would become a regular round of tours for the Methodist Episcopal Church, quickly emerging as a talented organizer and personable speaker of rare poise and cheer—and determination. Although prim and sunny, Juanita Jackson was no less canny and confident, unwilling to placidly embody respectable Negro womanhood. In Baltimore, she, her mother, and her older sister, Virginia, founded the City-Wide Young People's Forum, intending to productively organize the city's young people. Juanita served as Forum president and in early October 1931 offered the first program at Sharp Street ME Church, where Lillie Jackson had become a trustee. The Forum's weekly Friday evening meetings became instantly popular social gatherings, but a wave of racial violence on Maryland's Eastern Shore in December 1931 swiftly inspired more serious dedication. During the next three years, the Forum became the most active civil rights organization in the city—and Jackson among the most visible leaders of the local struggle in Baltimore. When she returned from another year of graduate study at the University of Pennsylvania in 1935 to lead the Baltimore membership drive, the NAACP's new special assistant—and renewed Association spirit—were both welcomed back in the community.[8]

"Baltimore is most enthusiastic," Juanita Jackson wrote Walter White in September 1935, while preparing to launch the local NAACP's membership campaign. "The University of Maryland case has paved the way for the drive." News of the case had recently filled the pages of the *Baltimore Afro-American*. Baltimore's Donald Murray, an Amherst College graduate who had been denied admittance into the University of Maryland Law School on the grounds of his race, had just that September entered the school. The victory had come after a months-long effort by NAACP lawyers led by another Baltimorean, twenty-seven-year-old Thurgood Marshall (under the careful supervision of Charles Houston). Hoping to harness the city's passion for the case during the ten-day membership campaign she was directing, Jackson had arranged for Marshall to speak about the case and the Association's legal program. Veteran branch coordinator Daisy Lampkin was scheduled to arrive late in the month to help with organization, but Jackson had already secured a network of volunteers to canvass churches, businesses, and households throughout northwest Baltimore. She expected Thurgood Marshall, especially, to succeed in "firing up the people on the school situation," which now expanded beyond the University of Maryland to challenges to Jim Crow at the other public schools in Baltimore County. Lillie Jackson would serve as captain of the women's division, and Carl Murphy, branch official and editor of the *Baltimore Afro-American*, would publicize the campaign. Beginning on the first of October, nightly meetings were to be held at Grace Presbyterian Church, where Jackson and speakers such as former branch president Rev. C. Y. Trigg would give pep talks during nightly reports on the drive.[9]

The drive began with a welcome gesture by the city. On the first day of the campaign the mayor of Baltimore pledged $25 to the NAACP, and the *Afro* printed a photograph of Daisy Lampkin and Juanita Jackson among the small contingent accepting the check in the mayor's office—a remarkable expression of support in a border state that continued to uphold the right to segregate, and which had not witnessed its last lynching. This validation of the NAACP's program, though, was not to be interpreted as evidence of accommodation, of moderation calculated to elicit white support. That night, Lampkin insisted to the audience gathered at Sharp Street ME that "the program of the NAACP is now an offensive one," citing the current Maryland legal cases as proof of the Association's ongoing efforts to undermine racial segregation. Appreciating the size and enthusiasm of the group crowding into Sharp Street ME, Rev. G. R. Waller, the original founder of the Baltimore NAACP, beamed. It had taken him a year, he mused, to convince just four others to join the original branch nearly twenty-five years earlier. Now, on the first night of the campaign, he marveled at the community's participation. Obviously the branch's recent torpor did not reflect the actual interest in advocating for civil rights in Baltimore. From her vantage, Juanita Jackson was equally pleased. Even these first efforts, she reported to Walter White, assured her that the membership drive "will mean the beginning of a REAL branch here in Baltimore."[10]

White witnessed the revival firsthand when he arrived on the final night of the campaign to deliver a speech before the closing mass meeting at the Bethel AME Church, among the most prestigious of the congregations in black Baltimore. The evening demonstrated that the city's Talented Tenth had been effectively marshaled behind the NAACP. Drive volunteers and members of the Elks, the City-Wide Young People's Forum, and the Knights of Pythias each had marched behind an American Legion drum and bugle corps in a parade through the city's northwest neighborhoods ending on Druid Hill Avenue with a procession into Bethel AME. Inside the church, *Afro* columnist Ralph Matthews directed a dramatized rendition of the Ossian Sweet case. He had originally written the sketch for broadcast over WCAO, a local radio station, earlier in the week.

The broadcast, however, had not aired. When the station learned that Matthews' production was not a selection of Negro spirituals but rather an account of the NAACP's celebrated 1925 defense of a black Detroit doctor accused of murder while protecting his home from mob violence, it cancelled the broadcast, claiming fear of "reprisals from members of the Ku Klux Klan and other white organizations." Instead, Matthews's script was read live as the centerpiece of the evening's program. The performance moved White to challenge the WCAO ban, remarking, "I wish that white Marylanders had had the courage to listen." But the skit also offered White the opportunity to describe the potential power local NAACP branches had when working with the national office. The success of recent efforts to open the University of Maryland Law School was as profound an example of this as the defense of Ossian Sweet had been a decade earlier. Of course, the Association needed both active members and ample funds to undertake such efforts. Baltimore would not disappoint. Juanita Jackson's first campaign resulted in over $2,000 in pledges, hundreds of new members, and new leadership for the local branch—Lillie Jackson, the incoming president, was sure to lead the Baltimore NAACP to a successful 1936.[11]

Jackson having recharged the Baltimore branch, White hoped his new special assistant would repeat her success in New York. White assigned Jackson the responsibility of directing the Association's Christmas Seal drive and a fundraising appeal for the NAACP's twenty-seventh anniversary. She accomplished these tasks with aplomb, if not with her customary alacrity. She was anxious to begin organizing youth councils under the auspices of the Association. Becoming a popular speaker among local NAACP groups within a short train ride from New York between Connecticut and New Jersey, Jackson's rising profile in New York earned her an invitation to a December 1935 conference of Mary McLeod Bethune's National Council of Negro Women, a newly founded organization amalgamating a host of black women's clubs into a group that extended the traditional movement among the women of the Talented Tenth. Although invited to join the council for a luncheon at the Harlem YWCA, Jackson devoted her attention to working closely with young branch members in Harlem, intending to inaugurate a youth council of the New York City NAACP. After coordinating an anti-lynching picket in Brooklyn, which continued the direct-action strategy the City-Wide Young People's Forum had employed in Baltimore, Jackson was encouraged to press for an expanded responsibility. In March 1936, she requested that Walter White authorize the formation of a Youth Division of the national NAACP with the board of directors.[12]

The NAACP had long promoted the organization of junior divisions (for members between fourteen and twenty-one years of age) and student chapters on college campuses, but it had yet to sustain a successful youth program. Field secretary Robert Bagnall had raised the issue in 1931: "Our branches are decidedly middle-aged," he reported, leaving "many able young adults" feeling unwelcome to "give full play to their activities." Walter White had come to the same conclusion, writing in 1933, as the New York office prepared for the Amenia Conference,

> One of the greatest weaknesses of the Association's program is the lack of a definite program for activity by Junior Branches and younger people. Many of our branches are officered by loyal and faithful, but elderly, people who in an uncomfortably large number of instances discourage initiative on the part of young people. In the meantime other activities and movements are occupying the attention of young people and gaining their support, though many of these others do not have as fundamental appeal as the work of the NAACP.

What Juanita Jackson proposed, then, might transform the Association's relationship with its network of local branches, a number of which were experiencing the languor of an entrenched and less than energetic older leadership. As the Baltimore drive showed, inertia could be overcome. But there was more to branch work than mobilizing members of a community to contribute annual dues, no matter how crucial such funds were to the continuing viability of the Association. A local legacy of activism could be restored by convincing communities that the NAACP wished to collaborate with local supporters in a civil rights movement that pursued an end to the Jim Crow order. Winning young people to the NAACP's cause, which Jackson ardently wished to achieve, would ensure a healthy future for the Association—but it meant blending activism with fund-raising.[13]

When Walter White appealed to the board in the spring of 1936, the prospect of securing greater support for the Association was all the more important, coming just weeks after the February inauguration of John P. Davis's National Negro Congress. The National Negro Congress might prove competition for resources his own Association depended on; with its radical activist agenda, it might subvert the NAACP's position on the vanguard of the civil rights struggle. Convening hundreds of supporters in Chicago on the anniversary of Frederick Douglass's birthday, the National Negro Congress sought to foster a social movement whose attention to workers' rights and express concern for the masses contrasted with the NAACP's middle-class, legalistic outlook. Taking up the economics of the race problem—with participation from black unionists, such as members of A. Philip Randolph's Brotherhood of Sleeping Car Porters, and overtures to the new, integrated Congress of Industrial Organizations—the National Negro Congress embraced the same suggestions outlined in the Harris report, the impact of which White had carefully maneuvered to downplay.

Establishing a clutch of NAACP youth councils in key cities just might parry this challenge. With Juanita Jackson now in place to launch and direct an Association youth program, the board readily approved of the idea. And if any were hesitant to hand the reins to White's young special assistant, her coordination of a critical membership campaign in Boston and calming influence in a squabble with Philadelphia suggested the scope of her talents.

In April 1936, Juanita Jackson arrived at the Robert Gould Shaw Settlement House on Windsor Street in Roxbury, a neighborhood south of downtown Boston that had become home to most of the city's African Americans. Shaw House was named for the youthful white Bostonian who commanded the colored 54th Massachusetts Regiment during the Civil War. Falling during the bloody assault on Fort Wagner in July 1863, Shaw was also memorialized in a bas-relief monument placed at the corner of Beacon and Park near the Common. A lasting abolitionist spirit had inspired Bostonians to erect such a memorial to the 54th in 1897, a spirit Jackson hoped to tap into during the upcoming membership campaign. The director of the Shaw House was Julian Steele, an African American graduate of the Harvard University class of 1929, who had also studied at the New York School of Social Work before assuming the directorship in 1930. In the past five years, Steele had become a frequent lecturer around Boston and New England, and as one of Boston's younger civil rights leaders he was hopeful of reviving the local NAACP branch. Steele had recently been elected vice president of the Association, and, knowing that the branch did not have a permanent home, he offered Jackson use of Shaw House as campaign headquarters.[14]

Like the Baltimore branch, the Boston NAACP had significantly declined in the past twenty years since its heralded protests of "The Birth of a Nation" during the mid-1910s. Back then, Butler Wilson, the branch's secretary and a black Boston University Law School-trained attorney, had been a driving force. By 1936, Wilson had been branch president for ten years, and, aside from his well-publicized handling of the George Crawford extradition case in the winter of 1933, he had presided over the disintegration of the Boston NAACP.[15] The problem was not that Bostonians' interest in civil rights had waned; the problem, Walter White thought, was with the unpopular and "caustic" seventy-six-year-old Wilson. Indeed, the city had witnessed a vibrant local movement composed of a coalition of such groups as the Scottsboro Defense League, the International Labor Defense, the League of Struggle for Negro Rights, and the Boston Urban League during the early 1930s. Demonstrations peaked between the fall of 1933 and spring of 1934 during a successful "Don't Buy Where You Can't Work" campaign and during protests against police violence in the summer of 1934.[16] But with tensions between a reluctant branch president and younger, more active members, the NAACP remained in an awkward position. When Wilson decided to retire in early 1936, leaving the branch to Irwin Dorch, an ambitious, and much younger, African American lawyer, White was eager to task Juanita Jackson with the branch's spring membership drive.[17]

In part because Butler Wilson had refused offers of assistance from the national office, the previous year's campaign had yielded meager results, despite the imprimatur of the *Boston Chronicle*, a local black weekly. And when Jackson arrived at Shaw House she found hostility to Wilson still lingering, months after his resignation. The new guard of local Association leaders welcomed her direction, but she wrote White, "I hope you and Roy realize the *job* you've given me." Keeping a schedule of campaign work from nine in the morning to between one and two at night, she paused to report in a breathless longhand, "We must face the facts. Boston has not been interested in the NAACP. They don't know what we're doing nationally—and the branch has done *nothing* locally. So the people simply haven't cared anything about the NAACP. More than that I have encountered antipathy to the Association because of Butler Wilson's policies." Her campaign's job, she wrote, "has been to *stab* them awake. We are working night and day to arouse them. There are only three weeks in which to do it."[18]

To "stab" Boston awake, Jackson relied on dozens of volunteers, emphasized the economic dimension of the civil rights struggle, and drew upon the example of the Baltimore revival. Throughout April, she organized over two hundred workers and coordinated with church, lodge, and social groups to boost membership by over fifteen hundred members. The campaign ended with a monster mass meeting at the Columbus Avenue AME Zion Church in Roxbury during the first week of May. The evening featured attention to the radical causes that had recently enflamed black Bostonians, further suggesting the Association's willingness to address issues of economic justice. Howard Kester, a southern white socialist cofounder of the Southern Tenant Farmers' Union who had investigated a spate of recent lynchings, spoke on "Racial and Economic Justice." An ally in Walter White's anti-lynching crusade, Kester was a willing advocate, encouraged by the increasing interest the NAACP paid to workers' rights. Testifying to the NAACP's broadening outlook, Ernest Rice McKinney, a black Communist and vice president of the union, was also invited to deliver an address—an appearance intended to allay concerns that the Association was overly conservative. The tenor struck that night seemed especially propitious to the younger supporters of the Boston NAACP frustrated with the branch's past parochialism. If some squirmed in the presence of such radicals, the appearance of Lillie Jackson redirected attention to the reward of assiduous, unremitting action. "In a dramatic outburst," reported the *Boston Chronicle*, Jackson related "how Baltimore had been in a state of lethargy, doing little about discrimination and prejudices until the NAACP fought and won the University of Maryland case, and showed what is possible when a group of people decides to fight."

Following the example set in Baltimore, Boston determined to fight, joining the roster of reinvigorated NAACP branches.[19]

Juanita Jackson left Bostonians impressed with her "dynamic personality," departing in early May to speak at NAACP branches in Montclair and Newark, New Jersey, and eager to begin organizing the Association's youth division. To start, Jackson would return to familiar ground in Baltimore and Philadelphia. That June, during the annual convention, Baltimore was to host the Association's first youth section of the conference. But if Baltimore and Boston had proven willing to revive branch missions in line with national office, the Philadelphia leadership displayed the sense of territoriality and proprietorship Jackson would need to assuage if she was to build a national network of NAACP youth councils.[20]

Jackson planned to visit Philadelphia in early June, but when the news reached I. Maximilian Martin, the city's NAACP secretary, he was incensed. The "so-called NAACP Youth Council of the NAACP," Martin wrote snippily to Jackson before her arrival, had "ceased functioning in December, 1935 when the Philadelphia Branch became first aware that such a group was functioning in the city." At the time, the disgruntled Martin recounted, "the circumstances surrounding the encouragement and establishment of this group by the national office almost resulted in the complete disruption of the NAACP work in Philadelphia." Only after the board of directors of the NAACP had sponsored a special investigation addressing local members' frustration did the branch avert complete dissolution. In the months since, he wrote, "although the scars of that incident were so deep they took a long time to heal, we have been trying to build up the work again." Such efforts, Martin claimed, had included renewed cooperation "with the group of people who were in the so-called Youth Council." This was a charitable concession, one he could not stomach repeating with Ms. Juanita Jackson. "I might say," Martin wrote, turning to Jackson herself, "that the things I have learned about your activities in connection with this group last year when you were in school here are almost unbelievable for one who even then had been engaged to start on the national staff." Juanita Jackson, Martin claimed, was an aggressive usurper. Several anonymous informants, he revealed, had named Jackson as a "prime mover" in a group that had sought to supplant the local branch, telling Walter White that it was "'dead,' 'inactive' and composed of 'old fossils.'" Despite his every attempt to work with her group, Martin alleged, he had been repeatedly rebuffed. Now, Martin asked Jackson, "Just why you should interfere with the work of the Philadelphia Branch"?[21]

I. Maximilian Martin's bile traced back to several years of tension between the Philadelphia branch and the national office. Martin and his fellow branch officers had nearly revolted in 1933 when it was rumored that the national office had given a group permission to establish a separate branch in north Philadelphia. At stake was the branch's relative autonomy. In all candor, Association friends (including former official Robert Bagnall, who led a prominent Philadelphia congregation, and the lawyer Raymond Pace Alexander) had warned that the Philadelphia NAACP was widely perceived to be a preserve of the socially connected elite, whose leadership had little intention of maintaining an activist agenda. Tellingly, in 1932, the group had refused to support Alexander's defense of a sixteen-year-old black boy accused of rape and murder, wary of sullying connections with white friends whose beneficence helped keep the branch afloat. When Walter White's office approved of a new branch, Philadelphians such as Maximilian Martin considered it a bald affront. And when a number of Young Turks appeared poised to challenge the authority of the branch in December 1935 (again, with the tacit approval of the national office), Martin and all of the Philadelphia NAACP's leaders tendered their resignation, accusing Walter White of personal interference. The NAACP's board of directors appeased the branch by effectively dissolving the youth group, but even this arbitration merely masked the friction between Philadelphia and New York. By the following March, Walter White still harbored bitter feelings about the failure of his "laboratory experiment." He conveyed to Martin, with a tone more of venom than regret, that due to the botched attempt to organize a youth council in Philadelphia, the Association had "lost irretrievably the enthusiasm of these young people and the fine work and spirit which they were willing to devote to the NAACP." Most members of the city's former youth council, White had been galled to learn, had recently declared their allegiance to the National Negro Congress. And he deemed the loss all the greater because "young people today are thinking more deeply and intelligently about race and other problems than at any other time with which I am familiar." White was not finished. "A movement like the NAACP cannot hope to continue to function, or even to exist, nor has it any right to demand that it be permitted to continue in existence, unless there is constantly being added to it new blood, new ideas, new enthusiasm and new workers." Crossed again, Martin responded with an insult of his own. When, in May, White planned to speak in Philadelphia concerning the Costigan-Wagner anti-lynching bill, Martin tartly forbade any local NAACP support of the event. Rather than provoke further furor, which he would have to again bring to the board, White remained fuming in New York.[22]

Drawn directly into this intramural feud, Jackson acted with earnest diplomacy. Deflecting Martin's allegation that a coup was afoot, and ignoring his blatantly insulting tone, she explained that the Association had already organized more than thirty youth councils that spring—the Philadelphia branch was in no way being singled out for surreptitious infiltration. Far from implying something slanderous, she expressed the hope that Philadelphia would make an exemplary partner in the development of a strong youth section of the NAACP.

Insisting on immediately meeting with Martin in person, she traveled by train to Philadelphia. A forty-five-minute conversation with the rankled branch secretary at the train station seemed to ease his irritation. Moreover, the trip was a success, she reported to Walter White, because she had also arranged for two meetings with potential young Philadelphia NAACP members. Despite the Philadelphia leadership's machinations, Jackson anticipated that the annual convention in Baltimore that June would launch a promising youth movement.[23]

Over two hundred young delegates congregated in the Community House of Sharp Street ME Church on the evening of Monday, June 29, 1936. With Juanita Jackson presiding, the president of the Baltimore youth council offered greetings, and Walter White provided a charge, asking the inaugural youth section of the Association's annual conference to "help us map out a program that will make the NAACP the kind of militant, uncompromising, fighting organization that you and I want it to be." The youth contingent cheering White's remarks helped make the convention attendance the largest ever, and they joined an audience of fifteen hundred inside Sharp Street ME for New Dealer Harold Ickes's opening address. Serving as an ambassador for the Roosevelt administration during this presidential election year, the secretary of the interior emphasized the promise the New Deal held for African Americans. In a nationally broadcast address, Ickes linked Roosevelt to the tradition of racial justice initiated by Abraham Lincoln, an unmistakable overture to black voters just two weeks after the Democratic National Convention. The NAACP delegates gathered before him represented an electorate that the progressive elements in the party deemed crucial to the future of the administration's legislative ambitions. Walter White, for one, hoped that Democrats' increasing dependence on black votes would lead to greater support for the NAACP's legal and legislative programs. To effectively thwart Jim Crow education, and to shepherd an effective anti-lynching bill through the legislature, it was pivotal then that the Association maintain vigilance. Breathing life back into the Baltimore and Boston branches and energizing an NAACP youth movement just might be steps toward unprecedented advances in the civil rights struggle.[24]

Aware of the promise the 1936 convention held, Juanita Jackson coordinated a program meant to launch a full-fledged youth council movement. She had spent much of the past several weeks encouraging local branches to raise the funds necessary to send youth delegates to the annual conference in Baltimore. "Since the youth work of the Association is at present just in the process of development," she wrote in a letter sent to branches from Muskogee, Oklahoma, to Mobile, Alabama, "it is at this Conference that we shall plan our national youth program and discuss our permanent organizational setup." Her appeal succeeded. Nearly half of all of the NAACP conferees attending were youth delegates, their week's program captured in an emphatic, nearly evangelical, slogan: "Youth, Let Us Awake!!" Through Friday, the delegates met twice a day at Grace Presbyterian and Sharp Street ME's Community House, then separated into discussion groups dedicated to topics ranging from "work and relief" to "organization, promotion and publicity," and from "educational opportunities" to "civil liberties." There was practical advice for creating and administering a youth council, as well as the opportunity to establish contacts and become acquainted with the central civil rights issues of the day. Seeking to introduce the delegates to exemplary black professionals from the younger set, Jackson arranged for J. St. Clair Drake, a twenty-five-year-old instructor of sociology at Dillard University, to lead discussion about developing a national program on lynching. From New York, Ella Baker, a well known thirty-two-year-old activist, explained the "Consumers Cooperatives" she and George Schuyler had organized in the Harlem-based Young Negroes' Cooperative League. Surveying the week, there was reason to expect the experience might mobilize an effective movement.[25]

Wednesday night was Youth Night, a showcase for the young delegates and an opportunity to define the youth council movement. Sixteen hundred audience members came together in Sharp Street ME on the third night of the convention to hear the symposium "Youth Hurls a Challenge." Clarence Mitchell, an *Afro* reporter and a former vice president of the City-Wide Young People's Forum (to whom Juanita Jackson had been quietly engaged since 1934), moderated a discussion among four young speakers who envisioned a forceful civil rights program. Jackson responded with a keynote speech: "The NAACP Challenges Youth," a statement establishing the broad outlines of a national youth council program, and calling on young people to take an active part. The NAACP's youth division, she asserted, could fight to "secure the full constitutional rights of the American Negro"—for the freedom to vote, for rights in court, for freedom from mob violence and segregation, for the right to educational opportunity, and for economic equality. Like the national office, the youth councils could sway public opinion, use legal test cases, assert suffrage rights, and push for legislation. Calling on young activists themselves to initiate these measures, the NAACP offered the youth councils as an alternative to the ad hoc groups they might otherwise form—or the more radical organizations they might join—with all the esteem and resources the national Association could offer. Youth had a voice; they had the backing of a respected national organization; now they needed to act.[26]

The following morning, the youth delegates assembled in a "fiery discussion period" to contemplate their challenge. Composing a declaration to be read during the closing meeting, they vowed "to fight relentlessly with the ballot, in the courts, with education of public opinion and the enactment of legislation for equal opportunities in all spheres, for protection and extension of civil liberties, and against the insane fury of the mob." The delegation assented to upholding the national program Jackson had proposed for the coming year, with an emphasis on direct action. Returning home, the delegates would endeavor to organize local youth councils with a militant tinge. Unembarrassed to align with causes championed by the radical left, they pledged to uphold the defenses of the Scottsboro Boys and Angelo Herndon, a young black Communist who had been jailed in Georgia. They endorsed "Don't Buy Where You Can't Work" campaigns, such as had taken place in Baltimore and Harlem, Boston and Washington, DC—boycotts to pressure businesses to integrate that some in the NAACP old guard considered imprudent but which suggested the delegates' insistence on economic rights. It was an agenda calibrated to co-opt support that might otherwise drift leftward—toward the National Negro Congress, to name but one competitor—but the youth councils would also heed the NAACP's emphasis on ending segregation in schools and seeing anti-lynching legislation through the senate. With national elections at stake in November, the delegates agreed to hold nationwide mass meetings condemning educational inequalities. In February 1937, the councils planned to commemorate Lincoln's Birthday and Negro History Week by staging large demonstrations against lynching, coordinating local movements in a national denunciation of white terror.[27]

As the Baltimore conference ended, both youth and adult delegates were impressed with the results. "Hats off to Juanita Jackson!" wrote one Cleveland NAACP branch member to Walter White following the annual conference, appending a request that Jackson visit his branch that fall. Oklahoma City's Roscoe Dunjee led a caravan of cars thirteen hundred miles home, enthusiastic about Jackson's youth councils and intent on developing such a movement in his home state. For her part, Jackson returned to 69 Fifth Avenue absorbed in the task of translating the heady promise of the convention into an actual movement. Following the conference, an advisory committee of the youth section of the conference planned to meet weekly in New York, alternating between the Harlem YWCA on 137th Street and the YMCA on 135th. To better maintain momentum, Jackson sought release from her fundraising duties to work solely on building the NAACP youth movement. "The time is ripe," she wrote to her fellow Association officers, explaining that several other organizations, including the National Negro Congress, had already begun moving in the same direction. The NAACP needed to act immediately, she stressed, to sponsor the kind of militancy White had encouraged at Baltimore. "The NAACP which has by far the most challenging program in the field of race relations for Negro and white youth," she contended, "must concentrate and throw its strength and resources immediately into this field." Jackson envisioned a national network of youth groups who could bolster the Association's standing—the planned anti-lynching demonstrations and mass meetings for educational equality might just be the beginning. She hoped to start that fall with an organizing tour in the Midwest.[28]

"We have counseled together," Jackson wrote to the youth members of the NAACP during the first week of August 1936. "We have come to grips with the problems of insecurity, education, inequalities, political injustices, and mob violence. We are aware of the long arm of poverty, Jim Crowism, lynching and oppression, as it seeks to tighten its fascist hold upon twelve million of Negro Americans." During the Baltimore convention they had "built a national program of action around four basic problems—education, jobs, civil liberties, lynching." In the coming year she wanted the NAACP's young leaders "to plunge into the struggle for the equal right to learn, to work, to live." "Remember," she prodded, "it is not enough to awaken; it is not enough to understand. We must act—and act now!"[29]

"These past two weeks have been a continual round of activity for me," wrote Jackson on a train from Flint to Lansing, Michigan, in early October 1936. She had been on a tour of local NAACP branches in the Midwest since mid-September, and had already stopped in Harrisburg, Pennsylvania; Akron, Cincinnati, Youngstown, and Cleveland, Ohio; Indianapolis and Gary, Indiana; and Detroit. Leaving Flint early that morning, she reported to the national office in New York, she expected to follow the usual itinerary in Lansing. Upon arrival she would undertake "a visit of Negro institutions and other agencies of interest, in order that I might make contacts for the Association." Afterward, she would meet with local "young people for the purpose of beginning a Youth Council," then, following dinner, deliver an address before an Association mass meeting, likely in one of the larger churches. There would be "people to meet until 11pm," and then she would leave with her hostess, who was "usually such a dear," but who would also invariably be "*so* interested in the Association" that she "must talk with her until 12:30 or 1am." She would arise early the next morning, before she had gotten nearly enough sleep, in order to catch the next train. Nearing the end of her trip, Jackson felt she could "sleep a thousand years."[30]

Although the Midwestern tour had left her drained, she had left local NAACP branches from Gary to Detroit bestirred in her wake, an effervescent emissary linking communities' branch work with the national educational and anti-lynching programs. Jackson began the tour in the middle of September with an appearance at the Pennsylvania State Conference of Branches in Media, where she led discussion groups on youth work. From Media, she traveled west to the state capital, but was disappointed in the lack of NAACP spirit in Harrisburg, even as important civil rights legislation was being ushered through the state legislature. She met with better success the next day at Centenary Church in Youngstown, Ohio, and during an evening spent in Akron. Jackson next toured

Cleveland, appeared at Phillips Christian Methodist Episcopal (CME) Church in Indianapolis, and then rallied over 250 enthusiasts at the Israel CME Church in Gary, urging the group to "organize and fight for educational, economic, political and social advancement" while "citing cases of jim-crowism throughout the United States." To Jackson's delight, members of the Gary youth council had already begun a picketing campaign of local stores that had not been willing to hire black workers. Spending the next several days in Detroit, she was similarly impressed—and impressive. Jackson "made a great impression upon the Detroiters," the branch president raved in a note to Walter White. "She is going places and doing things. The young people here rally to her 100%, while the adults seemingly worship the ground upon which she walks, in other words, I just can't tell you what kind of impression she made." Gloster Current, the Detroit youth council leader, found that her "effervescent spirit" had "instilled in me an enthusiasm that will long keep me active in the work of the NAACP." Jackson went on to Lansing and then to Flint, where she finished her September tour with a talk on "The Promotion of Youth" at Mt. Olive Baptist Church.[31]

After she returned from Michigan, a busy fall campaign beckoned. A friend expressed concern that Jackson had seemed quite worn during the trip, but after a few nights' recuperation on Druid Hill Avenue the NAACP special assistant was eager to forge on. She arranged for an appearance across the city at Morgan College and, with NAACP field secretary (and former Morgan College dean) William Pickens, organized a new chapter on the east Baltimore campus. The following week found Jackson in Richmond, Virginia. She spoke at Second Baptist Church to help the local NAACP inaugurate its membership campaign and organize a youth council. She also formed a college chapter at Virginia Union University, then traveled north to Cheyney, Pennsylvania, to address the NAACP chapter at Cheyney State Teachers College. With so much recent success, by the time she reached New York again in mid-October, Jackson was determined to renew efforts to revive the youth council in Philadelphia, the only major city in the northeast without activity. In June, she had alerted I. Maximilian Martin of the NAACP youth divisions' plans for the year after the Baltimore conference, but he had only responded with the suggestion that Philadelphia wait until the fall to begin work. In October Martin remained reluctant to cooperate, even after Jackson phoned long-distance from 69 Fifth Avenue, offering to travel to Philadelphia to help with organizing the council. "As far as I am concerned," he told Jackson, "at this time I have more than my hands full with branch matters" and "could not spare the time necessary to get the group going properly as much as I would like to." Stymied, Jackson brought the matter to Walter White. "For the last seven months," she explained to the executive secretary, "I have been trying to get a youth council in Philadelphia under way." She thought the matter had been resolved in June during their conversation at the Philadelphia train station, but Martin had continued to obstruct her efforts. "I can't help but feel that this is tragic," she wrote. The young people there, she could report, were ready to organize, but they were "simply being kept back by the apathy and indifference of Mr. Martin." White felt equally at a loss about proceeding and asked for the advice of several board members. During the November board meeting, Jackson reported on the situation. Isadore Martin, a longtime board member (and Maximilian's father), agreed to intervene. By the time the elder Martin sent an appreciative note to Jackson for arranging a list of potential youth members, however, she had embarked on a tour of southern NAACP branches.[32]

Jackson timed the tour to begin just after a nationwide series of youth council mass meetings decrying educational inequalities, all the better to sustain the enthusiasm initiated at the Baltimore convention and during her late-summer tour of the Midwest. Groups she had rallied with in recent weeks carried on successful November 12th programs. The youth council of Indianapolis hosted a forum featuring an address by the president of the State Conference of Branches; as a result of the mass meeting in Cleveland, the youth council began a survey of conditions in local schools to ensure that discrimination not pass unheeded. From hailing distance of 69 Fifth Avenue, the Jersey City group convening at Thirkfield Methodist Episcopal Church welcomed an appearance by the branch president of the New York NAACP, and the Staten Island youth council arranged for the endorsement of the borough president in its protest of Jim Crow conditions in schools—their contribution of $5 to the national fund to end such segregation coming at a moment when every pledge counted and when the NAACP hoped to keep the nation on the alert. Encouragingly, though such events were intended to highlight the national Association's signature programs, the attentions aroused also spurred local action. After Thurgood Marshall, for instance, spoke at the Lincoln University November 12th mass meeting, the college chapter resolved to bring suit against a local movie theater that segregated in defiance of the state's new civil rights law. With the new council in Richmond, Virginia, also participating in the November 12th mass meetings, Jackson could hold out hope for a similar impact following the tour that would take her southward through Thanksgiving.[33]

While initial reports of the November 12th events from Rochester, Pennsylvania, to Augusta, Georgia, arrived at 69 Fifth Avenue, Jackson embarked for Baltimore, where the *Afro-American* announced her plans to meet with the youth council, and for Washington, DC, where she spoke at Howard University. Traveling on the next day to West Virginia, Jackson participated in morning services and a mass meeting at First Baptist Church in Montgomery, and was in Charleston, thirty miles to the west, in time for one of the largest meetings the local branch had reportedly witnessed in several years. "She was simply marvelous," gushed the branch president in a note to Walter White, "and captivated that vast audience. We secured fifty-two new members in about fifteen minutes, and at least the hands of a hundred others went up indicating that they would join. It was one of the most effective meetings we have ever held." The next morning, Jackson met with students at Phillips High School, then found the "response amazing" at the State College campus in Institute. The group of three hundred students greeting her arrival had been forced to move from their scheduled location to one of the largest classrooms on campus. Even then "students were standing all around the room, many unable to get in." With success assured in the Kanawha River valley, Jackson traveled next to Cincinnati, Ohio, to spend the evening with branch leaders and organizing a youth council. The next afternoon, she was three hundred miles south in Nashville, Tennessee. "Nashville was a problem child," Jackson complained. The local branch was ill prepared for her arrival and seemed dismal in spirit—yet she still succeeded in getting college chapters underway at Fisk University, Agricultural and Industrial State College, and Meharry Medical College. Together, she predicted, these groups "will put new energy into senior branch."[34]

In two days Jackson was in Birmingham, that crucible of Jim Crow in central Alabama. She spoke at Miles College, where her encouragement to inaugurate an NAACP chapter inspired three-quarters of the student body to organize on the spot. She also appeared at two of the city's high schools, gaining pledges of support from over a hundred students, and enthralled the local branch during a mass meeting. "She has really resold the NAACP to Colored Birmingham," enthused branch secretary Charles McPherson, who shared a medical practice on Fourth Street with branch president E. W. Taggart, as well as a willingness to disobey the strictures of segregation. The previous winter, McPherson had gathered information on several southern lynchings for Walter White. Weeks later, in early March, Taggart had been arrested while distributing pamphlets on the NAACP's anti-lynching platform. That fall their branch was leading a challenge of the Birmingham Housing Authority to alleviate the city's slum conditions. Jackson's appearance helped bolster the campaign. "The old reactionaries," McPherson reported, "are restless in their boots for the want of something with which to combat the far reaching program she so clearly outlined." Of course, she also "captivated the youth." But her priority, as Jackson had explained to the Birmingham branch president, was to visit with the defendants in the Scottsboro trials, then being held in Jefferson County jail. After more than five years in prison, the Scottsboro Boys were now young men. In 1932 and 1935, the Scottsboro defense had won Supreme Court reversals of convictions that also resulted in landmark legal precedents: *Powell v. Alabama* guaranteed defendants access to adequate counsel, and *Norris v. Alabama* ended all-white juries. By 1936, though, the Scottsboro Boys remained imprisoned, worn out from months of unofficial solitary confinement and facing the prospect of new trials for their lives in 1937. While the nine young men suffered in limbo, Jackson visited, accompanied by branch president Taggart and youth council member Laura Kellum. Jackson wished to convey the support of the NAACP's new youth movement, but the youngest defendant, a dispirited Roy Wright, refused to participate in the visit: "Talk, talk, talk and we are still in jail." Willie Roberson was more expressive: "I'm appreciating everything you all have done. I'm glad you're still going to do everything you can to get us out. I've been feeling downhearted for a long time, but I try to keep my hope up. I'm so tired of jail." Assembling in a brightly lit corridor, the neatly dressed defendants posed with Jackson, Kellum, and Taggart for a photograph to appear in the next issue of the *Crisis,* along with a request that young people forward correspondence and tokens of support. In the center of the frame were Clarence Norris and Heywood Patterson, whose retrials had been scheduled for January. On the right, Patterson held Kellum's hand with a gesture of striking timidity, if his notoriety was to be believed; on the left, Jackson grasped Norris's hand with an expression of steadfast poise, affirming an unbending devotion to their cause.[35]

From the Jefferson County jail, Jackson forged eastward toward Atlanta, Georgia, home to a renascent NAACP branch. First, it was fifty miles to Talladega, where attendance for her speech at Talladega College was diminished because many students had traveled to Nashville for the school's football game with Fisk University. Brushing off this minor disappointment, she stopped next in Anniston, Alabama, where that night she addressed nearly two hundred young people at the Seventeenth Street Baptist Church, then appeared at the

Juanita Jackson and representatives of the Birmingham branch of the NAACP visiting the Scottsboro defendants in November 1936. Library of Congress, Prints and Photographs Division, Visual Materials from the NAACP Records.

local branch's mass meeting. The "surprising attendance" in Anniston matched Jackson's satisfaction with the newly organized youth council's plan to protest discrimination at the local library. By the following afternoon, Jackson was ninety miles away, across the Georgia line, in Atlanta, where her fiancé, Clarence Mitchell, had taken an Urban League fellowship to study at the Atlanta School of Social Work, and was also reporting for the black weekly the *Atlanta World*. Atlanta was home to a half dozen black colleges, a large and revitalized NAACP branch, and a host of youth council members ready to engage in the work of the Association's year-long program. Jackson spoke at nine meetings over the course of the November weekend she spent in the city. She visited the campuses of Morehouse College, Spellman College, Morris Brown University, and Clark University, forming NAACP chapters at each, and addressed a branch audience at the YWCA that included over three hundred young people. The new youth council agreed to help the senior branch with upkeep of its office in the Herndon Building, but also made bold plans of its own to bring the sort of direct-action protest that marked the youth movement in Baltimore and Gary to the seat of the modern South. The Atlanta youth council would boycott several local chain stores that refused to hire blacks, stage protests against the recent assault of a female high school student on a street car, and maintain a vigilant stance against lynching—critical in a state that had witnessed six of the eight lynchings counted in 1936. While Jackson was pleased with her visit—with the number of council members organized, with the relative militancy of their planned protests—several Atlanta leaders were just as happy with her efforts. The youth council's decision to engage in "mass action against lynching," the thoroughly biased Clarence Mitchell thought, "promises to be a real sensation." Such activism would further cure the branch of its former malaise. Indeed, the Sunday meeting, the new branch president and Atlanta School of Social Work director Forrester Washington boasted, had been discussed among Association members as the best "held in Atlanta in a great many years." Jackson's speech was "remarkable," said Washington. She "not only put added life into the Youth Movement which we have just started here, but she gave great stimulation to the whole local movement." In fact, Washington hoped for her quick return to the city, he told Walter White, because "all classes of people heard her speak on her recent visit and have asked me to have her come back and speak at a larger church."[36]

Before returning to Baltimore, Jackson stopped in Columbia, South Carolina. The NAACP had only been fitfully active in the Palmetto State during the previous several years, but she organized college chapters at Benedict College and Allen University and met with a group interested in reviving the Columbia NAACP, before boarding a Jim Crow train car for Maryland. She reached Druid Hill Avenue the day before Thanksgiving, exhausted but satisfied. She wrote

Walter White, "I can't help feeling a wee bit proud of the success of this last tour." After visiting with many hundreds of young people from Charleston to Columbia, she found "the most inspiring thing has been the ready and enthusiastic response of young Negroes. They are ready for action—what they need is leadership, a program, and an organization through which to channel their activities. *WE* have it!"[37]

After an autumn on tour, Jackson was back at 69 Fifth Avenue in December 1936, while the newly founded youth councils were fashioning a national movement that supported the NAACP's national programs even as they pursued the improvement of local conditions. With the February 12th anti-lynching demonstrations looming, Jackson again attended the winter meeting of the National Council of Negro Women, maintaining an important tie between the youth councils and Mary McLeod Bethune's formidable organization. That Bethune had just received a position within the Roosevelt administration—as a director of Negro Affairs in the National Youth Administration, Bethune was a keystone in the Black Cabinet—only heightened the significance of this relationship.[38] If the 1935 Christmas seal campaign had portended tedium in the coming year, this December it offered creative approaches to entwining the national fundraising efforts with local holiday social seasons. The Detroit youth council took up the challenge with gusto. Willing to include proper entertainment in their movement's repertoire, the group hosted a Christmas seal dance and frolic featuring the crowning of a Seal Queen and music provided by no fewer than three orchestras that had volunteered their services. A musical Christmas tea requiring the purchase of ten seals (they were a penny apiece) for admittance made a dainty, and profitable, addition to the holiday schedule. Such events in Detroit netted the sale of 16,300 seals, and the Boston youth council was not too much further behind. With contributions to fund the NAACP's upcoming programs in 1937, Jackson welcomed the news from Boston, and beyond. In New Rochelle, New York, the youth council had founded a lecture series and reported hosting a "symposium on politics." Council members in Gary, Indiana, had continued their boycott campaign, and had now picketed over fifty stores, convincing at least thirty-five to hire black workers. Rallies had been held in Staten Island, New York, Chicago, and on the campus of Lincoln University, in Lincoln, Pennsylvania. Lansing, Michigan, had begun a "fight against barring of Negro teachers in the public school system"; Atlantans had begun planning to boycott local discriminating chain stores. The Albany, New York, youth council was protesting segregation in area nursing and business schools, and in Chester, Pennsylvania, council members were organizing protests for open employment in the local Ford assembly plant. In Philadelphia, a youth council was at last in action: basing their meetings at the YWCA, the council planned to challenge discrimination in the city's theaters, a violation of the civil rights law recently passed in the state.

Like in Cleveland, the Brooklyn youth council had started a survey of conditions in its public schools.[39]

With the new year, Jackson entered into this swirl of activity—visiting youth branches in Chester, Pennsylvania, and addressing mass meetings in Mt. Vernon and White Plains, New York—but her attention was rooted to planning for the Association's national Anti-Lynching Day to be held on February 12th, Lincoln's Birthday and the anniversary of the founding of the NAACP. Following the demise of the Costigan-Wagner bill, Walter White maneuvered new legislation into the House from the office of Harlem's Democratic representative, Joseph Gavagan. A recent $5,000 contribution to the Association's anti-lynching fund would help endow the coming campaign in 1937, including the mobilization of grassroots support for the measure—which the youth movement might furnish. "There have been twelve lynchings in 1936," Jackson explained to members of NAACP youth councils at the end of December, and "the youth movement is redoubling its energy to get a federal anti-lynching bill through the 75th Congress," which was set to open in January. In October, the Crisis had featured a photograph of a new black flag, measuring six by ten feet, hanging from the window at 69 Fifth Avenue—it bore, in white letters, a grim announcement: "A Man Was Lynched Yesterday." The NAACP had first raised the "Death Flag" in September, and from then on the Association planned to fly it over Fifth Avenue after each reported lynching. The November Crisis had printed Dillard University sociologist J. St. Clair Drake's pamphlet on lynching, and the December issue elaborated on the plans to hold nationwide youth demonstrations against lynching. The demonstration in February 1937 would include "No More Lynching" parades, mass meetings, soapbox orations, student rallies on campuses, and radio broadcasts. The national office was taking orders for "Stop Lynching" buttons, with the initial expectation of selling ten thousand having already been surpassed by the Harlem NAACP's request of eighteen thousand. Demonstrators, too, would wear black armbands that day to mourn victims of lynching. As Jackson reminded youth council members, the purposes of this activism was

> To enlist youth groups in a national demonstration of their solidarity in the fight for Negro rights; To demonstrate to legislators and the general public that a large number of people are serious in their demands for anti-lynching legislation, and that they wish to make a determined protest against the measures used to defeat such legislation; To offer a channel through which the voice of black and white youths throughout the country might be heard in a demand for a lynchless America.

With Walter White orchestrating the NAACP's legislative lobbying, the youth councils could create a mighty upswell.[40]

Jackson began mobilizing in New York after the beginning of the new year, speaking during the first week of January at the Harlem YWCA about the importance of staging the anti-lynching demonstration in February. Two nights later, she hosted a meeting two blocks away at the YMCA on 135th Street to plan the demonstration and forming, with Dorothy Height, the United Youth Committee against Lynching, a network of over one hundred local youth groups. While the Committee brought together a spectrum of supporters in New York, from the radical left to Christian activists, Jackson endeavored to make the night a truly nationwide protest. Mailing detailed suggestions for planning local anti-lynching demonstrations to youth council leaders, she included a fact sheet for speakers on the history of lynching and on the NAACP's longstanding fight against lynching, and described the program for the upcoming monster meeting in Harlem, featuring Adam Clayton Powell, Jr., the "militant assistant pastor of Abyssinian Baptist Church." Jackson also hoped to line up New York's Democratic senator Robert Wagner, an advocate of the anti-lynching legislation currently in Congress, for a national broadcast on NBC radio. By mid-January, she reported to Walter White, "We are working at top speed on the preparation for our National Youth Demonstration Against Lynching." Newspapers had begun to publicize the event, and youth groups in Brooklyn and Jamaica, Queens, had joined Harlem in making demonstration plans. Through the end of the month, she traveled between Philadelphia, Baltimore, and Washington to promote the demonstrations. In Baltimore she met with youth council members to assist with preparations for a demonstration and parade, arranged for coordination with Morgan College, and made certain that the *Baltimore Afro-American* had begun to publicize the event. Jackson found the Howard University chapter in the midst of preparations, and offered help in recommending high-profile speakers. Back in New York, Jackson continued planning and publicizing the Harlem event through early February. Volunteers launched a drive to sell "Stop Lynching" flyers, posters, and car stickers. As Harlem became the hub of the anti-lynching campaign, the *New York Amsterdam News* observed a populace "showing an interest in the drive to end lynching that it has not shown in a long time," fully anticipating the "mammoth youth demonstration" at Mother AME Zion Church on Lincoln's Birthday.[41]

The February 12th event began at 6:15 PM with Senator Wagner's address on "The Lynching Problem Viewed on Lincoln's Birthday," heard on NBC radio over loudspeakers rigged outside Mother AME Zion on 137th Street, near Seventh Avenue. Following the broadcast, a parade featuring nine young men dressed in striped prison outfits to represent the Scottsboro defendants, wound through "the Campus" between 135th and 137th Streets, finishing back at Mother AME Zion. Inside, Juanita Jackson presided as over 2,500 audience members crowded into the church. She had arranged for an impressive roster of civil rights leaders to speak in support of the cause. Former NAACP board president Mary White Ovington opened the program with a bit of history. "It is twenty-six years," she said, since she and another activist had "edited the first anti-lynching pamphlet issued by the NAACP. Since then lynchings have decreased in number but the crime continues and the methods of torture are as horrible as ever." Now, she acknowledged, "another generation is working to end this disgrace of America." Ovington wished "all honor to its courage and determined effort, which must succeed before many years." Dorothy Height, chairman of the United Youth Committee against Lynching, and at twenty-five a member of this younger generation seeking to abolish this disgrace, detailed her committee's work. Association field secretary Daisy Lampkin reported on the fundraising successes of "The 'Stop Lynching' Button Campaign." Allan Knight Chalmers, head of the Scottsboro Defense Committee, spoke on Scottsboro— his presence, like the costumed marchers, emphasizing the NAACP's contribution to the fight to end legal lynching. Angelo Herndon, the twenty-four-year-old black Communist imprisoned in Georgia for leading an interracial workers' demonstration in 1932, whom the youth councils had pledged to support during the Baltimore convention, sent a plea to be read titled "Let Me Live." Walter White arrived from Washington, where the fight for anti-lynching legislation was hung up—in the Senate, southern legislators were refusing to allow a vote on the Gavagan bill. White described the legislative challenge the Association faced and told the group that mass appeal could help maintain pressure on the legislature, enough perhaps to convince the president to intervene. Joining these important national figures, two of Harlem's African American leaders also appeared, reflecting the range of support the anti-lynching campaign had engendered in the community, and demonstrating the NAACP's intention to foster a wide appeal for this program. Frank Crosswaith, the black Socialist founder of the Negro Labor Committee, supplemented White's address with an explanation of "The Economic Basis of Lynching." Adam Clayton Powell, Jr., the newly appointed activist pastor of the prestigious Abyssinian Baptist Church, ended the evening, testifying to the role the church could play in bringing an end to lynching. It was a point underscored by the very venue chosen to host the Anti-Lynching Day program: Mother Zion AME, whose abolitionist pedigree spoke of an enduring devotion to black freedom, whether from enslavement or from the "rope and faggot."[42]

Mother AME Zion was not the only church to host an Anti-Lynching Day program that February. The Harlem rally had been only the largest in a series of events nationwide. During the next week, news of local demonstrations arrived at 69 Fifth Avenue from across the country. In Cleveland, the youth council organized a demonstration and meeting at St. James AME Church, where members staged the Langston Hughes play *Scottsboro Limited*. In Chicago, the youth

On February 12, 1937, NAACP Youth Councils mobilized against lynching, including in Harlem (top) and Chicago (bottom). Special Collections and University Archives, W. E. B. Du Bois Library, University of Massachusetts Amherst, reprinted with the permission of the Crisis Publishing Company.

council held a "No More Lynching Parade" through the Loop, before convening at Good Shepherd Church for their mass meeting. Detroiters arranged a radio broadcast and held one of the nation's largest demonstrations. Beyond the urban Midwest, where Jackson had organized branches the previous fall, dozens of smaller youth council–sponsored events gave Anti-Lynching Day a national complexion. A "motor cavalcade" marked the day in Orange, New Jersey. A mass meeting was held at the Leigh Street Methodist Church in Richmond, Virginia. Baltimore attorney Thurgood Marshall spoke at the demonstration in Pough-keepsie, New York. The Houston College for Negroes sold buttons on campus. Two hundred youth council members wore black armbands in Lansing, Michi-gan. Chapter members organized campus rallies at Talladega College in Ala-bama, Allen University in South Carolina, and Morris Brown University in Atlanta. The youth council of Marion, Indiana, held its anti-lynching meeting at the YMCA. Members in Jersey City, New Jersey, convened at Metropolitan AME Zion Church for a speech on "The Fury of the Mob." Charles Houston spoke at Morgan College in Baltimore. The Columbus, Ohio, youth council issued telegrams to President Roosevelt asking for his support in passing anti-lynching legislation.[43]

Receiving this correspondence at the NAACP headquarters, Juanita Jackson had clear evidence that her fall tours of the Midwest and South had helped lay the foundation not only of a network of stronger branches but also of a vital movement among young African Americans. The success of Anti-Lynching Day instilled an even greater determination as she readied for another long trip that March that would take her from St. Louis to New Orleans, by way of Oklahoma and Texas, before returning east for the spring membership drives and prepara-tion for the annual convention in Detroit.[44]

Jackson arrived at the downtown offices of the St. Louis NAACP at the end of February 1937. Branch president and attorney Sidney Redmond welcomed Jackson to what the former Mississippi lawyer considered "just a big Southern city"; a youth council member had arranged a tour of the city for her. It was sev-eral blocks west from the local branch on North Jefferson Street to the Pine Street YMCA, where the youth council had recently held its "Youth Day," and it was two more miles to "the Ville," the African American neighborhood that had taken shape in northwest St. Louis. There, on a bluff offering vistas of the Missis-sippi River, Jackson found Antioch Baptist Church, Sumner High School (among the country's oldest black high schools), St. James AME Church, Stowe Teachers College, and the nearly finished Homer G. Phillips Hospital. Having noted the city's respectable colored institutions, Jackson met with branch members that evening and congratulated the youth council on its recent anti-lynching efforts. Even as the southern Democrats' obstructionist tactics blocked the Gavagan bill, such expressions of support maintained awareness and inspired continuing civil rights advocacy—for instance, for the NAACP's ongoing *Gaines* suit to desegregate the University of Missouri Law School. Redmond, a graduate of Harvard Law School (and old friend of Charles Houston), had been a key ally in that fight and could attest to the significance of the Association's incremental progress in defeating the "separate but equal" doctrine in the realm of education. After an evening of doting attention in the home of an NAACP benefactor, the next day Jackson ventured 250 miles west across the state to Kansas City, where she convinced members of the nearly defunct NAACP branch to pool "all their efforts to rehabilitate it." Then she was on to Oklahoma.[45]

Roscoe Dunjee met Jackson on the first of March, when she arrived from the train ride across flat Kansas to the capital of Oklahoma. Oklahoma City's indefatigable fifty-four-year-old editor of the *Black Dispatch* and NAACP proponent had begun promoting her arrival in January. "I wish every member of your branch could have been in Baltimore," he wrote members of the Oklahoma State Conference of Branches, "and have seen the inspiring youth program staged by Miss Jackson. She is one of the most dynamic young women of our race in America and your community cannot afford to have her enter this state without visiting your branch." Jackson planned to spend two weeks in the state, and there was no better host than Dunjee, whose unsurpassed network of contacts and knowledge of civil rights in the state would help evangelize the NAACP's programs to black Oklahomans. While in Oklahoma City, with a blend of paternal and political care, Dunjee arranged for the twenty-four-year-old special assistant to stay with leading Association families, revising the itinerary Jackson had originally planned because he did not deem her chosen host a strong enough NAACP supporter. The duo then hopped into Dunjee's automobile and, commencing a circle over the eastern half of the state, drove forty miles north to Langston, originally founded in the 1890s as an all-black town on the south bank of the Cimarron River. Jackson addressed an audience of seven hundred at Langston University, and then the pair drove several hours northeast to Tulsa, the bustling oil city just east of the confluence of the Arkansas and Cimarron Rivers. Greenwood, the heart of colored Tulsa, had been flattened during a race riot in 1921, and while the black community had since rebounded, scars remained. From Tulsa, it was a short trip southeast along the Arkansas to the river port community of Muskogee, where the local youth council had reportedly "dared to sell 50 'Stop Lynching' buttons in the prejudiced" town. Further evincing the protest spirit that linked stalwart locals to national campaigns, Muskogee agreed to challenge discrimination in local schools, a handy addition to the NAACP special counsel's quiver in the fight for desegregated education. Idabel was a longer drive away, 180 miles to the south, on the Red River in the far southeastern corner of the state; then Jackson and Dunjee doubled back 120 miles northwest to McAlester, home to the state penitentiary where Jess Hollins, convicted of raping a white woman, languished. Dunjee had been integral in the defense that saved Hollins from execution, but no one had yet been able to free him from a lifelong sentence; he was the state's equivalent to the Scottsboro Boys. Next, it was west to Chickasha, a prairie depot along the Rock Island Railroad, before turning back northeast to Oklahoma City. The Association's campaign for equal education, Jackson found, went over especially well with Oklahomans. But clearly Dunjee had sowed the seeds of the NAACP's popularity in the state. "Roscoe Dunjee is a jewel!" she wrote Walter White of her kindred-spirited companion in the midst of her tour. "It is amazing how NAACP conscious Oklahoma is—and because of his efforts." The admiration was mutual. Dunjee eagerly gave voice to Oklahomans' enthusiasm for the national office's special assistant. "Jackson is in my judgment the greatest find of the Association," he told Charles Houston, with whom he had worked in the Hollins case. Indeed, she "is very effective in her work," he reported to Walter White, "and I am writing right now to say that every day you keep her in the office is a mistake. She simply swept the young folk in this state off their feet, both black and white."[46]

It would be difficult to surpass her weeks with Roscoe Dunjee, but branch work in the South demanded attention. After the vitality she had witnessed in Oklahoma, the tepid interest in Texas presented a significant contrast. Yet, in her four days in the eastern half of the state, she helped to completely reorganize the Dallas and Houston branches, the latter gaining over one hundred members following her visit. It was, she thought, "the most significant job of my whole tour," firming up the NAACP presence in the state. She formed several college chapters, and was pleased to boast that the state conference of branches had determined to take up the fight to desegregate the University of Texas at Austin, creating another regional link to the NAACP's national education program. With this encouragement, Jackson departed east Texas for the 350-mile train ride along the Gulf of Mexico to New Orleans, where she launched the local branch's spring membership campaign and organized college chapters at Xavier and Dillard Universities. There she could catch up with J. St. Clair Drake; her collaborator in the anti-lynching campaign was undertaking a sociological survey of the city's churches and voluntary associations, the very institutions the New Orleans NAACP depended upon. Jackson ended her month-long tour with a return visit to Atlanta, and then was back in New York by the first week of April. Her enthusiasm had clearly not evaporated in the past weeks, despite the rigors of the tour. "I consider Juanita Jackson one of the most dynamic young women that I have ever met," wrote one Atlantan effusively to the New York office following her appearance. "The greatness of rhythm and spirit of her addresses measure in greatness with the nobility of the cause itself."[47]

The well-traveled special assistant would need whatever energy she had in reserve, for she was soon due back in Boston for the branch's annual membership drive. The Association, still lacking a large enough office, had again arranged for the use of Shaw House as campaign headquarters. What it lacked in office space the branch made up for in renewed vigor. That April, Jackson arrived to a Boston emboldened by an active youth council. In the past year, the branch council had instituted a regular lecture forum, begun a campaign to end discrimination among local insurance companies, and had coordinated with the local Urban League to develop economic and employment programs—an agenda that spoke to the initiative the organization was taking to address local conditions. During the April membership drive, the city's youth leaders again took a significant role, reemphasizing the invigorating influence a vital youth council could have on a local branch. Members of the council appeared on area university campuses, met with lodges, sororities, and social clubs, and installed speakers at weekly church services and public meetings, all in an effort to boost membership and awareness of the NAACP's program. In line with the national headquarters' attention to eliminating racial violence, the Association's anti-lynching efforts served as an inspiring rallying point during the campaign, a central focus of activity between Jackson's opening address at Union Baptist Church and *Crisis* editor Roy Wilkins's remarks at the closing meeting at Columbus Avenue AME Zion Church at the end of the month.[48]

Even though the anti-lynching drive of 1937 had failed to secure actual legislation, it was stimulating a nascent national civil rights movement that linked the constellation of communities Juanita Jackson rallied with that spring—St. Louis, Tulsa, Houston, Boston—to a broader campaign for racial justice. After two months on tour, Jackson made a final stop in the Connecticut River city of Springfield, Massachusetts. The constant branch visits, membership campaigns, and speaking engagements had tested the twenty-four-year-old's endurance, but back at 69 Fifth Avenue, the results were palpable. It was gratifying to learn that the Philadelphia youth council had finally been officially launched in April, no longer the object of branch leaders' derision. Elsewhere, youth councils followed the February 12th demonstrations with an eclectic and energetic challenge to Jim Crow. In the correspondence awaiting her when she returned, Jackson was apprised of the Columbus, Ohio, council's new speaker series and attempts to attack discrimination in the city's theaters and restaurants. In Kansas City, where she had visited just the month before, council members had initiated an "Occupational Conference" to address issues of African American labor and employment. The branch in Titusville-Mims, Florida, had begun a survey of local Negro history, and members in Albany, New York, had continued forums on lynching, including an evening with a witness to the 1908 Springfield, Illinois, riots that had inspired the founding of the NAACP. Eager to observe such activity, at the end of May, Jackson traveled to Philadelphia to speak before the new youth council. She arrived at the YWCA branch on Catherine Street, offering "brief accounts of the present fight for the passage of the federal anti-lynching bill and for equal educational opportunities," and attempting to build enthusiasm for the upcoming annual conference in Detroit. She also spent an afternoon at the First African Baptist Church, and a weekend making appearances at Bryn Mawr College and the Media, Pennsylvania, NAACP branch. By June of 1937, she could tell her audiences, more than seventy-five officially chartered youth councils had collectively participated in education rallies and Anti-Lynching Day. They had demonstrated in support of the Angelo Herndon and Scottsboro cases, and had launched local "Don't Buy Where You Can't Work" campaigns. Together, they had come to bolster a national network of vital local civil rights struggles, each with its own circumstances and challenges. In Detroit, later that month, they could share experiences and plot the coming year's program.[49]

Those who missed Jackson's May appearances, and her encouragements to answer the call to Detroit, received her correspondence through June. That month, the *Crisis* also carried the message. "The Detroit youth councils look forward to meeting the militant young people from other parts of America at the national conference," wrote one leading council member in the June *Crisis*. The city actually boasted five councils (East Side, West Side, North End, Eight Mile Road, and Twin Cities) whose coordination was the principal responsibility of Gloster Current, the twenty-four-year-old council president and a local jazz orchestra leader. Since Jackson's visit in 1936, the Detroit youth councils had embarked on an active program, becoming a visible part of the city's NAACP branch. As in Philadelphia, there were misgivings among the established branch leadership about the rising youth movement. At the moment, the Detroit NAACP was struggling over whether or not to support the sit-down strikes that had been taking place under the leadership of the United Auto Workers (UAW) union. The UAW was an affiliate of the Committee of Industrial Organizations (CIO), which had splintered from the AFL in 1935 over, among other issues, willingness to represent an interracial membership. In theory, supporting the UAW was a chance for the Association to strengthen its economic program, now that several unions were open to black workers. Members of the youth council were amenable to the idea, but frustration with the city's unions (and the AFL, in particular) had long ago spoiled the idea of cooperating with labor for most of the senior branch. A number had even cultivated the patronage of such vigorously anti-union industry leaders as Henry Ford. Professions of support for the UAW would come at a substantial cost. But over the past year the NAACP youth councils had come to embrace an activist economic agenda and wished to pursue such ends, even as the national office coordinated the anti-lynching and legal efforts. The challenge was to square these interests during the Detroit convention.[50]

As the NAACP's annual convention opened in Detroit at the end of June, the youth delegates gathered downtown at Ebenezer AME Church, at the corner of Willis and Brush Streets. The doors of Ebenezer AME opened to the piano playing of Detroit youth council member Louise Blackman accompanying singing by Juanita Jackson. A welcome from Gloster Current was followed by an address from Jackson and the introduction of the week's group discussion leaders. Jackson would lead discussion on building and sustaining interest in local youth councils. James Robinson, a divinity student at the Union Theological Seminary and member of the Harlem youth council, had been a participant in the Baltimore conference, and would facilitate conversation during the week on "Rural and Urban Job Opportunities." Union graduate Moran Weston was tall, rod-thin, and further distinguished by wire-rimmed glasses and a finely cropped moustache. Weston, a delegate at the Amenia Conference in 1933 now at work for the city of New York, had led a caravan of about two dozen delegates from Harlem and arrived to discuss "The Government and the Negro Worker." Leon Ransom was a Howard Law professor and veteran NAACP attorney (in 1933 he had joined Charles Houston on the George Crawford defense) who would consider "Education" in a broad context with the delegates. J. St. Clair Drake had traveled from New Orleans to lead discussion of "Problems of Civil Liberties and Lynching." And budding Negro historian L. D. Reddick, a doctoral candidate at the University of Chicago, would discuss "Problems of the Young Negro Citizen." Walter White welcomed the youth delegates to Detroit and, in a nod to the flap in Philadelphia, encouraged them to participate in tandem with older Association members—both during the annual conference and once they returned home. Together, they closed the session by singing the "Negro national anthem," James Weldon Johnson's turn-of-the-century composition, "Lift Every Voice and Sing." Then the 350 youth delegates together walked several blocks to the Technical High School on Cass Avenue for the opening addresses of a convention that would focus largely on the status of African Americans in the New Deal.[51]

Members of the NAACP youth councils were as cheered as any by the progress blacks experienced during the Roosevelt presidency, yet in Detroit they pressed for further economic advances. After a morning prayer, the youth delegates endorsed the fight for desegregated education and an end to lynching, but also sought to collaborate with the CIO. Sensitive to the youth movement's perspective, but also realizing that Walter White was reluctant to diverge from the Association's ongoing legislative and legal efforts, Juanita Jackson stressed the necessity of considering the fight for economic equality and the struggle to protect blacks' constitutional rights as part of a common endeavor. With like-minded

pragmatism, J. St. Clair Drake offered a probing analysis of the causes of lynching, explaining that "white supremacy, the protection of white womanhood
against insane Negro rapists, and the expediting of justice" were reasons that
merely masked the more powerful operators of "the social pattern of living, economic conditions, and personal frustrations." The NAACP's anti-lynching platform was no quixotic pursuit of legislation that might only peripherally allay
African Americans' plight during the Depression; the campaign addressed conditions fundamental to black exploitation. Moreover, as the past months had
shown (particularly since February 12th), the anti-lynching movement had
proven powerfully galvanizing, bringing local struggles together in "a dramatic
spectacle" that was creating "a sense of solidarity among Negroes." Inspired by
this show of unity, Drake asserted: "It gives us a chance to test our powers and
find out how far we can go."[52]

If the youth delegation appreciated this outlook, they remained willing to
risk discord for the sake of an aggressive program that attacked all forms of discrimination. When Homer Martin, president of the UAW appeared at the convention, the divisiveness of the union question was especially apparent. Invited
to speak on "The CIO and the Negro Worker," Martin had earlier pledged his
support of the "full protection of Negro workers in every way." Yet he was met
with "very audible boos and cat calls" from older delegates as Juanita Jackson
introduced him to the general convention. When Martin finally left the podium, Moran Weston recalled that several youth delegates felt compelled to
protectively guide him from the auditorium. Offering further rhetorical guard,
John P. Davis rose to make "a call for the critical appraisal of the motives and
practices of all labor unions and a full sharing of activity and responsibility in
the building of a more intelligent labor movement." Davis, the force behind the
National Negro Congress, advocated recognizing the CIO as an important
step, a position with which the NAACP youth delegates noisily agreed, in a
rebuke of the reception Martin had received. The tension over collaboration
with the CIO made for a controversy that was described in leading black newspapers; it also indicated the youth delegates' resolve to command a broadly
encompassing movement.[53]

The rift over Martin's appearance did not leave the youth delegates cowed.
"Youth Day," the occasion for the convention to celebrate the work of the Association's youth councils, brought reverie, with music provided by the Ford Dixie
Eight, and a wide-ranging discussion on "Negro Youth and the World Today"
that was broadcast on Detroit's WJR. When word circulated that some restaurants had refused service to conventioneers despite the civil rights law that was to
go into effect in September, members of the youth delegation were dispatched to
investigate. Returning for a Fellowship Dinner that evening at the four-year-old
Lucy Thurman YWCA, squads reported back with the good news that they had

been served at the offending restaurants. Toasts and pep songs followed; word of Walter White's birthday brought the house down. Smiling, White made a short speech, as did Joel Spingarn, Roy Wilkins, William Pickens, Daisy Lampkin, Cleveland national board member L. Pearl Mitchell, and L. C. Blount, president of the Detroit NAACP. Then they hustled several blocks north to Ebenezer AME, where the group was due back by eight to perform for the convention. Detroit youth council president Gloster Current began the evening session by performing two vibraphone solos. Moran Weston directed a dramatic skit on the Negro in America featuring L. D. Reddick as Scottsboro defendant Heywood Patterson, and highlighted by an emotional performance from John Hancock, an Arkansas sharecropper who could not return south because of his efforts to organize sharecroppers—just the sort of conflict that had inspired Joel Spingarn to join the NAACP a generation earlier. After Hancock read an original poem titled "Freedom," Spingarn followed with the rousing address "What the NAACP Expects of its Youth." Noting the militancy of the organization that had saved the lives of such sharecroppers as Pink Franklin and Steve Green, Spingarn said the Association expected youth "to be at least as militant as we have been all these twenty-seven years. We expect them to carry on the fire which has burned in the Association, especially in its early years. We expect you youth of America to be militant in the demands for your rights under the American way of life."[54]

As the convention closed, the youth delegates were assuredly committed to such a vigorous pursuit of the ideals of American democracy, with attention to economic justice as well as to civil liberties. After a celebratory evening at the Belle Isle Casino, a fashionable nightspot on an island in the middle of the Detroit River, they engaged in a final day of discussion sections, establishing a program for the coming year embodying the militancy Spingarn had stressed the night before. Mary McLeod Bethune, representing the National Youth Administration, issued "A Challenge to Youth," remarking on the importance of the ballot and impressing upon the conferees of the need to persevere in the face of any challenge. With Bethune's words still ringing, a group of delegates traveled to the Ford Motor Plant for a tour and interviews of workers, all the better to assess economic conditions. Upon return, Juanita Jackson addressed the "Integration of Youth Councils," especially important if the youth councils were to align with the labor movement, then joined the youth section's steering committee to draft the conference resolutions. With no remaining formal sessions scheduled, the youth delegates gathered at Belvedere Park for more dancing and music furnished by Gloster Current's orchestra, then dispersed. "Our conference was a huge success," Jackson wrote Julian Steele in Boston, a week after returning to New York. "The elders were a bit touchy—more youth delegates than adult delegates. They, however, came across in great shape," and had resolved to continue to support the Association's education and anti-lynching campaigns.[55]

The Harlem youth council was quick to demonstrate such resolve. Meeting regularly at the Harlem YMCA, the council had a "full agenda," Dorothy Height, one of its founding members, remembered. "We took on problems of the community. Fortified with the help of eighty-eight other youth groups that cooperated when we needed massive social action, we tackled any form of discrimination we found." One such opportunity came in the weeks following the Detroit convention. In a move reminiscent of the *Birth of a Nation* protests during the 1910s, the Harlem youth council used the showing of a moving picture to forward momentum for anti-lynching legislation. The Strand Theater in Manhattan was screening *They Won't Forget*, a Claude Rains and Lana Turner vehicle based on the lynching of Leo Frank, a Jewish man accused of murdering a teenage white girl in Atlanta, Georgia, on Confederate Memorial Day. Depicting the frenzy that led to the mob rule meted out in August 1915, the film made for an obvious rallying point for the NAACP's anti-lynching campaign (and one that, fittingly, pivoted around a holiday—Decoration Day—whose forgotten origins lay in the celebrations among emancipated slaves and their northern supporters marking the fall of the Confederacy). As the *New York Amsterdam News* observed, the youth council was "swinging into a drive to

PICKETING TO "STOP LYNCHING" IN NEW YORK CITY, AUGUST 1937. Library of Congress, Prints and Photographs Division, Visual Materials from the NAACP Records.

mobilize public opinion behind a demand for the passage of the anti-lynching bill before adjournment of Congress." Members of the youth council, along with the United Youth Committee against Lynching (which Jackson and Height had formed in January), donned black arm bands, pinned on "Stop Lynching" buttons, and spent four days in the midsummer heat marching before the Strand on Broadway near Forty-Seventh Street and chanting "Stop the Lynching" in Times Square, "the busiest square in the world."[56]

Juanita Jackson joined the pickets on Broadway, passed out handbills, and then, after spending the late summer at 69 Fifth Avenue, swung back into fund-raising for the fall. She returned to Druid Hill Avenue in Baltimore in mid-September for a month-long membership drive. There NAACP-led efforts to raise black teachers' salaries in Montgomery County bolstered both the local branch and the campaign against Jim Crow education. Jackson's third major drive was the city's most successful yet: after garnering nearly $3,200 in pledges, the branch presented her with a silver loving cup to commemorate her work. Trumping that honor, though, were the reports of youth council activity that continued to come in, suggesting the grassroots mobilization underway among the branches she had recently rallied. Columbus had begun protests of discrimination at Ohio State University. Boston was engaged in a letter-writing campaign, petitioning Massachusetts' two senators to back federal anti-lynching legislation. The council there had also initiated efforts to gain employment for African Americans at local M&P theaters, had begun a weekly radio broadcast on "problems of Negro youth," and was publicizing the recent state civil rights bill prohibiting discrimination. Youngstown, Ohio, members had integrated the city swimming pool for the first time in fourteen years. Muskogee, Oklahoma, was staging a campaign to open jobs at local J.C. Penny and Shouse Brothers stores. The plight of black domestic workers had gained attention at Talladega College, as well as from the youth section of the Oklahoma State Conference of Branches.[57]

Autumn would be dedicated to maintaining such action. While the national office emphasized support for Charles Houston's ongoing legal efforts and the upcoming winter legislative session, local youth councils were building momentum of their own. Returning from Baltimore, Jackson oversaw arrangements for the second annual call for mass meetings against educational inequality to be held in November. With the *Gaines* case against the University of Missouri Law School pending, Walter White planned to give a radio address over CBS airwaves "to stimulate an awareness of education inequalities which Negro youth face, nationally and locally, and of the educational program of the NAACP, as a basis for local educational activity and for a greater support of the Association's program." The importance of youth councils' support of this issue was all the more crucial that month, as funding from one of the NAACP's most significant donors (the Garland Fund) was ending. The Gary, Indiana, youth council rallied to the cause, with members following their meeting by challenging discrimination in the city's public schools. But in Philadelphia, Cleveland, Houston, Boston, and elsewhere, efforts expanded beyond education to include focus on pressing local conditions, such as discrimination in employment, housing, and public places. Even as Juanita Jackson took to the field after Thanksgiving—returning, by request, to Charleston, West Virginia, and the State College up the river in Institute—the youth councils she had spent the many past months cultivating seemed to have become largely self-motivating. In Rochester, New York, the youth council had organized efforts to end employment discrimination at Eastman Kodak and in the offices of the municipal government, both of which would hire only unskilled black workers. Weekly radio broadcasts continued in Boston, and new campaigns had been begun in Talladega, Alabama, and Plainfield, New Jersey. At Talladega College, issues included Jim Crow movie houses, inequality in public education, and community pride; in Plainfield, the youth council had launched a "don't buy where you can't work" campaign after a series of fact-finding efforts and church-based mass meetings.[58]

The NAACP wished to direct this activism to the congressional session soon set to open. That December, while working closely with New York branches on the annual Christmas seal campaign, Juanita Jackson initiated planning for the second annual Anti-Lynching Day, set for February 11th. At first, there was optimism at 69 Fifth Avenue that 1938 would witness the passage of the first anti-lynching bill. Indicative of the empathy the NAACP had generated, *Time* placed Walter White on the cover of the January 24th issue. "Talk is long but the rope is short," read the caption appearing beneath the photograph of Walter White, captured in a pose of discernable determination. Looking directly into the camera, White stood in front of a large painting of a bare-chested victim hung from a tree branch; with his head tilted ever so slightly toward this gruesome memorial of mob brutality, the secretary gripped his left side, bending his arm at such an angle to open his suit jacket and reveal two pens poking from a pocket, a reminder of the Wagner–Van Nuys anti-lynching bill that must be signed into law. Making much of White's light complexion, the magazine relayed how the "Pale-faced Negro White" had infiltrated lynch mobs during the 1920s, won the commitment of such senators as Robert Wagner during the 1930s, and was now propelling the fight for anti-lynching legislation. "The gradual growth of the anti-lynching movement had by last week made spunky, dapper, 44-year-old Negro White the most potent leader of his race in the U.S." But, as *Time* reported, the NAACP faced recalcitrant opposition among segregationist senior senators. In the course of a month, the passage of anti-lynching legislation in Washington went from seemingly imminent to highly unlikely after a several-week-long filibuster in the Senate. Still, in New York, the United Youth Committee against

Lynching, spearheaded by the Harlem youth council, had again sponsored a number of activities during the winter. The aim this year, as Jackson endeavored to coordinate demonstrations in over seventy cities, was to protest (and, ultimately, help overcome) the current legislative obstacle. Of course, the *Crisis* noted, "if the anti-lynching bill passes the Senate before the date of the demonstration, the activities will take the form of a victory celebration." In the meantime, "in spite of the cold and snow," Jackson wrote Walter White in late January, "we have been demonstrating in the streets, reaching untouched people with our protests against the filibuster." She had arranged for publicity in the pages of the *New York Amsterdam News*, which reinforced the NAACP message that "these nation-wide meetings will come at a time when Negroes must demonstrate to America that they are not defeated, that they will continue to fight more vigorously than ever before for the passage of a federal anti-lynching bill." Writing to White just days before the event, Jackson assured him that "in New York City our demonstrations will reach unprecedented proportions." In fact, local events would extend beyond one evening's events—Roy Wilkins was to speak in Brooklyn the following night, and Jamaica, Queens, too, would hold its own large demonstration.[59]

What the *Amsterdam News* predicted would be "a tremendous nation-wide protest" centered in Harlem on February 11th. That night, the "No More Lynching" parade began by torchlight outside the West 135th Street YMCA, proceeded south to 116th Street, then wound back up Seventh Avenue to Mother AME Zion Church at 137th Street, once again host to the NAACP's Anti-Lynching Day program. A group of young women dressed in black, representing widows of the men lynched in the past year, led the march into the church. Inside, field secretary Daisy Lampkin described the campaign as "The New Crusade for Liberty," and Charles Houston offered a candid Association version of "The Inside Story of the Senate and the Anti-Lynch Bill," including a personal message sent from Walter White reporting "On the Washington Battlefront." While the two NAACP leaders outlined their response to resistance in the Capitol, inspiration came in the form of an address from Abyssinian Baptist Church pastor Adam Clayton Powell, Jr., and appearances by two recently freed Scottsboro defendants, Roy Wright and Olen Montgomery. Wright had refused to meet with Juanita Jackson when she visited Birmingham in November 1936, but he was now willing to embody the fight for civil liberties.[60]

If Anti-Lynching Day was an accurate barometer, that fight had indeed become a national one, representing a culmination of activity for many NAACP branches and youth councils. That night communities from Chicago to Tulsa, Oklahoma, and from Gary, Indiana, to Raleigh, North Carolina, witnessed parades, mass meetings, church services, radio broadcasts, street-corner speeches, and pickets. In many communities, too, the anti-lynching campaign had come to mesh with ongoing youth council and local branch efforts—including Brooklyn's efforts to study housing problems; the boycott of A&P stores in Plainfield, New Jersey; the speaker series and lecture forums sponsored in Cleveland and Mobile, Alabama; and Boston's challenge to discrimination in public utilities hiring. The NAACP's grassroots anti-lynching efforts had inspired enough activism even to draw the National Negro Congress into the arena. In the weeks after the February 11th demonstrations, John P. Davis proposed a multilateral movement joining the National Negro Congress, NAACP, and CIO, among other progressive organizations. Hesitant to cede even a measure of control, and ever suspicious of Davis, White rejected this partnership, preferring the NAACP to spearhead the drive for anti-lynching legislation.[61]

Juanita Jackson noted the result of the anti-lynching efforts at the end of March, as she left for several weeks of branch work. The impact was evident in Boston when she arrived for a third membership campaign in that city. In the previous year, the branch had opened a new headquarters at 464 Massachusetts Avenue in the city's South End, and had continued to benefit from its active youth council, which not only broadcast a weekly program on WEEI but had also been integral to the branch's recent challenges to employment discrimination. The drive began with an "Anti-Lynching Sunday" at the South End Church in cooperation with a handful of other civil rights organizations, including the Eastern New England Congress for Equal Opportunity, the New England (Negro) Congress, and the Scottsboro Defense League. Appearing for the closing meeting at Columbus Avenue AME Zion Church, Walter White spoke on "The Story of Lynching." The recent filibuster would not keep the NAACP from dedicating its resources to securing protective legislation. Indeed, White saw such invitations to speak as evidence of a growing mobilization against Jim Crow—it would be up to Boston, and other branches throughout the country, to keep up the fight. Juanita Jackson left Boston for Columbus, Ohio, where a membership drive was to precede the city's hosting of the annual NAACP convention. Based in Ohio for three weeks, she rallied with youth councils throughout the state, able to convey the national movement their fellow council members had created to attack discrimination wherever it appeared. In Richmond, Virginia, the group had begun efforts to establish cafeterias in the city's segregated schools. The Cleveland council had held a forum on the plight of southern black sharecroppers, and Detroit had instituted a similar speaker series on black labor, even as it launched a local job campaign. From Sacramento, California, came word of the new youth council's protest of discrimination in the state's civil service branches. Boston had kept up its weekly radio broadcasts as "a means of keeping the Boston community NAACP conscious." Encouragingly, the once embattled Philadelphia council had embarked on an equal-employment campaign, with effective legal counsel from the Association's stalwart member of its National Legal Committee, attorney Raymond Pace Alexander.[62]

The NAACP special assistant thought such reports a satisfying gauge of the youth movement's vitality and considered it an appropriate time to move on. That spring, Juanita Jackson was twenty-five, growing ever older than the young people she wished to organize, and ready to hand over leadership of the Association's youth movement. Of no little significance, she was also now openly engaged to marry Clarence Mitchell, who had secured a post as executive secretary of the Urban League branch in St. Paul. Jackson planned to join Mitchell in Minnesota, and her resignation would be effective by the end of August. There was inevitably a buzz concerning Jackson's planned departure at the annual conference in Columbus. (Her decision to "Quit To Marry" was fodder for several black newspapers.) But the delegates were still able to muster a productive session. The fight for equality in education and the pledge to strike a legislative blow against lynching remained key themes during the youth meetings held at Shiloh Baptist Church. Senator Robert Wagner, the NAACP's key anti-lynching ally in the legislature, addressed the youth delegates, emphasizing the significance of the movement. Charles Edward Russell, among the original founders of the NAACP, also convinced the youth councils to collectively institute a campaign to eliminate textbooks containing offensive depictions of African Americans from their communities' public schools. With an eye toward the 1940 presidential elections, the delegates further resolved to initiate local voter registration campaigns, an effort that would accord with the NAACP's hopes of seeing a voting rights bill through Congress.[63]

Before leaving the NAACP on the last day of August 1938, Jackson drafted "Negro Youth Awakes" to run in the September *Crisis*. In the three years since her portrait had appeared on the magazine's cover, over one hundred youth councils had been officially chartered, and new applications continued to arrive monthly at 69 Fifth Avenue. Anti-lynching and education campaigns had been crucial in linking the national office and community efforts, and, as Jackson wrote, she left for Druid Hill Avenue, and her wedding, fully confident that she had helped develop "a strong, well-coordinated youth program meeting local youth needs." She was leaving behind a vibrant and far-reaching movement. But if some worried her resignation signaled nonchalance about the cause ("Resigns To Wed" announced the *Baltimore Afro-American*), the soon-to-be Mrs. Mitchell in no way saw marriage to her "prince" as an abandonment of the civil rights struggle she had endeavored to foster these past several years.[64]

That much would be clear when Juanita Jackson Mitchell returned to Baltimore during the early 1940s, a moment when wartime invigorated the fight for the full rights of African American citizenship.

* * *

The buses had already lined Dolphin Street when Juanita Jackson Mitchell spoke to the crowd gathered outside Sharp Street ME Church on Friday morning, April 24, 1942. At twenty-nine, Jackson was still younger than many on hand that day, but she had been a fixture in Baltimore's civil rights struggle for more than a decade, beginning as the founding president of the City-Wide Young Peoples Forum and continuing even after taking her national post as special assistant in the NAACP. Not even her marriage to Clarence Mitchell in September 1938 and their move to the Midwest had kept her long from Druid Hill Avenue. During the month after she resigned from the NAACP, descriptions of the Jackson-Mitchell union had filled the *Afro-American* society pages. The couple married before fifteen hundred in Sharp Street ME, honeymooned in Bermuda, then took up residence in St. Paul. While Clarence directed the local Urban League branch, Juanita quickly became a popular speaker on the Twin City's meeting and luncheon circuit. As a member of the Urban League's Women's Auxiliary, that fall she organized a public memorial to James Weldon Johnson (the former NAACP executive secretary had died in an automobile accident while on vacation in Maine) and was also anxious to help resuscitate the Minneapolis-St. Paul NAACP. But even as Juanita Jackson Mitchell began a new life and family in Minnesota during the next two years, she remained close to happenings on Druid Hill Avenue. During the fall of 1940 she even returned to Baltimore at Walter White's behest to direct the local NAACP branch's membership campaign and celebrate the fifth anniversary of the branch's revival. When the Mitchells relocated back to Baltimore in May 1941 after Clarence had accepted a new position at the NAACP's Washington office, Juanita was thrilled to be back on Druid Hill. "I have to keep pinching myself to believe that I am really back in the East," she wrote Roy Wilkins in New York. "But here I am." Nearly five months pregnant with her second child, she did not intend to take a very active role with the Baltimore NAACP that summer and fall, though Walter White had asked. But she planned to regularly send along branch news to the *Crisis*. The following winter, a Baltimore policeman shot and killed a black soldier, the latest in a series of instances of police brutality that had outraged the city's African American community. By April 1942, Juanita Jackson Mitchell and the Baltimore NAACP had helped galvanize the inchoate protest into mass action.[65]

Sharp Street ME simply could not accommodate everyone who wished to attend the Thursday evening mass meeting on April 23, 1942. More than 1,200 crowded into the church, even filling the aisles of both the first floor and balcony. Outside, over four hundred gathered on the corner of Etting and Dolphin Streets, listening to the proceedings broadcast over loudspeakers. Branch president Lillie Jackson presided, and speakers included Leon Ransom, dean of How- •
ard University Law School, Carl Murphy, *Afro* editor and chairman of the

Citizens' Committee for Justice, and Baltimore attorney W. A. C. Hughes. After Hughes addressed the circumstances of the ten victims police officers had killed since 1939, Juanita Jackson Mitchell appealed for donations to the Citizens' Committee. The committee she directed represented not only the NAACP but also over 150 other local organizations. Contributions, she explained, would help defray the cost of transportation and expenses during the next day's march on the state capitol in Annapolis. When she finished, Adam Clayton Powell, Jr., the pastor of the Abyssinian Baptist Church who had been sworn in to the New York City Council that January and who had been a firm friend in the NAACP's fight for anti-lynching legislation, took the podium to describe the importance of the march.

"When you march on Annapolis," Powell intoned to the audience gathered in Sharp Street ME, "you're doing something history-making which will echo all over the world because colored people have said: 'To hell with the world we are not going to stand this any longer.'" Powell's forty-five-minute exhortation echoed the bellicosity of the March on Washington Movement that A. Philip Randolph had inaugurated in early 1941. That winter, when the Roosevelt administration stalled on promises to address discrimination in the defense industries, Randolph, the president of the Brotherhood of Sleeping Car Porters, announced plans for ten thousand black protestors to march on the capital. The march, he hoped, would force conciliations from the president. By June, after Roosevelt failed to pledge his administration's full cooperation, Randolph suggested that the march had grown tenfold: one hundred thousand, he claimed, now planned to join in protest at the Lincoln Memorial. With the march a week away, Roosevelt blinked. The president agreed to issue Executive Order 8802, an unprecedented statement authorizing the establishment of the Fair Employment Practices Committee (FEPC) to enforce equal employment in the defense industries. Satisfied, Randolph called off the march, but the March on Washington Movement continued. In fact, in June 1942 organizers in New York (including Adam Clayton Powell, Jr.) planned to hold a rally for twenty thousand in Madison Square Garden; the event portended a militant movement for racial justice sure to continue striking blows against Jim Crow. "There's a new Negro emerging today," Powell declared in Sharp Street ME. "Two years ago it would not have happened here in Baltimore but today we've had enough—we've gotten up the nerve to March on Annapolis and we don't give a damn what happens. We believe it is better to die fighting for freedom than to live a slave." Through the applause the church choir sang "Tramping for Justice," a song of spiritual action specially written to commemorate the next day's march.[66]

On Friday morning, the March on Annapolis began on the steps of Sharp Street ME Church. Participants packed the street corner that morning before the first buses left at eleven, with Juanita Jackson Mitchell leading the pep talks.

A caravan of chartered buses and private automobiles started from Dolphin Street and drove thirty miles south to the capital. The *Baltimore Afro-American* was on hand for their arrival at midday: "Two thousand serious, quiet and resolute citizens joined the March on Annapolis and crowded into every available space of both chambers in the State capitol Friday afternoon to hear and applaud as leaders of the Citizens' Committee for Justice urged Governor [Herbert] O'Connor to take steps to end police brutality in Baltimore." *Afro* photographers captured the group crowding both chambers of the state legislature, spilling onto the capitol steps and sidewalk. In the hearing room, leaders met with the governor for two hours. He sat at the center of the panel in a high-backed leather seat, flanked by the state comptroller and Maryland's secretary of state, listening to the appeals of the Citizens' Committee.

Thirteen spoke, in all. One after another, the black Baltimoreans rose, including attorney W. A. C. Hughes, Dr. Ralph Young, Dr. George Crawley, Linwood Koger, youth leader Harry Cole, and Edward S. Lewis, executive secretary of the Baltimore Urban League. Carl Murphy urged Maryland to follow the example of Roosevelt's Executive Order 8802 and end discrimination in the state, and he protested the epidemic of police brutality. Indeed, Lillie Jackson added, the march was a consequence of the governor's ignoring their recent correspondence requesting a hearing on police killings. They would be heard. Juanita Jackson Mitchell, the *Afro* reported, then "told the Governor that the March on Annapolis was born of desperation and that he must take steps to stop 'smart aleck' policemen's brutality." She went on to emphasize that the committee represented many more thousands of African American Baltimoreans who wanted answers, and action, now.

The march, as the *Afro* noted, impressed not only the African American "Annapolis oldsters" who "in fifty years did not recall an occasion like this." The governor, admitting his surprise at the size of the protest and acknowledging the character of its spokespeople, said that he was open to considering each of the issues the committee had addressed, including the formation of a Governor's Interracial Commission, the appointment of black police officers, and an investigation of police brutality. While "the appeal was made in every case on the basis that colored citizens are entitled by law to equal treatment," the *Afro* explained, "louder than all the speeches was the sight of that sea of intelligent, earnest, resolute faces." With this victory, even the most stoic visages broke into smiles as the marchers regrouped on the Capitol steps and spontaneously began singing "America." Those who read the account in the *Afro* the next week could be assured: "They sang one verse and then the second. They knew the words. They did not fumble them, and nobody who heard them sing 'From every mountain side let freedom ring,' will ever forget it."[67]

When the marchers ended "America," a clergy member stood to offer a benediction. The group bowed their heads in prayer; then they left the steps to join the caravan back to Baltimore. The buses returned to Sharp Street ME, depositing the marchers near the corner of Dolphin and Etting Streets. Stepping from the intersection where she had rallied black Baltimore to the NAACP cause seven years earlier, Juanita Jackson Mitchell walked around the corner and home to Druid Hill Avenue, the melodies of "America" and "Tramping for Justice" still in her ears.

6

In Moran Weston's Harlem

Stepping into the Fraternal Clubhouse, a capacious union hall on West Forty-Eighth Street in midtown Manhattan, Moran Weston found a seat among the dozens of check-clothed tables that had been arranged in long rows to accommodate the delegates arriving for the founding of the Negro Labor Victory Committee. At one end of the hall, an American-flag-draped podium stood at the head of the speakers' platform. A long white banner hanging above the rostrum encapsulated the theme of this "win-the-war conference" with brevity and bold-faced emphasis: **JOBS—FREEDOM** *And* **VICTORY**. The session was to open at ten o'clock that Saturday morning, June 27, 1942. The hundreds of delegates crowding into the Fraternal Clubhouse represented, as the *Daily Worker* reported, "nearly one hundred CIO, AFL and Negro community organizations." Moran Weston's credentials were from the International Workers Order, for which the thirty-one-year-old served as secretary of its National Negro Commission, and the National Negro Congress, with which he was a field organizer. He had recently returned to New York after a two-month stay in Baltimore, working to organize black glassblowers and stevedores into CIO locals. In Maryland that spring, the Citizens' Committee for Justice had led a rousing march on Annapolis to demand the full works of freedom for African Americans; back in New York for the founding of the Negro Labor Victory Committee, Weston had returned to a city in a similarly emboldened mood.[1]

That June, as the nation mobilized for the Second World War, New York was witnessing the coalescence of a civil rights movement using pageantry, mass protests, and interracial political coalitions to link the fight against fascism abroad with a fight for freedom on the home front. In advance of a March on Washington Movement "monster" rally to be held at Madison Square Garden in the middle of the month, exhortative broadsides plastered on storefronts and lampposts throughout Harlem fairly roared: "Wake Up, Negro America!" "Stop Hitler in Europe and Hitlerism Here in America!" "Winning Democracy for the Negro is Winning the War for Democracy!" "Stand Upon Your Feet and Mobilize! Organize! and Fight for Equal Rights!" The rhetoric emanating from the

MORAN WESTON, 1940s. M. Moran Weston Papers, Rare Book and Manuscript Library, Columbia University in the City of New York.

Roosevelt White House had invited such exhortations. Arguing before Congress in January 1941 that the United States ought to intercede on behalf of Nazi-controlled Europe, Franklin Roosevelt justified the costs of intervention by appealing to the tenets of American democracy. "Freedom," said the president, "means the supremacy of human rights everywhere." Understanding "everywhere" to include the United States, the March on Washington Movement deployed this rhetoric to pressure the administration into making a remarkable concession: an executive order banning discrimination in the defense industries. Following the outbreak of war at the end of 1941, events like the March on Annapolis and the Madison Square Garden rally suggested that the movement to enjoin the fights for victory over foreign and domestic foes of freedom had not dissipated with the mere creation of the Fair Employment Practices Committee. If anything, the movement the *Pittsburgh Courier* called the "Double V Campaign" (for victory over fascism at home and abroad) was establishing racial justice as a central precept of American liberalism. Just months after Pearl Harbor, Eleanor Roosevelt expressed this with a measure of candor, acknowledging in May of 1942 that "one of the phases of this war that we have to face is the question of race discrimination." Realizing that many Americans would struggle to overcome discriminatory "habits," the First Lady nevertheless contended that "we are fighting for freedom, and one of the freedoms we must establish is freedom from discrimination." She advocated a gradual approach, but was unequivocal. "I do not see how we can fight this war and deny . . . rights to any citizen in our own land."[2]

Nor could the advocates of African American freedom assembled that Saturday at the Fraternal Clubhouse. In Harlem, June 27th was being celebrated as National Negro Achievement Day, with a parade down Lenox Avenue celebrating the advances enjoyed nearly four score years after emancipation. The midtown parley Moran Weston was attending that day to found the Negro Labor Victory Committee offered one more measure of such progress. With typical Double V Campaign trappings of patriotism, the Victory Committee was distinguished in its emphasis on merging the labor and civil rights movements into a progressive front for political and economic justice. And as its "Unity for Victory" gala planned for the next evening suggested, the Victory Committee also reflected the wartime use of glamour, glitz, and spectacle to forward the fight for freedom on the home front. Just as entertainers had embodied the popular front during the Depression years, and just as celebrities were called upon to endorse the American "arsenal of democracy" during the war years, in Moran Weston's Harlem, musicians and athletes joined preachers and politicians to press for radical democratic advances.

Unlike Juanita Jackson, just three years his junior, Moran Weston had not arrived in Harlem, the hub of the national civil rights struggle, with a staunch commitment to the NAACP. While the Association strategized to end lynching, invigorate its membership, and litigate against the "separate but equal" doctrine, Weston wished to pursue one of the key goals addressed at the 1933 Amenia Conference—the creation of an interracial movement for social justice emerging out of the respective struggles of American workers and advocates of black civil rights. As the NAACP downplayed this cause, Weston looked to the radical left so active then in New York, finding in the civil rights–oriented National Negro Congress and labor organizations, like the International Workers Order, potential vehicles of interracial unity. The founding of the Negro Labor Victory Committee, which deliberately fused the two social movements, signaled an encouraging mark of progress. In the political and cultural ferment of wartime Harlem, Weston perceived in the Victory Committee an opportunity to impel the nation to accept economic and civic equality as fundamental freedoms worth fighting for—in Europe, across the Pacific, and in the United States.

Milton Moran Weston II hailed from Tarboro, North Carolina, and he had no intention of returning. The imposition of white supremacy had been fitfully achieved in the decades following the Civil War, but by 1910, the year Moran Weston was born, the color line seemed ineluctably etched throughout the state.

An emergent Jim Crow order followed the redemption of the state's Democratic Party in 1874, with legal statutes and terror used to effect racial separation. With the party of white supremacy in power, the state legislature steadily enacted measures to ensure the segregation of the races, from separate school systems to the prohibition of interracial marriage. As elsewhere in the South, African Americans' retention of the franchise became a source of violent turmoil during the last decade of the nineteenth century. In November 1898, in the northeastern port of Wilmington, hundreds of whites shot their way through the city in the wake of a venomous election season, destroying black property and businesses, leaving bodies of murdered colored citizens floating in the Cape Fear River, and compelling black officeholders, at gunpoint, to resign from positions of power. In the years after the Wilmington massacre, black men were stripped of suffrage rights, and white supremacy ascended triumphant. As North Carolina's George White, the last remaining black congressmen, lamented in a final, defiant peroration before the House of Representatives in 1901, "cold-blooded fraud and intimidation" had suppressed the black vote, leaving African Americans all the more vulnerable to degradation and physical harm. White terror did not utterly end traditions of black protest in the state, but without the vote the racial order was difficult to overturn, and the threat of mob violence made it dangerous to challenge.[3]

From an early age, Moran Weston envisioned a life beyond Tarboro, in the church, and in the North, but it would not mean an escape from racial strictures. Aspiring to join the Episcopal clergy, he hoped to enter St. Stephen's College in Annandale-on-Hudson, New York, during the fall of 1928, in time for his eighteenth birthday. Established in 1860 as a preparatory school for the Episcopalian seminaries, St. Stephen's had recently become an undergraduate affiliate of Columbia University. The small northern college promised to offer an education befitting the scion of a line of devout Episcopalians. Weston had first attended St. Luke's, the parochial school at which his mother taught, and which his maternal grandfather had founded in Tarboro in 1882. By sixteen he had moved to Raleigh, enrolling in St. Augustine's College, a former freedman's school the Episcopal clergy had founded during Reconstruction. Weston distinguished himself at St. Augustine's, netting honors during the school's annual oratory competition in 1926, and graduating first in the class of 1928. With two years of instruction in Raleigh, Weston hoped to enter St. Stephen's that September as a junior. The Annandale college, however, declined to admit the St. Augustine valedictorian, intimating that previously matriculated colored students had encountered problems due to a lack of "social life" in that hamlet along the Hudson River. Weston persisted, ignoring the discriminatory implications of his rejection. While he insisted that he wanted training at St. Stephen's no matter the experience of earlier students, the college instead arranged for his admittance to Columbia, presuming the proximity of the university's Morning-side Heights campus to Harlem a more appropriate environment for Weston. It was just the first hint of the Jim Crow order he would continually confront in his adopted state.[4]

Given little choice, Weston enrolled in Columbia that September with his parents' encouragement, a reluctant junior in the class of 1930. Despite the insulting circumstances of his matriculation, once in New York Weston chafed at the idea of even considering leaving. The prospect of eventually returning to Tar-boro and to the proscriptions of segregation especially unnerved him. Instead, he began to sample a life without the boundaries that had confronted him in North Carolina, feeding his interest, he later recalled, in "political ideas" and un-derstanding "how society was put together." Inclined toward the left, during the fall of 1929 and spring of 1930, as the Socialist Party in New York launched a citywide membership campaign, he became a familiar face at meetings of the newly founded Morningside Heights local. Long a "voracious reader," Weston also endeavored to establish his own voice in the most influential black monthly, submitting a spirited critique of cynicism among young black professionals to the *Crisis*, insisting that members of his generation "burn with enthusiasm for their work."[5]

His own passion strengthened by filial duty and an inner sense of commit-ment, Weston was intent on the clergy. After graduating from Columbia, he spent a year at the divinity school of the Protestant Episcopal Church in Phila-delphia, then returned to Morningside Heights to study for his bachelor's of di-vinity at Union Theological Seminary. A generation earlier Union had been renowned for its graduate training, and when Weston enrolled in 1932, the sem-inary had renewed its program to produce ministers. Enticing the celebrated, if humbly trained, Reinhold Niebuhr away from his Detroit pulpit in 1928, Union had hired one of the most prolific liberal Protestant theologians to help under-score the seminary's newly rejuvenated mission. Yet, with Harry F. Ward, nearly as Marxist as he was Methodist, already on the faculty, Niebuhr's arrival not only drew students to his energetic improvised lectures but also invited a radical di-mension to campus. Having witnessed Niebuhr's run for New York State Senate on the Socialist Party ticket in 1930, Moran Weston entered Union eager to sup-plement traditional seminary training with study of social and economic justice. Attracted to Niebuhr and Ward's progressive Christian gospel championing a commitment to the working class, Weston quickly took a seat in courses on the "Economic Aspects of Religion," "Modern Social Movements," and "Ethical Is-sues of Social Order."[6]

By the spring of his first year, Weston derived inspiration from Union faculty members' social action, and he committed to acting on his own as well. In April 1933 he coordinated a three-day Conference on Negro Student Problems held on the Columbia campus, the confab's keynote address given by E. Franklin Frazier after Weston insisted on the radical Fisk sociologist over Frazier's more conservative colleague Charles Johnson. Hoping to help define a program of action for his generation, Weston did not have to pause long before accepting the NAACP's invitation to the Amenia Conference that August. Association assistant secretary Roy Wilkins lent him the train fare, and once among the young African American leaders assembled at Troutbeck, Weston felt further emboldened to dedicate his seminary training to supporting social justice. In fact, exposure to the ferment of economic social thought among his contemporary African American intellectuals in Amenia nearly inspired him to devote his Union bachelor's thesis to the role "organized religion" might "play in the process of emancipating the Negro race in America," as well as in the struggle to forge class unity among black and white workers. Weston returned to his dormitory in Hastings Hall promising Joel Spingarn that he would be among those attending the conference who would "succeed in promoting tangible results, concrete action, based upon our discussions and findings." Naturally impressed with W. E. B. Du Bois during the conference, he solicited the *Crisis* editor's opinion on forwarding the Amenia Conference aims and requested a *tête-à-tête* to discuss how "to act wisely and most effectively." Roy Wilkins had already become an unspoken mentor, but he approached other fellow delegates for counsel as well. Reminding E. Franklin Frazier that he was the "tall, young person" among the conferees at Troutbeck, Weston sought the Fisk professor's advice about pursuing a doctorate in sociology in order to meld radical Christianity and civil rights activism. At Howard University, political scientist Ralph Bunche replied to a similarly eager inquiry with a brief tutorial in the formation of class consciousness.[7]

However Weston envisioned his individual role in the broader struggle for African American equality, he first had to finish his course work at Union and overcome discriminatory tendencies within the church. That year, Weston had happened across Clement Wood's 1931 historical novel *The Woman Who Was Pope*. Piqued by Wood's imagined life of a rumored ninth-century pope, Weston composed a thesis investigating the theory that Pope John VIII had actually been a woman. Fulfilling his thesis requirements early, Weston expected to spend the spring making final preparations for joining the clergy. Instead, he remembered, he was "thrown into the wilderness." Weston would indeed graduate from Union with a bachelor's in divinity, but not with a place in Bishop William Manning's New York diocese. Assuming Weston could only serve an African American congregation, of which he had none to offer, Manning (an Englishman who had completed his theology training in 1891 at the University of the South in Sewanee, Tennessee) suggested that Weston return to North Carolina, where he was also ordained. In Tarboro he could have represented his family's third generation of Episcopalian clergy members, but Weston instead left Hastings Hall for a rented room in Harlem, refusing to return to the South. He preferred to find a way "to survive in New York City with confidence" rather than accommodate himself to the bishop's prejudices. His ambitions in the church thwarted, Moran Weston decided to devote himself to more secular means of uplift. If his future was to include activism, Weston's final semester at Union set a fortuitous example. During the spring of 1934 a cohort believed (probably rightly) to be inspired by the progressive ministrations of Niebuhr and Ward joined picket lines in support of a service workers' strike at the Waldorf Hotel. Another group camped in in protest at the home of a New York minister who had publicly approved of lynching. On campus, the radicalized seminarians protested the low wages the refectory paid workers. And on May Day, a red flag appeared on the seminary flagpole, a commemoration of workers that neither the Union administration nor its trustees could stomach—the radical students were, in a word, ousted. [8]

Even if Weston did not count himself among this radical clique, he considered himself a compatriot. Out of Union, he joined the social ferment that characterized 1930s Harlem, where progressive Christians mingled comfortably with Communists, risking likely conservative political backlash to advance the prospects of progress for African Americans, workers, and the Depression's dispossessed. After graduation, he enrolled in classes at the New School for Social Research, discontented Columbia intellectuals' fifteen-year-old progressive Greenwich Village answer to illiberal university education. He also found employment in the New York Department of Social Welfare, acting first as a welfare caseworker, then quickly earning promotion to supervisor of a Harlem division. In the position, Weston soon pivoted between his two professed goals of social action, economic and racial equality. When members of the welfare department unionized, Weston was among the first to join. When John P. Davis issued his call for a National Negro Congress (NNC) in February 1936, Weston traveled to Chicago and nearly became its youth director. Attracted to the NNC's explicit endorsement of an economic program for the civil rights struggle, he arrived back in Harlem embracing duties with the newly formed Manhattan council of the NNC; by 1938 he served as secretary of the council. In New York, the local NNC council upheld the national congress's denunciation of police brutality, support for the passage of federal anti-lynching legislation, and persistence in securing economic equality for black workers. During the fall of 1940, the Manhattan NNC council sponsored a statewide emergency conference on black rights, the theme of which—"fight for jobs, jobs and more jobs for the Negro people"—Weston had heeded by becoming the organizational secretary of the New York State Public Employees Federation Local 75. That winter, several left-wing trade unions, including the National Maritime Union, met with the Brooklyn and Manhattan councils of the NNC to draft a comprehensive "Statement of

Problems of Negro Workers in New York State" calling for the organization of African American labor. But if Weston's participation had marked him as among Harlem's radical leaders, it had also drawn the scrutiny of the New York state legislature's Rapp-Coudert Committee, established during the fall of 1940 to investigate Communist activities in Harlem, a local incarnation of a national antiradical backlash most embodied by Texas congressman Martin Dies's House Un-American Activities Committee. In February 1941, Weston resigned his position as welfare supervisor, but not before ugly fabrications appeared in the city's daily newspapers. Weston responded, denying membership in the Communist Party, but he was not the only one targeted in Harlem that winter. Max Yergan, the former YMCA representative who had become NNC president, was forced from his position teaching African American history at City College. The poet Gwendolyn Bennett relinquished directorship of the Harlem Arts Center. Ewart Guinier was released from his job as examiner in welfare department.[9]

Such repercussions were serious, but the rising anti-Communist backlash failed to stymie radicalism in Harlem. Indeed, with the advent of World War II and a concomitant boom in the defense industries that threatened to leave black workers behind, the economic dimensions of the civil rights struggle only took on heightened importance. Nationally, civil rights organizations and black newspapers alike had mobilized to open defense industries, leading by 1941 to the formation of the March on Washington Movement. Even the NAACP had joined the fray. Walter White's appearance on a United Auto Workers picket line at Ford's River Rouge plant in Detroit signaled a long-awaited endorsement of the local NAACP youth council's five-year campaign to back union (and, especially, CIO) efforts. The pledge helped turn the powerful Detroit NAACP, long suspicious of labor, to embrace an economic agenda, and also forged a new alliance between the NAACP and the CIO. In New York, during the early months of 1941 the city's NNC councils challenged the hiring practices of local defense contractors, sought redress from city and state authorities, and, working with the Transport Workers Union, backed a bus boycott to agitate for the hiring of black workers. While members of the Rapp-Coudert Committee fretted over such radicalism, Governor Herbert Lehman established the Governor's Committee on Discrimination in Employment. Just as the March on Washington Movement led to the creation of the FEPC, the governor's committee was a response to the left, an overture that legitimized efforts of the NNC councils and gave the labor movement added impetus to open its unions to black workers.[10]

After resigning his post with the city, Moran Weston accepted a position as secretary of the International Workers Order's National Negro Commission, shrugging off charges of Communism by even more vigilantly pursuing economic justice within an organization newly attuned to the plight of black laborers. The IWO had originally been founded in 1930, growing out of the

Workmen's Circle, a mutual aid society for laborers, following a split between its socialist and Communist members. During its earliest years, Jewish Communists made up the largest contingent of the IWO, before it grew into the largest fraternal society providing affordable insurance to workingmen. By the late 1930s, the IWO had become a critical ally of the CIO, aiding in the organization of locals, and, like other popular front organizations, it felt compelled to address the status of African Americans. Adding Moran Weston to its newly created National Negro Commission was just one expression of the IWO's outreach to black workers; a more dramatic gesture was the anniversary pageant the IWO held in New York amid protests against industrial discrimination. Presented during February's Negro History Week, the IWO celebrated its eleventh anniversary with staged reenactments of the African American past. Employing the radical left's use of popular culture to arouse the support of the masses, the event starred Paul Robeson, the black actor whose career had reached a zenith following a recent turn in *Othello*, and who was willing to lend his celebrity (and sonorous singing voice) to a spectrum of progressive causes. After five thousand attended the initial performance downtown, the IWO and Manhattan NNC council cosponsored an encore in March at the Golden Gate Ballroom, a premier venue for black performers and political rallies in Harlem, on the corner of Lenox and 142nd Street.[11]

In the weeks following the Golden Gate encore, Moran Weston assumed his duties with the IWO hoping that tangible action would follow such pageantry and seeking to dovetail his National Negro Commission responsibilities with his commitment to the NNC. While the IWO, duly impressed with the success of its Robeson-headlined spectacles, discussed founding a national "celebration around [Frederick] Douglass or some other dramatic personality," Weston sought more than symbolic affirmation. He envisioned the implementation of a "concrete program of activities nationally and locally" to organize black workers. Spectacular pageants and celebrity appearances might be useful attractions, but they could not completely "be substituted for a concrete program of action around such problems as jobs [and] housing." Rather, Weston recommended further collaboration with civil rights organizations, like the National Negro Congress, and black fraternal groups, such as the Elks, in making Baltimore, Washington, DC, Chicago, Detroit, and New York "points of concentration for building the Order among the Negro people." There were promising signs of black unionization that spring, with the Brotherhood of Sleeping Car Porters and several CIO unions experiencing increased membership, but Weston did not simply "expect mass applications from Negroes." He anticipated that the IWO would best reach black workers "on the basis of effective political activity."[12]

Given the authority to direct the National Negro Commission as an independent arm of the IWO, Weston chose to coordinate a national program around the issue of the poll tax, which, in recent months, had served as a rallying cry on the left. In 1941, eight southern states used the poll tax to determine voters and jury pools. Excluded from the cash economy, poor southerners, black and white, were left without a civic voice (at the ballot box and in the jury box), with the consequence that elite white southerners were disproportionately represented in Congress, where they controlled key committees, safeguarded white supremacy, and curtailed radicalism. In the waning months of 1940, the plight of Odell Waller, a black Virginia sharecropper indicted by an all-white jury for murdering his landlord, invigorated the national anti–poll tax movement. Echoing a decades' old dilemma, Waller personified the problems the poll tax spawned and galvanized a range of groups to the cause, from the socialist Workers Defense League to the liberal National Committee to Abolish the Poll Tax. Moran Weston envisioned the IWO similarly mobilizing around the issue, maintaining "cultural activities as part of the national program," but also never losing track of the concrete political issues that would best arouse mass support. The Waller case offered one such compelling issue; the Double V campaign that grew with the United States' participation in World War II would offer another.[13]

As the nation increasingly tilted toward involvement in the Second World War, Weston was drawn into a Harlem-based movement challenging Hitlerism on the home front. Promoted to the position of the NNC's national field organizer, during the summer of 1941 Weston linked his IWO efforts to "develop a chain of lodges in nine cities from Hartford to Norfolk" with the Congress's confrontation of Jim Crow. In the fight against domestic fascism, even the commonplace use of a racial epithet was cause for outcry. When Noxzema employed the phrase "nigger in the woodpile" in a letter dunning delinquent druggists, and when A&P stores stocked "Niggerhead" stove polish, Weston coordinated with IWO and NNC members to boycott both companies, seeking public apologies and open job opportunities, each in the name of freedom. Meaning to "deliver a sock at Hitlerism," the boycotts typified the NNC's campaign for jobs and equality, a program which took on added urgency after the bombing of Pearl Harbor that December. With the nation's formal entrance into World War II, civil rights advocates in New York mobilized in patriotic support of the national defense even as they maintained a vigilant offensive against vestiges of Hitlerism at home. The NNC pamphlet Weston distributed during the first months of 1942 insisted that "Negro People Will Defend America," but was equally adamant that the nation allow African Americans' full participation in the war. From the front lines to the assembly lines, only total desegregation would suffice in the struggle against international fascism. In the aftermath of Pearl Harbor, Weston also joined an interracial summit of one hundred labor leaders in New York to discuss founding the Negro Labor Victory Committee, a new organization to back the war effort, establish a stronger bond between black and white laborers, and defeat Jim Crow. In April, Weston participated in the inauguration of the Victory Committee, a "victory dinner" at the Aldine Club downtown that convened two hundred supporters from AFL and CIO affiliates endorsing a program "furthering the more inclusive mobilization of the manpower of the Negro people in industry, particularly in the nation's war production efforts." Looking to the militant, interracial National Maritime Union "as a model of victorious achievement on the anti-discrimination front," the Victory Committee pledged to convince the community that, as keynote speaker Adam Clayton Powell, Jr., remarked, "by delaying the 100 percent participation of the Negro people in the war effort we are delaying democracy's victory over fascism."[14]

Opening its headquarters in Harlem, at 217 West 125th Street, the Victory Committee's four African American officers (cochairmen Ferdinand Smith, of the National Maritime Union, and Charles Collins, of the Hotel and Restaurant Employees Union, and secretaries Dorothy Funn, of the National Negro Congress, and Ewart Guinier, of the United Public Workers Union) reflected the unity the organization sought to foster between the labor and civil rights movements. Acting as an informal field secretary, Moran Weston helped publicize the Victory Committee from the outset. In May, he addressed a mass meeting of the Manhattan NNC on the need to immediately integrate the armed forces. He also spread word among his IWO contacts as he traveled between Newark, Baltimore, and Washington, DC, announcing the upcoming trade union conference to be held at the Fraternal Clubhouse in New York on June 27th and appealing to friends to "Pack the Gate on the 28th" for a "Unity for Victory" celebration planned for the following evening at the Golden Gate Ballroom in Harlem. The two events would publicly launch the Negro Labor Victory Committee. And they had been cannily scheduled to follow the March on Washington Movement's mass rally at Madison Square Garden.[15]

In June, after spending several weeks organizing for the IWO, Weston returned to a Harlem buzzing in anticipation of the Garden rally. Broadsides blared from storefronts along 125th Street; lampposts were pasted with posters; advertisements in the *New York Amsterdam News*, the *New York Age*, and Adam Clayton Powell's *People's Voice* promised a thunderous event. A. Philip Randolph, the march leader, boasted that the enormity and militancy of the movement to "Stop Hitler in Europe and Hitlerism Here in America" had President Roosevelt "very concerned" for a second summer running. The previous summer, the march had led to the issuance of Executive Order 8802. This June, it was time to keep the pressure on, for as recent FEPC hearings in New York revealed, it would take more than a presidential commission to integrate the nation's defense industries. Summoned to the Bar Association Building on West Forty-Fourth Street over two days in mid-February, representatives of major New York and New Jersey industries had appeared before the FEPC to account for their companies' hiring practices. On Long Island, Ford Instrument Company, a division of the Sperry Gyroscope Corporation, employed just six unskilled black workers—an elevator operator and five porters. While Sperry's entire workforce topped eleven thousand, the company could count but twenty-one unskilled black employees among its ranks. When questioned about such alarming disregard for the president's ban on racial discrimination in defense-related industries, some representatives simply shrugged, claiming ignorance of any mandate. Others were more candid. A Bayonne, New Jersey, plant that required knowledge of applicants' race during the hiring process unapologetically cited "recognized racial aptitudes" to justify screening out black candidates. Likewise lacking repentance, the personnel manager of Fairchild Aviation in Jamaica, Queens, suggested that he was uniquely able to evaluate applicants; his experience with the Boy Scouts, he explained, had imbued him with an uncanny eye for "character." With a total workforce approaching two thousand, Fairchild only employed four African Americans. That such smug prejudice was an openly admitted barrier to equal opportunity in the workplace left black observers seething; the Madison Square Garden rally would offer an opportunity to respond. While Randolph's estimate on the eve of the rally that fifty thousand would "storm" the Garden had the ring of hyperbole, the prospect of even half that number descending upon Madison Square had *Amsterdam News* columnist J. Robert Smith, for his part, eager for one of "the greatest mass meetings in the history of the Negro in America."[16]

Neither the columnist nor New York would be disappointed. Twenty thousand filled Madison Square Garden on the night of June 16th, with thousands more crowding the street outside, cheering the proceedings broadcast over loudspeakers along Seventh Avenue. Inside, the young black soprano Muriel Rahn opened the evening with "The Star-Spangled Banner," and a performance of the African American playwright Dick Campbell's *The Watchword Forward* followed. Depicting the degradation blacks faced under Jim Crow, Campbell's satiric sketch offered a light foil to the roll call of distinguished African American speakers who took the podium over the next four hours. Milton Webster of the Brotherhood of Sleeping Car Porters; Lester Granger, executive secretary of the Urban League; and the YMCA's Channing Tobias joined a chorus of solemn counterpoint. Ever a Washington insider, NAACP executive secretary Walter White, reported on the machinations of a southern bloc attacking the FEPC from within Congress. Representing the National Council of Negro Women, Mary McLeod Bethune read a brief but thrilling statement of solidarity praising the militancy of the Garden audience, urging them to "keep it persistent, keep it courageous." Rising to the stage, Adam Clayton Powell, Jr., graced "Negro America's First Lady" with a theatrical kiss, then took the podium to just as dramatically announce his candidacy for Congress in the newly created Twenty-Second Congressional District in Harlem. While Bethune had struck a tone of dignity, the New York city councilor raised the Garden crowd from their seats with the vivid exhortation that "now is the time to fight like hell!" He had been sworn into the city council that winter, he declared, "because we protested." Now the "new Negro"—or the "marching black," in Powell's turn of phrase—had another mission: electing the Abyssinian Baptist Church pastor to national office. "It doesn't matter what ticket or what party," Powell intoned as if from the pulpit, shaking a clenched fist, "my people demand a forthright, militant, anti–Uncle Tom congressman!" Striving to somehow trump Powell for the evening's keynote, Harlem socialist Frank Crosswaith, the head of the Negro Labor Committee who had just been named special assistant to New York mayor Fiorello La Guardia, mustered an emphatic elegy to "the 'old' Negro" that returned the Garden to the principles of the March on Washington Movement. The new Negro American, Crosswaith affirmed, would not only be "loyal to the government and determined to give every effort toward winning the war" against fascism, the new Negro American would also be "determined and insistent upon gaining the same rights and liberties" afforded to all other Americans. Witnessing the rise of the militant organization, the March on Washington Movement audience had not arrived simply to a rally, he announced, but to a funeral for Uncle Tom; they had come to Madison Square "to bury in the grave of forgetfulness the type of black man that America has too long known."[17]

By midnight, A. Philip Randolph had yet to deliver his remarks, but after five hours of pageantry and politics he released the Garden audience, confident they understood the potency of African American unity. Certainly, he explained to the *Amsterdam News* as twenty thousand spilled from the Garden onto Thirty-Second Street and Eighth Avenue, the rally upheld the March's program for unity and freedom. "The important thing was the assembling of the Negro people," said Randolph, inviting members of the press to his headquarters at the Hotel Theresa on 125th Street. "The whole objective was to corral the Negroes so that they might exemplify by their unity their desire to secure the eight points enunciated by the March-on-Washington Movement." For those who did not attend the Garden event, Randolph provided the March's eight-point program to end discrimination to run on the front page of the *Amsterdam News*. Along with the March on Washington program, accounts of the rally nearly rang from the front pages of the black weeklies on Saturday morning. By the following week, as Randolph readied to call another twenty thousand to action in Chicago, the *Amsterdam News* continued to champion a new era of action, exclaiming "We Hope, We Hope!"[18]

Opening the June 27th *Amsterdam News* to page six, Moran Weston might have smiled at the political cartoon depicting "Uncle Tom's Funeral," the generations-old personification of meek Negro acquiescence to oppression put to rest at last. But he could not support the March on Washington Movement's insistence on remaining an all-black organization, a tactic Randolph used to insulate the group from the intrusion of Communists, whom the socialist March Movement leader had long disdained. Though the rally provided an impressive show of black unity, Weston considered this emphasis on race self-defeating. In New York, where alliances had grown between black organizations, labor unions, and liberal politicians, it would take an interracial movement to secure actual social and economic gains. The previous fall, for instance, such collaboration with the left-wing American Labor Party had helped win a seat for Adam Clayton Powell, Jr., on the city council. As Harlem's leading black Communist Benjamin Davis argued, there was reason to worry about remaining aloof from such a broad-based progressive coalition. Commending the rally's strike against Jim Crow, but condemning its racial exclusivity, Davis contended that casting the movement in the most patriotic terms would win the support of white compatriots, whose backing could then be used to press for an extension of democratic rights. "It remains for the Negro people themselves to insist that this movement becomes in the first place a win the war movement," Davis wrote in pages of the *Daily Worker*, "thereby increasing the assistance of the broadest masses of white workers and other citizens to battle for Negro equality in the interest of national unity and winning the war. Their interest lies in closer solidarity than ever with labor and the broad mass of white fair-minded citizens in support of the war to smash Hitler." To shut out white comrades for fear of Communist infiltration would be to unnecessarily hobble this wartime fight for black freedom.[19]

By the end of June, Harlem could decide whom to support, the March on Washington Movement, the Negro Labor Victory Committee—or both. While A. Philip Randolph left Harlem for a second March on Washington Movement rally at the Chicago Coliseum, and a third at St. Louis's Convention Hall, the Negro Labor Victory Committee aimed to maintain momentum in New York, drawing support for its own grassroots fight for the full works of equality. It would be a "win the war" effort seeking to unite labor and civil rights advocates, Communist or not, in a patriotic antifascist movement in the name of democratic freedom. Indicative of this link with the left, the *Daily Worker* hailed the Victory Committee's public inauguration in a week of generous coverage leading to the formal launch of its freedom fight, a founding session at the Fraternal Clubhouse in midtown followed by a "Unity for Victory" rally at the Golden Gate Ballroom. Inviting Harlem to come "Hear and Honor Dorie Miller's Mother" (her son, a black Navy mess attendant, had just been awarded the Navy Cross for heroism at Pearl Harbor), Victory Committee cochairman Charles Collins attested to the significance of the evening program. "We are beating Hitler's theories right here at home as we fight him abroad," Collins avowed, encouraging the community to "Pack the Gate on the 28th," where patriotic zeal, interracial political outreach, and the dazzle of celebrity promised to set the tone for the Victory Committee's wartime campaign for freedom from fascism.[20]

"We are here because we have one main purpose, the abolition of all discrimination against the Negro people." On the morning of Saturday, June 27, 1942, the bustle in the Fraternal Clubhouse stilled to the Caribbean-inflected voice of Ferdinand Smith. On a stage festooned with red, white, and blue, the cochairman of the Victory Committee spoke from a podium adorned with an American flag, his welcome emphasizing the gathering's support for the war against Hitler, Hirohito, and Mussolini, and stressing also a second front in the fight to defeat fascism. "Winning the war is the paramount issue before the trade unions and Negro organizations that are supporting the conference and mass meeting," Smith told the trade unionists gathered in the midtown union hall. But to secure victory abroad, he said,

> it is necessary to unite the whole American people. That is why our conference will fight for full rights for the Negro people. We want to strengthen America against Hitler by bringing up the immense Negro reinforcements who are waiting to get jobs in the war industries. We want also to utilize the great fighting spirit of the Negro people to the full by removing all barriers against them in the armed forces.

It was an opportune moment to mobilize under the Victory Committee's banner of "jobs, freedom, and victory," Smith contended, considering the ongoing FEPC hearings, the outreach unions (including his own National Maritime Union) were making to black workers, and the recent display of mass support for the March on Washington Movement at Madison Square Garden. Indeed, that morning the black weeklies for sale on 125th Street offered headlines on the previous week's FEPC hearings in Birmingham, Alabama. It was perhaps unsurprising that the commission's most recent hearings had revealed incontrovertible evidence of rampant Jim Crowism in southern industry. But events in Birmingham seemed also to promise change. While the *Pittsburgh Courier* exclaimed, "FEPC Gets Results in Dixie," the *Baltimore Afro-American* was specific: "FEPC Forces 8 War Plants to Hire Men." That morning's *New York Age* reported, too, that the recent fair employment hearings in New York had made real headway in the state's defense industries. Glancing through the coverage in the Saturday editions suggested, if nothing else, that the FEPC had made an important mark by publicizing unchecked economic discrimination in both the

North and South. And such measures of progress were not a consequence of bureaucratic munificence but of mass pressure exerted by emboldened advocates of Negro rights. "The Negro people are in motion," Smith observed.

> They are determined, they are insistent about their rights. This determination and insistence is reflected by the huge gatherings of Negroes that are now taking place, in which they are demanding an opportunity fully to participate in the struggle of our nation. If we understand these things, we then recognize that the fight for equality of the Negro people is part of the fight of the nation to win the war.[21]

Taking turns at the lectern, several speakers amplified Smith's sentiments. The recent FEPC hearings had been moderately encouraging, and the appointment of a black economist, Robert Weaver, as head of the Negro Manpower Service reflected a welcome extension of the Roosevelt administration's Black Cabinet from the New Deal into wartime. Yet it remained critical to formulate "a program to consolidate and extend these gains so as to fully integrate the Negro people in the war effort." John A. Davis, a former leader in the Washington, DC–based civil rights group, the New Negro Alliance, had since become the assistant executive director of the New York Governor's Committee on Discrimination in Employment. "We must have full integration of this democracy now and for all time," Davis told the Clubhouse audience, striking a theme that both Elmer Carter (the former *Opportunity* editor had since been named to the New York State War Council) and the AFL's Sam Kramberg underscored. "Victory in 1942," Kramberg announced to cheers, "demands the FULL AND COMPLETE INTEGRATION of the Negro People into ALL war activities on an equal basis—NOW." With Vito Marcantonio, "the fighting congressman" from east Harlem, pledging to draft more potent antidiscrimination legislation for consideration in the House, Edward Lawson, field representative of the Labor Division of the War Production Board saw reason to be optimistic about growing acceptance of black workers in the labor movement. In fact, members of several local unions spoke from the floor, reporting "on the victories they have won in their shops against discrimination." Joining the National Maritime Union with news of such positive gains, the Greater New York Industrial Union Council, the Transport Workers Union, the United Furniture Workers, and the United Electrical, Radio & Machine Workers also agreed to take further action, vowing to make shop-floor integration their patriotic goal.[22]

As a body, the four hundred delegates assembled in the Fraternal Clubhouse adopted a twelve-point program, "based on national unity and the end of discrimination." To support the Negro Labor Victory Committee was to pledge to foster "complete unity behind" the nation's war effort in the name of a "speedy and total victory and a durable peace." The group wished to "throw open the doors of industry to all Americans regardless of race, creed or color" and would work especially "to encourage Negro workers to join trade unions and to assist unions in organizing them." Beyond the workplace, the Victory Committee was committed "to end jim crowism in all phases of American life," including "in the armed forces, in government, labor and industry." The group would endeavor "to make the fight for complete equality for Negroes and other minorities an integral part of the program of the organized labor movement" and "to work for passage of anti-poll tax legislation and for making the President's Fair Employment Practices Committee a permanent agency."[23]

From his seat, Moran Weston wished to approve. He found a sheet of IWO letterhead and penned a quick note endorsing the establishment of the Negro Labor Victory Committee. In broad, hasty longhand he promised the IWO's backing of the Victory Committee, and accompanied the note with a twenty-five-dollar donation. It was a modest pledge. Coupled with the support of the others in the Fraternal Clubhouse audience, however, it helped seal a formal bond between the labor and civil rights movements, distinguishing the Victory Committee among Double V efforts to employ patriotic rhetoric to press for progressive reforms. Auspiciously launched on National Negro Appreciation Day, the Victory Committee was formed at a moment when New York was the lodestar in a national coalition evolving between advocates of civil rights, laborers, and liberal politicians. It aimed, for however long the war lasted, to foster a movement stressing interracial unity and economic justice, political equality and cultural expression. While drawing donations from a range of trade unions, and depending upon the open support of elected officials, it would be up to a handful of African American activists, including Moran Weston, to actually organize the Victory Committee's activities.[24]

Following the session at the Fraternal Clubhouse, the Victory Committee aimed to establish its presence on 125th Street, offering an energetic program to a packed house at the Golden Gate Ballroom. Harlem hummed to electric excitements. To draw attention, the Victory Committee would have to dazzle. Striving to "Pack the Gate" indicated ambitions of mass appeal. When it had opened three years earlier, the Golden Gate had challenged the Savoy Ballroom for the swinging crowds, hiring big band stars such as Count Basie, Coleman Hawkins, and Teddy Wilson to headline house orchestras playing (on some nights, five at a time) to a vast ballroom built to accommodate five thousand dancers and several thousand more spectators. Not even the Savoy stomped every evening, though, so between Miss Harlem pageants and "Rhythm Rodeos" the Golden Gate played host to a range of cultural and political events, from an evening benefit featuring Paul Robeson and author Richard Wright to a thirty-first-anniversary bash for the NAACP. In its brief existence, celebrity and civil rights had come to blend at the Golden Gate, where Lena Horne sang at a New Year's Eve gala and where, just weeks before the Victory Committee rally, Adam Clayton Powell, Jr., had organized an event denouncing police brutality. Holding its first official muster in Harlem at the Golden Gate, the Victory Committee hoped its own program would draw a crowd and forward momentum in its movement for racial justice.[25]

"Unity for Victory" proved an appealing call. More than six thousand filled the ballroom despite stifling early summer humidity, and two thousand more crowded along the corner of 142nd Street and Lenox Avenue. The evening's program, broadcast on WJZ, carried out from apartment windows, storefronts, and passing automobiles. Inside the Golden Gate, Adam Clayton Powell, Jr., hosted, introducing speakers from Winifred Norman, chairman of the National Council of Negro Youth, to Olympic sprinter Eddie Tolan. An emotional appeal by Connie Miller set a determined tone. Grateful for the commemoration of her son's valor at Pearl Harbor, she stressed the national significance of Dorie's service in the Pacific theater. "Some people say we have nothing to fight for," she remarked, acknowledging the question of why African Americans ought to defend a nation that segregated its armed forces. "But we all know we have something to fight for—that is freedom." The presence of Eddie Tolan on the program reminded the audience of fellow sprinter Jesse Owens's spectacular showing at the 1936 games in Berlin, a thrashing of Aryan competition that vividly gave lie to Nazi racialism. African Americans like Dorie Miller could help hand Hitler and Hirohito an ultimate defeat, but only if allowed the opportunity—on the battlefront, and on the home front. Rejecting discrimination as a hindrance to the war effort, Paul McNutt, head of the newly formed War Manpower Commission, scolded: "America cannot stand this nonsense."[26] Vito Marcantonio, the congressman from East Harlem who frequently rose in defense of black rights, was equally adamant that "discrimination must go," pledging to append a "Harlem rider" strengthening the FEPC to each appropriations bill appearing before Congress that summer. Repeating his Madison Square Garden requiem for Uncle Tom, Powell thundered, "a new Negro is on the march . . . out front fighting for our rights together with labor." Looking to McNutt and Marcantonio, the rise of black militancy seemed to have also inspired the emergence of "a new white man" willing to consign Jim Crow to the past. The Negro Labor Victory Committee, he hoped, would maintain the fight.[27]

The dramatic appearances and fiery rhetoric of the "Unite for Victory" rally certainly suggested the Victory Committee's resolve. "In the old days at mass meetings such as the one Sunday," the *Amsterdam News* observed, "speakers hedged and hemmed, compromised and sparred but no such punch-pulling was in evidence" at the Golden Gate, much as the March on Washington Movement had heralded a new Negro offensive against Jim Crow. Noting that the groups' respective platforms formed "a comprehensive program for the integration of the Negroes in the war effort," columnist J. Robert Smith, wondered if a merger was in order. The prospect of this was quite faint. More separated the two groups than the several blocks between their respective headquarters on 125th Street. Although both organizations sought integration, the March on Washington Movement refused to admit white activists into its fold, while the Victory Committee, willing to accept aid from the CIO and Communists, insisted upon interracial cooperation. The latter approach earned the Victory Committee effusive praise and detailed coverage in the *Daily Worker*. Extolling the events that weekend as "a demonstration of the rising militancy of the Negro people [and] their determination to win nothing less than full and equal participation in the war effort and their full citizenship rights," the paper endorsed black freedom as morally just and as a wartime necessity.[28]

To some, the acclamation of a Communist newspaper implied a great deal about the Victory Committee. Writing in the *Amsterdam News*, Frank Crosswaith, a supporter of the March on Washington Movement, displayed typical socialist contempt for perceived Communist interference. The Victory Committee was a puppet organization, he charged, and quite obviously attempting to hinder the socialist movement. The Federal Bureau of Investigation made the same deduction, describing the Victory Committee as having been formed "to combat and destroy the popular appeal of the March on Washington Movement." (If the New York field office relied on an informant with an outlook like Frank Crosswaith, then it was no coincidence the FBI arrived at this conclusion.) In the aftermath of Pearl Harbor, the FBI was in the midst of a national survey of racial conditions, its investigators gathering evidence on individuals and organizations it deemed dissident, with particular attention to "Negroes and Negro groups" leaning dangerously toward sedition. In the Bureau's view, sentiments "inimical to the Nation's war effort" included agitation against the poll tax, anti-lynching demonstrations, and demands to end discrimination in the armed forces. After all, the FBI maintained, with its reflexive callousness regarding African Americans' civil liberties, these were issues that did not "directly or even remotely" affect most blacks; rather, clever instigators could use such propaganda to encourage "the idea of the new militancy or aggressiveness" among African Americans. In New York, where the FBI treated advocacy of civil rights with intense suspicion, few escaped investigators' attention. In 1942, the Bureau scrutinized organizations from the moderate National Urban League to the tiny outposts of black nationalism found along Lenox Avenue, like the African Patriotic League, the Ethiopian Pacific Movement, and the Ethiopian World Federation. For so vigorously condemning Jim Crow and consorting with reputed radicals, prominent figures like Adam Clayton Powell, Jr., and Vito Marcantonio were under FBI surveillance, their cooperation with the Negro Labor

Victory Committee considered telling evidence of subversion. But what the FBI described as "the Communist Party line of twisting and distorting facts in order to garner mass support" was the enunciation of a "Harlem Charter." Taking inspiration from the Atlantic Charter, the United States' and Great Britain's plan for a free postwar world, advocates of African American civil rights in New York envisioned a free and equal America forged out of the international fight for democracy. In Harlem, the Victory Committee was on the vanguard of that fight.[29]

While the FBI watched in the weeks and months following the "Unite for Victory" rally, the Negro Labor Victory Committee was "exceedingly active in holding meetings and agitating among the Negroes in Harlem," eager to collaborate with Adam Clayton Powell, Jr., and insistent that the wartime fight extend to the rights of African Americans. The execution of Odell Waller, whose plight had stirred recent anti-poll-tax agitation, and a lynching in Texarkana, Texas, prompted a Victory Committee meeting on July 15. About one hundred committee supporters, including CIO representatives from fur and furniture workers' locals, assembled at the Renaissance Casino at 138th Street and Seventh Avenue to condemn the continuation of racial violence, whether perpetrated by the state or the lynch mob. Attending to conditions in New York, discussion turned to Spring Products Corporation, a Long Island plant that employed four hundred black workers. The Victory Committee, it was agreed, would petition the War Production Board for an extension of its government contract, ensuring that those African American laborers retain their jobs. A week later, members of the Victory Committee gathered at the Uptown Fur Center, where committee secretary Ewart Guinier recounted his recent participation in a conference with the attorney general on "recent lynchings and injustices committed against the Negro people." The Geyer anti-poll-tax bill discussed that evening was also a central issue on August 12 at the Harlem Workers Club on 125th Street, when it was decided to lobby local congressmen for their support of the legislation in the House of Representatives. At the end of the month, the Victory Committee held a mass meeting at the Golden Gate Ballroom where two thousand audience members cheered speakers like Adam Clayton Powell, Jr., who decried the poll tax and equated the police harassment and slum conditions experienced in Harlem with Hitlerism. That fall, the Victory Committee returned to the Golden Gate to host a "Peoples Rally and Drama on the Four Freedoms," an evening presentation that used President Roosevelt's eloquent enumeration of the liberties at stake in the war—freedom of speech and expression; freedom of religion; freedom from want; freedom from fear—to emphasize how the international triumph over fascism ought to benefit all nations, all peoples, including African Americans subjected to mob violence and systematic discrimination. Taking the stage, Vito Marcantonio denounced the filibuster then blocking the Geyer Bill, a dispiriting scene a Victory Committee delegation witnessed for itself from the Senate gallery during a late-November trip to Washington to meet with the National Committee to Abolish the Poll Tax. Anti-poll-tax legislation faced dim prospects at the end of 1942, but, looking ahead to 1943, the Victory Committee endeavored to sustain the cause, as well as to preserve the FEPC.[30]

In January, Moran Weston joined the Negro Labor Victory Committee's efforts to secure the FEPC. For months, the Roosevelt administration's tepid commitment to the commission had left it vulnerable to southern legislators' determination to ensure its demise. That month, the FEPC was being reined in, with budget curtailments looming and the discontinuation of an investigation into discrimination in the railroad industries. In cooperation with Adam Clayton Powell, Jr.'s People's Committee, which he had formed, in part, to unite the disparate organizations pressing for black political and economic equality in New York, the Victory Committee dispatched a score of representatives to Washington to seek redress from the White House, declaring it imperative to reinstate FEPC funding and continue to probe claims of discrimination in all defense-related industries, and to make the commission a permanent, independent bureau insulated from congressional animosity. By March, with such hearings making little progress, the Victory Committee entertained notions of a national spectacle, proposing—in the manner of the March on Washington Movement—to undertake an enormous Negro Freedom Rally at Madison Square Garden "expressing the aspirations and contributions that the Negro people have made to the political and cultural life of our Nation."[31]

Moran Weston was quick to offer assistance. After two years, he was leaving the International Workers Order, and though he had had trepidations about the IWO's emphasis on cultural events at the outset of his tenure with the National Negro Commission, Weston was now less hesitant about using pageantry as part of a systematic program to end segregation. After all, employing cultural spectacles to forward progressive causes had become a mainstay on the left; in recent years, the likes of Duke Ellington, Billie Holiday, Paul Robeson, and Josh White had routinely lent their musical talents in support of the civil rights movement. The success of the March on Washington Movement rallies in 1942 and the Victory Committee's own experiences holding dramatic events at the Golden Gate Ballroom also offered promising precedents of using wartime rhetoric to press for democratic freedoms. Official wartime propaganda provided another benchmark. During the first year of war, administrators from bureaus such as the Office of War Information and the Office of Facts and Figures had come to rely on black celebrities to bolster morale, sell war bonds, and symbolize the fight for democracy. After volunteering for the army, Harlem's own "Bronx Bomber," Joe Louis, was swinging his way through a series of charitable bouts to prevent racial discord and promote wartime unity. The army's public relations bureau had similar aims for *Freedom's People*, a variety show airing on NBC radio (Paul Robeson sang during the first broadcast, the August 1941 special "America's Negro Soldiers"), and for *Jubilee*, among the most popular programs carried on the Armed Forces Radio Service. Taking cues from both the popular front and official propaganda, the Victory Committee planned to promote the progressive crusade to abolish the poll tax, bolster the FEPC, and ensure the fair treatment of black soldiers with its own dramatic spectacle, entitled *For This We Fight*; Langston Hughes would pen the script.[32]

Moran Weston considered the upcoming Negro Freedom Rally to be part of a broader movement that was taking hold during this second year of war. Beginning a syndicated newspaper column that spring, Weston called it the "FREE-DOM NOW MOVEMENT," with the capitalized letters expressing the bold resolve he perceived among advocates of black liberty across the nation. In New York that April, the National Negro Congress was holding a "Victory Conference on the Problems of the War and the Negro People." Activists were on the march in Detroit that month as well, in support of a "Cadillac Charter" demanding the full works of citizenship and economic opportunity. "ALL WHO BELIEVE IN WHAT IS DECENT AND DEMOCRATIC," Weston wrote, were taking part in a "TWENTIETH CENTURY ABOLITION MOVEMENT, to repeal the un-American Jim Crow laws." Not satisfied to simply stand in witness, Weston planned a Freedom Now Movement meeting at the Harlem YMCA on April 14, "the anniversary of the founding of the first Abolitionist Society in 1775," and he devoted "Labor Forum," the new column he had begun writing for $10 a week in the *New York Amsterdam News*, to demanding a "two fisted war at home and abroad" in the name of abolishing Jim Crow.[33]

While preparations for the Negro Freedom Rally continued most evenings at the Victory Committee offices, Weston used "Labor Forum" to herald, as he put it in a May column, the significance of the "ORGANIZED NEGRO." Unity in the fight against fascism and collaboration with the labor movement, Weston demonstrated, had led to encouraging developments, such as in Baltimore, where he had spent so much time as an organizer for the National Negro Congress and International Workers Order. In that city, he reported, "the war and the coming of age of several Negro union leaders in the CIO and AFL stimulated a remarkable development in the 1942 election campaign." Not only had an African American been elected to the Maryland state legislature the previous fall, but that campaign had also marked the first time the labor movement had supported a black candidate for public office in the state. Such efforts to "QUAR-ANTINE JIM CROW" had also been adopted beyond electoral politics, he argued, as a "battle cry against the home-bred fascism which is eating away at the roots of democratic life." Progressive union locals from Baltimore to New York were on the forefront, endeavoring to eradicate "all remnants of jim crow in the labor movement." In Baltimore, CIO Local 43 of the Marine and Shipyard Workers Union had openly declared itself an ally in the fight for black equality. In New York, members of a domestic workers local planned to switch allegiance to the CIO in protest of the AFL's refusal to prohibit segregation among its ranks. Warehouse laborers affiliated with the CIO had worked to "smash" discriminatory hiring practices; joining with the Urban League and the Negro Labor Victory Committee, the local had placed 1,500 African Americans with jobs, elected African Americans to leadership roles within the union, and pledged to support upholding Executive Order 8802. The local, Weston cheered, "represents NEW AMERICA organized, united, democratic, our front-line defense against fascism at home and abroad."[34]

The upcoming Negro Freedom Rally, to be held on June 7th, epitomized this emergent movement, and Weston penned his most exhortative "Labor Forum" columns to kindle enthusiasm for the event. "December 7 is Pearl Harbor Day," Weston wrote, drawing a parallel already reverberating throughout Harlem, but "June 7 this year is NEGRO FREEDOM DAY." Arriving for the Madison Square Garden spectacular, Negro Labor Victory Committee supporters would witness an event of "national significance" as they "demand that Negro Americans, that all Americans, shall have full citizenship, with no strings attached." Together, they would "let the jail-keepers of the Negro people know that jim crow, discrimination and race terror must go—NOW." Moreover, during the Negro Freedom Rally, Weston promised, "the organized labor movement" would accept the "golden opportunity to stand up and be counted on the side of unconditional democracy for Negro Americans" in a cooperative movement for "freedom, equality, and full citizenship NOW."[35]

While across Harlem copies of the *Age* and *Amsterdam News* bore Weston's columns, union halls throughout the city received the latest imperatives from the Negro Labor Victory Committee. "The fight against Negro discrimination," read the Victory Committee's call to action, "is one that must engage the attention of every trade unionist, for labor cannot remain free while 13 million Americans are unable to take their rightful place in the war against fascism. The Negro seeks only equality—only the opportunity to contribute to the war effort to the full extent of his ability." Though in late May the Roosevelt administration issued Executive Order 9346 to bolster the faltering FEPC, the mass dedication on display during the Negro Freedom Rally would demonstrate that only the full works of equality would suffice.[36]

While the cast of *For This We Fight* held nightly rehearsals during the first week of June, the Victory Committee engaged in vigorous promotion. Broadsheets publicizing the rally dotted the streets of New York. The posters expressed a militant insistence on freedom, demanding an immediate end to segregation in the military and the elimination of discrimination in the war industries. "Negro soldiers are being murdered in the South before they even see the battlefields," read the poster's bold typeface, betraying a barely concealed fury. "They are discriminated against. Beaten. Jimcrowed wherever they go. The barriers of Jim Crow must be smashed forever. Now is the time to do it." While this message decried the inequities faced by African Americans in uniform, the image above it illustrated the imprudence of segregating the military. A muscular black soldier, eager to defend the nation, strains at the shackles of Jim Crow. Held back, he nevertheless remains fixed on the fight, his gaze resolute and his rifle firmly gripped; he could bring the world closer to freedom, if given the opportunity. If it was unwise to segregate the armed forces, maintaining a color line in the nation's defense industries amounted to disloyalty: "THOUSANDS OF SKILLED NEGRO WORKERS ARE BARRED FROM JOBS IN THE SHOPS SHIP-YARDS AND ARMS PLANTS OF THE NATION. DISCRIMINATION IN WAR TIME IS TREASON AGAINST THE NATION." Victory ought to trump color lines in this fight for the four freedoms, and this shift needed to occur immediately: "WE CANNOT WAIT UNTIL 'AFTER THE WAR' FOR DEMOCRACY. VICTORY DEMANDS AN END TO JIM CROWISM NOW." For the price of forty-four cents, admission to the Negro Freedom Rally promised an evening of such Double V protest—and pageantry. In Harlem, those attending a mass meeting at the Abyssinian Baptist Church were assured, in the words of Adam Clayton Powell, Jr., "It's Either Uncle Tom or Fite!" Taking to the road, Moran Weston traveled across the state to rally enthusiasm for the event, including in Rochester, where he spoke from beneath a statue of Frederick Douglass in Lilac Park, insisting that "The Road to Victory is the Road to Freedom." While African Americans were "second to none in our loyalty" during "this great war against Hitlerism," Weston contended, "we know that unconditional victory and lasting peace can be won only if all Americans unite, undivided by lines of race, class, religion or nationality." The Negro Labor Victory Committee had "a program to help build this unity," Weston insisted, and "to help win this war."[37]

Heeding this call, twenty thousand assembled in Madison Square Garden on the evening of June 7, 1943, and another twelve thousand massed outside along Eighth Avenue. From the seats and the street, they heard Victory Committee cochairman Ferdinand Smith open the Negro Freedom Rally. At the center of a large star-shaped stage, Smith declared that patriotic unity was imperative "to preserve our national independence and together with our Allies to liberate oppressed humanity everywhere." At no point was "the desire of the Negro people to help win this war against fascism" more evident than now, with so many thousands gathered at the Garden in the name of freedom. And yet this assemblage also embodied a mass movement demanding the liberation of oppressed Americans. "Out of this meeting," Smith said, "must come concrete measures which will serve to eliminate from the American way of life the system of Jim

Crow." Indeed, Channing Tobias, of the YMCA, marveled from behind the microphones that the evening marked "the biggest meeting for Negro freedom ever held in the world." Taking his turn, Congressman Vito Marcantonio looked to the rafters and pumped both his fists in pugilistic accompaniment as he recounted the recent legislative fight for an anti-poll-tax bill. To Charles Collins, the Victory Committee's "tall, forceful-speaking" other cochairman, Congressman Marcantonio exemplified the potential of interracial cooperation. Explicitly challenging the March on Washington Movement, Collins exhorted African Americans to "no longer seek a solution to their problems along the lines of narrow nationalism," encouraging the thousands listening that night to dispose of the notion "that the Negro problem is his own and that he must fight to organize by himself." Michael Quill, president of the Transport Workers Union, was in agreement, arguing that the progressive labor movement was proving a powerful ally in the struggle for black equality being waged in workplaces from Mobile to Detroit, where the CIO acted on the belief that "there cannot be a free American labor movement as long as discrimination is practiced." A deafening roar greeted the Urban League's Lester Granger, whose corollary challenging segregation in the armed forces brought to mind the image of the black soldier chained back by Jim Crow. "It is not the white man's responsibility alone," Granger insisted, to "smash the Axis and make this world really safe for democracy." Adam Clayton Powell, Jr., the final speaker, made this sentiment a patriotic refrain. "We are here because America needs us," Powell announced to cheers.

> We are here because America cannot win the peace without us. We are here for victory over Hitlerism abroad and at home. This is the New Negro that is present tonight. The New Negro who was born during the bitter days when he walked through the valley of the shadow of the depression.
>   The New Negro is united—One People!
>   The New Negro is fighting—One Purpose!
>   The New Negro is following—One Leadership!
>   The New Negro is willing to die—For One Victory![38]

This rousing peroration was a fitting prelude to the evening's pageant, *For This We Fight*. Langston Hughes's twelve-scene drama opened with a modestly staged—if immodestly didactic—prologue set in a Seventh Avenue flat in Harlem that same night. The New Negro that Powell had hailed was depicted on the star-shaped stage in the character of Pvt. Henry Jackson, "an ordinary citizen of Harlem," in the words of Hughes, "a plain American, one of those Common Men by whom, and for whom, this war is being fought." Pvt. Jackson, a recent army inductee, had just returned home on furlough, having traveled by a Jim Crow

Prominent political figures such as Adam Clayton Powell, Jr., participated in the Negro Freedom Rallies. This photograph captures Powell exhorting the crowd at Madison Square Garden during the 1945 rally. M. Moran Weston Papers, Rare Book and Manuscript Library, Columbia University in the City of New York.

train car from Fort Bragg in South Carolina. At home, his wife embodied the contributions black women were making on the home front, caring for their son and working for Sperry Gyroscope Corporation, the defense contractor the FEPC had recently scrutinized for discriminatory hiring practices. Hughes left the significance of this particular detail implied, but the script did not allow nuance to obscure the central messages of the performance. Alternating between a dialogue between Pvt. Jackson and his son and a series of historical episodes, *For This We Fight* emphasized the long, entwined history of liberty and oppression in the United States and cast African Americans as traditional freedom fighters, from Crispus Attucks, martyred during the Boston Massacre, to the ordinary heroism of Harlem's Henry Jackson, who chose to defend the nation with his life at a time when freedom was imperiled.

The play opened with the three members of the Jackson family alone on the stage. While Mrs. Jackson doted, the couple's son wanted to talk with Pvt. Jackson about the big rally that night at the Garden. More pressingly, he wants to ask why a black man would ever serve in the armed forces. A classmate, the son explained, had said he "didn't see no sense in colored folks fighting this war—cause his father told him we don't have anything now—and we won't have anything after the war either, but Jim Crow!" Pvt. Jackson himself had experienced the degradations of Jim Crow, his son pointed out. Despite his uniform, he had been compelled to travel in a segregated train car during his trip home to Harlem. Now the young boy wondered from under the spotlight in the middle of Madison Square Garden: Is this really a nation worth defending to the death? Asking his wife and son to listen closely, Pvt. Jackson acknowledged this frustration but insisted that their patriotism was necessary in the fight against fascism. Their sacrifices now could help defeat fascism forever. Failing to act would be too dangerous to contemplate, Jackson argued, saying "If we ever give up hope, and don't work and don't try, and don't fight—we *never* will have anything!" Looking from his wife to his son and then into the vast, darkened audience surrounding him, Jackson declared that "liberty and freedom and democracy and all the good things in American life are here for us, just like everybody else—but they are *seeds* not yet grown into big plants. We have to help them grow."

As the Jackson family stepped aside, a series of seven dramatic scenes demonstrated that the "seeds of freedom" had long been germinating in American soil, planted by African Americans and their white compatriots since the very founding of the nation. "A Negro's blood made the first red stripes in our flag, and the freedom seed was planted," said Pvt. Jackson, referring to Crispus Attucks. And, yes, Jackson confirmed for his vigilantly inquisitive son, though the nation sprang from the spirit of liberty and justice, enslavement had nonetheless remained in place. On cue, the shouts and shrieks of an early-nineteenth-century New Orleans slave auction rang out, with Pvt. Jackson explaining that slavery had underwritten national prosperity even as it clashed with the nation's founding principles. Yet the slave driver's lash had not impelled obedience, as the following scene demonstrated; rather, slaves joined in another fight for freedom, though, Pvt. Jackson explained, their rebellions did not lead to liberty. Asked why slaves had persisted in their struggle when there was so little hope, Pvt. Jackson exclaimed: "Freedom has no end, son! It's so deep in the hearts of the people nothing can stop it!" Indeed, as the following scenes depicted, with the assistance of white abolitionists from pacifist William Lloyd Garrison to the wrathful John Brown, the struggle to end slavery culminated in the direst of national crises—the Civil War. Ordinary black citizens clamored to enter the fray and were finally allowed to enlist in such celebrated colored regiments as the 54th Massachusetts Volunteer Infantry. Despite the demeaning duties colored soldiers were forced to perform (and for partial pay, moreover), the singular black leader of the day, Frederick Douglass, encouraged patriotic support of the Union. Taking the Garden stage with Abraham Lincoln, Douglass addressed the president: "I am deeply grieved at the inequalities put upon my race. Nevertheless, I have urged every colored man to enlist, get an eagle on his button, and a musket on his shoulder." While Lincoln equivocated at first, he was convinced when two slaves affirmed their intention to fight on behalf of the Union. "All America must—and shall be free," exclaimed Lincoln as the spotlight dimmed and strains of "John Brown's Body" rose.

As the cast made way for an interlude between the American past and present—a cultural sequence of "Negro music" and dance, featuring Paul Robeson, Pearl Primus, and W. C. Handy—the Garden audience was left to ponder the parallels between 1863 and 1943. Then, colored soldiers had served in a segregated, discriminatory military; now, black men faced the same circumstance. Then, Frederick Douglass had pressed President Lincoln to transform a war to repair the nation's sectional divisions into a "new birth of freedom"; on this night, the Negro Freedom Rally urged President Roosevelt to ensure that the war to save the world from fascism extend the Four Freedoms to black Americans. Then, with the stroke of a pen, President Lincoln had proclaimed an end to slavery; now, with an executive order, President Roosevelt could announce an end to Jim Crow.

If Frederick Douglass had stood for 1863, Paul Robeson now stood for 1943. The tall, muscular, and internationally renowned "voice for democracy" took center stage, to the delight of Pvt. Jackson and his son. Asked if this Robeson is the same as the all-American footballer from Rutgers, Henry Jackson beamed: "That's also what he is as a man—ALL-AMERICAN! He uses his songs as a weapon for freedom." A month earlier, Robeson, a dedicated supporter of both the National Negro Congress and the CIO, had spoken before the Labor for Victory rally at Yankee Stadium. His rendition of the labor ballad "Joe Hill" this evening similarly underscored the theme of interracial unity that, like the black freedom struggle, recurred throughout the Hughes pageant. The choreographer and dancer Pearl Primus followed, performing "Jim Crow Train," the title a reference to the undignified treatment Pvt. Jackson had endured during his return trip to Harlem, and then W. C. Handy led a rendition of his composition "St. Louis Blues" that brought the musical performances to an end. "The blues," Henry Jackson mused as the musical interlude ended, "those great, sad, strong, determined songs of the Negro people, warm as the beat of the human heart, a real part of Negro culture," was but one contribution African Americans had made to American society—and could continue to make with the abolition of domestic fascism.

As the cast returned to the stage, the evening's pageantry closed with a set of three moralistic scenes depicting the American dilemma in 1943. A portrayal of Hitlerism on American shores equated fascism with segregation, suggesting the Führer's satisfaction with the divisions wrought by white supremacy. "Hitler knows Jimcrowism weakens the war effort," Pvt. Jackson observed with palpable consternation while the actors assembled into an all-too-familiar scene: "Discrimination in Industry." The frustrating fact was that companies continued to reject black workers to the detriment of the war effort and despite the

The Negro Freedom Rallies featured African American celebrity entertainers, such as Paul Robeson, photographed here while performing during the 1945 rally. M. Moran Weston Papers, Rare Book and Manuscript Library, Columbia University in the City of New York.

president's mandate of integration in defense-related industries. Dismissed from an employment line despite a dearth of able laborers, a "union Negro" gave voice to a common question: "Say, listen, I'm a citizen. I got two brothers fighting in New Guinea. How come I can't work?" A white worker came to his defense, challenging such discrimination as a betrayal of the very aims of the war, and offering a heartening example of interracial unity to the trade unionists gathered at the Garden. To further underscore the patriotic contributions black workers were making to the war effort, Hughes crafted a monologue for Canada Lee, a thirty-six-year-old former boxer whose participation in the Federal Theater Project had led to a stellar acting career. The most prominent black actor of the day took the stage as a merchant marine (a nod to the support the National Maritime Union had lent to the Negro Labor Victory Committee) who was returning from service, like Henry Jackson, to his home in Harlem. Soldiers like Pvt. Jackson endured the indignities of a Jim Crow military; merchant marines confronted the Nazi threat while moving supplies across the seas; each attested to the patriotic contributions of black Americans.

After Lee recounted the demands that service to the nation has required, in the pageant's closing moments Pvt. Henry Jackson articulated the demands the New Negro now made of the nation. While he and his fellow soldiers had pledged to "carry on against fascism Over There," he told the Garden audience he counted on them "to battle at home against fascism in American life"—to convince the nation's leaders to abolish the poll tax, to pass an anti-lynching bill, and to end segregation in the armed forces and defense industries. "It's up to all those people out there in this audience tonight," Jackson shouted, "to you—and you—and you! You can do something about it! And it's up to millions of Americans who believe in liberty throughout the nation who know these things are wrong." And it was time for the president to take a stand. "Tell America, Mr. Roosevelt, this nation can't fight with all its strength with its black arm chained by the color bar. Tell the world Mr. Roosevelt, that when we say *democracy*, we mean DEMOCRACY!" There would be no more waiting, Jackson assured the Garden crowd. "Now the day has come to put a Time Limit on Freedom. We want it NOW! Not fifty years from today—but NOW! Freedom is not just something to talk about. Freedom has to be real—as a man is real! Tonight American Negro soldiers are stationed all over the world . . . fighting for the liberty of the whole world. They won't be cheated of the Victory." As Jackson's voice swelled, a black soldier appeared at each corner of the stage holding an American flag. "At home we're tired of being Jim Crowed! We want to win this war, we want to fight shoulder to shoulder with everybody else—but we also want to train together, vote together, work together, fight together till fascism is conquered and be Americans together! We want Hitler not only out of Europe, but out of the USA!" This, said Pvt. Jackson, quieter now but still firm in his intonation, is the meaning of the war. "Jim Crow started its Last Stand" at Pearl Harbor when Mess Attendant Dorie Miller manned the antiaircraft guns on the deck of the USS *West Virginia.* "Things can't be the same again," Jackson vowed, "and WON'T be!" Standing amid five flag-bearing black soldiers, Jackson adopted a poetic cadence: "To break the power of Hitlerism and Jim Crowism all over the earth, folks—for this we fight!"

America, our homeland,
Ever dear will be,
That's why we want America
For ALL men to be free!
Let's put an end to the color bar!
Let's put an end to the Jim Crow car!
For the right to be men
In this land we defend—
For this we fight!

"For this we fight!" repeated the rapturous Garden crowd, the words reverberating from the rafters to the floor. "For this we fight!" responded the cast of
two hundred, Paul Robeson's resonant baritone, all-American voice of democracy among them. "For this we fight!" Pvt. Henry Jackson's call to arms echoed
above the thousands massed along Eighth Avenue. "For this we fight!" The emphatic hymn of the New Negro resounded from stage to audience to street as the
pageant came to a climactic end. "For this we fight!"[39]

"We're not alone. We've got power." Moran Weston summarized the Negro Freedom Rally in these two simple, significant sentences. Still, despite the excitement that "ran through the minds and hearts" of the thousands at Madison
Square Garden, Weston observed, "fine speeches and splendid turn-outs never
won a battle. Organization and action will decide the issue." The Negro Freedom
Rally promised each. "It was," he wrote, "a new kind of organization for equality
and liberty." As important to the labor movement as to "the Negro people," the
June 7th rally

> proved, as only action can prove, that there is a new and more mature
> unity among Negroes; that the Negro people know that their fight for
> equality and the war are one fight; that there is a new leadership coming
> of age among the Negro people—from the ranks of organized labor;
> that organized labor will unite with the Negro organizations to win a
> people's victory and a people's peace; that friendship between white
> and black America has been strengthened through the trade unions and
> is now a real power for democracy, for victory over fascism, . . . that the
> Negro people are on the march for freedom now and all the powers of
> hell cannot stop it.

Catching his breath, Weston contended that while "the people themselves must
close ranks behind the militant program of the rally," a "heavy responsibility"
also weighed "upon the leaders who directed this rally. They must work in a spirit
of devotion and self-sacrifice as never before. They must weld this unity and
power revealed in the rally into a powerful, organized movement to blast away
those discriminations, those humiliations, those Jim Crow evils which slow
down our progress on the road to victory which is the only road to freedom."[40]
    Indeed, the Negro Labor Victory Committee hoped momentum from the
rally would boost its ranks and strengthen its program. To ensure a growing
membership, following the Garden rally the Victory Committee hired Moran
Weston as a full-time salaried field secretary. In several weeks he had cultivated connections in Buffalo, Washington, and Baltimore; in New Jersey, a
new Victory Committee affiliate planned to hold a Negro Victory Rally at

Newark Stadium on Independence Day. In print, Weston scolded the Justice Department for failing to protect African Americans during the riots that flared in Detroit in June, demanding that the attorney general order FBI investigators to arrest "KKK" instigators. (The Bureau, for its part, was rather intent on maintaining surveillance of Adam Clayton Powell, Jr., and collecting news clippings to document reaction to the Negro Freedom Rally.) Decrying the wave of racial violence that saw uniformed black men targeted, the Victory Committee coordinated with the People's Committee to hold a mass meeting at the Golden Gate Ballroom to denounce the recent outrages in Los Angeles; Detroit; Mobile, Alabama; and Beaumont, Texas. Declaring "It Must Not Happen Again!" the Victory Committee staged a repeat performance of *For This We Fight*, whose themes only resonated more loudly now. Committed to reversing the structural inequalities leading to violent uprisings, that night the Victory Committee pledged to make such incidents an issue during the fall elections. Meanwhile, it would organize a delegation to travel to Washington to press the administration on fair employment.[41]

Moran Weston planned to accompany the group to Washington, but he was also attentive to events elsewhere in the nation. That workers at the Sun Shipyard in Chester, Pennsylvania, had voted to allow the CIO to represent them, thus opening their ranks to black workers, boded well; as did the FEPC's announcement that it would investigate the railroad industry and unions in September. Yet with lagging unions (particularly those affiliated with the AFL) continuing to recognize a difference between "white jobs and Negro jobs," Weston considered the need for a national conference among labor groups obvious. Between columns, he traveled to Baltimore to collaborate with the local "equivalent of the NLVC," returned to New York for an open air rally of the Upper West Side Victory Council, and then led the Victory Committee delegation to Washington to confer with FEPC officials. Weston left Washington assured the commission would investigate the Victory Committee's complaints, and returned to a Harlem in uproar.[42]

On the evening of August 1, Harlem erupted after a police officer shot an off-duty black soldier. As rumor spread that the soldier had been killed defending his mother (fortunately, he actually survived the shooting), a melee ensued, concentrated along 125th Street. That evening Victory Committee officials toured the scene of the riot with Mayor La Guardia and a contingent of black leaders, then conferred to state their position. It was the very sort of incident Adam Clayton Powell, Jr., and the Victory Committee had been warning about—and had been diligently trying to prevent. "The grave disturbance that occurred in the Harlem community on Sunday night, August 1st," the Victory Committee pronounced, "were in no way race riots as some newspapers and misguided persons tried to imply. This outbreak was due to the underlying resentments of the Negro people against indignities to which they have been subjected—discrimination in job placement, segregation in the armed forces, lack of rent and price control, inadequate playground facilities, poor housing conditions." Calling for prompt action by Mayor La Guardia, the Victory Committee declared its dedication to eliminating the root cause of the outbreak: Jim Crow. Writing in "Labor Forum," Moran Weston was equally unequivocal. "The major responsibility for the unfortunate outbreak of violence must be PLACED ON THE DOORSTEPS OF THE PUBLIC OFFICIALS WHO HAVE FAILED TO END THE VICIOUS DISCRIMINATION AND JIM CROW WHICH DAILY HUMILIATE, PAIN AND OPPRESS NEGROES."[43]

Acknowledging that it was necessary to take action to assure change, in the weeks following the Harlem riot Weston endeavored to forward the Victory Committee's program throughout metropolitan New York. In August, Weston assisted in the production of the Brooklyn Freedom Rally at the Brooklyn Academy of Music, addressed a CIO council in Washington Heights, met with bakers and hotel, restaurant, and confectionary workers, and helped established affiliate committees in Newark and Elizabeth, New Jersey, making progress toward a goal of creating one hundred local Victory Committees by September. This may have seemed a lofty ambition for a single field secretary to achieve, but by the end of the month, as Weston coordinated a meeting of affiliates in New Jersey, he could report with satisfaction that the Victory Committee had placed roughly six thousand workers "largely in industries where they had not worked in the past." The Victory Committee affiliates, such as those recently inaugurated in New Jersey, could further bolster a program dedicated to supporting "the anti-discrimination drive of the President's Fair Employment Practices Committee, eliminating discrimination and segregation in the armed forces." These were the types of measures necessary to bury Jim Crow once and for all, and to forestall future outbreaks like the August riot in Harlem.[44] The problem of discrimination, however, remained especially rampant in the AFL, as Weston detailed in "Labor Forum." He admonished the New York state convention of the AFL for failing to accomplish much to be "distinguished by liberality or positive action in public affairs," urging the organization to follow the CIO's example of establishing antidiscrimination committees within unions. Weston also encouraged black workers to seek out advanced training, as the prospect of qualified laborers would make it even difficult for the most recalcitrant unions or companies to justify racial discrimination. Such recommendations fit the message the Victory Committee put forth during its general meetings held monthly at the 135th Street YMCA. During the September assembly, Weston reported that the Victory Committee now had fifty-one affiliates, each of which could rally mass support for the FEPC's railroad hearings underway that month in Washington. Reassuringly, there was growing validation for this antidiscriminatory zeal: the

War Labor Board had ruled that the AFL could not discriminate while organizing workers. As many hoped, persistence had led to an incremental but
important advance. And, as the November elections loomed, the Victory Committee sought to gain even more, supporting a newly opened workers' school,
appealing to members of the Judiciary Committee to facilitate the passage of
anti-poll-tax legislation, and calling on the New York district attorney to investigate discriminatory policies in the city's hotels.[45]

Among all its endeavors that fall, the Negro Labor Victory Committee planned
a vigorous electoral agenda. While Moran Weston used "Labor Forum" to insist
that it was imperative that the "ORGANIZED NEGRO" register to vote, the
Victory Committee arranged with the American Labor Party to form a "political
action group" in support of a left-wing ticket that included black candidates for
city office. The American Labor Party (ALP) was less an actual political party
than an influential vehicle for leftist politics in the city. Originally formed in
1936, the ALP had initially offered voters opposed to atavistic elements in the
Democratic Party (namely, corrupt Tammany Hall hacks and segregationist
southerners) an opportunity to support the presidential and gubernatorial candidacies of Franklin Roosevelt and Herbert Lehman without actually having to
vote for Democrats. When the ALP named Roosevelt and Lehman its candidates, a progressive New Yorker could vote them in with a clear conscience.
Since the 1936 campaign, the ALP had become a vital electoral influence in New
York; in some quarters of the city it was strong enough to swing an entire district, even as it supported open members of the Communist Party. The Victory
Committee's collaboration with the group that in recent years had helped elect
friends Vito Marcantonio to Congress and Adam Clayton Powell, Jr., to the city
council elicited red-baiting barbs from supporters of the faded March on Washington Movement, but Moran Weston paid little heed to internecine jousting,
concentrating on organizing the campaign for the Nineteenth and Twenty-First
Assembly Districts.[46]

After renting an office on Seventh Avenue, just above 139th Street, Weston
opened the Victory Committee and ALP Club campaign with a rally on the first
of October. By day, Weston penned a series of columns trumpeting the Victory
Committee's electoral commitment to ensure that African Americans become
"A PART OF THE **MAJORITY** IN AMERICA." By night, Weston met with
campaign captains over the next five weeks at the Harlem headquarters to coordinate the house-to-house canvasses and to arrange for dozens of outdoor rallies,
ending with a Halloween blowout at the Golden Gate Ballroom.[47] The Victory
Committee backed an interracial slate of left-wing candidates, seeking to return
Vito Marcantonio to the House of Representatives and to place two black aspi-
rants in city offices: Francis Rivers on the bench as a city judge, and Benjamin
Davis, Jr., on the city council. Davis, a Georgia-born Communist, was a Harvard

Law–trained attorney who had defended Angelo Herndon before relocating to Harlem in the mid-1930s; the Victory Committee hoped he would replace the outgoing Adam Clayton Powell, Jr., who was already eyeing a run for Congress in 1944.

Taking special notice of the Benjamin Davis campaign, the *Daily Worker* observed with unabashed partisan approval that the Victory Committee was engaged in "perhaps the most intensive campaign ever launched to get out the Negro vote." Beyond the Victory Committee's street-corner stumping, the ALP ticket had the backing of a coterie of influential Harlem ministers; city buses carried placards through the district, and campaign trailers were showing in Harlem movie houses. Calling his candidacy for city council a challenge to Jim Crow, Benjamin Davis watched as his "campaign spread like wildfire." Building his campaign, as he put it, "upon the theme of winning the war and demonstrating against Hitler racism by advancing the cause of Negro representation at home," his avowed Communism did little to dissuade support. Rather than espousing narrow doctrine, Davis typified the ALP ticket's pledge to uphold a spectrum of progressive causes. Fashioning himself as a "people's candidate," Davis promised to use his place on the city council to challenge housing discrimination and slum conditions, to ensure that a black representative be appointed to the Board of Education, and to address the issue that had sparked the August riot—police brutality. It was, he called it, an "all-people's . . . movement against the jim-crow ghetto system." Even conservative "old-timers," Davis would later recount, offered their support. "Some of them would slap me on the back and say: 'Davis, your father was a Lincoln Republican. You must be a Lincoln Communist. I'm going to vote for you.'" Near the end of October, backslapping supporters could even sing the lyrics printed in the *Daily Worker*:

> Ben, Ben we're voting for you,
> When you get into the Council,
> Here's what you do,
> Let the whole world know,
> New York City's gonna end Jim Crow,
> Yes, yes, end Jim Crow,
> Yes, yes end Jim Crow,
> Democracy has got to grow,
> New York City's gonna end Jim Crow.

During the final days of the campaign, while local clergy members were called upon to preach the power of the ballot from their Sunday pulpits and the Victory Committee readied for the Halloween bash at the Golden Gate Ballroom, Weston led an "IT'S NOW OR NEVER" drive throughout the Twenty-First

District. "Economic equality is the corner-stone of democracy," Weston wrote in an October column, but suffrage was equally indispensible. "Voting and voting wisely is the only way Negroes can prove they mean business about getting equality, economic security, and full citizenship." When it came time to vote, Weston urged readers to remember that "organized labor and the Negro people have a common destiny." Working with the labor movement, the Victory Committee intended "to make sure that every Negro community has Negro candidates for public office and that they are elected in cooperation with the organizations of the Negro people."[48] The backing of Harlem's luminaries helped too. At the late-October evening at the Golden Gate, the support of politically conscious black celebrities lent immeasurable vitality to the campaign. As Benjamin Davis attested, "There was scarcely a name band or popular entertainer who did not volunteer their services." The jazz pianist Teddy Wilson, who had integrated the big band scene during the 1930s by joining Benny Goodman's orchestra, chaired the Artist's Committee for Davis, which solicited donations, performed during street corner rallies, and agreed to headline the Halloween election bash at the Golden Gate. The contributions of such figures as Count Basie, Ella Fitzgerald, Lena Horne, and Duke Ellington helped explain why the fête at the Harlem ballroom was sold out more than a week in advance, even though reserved seats cost an unheard of $2.75 and general admission went for fifty cents. Still, so many massed outside that another hall had to be opened several blocks away—not an inauspicious portent for ALP candidates Davis, Marcantonio, and Rivers.

Less propitious was the rain that poured down during the busiest hours of Election Day. During another year rain might have kept people from the polls. This November, however, workers returning home defied the downpour and made certain to cast their ballots. "Many elderly Negroes," Benjamin Davis realized, had "voted for the first time in their lives." The Victory Committee's coordination was one reason for this, with members of the National Maritime Union, CIO furriers, and AFL food workers volunteering their efforts on the day of the election. So, too, was the rhetoric the campaign used to link the election of the local ALP slate with the defeat of international fascism. To vote the ALP ticket was to strike a patriotic blow against Jim Crow. It was also an opportunity to participate in a new era of interracial, progressive politics. "The solid vote of Harlem was not enough to elect me," recalled Davis, nor could he rely on the meager numbers of New York Communists. He required "the trade union and white progressive vote" to win a place on the city council. Despite the rain, the Victory Committee helped deliver each bloc to the ALP candidates. Ebullient, Davis remarked that "white supremacy had taken a licking," calling his election to city council, Francis Rivers' new judicial position, and Vito Marcantonio's return to Washington a "high-water mark in the achievement of the labor-Negro people's progressive coalition." The election was a clear measure of the Double V commitment during the fall of 1943. "The Negro people of Harlem," Davis later recounted, "demonstrating tremendous political maturity, had fired a shot that was heard not only in the sharecropper's cabin in Mississippi, but in the trenches in Europe and the Far East. It was, above all, a victory for unity behind our country's patriotic, national war to defeat the Rome-Berlin-Tokyo axis." The black journalist Roi Ottley agreed, portraying the shift "taking place in Negro life" as a "transfer of power from the politicians to the leaders of the labor and militant civil rights organizations, and the emergence of new types of men who are taking positions toward the left." Moran Weston, among them, likewise took satisfaction with the results, writing "the elections proved in short that it is possible to organize UNITED ACTION between labor, the Negro people and liberals." Now, it remained to maintain such action.[49]

Eager to continue, the Negro Labor Victory Committee announced a celebratory postelection swing dance at the Golden Gate to benefit its winter agenda. Following the campaign, the Victory Committee wished to make rapid progress on new fronts requiring action from two of the candidates it had supported. On the city council, Benjamin Davis would press for legislation outlawing housing discrimination. In the House of Representatives, Vito Marcantonio would sponsor a measure to "put teeth" into the FEPC by authorizing its punishment of violators. Following the maxim that legislative measures required mass pressure, Moran Weston returned to the field, with support from friends in several industrial cities in the northeast and mid-Atlantic. He spoke first at the John Street YMCA in downtown Bridgeport, Connecticut, then traveled to Philadelphia to attend the annual CIO convention. There, Victory Committee cochairman Ferdinand Smith was elected to the National Maritime Union's executive board, an event Weston compared to the recent Harlem elections. It was evidence, he informed his "Labor Forum" readers, of "the growing determination of the Negro people to get representation in the labor movement, in politics, in industry—in all phases of American life." In Philadelphia he also attended a meeting of trade unionists and National Negro Congress members at the Catherine Street YMCA, a center of progressive political action in the city (the local NAACP youth council met there, too). Working to establish a new Victory Committee affiliate in Philadelphia, Weston expressed what he felt was so evident following the Negro Freedom Rally and 1943 elections, encouraging a continuing interracial movement to strengthen the FEPC and describing unions as the best place for black and white folk to come together "on a basis of equality." If the nation was to integrate, a local Victory Committee affiliate would provide a welcome example.[50]

Back at the Negro Labor Victory Committee headquarters in December, Moran Weston returned to a growing stream of letters documenting employment discrimination in area industries. More had begun dialing ATwater 9-4630 to reach the headquarters, too, and so many had appeared in the office on 125th Street that the Victory Committee arranged to lease a new, larger suite nearby. If it was frustrating to receive such complaints of job discrimination, it was nonetheless encouraging to realize that African Americans in New York felt emboldened enough to claim their right to equal opportunity—and that they chose to reach out to the Negro Labor Victory Committee for assistance. Amid the complaints he received, Weston considered one trend especially grievous. Disturbingly, on the second anniversary of Pearl Harbor, black veterans faced trouble finding work once back from overseas. "It requires no imagination," he fumed, "to understand what bitterness arises in the hearts of these Negro veterans." Before long, bitterness might turn to rage and the riots of 1943 might return on a furious home front in 1944. Weston applauded the fact that the FEPC had opened an office in Atlanta to monitor complaints; this development brought federal oversight to a southern city and might aid in securing employment for returning black soldiers. But it was a minor balm. With the New Year approaching—and with it, a new congress—Weston urged united action among African Americans and organized labor to muster mass support to make the FEPC a permanent bureau, not simply a wartime one. "It works," Weston insisted. "Make it permanent."[51]

In January 1944, reporters from the *New York Age* and *Pittsburgh Courier* visited the Negro Labor Victory Committee's new office at 308 Lenox Avenue, just above 125th Street. It "hums with activity," observed the *Age*, "every day taking care of the complaints and needs of hundreds who come there every day of the week." Among an office staff of six, Moran Weston, a former city caseworker, ably took the lead listening to concerns about jobs and deciding which complaints to formally forward to the FEPC. The Victory Committee was, according to the *Courier*, "learning to talk with more firmness and assurance and [was] establishing a strong foothold in an increasingly labor-conscious Harlem."[52]

No longer merely the darling of the *Daily Worker*, the Victory Committee drew the attention in the black press, reflecting the rising profile it enjoyed at the outset of 1944, as it sought an influence beyond New York's progressive left. The Harlem upstart had national ambitions. Job discrimination had been a crucial focus of the Negro Labor Victory Committee during its first year, with the organization creating affiliates in the industrial cities of Buffalo, Newark, Baltimore, Detroit, Washington, Bridgeport, Philadelphia, and St. Louis. Appropriately, with the new year the Victory Committee launched a full-fledged campaign to back legislation for a permanent FEPC, to compel the railroads to comply with antidiscriminatory regulations, to secure passage of an anti-poll-tax bill, and to end discrimination in the military. With this platform, Moran Weston contended, the Victory Committee stood poised to challenge the "invasion from within"; to confront those vestiges of American fascism—segregation and race hatred—was as imperative as repelling the Axis powers abroad. Regionally, the Victory Committee had similarly robust intentions, endorsing the measures Benjamin Davis brought before the city council, including legislation to prohibit housing discrimination, to recognize Negro History Week throughout the city, and to end the Jim Crow conditions black firemen endured. The Victory Committee also marshaled union support for the antidiscrimination bills addressing housing and education that Harlem state assemblyman Hulan Jack sponsored in Albany. Its members participated in a letter-writing campaign to Governor Thomas Dewey, and challenged the constitutionality of congressional committees on un-American activities—such as the Dies Committee in Washington and the Rapp-Coudert Committee in New York. Although not every action succeeded, the Victory Committee nonetheless asserted pressure on manifestations of Jim Crow. And when petitions proved insufficient (such as an unfulfilled request that the AFL's largest boilermakers union desegregate), the Victory Committee maintained its faith in the power of spectacular mass mobilization. Looking ahead to June, it announced another "gigantic peoples rally" to exhibit the fighting spirit at Madison Square Garden.[53]

Responsible for organizing the rally, Moran Weston began by creating the Freedom Fighters campaign that winter. The Freedom Fighters ran a membership drive timed to end on February 14, Frederick Douglass's birthday, then met regularly at 308 Lenox Avenue to discuss how best to promote the Victory Committee's program. Flyers were produced enumerating recent efforts such as forwarding over two hundred documented cases of discrimination to the FEPC, helping place more than eight thousand African American workers in area industries, and organizing campaigns to support civil rights legislation and establish union-based antidiscrimination committees. Hoping to build on this record, Weston wished the Victory Committee not only to persist in attaining anti-poll-tax legislation, and in keeping the issue of police brutality on Mayor Fiorello La Guardia's desk, but also to address the issue of reconversion: the prospects of postwar employment, about which, he observed, a "sense of uneasiness stirs the hearts from barbershop philosopher to professional politician." To effect this, through late February Weston looped from Buffalo, Detroit, and Chicago back to Cleveland, Pittsburgh, and Philadelphia, then traveled south to Baltimore and Washington to impress upon Victory Committee affiliates the need to be ready for the looming economic transition from wartime boom to peacetime doldrums. African American workers simply had to be protected from mass layoffs after the war. According to most unions' seniority policies, recently hired black workers would be the first fired when industry production slowed. This, clearly, would run counter to progressive labor's commitment to integrate the workplace, but union locals often balked at instituting the kind of affirmative action necessary to retain the wartime level of African American employment. When the Freedom Fighters met on March 1 in Harlem, Weston sought to ensure a central place for reconversion in the upcoming primary campaigns later that month. Hosting a guest speaker from the American Labor Party, Weston argued that when "the majority of Negro workers are not . . . anywhere near the goal of job security," and when the railroads were persisting in refusing to hire black workers "except by the handful and in the lowest paying jobs," the importance of gaining political power to effect change was only heightened.[54]

With the end of the war not yet imminent, Moran Weston and the Freedom Fighters faced the more immediate issue of the poll tax. Organizing a meeting of the New York State Committee to Abolish the Poll Tax at the Hotel Capitol in midtown, the Victory Committee initiated a renewed campaign to eliminate the restriction that kept thousands of African Americans from the ballot box and allowed segregationist senators to enjoy the safety of their seats in Washington. Taking heart from *Smith v. Allwright*, the decision the Supreme Court announced earlier that month to outlaw the white Democratic primary in Texas, a coalition of politicians, community activists, and union members pledged themselves to the poll-tax fight and offered to dedicate even more resources to support the upcoming Negro Freedom Rally, which would make the poll tax a central issue. While the Victory Committee reached out to New York senator Robert Wagner, the reliable advocate of anti-lynching legislation, members of the Freedom Fighters campaign solicited contributions throughout Harlem. From the pulse of activity that April, and the promise of another stellar night at Madison Square Garden, Weston predicted the impending demise of the poll tax.[55]

The sanguine outlook Moran Weston expressed in "Labor Forum" that April harmonized with the optimism of *New World Coming,* the centerpiece of the 1944 Negro Freedom Rally. That month Weston arranged for the twenty-nine-year-old Brooklyn poet, playwright, and navy veteran Owen Dodson to write and direct the rally pageant, which borrowed its title from *New World A-Coming,* an impressionistic survey of Harlem and the state of contemporary race relations by the black journalist Roi Ottley. Published in 1943, Ottley's book set the tenor for 1944. On Saturday mornings that spring, a serialization of the work appeared in the *Amsterdam News;* on Sunday afternoons, the liberal independent radio station WMCA aired *New World A'Coming,* a program in which narrator Canada Lee gave strident voice to the Harlem Double V campaign, stressing black patriotism while candidly identifying the constraints of Jim Crow. That June, the Negro Freedom Rally would provide a climactic expression of this at the Garden. After an initial meeting at Adam Clayton Powell, Jr.'s home on St. Nicholas Avenue on a Saturday afternoon in late April, playwright Dodson went swiftly to work. He had a draft completed by May 1st, bearing the subtitle "An Original Pageant of Hope."[56] Weston attempted to work just as efficiently, publishing a three-part "Labor Forum" series outlining necessary civil improvements in Harlem, and arranging to have Duke Ellington, the premier African American band leader, perform for the rally. The year before, Ellington, a dependable defender of black causes, had debuted *Black, Brown, and Beige* at Carnegie Hall, an expressive interpretation of the African American historical experience; in December, he had even been moved to name a new piece *New World A-Comin,'* which also served as the introductory theme of the radio broadcast. By the end of the month, as pageant rehearsals were held downtown at the Institute for International Democracy and in Harlem at the Ethiopian World Federation Hall, Weston secured the cooperation of the Freedom Fighters and radical labor organizers in distributing thousands of flyers advertising the rally and for "mobilizing the people." The *Amsterdam News, Age, People's Voice,* and *Daily Worker* each kept close tabs on rally preparation, the articles serving as welcome publicity for the June 26 extravaganza.[57]

In early June, news from the warfront deepened this hopeful mood, even as it underscored the need for organizations like the Negro Labor Victory Committee to maintain a vigilant domestic fight for freedom. New Yorkers, black and white, celebrated word of the allied invasion of Normandy, a massive, long-in-planning amphibious assault across the English Channel to free German-controlled France that was called, simply, "D-Day." Reports of the invasion heralded the opening of a new western front, kindling hope of a quickening end to the conflagration. Duly moved to patriotic jubilance, members of the Victory Committee could also be expected to notice that there was little mention of black soldiers' participation in the invasion, for Negro men in uniform had been kept from combat during D-Day, relegated to support duties: manning barrage balloons, transporting supplies, preparing food. (On *New World A'Coming*, listeners were reminded that discrimination also remained prevalent in the nation's industries.) This segregated reality contrasted with the integrated ideal the labor political cartoonist Ben Yomen conjured to illustrate the "New World A-Coming." In the advertisements and publicity posters for the 1944 Negro Freedom Rally, a black and white soldier are on the warfront, standing shoulder to shoulder, with no color line to divide them and only democratic aspirations to unite them. Bearing rifles with bayonets, the two infantrymen are poised to reach a liberated global postwar order; barring their way is the barbed wire of "Hitlerism," "Jim Crow," and "Anti-Semitism." Their visages are determined and their eyes are trained on the word "FREEDOM," rising as a sun on a distant horizon. With the combination of patriotic unity and a commitment to equality, the imagery implied, victory over fascist foes was inevitable, freedom as certain as the dawn. Bringing this hopeful theme to Madison Square Garden, the rally promised a program of unity "Behind our Commander-in-Chief for a speedy victory—a just and lasting peace," with notable speakers demanding that equality reach ballot boxes as well as Army battalions, and "a colorful pageant" featuring Duke Ellington and Pearl Primus. While Harlem churches and union locals sold tickets, a week before the rally the Victory Committee celebrated D-Day during Negro Freedom Sunday. A Freedom Parade winding up Lenox Avenue from 127th Street to Dorrance Brooks Square at St. Nicholas and 136th Street—a symbolically appropriate choice, named for a member of the 369th Infantry Regiment, the Harlem Hell-fighters, killed in battle in France during World War I—ended with speeches and prayers in recognition of the allied invasion and demands for a domestic D-Day. The event marked the beginning of a week of pageant rehearsals and announcements meant to heighten anticipation for the 26th, festivities that even included the naming of two "Miss Negro Victory Workers."[58]

Covering the night of the rally, the *People's Voice* estimated an attendance topping twenty-five thousand. It was only a modest exaggeration. As they filled Madison Square Garden, the audience members looked down at a characteristic patriotic setting: a blue stage with a raised, red star-shaped platform at its center. Above, a banner hanging from the rafters indicated both wartime unity and political aspirations: "With FDR for victory in 1944!" The place of Benjamin Davis, Jr., on the speaker's program served as an appropriate reminder of African Americans' potential political influence. Following the 1943 rally, the Victory Committee had helped elect Davis to the city council; this summer, Adam Clayton Powell, Jr., was seeking a congressional seat. The eminent figures speaking that night demonstrated the interracial support the Victory Committee could muster in support of the war, candidate Powell, and the effort to smash the triple Axis of segregation, discrimination, and racism in the United States. From the National Council of Negro Women came Charlotte Hawkins Brown; from the American Jewish Congress came Steven Wise. Elected officials and union officers also stepped up to the microphones and offered a chorus to Powell's welling appraisal of their moment in history. Between a Pearl Primus "blues dance" and a Josh White guitar ballad, Powell took the stage demanding—in a phrase taken from his congressional campaign—that America "Let My People Go—NOW!" Turning as he spoke to face each side of the Garden audience, Powell exhorted, "We serve notice that the day has finally arrived on the American scene when no bigoted, race-hating, anti-Semitic, labor-baiting, jimcrow-ing un-American minority is going to be able to stand up against the righteous wrath of a united American people." When this elicited a roar, Powell shouted back, "If we are good enough to fight to make the world safe for democracy then, by the grace of God and the power of a united mass, we are going to have a full Democracy—Right Now!"

"The rafters rang with the blast of applause," one observer noted, as Powell returned to his seat, "mopping his brow and overcome with the intensity of his own deliverance of . . . one of the most forceful speeches of the evening." Following Powell, a Broadway Salute, featuring Paul Robeson and the members of the cast of

Othello, among other plays, took a bow and offered their commitment. Duke Ellington's orchestra sounded the chords of the original pageant theme *New World A-Comin,'* accompanying Owen Dodson's eight-scene dramatization of the international struggle against fascism. The pageant brought the Negro Freedom Rally poster to life: an interracial, multinational alliance embodied in the soldiers and workers pledged to defeat Hitlerism, anti-Semitism, and Jim Crow. Attempting a poetic pastiche, Dodson had one character speak the mournful lines of his own widely known piece, "Black Mother Praying in the Summer of 1943," a condemnation of race riots. Another, standing for the segregationist Speaker of the House, intoned the words of the poet Countee Cullen:

> Before I'd let a nigger vote
> Or match me place for place
> With my own hands I'd slash my throat
> To spite that nigger's face.
> I'd raise my hand in holy heil,
> March with the Germans knee for knee.
> Niggers may be American
> But Hitler's white like me!

In contrast to this dark ode to white supremacy, the pageant provided a more convivial chorus, giving 1944 a theme to sing along to:

> There's a new world a-coming, come on
> We've buried Jim Crow, we'll keep him down
> White supremacy has no crown
> Come on, come on
> and on and on and on!

When the singing ended and the pageant lights dimmed, Moran Weston intended to conclude the evening by reading the rally's twelve-point resolution. But as he finished, Mayor Fiorello La Guardia and Congressman Vito Marcantonio, both arriving late to the Garden, each insisted on taking the microphone to praise the pageant, to uphold the principles of the rally, and to pledge their ongoing support to the cause of Negro Freedom.[59]

"There's a new world a coming," Moran Weston wrote a week later, "and it will get here pretty fast if the 25,000 people who were at the Negro Freedom Rally at Madison Square Garden last week have anything to do with it." Statements of enthusiasm from two of the city's most powerful politicians was perhaps the smallest indication of the rally's potential. With "the center of power among the Negro people . . . rapidly shifting to the trade unions," he predicted, African

Americans indeed stood on the brink of freedom. Weston did not reserve his expression of enthusiasm for his column. Addressing Victory Committee meetings in Elizabeth, New Jersey, and Harlem in early July, he declared the rally "a success on every point." Weston's efforts earned him a welcome raise in salary and lent strength to the political campaign the Victory Committee launched that month for Adam Clayton Powell, Jr., and Vito Marcantonio. Using the rally momentum to prepare for the citywide primary elections on August 1st, the Victory Committee held the first of its open-air rallies in July outside the Harlem YWCA. While "brazen threats of violence" had kept thousands of African American voters from the July primaries in Georgia, despite the *Smith v. Allwright* decision, Weston commended the CIO in Texas and Arkansas for setting "in motion the most extensive political action program in history" in each state. In New York, too, Weston argued, noting the anniversary of the Harlem Riot of 1943, "the people of Harlem have an opportunity to do something in an **organized way**. They have an opportunity to nominate the first Negro Congressman from New York. This will make a real blow at jim crow. Rioting is the wrong way. VOTING IS THE RIGHT WAY"—a point underscored when Powell and Marcantonio both made the November ballot.[60]

Turning to the transit workers' strike wracking Philadelphia during the first week of August, Weston contended that the labor–civil rights alliance was essential for fostering progress now, after the November elections, and in the rapidly approaching postwar era. At the same time the CIO boosted black electoral power in the South, Weston pointed out, the union was also challenging segregation in such northern workplaces as the Philadelphia transit system. After years of attempts to secure better jobs for blacks with the Philadelphia Transportation Company, that summer the newly formed CIO Transit Workers Union had set new nondiscrimination policies in motion. But when the company chose eight black porters to train to become streetcar conductors, six thousand white employees struck in protest, effectively shutting down commuter service in Philadelphia. Joining the NAACP and the National Negro Congress, the Victory Committee angrily petitioned President Roosevelt to act. Convinced, rather, by the mayor of Philadelphia (who feared a riot), the Roosevelt administration interceded, sending in the army to quell the strike and return the city's streetcars to service. Advocates of integration declared it a victory. "It was the first time since Reconstruction Days," wrote Weston triumphantly, "that the Federal Government had used troops to protect the rights of Negroes."[61] While desegregation of the transit system began in Philadelphia, the Victory Committee scheduled a fall program dedicated to continued agitation for desegregation in AFL unions and the armed forces, addressing postwar job security, and to the November elections. In "Labor Forum," Weston repeated what had become an annual call for the New York AFL to integrate its leadership positions during its statewide convention. Though the AFL did not respond as hoped, the Victory Committee determined to maintain pressure, calling upon both the president and the secretary of the navy to desegregate the military. Victory Committee officials received an assuaging response, but they wanted civil rights, not civil replies. Acknowledging that this would require political pressure, Weston offered his yearly September instructions on how to register to vote. He also reserved his "Labor Forum" column that month to describing reconversion as a major postwar political issue. Black workers would likely face a crisis after the war if segregation was allowed to persist and if industry followed "last hired, first fired" seniority policies.[62]

Moran Weston devoted himself to another season of electioneering. Coordinating again with the American Labor Party, "during Registration Week and the week before," Weston noted, the Victory Committee held fifty-eight outdoor rallies "on the street corners from 110th Street to 155th Street on Sugar Hill." Canvassing resulted in the registration of thousands of new voters, which the ALP and Victory Committee understood to mean that Harlem would "hold the potential balance of power in New York State." Urging "a new approach" come election time, Weston encouraged the community not to dwell on party affiliation but to vote according to which candidate "is most likely to continue to fight against discrimination in employment, in the armed forces and in politics." Five ALP clubs in Harlem promoted the candidacies of Adam Clayton Powell, Jr., and Vito Marcantonio, culminating with a Victory Committee–sponsored parade and November 1st rally of six thousand at the Golden Gate Ballroom. It had been more than two years since Powell first announced his run, during the March on Washington Movement's June 1942 rally at Madison Square Garden, and he was now on the verge of becoming a congressman.[63]

The election of Powell to the House of Representatives encouraged Moran Weston, but now was no time to relent. Contending that the road to victory did not end with the elections, Weston returned to Victory Committee fieldwork, preaching, as he traveled between Buffalo, Detroit, and Chicago, the same points he argued in "Labor Forum." The war "still requires everything we've got as a nation," he explained. "The poll tax, jim crow, discrimination against minorities, post-war employment and security," each a roadblock to full victory, "are still on the order of the day." In New York, if not across the nation, this meant taking an active role in legislative hearings the New York State Commission Against Discrimination planned to hold in early December. At 308 Lenox Avenue, the Victory Committee executives studied two proposed bills outlawing discrimination in employment. Weston arranged for Charles Collins's participation in the Commission's three-day hearings, arguing that the Victory Committee had "carried on an extensive campaign in support of antidiscrimination legislation relating particularly to employment" and that "any legislation proposed by the Commission" ought to have its endorsement. And any positive developments in New York also ought to set national precedent. The CIO, as Weston affirmed in "Labor Forum," had long called for "labor to take the lead in the fight to end discrimination and segregation in America." The New York hearings were a good start, and, as he outlined in several columns through December, the next step needed to be the establishment of a permanent FEPC.[64]

What the Victory Committee had called for in 1944 Weston hoped to achieve in 1945. Teaching an adult education course concerning labor issues at the progressive Carver School on Tuesday nights and participating in the Harlem-based Carver Democratic Club left him optimistic about the potential for grassroots activism above 125th Street. His record—with the Victory Committee, on the 1943 and 1944 election campaigns, in "Labor Forum"—had even led to gossip about his challenging incumbent Benjamin Davis, Jr., for a seat on the city council in 1945. For his part, though, Weston was intent on pursuing the Victory Committee's program. In January, he helped arrange the Victory Committee's Harlem Ball in celebration of Adam Clayton Powell, Jr.'s inauguration to Congress. That night the committee announced it would send delegates to the National Conference on the Negro and Postwar Employment in Chicago, which Weston would report on in early February during the Carver Democratic Club's Conference on Harlem's Post-War Problems, and again in March during the Victory Committee's own conference on reconversion. While planning the March meeting, though, Weston kept keen watch on the hearings in Albany concerning the Ives-Quinn Bill, legislation prohibiting employment discrimination that had evolved from the New York State Commission Against Discrimination hearings in December. Using "Labor Forum" to urge Harlem to unite and stymie potential opposition to the bill, he advised, "The road to victory over discrimination in employment in New York State . . . is for the people themselves to get on the warpath and smother the opposition with an avalanche of letters, telegrams, postcards, meetings and delegations in Albany in support of the bills."[65]

When the landmark Ives-Quinn Bill for a permanent New York State FEPC passed in March, Weston drew a lesson. "The overwhelming majority of the American people and their leaders," he maintained, "can be united behind a realistic legislative program to protect the democratic rights of all Americans." Still, he contended, "the job is not finished." Civil rights and labor leaders still needed to force the founding of a permanent FEPC in Washington and to "rally in support of legislation to outlaw discrimination in the field of housing." New York could serve as a national model—in fact, he noted after visits with Victory Committee affiliates outside Harlem, similar bills were pending in New Jersey and Pennsylvania. Yet organized labor also needed to ensure the protection of black workers' rights during the reconversion to a peacetime economy. Asking that "the labor movement see to it that gains made by Negroes during the war are safeguarded and extended," Moran Weston chaired the Metropolitan Area Labor Conference on Reconversion and Related Problems that the NLVC convened for two hundred delegates over two days at the Fraternal Clubhouse. The Victory Committee had rallied for Negro Freedom during the war, helping elect black politicians, supporting the FEPC, testifying at antidiscrimination hearings, creating antidiscrimination committees within unions, and sending delegations to Washington. But the Victory Committee would also need to adjust its program to address postwar concerns, both international and domestic. During the Fraternal Clubhouse meetings, the Victory Committee announced it would dedicate the third annual Negro Freedom Rally to this program, renewing, as Weston put it both in "Labor Forum," and in Detroit while speaking at a Ford workers meeting, the message that "labor must take the lead in the abolition movement of today"—starting with the abolition of Jim Crow in employment.[66]

That spring, however, while the fall of Germany appeared inevitable, that the FEPC would be made permanent seemed improbable. The commission, Weston lamented, had yet to gain the support of the AFL and faced stiff opposition from "clever reactionaries" in the Capitol. Nevertheless, he insisted, "the closer we come to V-E Day, the more urgent it becomes that we have a permanent federal FEPC ready to protect the job gains of minorities, especially Negroes." Through May, as the wartime imperative of the commission faded, the Victory Committee spearheaded local efforts to save the FEPC. As the Victory Committee organized the June Negro Freedom Rally to bring thousands together in support of a permanent FEPC, the Manhattan council of the National Negro Congress (which, tellingly, had opened a new office near the Victory Committee on Lenox Avenue) prepared an eight-page pamphlet on the implications of the Ives-Quinn antidiscrimination law. The pamphlet made a fine educational supplement to the rally preparations, Weston thought, and President Roosevelt's death that April added poignancy to the rally's postwar theme: "Carry on, America." That spring, the Freedom Rally posters featured the former president smiling from the heavens as black and white hands grasp each other in solidarity.[67]

The Victory Committee was not content to simply appeal to the late president's memory. Hoping to make the Negro Freedom Rally a vehicle for ongoing activity, the Victory Committee held rally meetings each Friday through May and June at the 135th Street YMCA and, in the Bronx, at St. Augustine Church on Prospect Avenue and 165th Street. With the FEPC's appropriations in danger of being withheld, Weston wrote, "the time has come for labor to organize mass delegations from the districts of these backsliding Congressmen to pin them down in support of the FEPC. Letters, telegrams, petitions are important. But they are not enough in this crisis. People must make known their determination to keep the FEPC by demonstrating their support in person." The Bronx committee leader echoed this statement, reminding rally supporters that "these are critical times, and it is most urgent that we have this great mass demonstration to impress upon those forces of reaction within our midst that we will no longer tolerate their sabotage of such progressive measures as the FEPC, and Anti-Poll Tax Bills." To better broadcast this appeal, in June the Victory Committee organized street-corner meetings to support the preservation of the FEPC. In the weeks leading up to the Madison Square Garden rally, "prominent labor, church and civil leaders" appeared each night between 112th and 137th Streets along Fifth, Lenox, Seventh, Eighth, and St. Nicholas Avenues. Announcing it planned to honor an industrial corporation with an FEPC Merit Award for distinguished compliance with antidiscrimination policies, the Victory Committee also demanded that pressure be put on the New York State Committee Against Discrimination to avoid "staging a make-believe fight against discrimination." No token committee would be acceptable. Like the NAACP, which had organized a mass civil rights protest in Washington on June 22, the Victory Committee intended the Negro Freedom Rally to galvanize support for the FEPC with an eye toward the summer primaries and fall elections. "Congress," Moran Weston wrote, "needs a good housecleaning."[68]

With Madison Square Garden again filled to capacity on June 25, and a "million dollars" of entertainment (in the words of the *Amsterdam News*), Adam Clayton Powell, Jr., could speak to this assessment from experience. Reporting on his first six months in Congress, Powell remarked, "I am proud to stand here tonight and say that time has vindicated us, that the concept of democracy has become enriched by virtue of the righteous indignation and the disciplined resentment of the Negro men." Still, he asserted, "two things face the Negro people today of paramount importance. One, the problem of jobs in the post-war world, and two, the problem of Jim Crow in the United States Army now—in wartime— and later—in peacetime." Powell had recently offered a House resolution to end segregation in the armed forces, but he also urged that "unless the FEPC bill is passed . . . Negroes and their white allies in New York, Detroit, Chicago, and Los Angeles [should] take to the streets again on the picket lines and win freedom." Victory Committee cochairmen Ferdinand Smith and Charles Collins, the National Council of Negro Women's Mary McLeod Bethune, and FEPC chairman Malcolm Ross joined Powell in appealing for mass action to "aid in the fight to save the FEPC." The FEPC "has many and powerful enemies," Ross admitted, but it "must not be abandoned." Councilman Benjamin Davis, Jr., engaged in his own citywide challenge of Jim Crow, added the need for a strong New York FEPC, arguing that African Americans "will not be satisfied with less than full and unconditional citizenship." This sentiment pervaded the dramatic revue *Carry On—America*, cowritten by Langston Hughes, and featuring a familiar cast of black stars, including Paul Robeson, Canada Lee, Hazel Scott, Muriel Rahn, Josh White, and Pearl Primus. With the Nazi surrender, the allied triumph over fascism was assured, but victory on the home front remained unfinished. "Victory is what you make it," the pageant of 1945 encouraged, stressing that Roosevelt's Four Freedoms remained attainable through concerted action. Roosevelt had passed on but, encouragingly, a telegram from President Truman greeted the rally. After reading this welcome recognition, Moran Weston repeated the evening's appeal, setting "the keynote in a brilliant address," and ending, in the view of the *Daily Worker*, the most inspiring Negro Freedom Rally yet held.[69]

Plaudits did little to dispel the frustration Moran Weston felt that summer. After the rally he could summon neither enthusiasm nor optimism in "Labor Forum." While the New York State Commission Against Discrimination opened its doors on July 1, Congress crippled the FEPC, voting to sustain its funding through June 30, 1946, but with only half its budget intact. With the end of the war in Europe, fair employment was deemed expendable. This was a consequence of conservative opposition to integration, but in Weston's estimation, the defeat of the FEPC also stemmed from fundamental weaknesses in the labor movement. The AFL, CIO, and railroad brotherhoods had simply been unable

The Negro Freedom Rally pageants emphasized the contribution of African American soldiers during World War II, as depicted here during the 1945 rally. M. Moran Weston Papers, Rare Book and Manuscript Library, Columbia University in the City of New York.

to find an antidiscriminatory common ground and combine in a potent pressure group. This meant reconversion would demand a united fight no less committed than the wartime Double V campaigns. The CIO had a plan for the postwar era, but realizing the AFL would not willingly abolish Jim Crow among its own ranks, Weston urged greater initiative and organization among African Americans. Whether in "unions, fraternal organizations, churches, political clubs and civic organizations," he advised that African Americans "must find a way to work together on a national and local basis." Such groups, in cooperation "with powerful regional organizations, such as the Negro Labor Victory Committee of Greater New York," he insisted, simply must "carry on the fight against American fascism."[70]

This imperative was all the more apparent later that summer. Visiting Buffalo in early August, Weston found the city rife with rumors of impending mass unemployment for African American workers. Recent layoffs, he suspected, justified the fear, as did the abrupt end of the war in Japan. After warning of an interminable siege, the Truman administration instead dropped atomic weapons on Hiroshima and Nagasaki, achieving swift surrender. In Harlem, reticence accompanied jubilation. In the weeks following V-J Day, two dozen New York industries laid off thousands of black laborers—nearly 45 percent of their black workforce. And the implications of peacetime for the future of the Victory Committee, created as a wartime organization, were unclear. Even without a war abroad, the committee wished to pursue the fight for full and fair employment on the home front and considered African American political power crucial to the future of American democracy.[71]

In September, as the war in the Pacific came to an official end, Weston assumed responsibilities for organizing the Victory Committee's political campaign. The electoral work that fall, which Weston launched with a speech on the corner of 145th Street and Amsterdam Avenue, focused on reelecting Benjamin Davis, Jr., to city council and addressing reconversion. Over the past two years, Davis had earned this support, offering steadfast commitment to confronting Jim Crow in New York; in the next two years he would prove a welcome ally, challenging discrimination in the workplace. In October, the electoral campaign intersected with that month's two-day Emergency Job Conference held at the Harlem YWCA and the Golden Gate Ballroom, sponsored by a coalition of labor groups and civil rights organizations including the New York branch of the NAACP, the National Negro Congress, and the Victory Committee. Between organizing outdoor rallies and voter canvassing, Weston observed that the conference "represents the first attempts by labor and civic organizations in this community since V-J Day to get together and do something about the vital problem of jobs for the millions of veterans returning from the battle fronts." Meetings, however, could only begin to provide for an equitable reconversion process.

"Political action by the people is necessary to win their crusade for jobs for all without discrimination." The Victory Committee aimed to facilitate such action as it campaigned throughout Harlem. Coordinating nearly sixty rallies through early November, the Victory Committee and ALP together distributed fifty thousand leaflets, placed advertisements in papers, erected outdoor signs, held torchlight parades, and hired two trucks towing nine-by-fifteen-foot wooden billboards to drive throughout the assembly district. In late October, they sponsored a Café Show and Reception for Benjamin Davis, Jr., at Small's Paradise: Paul Robeson's baritone boomed, Imogene Coca cracked wise, and Duke Ellington, Josh White, and Teddy Wilson each performed selections from the contemporary canon of jazz and blues. The same combination of progressive politics, public agitation, and cultural spectacle that had defined the Victory Committee's program during war years would help return Davis to the city council. It made for a fine valediction for the Victory Committee.[72]

In the weeks after the November 1945 elections, the Victory Committee quietly dissolved. Inaugurated with such fanfare in 1942, the organization enjoyed no final fete at the end of 1945. With the end of the war, the Victory Committee's Double V rhetoric had become less meaningful and its programs less distinguishable from those of the National Negro Congress. Revitalized nationally in recent months to deal a "death blow to Jim Crow," the NNC absorbed the Victory Committee in Harlem in the winter of 1946, placing Ferdinand Smith on its executive staff and taking up its plans to picket the White House demanding a permanent FEPC. The legacy of the Victory Committee in New York, however, would be evident in the postwar years as the radical left continued to make agitation against police brutality, segregated housing, and discriminatory employment the critical foci of a bellwether regional civil rights struggle—and the object of conservative scorn. The politics of the progressive wartime front plagued former Victory Committee participants. In several years, the attorney general would declare any association with the Victory Committee evidence of treason. Even having performed during the 1944 Negro Freedom Rally, as one distinguished actor discovered during an early-1950s investigation of un-American activities, was tantamount to disloyalty.[73]

After several peripatetic years of organizing, Moran Weston was becoming increasingly rooted in Harlem. No longer the Victory Committee field secretary, Weston nonetheless continued to press for African Americans' economic and civil rights in the postwar years. "Labor Forum" would still appear every Saturday in the *Amsterdam News*. And there were rumors that he would next seek elected office. His new position (deputy commissioner in the New York City Department of Water Supply, Gas, and Electricity) and his vice presidency of the Eleventh Assembly District Democratic Club seemed to give credence to reports that Weston was "quietly seeking labor's support for the State Senate nomination." Yet the pulpit beckoned more enticingly than public office. More than a decade since Bishop Manning's casual prejudice had flung him "into the wilderness" after his graduation from Union Theological Seminar, Weston found new sanctuary on 134th Street at St. Philip's Episcopal Church, among the oldest and most distinguished African American congregations in New York.[74]

At thirty-five, Milton Moran Weston II was returning to his Tarboro roots, if not to North Carolina. During Reconstruction his family had found faith in the Episcopal Church; in the coming years, as the nation lurched toward a second Reconstruction, Weston wished to reembark on his path toward ordination, keeping racial equity and economic justice at the heart of his personal gospel even as the postwar civil rights movement promised to transform the nation.

The Question of Ralph
Bunche's Loyalty

After it was over, Ralph Bunche read his mail. From an envelope postmarked May 29, 1954, Howard University, Washington, DC, he took out a handwritten note. On it, two lines of thin cursive congratulated him: "Dear Doctoré, We glad you win." Dashed off at one in the morning by a half dozen of Bunche's friends and former colleagues, the note was signed "Sincerely, the Thinkers and Drinkers." After a Friday evening of highballs and poker, Sterling the Dutchman, Frank F., Sam Dorsey, Mau Mau, Rabbit, and John Hope Franklin had each raised their tumblers in a toast to Ralph Bunche, the test of whose mettle had just come to an end after two days of testimony before a loyalty board in New York City.[1]

The first news of the hearings had appeared in the Wednesday dailies. The *New York Times* reported that "Dr. Ralph J. Bunche, one of the United Nation's top officials," had been called before the International Organizations Employees Loyalty Board after "a full Federal Bureau of Investigation inquiry." The *Times* revealed nothing more of the content or the context of the investigation, but the following day careful *Times* readers could infer the charge. Two witnesses, each "admitted former Communists," had testified.[2]

Even the appearance of "Communist connections," as the *Times* put it, tainted Bunche, who in May 1954 was perhaps the most renowned African American of his generation. The details of his life were well known. Raised in Los Angeles, Bunche graduated with distinction from the University of California, Los Angeles, in 1927 and earned his doctorate at Harvard University in 1934. During the 1930s and early 1940s he helped modernize the Howard University political science department and served as the Swedish social scientist Gunnar Myrdal's lead research assistant for the Carnegie Corporation survey of African American life, published in 1944 as *An American Dilemma*. During World War II the Office of Strategic Services (OSS) employed Bunche as a specialist on African affairs, which led to a post with the State Department, where Bunche proved instrumental in launching the United Nations (UN). His role as the UN's mediator for

RALPH BUNCHE, 1950s. Library of Congress, Prints and Photographs Division, Carl Van Vechten Collection.

negotiating peace between Israel and several Arab states over Palestine gained him both international prominence and the 1950 Nobel Peace Prize.[3]

Yet Bunche's position in 1954 as the UN's highest ranking American earned him no reprieve from questioning concerning his past. Indeed, his reputation likely only made the allegations of his sympathy to Communism more pressing to investigate. Naturally, Bunche deplored the insinuation. But with witnesses "clamoring to be heard," the loyalty board claimed it simply "had to hear them." If it did not pursue the accusations, "in view of the atmosphere of today" the board would otherwise "lay itself open to [the] possible charge that it was 'protecting Communists.'" Bunche had little choice but to acquiesce.[4]

He was not alone. Legitimized in national politics during the onset of the Cold War, anti-Communism had come to affect a vast number of Americans. The House Un-American Activities Committee, long a device to suppress the left, became permanent in 1945. In 1947, the Taft-Hartley Act requiring union leaders to renounce Communism in order to use the National Labor Relations

Board survived President Truman's veto and protest among labor and civil rights leaders. Despite his veto, though, Truman was committed to containing the Communist threat purportedly posed both by the Soviet Union abroad and by "front" organizations at home. In March 1947 he signed an executive order establishing a Federal Employee Loyalty Program to investigate suspect individuals; it also authorized the investigation of organizations deemed subversive. The Justice Department and FBI made extensive use of this latitude.[5]

By the early 1950s, the impact on the labor and civil rights movement was unmistakable. The AFL, already hostile toward the left, quickly complied with Taft-Hartley. The CIO, too, targeted Communists and suspected Communists within its ranks, even revoking the charters of entire unions. Among Ralph Bunche's generation of African American leaders, those who had pressed for black economic equality were most at risk for scrutiny and persecution. Indeed, Bunche himself had already answered to investigators about his past. In 1943 he had reported to a formal civil service investigation during his appointment to the OSS. In New York after the war, former Victory Committee executives Charles Collins and Ferdinand Smith faced union expulsion and, because they had both been born in the West Indies, deportation. Benjamin Davis, Jr., an avowed Communist, endured a nine-month trial, then served four years in prison. While members of the black left in New York were a particular target, national figures were not immune. The FBI had long followed Adam Clayton Powell, Jr., and the State Department revoked the passports of both Paul Robeson and W. E. B. Du Bois. Rather than protest, even with Du Bois in handcuffs at eighty-two, the national NAACP responded to anti-Communism much as organized labor had. During its annual convention in June 1950, the Association resolved to purge its branches of Communists. By the early 1950s, such repression had stifled the dynamic movement to link labor and civil rights activism in a broader program of economic transformation, leaving former activists wondering if—or when—they might be next.[6]

For Ralph Bunche, it began with a phone call—long distance—from the White House on Saturday, January 9, 1954. On the other end of the line, Maxwell Rabb introduced himself. Bunche did not know President Eisenhower's aide but he "immediately suspected" that the call "might mean trouble." He had not heard anything about his security clearance since submitting the requisite paperwork the previous winter. When Rabb explained that he would be in New York on Monday, Bunche could not help suspect the reason for the visit.[7]

Bunche had addressed questions about his background the previous March, submitting to a "regular third degree" by two members of a loyalty committee empowered by an executive order that President Truman had signed shortly before leaving office. The events that most interested Bunche's inquisitors had occurred nearly twenty years earlier. They wanted to know the extent of his involvement in the founding of the National Negro Congress, and more specifically, they wished to understand the circumstances surrounding a May 1935 Howard University conference on the Negro and the New Deal. Bunche explained that he had taken part in both the formation of the NNC and the Howard conference, but he also stressed that he had never been involved with the Communist Party. Even as he offered his explanation, though, he suspected that his answers had not satisfied the investigators. When, after ten months of silence, Maxwell Rabb phoned him, expectation of such a call had never been far from his mind.[8]

Two days later, Rabb arrived at Bunche's office at the United Nations with Pierce Gerety, an attorney from Bridgeport, Connecticut, who was the chairman of the International Organizations Employees Loyalty Board. Rabb began the conversation amiably, offering that President Eisenhower "thought very highly" of America's top man in the UN. Even so, Gerety's board could not ignore the "derogatory information" it had in their files on Bunche. Gerety was oblique, wondering aloud what the board ought to do about the allegations. Bunche stopped himself from suggesting that they, as he later wrote, "stick it up etc." Instead, he "kept cool" and told his visitors exactly what they hoped to hear, replying "that in view of the information given on my questionnaire" the previous March he had "been anticipating an interrogatory from the Board," especially since he fully "expected to be treated like every other American employed in the UN—no better and no worse." Visibly relieved, Gerety explained the accusations against Bunche in more detail.[9]

It was just as Bunche had guessed. The board members could not square his avowed distance from Communism with his acknowledged involvement with the National Negro Congress, a recognized Communist front organization. Bunche knew different, but rather than challenge their interpretation by explaining the roots of the NNC, he struck upon a different tack. To parry their implied accusation he would show them that he had been on their side all along. Bunche asked if Gerety knew that he himself had exposed the Communist's "capture" of the NNC in 1940; he had written about it at length, he said, in a research memorandum for the Myrdal-Carnegie study. Gerety shook his head: "He didn't." The memorandum had never been published, but Bunche had a bound copy of the typescript in his office. He pulled it from the shelf and flipped to page 319, where his fifty-page chapter on the National Negro Congress began. Next, he took down sociologist Wilson Record's 1951 study, the definitively anti-Communist *The Negro and the Communist Party*, which described Bunche's work as "the most incisive evaluation of the first meeting of the Congress and the whole movement over a four-year period." Gerety, Bunche could tell, "was much interested." Yet, Gerety explained, his board would still need to pursue the matter. He told Bunche to expect the formal interrogatory in the mail "in a few days." Normally, responses were expected within ten days, but Bunche could take longer if he needed. Bunche remained composed and said flatly that he "would welcome the opportunity to answer any and all derogatory information," even though he believed that his "open record ought to be answer enough." The meeting ended with pleasantries; then, Bunche waited.[10]

The interrogatory arrived at his office in the UN the following weekend. When Bunche signed for the "big fat Civil Service envelope" that been delivered by special post, he realized why Gerety had suggested that he take his time responding. The cover letter enumerated fourteen allegations against him. A few Bunche had expected, but others came "very much [as] a surprise." Reading the letter, he found that the "basic and most startling allegation" was that he had "been and may still be a concealed member of the Communist Party." Allegation number fourteen put it the most bluntly: "The Communists are in a position to control you." This conclusion, the board submitted, could be traced back to their information that "on or about May 17, 1935" he had joined a secret Communist Party meeting in John P. Davis's Florida Avenue office in Washington, DC. That day, the board asserted, Bunche had helped plot a Communist takeover of the National Negro Congress. The interrogatory made several other points, as well, that may have seemed innocuous on their own but suggested a disquieting pattern in sum. During the late 1930s Bunche's name had appeared in the masthead of *Science and Society*, a journal since designated by the attorney general as a Communist organ. A staff member at the OSS whose hiring Bunche had supported during the 1940s had since been investigated as a suspected Communist. It seemed to Bunche, though, that each such allegation traced back to the "basic one" claiming that in May of 1935 he had become a "concealed" member of the Communist Party, planning the penetration of the National Negro Congress.[11]

Bunche acknowledged receipt of the interrogatory and requested the extension that Gerety had offered. His mind spun. Because "the basic allegation and the item about the Communist Party meeting were so patently false," it seemed obvious to Bunche "that whoever had made them had done so quite deliberately with malicious intent." But he could not dwell on intent; he "saw immediately" that he faced "a big and most serious job." The trick would be demonstrating what had never happened, what he had never felt. Of course, it would be hard enough to overcome the gaps in time and memory to show what *had* happened, what he *had* felt. His "first task," he decided, "and a tough one, was to take a couple of weeks—nights and week-ends—to search through [his] files at home and at the office" for sources to document his movements and mindset during May 1935—anything, he thought, to "refresh" his "memory on events of nearly a score of years ago."[12]

Bunche quickly exhausted the material in his office at the United Nations. He had his research memoranda for the Carnegie-Myrdal study and the Wilson Record monograph on his shelves, but little else of use. At work, his oldest personal files dated to the 1940s, nothing old enough to refute charges of Communist affiliation during the mid-1930s. That night, however, he searched his basement at home in Kew Gardens in Queens and found amid the domestic clutter "a half dozen big packing boxes and locker trunks full of old dusty papers." He "developed painful hangnails and an aching back" while unpacking these, but even at first glimpse he knew he had uncovered "a gold mine." He found that "almost miraculously" he had "kept and carted" during his move from Washington, DC, to New York "virtually everything" he had ever written. If he regretted that his past at Howard had followed him to the United Nations, finding actual evidence of that past proved to be a coup. Paging through what just a year before might have seemed ephemera—"mimeographed notices of Howard University Social Science Division meetings, conference programs, old letters etc."—Bunche began to place himself back in 1935.[13]

May 17, 1935. He spent several "sleepless nights of cellar exploration" trying to answer what had happened that day. Sorting through his papers, he could not track his movements precisely to the day, but he "gradually began to dig out a good deal of very useful information" that put the moment in context. Several sets of documents seemed most relevant. His response to a 1943 government clearance interview explained his involvement in the Howard University conference and the initial discussions about forming a National Negro Congress. An article on black Washington, DC, that John P. Davis had written for *Fortune* magazine in 1934 described the contemporary intellectual milieu in the "Secret City." Several letters Davis had sent him established their relationship between 1933 and 1936. Memoranda he had written as head of the Social Science Division at Howard disclosed his part in organizing the university's May 1935 symposium on the Negro and the New Deal. A copy of the conference program depicted the scope of the discussions. The *Journal of Negro Education* had published many of the conference papers in January 1936, allowing for a close focus on the main ideas discussed. A selection of his own writings from the period, including a handful of articles from the mid-1930s and his 1936 book *A World View of Race* revealed the particular contours of his own thoughts. Together, Bunche realized, these sources could help him compose—in both broad strokes and in close detail—an intellectual autobiography that put himself, and the Depression-era radicalism the loyalty board in 1954 found so suspect, in careful historical context.[14]

By the end of January, Bunche felt he had identified "an imposing mass" of documents to draw from. With two weeks remaining to write, he gathered these up and took them to his office at the UN. There he would compose his response in private. He "really had to dig in," he wrote later. At once "incensed, disgusted and also frightened at the necessity of doing the reply," he knew that no matter the absurdity of the charges he faced, he stood to have his "entire career and future shattered with immeasurable hardship" to his family. Those evenings he "worked with determination," feeling "grim and angry, and at times almost desperate." But the writing progressed quickly as both adrenaline and the wealth of material he had unearthed helped him along. Soon after he put pen to lined paper he had filled his notepad with his hasty cursive.[15]

He began with a denial.

> I am not now, nor have I ever been a member of the Communist Party, "concealed" or otherwise. Moreover, I have never been a supporter of that party, its candidates or officers. I have never in public or private, in oral or written statement, endorsed the Communist Party, espoused its cause or supported its ends. Its tactics and its revolutionary philosophy and objectives are, and have always been, repugnant to me.[16]

Furthermore, he denied the specific allegation that he had visited John P. Davis's office and participated in a secret Party strategy session to infiltrate the National Negro Congress, writing "I am certain that I did *not* attend" any such meeting. He had, in fact, visited Davis's office that spring, but never as part of a "discussion with anyone, at any time, on the procedures and policies which the Communist Party might employ to take control of the National Negro Congress." Indeed, "On May 17, 1935, there was in existence no 'National Negro Congress'; I knew nothing of any such idea." Bunche would explain further. "I can best deal with" the allegation, he wrote, "by sketching the history of the formation of the National Negro Congress, which I am well qualified to do, since I was active in bringing it about." To answer accusations about events that had never happened and circumstances that had never existed, he would reconstruct what had actually occurred. He knew that his accusers—unnamed, unknown—had the advantage, having made their ugly assertions. He could respond only with what he had uncovered: the context of a young black intellectual who hoped to play a role in expanding the struggle for African American citizenship rights during the 1930s to include the fight to achieve economic equality.[17]

On Saturday morning, May 18, 1935, 250 delegates convened at Frederick Douglass Memorial Hall, the newest building on the Howard University campus, for the opening session of the three-day conference "The Position of the Negro in Our National Economic Crisis." Among them were African American academics and civil rights leaders, white New Dealers and social scientists, and black trade and agricultural workers from the rural South and urban North. After registration, the conferees filled the auditorium, exchanging introductions, renewing acquaintances, and checking programs for the first speaker. He was John P. Davis, scheduled to offer "A Survey of the Problems of the Negro under the New Deal." Davis, most knew, was uniquely positioned to speak on this topic. As chairman of the Joint Committee on National Recovery, he had worked since 1933—at times, single-handedly—to ensure equal treatment for black workers under the alphabet soup of New Deal agencies. Many in the audience that morning had read his exposés on the New Deal, reported in a series of articles published in the *Crisis* and the *New Republic*. In large part, the conference had been Davis's idea; the other organizer was Ralph Bunche.[18]

In early 1935, Ralph Bunche's name was less familiar than that of John P. Davis. Bunche had published modestly (including two pieces in the Urban League's *Opportunity* and an article in the *Journal of Negro Education* derived from his dissertation) and may have seemed overshadowed by such colleagues at Howard as the economist Abram Harris, coauthor of the landmark monograph *The Black Worker*, sociologist E. Franklin Frazier, author of *The Negro Family in Chicago*, and Alain Locke, black America's first Rhodes scholar and editor of the renowned 1925 anthology *The New Negro*. Yet at thirty years old Bunche could stake as clear a claim on the label "emerging young black intellectual" as any in Douglass Hall that morning. The previous June his dissertation, "French Administration in Togoland and Dahomey," had been awarded Harvard University's Toppan Prize for best dissertation completed at the university that year. Later, during the fall of 1934, he had joined a number of black leaders at Shaw University, in North Carolina, for the Conference on Social and Economic Aspects of the Race Problem that would result in the electric but short-lived magazine *Race*. He returned home to Washington, DC, to help organize a December 1934 picket in front of the Justice Department; among a group that included over seventy Howard students, Bunche marched, carried a placard, and wore a noose from his neck, all to protest the National Crime Conference's refusal to condemn lynching. Well known on the Howard campus, by 1935 Bunche had also earned a reputation among Washington activists for his strong stand against "racialism," such as he saw pervading the local New Negro Alliance's boycott campaign, and which he believed would ultimately undermine such civil rights efforts. In March 1935, he addressed the Alliance on "The Tragedy of Racial Introversion," warning the group, "Race is not the basic factor in social causation, it is economic."[19]

Bunche hoped the May conference at Howard would both further enunciate how economic factors could explain "the Negro problem" and also demonstrate the necessity of interracial working-class unity in order for any fight for black civil rights to succeed. Initially, the event had been conceived as several sessions of panel discussion devoted to "The Economic Position of the Negro at Present, with particular reference to the policies of the New Deal." Howard's Social Science Division was to sponsor it as its annual spring conference. Bunche, who had been nominated chair of the division's program committee for the 1934–35 academic year, was responsible for organizing the event. He envisioned a mix of black leaders and New Deal officials, and began arranging for representative speakers. But as he did, each offered the same excuse: John P. Davis had already requested their participation in his own conference on the New Deal's effects on black America.[20]

A phone call to Davis's Florida Avenue office found the head of the Joint Committee on National Recovery amenable to joining forces in a more ambitious collaborative effort. Over the previous two years, Davis had become quite familiar with Bunche and his colleagues at Howard—familiar enough, in fact, to sketch their group portrait, which was printed in a sidebar to a feature on black Washington, DC, in *Fortune*. Bunche's Howard cohort was one reason Davis posited in "The Negroes in Washington" that the capital city was "the US center of Negro culture." Howard, the acme of African American higher education, tipped the balance away from black Manhattan, and its younger faculty members did most of the tipping. They were, in Davis's estimation, as "vigorous minded a group of political scientists and economists as you will find anywhere." They included Abram Harris, the "robust Dr. Ralph Bunche," and "a coming young instructor, Emmett Edward ("Sam") Dorsey, who [stood] six-feet-four and used to be an able-bodied seaman." Davis singled out Harris, who was "recognized as one of the outstanding experts on Marxian theory," as the exemplar. Harris "not only sets the tone of the Howard group," Davis wrote, "but is the national leader of that strong, growing wing of Negro opinion that views the race problem in the light of a class problem and holds that the most important, immediate need of the Negroes is the consolidation of the black and white labor movements." Harris, Davis knew, had just drafted a "Future Plan and Program for the NAACP" that attempted to put these ideas into action. Harris's plan suggested significant changes in how the Association construed the struggle for civil rights and how it oversaw its dozens of branches. Harris's vision of a democratic network of local branches that might provide the base of an interracial, class-based movement for both full citizenship and economic rights struck Davis as the latest significant development in black political and intellectual history. "The Harris wing," he asserted, "is as prominent today as the two great Negro movements" that Booker T. Washington and W. E. B. Du Bois had led a generation earlier. But while members of this group believed "that since most Negroes are workingmen their best chance for social progress lies with the progress of the working-class movement," they should be differentiated from Communists. Their "Marxism," explained Davis, "remains academic, educational rather than political," as they "have no party affiliations and little faith in the influence of any of the existing Marxian political groups." In fact, Davis might have mentioned that Harris, Bunche, Dorsey, and similar thinkers were critical of predictions of class-consciousness rising among African Americans. Most blacks, they argued, had long believed in both the significance of race and the virtues of capitalism, both of which would foil class-consciousness as well as significant civil rights victories.[21]

That Bunche represented this vanguard group of black intellectuals made his offer to combine efforts all the more appealing to Davis. Davis and Bunche, each connected to the city's most influential young black leaders, would have an advantage in recruiting an impressive array of participants for the conference. They began by announcing that they sought "to perform the much needed task of bringing together for careful analysis the factual material of social scientists in various fields who have studied some particular phase of the Negro citizen in the nation's social and economic life." But they also made clear that their conference would not be dedicated to "research for research's sake." Indeed, they explained, "Our purpose is to find out the present social and economic condition of the Negro in America, to determine its effect on our whole national economy and to act on the basis on this data." Inspiring action, they hoped, would differentiate this gathering from previous, less fruitful, social science confabs.[22]

For his part, Davis already had an inkling of the kind of action he would sponsor. Shortly after he mailed invitations to participate in the conference, his article "A Black Inventory of the New Deal" appeared on the newsstands in the May issue of the *Crisis*. The piece lived up to its title, offering an appraisal of the national economic recovery program the Roosevelt administration had implemented, and kept a keen eye on the New Deal's implications for black America. In it, Davis also mentioned the upcoming Howard conference and noted a potential outgrowth of the proceedings—a National Negro Congress. While the meeting sessions would offer the chance for "a candid and intelligent survey of the social and economic condition of the Negro," the result would not simply be "a talk-fest." Analysis, he believed, would "furnish a base for action," and he envisioned convening this Congress as "throughout America as never before Negroes awake to the need for a unity of action on vital economic problems."[23]

For those in Frederick Douglass Memorial Hall that morning who had missed Davis's article, his forty-minute address set the agenda. "This session," he began, "marks for us the beginning of three days of candid inventory of the position of the Negro in our national economic crisis." Abram Harris offered the first rejoinder to Davis's comments, and then responses followed from the floor. From that moment, the conference did not lack for viewpoints or proposed solutions. During the afternoon session on "The Negro Industrial Worker," A. Howard Meyers, the executive director of the Labor Advisory Board of the National Recovery Administration; T. Arnold Hill, executive secretary of the Urban League; and A. Philip Randolph, president of the Brotherhood of Sleeping Car Porters each spoke. That evening delegates heard from eight workers themselves during a "Symposium of Negro Workers and Farmers on the 'New Deal.'" The next morning, discussions were dedicated to "America's Negro Farm Population," and the remainder of Sunday took up "'New Deal' Social Planning and the Negro." In the first session that afternoon, Ralph Bunche presented a "Critique of New Deal Social Planning as It Affects Negroes," his conclusion echoing the position of his Howard colleagues. "New Deal planning," he told his audience, "only serves to crystallize those abuses and oppressions which the exploited Negro citizenry and America have long suffered under laissez-faire capitalism." Following Bunche, W. E. B. Du Bois and Abram Harris considered "What Kind of Social Planning Best Suits the Needs of the Negro," with Du Bois offering an interpretation of past and present options and Harris describing the future outlook.[24]

By the end of Sunday, Bunche believed the conferees had been treated to a wide range of opinions, but he perceived a real "confusion in thinking" and a "lack of any consensus among the Negroes at the Conference as to the ways and means of attacking the Negro problem." Davis agreed. Together they "began to think and talk about the possibility of a further step which might achieve agreement among Negro leaders on a minimum program of action," and they decided to convene a smaller number of delegates to discuss future plans on the final day of the conference at Bunche's home. Davis mimeographed a typed invitation explaining that he and Bunche were "anxious" to confer "with a small group of persons to discuss the possibility of a National Congress for Negro Rights." The smaller meeting, he wrote, "will be held at Dr. Bunche's residence on the campus of Howard University directly after the final adjournment of the conference on the economic status of the Negro on Monday afternoon. We shall have a brief discussion lasting not more than one hour, during which time it is hoped that we will thoroughly canvass the proposal."[25]

Davis passed out invitations during Monday morning sessions on "The Plight of Domestic Labor" and "Unemployment and Relief." Then, after Norman Thomas, the 1932 Socialist candidate for president, laid out "The Answer of the Socialist Party," and James Ford, the Communist Party's 1932 candidate for vice president, argued for "The Answer of the Communist Party" to end the afternoon panel, talk of the conference topic "Next Steps in Light of Present Problems" continued among delegates repairing to Bunche's home just a short walk from Douglass Hall. Bunche's "living room was crowded and the discussion was vigorous," and soon "the idea of the National Negro Congress emerged and began to take shape." As Davis described his vision of a large NNC made up of hundreds of groups and thousands of delegates, Bunche found himself "in strong disagreement over the question" of whether or not "the basis for a National Negro Congress would be more fruitful if it were selective." Bunche thought the scope of Davis's plan was unworkable and suggested a compromise to unwieldy democracy—that the NNC be "confined to a homogeneous group of Negro leaders who could more readily agree on a common program. Then this program could gradually be 'sold' to leaders in other walks in life." To most in the room, Bunche's motion clearly smacked of elitism. Davis's idea "to proceed on the broadest possible front, by calling together leaders of all kinds," won the group's favor. Bunche harbored no ill will for Davis's brainchild, "for the need was great." Still, he doubted its potential effectiveness. The result of such a broad program, he predicted, "would merely reproduce the confusion pathetically apparent at the Howard Conference." Given his position, Bunche would not be asked to take "a prominent role in the planning for the first Congress or in the Congress itself." Yet he remained a sympathetic observer whose interests, in fact, did not diverge very far from those of Davis and his National Negro Congress.[26]

The conference provoked Kelly Miller, the agitated former Howard dean, to claim many among the university's professors had fallen under the charm of Moscow. The ensuing squabble along Georgia Avenue (and in the black press) gave way to a congressional investigation of Miller's "alleged communistic activities" at Howard. But neither gave pause to the conference co-organizers. That summer, as Davis worked to found the National Negro Congress, Bunche offered intellectual direction to the civil rights struggle, seeing "A Critical Analysis of the Tactics and Programs of Minority Groups" into print in the July issue of the *Journal of Negro Education*. "Throughout the world today," Bunche posited in this article, "wherever whites and blacks are present in any significant numbers in the same community, democracy becomes the tool of the dominant elements in the white population in their ruthless determination to keep the blacks suppressed." Of course, he blamed not the institution of democracy but rather the "capitalistic society which fathered it." Turning to the case of the United States, Bunche asserted that "much of what is called prejudice against the Negro can be explained in economic terms." While he and his contemporary African American intellectuals recognized this, "Negro leadership, however, has traditionally put its stress on the element of race; it has attributed the plight of the Negro to a peculiar racial condition." Because of this narrow vision, traditional tactics for achieving full citizenship rights, as Bunche saw it, would be "essentially inefficacious in the long run." He did not mean to suggest that black America "relent in the most determined fight for its rights"; he explained that he hoped black leaders would supplement these efforts by developing broader programs that considered interracial working-class unity paramount in the struggle for full citizenship.[27]

Bunche elaborated on this point that summer, when he addressed the Institution of Race Relations at Swarthmore College outside Philadelphia, presenting an "Economic Analysis of the American Negro Population." In this talk, as in the short book Alain Locke had commissioned him to write, he stressed the economic underpinnings of the "race problem," and also attempted to develop an international perspective. Writing *A World View of Race* occupied Bunche throughout the fall and winter, by which time he traveled to the first National Negro Congress, held in Chicago in February 1936. He served as a discussion leader for one of the smaller panels during the four-day assemblage, and also observed most of the sessions. Counting "three major points of significance," he thought it was "the most interesting event in recent years in the Negro race, from the point of view of the social scientist." To Bunche, the number of people attending the first National Negro Congress indicated the "intense interest and unusual enthusiasm" in the proceedings—it seemed as if, as Davis had written the previous spring, African Americans "as never before" had awoken "to the need for unity." While nearly eight hundred had registered as delegates, during one session Bunche estimated an audience topping eight thousand. And not only how many, but also who had attended the Chicago Congress, impressed Bunche. "For the first time, to my knowledge, this Congress brought together on a large scale Negro leaders, Negro intellectuals, organizers of Negro workers and workers themselves," bridging the distance between intelligentsia and "the masses." Finally, the conference participants' commitment to pursue the National Negro Congress resolutions seemed remarkable. Bunche acknowledged the inevitable conflicts in opinion and personality that arose over the course of the sessions, and also detected flaws in the Congress's organization, but given that "this was an initial effort" made without significant financial backing, he thought the first National Negro Congress a success.[28]

Bunche amplified these impressions in "Triumph?—or Fiasco?" an overview of the National Negro Congress to be published in the summer 1936 issue of *Race*. "The next Congress, in Philadelphia in 1937," he predicted, "should prove a better test of the ability of such a national movement to reach the Negro masses, and, battering down all obstacles, unite them solidly behind the American labor movement." He would look forward to the NNC making progress in the next year as "an effective means of drawing the Negro masses into the mainstream of American organized labor." In the meantime, however, he had another Howard conference to organize for May on "The Crisis of Modern Imperialism in Africa" and an address to deliver before the annual NAACP convention in Baltimore on "Fascism and Minority Groups" in early July, and he was also scheduled to return to Philadelphia that summer to serve as codirector of the Institute of Race Relations.[29]

If this flurry of activity in the past year had not placed him among the most recognized young black intellectuals, then publication of *A World View of Race* would. In this monograph, Bunche situated himself among contemporary political scientists and anthropologists such as Franz Boas, Melville Herskovits, Donald Young, and Otto Klineberg, and engaged in conversation with leading black scholars like W. E. B. Du Bois, Carter Woodson, Abram Harris, Ira de Augustine Reid, George Padmore, Charles Wesley, and E. Franklin Frazier. Here Bunche described race as an impermanent and shifting concept and discussed how it had "become an effective instrument in national politics," offering a close reading of the American case. "Race prejudice" in America, as elsewhere, he wrote, had "deep economic roots" and had been "woven" so "deeply into the fabric of American civilization" that it had become "the great American shibboleth." Although, as Bunche wrote, "it is widely accepted that the 'race problem' is one of the fundamental problems of our society," this single-minded fixation on race had obscured "the fundamental conflicts and issues confronting society" and had become "one of the most serious obstructions in the alignment of the population along the lines of natural class interests." Previous black leaders, he argued, had encouraged "'racial' interpretations" that had hindered "a clear understanding of the true group and class status of the Negro in American society." Such leaders "shy away from any realistic analysis of the population of the Negro in the American social, political and economic structure" and "lead Negroes up the dark, blind alley of black chauvinism." Bunche charged black leadership not just with the task of solving "the so-called 'race problem'" but also with the responsibility of reducing the importance of race itself to allow for "a consciousness of class interest and purpose." African Americans, he wrote, "must strive for an alliance with the white working classes in a common struggle for economic and political equality and justice," because, he wrote, "if the fundamental ailments of the American economy are remedied, the 'race question' will loom less large."[30]

In *A World View of Race* Bunche articulated much the same vision of a civil rights struggle that Davis had described two years earlier as "the Harris wing" centered at Howard University. But while Bunche's Howard colleagues focused most closely on the class dimension of the "race problem," Bunche also hoped to develop an even clearer analysis of the international perspective. In the fall of 1936, while John P. Davis was organizing the second National Negro Congress, Bunche accepted a two-year postdoctoral fellowship funded by the Social Science Research Center, beginning with coursework at Northwestern University with anthropologist Melville Herskovits. Over next two years he studied at the London School of Economics and the University of Cape Town in South Africa, and conducted anthropological field research for a book he envisioned writing on contemporary Africa upon returning to Howard in the fall of 1938. During the spring of 1939, however, he put off his immediate academic plans to join Carnegie-Myrdal study of the Negro in America. That fall, as Davis readied for the third National Negro Congress in Washington, DC, Bunche accompanied Myrdal on a trip through the South, preparing what would become four lengthy monographs on the status of blacks in America.[31]

April 1940 found Bunche, four years removed from the first National Negro Congress in Chicago, attended the third in Washington. There, he witnessed a significant point in the history of the NNC—as he would describe it, the moment of "its capture by the Communists." He first noticed the shift during the opening evening address, when NNC president A. Philip Randolph cautioned members against forging too close a relationship with the Soviet Union. As Randolph called for nonpartisanship, Bunche took note of the number of audience members who left the auditorium in protest. Given this reception, and the subsequent tenor of the conference, Bunche concluded that he had observed "a blind acceptance of the Communist party line." When Randolph resigned on the last day of the conference, Bunche marked "an embarrassing silence and no applause." What had begun in his living room in May 1935 as a plan to redirect the civil rights struggle seemed to him to have been "reduced to a Communist cell." He predicted the National Negro Congress's quick demise.[32]

Writing in his United Nations office in February 1954, Ralph Bunche remembered his reaction to the events of 1940. "My *hopes* for the National Negro Congress," Bunche explained in his reply to the loyalty board, "died with the actions of the Third Congress" in Washington. It was true that between 1935 and 1940, Bunche, like other contemporary black intellectuals, had described race as socially and, more fundamentally, economically constructed. Bunche and his intellectual cohort had hoped this understanding of race would open civil rights efforts to include interracial agitation for economic equality. But their vision was not based on dogmatic theory, as their misgivings about the radicalization of the "Negro masses" demonstrated. They had read Marx, certainly, but they relied, too, on their own experience and on the pragmatic realization that blacks could not expect to gain full, equal citizenship without working to improve the lot of every disadvantaged American, regardless of race. Bunche himself supported steps such as increased involvement in unions and organized labor, but was never willing to trade intellectual flexibility for a rigid party line.[33]

Above all, Bunche wished to highlight his commitment to independent thinking during the 1930s and 1940s in his response to the loyalty board. His Carnegie-Myrdal research memorandum offered the perfect source to draw from. Bunche called his readers' attention to several passages condemning the National Negro Congress's drift leftward. His research, he wrote, presented "very clearly my appraisal of, attitudes toward and conclusions about the National Negro Congress and the finally successful effort of the Communist Party to dominate it." His interpretations, he noted, had even been endorsed by scholarship, having been incorporated into Wilson Record's studiously anti-Communist book *The Negro and the Communist Party*. Yet, even as he cited his objections to Communism in his 1940 memorandum, Bunche wondered whether this and his sketch of his place among the black intelligentsia during the 1930s would adequately rebut the blunt assertion that Communists had been and may still be in a position to control him.[34]

When Bunche finished the first draft of his reply to the loyalty board in early February 1954, he decided to get the opinion of a friend, William Hastie, a federal judge and former governor of the Virgin Islands. Judge Hastie had been one of Bunche's black classmates at Harvard in the late 1920s and was an old friend from Washington since the 1930s. Together, Bunche and Hastie pored over the typescript until well after midnight one evening at the Bunche home in Kew Gardens. Hastie "offered excellent advice on the draft," Bunche thought, and although, ever the lawyer, he suggested "many revisions and advised eliminating some passages not called for in the interrogatory," he believed the "replies could not be more convincing or better documented." Bunche spent the next several days on revisions, then asked Donald Young, a white social scientist and former colleague on the Myrdal-Carnegie project, to give his "draft a critical reading." Young, too, believed Bunche's self-defense "could not be stronger than it was." Bunche made final cosmetic revisions and arranged for the delivery of his annotated reply to the loyalty board on February 12th. "Lincoln's birthday," he thought—"what a day for me to deliver myself of a document like that!"[35]

He heard nothing for a month. Then, at the NAACP's Fight for Freedom Conference in Washington, where both he and President Eisenhower spoke, Bunche bumped into Maxwell Rabb, who urged him to "forget about" the loyalty board. Bunche took some encouragement from the exchange but was not completely reassured. Several days later, Bunche inquired about his status to the board and was told to be patient, that the hundred-page reply and cache of supporting material he had provided would keep the board members busy for several more weeks. Indeed, a date for his hearing was soon set: May 25, 1954, chosen to accommodate the two witnesses who had stepped forward to testify that Bunche had been a "concealed" Communist on May 17, 1935.[36]

The hearing began at ten. The six members of the loyalty board met Bunche and Ernie Gross, a friend and lawyer from the United Nations, in a private room at the Foley Square Courthouse. The board members—Pierce Gerety, two attorneys, a school superintendent, a businessman, and a real estate agent—listened to the 1950 Nobel laureate answer preliminary questions, then heard two witnesses provide an alternate history of the origins of National Negro Congress and of Ralph Bunche's radicalism. Manning Johnson, an African American active in the Communist Party during the 1930s, testified first. Johnson, a Justice Department informant who several years earlier had testified against such black figures as Paul Robeson and W. E. B. Du Bois, claimed that the Communist Party had ordered the launch of the National Negro Congress. Bunche, he said, had in fact been part of a secret cell operating among the faculty at Howard University; the cell members had been identified to him by James Ford, the nation's leading black Communist. In fact, during the May 1935 conference Ford had privately introduced Johnson to Bunche with incriminating identifiers: "Comrade Bunche," he had said, "meet comrade Johnson." During conference sessions, Johnson testified, Bunche had acted "like all of us under orders of the CP." Indeed, he explained, Bunche had to obey party directives, "otherwise he would never have been entrusted with the vital responsibility of launching the Congress." This depiction of Bunche following Communist strategy provoked a blunt question from the board. Had Johnson any doubt that Bunche was a member of the Communist Party? No doubt in his mind, the professional witness replied, as Bunche looked on, furiously taking notes. Bunche's membership was "a closely guarded secret," Johnson allowed, but if his sponsorship of the Howard conference was not evidence enough, he suggested that Bunche had also betrayed his clear embrace of Communist doctrine in publications like *A World View of Race*.[37]

The next witness, Leonard Patterson, another black Communist active during the 1930s, corroborated Johnson's testimony. Like Johnson, Patterson explained that James Ford had told him that Bunche was an "undercover" Communist. Patterson believed he had seen evidence of this himself when he watched Bunche run the Howard conference as a "pretty orderly" affair—much as one would expect a party function to proceed when members simply carried out their instructions. Patterson, too, had detected clear signals from Bunche's writings. They "were communist slanted," he told the board; all of his "writings prior to 1939 followed the CP line."[38]

Ralph Bunche fumed. While the witnesses had fabricated his connection to the Communist Party, they had done so cleverly, weaving the perspective of the party with details he could not deny, such as his participation in the Howard conference. To Bunche, all the testimony seemed to amount to was guilt by association, and evidence of this even appeared tenuous. But considering James Ford's alleged statements, Bunche wrote that he was "helpless in trying to refute what one former party member told" another except to say that he had "done many foolish things but nothing so foolish as joining the CP." He was not in position to "disprove what Ford said," Bunche scribbled in his notepad; he faced "a diabolical trick—all based on hearsay from Ford and other communists. I obviously cannot call them as witnesses."[39]

His self-defense, instead, hinged on his ability to further probe the historical context of the 1930s. For instance, if the Communists controlled the Howard conference, he wanted to know of Johnson and Patterson whether they would have put archrival socialist "Norman Thomas on program to attack Communist program?" or, for that matter, "*other* non-communists on program?" Bunche pushed for details concerning his supposed party involvement, the timing of the alleged secret meetings, and who was present, and wondered why "you say your memory after 19 yrs. is not certain, you cannot remember all who were present at meeting in Davis' office, but you are *certain* I was there (yet I didn't say anything)—why is your memory so certain on this point?"

Bunche also wanted clarification concerning contemporary black politics. While he conceded his interest in the Scottsboro trials, during which the party-affiliated International Labor Defense had represented the nine black teenagers, he asked, "Is it your view that everyone interested in the Scottsboro case was CP?" Following this logic would have made the entirety of black America Communist Party members. In fact, he explained, he had openly criticized the party's slogan "Self-determination for Negroes in [the] Black Belt" during the 1930s. Could "any Party member, and especially any 'top leader' of the Party," he asked, "be opposed to that line?" As for the National Negro Congress, Bunche again wanted more perspective. Did the witnesses "know of *any* leading Negroes or leading Negro organizations who *opposed* the Negro congress?" The NAACP, the National Urban League, the national board of the Young Women's Christian Association, among other groups, had also supported the NNC. Likewise, concerning his published work, "did it follow that anyone who in [the] '30s spoke or wrote of class divisions in society or class conflict or colonial imperialism was a communist?"[40]

The implicit answer, of course, was no, Bunche tried to convince the loyalty board. Even if the "CP plot at the early stage of 1935" that Johnson and Patterson described was true, Bunche said, he submitted that "something like NNC wd. have come into being without CP effort—need was so great—support so readily forthcoming." The "joint sponsorship of Howard Confer. [was] purely a coincidence," he explained, not part of a broad scheme, but had grown out of the "belief that N[egroes] had to become part of Amer. Labor" and that the "'talented tenth'—N[egro] organizations had to have a mass basis." This belief, too, had infused his publications. Although he was "not proud" of *A World View of Race* in retrospect (he believed it hastily written, not errant in interpretation), during the 1930s his was not an unusual view. And it was certainly not a Communist position. "In [the] thirties," Bunche explained, "we Negroes knew communism chiefly through Negro reps. of American C.P." like James Ford, and "we didn't take Ford seriously—he was so ignorant & so clearly imprisoned intellectually by the CP line that N[egro] intellectuals were amused by him." Instead, Bunche said, he thought of himself as "a Young Turk and proud of it—wd. never submit myself to any intell. discipline as CP requires—I wrote as I thot & believed without regard to obligation to anybody's 'line.'"[41]

The hearing adjourned after twelve hours of questions and testimony, but with a second round scheduled for two days later. Hoping to counter Johnson and Patterson's caricature of him as an undercover Communist, the next morning Bunche called John P. Davis, now editor of the glossy black monthly *Our World*, and Walter White, executive secretary of the NAACP, for help. Rather than simply write a statement, Davis offered (over Bunche's initial objection) to travel from Washington to New York the next day and personally testify on his behalf, regardless of any potential repercussions. Walter White agreed to do the same, and also made his intentions public, releasing an NAACP press statement saying what Bunche could not openly suggest. Any "question of the loyalty of Dr. Bunche or of his devotion to his country and the democratic process is shocking," said White, dismissing the hearing out of hand as "an unseemly farce." He declared Bunche to be "not only a great and distinguished American" but also "a great and distinguished citizen of the world whose entire career has been dedicated to the preservation and enlargement of human liberty. To achieve that status he has had to overcome, because of race, great handicaps." White would, he said, "gladly stake whatever reputation I may possess on Dr. Bunche's unqualified loyalty and integrity." He would get the chance to do so the next day.[42]

When Walter White appeared before the loyalty board, he spoke unequivocally of Bunche's integrity. He had known Bunche for twenty-three years, since 1931 when he consulted the young intellectual concerning strategy for resisting the pressure the Communist Party had put on the NAACP during the Scottsboro trials. In the intervening years, as Bunche had published and become an important public figure, White had kept abreast of all of Bunche's writings and was also familiar with his speeches. Neither, in White's estimation, showed any connection to the tenets of Communism. In fact, White averred, the United States should regard Bunche as "one of the most effective opponents of communism." After all, what better symbol of American democracy could there be than Ralph Bunche, who despite his race had risen higher than any other American in the United Nations?[43]

While White served as a character witness, John P. Davis, in whose office Ralph Bunche's alleged record of treason had originated, appeared before the board in order to actually settle the matter of Bunche's "loyalty." After founding the Joint Committee on National Recovery to represent African American interests during New Deal hearings in Washington, Davis's watchdog group quickly gained the backing of leading organizations, whose small contributions financed the endeavor. But none had come from the Communist Party, Davis said, and certainly none from any source had exceeded one thousand dollars. On several occasions, Davis mentioned, he had invited Bunche, whom he had known since their days together at Harvard in the late 1920s, to participate in Joint Committee meetings. They never collaborated, however, until they cosponsored the Howard conference in 1935. That Bunche had been a Communist at the time, or ever, Davis considered laughable—and he would know. Between 1935 and 1942, Davis revealed, he had worked, sometimes closely, with Communists. During this time he never had any reason to believe that Bunche was a "concealed" Party member, though he had heard of such people. Davis's admission prompted even closer scrutiny from the loyalty board, which he satisfied with answers candidly demonstrating a fluency in the character of the Depression-era left. Bunche remained at the Foley Square Courthouse after midnight answering ludicrous question after ludicrous question "categorically no," but the danger had effectively passed. To the loyalty board, Davis's self-incriminating statements validated the written and oral testimony Bunche offered during the hearings.[44]

The next morning, during a press conference at the United Nations, the board announced its unanimous decision to dismiss all of the allegations against Bunche. Reporters on hand spoke with board chairman Pierce Gerety and Bunche's attorney, Ernie Gross, but gathered very few quotes from Ralph Bunche himself. Bunche offered only the tersest public comment, then left to lunch with the United Nations secretary general, hoping to remain politic and clearly eager to put the entire episode behind him. He kept his reactions private, as when that weekend he tipped a glass in response to that letter the "Thinkers and Drinkers" had mailed him from Howard saying "We glad you win." So was the "Doctoré."[45]

Louis Redding let out a whoop. He was driving in Manhattan on a Monday afternoon in May 1954 when a voice over his car radio announced the Supreme Court's *Brown v. Board of Education* decision. In late 1952, and again a year later, in December 1953, NAACP lawyers representing Kansas, the District of Columbia, South Carolina, Virginia, and Delaware had brought their joint cases to end school segregation before the Supreme Court. Redding had represented Delaware. The Court's decision was long delayed and was not yet expected on May 17th—but the NAACP had won. "Oh, boy," Redding said to himself as he steered through downtown New York. "Terrific."[46]

As civil rights news, the May 1954 announcement of the Supreme Court's *Brown v. Board of Education*—the decision prohibiting segregation in the nation's schools—quickly overshadowed the question of Ralph Bunche's loyalty. Even as the nation's leading African American newspapers detailed the news concerning "perhaps Negro America's top spokesman," the overriding significance of *Brown* was clear. The *Chicago Defender* published a political cartoon depicting the *Brown* decision as equivalent to the Emancipation Proclamation: a hammer and chisel breaking the chains of black bondage. Beyond the black weeklies, the *New York Times* reprinted editorials from across the nation indicating the profound sense of change wrought by the new Supreme Court precedent. Next to its coverage of the Bunche hearings, the *Pittsburgh Courier* printed a headline declaring another strike against segregation: "Supreme Court Strikes Again—Segregation in Colleges, Theatres, Public Recreation, and on Golf Courses Outlawed by Court's Second Big Decision." An impending era of integration appeared imminent.[47]

As the struggle over integration enveloped the nation over the next decade, many perceived the *Brown* decision as having inspired a "Negro revolution," a fight for civic equality culminating in the passage of the Civil Rights Act of 1964 and Voting Rights Act of 1965. Even at the time, however, it was evident that this movement was rooted in the past. When Ralph Bunche strode the length of the National Mall in August 1963, his place at the steps of the Lincoln Memorial alongside Martin Luther King, Jr., testified to the significance of his generation in this long march toward freedom.

Yet the anti-Communist fervor of the postwar years muted—if not entirely silenced—a singular legacy. Thirty summers before the March on Washington, when a quarter million thrilled to King's "dream," twenty-six young black leaders had agreed that the civil rights movement required a program to attain economic equality. They represented a young generation of elite black leadership—the label of the day, the Talented Tenth, was by 1963 a relic of the past—who, in the midst of the economic and political tumult of the early 1930s, had eschewed accommodationism and embraced a radical agenda that gave shape to their civil rights struggle. Lawyers like Charles Houston, Edward Lovett, and Louis Redding, who left the Amenia Conference to challenge the legality of Jim Crow, had gradually brought an end to the "separate but equal" doctrine. But the participants in the Amenia Conference had also endorsed the economic argument that Abram Harris and Ralph Bunche posited during the conference and that activists like Juanita Jackson and Moran Weston sought to achieve in the years following those three days at Troutbeck.

When Ralph Bunche, among the most respected Americans of the day, could no longer safely, reasonably recount his part in this period of the civil rights struggle, that radical past was elided, that legacy eclipsed by the freedom movement that transformed the nation during the years that followed the *Brown* decision.

Epilogue

Langston Hughes needed a favor. It was February 1962, and black America's sixty-year-old poet laureate was finishing final revisions on his manuscript *Fight for Freedom*, a history of the NAACP to be published later that year. He held in hand a group portrait of the 1933 Amenia Conference. He wished to include it in his book, but he was unable to identify each of the figures in the photograph.

A dozen images would illustrate his story of the NAACP, which he described as "the most *damned* group of respectable citizens and, on the other hand, one of the most praised groups in America." A few photographs were chosen to depict brazen white supremacy. Members of the Ku Klux Klan parading near the Capitol Building in Washington, DC, in 1925, carrying American flags and outfitted in white robes and conical headpieces. A mob of white men crowding around the smoking, charred corpse of a black man lynched in St. Joseph, Missouri, in 1933. A black farmer in Tennessee, evicted from his tenancy for attempting to vote, standing beside the tent he now shared with his wife and five children. Several other images portrayed Association officials whose work had helped make NAACP "the most *famous* initials in America." To consider each of these portraits in the order Hughes arranged was to appreciate the gradual arc toward justice the Association had forged. W. E. B. Du Bois, reading intently in the offices of the *Crisis*. A grim-faced Walter White in Florida, surveying the bombed home of an NAACP official murdered in 1951 for his role in registering black voters. NAACP special counsel Thurgood Marshall wearing a jubilant smile on the steps of the Supreme Court after the 1954 *Brown* decision. Daisy Bates, of the Little Rock, Arkansas, NAACP, posing proudly with the nine students chosen to integrate the city's Central High School in 1957. Roy Wilkins grinning broadly from both a picket line and the Kennedy White House, as the civil rights movement crested toward a second Reconstruction securing citizenship and voting rights for African Americans.[1]

Standing with Roy Wilkins in that last photograph was Arthur Spingarn, by 1962 an Association elder, serving his twenty-third year as president of the NAACP Board of Directors, the position his brother, Joel, had held until his death in 1937. The photograph of the Amenia Conference featured Joel Spingarn at the center, caught in an obviously informal pose, reaching toward the young woman sitting at his feet. Placing this image first would offer a subtle ode to the Spingarns' devotion to the civil rights movement: Joel hosting an NAACP gathering at Troutbeck in 1933, Arthur accompanying an NAACP delegation to the White House in 1961. The assemblage at Amenia, that group of well-comported advocates of African American rights, would also nicely embody the "respectable citizens," as Hughes put it, who had made the NAACP "the most *talked-about* non-political organization" and "the most *written-about* voluntary association in America."

But who were they?

Hughes had no trouble placing a number of faces. At Spingarn's left sat the round-faced Elmer Carter, at the time the editor of *Opportunity*, the Urban League's monthly magazine. Behind Carter's right shoulder was Mary White Ovington, a progressive cofounder of the NAACP, leaning forward with laughter. On her left, James Weldon Johnson, former NAACP executive secretary, casually regarded the camera, his head cocked beneath a charcoal hat. Behind him, partially obscured, was the sociologist Ira De Augustine Reid, looking to his right, toward the center of the group, where E. Franklin Frazier and Roy Wilkins stood in the back row. Below them sat Moran Weston, still a college student at the time, and to his right the beaming Juanita Jackson, only twenty years old. Behind her and to her right, in tweed and a bowtie, his hands in his pocket, was W. E. B. Du Bois. On his right, with a calm smile, stood Ralph Bunche; sitting two rows in front of him, near the bottom left of the photograph, was Hughes's fellow poet Sterling Brown. At the far right, in a white V-neck sweater, was Walter White, cigarette smoke in the air around his face.

How like Walter. His friend was gone now, having passed in 1955, the year after the *Brown* decision. As was his friend Charles Houston, whom Hughes credited with crafting the stratagem that had led to the Supreme Court's new integrationist precedent. The hard-driving Houston had died in 1950, four years before his plan to systematically challenge racial segregation in education reached its epochal fruition. Hughes noted that Houston's protégé, Thurgood Marshall, had refused to accept sole acclaim for the achievement—an indication that some had already begun to forget (if they ever knew of) Houston's pivotal role in the civil rights movement.[2]

"It should not be forgotten," wrote Arthur Spingarn in the foreword to *Fight for Freedom*, "that the NAACP first lit the torch which is now being carried by its spiritual sons and daughters." But by 1962, amid the civil rights ferment so swiftly evolving even in just the eight years since the *Brown* decision, it was apparently easy to neglect the legacy of aging or departed figures like Charles Houston.

At the end of 1955, a bus boycott began in Montgomery, Alabama, unexpectedly making an ambitious, if unknown, twenty-six-year-old Rev. Martin Luther King, Jr., the charismatic face of the black freedom struggle. While states like

Alabama effectively crippled local NAACP branches (they were deemed part of a Communist conspiracy), the Southern Christian Leadership Conference emerged after the Montgomery bus boycott putting forth a program to overturn segregation throughout the South. In 1957, the showdown over desegregation in Little Rock saw members of the 101st Airborne patrolling the halls of Central High School to assure integration. The lunch counter sit-ins that swept out of Greensboro, North Carolina, led in 1960 to the formation of the Student Nonviolent Coordinating Committee. In collaboration with the Congress of Racial Equality, SNCC members avowed their dedication to democracy and civil disobedience, joined in the "freedom rides" of 1961, and by 1962 were collaborating in a painstaking, perilous effort to register black voters in regions of the nation like the Mississippi Delta where the grip of white supremacy seemed to have altered little in a half century, since the earliest issues of the *Crisis* recounted the national shames of vigilantism and peonage in places like Crittenden County, Arkansas, where Steve Green shot his former landlord in defense of his life and then fled to Chicago. If, in 1962, Rev. Martin Luther King, Jr., disavowed armed resistance, figures like North Carolina's Robert F. Williams, a veteran of the World War II fight against fascism, brandished rifles in unapologetic defiance of white terror, lending the "Negro revolution" a militancy that seemed far removed from the comparatively conservative posture of the NAACP and its respectable representatives.

In the flush of such a rapidly transforming civil rights movement, it was all too possible to lose sight of the present's connections with the past. When Fred Shuttlesworth led an armed caravan out of Birmingham to rescue bloodied freedom riders in 1961, who remembered that W. E. B. Du Bois had sanctioned armed self-defense a half century earlier? In the October 1911 number of the *Crisis*, to cite one instance, he had answered the question of how best to meet the "reign of terror" lynching wrought that year by quoting the "pithy" reminiscences of a wizened veteran of the racial violence that had raged a generation earlier, during the years of Reconstruction: "In Arkansas, 1873, we adopted a remedy for lynching that was to kill the lynchers. Therefore we had no lynching in that end of Pulaski County." What had been effective in 1873 seemed to work in 1911 too. A few pages later, Du Bois had offered a curious little item for his readers to consider, culled from the Wagoner (Oklahoma) *American*. A pair of colored men, Du Bois recounted, armed with revolvers and automatic Winchester rifles, had held off a mob of more than thirty men dressed as "mother hubbards." In the face of spirited fire, the white mob had made a comical retreat, confirming the cowardice of those "willing to take life but unwilling to give up their own."[3]

The staunch defense of black freedom had long roots, and innumerable incarnations. But when communities such as Montgomery, Alabama, united in 1955 to end the segregation of city busses, who remembered the neighbors on Tenth Street Hill in Wilmington, Delaware, who had come together during the 1920s to integrate their city's courtrooms? When leaders like Martin Luther King, Jr., writing in such works as *Why We Can't Wait*, insisted that the civil rights revolution consider economic equality necessary for the full works of freedom, who remembered that Abram Harris had argued during the NAACP's annual convention in 1932 that the civil rights movement needed to develop a full-fledged economic program? When, in the spring of 1960, Ella Baker, of the Southern Christian Leadership Conference, urged youthful activists to create an independent, student-led nonviolent coordinating committee, who remembered the NAACP youth council movement that Juanita Jackson had coordinated during the Great Depression? When entertainers like Harry Belafonte, Nina Simone, Dick Gregory, and Josephine Baker raised funds, performed, and appeared on behalf of the civil rights movement, who remembered the Negro Freedom Rallies and Golden Gate Ballroom bashes that the Negro Labor Victory Committee held during the 1940s, when Duke Ellington, Lena Horne, Paul Robeson, and Pearl Primus had offered their talents to the fight for freedom? When young writers during the early 1960s contended that the Negro revolution belonged to a global anticolonial movement intent on smashing white cultural, political, and economic hegemony, who remembered *A World View of Race*, the short book Ralph Bunche had written in 1936?

Hughes felt it was imperative to remember this past. In writing *Fight for Freedom* he meant to preserve the remarkable legacy of the NAACP, ensuring that the militancy of the Association's endeavors would be appreciated as a forerunner of the contemporary vanguard for black freedom. He meant to imbue the story of the NAACP—to which Joel Spingarn (now dead twenty-five years), Charles Houston (dead twelve years), Walter White (dead seven), and W. E. B. Du Bois (remarkably, still alive, in Ghana) had so dedicated their lives—with drama enough to impress readers in the midst of the early 1960s civil rights revolution. And he meant to include the photograph of the 1933 Amenia Conference, illustrative of his own generation of elite black leadership's distinct contribution to the freedom struggle.

Hughes's generation had been born at the turn of the twentieth century, when the legal, political, cultural, and economic dimensions of the Jim Crow order had combined in such an imposing edifice. But figures such as those gathered in Amenia had disdained the prospect of accommodating white supremacy. From the vantage of 1962, the young men and women posing for Amy Spingarn at that secluded August retreat twenty-nine summers earlier might have seemed quite a genteel cohort. Their manifesto espousing an interracial movement for political and economic equality, however, bespoke a radical outlook that Hughes himself had avowed and projected as he wrote the 1943 Negro Freedom Rally pageant

For This We Fight, and which had come to inform the contemporary civil rights movement. Three decades after Amenia, their vision remained central in such places as New York City, where advocates of black civil rights considered equal economic opportunity a cornerstone of freedom. A year later, Anna Arnold Hedgeman, an Amenia participant, would even help organize the August 1963 March on Washington for Jobs and Freedom, a collaboration of the civil rights and labor movements of the sort envisioned at Troutbeck but most vividly remembered as the event at which Martin Luther King, Jr., repeated, "I have a dream." No mere afterthought, inclusion of a group portrait of those invited to the Spingarns' home would offer acknowledgment and commemoration of a generation's role in the long civil rights movement.

But Hughes struggled to identify them all. In the photograph hats and shadows conspired to hide otherwise familiar faces; postures and the passage of nearly three decades obscured those who had convened at Troutbeck in August of 1933. Seeking help, Hughes made copies of the photograph and forwarded them to Frank Frazier and Ira Reid. Could they match names with faces? The photograph jogged memories, but not entirely. Frazier urged Hughes to contact the former Mabel Byrd, now of St. Louis, whom he remembered as a fellow conferee; Reid encouraged Hughes to check with Emmett Dorsey, now an affable political science professor at Howard University. Appreciative of these leads, but with his publication deadline looming, Hughes accepted an editorial compromise. He included the conference photograph, placing it as the first of twelve images at the center of his book—but without their names.[4]

Left unidentified by Langston Hughes, few of the Amenia delegates were actually obscure, and much has been written about their lives since Hughes completed *Fight for Freedom*.

Considered representatives of their race in 1933, many of those who gathered at Troutbeck lived lives typical of their generation. Ira Reid and E. Franklin Frazier, as sociologists; Emmett Dorsey, Hazel Browne, and Harry Greene, as educators; Frances Williams and Marion Cuthbert, as YWCA officials; Pauline Young, as a librarian; Anna Arnold, as an activist. A few, like Truly Hayes and Virginia Alexander, passed away early, Hayes in 1937, after a terrible accident at the Hampton Institute, where he was an instructor, and Alexander in 1949, after a long struggle with lupus. Others, like Frances Williams and Sterling Brown, lived nearly the length of the century.

When Ralph Bunche died in 1972, the Nobel Peace Prize and Spingarn Medal winner was certainly the most widely known of the group, his academic career and public service considered a gauge of twentieth-century Negro achievement. Yet his friend Sterling Brown regretted that more had not realized the full dimensions of Bunche's life. "He was a skilled raconteur," Brown eulogized in the *Crisis* in January 1972, who "frequently used anecdotes in his lectures" and entertained friends and colleagues alike with "tales [that] were broad and ironic, most often with a social point." He favored autobiographical episodes. Bunche liked best to tell stories about "his tough boyhood experiences in Detroit and Albuquerque" before moving to Los Angeles; "a teacher's belated concession about his exclusion from his high school's honor society, though he had finished valedictorian"; and "an experience with Gunnar Myrdal in the deepest South where Gunnar's candid questioning of a Confederate daughter" about interracial relationships "forced them to leave town early." Bunche, said Brown, had "a great store of these yarns that made for both laughter and thought."[5] That he never composed an autobiography is a loss, a lacuna in the long civil rights movement, perhaps attributable to the harassment he experienced during his 1954 loyalty hearing.

Moran Weston lived for more than three decades after Ralph Bunche died, passing away in May 2002. He had first moved to New York in 1928 to prepare for a life in the clergy, and when the Negro Labor Victory Committee dissolved after the end of World War II, Weston returned to the church. "Labor Forum" appeared each week through the late 1940s, as Weston continued to address the need for a united struggle among black and white workers. In 1948 he helped found Carver Federal Savings Bank on 125th Street in Harlem, which soon became the nation's largest African American–owned bank, offering black clientele an option when financial institutions routinely discriminated against them. At St. Philip's Episcopal Church, among Harlem's most distinguished congregations, he served first as business manager; then, in 1951, he joined the National Council of the Protestant Episcopal Church. After earning his doctorate in social history from Columbia University in 1954, authoring a dissertation on the twentieth-century social policies of the Protestant Episcopal Church, Weston returned again to St. Philip's in 1957, where, during the 1960s, he launched a major church-based housing initiative in Harlem. In 1968 Columbia University named Weston the first African American member of its board of trustees. That year he also began teaching black studies at the State University of New York in Albany, a position lasting until 1977. In 1982, the sixth rector in the history of St. Philip's Episcopal Church retired after serving the 134th Street congregation for twenty-five years.

When she passed away in the summer of 1992, Juanita Jackson Mitchell's services were held at Sharp Street ME Church, where, sixty-one years earlier, she had first launched the City-Wide Young People's Forum. After returning home to Baltimore during the 1940s, she entered the recently desegregated University of Maryland Law School. Graduating in 1950, Mitchell was the first African American woman to receive a law degree from the school and then the first African American woman to practice law in Maryland. Not satisfied with "firsts," she quickly became one of the most active civil rights lawyers in the state. Soon after she won admittance to the bar in 1950, Mitchell sued to desegregate Maryland state beaches and swimming pools, arguing the case to a successful 1955 decision before the Supreme Court. After joining the effort to desegregate Baltimore schools following *Brown*, Mitchell returned to the Supreme Court in 1965, winning a case outlawing Jim Crow in Maryland restaurants. While Mitchell's legal record included numerous civil rights victories, she also remained active within the Baltimore and Maryland state chapters of the NAACP, directing voter registration drives during the 1950s and early 1960s, and serving as president of the state convention of branches during the 1970s. Soon after spending the 1981–82 academic year as a Dean's Visiting Fellow at her alma mater, the University of Pennsylvania, Mitchell retired to her home on Druid Hill Avenue.

Abram Harris died in November 1963, with a book on the nineteenth-century English philosopher John Stuart Mill remaining to be finished. After spending more than fifteen years thinking, writing, and lecturing about the "economics of the race problem," in 1935 Harris had returned to his scholarship, which, true to the pledge he had made to V. F. Calverton in the 1920s to look beyond "the Negro problem," had become more and more theoretical and much less specific to the African American experience. While the NAACP declined to accept his prescription for change, Harris took a Guggenheim Fellowship and went abroad, studying at the London School of Economics and traveling to the Soviet Union. Back in Washington, DC, he was restless at Howard University, and accepted short-term visiting professorships, hoping to sustain a life near New York City. When he permanently left Howard to teach economics at the University of Chicago in 1946, Harris was among the first African American scholars hired outside black academia. Chairing panels in the field's most prestigious national conferences, and producing well-regarded articles and monographs at Chicago through the 1950s and 1960s, Harris sought to shed the label "Negro intellectual," and to instead hone a reputation as an influential economist, regardless of race.

When he died in September 1998, Louis Redding had become a dean among Delaware lawyers. Returning from the Amenia Conference in 1933, Redding kept his one-man practice on French Street until World War II, when he accepted a position with the Office of Price Administration in New York. After reopening a larger office on Market Street in downtown Wilmington after the war, Redding challenged segregation in the state's public schools. In 1950 he won *Parker v. University of Delaware*, the Delaware Chancery Court decision to desegregate the state university; the following year he began new suits challenging Jim Crow in Delaware secondary schools. By 1952, Redding's cases were joined with several other state challenges in *Brown v. Board of Education*, the broader NAACP suit brought to the Supreme Court. Redding continued to practice privately until 1964, even returning to the Supreme Court in 1961 with a successful antidiscrimination suit. He ended his career in 1984 after twenty years with the Wilmington Public Defender's office.

In May 1992 the city of Wilmington, Delaware, erected a statue of Louis Redding in front of the newly renamed Louis L. Redding City/County Building. Celebrating his work to desegregate the state's schools, the statue of Redding, cast in bronze, stands between two school children, a black boy and a white girl. Beyond the statue, the nine-story Redding Building houses most of Wilmington's municipal offices, from Register of Wills to Clerk of the Peace, as well as the regular meeting of the New Castle County Council. Both statue and building stand just two blocks from the one-room, second-floor law office at 1002 French Street, from which, fifty-nine summers earlier, Louis Redding left to begin driving to Amenia, New York.

NOTES

Introduction

1. "Amenia Conference, Important Notice No. 3, end of July 1933," Bunche Papers, box 25, folder 10, Schomburg Center for Research in Black Culture, New York Public Library (hereafter SCRBC); Lewis Mumford, "The Story of Troutbeck," unpublished typescript, Troutbeck History album, Troutbeck Inn, Amenia, New York; "The Amenia Conference, Amenia, NY, August 18–21, 1933," *Papers of the National Association for the Advancement of Colored People*, microfilm (Frederick, MD: University Publications of America, 1982–)part 11, series A, reel 18; Amenia Conference, box 95–13, folder 524, Joel Spingarn Papers, Moorland-Spingarn Collection, Howard University; Lewis Mumford to Catherine Bauer, August 20, 1933, in Lewis Mumford, *My Work and Days* (New York: Harcourt Brace Jovanovich, 1979), 310–11; Charles E. Benton, *Troutbeck: A Dutchess County Homestead* (Dutchess County, NY: Dutchess County Historical Society, 1916); Donald L. Miller, *Lewis Mumford: A Life* (New York: Weidenfeld & Nicholson, 1989), 244; W. E. B. Du Bois, "Youth and Age at Amenia," *Crisis*, October 1933, 226–27; "The Weather," *New York Times*, August 19, 1933; Joel Spingarn to Ralph Bunche, April 12, 1933, Bunche Papers, box 25, folder 10, SCRBC.
2. Langston Hughes, *Fight for Freedom: The Story of the NAACP* (New York: Norton, 1962); Du Bois, "Youth and Age."
3. Lewis Mumford to Catherine Bauer, August 20, 1933, in Mumford, *My Work and Days*, 310–11; Louis Redding to Roy Wilkins, September 2, 1933, *NAACP Papers*, 11:A:18; Ralph Bunche, "The Programs, Ideologies, Tactics and Achievements of Negro Betterment and Interracial Organizations," Carnegie-Myrdal Study Research Memorandum for *The Negro in America*, 210–11, reel 1, Ralph Bunche Papers, microfilm, Lamont Library, Harvard University; W. E. B. Du Bois, *Dusk of Dawn: An Essay Toward an Autobiography of a Race Concept* (New York: Harcourt, Brace, 1940); interview with Moran Weston, Heathrow, FL, July 22, 2000.
4. For a synthesis of civil rights scholarship that emphasizes the economic dimensions of the twentieth-century civil rights struggle, suggests its duration and evolution over the course of several decades, and emphasizes the intersection between grassroots communities and national civil rights organizations in the creation of a national civil rights movement, see Jacquelyn Dowd Hall, "The Long Civil Rights Movement and the Political Uses of the Past," *Journal of American History* 91, no. 4 (March 2005): 1233–63. For criticism of this interpretation, see Eric Arnesen, "Reconsidering the 'Long Civil Rights Movement,'" *Historically Speaking* 10, no. 2 (April 2009): 31–34; and Sundiata Keita Cha-Jua and Clarence Lang, "The 'Long' Movement as Vampire: Temporal and Spatial Fallacies in Recent Black Freedom Studies," *Journal of African American History* 92, no. 1 (Winter 2007): 265–88. For further entry into the voluminous literature on civil rights history, see also Adam

Fairclough, "Historians and the Civil Rights Movement," *Journal of American Studies* 24, no. 3 (December 1990): 387–98; Steven F. Lawson, "Freedom Then, Freedom Now: The Historiography of the Civil Rights Movement," *American Historical Review* 96, no. 2 (April 1991): 456–71; Kevin Gaines, "Rethinking Race and Class in African-American Struggles for Equality, 1885–1941," *American Historical Review* 102, no. 2 (April 1997): 378–87; Charles Eagles, "Toward New Histories of the Civil Rights Era," *Journal of Southern History* 66, no. 4 (November 2000): 815–48.

Chapter 1

1. This sketch is based primarily on the oral histories Annette Woolard conducted with Louis Redding. See Louis Redding to Annette Woolard, May 18, 1990; June 5, 1990; July 26, 1990; January 18, 1991; interviews, Delaware Historical Society, Wilmington, Delaware. See also Annette Woolard, "A Family of Firsts: The Reddings of Delaware" (Ph.D. diss., University of Delaware, 1993); "Louis Redding: 'black and white are getting to know one another,'" *Brown Alumni Monthly*, April 1972, 69; Jube Shriver, Jr., "Redding, State's First Black Lawyer, Recalls His 50-Year Fight for Equality," *Wilmington Evening Journal*, January 16, 1979; Bill Frank, "Historic Event at the Bar," newspaper clipping, January 18, 1979, Louis Redding biographical file, Brown University Archives, Brown University; Laurie Hays, "Louis Redding's Fight for Dignity and Decency," *Brown Alumni Monthly*, May 1986, 38–43, 60; Chris Barrish, "A Legal Legend," *Brown Alumni Monthly*, March 1993, 39; Louis Redding to Roy Wilkins, September 2, 1933; "The Amenia Conference, Amenia, NY, August 18–21, 1933," *Papers of the National Association for the Advancement of Colored People*, microfilm (Frederick, MD: University Publications of America, 1982–) part 11, series A, reel 18; Louis Redding to Joel Spingarn, April 17, 1933, box 95–9, folder 377; Attendance Card, Louis Redding, box 95–13, folder 524, Joel Spingarn Papers, Moorland-Spingarn Collection, Howard University; Carol Hoffecker, *Corporate Capital: Wilmington in the Twentieth Century* (Philadelphia: Temple University Press, 1983); "The Weather," *New York Times*, August 19, 1933.
2. Joel Spingarn to Ralph Bunche, April 12, 1933, box 25, folder 10, Ralph Bunche Papers, Schomburg Center for Research in Black Culture, New York Public Library (hereafter SCRBC).
3. "The Amenia Conference, Amenia, NY, August 18–21, 1933"; "Second Amenia Conference on a New Programme for the Negro (or on the Aspirations of Negro Youth, etc.?)," *NAACP Papers*, 11:A:18.
4. "The Amenia Conference, Amenia, NY, August 18–21, 1933," *NAACP Papers*, 11:A:18.
5. Hoffecker, *Corporate Capital*, 28.
6. Dan Carter, *Scottsboro: A Tragedy of the American South* (Baton Rouge: Louisiana State University Press, 1969); Mark D. Naison, *Communists in Harlem during the Depression* (Urbana: University of Illinois Press, 1983), 57–94; Pauline Young to Walter White, February 3, 1932, *NAACP Papers*, 12:B:1.
7. Alice Baldwin to Robert Bagnall, December 12, 1928; Robert Bagnall to Alice Baldwin, June 15, 1929; Alice Baldwin to Robert Bagnall, December 4, 1929, *NAACP Papers*, 12:B:1.
8. "The Amenia Conference, Amenia, NY, August 18–21, 1933," *NAACP Papers*, 11:A:18; Charles Flint Kellogg, *NAACP: A History of the National Association for the Advancement of Colored People*, vol. 1, *1909–1920* (Baltimore: Johns Hopkins University Press, 1967). For the New Haven and Durham conferences, see files of the Negro Problem Conference, Laura Spellman Rockefeller Memorial Archives, 3.8, 101–2, 1023–24 [hereafter LSRM]; files of the Durham Conference, LSRM, 3.8, 97, 981–83, Rockefeller Archives Center, Sleepy Hollow, New York. On the NAACP's 1932 annual convention, see "1932 NAACP Annual Convention Conference Program," *NAACP Papers*, 1:A:9; "NAACP Opens Meet

in D.C.," *Baltimore Afro-American*, May 21, 1932, 13, 7; "NAACP Washington Meeting Delivers Address to Nation," *Washington Tribune*, June 3, 1932, 1, 2; "The 23d Conference, NAACP," *Crisis*, July 1932, 219, 236.

9. Louis Redding to Joel Spingarn, April 17, 1933, box 95–9, folder 377, Spingarn Papers; "Memorandum No. 2," May 27, 1933, box 25, folder 10, Bunche Papers, SCRBC.

10. The *Afro-American* carried extensive coverage of the conference. See, for instance, "Reds Slip into Rosenwald Meeting," *Baltimore Afro-American*, May 20, 1933, 1, 2. "NAACP Cuts Annual Session to 4 Days," *Baltimore Afro-American*, May 20, 1933, 2; "Along the Color Line," *Crisis*, July 1933, 159. See also "The Rosenwald Conference," *Crisis*, July 1933, 156–57.

11. "Along the Color Line," *Crisis*, August 1933, 186–87. Rayford Logan, "The Growth of Liberal and Radical Thought among Negroes"; Charles Houston, "Closing Remarks," *NAACP Papers*, 1:A:9. See also "NAACP Conference Resolution Reflects Economic Status Worry," *Baltimore Afro-American*, July 15, 1933, 4.

12. Attendance Card, Louis Redding, box 95–13, folder 524, Spingarn Papers; "Amenia Conference, Important Notice, No. 3, end of July, 1933," *NAACP Papers*, 11:A:18. Reference to "snake hunting," in the same breath as canoeing and swimming, may seem at first a bit unusual. But, on the authority of my grandfather, lifelong Dutchess County resident John C. Miller, it was not. During the Depression, boys in the Civilian Conservation Corps, like his brother-in-law, had sometimes led visitors from Manhattan on snake hunts, earning pay for the good time, certainly, but also for the capture of what was then a fashionable dinner item. Conversation with John C. Miller, Millerton, NY, March 15, 2001.

13. "The Amenia Conference, Amenia, NY, August 18–21, 1933," *NAACP Papers*, 11:A:18; "The Late Booker T. Washington," *Crisis*, December 1915, 82; "Amenia," *Crisis*, October 1916, 276–77; "Amenia," *Crisis*, November 1916, 18, 19; David Levering Lewis, *W. E. B. Du Bois: Biography of a Race, 1868–1919* (New York: Henry Holt, 1993), 517–22; "Second Amenia Conference on a New Programme for the Negro (or on the Aspirations of Negro Youth, etc.?)," *NAACP Papers*, 11:A:18; W. E. B. Du Bois, "The Amenia Conference," in *Pamphlets and Leaflets by W. E. B. Du Bois*, ed. Herbert Aptheker (White Plains, NY: Kraus-Thomson, 1986), 210–16.

14. Jay Saunders Redding, *On Being Negro in America* (Indianapolis: Bobbs-Merrill, 1951), 38; W. E. B. Du Bois, "The Talented Tenth," in *The Negro Problem: A Series of Articles by Representative American Negroes of Today* (New York: Potts, 1903). Du Bois employed a similar perspective in "Of Booker T. Washington and Others," in *The Souls of Black Folk* (Chicago: McClurg, 1903), chap. 3.

15. Du Bois, "The Amenia Conference," 210–11; "The Niagara Movement Declaration of Principles, 1905," in Aptheker, *Pamphlets and Leaflets*, 55–58.

16. "The Call," reprinted in Kellogg, *NAACP*, 1:297–99; Patricia Sullivan, *Lift Every Voice: The NAACP and the Making of the Civil Rights Movement* (New York: New Press, 2009).

17. "Along the Color Line," *Crisis*, January 1911, 8; "Along the Color Line," *Crisis*, February 1911, 5, 9; "Along the Color Line," *Crisis*, November 1910, 6; "Along the Color Line," *Crisis*, December 1911, 9; "Along the Color Line," *Crisis*, January 1911, 6–7; *Crisis*, February 1911; "Concerning Parks," *Crisis*, March 1911, 28; "Along the Color Line," *Crisis*, March 1911, 8; *Crisis*, April 1911.

18. "Agitation," *Crisis*, November 1910, 11; "NAACP," *Crisis*, December 1910, 16; "Along the Color Line," *Crisis*, February 1911, 10; "Along the Color Line," *Crisis*, March 1911, 9–10; "Emigration to Canada," *Crisis*, May 1911, 13–14; "Along the Color Line," *Crisis*, December 1910, 9; "Along the Color Line," *Crisis*, February 1911, 10; "Along the Color Line," *Crisis*, December 1910, 10; "The NAACP," *Crisis*, June 1911; "The Burden," *Crisis*, July 1911, 123–24; "The Burden," *Crisis*, December 1910, 26; "The Burden," *Crisis*, February 1911, 29; "The National Pastime," *Crisis*, January 1911, 18–19.

19. "The NAACP," *Crisis*, August 1911, 153–54; "Along the Color Line," *Crisis*, October 1911, 233. The Coatesville lynching, as the *Crisis* recorded, provoked an outcry in the northern

press as evidence of "a broadly national shame" and not just a southern peculiarity. That not everyone shared this sense of indignation was similarly clear. While newspapers published incensed editorials, one man traveled across much of the state from Waynesboro to Coatesville to collect charred shards of bone. "Lynching," *Crisis*, August 1911, 158–59; "The Coatesville Lynching," *Crisis*, September 1911, 188; "Along the Color Line," *Crisis*, October 1911, 233.

20. Franklin was eventually paroled in 1919. "Pink Franklin," *Crisis*, December 1910, 26; "Pink Franklin's Reprieve," *Crisis*, February 1911, 15; "Pink Franklin," *Crisis*, February 1911, 17. The newspaper was the *Providence Journal*. "A Latter-Day Dred Scott," *Crisis*, February 1911, 13.

21. "Steve Green's Story," *Crisis*, November 1910, 14; Kellogg, *NAACP*, 1:62–64; Barbara Joyce Ross, *J. E. Spingarn and the Rise of the NAACP, 1911–1939* (New York: Atheneum, 1972), 20–21.

22. Alice M. (Mrs. Paul Lawrence) Dunbar, letter to the editor, *Crisis*, April 1911, 3.

23. Several sources state that the branch formed in 1912, but the NAACP's administrative files show that it did not officially associate until 1914. Pauline A. Young, "The Negro in Delaware: Past and Present," in *Delaware: History of the First State*, ed. H. Clay Reed (New York: Lewis Historical Publishing, 1947), 2:581–607; John A. Munroe, *History of Delaware* (Newark: University of Delaware Press, 1979), 211; Alice M. Dunbar to W. E. B. Du Bois, December 1, 1912; "Application," November 30, 1914; Edwina Kruse to Mary Childs Nerny, September 17, 1915, *NAACP Papers*, 12:B:1; Redding, *On Being Negro*, 38; Mark Schneider, "The Boston NAACP and the Decline of the Abolitionist Impulse," *Massachusetts Historical Review* 1 (1999): 95–114; Christopher Robert Reed, *The Chicago NAACP and the Rise of Black Professional Leadership, 1910–1966* (Bloomington: Indiana University Press), 37. Prior to regular publication of NAACP branch news in March 1913, branch information was regularly reported in the *Crisis*'s monthly column "The NAACP." See the note in "NAACP," *Crisis*, March 1913, 245. On the founding of the local branches, see also Kellogg, *NAACP*, 1:117–38.

24. Alice Dunbar-Nelson, "These 'Colored' United States: No. 16—Delaware: A Jewel of Inconsistencies," part 2, *Messenger*, September 1924, 276–79; Eric Foner, *Reconstruction: America's Unfinished Revolution, 1863–1877* (New York: Harper & Row, 1988), 421–22; Harold Hancock, "The Status of the Negro in Delaware after the Civil War, 1865–1875," *Delaware History* 13, no. 1 (April 1968): 57–67; Amy Hiller, "The Disfranchisement of Delaware Negroes in the Late Nineteenth Century," *Delaware History* 13, no. 2 (October 1968): 124–53; Carol E. Hoffecker, "The Politics of Exclusion: Blacks in Late Nineteenth Century Wilmington, Delaware," *Delaware History* 16, no. 1 (April 1974): 65. Between 1890 and 1940, more than nine in ten African American laborers were employed as unskilled agricultural workers, as teamsters, as manual laborers, and as servants. Harold C. Livesay, "The Delaware Negro, 1865–1915," *Delaware History* 13, no. 2 (October 1968): 99–102.

25. Dennis Downey, "'Mercy Master Mercy': Racial Politics and the Lynching of George White," *Delaware History* 30, no. 3 (Spring–Summer 2003): 189–210; "The NAACP," *Crisis*, June 1911, 61.

26. Mary Nerny to Mrs. E. Williams America, November 25, 1924, *NAACP Papers*, 12:B:1; "Meetings," *Crisis*, January 1915, 135; Ross, *J. E. Spingarn*, 34; "Application," November 30, 1914, *NAACP Papers*, 12:B:1. In coming years the branch officers would change, but the women of Tenth Street Hill continued to constitute its core leadership. The prominence of black women in a local branch was remarkable but not unique. The NAACP's traveling secretary, Mary Nerney, noted that women similarly energized the Indianapolis NAACP during the mid-1910s. Indeed, by taking crucial leadership roles, the women of Wilmington's Talented Tenth fit into a broader pattern of African American women's activism at the turn of the century. Without access to the vote, during the early 1900s black women like those who joined the Wilmington branch pursued political change instead through social

organizations. Through such groups as the NAACP, black women lobbied local and state governments and pressured men who held the franchise to employ their votes responsibly. In Delaware, where black voters could sway the fortunes of the Republican Party, this political leverage proved critical. "Application," November 30, 1914; Edwina Kruse to Mary Nerney, September 17, 1915, *NAACP Papers*, 12:B:1. On the role of African American women during the Jim Crow era, see, for instance, Elsa Barkley Brown, "Negotiating and Transforming the Public Sphere: African American Political Life in the Transition from Slavery to Freedom," *Public Culture* 7, no. 1 (Fall 1994): 107–46; Glenda Elizabeth Gilmore, *Gender and Jim Crow: Women and the Politics of White Supremacy in North Carolina, 1896–1920* (Chapel Hill: University of North Carolina Press, 1996); Deborah Gray White, *Too Heavy a Load: Black Women in Defense of Themselves, 1894–1994* (New York: Norton, 1999); Lisa Materson, *For the Freedom of Her Race: Black Women and Electoral Politics in Illinois, 1877–1932* (Chapel Hill: University of North Carolina Press, 2009).

27. Thomas R. Cripps, "The Reaction of the Negro to the Motion Picture 'Birth of a Nation,'" *Historian* 25, no. 3 (May 1963): 344–62; Adam Fairclough, *Better Day Coming: Blacks and Equality, 1890–2000* (New York: Viking, 2001), 83; Lewis, *W. E. B. Du Bois*, 507.

28. "The Clansman," *Crisis*, May 1915, 33; "Fighting Race Calumny," *Crisis*, May 1915, 40–42; "Fighting Race Calumny, Part II," *Crisis*, June 1915, 87–88; "Branches," *Crisis*, June 1915, 85; Mary Nerney to Edwina Kruse, May 25, 1915; Edwina Kruse to Mary Nerney, June 1, 1915; Edwina Kruse to Mary Nerney, June 4, 1915; Alice Baldwin to Mary Nerney, December 18, 1915, *NAACP Papers*, 12:B:1; "Branches," *Crisis*, July 1915, 147–48.

29. "Branches," *Crisis*, May 1915, 39; Alice Baldwin to Mary Nerney, December 18, 1915, *NAACP Papers*, 12:B:1. On Wilson, see, for instance, "Branches," *Crisis*, April 1915, 300; and "Meetings," *Crisis*, December 1915, 86.

30. "Says Negroes Must Help Themselves," *Wilmington Morning News*, undated newspaper clipping, ca. December 18, 1916, *NAACP Papers*, 12:B:1; W. E. B. Du Bois, *The Negro* (New York: Henry Holt, 1915). For the advertisement of *The Negro*, see *Crisis*, April 1915, 324. On Leslie Pinkney Hill, see Werner Sollors, Caldwell Titcomb, and Thomas Underwood, eds., *Blacks at Harvard: A Documentary History of African-American Experience at Harvard and Radcliffe* (New York: New York University Press, 1993), 123; Kellogg, *NAACP*, 1:36.

31. Alice Baldwin to Mary White Ovington, February 3, 1916; Alice Baldwin to Mary White Ovington, March 14, 1916, *NAACP Papers*, 12:B:1; "That Capital 'N,'" *Crisis*, February 1916, 184; Donald L. Grant and Mildred Bricker Grant, "Some Notes on the Capital 'N,'" *Phylon* 36, no. 4 (1975): 435–43.

32. Alice Baldwin to Mary Nerny, ca. December 1915; Alice Baldwin to Mary Nerny, December 12, 1915, *NAACP Papers*, 12:B:1; Jay Saunders Redding, *No Day of Triumph* (New York: Harpers, 1942), 10. On Redding's parents, see Redding interview, May 18, 1990; Woolard, "Family of Firsts," 27, 41–42; Redding, *No Day of Triumph*, 3.

33. Redding vividly remembered the neighborhood YMCA, which prohibited black members, and which he passed every school day. The old Howard High was located between Twelfth and Thirteenth on Orange; it moved to Thirteenth and Poplar late in the 1920s. Redding interview, May 18, 1990; "Education," *Crisis*, February 1915, 165; Dunbar-Nelson, "Jewel of Inconsistencies"; Hancock, "Status of the Negro," 60; Jacqueline Halstead, "The Delaware Association for the Moral Improvement and Education of Colored People," *Delaware History* 15, no. 1 (April 1973): 19–40; "The Pierre Du Pont Schools," *Crisis*, January 1923, 107–11. In the end, it was Du Pont's overwhelming largesse, not the sudden enlightenment of the Delaware General Assembly, that afforded the construction of several dozen new schools for African Americans throughout the state. Yet the "Pierre Du Pont Schools," as showcased in the pages of the *Crisis* in January 1923, constituted only a partial blow to the Jim Crow order in Delaware. The fifty-one schools constructed "for Negro children" through 1922 and the twenty-six new schools that remained to be built were just that: "for Negro children." The movement to revamp the education system in

Delaware adhered to the precedent of separate but equal expressed in the 1896 *Plessy* decision. It made the pretense of offering equal education to African American children while keeping the races decidedly separate. In the Jim Crow era even Pierre du Pont's munificence had its limit.

34. Redding interview, May 18, 1990; Young, "Negro in Delaware," 593. Contemporary reports in the *Crisis* corroborate Young's firsthand account of small class sizes. Howard High School graduated twelve students in 1913, twenty in 1915, seven in 1916, nineteen in 1917, thirteen in 1918, and thirteen in 1919. "Along the Color Line," *Crisis*, July 1913, 111; "The Colored High School," *Crisis*, July 1915, 143; "Leading Colored High Schools," *Crisis*, July 1916, 127; "Colored High Schools," *Crisis*, July 1917, 124; "High School Graduates," *Crisis*, July 1918, 120; "The Year in Negro Education," *Crisis*, July 1919, 137.

35. Alice Baldwin to Roy Nash, January 3, 1917; Alice Baldwin to Roy Nash, February 8, 1917, *NAACP Papers*, 12:B:1.

36. Rev. H. Y. Arnett, "Wilmington, Del.," undated typescript, ca. 1917–18; H. Y. Arnett, untitled typescript, December 17, 1918, *NAACP Papers*, 12:B:1.

37. Alice Baldwin to Roy Nash, February 8, 1917; Alice Baldwin to John Shilladay, December 4, 1918, *NAACP Papers*, 12:B:1.

38. Woolard, "Family of Firsts," 119, 158; Redding, *On Being Negro*, 43; Undergraduate Statistics, January 14, 1921, Redding biographical file; Redding interview, May 18, 1990.

39. "Report of Election of Officers," December 1922, *NAACP Papers*, 12:B:1; Robert Zangrando, *The NAACP Crusade Against Lynching, 1909–1950* (Philadelphia: Temple University Press, 1980), 51–71; "Opinion of W. E. B. Du Bois," *Crisis*, September 1922, 193; "The Dyer Bill," *Crisis*, October 1922, 261.

40. "The Dyer Bill," *Crisis*, October 1922, 261–65; "Opinion of W. E. B. Du Bois," *Crisis*, January 1923, 104; "Colored Votes," *Crisis*, January 1923, 117; Alice Dunbar-Nelson, *Give Us Each Day: The Diary of Alice Dunbar-Nelson*, ed. Gloria Hull (New York: Norton, 1984), 16; "Colored Votes," *Crisis*, January 1923, 117. Although Massachusetts leaders were not defeated in the wake of the Dyer bill, Mark Schneider argues that 1922 elections marked a similar turning point in black Bostonians' shift in political allegiance from the Republican to Democratic Party. Schneider, "Boston NAACP." For African American women's participation in this ongoing political shift, see Glenda Elizabeth Gilmore, "False Friends and Avowed Enemies: Southern African Americans and Party Allegiances in the 1920s," in *Jumpin' Jim Crow: Southern Politics from Civil War to Civil Rights*, ed. Jane Dailey (Princeton, NJ: Princeton University Press), 219–38; Evelyn Brooks Higginbotham, "Clubwomen and Electoral Politics in the 1920s," in *African-American Women and the Vote, 1837–1965*, ed. Ann Gordon (Amherst: University of Massachusetts Press, 1997), 134–55; Materson, *For the Freedom of Her Race*.

41. "Negro May Pass Bar in Delaware," *Providence Journal*, July 12, 1928, Redding biographical file; "Colored Students and Graduates of 1923," *Crisis*, July 1923, 112; "Biography of Louis Lorenzo Redding '23," ca. 1973; "Competition for Gaston Medal Tuesday Evening," undated newspaper clipping, Redding biographical file.

42. Woolard, "Family of Firsts," 153; "Biography of Louis Lorenzo Redding '23," ca. 1973, Redding biographical file.

43. "Delaware NAACP Opposes Ku Klux Meeting in Wilmington," August 10, 1923; Alice Dunbar-Nelson to Walter White, August 10, 1923; Alice Baldwin to Robert Bagnall, December 13, 1923, *NAACP Papers*, 12:B:1; David Chalmers, *Hooded Americanism: The History of the Ku Klux Klan* (New York: Watts, 1981), 158–59.

44. "Colored Students and Graduates of 1923," *Crisis*, July 1923, 112; Redding interview, May 18, 1990. His graduation portrait appeared the following month in "The Horizon," *Crisis*, August 1923, 180.

45. Joe M. Richardson, "Joseph L. Wiley: A Black Florida Educator," *Florida Historical Quarterly* 71, no. 4 (April 1993): 458–72; Louis Redding, "A Florida Sunday—A Sketch," *Opportunity*, October 1925, 301–3.

46. Louis Redding to Roy Wilkins, September 2, 1933, *NAACP Papers*, 11:A:18; Redding interview, January 18, 1991. On the Big Quarterly, see Lewis J. Baldwin, "Festivity and Celebration: A Profile of Wilmington's Big Quarterly," *Delaware History* 19, no. 4 (Winter 1981): 197–211; Redding, "A Florida Sunday," 302; Redding interview, June 5, 1990.

47. Clarence Bacote, *The Story of Atlanta University: A Century of Service, 1865–1965* (Atlanta: Atlanta University Press, 1969); Redding interview, June 5, 1990; Ben Mays, *Born to Rebel: An Autobiography* (New York: Scribner, 1971), 66–98; David Levering Lewis, *When Harlem was in Vogue* (New York: Oxford University Press, 1979), 97.

48. Dunbar-Nelson, "Jewel of Inconsistencies," part 2, 279; Dunbar-Nelson, "Politics in Delaware," *Opportunity*, November 1924, 339.

49. Alice Baldwin to Robert Bagnall, May 25, 1924; Walter White to Alice Baldwin, May 27, 1924, *NAACP Papers*, 12:B:1. For the September 1924 case, see Lewis Redding to Walter White, September 17, 1924; Walter White to Lewis Redding, September 19, 1924; L. A. Redding to "Dear Son," September 20, 1924; Walter White to Lewis Redding, September 22, 1924; Lewis Redding to Walter White, September 23, 1924; Arthur Chippey to Daniel Hastings, September 25, 1924; Arthur Chippey to Sylvester Townsend, September 25, 1924; Walter White to Lewis Redding, September 26, 1924; Lewis Redding to Walter White, September 30, 1924; NAACP Press Release, "Delaware Attorney General Denies Laxity in Assault Case," October 3, 1924, *NAACP Papers*, 12:B:1.

50. Alice Baldwin to Robert Bagnall, December 11, 1924; Alice Baldwin to Robert Bagnall, October 19, 1925, *NAACP Papers*, 12:B:1. On Hastings, see the obituary in the *New York Times*, May 11, 1966.

51. "Contest Awards," *Opportunity*, May 1925, 142–43; Redding, "A Florida Sunday"; Redding, "A Christmas Journey," *Opportunity*, December 1925, 366–68; Alumni Card/Questionnaire, undated, Redding biographical file; Walter White to James Cobb, June 1, 1933, *NAACP Papers*, 16:A:7; Arthur E. Sutherland, *The Law at Harvard: A History of Ideas and Men, 1817–1967* (Cambridge, MA: Harvard University Press, 1967), 242.

52. NAACP Press Release, "White Man Attacks Colored Woman, No Action in Delaware," March 19, 1926; "Rape Case Recalled," undated broadsheet; Alice Baldwin to Robert Bagnall, December 24, 1927, *NAACP Papers*, 12:B:1.

53. Hays, "Louis Redding's Fight for Dignity and Decency," 39–40; "Membership Report," June 3, 1928, *NAACP Papers*, 12:B:1; "Along the Color Line," *Crisis*, June 1929, 199.

54. Alice Dunbar-Nelson, "As in a Looking Glass," syndicated column, July 6, 1928, box 13, Alice Dunbar-Nelson Papers, Special Collections, University of Delaware. Though she did not go into detail here, in a letter four years later she mentioned that the "1922 calamity" influenced Hastings' decision, referring to the defeat of the Republicans following demise of the Dyer bill. Alice Dunbar-Nelson to Walter White, July 1, 1932, *NAACP Papers*, 16:A:7.

55. "First Delaware Negro Lawyer in Making," *Wilmington Star*, July 1, 1928, Redding biographical file. When his office received the clipping from the news service, Brown's alumni secretary "showed it to one of my reporter friends on the Providence *Journal* and he rewrote" it for publication. Alfred Gurney to Louis Redding, August 1, 1928, Redding biographical file.

56. "First Delaware Negro Lawyer in Making"; Louis Redding to Alfred Gurney, September 2, 1928, Redding biographical file; "Along the Color Line," *Crisis*, June 1929, 199; Dunbar-Nelson, *Give Us Now*, 266.

57. Redding interview, January 18, 1991; Louis Redding to Elisabeth Strother, August 3, 1939, *NAACP Papers*, 11:B:2.

58. Redding interview, January 18, 1991; Louis Redding to Roy Wilkins, September 2, 1933, *NAACP Papers*, 11:A:18; "Wilmington Group Quizzes Afro Editor," *Baltimore Afro-American*, March 23, 1929, 7.

59. "Delaware City to Get First Race Lawyer," *Baltimore Afro-American*, March 23, 1929, 11.

60. Woolard, "Family of Firsts," 207; "To Admit Negro as Lawyer Here," *Wilmington Evening Journal*, March 19, 1929, Redding biographical file.

61. Louis Redding, "I Become a Party Man," *Opportunity*, November 1929, 348; Redding interview, May 18, 1990; Redding interview, January 18, 1991. The phrase "the burden," still resonant to Redding in his ninetieth year, was the name of the monthly feature the *Crisis* ran on segregation during the 1910s.

62. "Memorandum from Mr. Andrews to Mr. White," July 28, 1930, *NAACP Papers*, 12:B:1.

63. "Memorandum from Mr. Andrews to Mr. White," July 28, 1930, *NAACP Papers*, 12:B:1.

64. Dunbar-Nelson, *Give Us Now*, 376–79; Alice Dunbar-Nelson to Walter White, July 9, 1930; Alice Dunbar to Alice Baldwin, July 11, 1930; Alice Dunbar-Nelson to Walter White, July 12, 1930; Walter White to Alice Dunbar-Nelson, July 14, 1930; Walter White to William T. Andrews, July 14, 1930; William T. Andrews to Thomas Fraim [*sic*], July 17, 1930; William T. Andrews to Alice Dunbar-Nelson, July 19, 1930; Thomas Frame to NAACP, July 19, 1930; Walter White to William T. Andrews, July 21, 1930; Alice Dunbar-Nelson to William T. Andrews, July 21, 1930; William T. Andrews to Alice Dunbar-Nelson, July 22, 1930; Alice Dunbar-Nelson to William T. Andrews, July 23, 1930; William T. Andrews to Walter White, July 23, 1930; William H. Slockum to William T. Andrews, July 24, 1930; William T. Andrews to William H. Slockum, July 25, 1930; William H. Slockum to William T. Andrews, July 26, 1930; "Memorandum from Mr. Andrews to Mr. White," July 28, 1930, *NAACP Papers*, 12:B:1.

65. Dunbar-Nelson, *Give Us Now*, 379–82; "Memorandum from Mr. Andrews to Mr. White," July 28, 1930, *NAACP Papers*, 12:B:1.

66. Dunbar-Nelson, *Give Us Now*, 382.

67. "Negroes for Advancement," *Wilmington Evening Journal*, December 18, 1931; Pauline Young to Walter White, February 3, 1932; Pauline Young to Walter White, February 15, 1932; Walter White to Pauline Young, February 18, 1932, *NAACP Papers*, 12:B:1.

68. Walter White to Alice Dunbar-Nelson, June 24, 1932, *NAACP Papers*, 16:A:7. In January 1933 the International Labor Defense also asked Redding to join its legal staff. "Alumni Report," January 15, 1934, Redding biographical file; Walter White to James Cobb, June 1, 1932; Walter White to Louis Redding, June 1, 1932; Walter White to Arthur Spingarn, June 3, 1932; Arthur Spingarn to Walter White, June 15, 1932; Walter White to Louis Redding, June 21, 1932; Louis Redding to Walter White, June 23, 1932; Walter White to Alice Dunbar-Nelson, June 24, 1932; Walter White to Louis Redding, June 24, 1932, *NAACP Papers*, 16:A:7.

69. "1932 Annual Convention Conference Program," *NAACP Papers*, 1:A:9; "NAACP Opens Meet in D.C.," *Baltimore Afro-American*, May 21, 1932, 13, 7; "NAACP Washington Meeting Delivers Address to Nation," *Washington Tribune*, June 3, 1932, 1, 2; Walter White to Louis Redding, August 6, 1932; Louis Redding to Walter White, August 9, 1932; "Questionnaire," September 14, 1932, *NAACP Papers*, 11:B:27; Redding, "Party Man," 347; Walter White to F. Katherine Bailey, November 7, 1932; Louis Redding to Walter White, November 11, 1932; Walter White to Louis Redding, November 14, 1932, *NAACP Papers*, 11:B:21.

70. Office Diary of Walter White, entries for February 28, March 3, March 6, 1933, *NAACP Papers*, 2:A:16; W. E. B. Du Bois to J. E. Spingarn, March 28, 1933; J. E. Spingarn to W. E. B. Du Bois, April 7, 1933, reel 40, *The Papers of W. E. B. Du Bois*, microfilm (Sanford, NC: Microfilming Corp. of America, 1980–1981); Walter White to W. E. B. Du Bois, April 8, 1933; J. E. Spingarn to Walter White, April 12, 1933, *NAACP Papers*, 11:A:18.

71. W. E. B. Du Bois, "Youth and Age at Amenia," *Crisis*, October 1933, 226–27.

72. "Can a Colored Woman be a Physician?" *Crisis*, February 1933, 33–34. On their friendship, see W. E. B. Du Bois to Pauline Young, August 14, 1933, reel 40, *Du Bois Papers*. Alexander and Young graduated from Penn in succeeding years. "Education," *Crisis*, August 1920, 194; "The Higher Training of Negroes," *Crisis*, July 1921, 106. See also the biographical file in Alexander Papers and the Pauline Young Papers, Special Collections, University of Delaware.

73. Harris, "The Plight of Negro Miners," *Opportunity*, October 1925, 303–4.

74. Because little has been written about many of the following Amenia delegates, I will offer below a brief list of sources giving biographical detail. These are by no means exhaustive references; they are, rather, simply supportive of the text. **Edward Lovett**: Edward Lovett Papers, Moorland-Spingarn Research Center, Howard University. **Roy Ellis**: Roy Ellis to Walter White, June 8, 1932, *NAACP Papers*, 11:B:1; Roy Ellis to W. E. B. Du Bois, March 13, 1934, reel 42, *Du Bois Papers*. **Juanita Jackson**: "Along the Color Line," *Crisis*, April 1933, 89. **Truly Hayes**: biographical file in Hampton University Archives. See also "Flying Blade Kills Hampton Shop Teacher," *Norfolk Journal and Guide*, September 25, 1937, 1. **Thelma Taylor**: "New Negro Libraries," *Crisis*, September 1932, 285; and biographical file in the Cleveland Public Library Archives. **Howard Shaw**: "The Horizon," *Crisis*, August 1922, 171; Howard Shaw to Joel Spingarn, June 18, 1933, box 95–10, folder 401, Spingarn Papers; P. L. Prattis, "Engineers Who Wash Air," *Crisis*, September 1935, 269, 283–84. **Mabel Byrd**: "Survey of the Month," *Opportunity*, August 1926, 266; "Along the Color Line," *Crisis*, December 1927, 340; "Along the Color Line," *Crisis*, February 1928, 53–54; Byrd, "The League of Nations and the Negro Peoples," *Crisis*, July 1928, 223–24, 242; "The Negro in American Colleges," *Crisis*, August 1932, 250; Byrd, "The Black and Red Convention," *Crisis*, September 1932, 279–80, 300. **Hazel Browne**: "Along the Color Line," *Crisis*, March 1930, 97; Hazel Browne Williams, "Vita," in Hazel Browne Williams Papers, University Archives, University of Missouri-Kansas City. **Harry Greene**: s.v. Greene, Harry Washington, *Who's Who in Colored America, 1933–1938*, 219. **Frank Wilson**: "Along the Color Line," *Crisis*, September 1929, 310; "The YMCA," *Crisis*, March 1930, 87; Frank T. Wilson biographical file, Presbyterian Historical Society, Philadelphia, Pennsylvania. **Marion Cuthbert**: biographical file in Marion Cuthbert Papers, Special Collections, Atlanta University. **Frances Williams**: biographical file in Mount Holyoke College Archives & Special Collections. **Anna Arnold**: Anna Arnold Hedgeman, *The Trumpet Sounds: A Memoir of Negro Leadership* (New York: Holt, Rinehart & Winston, 1964). **Wenonah Bond**: Adele Logan Alexander, *Homeland and Waterways: The American Journey of the Bond Family, 1846–1926* (New York: Pantheon, 1999). **Sara Reid**: "Along the Color Line," *Crisis*, November 1930, 382; "Along the Color Line," *Crisis*, July 1931, 237; "Survey of the Month," *Opportunity*, February 1932, 60; "Survey of the Month," *Opportunity*, June 1933, 189. **Moran Weston**: M. Moran Weston Papers, Rare Book and Manuscript Library, Columbia University in the City of New York. I was fortunate to interview Rev. Weston by telephone on June 14 and July 21 and 22, 2000, in Heathrow, Florida.

75. Louis Redding to Roy Wilkins, September 2, 1933, *NAACP Papers*, 11:A:18.

Chapter 2

1. Amenia Conference Menu, *Papers of the National Association for the Advancement of Colored People*, microfilm (Frederick, MD: University Publications of America, 1982–) part 11, series A, reel 18; Abram Harris to V. F. Calverton, February 11, 1925; Abram Harris to V. F. Calverton, ca. late November 1925, V. F. Calverton Papers, New York Public Library; Abram Harris to Ernest Just, November 17, 1935, Ernest Just Papers, Moorland-Spingarn Research Center, Howard University; "Amenia Conference, Important Notice, no. 3, end of July, 1933," *NAACP Papers*, 11:A:18; W. E. B. Du Bois, review of *The Black Worker: The Negro and the Labor Movement*, by Sterling D. Spero and Abram L. Harris in *Nation*, April 8, 1931; Abram Harris to Joel Spingarn, April 24, 1933, box 95–5, folder 192, Joel Spingarn Papers, Moorland-Spingarn Collection, Howard University.

2. On the Harris family, see E. A. Topin, *A Biographical History of Blacks in America* (New York: McKay, 1971), 313. Mary Harris likely graduated from Richmond Colored Normal and High School.

3. Ann Field Alexander, "Black Protest in the New South: John Mitchell, Jr., (1863–1929) and the Richmond *Planet*" (Ph.D. diss., Duke University, 1973), 267, 331; Raymond Gavins, "Urbanization and Segregation: Black Leadership Patterns in Richmond, Virginia, 1900–1920," *South Atlantic Quarterly* 79, no. 3 (Summer 1980): 259; Abram Harris, *The Negro as Capitalist: A Study of Banking and Business among American Negroes* (Philadelphia: American Academy of Political and Social Science, 1936), 74–75.

4. Gavins, "Urbanization and Segregation"; Charles E. Wynes, "The Evolution of Jim Crow Laws in Twentieth Century Virginia," *Phylon* 28, no. 4 (1967): 416–25; Andrew Buni, *The Negro in Virginia Politics, 1902–1965* (Charlottesville: University of Virginia Press, 1967); Suzanne Lebsock, *A Murder in Virginia: Southern Justice on Trial* (New York: Norton, 2003), 306; *Richmond Planet*, April 9, 1904.

5. "The High School Ends Term," *Richmond Planet*, June 29, 1918, 1; Cecil Raynard Taliaferro, "Virginia Union University, The First One Hundred Years—1865 to 1965" (Ph.D. diss., University of Pittsburgh, 1975).

6. "Editor Trotter Here," *Richmond Planet*, October 25, 1919, 4; "The Redoubtable Boston Editor Succumbs to Southern 'Hospitality,'" *Richmond Planet*, November 1, 1919, 1, 3.

7. Abram Harris to the Chief of Police and whom it may concern, October 27, 1919, in Abram Harris to W. E. B. Du Bois, October 31, 1919, reel 8, *The Papers of W. E. B. Du Bois*, microfilm (Sanford, NC: Microfilming Corp. of America, 1980–1981). On the change in Mitchell, see Alexander, "Black Protest," 332.

8. Buni, *Negro in Virginia Politics*, 87; Abram Harris, "Black Communists in Dixie," *Opportunity*, January 1925, 26–27. On the Richmond Klan, see "Ku Klux Klan Meets in Richmond Tonight," *Richmond Planet*, October 2, 1920, 2; "Ku-Klux Klan is Resurrected in Nine States of South Under Charter from Georgia Court," *Richmond Planet*, October 30, 1920, 1.

9. Harris, "Black Communists in Dixie," 26–27.

10. Raymond Gavins, *The Perils and Prospects of Southern Black Leadership: Gordon Blain Hancock, 1884–1970* (Durham, NC: Duke University Press, 1977), 30; Henry Jared McGuinn, "Phylon Profile V: Joshua Baker Simpson," *Phylon* 6, no. 3 (1945): 219–24. For Harris's degree and position after graduation, see "Social Progress," *Opportunity*, September 1925, 286. Francille Wilson asserts that Harris had an "in" at both the Urban League and the *Messenger* because League officials Charles Johnson and Eugene Kinkle Jones and *Messenger* editor Chandler Owen had each graduated from Virginia Union. Francille Rusan Wilson, "The Segregated Scholars: Black Labor Historians, 1895–1950" (Ph.D. diss., University of Pennsylvania, 1988), 320–21. On Johnson, see Richard Robbins, *Sidelines Activist: Charles S. Johnson and the Struggle for Civil Rights* (Jackson: University Press of Mississippi), 29. For Harris's graduation, see "Haynes Says Good Will, Not Violence, Basis of Race Adjustment," *Norfolk Journal and Guide*, June 17, 1922, 1; "Virginia Union Commencement Program," *Richmond Planet*, June 3, 1922, 1.

11. For his address, see Abram Harris to Alain Locke, April 22, 1923, box 164–34, folder 1, Alain Locke Papers, Moorland-Spingarn Research Center, Howard University. A photograph of the Abyssinian Baptist Church's April 1922 ceremony is in Gilbert Osofsky, *Harlem: The Making of a Ghetto* (New York: Harper & Row, 1966), following page 148.

12. James Weldon Johnson, *Black Manhattan* (New York: Knopf, 1930); Osofsky, *Harlem*; David Levering Lewis, *When Harlem was in Vogue* (New York: Oxford University Press, 1979); Jervis Anderson, *This Was Harlem: A Cultural Portrait, 1900–1950* (New York: Farrar, Straus, Giroux, 1981).

13. Arthur P. Davis, "Growing Up in the New Negro Renaissance: 1920–1935," *Negro American Literature Forum* 2, no. 3 (Autumn 1968): 53–59. See also Lewis, *When Harlem was in Vogue*, 104; Kevin Gaines, *Uplifting the Race: Black Leadership, Politics, and Culture in the Twentieth Century* (Chapel Hill: University of North Carolina Press, 1996), 239.

14. Abram Harris, review of *The Modern Ku Klux Klan*, by H. P. Fry, *Opportunity*, January 1923, 28–29; Harris, review of *The New Social Order*, by Harry F. Ward, *Opportunity*, February 1923, 29–30; Harris, review of *Christianity and the Race Problem*, by Robert Edwin Smith,

Opportunity, May 1923, 29–30; Theodore Kornweibel, Jr., *No Crystal Stair: Black Life and the* Messenger, *1917–1928* (Westport, CT: Greenwood, 1975), 58; Harris, review of *The New Social Order*, by Harry F. Ward, *Messenger*, May 1923, 703, 724–25.

15. "Our Contributors," *Messenger*, July 1923, 756; Harris, "The Negro Problem," 410–18. Beginning that summer Harris appeared as "Contributing Editor" on the *Messenger*'s masthead. See *Messenger*, July 1923.

16. Matthew Guterl, *The Color of Race in America, 1900–1940* (Cambridge, MA: Harvard University Press, 2001); Abram Harris, "The Ethiopian Art Players and the Nordic Complex," *Messenger*, July 1923, 774–75, 777; Abram Harris, review of *The Black Man's Place in South Africa*, by Peter Nielsen, *Crisis*, September 1923, 209–11.

17. Abram Harris to V. F. Calverton, March 25, 1925, Calverton Papers; Andrew Buni, *Robert L. Vann of the Pittsburgh Courier: Politics and Black Journalism* (Pittsburgh: University of Pittsburgh Press, 1974); Peter Gottlieb, *Making Their Own Way: Southern Blacks' Migration to Pittsburgh, 1916–1930* (Urbana: University of Illinois Press, 1987); Scott Smith, "Pittsburgh's African-American Neighborhoods, 1900–1920," *Pittsburgh History* 78, no. 4 (Winter 1995–1996): 158–62; Abram Harris, review of *Sidelights on Negro Soldiers*, by Charles H. Williams, *Crisis*, February 1924, 174–75; Abram Harris to W. E. B. Du Bois, October 28, 1924, reel 14, *Du Bois Papers*.

18. Harris, "The New Negro Worker in Pittsburgh" (M.A. thesis, University of Pittsburgh, 1924), 1; W. E. B. Du Bois, *The Souls of Black Folk*, ed. David Blight and Robert Gooding-Williams (Boston: Bedford/St. Martin's, 1997), 134.

19. Emmett J. Scott, "Letters of Negro Migrants of 1916–1918," *Journal of Negro History* 4, no. 3 (July 1919): 290–340; Emmett J. Scott, "More Letters of Negro Migrants of 1916–1918," *Journal of Negro History* 4, no. 4 (October 1919): 412–65.

20. Harris, "The New Negro Worker," 5–6, 12–18, 47.

21. Harris, "The New Negro Worker," 49–50.

22. Du Bois, *Souls of Black Folk*, 135; Harris, "The New Negro Worker," 71–78.

23. "Social Progress," *Opportunity*, September 1925, 286.

24. "Some Male Members of the Faculty," *Institute Monthly*, October 1924, 6; "Social Progress," *Opportunity*, September 1925, 286; Charles H. Ambler and Festus P. Summers, eds., *West Virginia: The Mountain State* (Englewood Cliffs, NJ: Prentice-Hall, 1940), 414; William P. Jackameit, "A Short History of Negro Public Higher Education in West Virginia, 1890–1965," *West Virginia History* 37, no. 4 (July 1976): 309–25. See also T. Gillis Nutter, "These Colored United States, X: West Virginia," *Messenger*, February 1924, 44–48; Joe William Trotter, Jr., *Coal, Class, and Color: Blacks in Southern West Virginia, 1915–1932* (Urbana: University of Illinois Press, 1990), 220–21, 246–47.

25. Abram Harris to V. F. Calverton, October 3, 1924; Abram Harris to V. F. Calverton, October 28, 1924; Abram Harris to V. F. Calverton, ca. late October 1924, Calverton Papers.

26. Abram Harris to V. F. Calverton, October 3, 1924; Abram Harris, "Negro Migration to the North," *Current History*, September 1924, 921–25.

27. Abram Harris to V. F. Calverton, May 12, 1925; Abram Harris to V. F. Calverton, October 3, 1924, Calverton Papers.

28. Abram Harris to V. F. Calverton, ca. fall 1924; Abram Harris to V. F. Calverton, October 3, 1924; Abram Harris to V. F. Calverton, ca. October 11–12, 1924; Abram Harris to V. F. Calverton, ca. late October 1924; Abram Harris to V. F. Calverton, November 4, 1924, Calverton Papers; Abram Harris to W. E. B. Du Bois, November 7, 1924, reel 14, *Du Bois Papers*; Abram Harris to V. F. Calverton, December 12, 1924, Calverton Papers.

29. Abram Harris to V. F. Calverton, December 12, 1924, Calverton Papers. Johnson, who earned an advanced degree in divinity at Harvard in 1922, had been the first president of the Charleston NAACP, founded in 1918. See Mordecai Johnson to Walter White, March 23, 1918, in *NAACP Papers*, 12:C:26; Richard I. McKinney, *Mordecai, The Man and His Message: The Story of Mordecai Wyatt Johnson* (Washington, DC: Howard University Press, 1997).

30. Abram Harris to V. F. Calverton, January 19, 1925, Calverton Papers; Leonard Wilcox, *V. F. Calverton: Radical in the American Grain* (Philadelphia: Temple University Press, 1992), 2. See also Philip Abbot, *Leftward Ho!: V. F. Calverton and American Radicalism* (Westport, CT: Greenwood, 1993); Haim Genizi, "V. F. Calverton, a Radical Magazinist for Black Intellectuals," *Journal of Negro History* 57, no. 3 (July 1972): 241–53. For an evocative recollection of Calverton's Pratt Street salon, see James Farmer, *Lay Bare the Heart: An Autobiography of the Civil Rights Movement* (New York: Arbor House, 1985).

31. Abram Harris, "Defining the Negro Problem," review of *A Review of Society and its Problems: An Introduction to the Principles of Sociology*, by Grove S. Dow, *Opportunity*, January 1925, 26–27; Harris, "The Negro and Economic Radicalism," *Modern Quarterly*, February 1925, 198–208.

32. Abram Harris to V. F. Calverton, February 10, 1925; Abram Harris to V. F. Calverton, February 11, 1925; Abram Harris to V. F. Calverton, February 20, 1925; Abram Harris to V. F. Calverton, ca. March 1925; Abram Harris to V. F. Calverton, March 25, 1925; Abram Harris to V. F. Calverton, April 6, 1925, Calverton Papers. Harris was vague, but here he seems to hint at a spirit of Black Nationalism, perhaps derived from Garveyism or the New Negro student movement, although these movements would have rejected his insistence on the insignificance of race. Abram Harris to V. F. Calverton, ca. March 1925, Calverton Papers. See Judith Stein, *The World of Marcus Garvey: Race and Class in Modern Society* (Baton Rouge: Louisiana State University Press, 1986); Raymond Wolters, *The New Negro on Campus: Black College Rebellions of the 1920s* (Princeton, NJ: Princeton University Press, 1975).

33. Abram Harris to W. E. B. Du Bois, March 10, 1925; W. E. B. Du Bois to Abram Harris, March 14, 1925; Abram Harris to W. E. B. Du Bois, March 25, 1925, reel 17, *Du Bois Papers*; Abram Harris to V. F. Calverton, April 20, 1925, Calverton Papers.

34. Abram Harris to Alain Locke, ca. April 1925; Abram Harris to Alain Locke, April 16, 1925, box 164–34, folder 1, Locke Papers. Rayford Logan, *Howard University: The First Hundred Years, 1867–1967* (New York: New York University Press, 1969), 228–29. The "criticism" Harris mentioned likely referred to an unsigned note in the May *Crisis* chiding him for not mentioning the NAACP's 1924 platform on strikes. In response, Harris mounted a confident self-defense in correspondence with Association executive secretary James Weldon Johnson. "The Looking Glass," *Crisis*, May 1925, 38; Abram Harris to James Weldon Johnson, April 22, 1925; W. E. B. Du Bois to Abram Harris, May 14, 1925, reel 17, *Du Bois Papers*.

35. Abram Harris to V. F. Calverton, ca. spring 1925; Abram Harris to V. F. Calverton, April 20, 1925, Calverton Papers.

36. Abram Harris to V. F. Calverton, May 12, 1925; Abram Harris to V. F. Calverton, May 14, 1925, Calverton Papers; Harris, "Negro Miners in the Coal Strike," *Opportunity*, July 1925, 195; Harris, "The Negro in the Coal Mining Industry," *Opportunity*, February 1926, 45–47.

37. Abram Harris to V. F. Calverton, May 26, 1925; Abram Harris to V. F. Calverton, June 18, 1925, Calverton Papers.

38. Abram Harris to Alain Locke, June 29, 1925, box 164–34, folder 1, Locke Papers; Abram Harris to V. F. Calverton, ca. June 1925, Calverton Papers.

39. "Minnesota," *Chicago Defender*, October 31, 1925, 13. On south Minneapolis, see Michiko Hase, "W. Gertrude Brown's Struggle for Racial Justice: Female Leadership and Community in Black Minneapolis, 1920–1940" (Ph.D. diss., University of Minnesota, 1994), 35; Eugene Kinckle Jones, "The Executive Secretary Speaks," *Opportunity*, August 1925, 244; Howard Jacob Karger, "Phyllis Wheatley House: A History of the Minneapolis Black Settlement House, 1924 to 1940," *Phylon* 47, no. 1 (1986), 81; "Minnesota," *Chicago Defender*, July 11, 1925, 6.

40. Abram Harris to V. F. Calverton, July 2, 1925, Calverton Papers.

41. Abram Harris to V. F. Calverton, ca. summer 1925, Calverton Papers; "Minnesota," *Chicago Defender*, August 1, 1925, 8.

42. Abram Harris, review of *The Newer Spirit: A Sociological Criticism of Literature,* by V. F. Calverton, *Opportunity,* August 1925, 250–51; "A New Book," *Opportunity,* August 1925, 251; Abram Harris to V. F. Calverton, ca. 1925, Calverton Papers. For a close reading of this correspondence, see Jonathan Scott Holloway, *Confronting the Veil: Abram Harris, Jr., E. Franklin Frazier, and Ralph Bunche, 1919–1941* (Chapel Hill: University of North Carolina Press, 2002), 115–16.

43. "Minnesota," *Chicago Defender,* September 5, 1925, 11; "Minnesota," *Chicago Defender,* September 12, 1925, 5; "Minnesota," *Chicago Defender,* October 3, 1925, 7.

44. "Proceedings of the Annual Meeting," *Journal of Negro History* 10, no. 4 (October 1925): 583–89; Abram Harris to V. F. Calverton, September 17, 1925, Calverton Papers; "A Suggested Outline for a Study Book on Race Relations in Industry," October 7, 1925, box 43–1, folder 15, Abram Harris Papers, Moorland-Spingarn Research Center, Howard University; "Minnesota," *Chicago Defender,* October 10, 1925, 11; "Minnesota," *Chicago Defender,* October 24, 1925, 10.

45. Harris, "The Plight of Negro Miners," *Opportunity,* October 1925, 303–4.

46. Abram Harris to V. F. Calverton, October 8, 1925; Abram Harris to V. F. Calverton, ca. November 1925, Calverton Papers; "Labor Congress Closes Sessions," *Chicago Defender,* November 7, 1925, 2; "That Labor Congress," *Chicago Defender,* November 7, 1925, 10; Harris, "Lenin Casts His Shadow Upon Africa," *Crisis,* April 1926, 272–75.

47. Abram Harris to V. F. Calverton, ca. fall 1925; Abram Harris to V. F. Calverton, ca. November 1925; Abram Harris to V. F. Calverton, ca. late November 1925, Calverton Papers; Abram Harris to W. E. B. Du Bois, November 21, 1925, reel 15, *Du Bois Papers.*

48. Abram Harris to V. F. Calverton, December 8, 1925; Abram Harris to V. F. Calverton, ca. 1925, Calverton Papers; "Minnesota," *Chicago Defender,* December 19, 1925, 11; "Minnesota," *Chicago Defender,* December 26, 1925, 11. On the BSCP, see "Minnesota," *Chicago Defender,* January 16, 1926, 10.

49. Abram Harris to V. F. Calverton, ca. December 1925; Abram Harris to V. F. Calverton, December 8, 1925; Abram Harris to V. F. Calverton, December 15, 1925; Abram Harris to V. F. Calverton, ca. late 1925, Calverton Papers.

50. Abram Harris to V. F. Calverton, December 25, 1925; Harris, "A White and Black World in American Labor and Politics," *Social Forces* 4, no. 2 (December 1925): 376–83.

51. W. E. B. Du Bois to Abram Harris, January 20, 1926, reel 20, *Du Bois Papers*; Abram Harris, "The Negro in the Coal Mining Industry," *Opportunity,* February 1926, 45–47; Abram Harris to V. F. Calverton, ca. February 1926, Calverton Papers; Harris, *The Negro Population in Minneapolis: A Study of Race Relations* (Minneapolis: Minneapolis Urban League and Phyllis Wheatley Settlement House, 1926). As it identified issues affecting black Minneapolis, the survey shaped the local branch's work over the next several years. See "Historical Sketch of the Minneapolis Urban League," ca. 1934, box 1, Minneapolis Urban League Organization Records, Minnesota Historical Society, Minneapolis, Minnesota; "Minnesota," *Chicago Defender,* February 13, 1926, 9.

52. Abram Harris to V. F. Calverton, ca. February 1926; Abram Harris to V. F. Calverton, March 8, 1926; Abram Harris to V. F. Calverton, March 16, 1926, Calverton Papers; "Minnesota," *Chicago Defender,* March 6, 1926, 9; "Minnesota," *Chicago Defender,* April 17, 1926, 5; "Minnesota," *Chicago Defender,* July 17, 1926, 12; "Minnesota," *Chicago Defender,* August 7, 1926, 4; Abram Harris to E. Franklin Frazier, June 28, 1926; Abram Harris to E. Franklin Frazier, July 30, 1926, box 131–10, folder 14, E. Franklin Frazier Papers, Moorland-Spingarn Research Center, Howard University; Harris, "Negro Labor's Quarrel with White Workingmen," *Current History,* September 1926, 903–8.

53. Abram Harris to W. E. B. Du Bois, October 18, 1930, reel 33, *Du Bois Papers*; Abram L. Harris, *Race, Radicalism, and Reform: Selected Papers,* ed. William Darity (New Brunswick, NJ: Transaction, 1989), 10; "Horizon," *Crisis,* December 1926, 87. For arranging Harris's employment, see Abram Harris to Melville Herskovits, September 2, 1926; Melville Herskovits to Abram Harris, September 7, 1926; Abram Harris to Melville Herskovits, September 16, 1926, Melville

Herskovits Papers, University Archives, Northwestern University. Herskovitz was a white Africanist who had contributed to Locke's *The New Negro*. Melville Herskovits, "The Negro's Americanism," in *The New Negro*, ed. Alain Locke (New York: Boni, 1925), 353–60. W. E. B. Du Bois to Abram Harris, February 8, 1927, reel 22, *Du Bois Papers*; Abram Harris to V. F. Calverton, ca. February 1927; Abram Harris to V. F. Calverton, ca. February 1927; Abram Harris to V. F. Calverton, April 29, 1927, Calverton Papers; Helen G. Norton, "The Brookwood Conference on Negro Labor," *Opportunity*, August 1927, 244–45.

54. Charles F. Howlett, *Brookwood Labor College and the Struggle for Peace and Justice in America* (Lewiston, NY: Mellen, 1993); Nat Hentoff, *Peace Agitator: The Story of A. J. Muste* (New York: A. J. Muste Memorial Institute, 1962), 58–72; Jo Ann Ooiman Robinson, *Abraham Went Out: A Biography of A. J. Muste* (Philadelphia: Temple University Press, 1981), 31–34; Abram Harris, "Economic Foundations of American Race Division," *Social Forces* 5, no. 3 (March 1927): 468–78; Harris, "Brookwood's Symposium on Negro Labor," *Crisis*, September 1927, 226.

55. "Along the Color Line," *Crisis*, October 1927, 270; Johnson quoted in Kenneth R. Manning, *Black Apollo of Science: The Life of Ernest Everett Just* (New York: Oxford University Press, 1983), 208; Logan, *Howard University*, 243, 247–58.

56. Abram Harris to W. E. B. Du Bois, July 13, 1927, reel 22, *Du Bois Papers*; "Doctoral Dissertations in Political Economy in Programs," *American Economic Review* 17, no. 3 (September 1927): 576; Abram Harris to W. E. B. Du Bois, June 11, 1930, reel 33, *Du Bois Papers*. Francille Wilson suggests that Harris and Spero intended the collaboration between black and white scholars to underscore the potential of interracial unity, with hopes of extending the example to workers. Wilson, "The Segregated Scholars," 328; Abram Harris, *Economics and Social Reform* (New York: Harper, 1958), xiv–xv; Abram Harris to Melville Herskovits, October 22, 1927, Herskovits Papers; "The Secret City: An Impression of Colored Washington," *Crisis*, June 1932, 185–87; "Sleeping Car Porters in Mass Meeting," *Washington Tribune*, September 9, 1927, 2; advertisement for Murray Palace Casino, *Washington Tribune*, September 9, 1927, 6; Samuel H. Lacey, "Howard University May Cancel All Its Football Games," *Washington Tribune*, October 7, 1927, 1, 7; Abram Harris to Melville Herskovits, ca. November 10, 1927; Melville Herskovits to Abram Harris, November 16, 1927, Herskovits Papers.

57. Harris, "The Prospects of Black Bourgeoisie," in *Ebony and Topaz: A Collectanea*, ed. Charles Johnson (New York: National Urban League, 1927), 131–34; Abram Harris to Melville Herskovits, January 7, 1928; Abram Harris to Melville Herskovits, January 20, 1928; Abram Harris to Melville Herskovits, February 29, 1928; Abram Harris to Melville Herskovits, May 12, 1928, Herskovits Papers; Abram Harris to W. E. B. Du Bois, August 5, 1928, reel 25, *Du Bois Papers*; Abram Harris to V. F. Calverton, August 5, 1928, Calverton Papers; Davis, "Growing Up," 54; Anderson, *This Was Harlem*, 343; Abram Harris to W. E. B. Du Bois, August 5, 1928; W. E. B. Du Bois to Abram Harris, August 10, 1928, reel 25; Ira Reid to W. E. B. Du Bois, September 28, 1928, reel 26, *Du Bois Papers*. Harris described Howard as "prosaic" in Abram Harris to Melville Herskovits, May 12, 1928, Herskovits Papers. See also Abram Harris to W. E. B. Du Bois, November 25, 1928, reel 25, *Du Bois Papers*. In addition to Bunche, Francis Summer, a former colleague of Harris's at Institute, joined the psychology department, and Mortimer Weaver, another recent Harvard M.A., entered the English department. "Thirteen New Instructors Will Start Work When Howard U. Opens Monday," *Washington Tribune*, September 28, 1928, 2. Abram Harris to Franz Boas, March 6, 1929, in *The Professional Correspondence of Franz Boas*, microfilm (Wilmington, DE: Scholarly Resources, 1972); Harris, "The Negro and the New Economic Life," in *Anthology of American Negro Literature*, ed. V. F. Calverton (New York: Modern Library, 1929), 324–38; "H.U. Profs to Study Abroad," *Washington Tribune*, June 14, 1929, 6; "Along the Color Line" *Crisis*, August 1929, 275; Abram Harris to W. E. B. Du Bois, July 6, 1929, reel 28, *Du Bois Papers*; "Twenty-Sixth List of Doctoral Dissertations in Political Economy in Progress in American Universities and Colleges," *American Economic Review* 19, no. 3 (September 1929): 555;

Joanne V. Gabbin, *Sterling A. Brown: Building the Black Aesthetic Tradition* (Westport, CT: Greenwood, 1985), 49; Emmett Dorsey, Alumni Questionnaire, July 1, 1959, in biographical file, Oberlin College Archives, Oberlin College, Oberlin, Ohio; Abram Harris to Melville Herskovits, November 30, 1929, Herskovits Papers.

58. A. J. Muste to W. E. B. Du Bois, December 12, 1929, reel 29, *Du Bois Papers*; Robinson, *Abraham Went Out*, 42–45; Harris, "The Negro Worker: A Problem of Progressive Labor Action," *Crisis*, March 1930, 83–85.

59. "Asks A.F.L. to Aid Negro," *New York Times*, February 3, 1930; Harris, "The Negro Worker," 83–85; Abram Harris to W. E. B. Du Bois, December 20, 1929, reel 29; W. E. B. Du Bois to Abram Harris, January 15, 1930; W. E. B. Du Bois to Abram Harris, April 10, 1930, reel 33, *Du Bois Papers*; "National Urban League Conference," *Opportunity*, June 1930, 166–67; Abram Harris to W. E. B. Du Bois, June 11, 1930, reel 33, *Du Bois Papers*; Abram Harris to Melville Herskovits, October 28, 1930, Herskovits Papers; "Negro Educator Wins Columbia Doctorate," *New York Times*, October 12, 1930; Abram Harris to W. E. B. Du Bois, October 18, 1930; W. E. B. Du Bois to Abram Harris, October 21, 1930, reel 33; Abram Harris to W. E. B. Du Bois, October 30, 1930; Abram Harris to W. E. B. Du Bois, November 5, 1930, reel 31, *Du Bois Papers*.

60. Abram Harris to Benjamin Stolberg, November 12, 1930, Benjamin Stolberg Papers, Manuscripts and Rare Books Library, Butler Library, Columbia University; "Along the Color Line," *Crisis*, December 1930, 419–20; W. E. B. Du Bois, "Woofterism," *Crisis*, March 1931, 81–83. It is tempting to compare Harris's criticism to the tone in Benjamin Stolberg, "Classic Music and Virtuous Ladies," *Crisis*, January 1931, 23–24.

61. Melville Herskovits to Abram Harris, October 22, 1930, Herskovits Papers; A. J. Muste to W. E. B. Du Bois, December 1, 1930, reel 30; Abram Harris to W. E. B. Du Bois, December 9, 1930, reel 33, *Du Bois Papers*; "Along the Color Line," *Crisis*, March 1931, 93; "Along the Color Line," *Crisis*, December 1930, 419, 420; "The Crisis Recommends," *Crisis*, February 1931, 67.

62. Abram Harris to Benjamin Stolberg, ca. early 1931, Stolberg Papers.

63. W. E. B. Du Bois to Abram Harris, January 27, 1931; Abram Harris to W. E. B. Du Bois, January 28, 1931, reel 36, *Du Bois Papers*. Harris had been mulling this specific project as early as 1927. Abram Harris to Franz Boas, February 26, 1930; Abram Harris to Franz Boas, February 5, 1931, *The Professional Correspondence of Franz Boas*; "Survey of the Month," *Opportunity*, May 1931, 156; "Along the Color Line," *Crisis*, June 1931, 202; Abram Harris to W. E. B. Du Bois, July 24, 1931, *Du Bois Papers*; Abram Harris to Benjamin Stolberg, August 3, 1931, Stolberg Papers.

64. Abram Harris to V. F. Calverton, September 2, 1931, Calverton Papers; W. E. B. Du Bois to Abram Harris, September 16, 1931, Abram Harris to W. E. B. Du Bois, September 17, 1931, reel 36, *Du Bois Papers*; Abram Harris to Sterling Brown, November 12, 1931, correspondence box 6, Sterling Brown Papers, Moorland-Spingarn Research Center, Howard University; Abram Harris to Benjamin Stolberg, November 20, 1931, Stolberg Papers; Abram Harris, review of *The Brown American*, by Edwin Embree, *Nation*, January 6, 1932, 23–24. For Embree's enthusiastic reaction to what was ultimately a biting review, see Edwin Embree to Abram Harris, January 8, 1932, box 125–9, folder 173, Just Papers. Abram Harris to Benjamin Stolberg, December 9, 1931; Abram Harris to Benjamin Stolberg, December 21, 1931; Abram Harris to Benjamin Stolberg, January 4, 1932, Stolberg Papers.

65. Abram Harris to Benjamin Stolberg, ca. February 1932; Abram Harris to Benjamin Stolberg, February 18, 1932; Abram Harris to Benjamin Stolberg, April 7, 1932, Stolberg Papers; W. E. B. Du Bois, "The Browsing Reader," *Crisis*, March 1932, 102.

66. "Du Bois and Buell to Address H.U. Economic Clubs," *Washington Tribune*, April 22, 1932, 9; "Bellegarde, Haitian Minister, and Woodson to Address NAACP," *Washington Tribune*, April 29, 1932, 1, 2; "Gives Program for NAACP Meet in D.C.," *Baltimore Afro-American*, May 7, 1932, 4; "1932 NAACP Annual Convention Conference Program," *NAACP Papers*,

1:A:9; Abram Harris to Benjamin Stolberg, ca. April 1932, Stolberg Papers. For his suspicions of Woodson, see Abram Harris to Franz Boas, February 26, 1930, *The Professional Correspondence of Franz Boas*; "NAACP Opens Meet in D.C.," *Baltimore Afro-American*, May 21, 1932, 13, 7; "The 23d Conference, NAACP," *Crisis*, July 1932, 218; Abram Harris to Benjamin Stolberg, May 18, 1932, Benjamin Stolberg Papers; Walter White to Roy Wilkins, June 15, 1932, *NAACP Papers*, 11:A:18; Abram Harris to Benjamin Stolberg, July 7, 1932, Stolberg Papers; "The 23d Conference, NAACP," *Crisis*, July 1932, 219; NAACP Press Release, "Era of Special 'Negro' Jobs Past Says Schuyler Urging Consumer Cooperation," *NAACP Papers*, 1:A:9.

67. Abram Harris to Benjamin Stolberg, May 18, 1932, Abram Harris to Benjamin Stolberg, ca. May, 1932; Abram Harris to Benjamin Stolberg, ca. July, 1932; Abram Harris to Benjamin Stolberg, July 2, 1932; Abram Harris to Benjamin Stolberg, July 7, 1932; Abram Harris to Benjamin Stolberg, ca. mid July, 1932; Abram Harris to Benjamin Stolberg, August 25, 1932, Stolberg Papers; Abram Harris to Frank Knight, July 19, 1932, Frank Knight Papers, Special Collections Research Center, University of Chicago Library, University of Chicago; Abram Harris to Benjamin Stolberg, October 11, 1932; Abram Harris to Benjamin Stolberg, October 15, 1932; Guy Pearce to Benjamin Stolberg, October 18, 1932; Abram Harris to Benjamin Stolberg, October 20, 1932; Abram Harris to Benjamin Stolberg, November 1, 1932, Stolberg Papers; Abram Harris to Melville Herskovits, November 8, 1932, Herskovits Papers; Rayford Logan, *Howard University: The First Hundred Years, 1867–1967* (Washington, DC: Howard University Press, 1968), 281; Abram Harris to V. F. Calverton, November 18, 1932, Calverton Papers.

68. Abram Harris to Benjamin Stolberg, ca. December 1932, Stolberg Papers. For a corroborating account of Richmond in December 1932, see Daisy Lampkin, "The NAACP as Work, I. Richmond," *Crisis*, February 1933, 34–35.

69. Harris, "Types of Institutionalism," *Journal of Political Economy* 40, no. 6 (December 1932): 721–49; Abram Harris to Benjamin Stolberg, ca. December 1932; Abram Harris to Benjamin Stolberg, December 23, 1932, Abram Harris to Benjamin Stolberg, ca. January 1932, Stolberg Papers; Abram Harris to Frank Knight, January 13, 1932, Knight Papers; "Two Educators Get Fellowships," December 30, 1932, *New York Times*; "Scholarship: Awarded to HU Professor to Study Negro Finance," *Washington Tribune*, January 6, 1933, 9; "University of Chicago Publishes Article by Prof. Abram L. Harris," *Washington Tribune*, January 13, 1933, 11.

70. W. E. B. Du Bois, "Toward a New Racial Philosophy," *Crisis*, January 1933, 20–22; W. E. B. Du Bois to Abram Harris, January 6, 1933; Abram Harris to Du Bois, January 7, 1933; W. E. B. Du Bois to Abram Harris, February 2, 1933; W. E. B. Du Bois to Abram Harris, March 9, 1933; Abram Harris to W. E. B. Du Bois, March 13, 1933, reel 40, *Du Bois Papers*; "Along the Color Line," *Crisis*, March 1933, 64–65.

71. Abram Harris to Frank Knight, March 19, 1933, Knight Papers; W. E. B. Du Bois, "Karl Marx and the Negro," *Crisis*, March 1933, 55–56; Du Bois, "Marxism and the Negro Problem," *Crisis*, May 1933, 103–4, 118; Abram Harris to W. E. B. Du Bois, March 30, 1933, reel 41, *Du Bois Papers*; Abram Harris to Melville Herskovits, ca. February 1933, Herskovits Papers; Abram Harris to Frank Knight, February 17, 1933, Knight Papers; Abram Harris and Sterling Spero, "Negro Problem," in *Encyclopedia of the Social Sciences*, ed. E. R. A. Seligman and A. Johnson (New York: Macmillan, 1933), 11:335–57; Abram Harris to Joel Spingarn, April 24, 1933, box 95–5, folder 192, Spingarn Papers.

72. Abram Harris to Benjamin Stolberg, April 4, 1933; Abram Harris to Benjamin Stolberg, April 15, 1933, Stolberg Papers; Abram Harris to Melville Herskovits, May 2, 1933, Herskovits Papers; W. E. B. Du Bois to Abram Harris, May 18, 1933; Abram Harris to W. E. B. Du Bois, May 22, 1933, reel 40, *Du Bois Papers*; "Survey of the Month," *Opportunity*, June 1933, 190; Abram Harris to Benjamin Stolberg, June 28, 1933, Stolberg Papers; Abram Harris to Sterling Brown, July 12, 1933, correspondence box 6, Brown Papers; Harris, "America's Forced Labor," *Nation*, August 9, 1933, 165–66.

73. Abram Harris to Ralph Bunche, ca. July 1933, box 1, folder 7, Ralph Bunche Papers, Special Collections, Young Research Library, University of California at Los Angeles; "Education Ills Labeled Racial at NY Confab," *Baltimore Afro-American*, August 19, 1933, 9.

74. Abram Harris to W. E. B. Du Bois, July 24, 1933; W. E. B. Du Bois to Abram Harris, August 4, 1933; W. E. B. Du Bois to Joel Spingarn, August 8, 1933; W. E. B. Du Bois to Pauline Young, August 16, 1933, reel 40, *Du Bois Papers*; Attendance cards, box 95–13, folder 524, Spingarn Papers; W. E. B. Du Bois, *Dusk of Dawn: An Essay Toward an Autobiography of a Race Concept* (New York: Harcourt, Brace, 1940), 302; Roy Wilkins, *Standing Fast: The Autobiography of Roy Wilkins* (New York: Viking, 1982), 149; "President Spingarn Dies," *Crisis*, September 1939, 269; Barbara Joyce Ross, *J. E. Spingarn and the Rise of the NAACP, 1911–1939* (New York: Atheneum, 1972), 97–98; Joel Spingarn, *The Climbing Clematis* (Amenia, NY: Troutbeck, 1932); Spingarn, *American Clematis for American Gardens* (Takoma Park, MD: American Horticultural Society, 1934).

75. Wenonah Bond, "Impressions," no date, box 95–2, folder 50, Spingarn Papers.

Chapter 3

1. "The Twenty-Second Annual Conference, NAACP," *Crisis*, August 1931, 271, 284; Mark V. Tushnet, *The NAACP's Legal Strategy Against Segregated Education, 1925–1950* (Chapel Hill: University of North Carolina Press, 1987), 15–16; Harvard Sitkoff, *A New Deal for Blacks: The Emergence of Civil Rights as a National Issue* (New York: Oxford University Press, 1978), 85–86; Robert Zangrando, *The NAACP Crusade Against Lynching, 1909–1950* (Philadelphia: Temple University Press, 1980), 96–97; August Meier and John H. Bracey, Jr., "The NAACP as a Reform Movement, 1909–1965: 'To reach the conscience of America,'" *Journal of Southern History* 59, no. 1 (February 1993): 14–17; Raymond Wolters, *Negroes and the Great Depression: The Problem of Economic Recovery* (Westport, CT: Greenwood, 1970), 267–70; Barbara Joyce Ross, *J. E. Spingarn and the Rise of the NAACP, 1911–1939* (New York: Atheneum, 1972), 141–43; Charles H. Martin, "Oklahoma's 'Scottsboro' Affair: The Jess Hollins Rape Case, 1931–1936," *South Atlantic Quarterly* 79, no. 2 (Spring 1980): 175–88.

2. W. E. B. Du Bois, Memorandum to the Chairman and Secretary, January 6, 1932; January 9, 1932, reel 37, *The Papers of W. E. B. Du Bois*, microfilm (Sanford, NC: Microfilming Corp. of America, 1980–1981).

3. Sitkoff, *New Deal for Blacks*, 148; Zangrando, *NAACP Crusade Against Lynching*, 97; Board minutes, January 4; March 14; March 29, 1932, *Papers of the National Association for the Advancement of Colored People*, microfilm (Frederick, MD: University Publications of America, 1982–) part 1, series A, reel 2; "Negro Editors on Communism," *Crisis*, April 1932, 117–18; "Negro Editors on Communism," *Crisis*, May 1932, 154–56, 170. The editors represented the *Baltimore Afro-American, Norfolk Journal and Guide, New York Amsterdam News, Philadelphia Tribune, Houston Informer, Atlanta World, Houston Defender, Cincinnati Union, Kansas City Call, Oklahoma City Black Dispatch, Pittsburgh Courier, St. Louis Argus, New York Age*, and *Louisville Leader*.

4. Board minutes, April 11, 1932; "Dr. Wright's Suggestion as to Means of Increasing Interest in the NAACP," Board minutes, May 9, 1932, *NAACP Papers*, 1:A:2.

5. Board minutes, May 9, 1932, *NAACP Papers*, 1:A:2.

6. Joel Spingarn, "Race and Social Equality," typescript, *NAACP Papers*, 1:A:9; reprinted in *Baltimore Afro-American*, "U.S. to Erase Color Lines," June 4, 1932, 24.

7. W. E. B. Du Bois, "What Is Wrong with the NAACP?" typescript, *NAACP Papers*, 1:A:9.

8. W. E. B. Du Bois, "What Is Wrong with the NAACP?" typescript, *NAACP Papers*, 1:A:9.

9. W. E. B. Du Bois, "The NAACP in Washington," *Crisis*, May 1932, 159, 171; Abram Harris to Benjamin Stolberg, May 18, 1932, Benjamin Stolberg Papers, Manuscripts and Rare Books Library, Butler Library, Columbia University; "The 23d Conference, NAACP," *Crisis*, July 1932, 218.

10. Abram Harris to Benjamin Stolberg, May 18, 1932, Stolberg Papers.

11. "The 23d Conference, NAACP," *Crisis*, July 1932, 219; "Gives Program for NAACP Meet in D.C.," *Baltimore Afro-American*, May 7, 1932, 4; "NAACP Opens Meet in D.C.," *Baltimore Afro-American*, May 21, 1932, 7, 13; Abram Harris to Benjamin Stolberg, ca. May 1932, Stolberg Papers; Press Release, "Era of Special 'Negro' Jobs Past Says Schuyler Urging Consumer Cooperation," *NAACP Papers*, 1:A:9.

12. Abram Harris to Benjamin Stolberg, May 18, 1932, Stolberg Papers; "NAACP Washington Meeting Delivers Address to Nation," *Washington Tribune*, June 3, 1932, 1, 2; "The 23d Conference, NAACP," *Crisis*, July 1932, 218–19, 236.

13. Joel Spingarn to William Pickens, ca. May/June 1932, *NAACP Papers*, 11:A:18; Board minutes, June 13, 1932, *NAACP Papers*, 1:A:2; Walter White to Roy Wilkins, June 15, 1932, *NAACP Papers*, 11:A:18.

14. Roy Wilkins to Walter White, June 16, 1932, *NAACP Papers*, 11:A:18. Roy Wilkins, *Standing Fast: The Autobiography of Roy Wilkins* (New York: Viking, 1982), 116. For Wilkins's status in St. Paul, see also Anna Arnold Hedgeman, interview with Ellen Craft Dammond, December 6, 1978, Black Women Oral History Collection, Schlesinger Library, Radcliffe Institute, Cambridge, MA; Walter White to Joel Spingarn, June 29, 1932; Joel Spingarn to Roy Wilkins, June 30, 1932, *NAACP Papers*, 11:A:18.

15. Joel Spingarn to Roy Wilkins, June 30, 1932; Roy Wilkins to Walter White, July 1, 1932, *NAACP Papers*, 11:A:18; Board minutes, July 11, 1932, *NAACP Papers*, 1:A:2.

16. Abram Harris to W. E. B. Du Bois, July 24, 1931, reel 34, *Du Bois Papers*; W. E. B. Du Bois to Roy Wilkins, July 12, 1932, *NAACP Papers*, 11:A:18. Walter White's lone suggestion was to add Benjamin E. Mays, a product of Bates College and the University of Chicago, then in the midst of writing *The Negro's Church*. Walter White to Roy Wilkins, July 14, 1933; Roy Wilkins to Joel Spingarn, July 16, 1932; Roy Wilkins note, July 18, 1932, *NAACP Papers*, 11:A:18.

17. Roy Wilkins to George Schuyler, July 16, 1932, *NAACP Papers*, 11:A:18.

18. Raymond Pace Alexander to Robert Bagnall, July 25, 1932, *NAACP Papers*, 11:A:18. See, for instance, Abram Harris to Roy Wilkins, July 16, 1932; Charles Houston to Roy Wilkins, July 16, 1932; George Schulyer to Roy Wilkins, July 16, 1932; J. Gordon Baugh to Roy Wilkins, July 18, 1932; B. E. Mays to Roy Wilkins, July 20, 1932; Robert Bagnall, Memo, July 21, 1932, *NAACP Papers*, 11:A:18; Board minutes, August 1932, *NAACP Papers*, 1:A:2.

19. Nancy J. Weiss, *Farewell to the Party of Lincoln: Black Politics in the Age of FDR* (Princeton, NJ: Princeton University Press, 1983), 17; Joel Spingarn to W. E. B. Du Bois and Walter White, December 22, 1932, *NAACP Papers*, 11:A:18; Walter White to Joel Spingarn, December 31, 1932, *NAACP Papers*, 1:A:25.

20. Ross, *J. E. Spingarn and the Rise of the NAACP*, 172–77; W. E. B. Du Bois to Joel Spingarn, March 28, 1933, reel 40, *Du Bois Papers*; Walter White to NAACP Board of Directors, February 2, 1933, *NAACP Papers*, 19:A:1; Walter White to Roy Wilkins, December 27, 1932; W. E. B. Du Bois to Walter White, March 14, 1933, *NAACP Papers*, 11:A:18; Board minutes, March 14, 1933, *NAACP Papers*, 1:A:2.

21. List of recommendations, *NAACP Papers*, 11:A:18; Mason Hawkins to Du Bois, March 21, 1933; W. E. B. Du Bois to J. E. Spingarn, March 28, 1933; W. E. B. Du Bois, Memorandum Concerning the Amenia Conference, ca. April 1933, reel 40, *Du Bois Papers*.

22. W. E. B. Du Bois to J. E. Spingarn, March 28, 1933; J. E. Spingarn to W. E. B. Du Bois, April 7, 1933, reel 40, *Du Bois Papers*; Walter White to W. E. B. Du Bois, April 8, 1933; J. E. Spingarn to Walter White, April 12, 1933, *NAACP Papers*, 11:A:18.

23. "Reds Slip into Rosenwald Meeting," *Baltimore Afro-American*, May 20, 1933, 1, 2; "Miller, Frazier in Clash over Heart Appeal," *Baltimore Afro-American*, May 20, 1933, 2; "Professional Group Seeking Market," *Baltimore Afro-American*, May 20, 1933, 2; "The Rosenwald Conference," *Crisis*, July 1933, 156–57. Representative articles by Ira Reid are: "Lily White Labor," *Opportunity*, June 1930, 215–17; "Some Aspects on the Negro Community,"

Opportunity, January 1932, 18–20; "Life and Death among Negroes in New Jersey," *Opportunity,* March 1933, 72. E. Franklin Frazier, "La Bourgeoisie Noire," *Modern Quarterly* 5 (1928–1930): 78–84.

24. Arthur P. Davis, "E. Franklin Frazier (1894–1962): A Profile," *Journal of Negro Education* 31, no. 4 (Autumn 1962): 429–35; Anthony Platt, *E. Franklin Frazier Reconsidered* (New Brunswick, NJ: Rutgers University Press, 1991), 74–81; "Miller, Frazier in Clash over Heart Appeal," *Baltimore Afro-American,* May 20, 1933, 2; E. Franklin Frazier, "How Edward F. Frazier Became E. Franklin Frazier," no date, box 131–1, folder 1, E. Franklin Frazier Papers, Moorland-Spingarn Research Center, Howard University; E. Franklin Frazier to W. E. B. Du Bois, September 23, 1924, reel 13; E. Franklin Frazier to W. E. B. Du Bois, January 18, 1927; W. E. B. Du Bois to E. Franklin Frazier, January 21, 1927; W. E. B. Du Bois to Thomas E. Jones, March 9, 1927; Thomas E. Jones to W. E. B. Du Bois, March 26, 1927; W. E. B. Du Bois to Thomas E. Jones, March 30, 1927; Thomas E. Jones to W. E. B. Du Bois, April 11, 1927, reel 22, *Du Bois Papers;* Leonard Outhwaite to John Hope, May 12, 1927; John Hope to Leonard Outhwaite, May 19, 1927, E. Franklin Frazier, Fellowship, Laura Spellman Rockefeller Memorial Archives, 3.8, 97, 982 (hereafter LSRM).

25. "Lawyer's Day," *Washington Tribune,* March 24, 1933, 8; "Education," *Crisis,* November 1921, 34; "Negro Higher Education, 1921–22," *Crisis,* July 1922, 110; "Colored Students and Graduates of 1923," *Crisis,* July 1923, 108; Charles Houston to Edward Lovett, October 5, 1935, *NAACP Papers,* 2:A:2; Charles Houston to Roscoe Pound, December 15, 1925, Roscoe Pound Papers, Special Collections, Langdell Hall, Harvard University Law School; Genna Rae McNeil, *Groundwork: Charles Hamilton Houston and the Struggle for Civil Rights* (Philadelphia: University of Pennsylvania Press, 1983), 67.

26. Leonard Outhwaite to Charles Houston, March 2, 1927; Leonard Outhwaite, memorandum of interview with Charles Houston, October 20, 1927; Leonard Outhwaite to Charles Houston, November 9, 1927; Charles Houston to Leonard Outhwaite, April 7, 1928; Charles Houston, "Report of Preliminary Survey on the Negro and His Contact with the Administration of Law," May 1928, LSRM, 3.8, 101, 1018; McNeil, *Groundwork,* 70; "Att'y Charles Houston Made Vice-Dean Law," *Washington Tribune,* June 7, 1929, 5.

27. "Commonwealth v. William Brown," *Opportunity,* April 1933, 109–11; "Howard Dean to Speak at Mass Meeting Sunday," *Washington Tribune,* May 26, 1933, 8. On the Crawford case, see Richard Kluger, *Simple Justice: The History of Brown v. Board of Education and Black America's Struggle for Equality* (New York: Knopf, 1975), 147–54; McNeil, *Groundwork,* 89–95.

28. "The Negro's Problems Justify Radical Attack, Says Houston," *Washington Tribune,* July 13, 1933, 3; "NAACP Conference Resolution Reflects Economic Status Worry," *Baltimore Afro-American,* July 15, 1933; "Address Delivered by Charles H. Houston Before the Twenty-Fourth Annual Conference of the National Association for the Advancement of Colored People—Chicago, Illinois, Sunday, July 2, 1933," *NAACP Papers,* 1:A:9; "Charles Houston Succeeds Bennett on School Board," *Washington Tribune,* July 7, 1933, 1; "A Gratifying Appointment," *Washington Tribune,* July 7, 1933, 4.

29. Walter White to Joel Spingarn, July 19, 1933; Walter White to Joel Spingarn, July 22, 1933, *NAACP Papers,* 11:A:18; Charles Houston to Ralph Bunche, July 21, 1933, box 1, folder 7, Ralph Bunche Papers, Special Collections, Young Research Library, University of California at Los Angeles; W. E. B. Du Bois to Emmett Dorsey, July 10, 1933; Emmett Dorsey to W. E. B. Du Bois, ca. summer 1933, reel 39, *Du Bois Papers.*

30. Sterling A. Brown, "The Negro Character as Seen by White Authors," *Journal of Negro Education* 2, no. 2 (April 1933): 179–203; Joanne V. Gabbin, *Sterling A. Brown: Building the Black Aesthetic Tradition* (Westport, CT: Greenwood, 1985), 187; "HU Professor Returns from African Tour," *Washington Tribune,* March 17, 1933, 7; Brian Urquhart, *Ralph Bunche: An American Life* (New York: Norton, 1993), 54; "Students Conference Meets at Columbia," *Baltimore Afro-American,* April 15, 1933, 21; Moran Weston to E. Franklin Frazier, April 21, 1933, box 131–16, folder 26, Frazier Papers; Pauline A. Young, "The American

Negro, A Bibliography for School Libraries," *Wilson Bulletin for Librarians* 8, no. 8 (May 1933): 563; "Along the Color Line," *Crisis*, July 1933, 163; "Now On Tour," *Baltimore Afro-American*, July 8, 1933, 21; *"Opportunity* in Industry Aired at Conference," *Baltimore Afro-American*, July 29, 1933, 14; "Race Relations Institute Ends Month's Work," *Baltimore Afro-American*, August 12, 1933, 6; Thomas E. Jones to E. Franklin Frazier, June 16, 1933, box 131–2, folder 2, Frazier Papers.

31. "Two Washington Attorneys Enter the Jupiter Case," *Washington Tribune*, July 13, 1933, 1; "Dr. Houston Studies Peterson Case," *Baltimore Afro-American*, August 19, 1933, 8.

32. Sterling D. Spero and Abram L. Harris, *The Black Worker: The Negro and the Labor Movement* (New York: Columbia University Press, 1931), 462–64.

33. Louis Redding to Roy Wilkins, September 2, 1933, *NAACP Papers*, 11:A:18; Ralph Bunche, "The Programs, Ideologies, Tactics and Achievements of Negro Betterment and Interracial Organizations," Carnegie-Myrdal Study Research Memorandum for *The Negro in America*, 210–11, reel 1, Ralph Bunche Papers, microfilm, Lamont Library, Harvard University.

34. W. E. B. Du Bois, "Youth and Age at Amenia," *Crisis*, October 1933, 226; Frank Wilson to W. E. B. Du Bois, March 16, 1934, reel 43; Roy Ellis to W. E. B. Du Bois, March 13, 1934, reel 42, *Du Bois Papers*; Wilkins, *Standing Fast*, 151–52.

35. Louis Redding to Roy Wilkins, September 2, 1933, *NAACP Papers*, 11:A:18.

36. Lewis Mumford to Catherine Bauer, August 20, 1933, in Mumford, *My Works and Days* (New York: Harcourt Brace Jovanovich, 1979), 310.

37. Charles E. Benton, *Troutbeck: A Dutchess County Homestead* (Dutchess County, NY: Dutchess County Historical Society, 1916); Donald L. Miller, *Lewis Mumford: A Life* (New York: Weidenfeld & Nicholson, 1989), 244.

38. Benton, *Troutbeck*. For a similar account of Indian practices in eighteenth-century New York, see Alan Taylor, *William Cooper's Town: Power and Persuasion on the Frontier of the Early American Republic* (New York: Knopf, 1995), 37–38. Lewis Mumford, "The Story of Troutbeck," unpublished typescript, Troutbeck History album, Troutbeck Inn, Amenia, New York; J. E. Spingarn, "Clematis Clan Climbs Into Favor," *New York Times*, August 4, 1935.

39. Mumford, "The Story of Troutbeck"; Mumford, *Sketches from Life: The Autobiography of Lewis Mumford, The Early Years* (New York: Dial, 1982), 481–87; Miller, *Lewis Mumford*, 243–45.

40. Hilmar Jensen convinced me that Emmett Dorsey was "Jones." W. E. B. Du Bois, *Dusk of Dawn: An Essay Toward an Autobiography of a Race Concept* (New York, Harcourt, Brace: 1940), 302. ABS [Arthur Spingarn], undated note in possession of the proprietors of Troutbeck.

41. Wenonah Bond, "Impressions," no date, box 95–2, folder 50, Joel Spingarn Papers, Moorland-Spingarn Collection, Howard University; Anna Arnold Hedgeman, *The Trumpet Sounds: A Memoir of Negro Leadership* (New York: Holt, Rinehart & Winston, 1964), 62; Louis Redding to Roy Wilkins, September 2, 1933, *NAACP Papers*, 11:A:18; Virginia Alexander to Joel Spingarn, September 2, 1933, box 95–1, folder 19; Amenia Conference Photographs, box 95–13, folder 527, Spingarn Papers.

42. Photograph of the 1933 Amenia Conference, Library of Congress, Prints and Photographs Division, Visual Materials from the NAACP Records.

43. Program, Amenia Conference Important Notice, no. 3, end of July, 1933, *NAACP Papers*, 11:A:18; "Along the Color Line," *Crisis*, February 1928, 53–54; Juliette A. Derricotte, "The Student Conference at Mysore, India," *Crisis*, August 1929, 267; "HU Professor Returns from African Tour," *Washington Tribune*, January 13, 1933, 7; Moran Weston, interview, July 22, 2000; Frazier quoted in Anthony Platt, *E. Franklin Frazier Reconsidered* (New Brunswick, NJ: Rutgers University Press, 1991), 178. Frazier's pseudonymous entry (by "Mbombu") to the Amy Spingarn Contest in Literature and Arts in 1925 was slated to appear in the *Crisis*, but never did. "Krigwa," *Crisis*, October 1925, 276. Instead, Frazier published two essays on Garvey in 1926: E. Franklin Frazier, "Garvey: A Mass Leader,"

Nation, August 18, 1926, 147–48; Frazier, "The Garvey Movement," *Opportunity*, November 1926, 346–48; E. Franklin Frazier to Walter White, May 17, 1934, box 131–16, folder 32, Frazier Papers. See also E. Franklin Frazier, "La Bourgeoisie Noire," *Modern Quarterly* 5 (1928–1930): 78–84.

44. Louis Redding to Roy Wilkins, September 2, 1933, *NAACP Papers*, 11:A:18.

45. Lewis Mumford to Catherine Bauer, August 20, 1933, in Mumford, *My Works and Days*, 310; Louis Redding to Roy Wilkins, September 2, 1933, *NAACP Papers*, 11:A:18; Du Bois, "Youth and Age," 227; Ralph Bunche to W. E. B. Du Bois, March 2, 1934, reel 41; Emmett Dorsey to W. E. B. Du Bois, March 8, 1934, reel 42, *Du Bois Papers*; Wenonah Bond, "Impressions," no date, box 95–2, folder 50, Spingarn Papers.

46. Thelma Taylor to Joel Spingarn, August 30, 1933, box 95–10, folder 401, Spingarn Papers. David Levering Lewis suggests the timing of Morgenthau's visit. Lewis, *W. E. B. Du Bois: The Fight for Equality and the American Century, 1919–1963* (New York: Holt, 2000), 321; Louis Redding to Roy Wilkins, September 2, 1933, *NAACP Papers*, 11:A:18; Elmer Carter to Joel Spingarn, September 20, 1933, box 95–3, folder 93, Spingarn Papers; M. Moran Weston I, to W. E. B. Du Bois, ca. August 28, 1933; Joel Spingarn to W. E. B. Du Bois, August 22, 1933, reel 40, *Du Bois Papers*. Ultimately, Morgenthau hired Henry Hunt, principle of the Fort Valley High and Industrial School in Fort Valley, Georgia. Donnie Bellamy, "Henry A. Hunt and Black Agricultural Leadership in the New South," *Journal of Negro History* 60, no. 4 (October 1975): 464–79.

47. Wenonah Bond, "Impressions," no date, box 95–2, folder 50; Louis Redding to Joel Spingarn, September 2, 1933, box 95–9, folder 377, Spingarn Papers; Moran Weston, interview, July 22, 2000.

48. Many years later, Moran Weston still recalled the suspicious looks he received while recording his notes. The conference, after all, had been billed as an opportunity for confidential expression; to foster honest discussion, no official record was to be kept of the delegates' comments. Anna Arnold borrowed Weston's notes, likely to aid the work of the conference Finding Committee, but they were never returned to him. Moran Weston, interview, July 22, 2000; Wilkins, *Standing Fast*, 151; Louis Redding to Roy Wilkins, September 2, 1933, *NAACP Papers*, 11:A:18.

49. W. E. B. Du Bois, "On Being Ashamed of Oneself: An Essay on Race Pride," *Crisis*, September 1933, 199–200 (his emphasis); Moran Weston, interview, July 22, 2000; Amy Spingarn to Langston Hughes, September 4, 1933, box 149, folder 2769, Langston Hughes Papers, James Weldon Johnson Collection in the Yale Collection of American Literature, Beinecke Rare Book and Manuscript Library, Yale University.

50. Louis Redding to Roy Wilkins, September 2, 1933, *NAACP Papers*, 11:A:18; Wilkins, *Standing Fast*, 123, 152.

51. Louis Redding to Roy Wilkins, September 2, 1933, *NAACP Papers*, 11:A:18.

52. Louis Redding to Roy Wilkins, September 2, 1933, *NAACP Papers*, 11:A:18; Emmett Dorsey to Joel Spingarn, September 6, 1933, box 95–4, folder 135, Spingarn Papers.

53. Ira Reid to Joel Spingarn, September 2, 1933, box 95–9, folder 380, Spingarn Papers; Louis Redding to Joel Spingarn, September 2, 1933, *NAACP Papers*, 11:A:18; Du Bois, *Dusk of Dawn*, 300.

54. Ira Reid to Roy Wilkins, August 30, 1933; Roy Wilkins to William N. Jones, September 7, 1933, *NAACP Papers*, 11:A:18; Harry Greene to Joel Spingarn, August 26, 1933, box 95–5, folder 175, Spingarn Papers; Elmer Carter to Roy Wilkins, August 30, 1933, *NAACP Papers*, 11:A:18. See also Elmer Carter to Joel Spingarn, September 20, 1933, box 93–3, folder 93, Spingarn Papers.

55. Roy Wilkins to William Hastie, August 22, 1933, reel 37, William Hastie Papers, microfilm, Langdell Hall, Harvard University Law School, Cambridge, MA; Louis Redding to Joel Spingarn, September 2, 1933, box 95–9, folder 377, Spingarn Papers; Moran Weston to W. E. B. Du Bois, ca. August 28, 1933, reel 40, *Du Bois Papers*; Marion Cuthbert to Joel Spingarn, September 11, 1933, box 95–4, folder 121, Spingarn Papers.

56. Joel Spingarn to W. E. B. Du Bois, August 24, 1933, reel 40, *Du Bois Papers*; Juanita Jackson to Joel Spingarn, August 29, 1933, box 95–6, folder 233; Harry Greene to Joel Spingarn, August 26, 1933, box 95–5, folder 175; Thelma Louise Taylor to Joel Spingarn, August 30, 1933, box 95–10, folder 441; Virginia Alexander to Joel Spingarn, September 2, 1933, box 95–1, folder 19; Pauline Young to Joel Spingarn, September 11, 1933, 95–12, folder 513; Edward Lovett to Joel Spingarn, August 26, 1933, box 95–7, folder 288; Frances Williams to Joel Spingarn, August 23, 1933, box 95–12, folder 494, Spingarn Papers; Frances Williams to Walter White, August 23, 1933, *NAACP Papers*, 11:A:18; Hazel Browne to Joel Spingarn, September 6, 1933, box 95–2, folder 72; Mabel Byrd to Joel Spingarn, September 6, 1933, box 95–2, folder 75; Emmett Dorsey to Joel Spingarn, September 6, 1933, box 95–4, folder 135; Wenonah Bond, "Impressions," no date, box 95–2, folder 50, Spingarn Papers.

Chapter 4

1. Abram Harris to W. E. B. Du Bois, September 4, 1933; September 14, 1933; October 2, 1933, reel 40, *The Papers of W. E. B. Du Bois*, microfilm (Sanford, NC: Microfilming Corp. of America, 1980–1981).

2. Abram Harris to W. E. B. Du Bois, September 4, 1933, reel 40, *Du Bois Papers*; "Findings Report of the Second Amenia Conference"; Elmer Carter to Roy Wilkins, August 30, 1933, *Papers of the National Association for the Advancement of Colored People*, microfilm (Frederick, MD: University Publications of America, 1982-), part 1, series A, reel 18.

3. "Findings—Second Amenia (N.Y.) Conference, August 18–21, 1933," *Journal of Negro Education* 2, no. 4 (October 1933): 516–17.

4. W. E. B. Du Bois, "Youth and Age at Amenia," *Crisis*, October 1933; Charles Thompson to Roy Wilkins, September 9, 1933, *NAACP Papers*, 11:A:18; "Findings—Second Amenia (N.Y.) Conference," 516–17; "The Amenia Conference," *New York Amsterdam News*, September 6, 1933, 6; George S. Schuyler, "Views and Reviews," *Pittsburgh Courier*, September 16, 1933, 10; Kelly Miller, "The Young Negro Brain Trust Takes Model from Moscow," *Washington Tribune*, September 21, 1933, 4; Roy Wilkins to Walter White, August 8, 1933, *NAACP Papers*, 1:A:26; Roy Wilkins to Charles Houston, September 6, 1933, *NAACP Papers*, 11:A:18. Positive coverage included "Spingarn Calls Youth to Shape New Program," *Baltimore Afro-American*, August 26, 1933, 9; "The Amenia Conference Findings," *Washington Tribune*, September 7, 1933, 4; "Howard Faculty Members Attend Amenia Conference," *Washington Tribune*, September 7, 1933, 2; "Text of Findings of Second Amenia Conference Held in New York, August 18–21," *Baltimore Afro-American*, September 9, 1933, 6; "Young Group Asks for New Labor Move," *Baltimore Afro-American*, September 9, 1933, 9; William N. Jones, "Youth Speaks at Amenia," *Baltimore Afro-American*, September 9, 1933, 16; "Conference Reports on Its Findings," *Norfolk Journal and Guide*, September 9, 1933, 1, 10; "Discuss Future of Race Labor at Conference," *Chicago Defender*, September 9, 1933, 2; "Amenia Conference Suggests New Union Labor Movement," *Washington Tribune*, September 14, 1933, 11; "Howard Men at Amenia Confab," *Baltimore Afro-American*, September 16, 1933, 11; "Findings, Amenia, New York, Conference, August 18–21," *Washington Tribune*, September 21, 1933, 4; Elmer Carter, "The Second Amenia Conference," *Opportunity*, October 1933.

5. Walter White to Joel Spingarn, September 8, 1933; Roy Wilkins to Charles Houston, September 22, 1933; Roy Wilkins to Elmer Carter, December 13, 1933, *NAACP Papers*, 11:A:18; Board minutes, October 9, 1933, *NAACP Papers*, 1:A:2; W. E. B. Du Bois to Joel Spingarn, October 16, 1933, reel 40, *Du Bois Papers*; "Miss Mabel Byrd Gets Appointment in NRA Research Division," *Washington Tribune*, September 7, 1933, 2. The other Amenia delegate discussed was Anna Arnold, who especially impressed Joel Spingarn during the conference. Indeed, the nominating committee took into account the actions of each of

these delegates they observed at Troutbeck as an important factor concerning their nomination. Joel Spingarn to W. E. B. Bois, October 25, 1933; W. E. B. Bois to Joel Spingarn, October 25, 1933; Joel Spingarn to W. E. B. Bois, October 27, 1933; W. E. B. Du Bois to Lillian Alexander, October 30, 1933; W. E. B. Du Bois to Lillian Alexander, November 3, 1933; Lillian Alexander to W. E. B. Du Bois, November 6, 1933; Walter White to Lillian Alexander, November 9, 1933, reel 40, *Du Bois Papers*; Board minutes, November 13, 1933, *NAACP Papers*, 1:A:2.

6. Walter White, *Rope and Faggot: A Biography of Judge Lynch* (New York: Knopf, 1929); Robert Zangrando, *The NAACP Crusade Against Lynching, 1909–1950* (Philadelphia: Temple University Press, 1980), 102–3, 111; Harvard Sitkoff, *A New Deal for Blacks: The Emergence of Civil Rights as a National Issue* (New York: Oxford University Press, 1978), 280–81; Walter White to Juanita Jackson, December 5, 1933, *NAACP Papers*, 12:A:16.

7. Abram Harris to Benjamin Stolberg, December 8, 1933, Abram Harris to Benjamin Stolberg, January 9, 1934, Benjamin Stolberg Papers, Manuscripts and Rare Books Library, Butler Library, Columbia University; W. E. B. Du Bois to Abram Harris, December 3, 1933, reel 40; W. E. B. Du Bois to Abram Harris, January 16, 1934, reel 42, *Du Bois Papers*; Walter White to Abram Harris, January 11, 1934, *NAACP Papers*, 16:A:3; Abram Harris to W. E. B. Du Bois, September 4, 1933; Abram Harris to W. E. B. Du Bois, September 14, 1933; Abram Harris to W. E. B. Du Bois, October 2, 1933, reel 40, *Du Bois Papers*; Abram Harris to Joel Spingarn, September 7, 1933, box 95–5, folder 192, Joel Spingarn Papers, Moorland-Spingarn Collection, Howard University; Abram Harris to Benjamin Stolberg, September 19, 1933, Stolberg Papers; Abram Harris to Melville Herskovits, October 3, 1933, Melville Herskovits Papers, University Archives, Northwestern University; Abram Harris to Frank Knight, November 23, 1933, Frank Knight Papers, Special Collections Research Center, University of Chicago Library, University of Chicago; Abram Harris to Benjamin Stolberg, December 8, 1933; Abram Harris to Benjamin Stolberg, January 9, 1934, Stolberg Papers.

8. John P. Davis, "What Price National Recovery?" *Crisis*, December 1933, 271–72.

9. Abram Harris to W. E. B. Du Bois, December 26, 1933, reel 40; W. E. B. Du Bois to Abram Harris, January 3, 1934; Abram Harris to W. E. B. Du Bois, January 6, 1934, reel 42, *Du Bois Papers*.

10. W. E. B. Du Bois to Abram Harris, January 16, 1934; W. E. B. Du Bois to Abram Harris, January 23, 1934; W. E. B. Du Bois to Abram Harris, February 1, 1934, reel 42, *Du Bois Papers*.

11. Abram Harris to Benjamin Stolberg, February 5, 1934, Abram Harris to Benjamin Stolberg, February 19, 1934, Stolberg Papers; Abram Harris to V. F. Calverton, March 12, 1934, V. F. Calverton Papers, New York Public Library; W. E. B. Du Bois to Virginia Alexander, February 1, 1934, reel 41, *Du Bois Papers*; Walter White to Abram Harris, January 15, 1934; Abram Harris to Mary White Ovington, January 17, 1934; Walter White to Abram Harris, January 19, 1934, *NAACP Papers*, 16:A:3; W. E. B. Du Bois to E. Franklin Frazier, February 20, 1934, box 131–9, folder 4, E. Franklin Frazier Papers, Moorland-Spingarn Research Center, Howard University. Representative responses to the Negro Youth Movement proposal are Sadie Alexander to W. E. B. Du Bois, February 27, 1934; Marion Cuthbert to W. E. B. Du Bois, March 3, 1934; Sterling Brown to W. E. B. Du Bois, March 31, 1934, reel 41, *Du Bois Papers*.

12. "NAACP Progress Traced in Radio Broadcast," *Washington Tribune*, February 15, 1934, 1; Walter White, "George Crawford—Symbol," *Crisis*, January 1934, 15; Mary White Ovington, "The Year of Jubilee," *Crisis*, January 1934, 7; William Pickens, "The Second Mile," *Crisis*, January 1934, 8.

13. W. E. B. Du Bois, "Segregation," *Crisis*, January 1934, 20; W. E. B. Du Bois, "The NAACP and Race Segregation," *Crisis*, February 1934, 52–53; "Segregation—A Symposium," *Crisis*, March 1934, 79–82; W. E. B. Du Bois, "Separation and Self-Respect," *Crisis*, March 1934, 85; "History of Segregation Philosophy," *Crisis*, March 1934, 85–86; "Segregation in

the North," *Crisis*, April 1934, 115–16; "No Segregation," *Crisis*, April 1934, 116; "Objects of Segregation," *Crisis*, April 1934, 116; "Boycott," *Crisis*, April 1934, 117; "Integration," *Crisis*, April 1934, 117; Board minutes, April 9, 1934, *NAACP Papers*, 1:A:2; Abram Harris to Benjamin Stolberg, April 10, 1934, Stolberg Papers; Board minutes, April 23, 1934, *NAACP Papers*, 1:A:2.

14. Abram Harris to Benjamin Stolberg, April 10, 1934; Abram Harris to Benjamin Stolberg, April 16, 1934; Abram Harris to Benjamin Stolberg, April 27, 1934; Abram Harris to Benjamin Stolberg, May 7, 1934, Stolberg Papers; Abram Harris to Frank Knight, May 2, 1934, Knight Papers; Joel Spingarn to Walter White, May 10, 1934, *NAACP Papers*, 1:A:23; Abram Harris to Walter White, May 7, 1934; Walter White to Abram Harris, May 9, 1934; Abram Harris to Walter White, May 12, 1934, *NAACP Papers*, 16:A:3; Walter White to Charles Houston, May 2, 1934, *NAACP Papers*, 1:A:26; "He Walks Out on NRA's Consumers' Advisory Board," *Baltimore Afro-American*, September 22, 1934, 1–2; Abram Harris to Benjamin Stolberg, ca. May/June 1934, Stolberg Papers; Rachel Davis DuBois to W. E. B. Du Bois, June 15, 1934; Abram Harris to W. E. B. Du Bois, May 7, 1934, reel 42, *Du Bois Papers*.

15. W. E. B. Du Bois, "Segregation," *Crisis*, May 1934, 147; "The Board of Directors on Segregation," *Crisis*, May 1934, 149; Board minutes, May 14, 1934, *NAACP Papers*, 1:A:2; Board minutes, June 11, 1934, *NAACP Papers*, 1:A:2. W. E. B. Du Bois, "The Crawford Case," *Crisis*, May 1934, 149. Though the published editorial was a muted version of the original, privately Charles Houston admitted that he felt Du Bois had personally attacked him. Charles Houston to Walter White, May 10, 1934; Charles Houston to Roy Wilkins, May 21, 1934, *NAACP Papers*, 1:A:16; David Levering Lewis, *W. E. B. Du Bois: The Fight for Equality and the American Century, 1919–1963* (New York: Holt, 2000), 333; Mark V. Tushnet, *The NAACP's Legal Strategy Against Segregated Education, 1925–1950* (Chapel Hill: University of North Carolina Press, 1987), 29. Du Bois parted from the NAACP, and the *Crisis*, with a final flurry of "segregation" essays in the June *Crisis*: "Counsels of Despair," 182; "The Anti-Segregation Campaign," 182; "Protest," 183; "The Conservation of Races," 183; "Methods of Attack," 183; "The New Negro Alliance," 183–84; "Negro Fraternities," 184. Abram Harris to Benjamin Stolberg, ca. June 1934, Stolberg Papers.

16. Board minutes, June 11, 1934, *NAACP Papers*, 1:A:2; Rachel Davis DuBois to W. E. B. Du Bois, June 15, 1934; W. E. B. Du Bois to Rachel Davis DuBois, June 26, 1934, reel 42, *Du Bois Papers*; "Board Holds Up Du Bois' Resignation," *Baltimore Afro-American*, June 16, 1934, 1, 2; "Du Bois Hints at Starting New Organization," *Washington Tribune*, June 28, 1934, 3; "Du Bois Quits Despite Refusal of Board to Consider Resignation," *Washington Tribune*, July 5, 1934, 1, 3; "Du Bois Rejects Olive Branch from NAACP," *Baltimore Afro-American*, July 7, 1934, 1, 2.

17. Kenneth Janken, *White: The Biography of Walter White, Mr. NAACP* (New York: Free Press, 2003), 191–93; Patricia Sullivan, *Lift Every Voice: The NAACP and the Making of the Civil Rights Movement* (New York: New Press, 2009), 202.

18. Walter White to E. Franklin Frazier, May 21, 1934; Walter White to E. Franklin Frazier, June 4, 1934; E. Franklin Frazier to Walter White, June 15, 1934, box 131–16, folder 26, Frazier Papers. For Frazier's move to Howard, see Emmett J. Scott to E. Franklin Frazier, April 14, 1934; E. Franklin Frazier to Emmett J. Scott, April 15, 1934, box 131–2, folder 2; E. Franklin Frazier to Walter White, May 17, 1934, box 131–16, folder 26, Frazier Papers.

19. "Charles Houston, 'An Approach to Better Race Relations,' National YWCA Convention, Philadelphia, May 5, 1934," in Charles Houston to Roscoe Pound, May 19, 1934, Pound Papers.

20. Zangrando, *NAACP Crusade against Lynching*, 120; Hilmar Jensen, "The Rise of an African American Left: John P. Davis and the National Negro Congress" (Ph.D. diss., Cornell University, 1997); "NAACP Opens 25th Annual Conference," *Baltimore Afro-American*, June 30, 1934, 14; "NAACP Hits Segregation," *Washington Tribune*, July 5, 1934, 1, 3; "Davis Says New Deal Has Not Aided Negroes," *Washington Tribune*, July 5, 1934, 9; "Davis Calls

Bluff of 300 Cotton Ginners," *Baltimore Afro-American*, July 7, 1934, 2; "White Urges an 'Unending War' on Segregation," *Baltimore Afro-American*, July 7, 1934, 3; "Okla. House Shocked by J. P. Davis," *Washington Tribune*, July 12, 1–2; "Critical Survey of Negro's Plight at NAACP Conference," press release, June 15, 1934; "An Address to the Country by the Twenty-Fifth Annual Conference of the NAACP, Oklahoma City, June 27 to July 1," July 1934; Walter White, address to annual convention, 1934; Conference Program, 1934; "Twenty-Five Years of Work," Mary White Ovington, *NAACP Papers*, 1:A:9.

21. "Along the Color Line," *Crisis*, April 1933, 89; "Charles Houston Speaks in Richmond and Baltimore," *Washington Tribune*, January 25, 1934, 3; Bruce A. Thompson, "The Civil Rights Vanguard: The NAACP and the Black Community in Baltimore, 1931–1942" (Ph.D. diss., University of Maryland, 1996), 52–53; Andor Skotnes, "'Buy Where You Can Work': Boycotting for Jobs in African-American Baltimore, 1933–1934," *Journal of Social History* 27, no. 4 (Summer 1994): 735–61; Juanita Jackson to Caroline Dunjee, October 26, 1936, *NAACP Papers*, 1:A:17.

22. Walter White to Juanita Jackson, November 28, 1933; Juanita Jackson to Walter White, November 29, 1933; Walter White to Juanita Jackson, November 29, 1933; Walter White to Juanita Jackson, December 5, 1933; Walter White to Rev. Charles Y. Trigg, January 26, 1934; Walter White to Juanita Jackson, February 8, 1934, *NAACP Papers*, 12:A:16. For a photograph of Jackson at the anti-lynching hearing, see Denton L. Watson, *Lion in the Lobby: Clarence Mitchell, Jr.'s Struggle for the Passage of Civil Rights Laws* (New York: Morrow, 1990), 261. Juanita Jackson to Walter White, May 29, 1934; Juanita Jackson to Roy Wilkins, June 4, 1934; Juanita Jackson to Roy Wilkins, June 7, 1934, *NAACP Papers*, 12:A:16; Juanita Jackson to Walter White, June 4, 1934, *NAACP Papers*, 1:A:16; Roy Wilkins, "The NAACP Meets in Oklahoma," *Crisis*, August 1934, 229–30.

23. Program, 25th Annual Conference of the NAACP, 1934, *NAACP Papers*, 1:A:9; "Houston, White and Davis Visit Flood Control Project," *Washington Tribune*, July 12, 1934, 15; Walter White to Abram Harris, November 27, 1934, *NAACP Papers*, 2:A:17; "Swarthmore to Open Institute," *Baltimore Afro-American*, July 14, 1934, 9.

24. Helen Boardman and Martha Gruening, "Is the NAACP Retreating?" *Nation*, June 27, 1934, 730–32. Charles Houston and Leon Ransom, co-counsel in the case, responded in the following issue. Charles Houston and Leon Ransom, "The George Crawford Case: An Experiment in Social Statesmanship," *Nation*, July 4, 1934, 17–19. For Harris, see "5 H.U. Professors Attending Race Relations Meet," *Washington Tribune*, July 19, 1934, 9.

25. Board minutes, July 9, 1934; Board minutes, July 19, 1934, *NAACP Papers*, 1:A:2; Walter White to Abram Harris, July 10, 1934, Abram Harris to Walter White, July 11, 1934; Walter White to Abram Harris, July 13, 1934, *NAACP Papers*, 16:A:4; Abram Harris to Walter White, July 14, 1934; Walter White to Abram Harris, July 20, 1934; Walter White to Charles Houston, August 7, 1934, *NAACP Papers*, 16:A:8.

26. Abram Harris to Walter White, July 18, 1934, *NAACP Papers*, 16:A:8; Jensen, "African American Left," 159. At first, Harris thought the convivial setting might hamper truly critical discussion of the NAACP. But when it became evident that older board members Mary White Ovington and James Weldon Johnson would have difficulty traveling the distance from their homes in Great Barrington, he agreed to leave the decision to the rest of the committee. Walter White to Abram Harris, July 20, 1934; Abram Harris to Walter White, July 28, 1934; Walter White to Abram Harris, July 30, 1934; Abram Harris to Walter White, August 4, 1934, *NAACP Papers*, 16:A:8.

27. Abram Harris to Walter White, July 28, 1934; Abram Harris to Walter White, August 4, 1934, *NAACP Papers*, 16:A:8; Abram Harris to W. E. B. Du Bois, August 6, 1934, reel 42, *Du Bois Papers*; Abram Harris to Benjamin Stolberg, August 11, 1934; Abram Harris to Benjamin Stolberg, August 21, 1934, Stolberg Papers; Abram Harris to Frank Knight, August 22, 1934, Knight Papers.

28. Walter White to Mr. Tunner, August 28, 1934; Abram Harris to the Board of Directors, September 6, 1934, *NAACP Papers*, 16:A:8; Board minutes, September 10, 1934, *NAACP*

Papers, 1:A:2. The logistics of getting committee members to commit to traveling to Amenia in time for the Spingarns to prepare their arrival necessitated that the meeting be at 69 Fifth Avenue instead. Roy Wilkins to Rinchetta Randolph, August 16, 1934; Walter White to Abram Harris, August 16, 1934; Abram Harris to Walter White, August 16, 1934; Joel Spingarn to Roy Wilkins, August 18, 1934; Walter White to Joel Spingarn, August 20, 1934, *NAACP Papers*, 16:A:8.

29. For instance, Memo, August 6, 1934; Abram Harris to Arthur Spingarn, August 28, 1934; Abram Harris to Ralph Bunche, August 28, 1934; William Pickens to Abram Harris, August 29, 1934; Roy Wilkins to Abram Harris, September 6, 1934, *NAACP Papers*, 16:A:8. See also Walter White to Benjamin Stolberg, August 29, 1934; Roy Wilkins to Walter White, August 30, 1934; Walter White to Benjamin Stolberg, August 30, 1934; Walter White to Lewis Gannett, August 30, 1934; Walter White to Abram Harris, August 31, 1934; Walter White to Mary White Ovington, September 5, 1934; Benjamin Stolberg to Walter White, September 5, 1934, *NAACP Papers*, 16:A:8.

30. Board minutes, September 10, 1934, *NAACP Papers*, 1:A:2; "He Walks Out on NRA's Consumers' Advisory Board," *Baltimore Afro-American*, September 22, 1934, 1–2; Abram Harris to the Board of Directors, NAACP, September 6, 1934; Abram Harris to Walter White, September 10, 1934; Walter White to Abram Harris, September 12, 1934; Abram Harris to Walter White, September 13, 1934; Walter White to Abram Harris, September 14, 1934; Walter White to Abram Harris, September 19, 1934; Abram Harris to Joel Spingarn, September 21, 1934; Abram Harris to T. Arnold Hill, January 2, 1935, *NAACP Papers*, 16:A:8.

31. "Preliminary Report of the Committee on Future Plan and Program of the NAACP," *NAACP Papers*, 16:A:8, 1–5.

32. "Preliminary Report of the Committee on Future Plan and Program of the NAACP," *NAACP Papers*, 16:A:8, 5–17.

33. Roy Wilkins to Walter White, September 19, 1934, *NAACP Papers*, 16:A:8.

34. Board minutes, September 25, 1934, *NAACP Papers*, 1:A:2; Harry Davis to Walter White, September 21, 1934; Joseph Prince Loud to Walter White, September 22, 1934; Isadore Martin to Joel Spingarn, September 24, 1934; Mary White Ovington to Walter White, September 23, 1934; Daisy Lampkin to Walter White, September 24, 1934; William Hastie to Walter White, September 24, 1934; Charles Houston to Walter White, September 24, 1934, *NAACP Papers*, 16:A:8.

35. Genna Rae McNeil, *Groundwork: Charles Hamilton Houston and the Struggle for Civil Rights* (Philadelphia: University of Pennsylvania Press, 1983), 116–17; Charles Houston, "Statement on Legal Activities of the NAACP," June 24, 1935, *NAACP Papers*, 1:A:9.

36. Ralph Bunche, Emmett Dorsey, and Abram Harris to The Editor, *Fortune*, October 30, 1934, reel 2, Ralph Bunche Papers, microfilm, Lamont Library, Harvard University; "The Negroes in Washington," *Fortune*, December 1934, 132.

37. Board minutes, September 25, 1934; October 8, 1934, *NAACP Papers*, 1:A:2; Walter White to Abram Harris, September 20, 1934; Walter White to Abram Harris, October 3, 1934; Walter White to Abram Harris, October 10, 1934; Abram Harris to Walter White, October 11, 1934, *NAACP Papers*, 16:A:8.

38. Jensen, "African American Left," 457; Charles Houston and John P. Davis, "TVA: Lily-White Reconstruction," *Crisis*, October 1934, 290–91, 311; John P. Davis, "NRA Codifies Wage Slavery," *Crisis*, October 1934, 298–99, 304.

39. Office Diary of Walter White, November 2, 1934, *NAACP Papers*, 2:A:17.

40. Charles Houston to Walter White, November 5, 1934, *NAACP Papers*, 1:A:16. For White's response, see Walter White to Charles Houston, November 8, 1934, *NAACP Papers*, 1:A:26.

41. Minutes of the Board of Directors, November 24, 1934, *NAACP Papers*, 16:A:4; Walter White to James Weldon Johnson, May 14, 1934, *NAACP Papers*, 16:A:3; Walter White to Carl Murphy, November 22, 1934; Carl Murphy to Walter White, November 23, 1934;

Walter White to Carl Murphy, November 27, 1934, *NAACP Papers*, 12:A:16; Walter White to Juanita Jackson, July 10, 1934, *NAACP Papers*, 1:A:26; Lillie May Jackson to Walter White, July 25, 1934, *NAACP Papers*, 12:A:16; Mary Jenness, *Twelve Negro Americans* (New York: Friendship, 1936), 126, 133; "National Vice-President of M.E. National Council," *Baltimore Afro-American*, September 15, 1934, 3; Walter White to Joel Spingarn, November 16, 1934; Joel Spingarn to Walter White, November 19, 1934, *NAACP Papers*, 1:A:23; Walter White to Charles Dorsey, October 23, 1934; Walter White to Charles Dorsey, December 12, 1934; Charles Dorsey to Walter White, January 7, 1935, *NAACP Papers*, 12:B:8; Walter White to Arthur Spingarn, November 26, 1934, *NAACP Papers*, 16:A:4.

42. Walter White to Abram Harris, November 27, 1934, *NAACP Papers*, 2:A:17; Charles Houston to Walter White, November 2, 1934, *NAACP Papers*, 1:A:16.

43. "Our Aims," *Race*, Winter 1935–36, 3; Jensen, "African American Left," 466–72; Abram Harris to Walter White, December 4, 1934, *NAACP Papers*, 16:A:4.

44. Abram Harris to Frank Knight, September 16, 1934, Knight Papers; Abram Harris to Benjamin Stolberg, January 15, 1934, Stolberg Papers; Abram Harris to Walter White, December 27, 1934, *NAACP Papers*, 16:A:4; W. E. B. Du Bois to Rachel Davis DuBois, June 26, 1934, reel 42, *Du Bois Papers*. It took Harris nearly three months to convince the NAACP his resignation was serious. See, for example, Walter White to Abram Harris, December 29, 1934, *NAACP Papers*, 16:A:4; Walter White to Abram Harris, January 10, 1935; Abram Harris to Walter White, *NAACP Papers*, 11:A:5; Board minutes, February 11, 1935; March 11, 1935, *NAACP Papers*, 1:A:2. Abram Harris to Benjamin Stolberg, January 15, 1935, Stolberg Papers.

45. Walter White to Joel Spingarn, December 27, 1934, *NAACP Papers*, 1:A:26; "Crime Pickets Arrested," *Baltimore Afro-American*, December 15, 1934, 1, 2; "Ropes Are Not Placards," *Baltimore Afro-American*, December 22, 1934, 1; Arthur M. Carter, "NAACP Pickets Make Silent Protest after Police Arrest Threats," *Washington Tribune*, December 22, 1934, 16; "Picket Crime Conference," *Crisis*, January 1935, 26; Wilkins, *Standing Fast: The Autobiography of Roy Wilkins* (New York: Viking, 1982), 133–36; Walter White to Ralph Bunche, December 20, 1934, reel 3, Bunche Papers, Harvard University.

46. August Meier and Elliott Rudwick, "Attorneys Black and White: A Case Study of Race Relations within the NAACP," *Journal of American History* 62, no. 4 (March 1976): 913–46; Charles Houston, "The Need for Negro Lawyers," *Journal of Negro Education* 4 (January 1935): 49–52; Charles Houston to Walter White, January 23, 1935, *NAACP Papers*, 1:A:16; Richard Kluger, *Simple Justice: The History of* Brown v. Board of Education *and Black America's Struggle for Equality* (New York: Knopf, 1975), 162–63.

47. Jenness, *Twelve Negro Americans*, 132; Juanita Jackson to Walter White, February 26, 1935; Marjorie Penney to Juanita Jackson, September 16, 1936, *NAACP Papers*, 1:A:16; Juanita Jackson to Robert Snead, March 25, 1936, *NAACP Papers*, 12:B:6. Jackson had been trying to arrange an appearance by Johnson since the fall of 1933, just after the second Amenia Conference. See, for instance, Juanita Jackson to James Weldon Johnson, February 19, 1934; Juanita Jackson to James Weldon Johnson, November 25, 1934, box 3, folder 35, James Weldon Johnson Correspondence Files, James Weldon Johnson Collection in the Yale Collection of American Literature, Beinecke Rare Book and Manuscripts Library, Yale University.

48. Walter White to Juanita Jackson, February 28, 1935; Walter White to Juanita Jackson, March 19, 1935; Walter White to Juanita Jackson, April 2, 1935; Walter White to Juanita Jackson, April 9, 1935; Walter White to Juanita Jackson, June 6, 1935, *NAACP Papers*, 1:A:26; "Memorandum from the Secretary to the Committee on Administration," April 1, 1935; Minutes of the Meeting of the Committee on Administration, April 1, 1935, *NAACP Papers*, 16:A:5; Juanita Jackson to Walter White, April 5, 1935; Juanita Jackson to Walter White, June 4, 1935, *NAACP Papers*, 1:A:16; Board minutes, March 11, 1935; April 8, 1935, *NAACP Papers*, 1:A:2; Mary White Ovington, "A Visit to Our National Office," *Crisis*, May 1936, 156.

49. Walter White to E. Franklin Frazier, March 25, 1935; E. Franklin Frazier to Walter White, March 30, 1935, box 131-16, folder 26, Frazier Papers; Walter White, "Statement to the Press on Harlem Riot of March 19th," *NAACP Papers*, 7:A:15; "Mayor Places Radicals' Foe on Riot Body," *New York Amsterdam News*, April 6, 1935, 1, 2.

50. "It's Your Job Now," *New York Amsterdam News*, June 8, 1935, 9; "Davis Seeks Opinions on Proposed National Congress," *Baltimore Afro-American*, June 15, 1935, 4.

51. Raymond Wolters, *Negroes and the Great Depression: The Problem of Economic Recovery* (Westport, CT: Greenwood, 1970), 377–78; "St. Louis Host to 26th Annual Conference," *Crisis*, August 1935, 248–50; Joel Spingarn, "The Second Quarter-Century of the NAACP," June 25, 1935; NAACP Press Release, June 30, 1935, *NAACP Papers*, 1:A:9; Janken, *White*, 194–95.

52. Sullivan, *Lift Every Voice*, 222–23; Charles Houston, "Statement on Legal Activities at the NAACP," June 24, 1935, *NAACP Papers*, 1:A:9; Charles Houston to Claude Barnett and P. L. Prattis, July 12, 1935, *NAACP Papers*, 2:A:2; Sitkoff, *New Deal for Blacks*, 221–22.

53. Juanita Jackson, "Young Colored America Awakes," *Crisis*, September 1938, 289; Thompson, "The Civil Rights Vanguard," 225–26; Juanita Jackson, "Share Cropper Talks, NAACP Weeps," *Baltimore Afro-American*, July 6, 1935, 1, 2; "Resolutions Committee, St. Louis Conference 1935," *NAACP Papers*, 1:A:9; "Roosevelt Says that NAACP Rendered Important Service," *Baltimore Afro-American*, July 6, 1935, 1, 2.

54. Juanita Jackson to Walter White, July 9, 1935, *NAACP Papers*, 1:A:16; Walter White to Juanita Jackson, July 18, 1935, *NAACP Papers*, 1:A:26; Virginia Alexander and George Simpson, "The Social, Economic and Health Problems of North Philadelphia Negroes and Their Relation to a Proposed Interracial Public Health Demonstration Center," typescript, 49, Alexander Papers. The study was published in summary form as "Negro Hospitalization," *Opportunity*, August 1937, 231–32. Juanita Jackson to Walter White, September 9, 1935, *NAACP Papers*, 1:A:16.

Chapter 5

1. "Baltimore Campaign," *Crisis*, December 1935, 374.

2. Recent works demonstrate that during the 1930s and 1940s such women as Juanita Jackson, Ella Baker, Anna Arnold Hedgeman, Dorothy Height, Pauli Murray, and Septima Clark, among many others, transcended traditional conventions of black women's leadership, moving beyond the "politics of respectability" that characterized the clubwomen's movements of the early twentieth century toward an outward embrace of militant activism with emphasis on radical social change and direct action protest. Prudence Cumberbatch, "What 'the Cause' Needs Is a 'Brainy and Energetic Woman': A Study of Female Charismatic Leadership in Baltimore," in *Want to Start a Revolution? Radical Women in the Black Freedom Struggle*, ed. Dayo Gore, Jeanne Theoharis, and Komozoi Woodard (New York: New York University Press, 2009), 47–70; Barbara Ransby, *Ella Baker and the Black Freedom Movement: A Radical Democratic Vision* (Chapel Hill: University of North Carolina Press); Thomas Sugrue, *Sweet Land of Liberty: The Forgotten Struggle for Civil Rights in the North* (New York: Random House, 2008), 3–31; Dorothy Height, *Open Wide the Freedom Gates* (New York: PublicAffairs, 2003); Glenda Gilmore, *Defying Dixie: The Radical Roots of Civil Rights, 1919–1950* (New York: Norton, 2008); Katherine Mellon Charron, *Freedom's Teacher: The Life of Septima Clark* (Chapel Hill: University of North Carolina Press, 2010).

3. "Baltimore Campaign Nets $2,314 in Memberships," *Crisis*, December 1935, 374–75; Bruce A. Thompson, "The Civil Rights Vanguard: The NAACP and the Black Community in Baltimore, 1931–1942" (Ph.D. diss., University of Maryland, 1996), 15–19; Dreck Spurlock Wilson, "Druid Hill Branch, Young Men's Christian Association: The First Hundred Years," *Maryland Historical Magazine* 84, no. 2 (1989): 135–46.

4. Willard Gatewood, *Aristocrats of Color: The Black Elite, 1880–1920* (Baton Rouge: Louisiana State University Press, 1990), 72–80, 227–28; "Economic," *Crisis*, November 1910, 6; "Opinion," *Crisis*, November 1910, 7; "Baltimore," *Crisis*, November 1910, 11; W. Ashbie Hawkins, "A Year of Segregation in Baltimore," *Crisis*, November 1911, 27–30.

5. *Crisis*, February 1911, 18–19.

6. "Along the Color Line," *Crisis*, November 1910, 3; "Judicial Decisions," *Crisis*, December 1910, 6; "The Maryland Decision," *Crisis*, December 1910, 12–13.

7. Juanita Jackson, "Biographical Sketch for Publicity Purposes," ca. 1936, *Papers of the National Association for the Advancement of Colored People*, microfilm (Frederick, MD: University Publications of America, 1982–), part 1, series A, reel 17; "Student Information, 1929–1930"; Juanita Jackson Mitchell to Vartan Gregorian, September 24, 1980; Black Centenary Celebration Questionnaire, "Biographical Sketch of Juanita Jackson Mitchell," ca. 1980, Juanita Jackson Mitchell biographical file, University Archives and Record Center, University of Pennsylvania; Mary Jenness, *Twelve Negro Americans* (New York: Friendship, 1936), 128–29; Andor Skotnes, "Narratives of Juanita Jackson Mitchell: The Making of a 1930s Freedom Movement Leader," *Maryland Historian* 1, no. 1 (Fall/Winter 2001): 44–66; Cumberbatch, "What 'the Cause' Needs."

8. "National Vice-President of M.E. National Council," *Baltimore Afro-American*, September 15, 1934, 3; Jenness, *Twelve Negro Americans*, 126–27; "Now on Tour," *Baltimore Afro-American*, July 8, 1933, 8; William N. Jones, "Day by Day," *Baltimore Afro-American*, August 26, 1933, 16; Thompson, "The Civil Rights Vanguard," 44, 50, 62–72. James Farmer remembered Jackson as a star within the Methodist Church's national youth movement. Farmer, *Lay Bare the Heart: An Autobiography of the Civil Rights Movement* (New York: Arbor House, 1985), 127–29.

9. Walter White to Juanita Jackson, July 18, 1935; Walter White to Daisy Lampkin, September 3, 1935; Walter White to Daisy Lampkin, September 11, 1935; Walter White to Juanita Jackson, September 11, 1935, *NAACP Papers*, 1:A:26; Juanita Jackson to Walter White, September 9, 1935, *NAACP Papers*, 1:A:16; "Murray Enters Md. U. Law School," *Baltimore Afro-American*, September 28, 1935, 1, 2; "Couldn't Keep Him Out," *Baltimore Afro-American*, September 28, 1935, 5; Ralph Matthews, "Watching the Big Parade," *Baltimore Afro-American*, September 28, 1935, 6; Charles Flint Kellogg, *NAACP: A History of the National Association for the Advancement of Colored People*, vol. 1, *1909–1920* (Baltimore: Johns Hopkins Press, 1967); Charles Houston, "Cracking Closed Doors," *Crisis*, December 1935, 364, 370, 374; Richard Kluger, *Simple Justice: The History of* Brown v. Board of Education *and Black America's Struggle for Equality* (New York: Knopf, 1975), 186–94; Juanita Jackson to Roy Wilkins, September 9, 1935, *NAACP Papers*, 1:A:16; W. Edward Orser, "Neither Separate Nor Equal: Foreshadowing *Brown* in Baltimore County, 1935–1937," *Maryland Historian* 92, no. 1 (Spring 1997): 5–35.

10. "NAACP Wades Into Problem of MD," *Baltimore Afro-American*, September 21, 1935, 1; "NAACP Workers Await Coming of Woman Leader," *Baltimore Afro-American*, September 28, 1935, 15; "Mayor Leads Off in NAACP Drive with $25 Gift," *Baltimore Afro-American*, October 5, 1935, 11; "Baltimore Mayor Gives $25," *Baltimore Afro-American*, October 5, 1935, 17; Juanita Jackson to Walter White, October 1, 1935, *NAACP Papers*, 12:A:16.

11. "Victory Speaker," *Baltimore Afro-American*, October 5, 1935, 15; "NAACP Campaign Jumps to 2,000 in Final Spurt," *Baltimore Afro-American*, October 19, 1935, 15.

12. Walter White to Juanita Jackson, October 11, 1935, *NAACP Papers*, 12:A:16; "Branch News," *Crisis*, December 1935, 377; Juanita Jackson to Daisy Lampkin, November 8, 1935; Juanita Jackson to Daisy Lampkin, November 8, 1935; Juanita Jackson, handwritten notes on "Report of the Special Assistant to the Secretary," February 1936; Juanita Jackson to Walter White, July 16, 1936, *NAACP Papers*, 1:A:16; "$2,000 Received from 1935 Christmas Seal Sale," *Crisis*, March 1936, 86–87; Mary McLeod Bethune to Juanita Jackson, November 27, 1935, *NAACP Papers*, 1:A:16; "Branch News," *Crisis*, March 1936, 88; "Branch News," *Crisis*, April 1936, 119; Juanita Jackson to Walter White, March 25, 1936,

NAACP Papers, 19:A:1; "Branch News," *Crisis*, May 1936, 154; Juanita Jackson to Daisy Lampkin, March 12, 1936, *NAACP Papers*, 1:A:16; Juanita Jackson to "Dear Friend," February 4, 1936; Juanita Jackson to James E. Allen, February 6, 1936; Juanita Jackson to James E. Allen, March 6, 1936; Juanita Jackson to James E. Allen, March 24, 1936, *NAACP Papers*, 12:B:5; Juanita Jackson to Robert Snead, March 25, 1936, *NAACP Papers*, 12:B:6; Juanita Jackson to Walter White, March 9, 1935; Juanita Jackson to Rinchetta Randolph, April 8, 1936, *NAACP Papers*, 1:A:16; Board minutes, March 9, 1936, *NAACP Papers*, 1:A:2.

13. "Chapters Already Established," ca. 1923; Robert Bagnall to C. H. Mason, February 14, 1923; "How to Form a Junior Division," ca. 1925; "Suggestion for a Program for College Chapters," ca. 1930; "What Can Youth Movement Do?" ca. 1931; Robert Bagnall to Walter White, September 29, 1931; Walter White, Memorandum to the Board of Directors, February 2, 1933, *NAACP Papers*, 19:A:1.

14. "Interracial Meet Here," *Boston Chronicle*, April 22, 1933, 1; "N.E. Negro Congress," *Boston Chronicle*, February 8, 1936, 1; "N.E. Congress Huge Success," *Boston Chronicle*, February 15, 1936, 1; "The Negro Congress," *Boston Chronicle*, February 15, 1936, 4; "National Negro Congress Makes History," *Boston Chronicle*, February 22, 1936, 1; "Julian Steele Gets Professorship," *Boston Guardian*, October 26, 1935, newspaper clipping; "Saltonstall Aids Drive for Negroes," *Boston Traveler*, April 17, 1936, box 3, scrapbook; John P. Davis to Julian D. Steele, April 9, 1936, box 5, folder 1; Alfred Baker Lewis to Julian Steele, February 4, 1936; Boston branch NAACP minutes, March 18, 1936; Boston branch NAACP minutes, April 1, 1936, box 20, folder 6, Julian D. Steele Papers, Special Collections, Mugar Library, Boston University.

15. "Butler R. Wilson and the Boston NAACP Branch," *Crisis*, December 1974, 346–48; "Crawford Will Be Extradited, *Boston Chronicle*, February 18, 1933, 1; "Continue Fight For Crawford," *Boston Chronicle*, February 25, 1933, 1; "Habeas Corpus Writ Issued," *Boston Chronicle*, March 4, 1933, 1; "Crawford Hearing Postponed," *Boston Chronicle*, March 18, 1933, 1; "Habeas Corpus Case in Court," *Boston Chronicle*, March 25, 1933, 1.

16. "No Negro Managers," *Boston Chronicle*, February 3, 1934, 1; "FINAST Chain Hires Negroes," *Boston Chronicle*, May 5, 1934, 1; Eben Simmons Miller, "'A New Day is Here': The Shooting of George Borden and 1930s Civil Rights Activism in Boston," *New England Quarterly* 73, no. 1 (March 2000): 3–31.

17. Jeffrey Thomas Sammons, "Boston Blacks in the Depression and New Deal" (M.A. thesis, Tufts University, 1974), 17–18; "Boston NAACP Holds Annual Meeting," *Boston Chronicle*, February 29, 1936, 1; "Atty. Has Fine Record," *Boston Chronicle*, February 29, 1936, 1; "Passing the Baton," *Boston Chronicle*, February 29, 1936, 4; "Dorch Makes Appeal," *Boston Chronicle*, March 7, 1936, 1.

18. "The Boston NAACP Appeals," *Boston Chronicle*, April 27, 1935, 4; "Holmes at NAACP Drive," *Boston Chronicle*, May 11, 1935, 1; Juanita Jackson to Roy Wilkins, April 16, 1936; Juanita Jackson to Roy Wilkins, April 18, 1936; Juanita Jackson to Walter White, April 21, 1936, *NAACP Papers*, 1:A:16.

19. Juanita Jackson to Walter White, April 21, 1936; Juanita Jackson, Memorandum, July 17, 1936, *NAACP Papers*, 1:A:16; Walter Wendell, "This & That," *Boston Chronicle*, April 18, 1936, 1; "Membership Drive by Boston NAACP," *Boston Chronicle*, April 18, 1936, 1; "NAACP Drive Under Way," *Boston Chronicle*, April 25, 1936, 1; "NAACP Drive Nears Close," *Boston Chronicle*, May 2, 1936, 1; "NAACP Drive Completed," *Boston Chronicle*, May 9, 1936, 1; "Boston Answers the Call," *Boston Chronicle*, May 9, 1936, 4. On Howard Kester's support for Walter White and the NAACP, see Kenneth Janken, *White: The Biography of Walter White, Mr. NAACP* (New York: Free Press, 2003), 195–96.

20. "Branch News," *Crisis*, June 1936, 185; "Branch News," *Crisis*, August 1936, 250.

21. I. Maximilian Martin to Juanita Jackson, June 5, 1936, *NAACP Papers*, 12:B:8.

22. I. Maximilian Martin to NAACP Board of Directors, December 3, 1935; Walter White to I. Maximilian Martin, December 7, 1935; "Digest of Correspondence with the Philadelphia

Branch and Mr. Homer Starks of North Philadelphia, re organizing a North Philadelphia Branch," December 13, 1935; "Conference Between the Philadelphia Branch and the Committee of the National Board of Directors," January 25, 1936; I. Maximilian Martin to Walter White, February 8, 1936; Walter White to I. Maximilian Martin, March 5, 1936, *NAACP Papers*, 12:B:8; H. Viscount Nelson, "The Philadelphia NAACP: Race Versus Class Consciousness During the Thirties," *Journal of Black Studies* 5, no. 3 (March 1975): 255–76.

23. Juanita Jackson to I. Maximilian Martin, June 9, 1936; Juanita Jackson to Walter White, June 12, 1936, *NAACP Papers*, 12:B:8.

24. "Youth Section of the 27th Annual Conference of the NAACP," *NAACP Papers*, 1:A:9; "Ickes Assails Lynching Mobs at NAACP Meet," *Baltimore Afro-American*, July 4, 1936, 1, 2; Patricia Sullivan, *Lift Every Voice: The NAACP and the Making of the Civil Rights Movement* (New York: New Press, 2009), 223–25.

25. Juanita Jackson to "Dear Youth Delegate," June 16, 1936, *NAACP Papers*, 19:A:1; "Youth, Let Us Awake!!" *NAACP Papers*, 1:A:9; Clarence M. Mitchell, Jr., "NAACP—Welcome to Baltimore!" *Crisis*, July 1936, 200–201, 208; "27th Annual Conference Best in Years," *Crisis*, August 1936, 246–49; Juanita Jackson to J. St. Clair Drake, June 20, 1936, *NAACP Papers*, 19:A:1; Ransby, *Ella Baker*, 75–91.

26. "Youth Section of the 27th Annual Conference of the NAACP," *NAACP Papers*, 1:A:9; Juanita Jackson, "The NAACP Challenges Youth," July 1, 1936, *NAACP Papers*, 19:A:2.

27. "Youth Section of the 27th Annual Conference of the NAACP"; "NAACP Youth March Forward! National Youth Program, September 1936–June 1937," *NAACP Papers*, 1:A:9; "NAACP Youth Councils for New Social Order," Press Release, July 10, 1936, *NAACP Papers*, 19:A:1; "Youth Council News," *Crisis*, December 1936, 378–79.

28. Robert E. Williams to Walter White, July 14, 1926, *NAACP Papers*, 12:C:26; "461 NAACP Delegates in Session," *Baltimore Afro-American*, July 4, 1936, 6; Roscoe Dunjee to Oklahoma Branches of the NAACP, ca. January 1937, *NAACP Papers*, 12:D:7; Juanita Jackson to William Sutherland, July 12, 1936; Juanita Jackson to [blank] form letter, July 17, 1936, *NAACP Papers*, 19:A:1; Juanita Jackson, Memorandum, July 17, 1936; Juanita Jackson to Walter White, August 27, 1936, *NAACP Papers*, 1:A:16; Juanita Jackson to Robert E. Williams, July 27, 1936, *NAACP Papers*, 12:C:26

29. Juanita Jackson to Youth Members of the NAACP, August 5, 1936, *NAACP Papers*, 19:A:1.

30. Juanita Jackson to Louise Rowe, ca. October 2, 1936, *NAACP Papers*, 1:A:17.

31. Juanita Jackson to Walter White, September 18, 1936, *NAACP Papers*, 1:A:16; "Youth Council News," *Crisis*, November 1936, 345; Juanita Jackson to E. M. Lancaster, July 30, 1936, *NAACP Papers*, 12:C:20; Juanita Jackson to Chester Gillespie, August 3, 1936, *NAACP Papers*, 12:C:25; Juanita Jackson to Arthur Womack, September 4, 1936, *NAACP Papers*, 12:C:10; "Youth Council News," *Crisis*, November 1936, 345; George Gatlin to Juanita Jackson, August 28, 1936; Juanita Jackson to George Gatlin, September 8, 1936; news clipping, "Says NAACP Seeks Abolition of Lynching and Discrimination"; "Activities of Gary's Youth Council of NAACP," typescript, 1936, *NAACP Papers*, 12:C:9; "Youth Council News," *Crisis*, November 1936, 344–45; Juanita Jackson to L. C. Blount, August 27, 1936; L. C. Blount to Walter White, September 30, 1936; Gloster Current to Juanita Jackson, July 15, 1937, *NAACP Papers*, 12:C:13. On the movement in Gary, Indiana, see Neil Butten and Raymond A. Mohl, "The Evolution of Racism in an Industrial City, 1906–1940: A Case Study of Gary, Indiana," *Journal of Negro History* 59, no. 1 (January 1974): 51–64. Gloster Current's words were prescient; he would indeed become a lifelong activist and administrator in the NAACP, rising from the Detroit youth council during the 1930s to the Association's national board during the 1980s. Mike Hurewitz, "Civil Rights Warrior: Gloster B. Current," *Crisis*, November 1976, 326–27; Lawrence Van Gelder, "Gloster B. Current, 84, Leader Who Helped Steer NAACP," *New York Times*, July 9, 1997.

32. Marjorie Penney to Juanita Jackson, October 2, 1936; Juanita Jackson to Walter White, October 8, 1936; Juanita Jackson to William Pickens, October 9, 1936; Juanita Jackson to

Louise Rowe, October 9, 1936; "Report of Visit to Richmond, Virginia," *NAACP Papers*, 1:A:17; "Branch News," *Crisis*, December 1936, 377; Juanita Jackson to Frances Rankin, October 13, 1936, *NAACP Papers*, 1:A:17; "Youth Council News," *Crisis*, December 1936, 379; Juanita Jackson to I. Maximilian Martin, August 3, 1936; Juanita Jackson to I. Maximilian Martin, September 3, 1936; I. Maximilian Martin to Juanita Jackson, September 9, 1936; Juanita Jackson to I. Maximilian Martin, October 21, 1936; I. Maximilian Martin to Juanita Jackson, October 26, 1936; Juanita Jackson to Walter White, October 27, 1936; Walter White, Memorandum, October 28, 1936; Isadore Martin to Juanita Jackson, November 19, 1936, *NAACP Papers*, 12:B:8; Board minutes, November 9, 1936, *NAACP Papers*, 1:A:2.

33. "NAACP Youth Council News," *Crisis*, December 1936, 379; "NAACP Youth Council News," *Crisis*, January 1937, 27.

34. *Baltimore Afro-American*, November 14, 1936, 6; "Youth Council News," *Crisis*, December 1936, 378–79; "Youth Council News," *Crisis*, January 1937, 27–28; "Engagements," ca. November 1936; "Report of Tour of Juanita E. Jackson, November, 1936," *NAACP Papers*, 1:A:17; Juanita Jackson to Sara Meriwether Nutter, November 4, 1936; T. G. Nutter to Walter White, December 1, 1936, *NAACP Papers*, 12:C:27.

35. Charles A. J. McPherson to Walter White, February 13, 1936; E. W. Taggart to Walter White, March 9, 1936; Birmingham NAACP to the Housing Authority of Birmingham District, September 21, 1936; "Report of Tour of Juanita E. Jackson, November, 1936," *NAACP Papers*, 1:A:17; Juanita Jackson to E. W. Taggart, November 4, 1936; Juanita Jackson to E. W. Taggart, November 7, 1936; Chas. A. J. McPherson to Walter White, December 5, 1936; Laura Kellum to Juanita Jackson, December 15, 1936, *NAACP Papers*, 12:A:2; "Birmingham Branch President Arrested," *Crisis*, April 1936, 118; "Youth Council News," *Crisis*, January 1937, 26, 28.

36. Juanita Jackson to Walter White, November 26, 1936, *NAACP Papers*, 1:A:17; "Youth Council News," *Crisis*, December 1936, 379; "Report of Tour of Juanita E. Jackson, November, 1936," *NAACP Papers*, 1:A:17; "Youth Council News," *Crisis*, January 1937, 27–28; Forrester Washington to Juanita Jackson, September 18, 1936; Juanita Jackson to Walter White, November 26, 1936, *NAACP Papers*, 1:A:17; Clarence Mitchell to Walter White, November 24, 1936; Forrester Washington to Walter White, November 30; Forrester Washington to Walter White, December 10, 1936, *NAACP Papers*, 12:A:10; Karen Ferguson, *Black Politics in New Deal Atlanta* (Chapel Hill: University of North Carolina Press, 2002), 148–52.

37. "Youth Council News," *Crisis*, January 1937, 28; Juanita Jackson to J. J. Starks, November 13, 1936, *NAACP Papers*, 12:A:19; Juanita Jackson to Walter White, November 26, 1936, *NAACP Papers*, 1:A:17; Edwin D. Hoffman, "The Genesis of the Modern Movement for Equal Rights in South Carolina, 1930–1939," *Journal of Negro History* 44, no. 4 (October 1959): 346–69.

38. B. Joyce Ross, "Mary Bethune and the National Youth Administration: A Case Study of Power Relationships in the Black Cabinet of Franklin Roosevelt," *Journal of Negro History* 60, no. 1 (January 1975): 1–28; Joyce Ann Hanson, *Mary McCleod Bethune and Black Women's Political Activism* (Columbia: University of Missouri Press, 2003).

39. "Detroit Council Leads Christmas Seal Sale," *Crisis*, February 1937, 56–57; "Youth Council News," *Crisis*, November 1936, 344–45; "Youth Council News," *Crisis*, December 1936, 378–79; "Youth Council News," *Crisis*, January 1937, 26–28; "Youth Council News," *Crisis*, February 1937, 56–58.

40. Mary McLeod Bethune to Juanita Jackson, December 4, 1936, *NAACP Papers*, 1:A:17; "Youth Council News," *Crisis*, January 1937, 27; "Youth Council News," *Crisis*, February 1937, 57–58; Juanita Jackson to Benjamin Parks, December 31, 1936, *NAACP Papers*, 19:A:1; "On the Cover," *Crisis*, October 1936; J. St. Clair Drake, "Along the Battlefront," *Crisis*, November 1936, 327, 345; "Youth Council News," *Crisis*, December 1936, 378; "Anti-lynching Button Sale Sweeps Country," *Crisis*, February 1937, 52; Janken, *White*, 222–23.

41. Miriam T. Magill to Juanita Jackson, January 7, 1937, *NAACP Papers*, 12:B:2; Juanita Jackson, form letter, December 28, 1936, *NAACP Papers*, 19:A:1; Height, *Open Wide*, 61; "Facts for Youth Speakers," ca. January 1937; Juanita Jackson to Phillips Carlin, January 5, 1937; Juanita Jackson to Phillips Carlin, January 15, 1937; Juanita Jackson to Phillips Carlin, February 2, 1937; Juanita Jackson to Walter White, January 15, 1937, *NAACP Papers*, 19:A:1; "100,000 Arm Bands to Mourn Lynch Victims," *New York Age*, January 16, 1937, 3; "Jamaica Jr. NAACP in Demonstration against Lynching," *New York Age*, January 16, 7; "Junior NAACP Anti-Lynch Move," *New York Age*, January 23, 1937, 7; Juanita Jackson, Memorandum, February 1, 1937, *NAACP Papers*, 1:A:17; Louise Rowe to Walter White, January 29, 1937, *NAACP Papers*, 12:A:17; "Harlem Youths Unite in Anti-Lynching Drive," *New York Amsterdam News*, February 6, 1937, 20.

42. Mary White Ovington, "Greetings to the Youth Movement Lincoln's Birthday Meeting to Protest Against Lynching," February 12, 1937; "Program," *NAACP Papers*, 19:A:1; "Youth Council News," *Crisis*, March 1937, 89; "Youth Council News," *Crisis*, April 1937, 121; "Present Walter White in Anti-Lynching Meeting," *New York Age*, February 13, 1937, 7; "Young and Old Unite against Lynching," *New York Amsterdam News*, February 20, 1937, 5; "Urges Masses to Back Lynch Bill," *New York Age*, February 20, 1937, 7; "Anti-Lynching Bill Seen Near Passage," *New York Times*, February 13, 1937.

43. "Youth Council News," *Crisis*, March 1937, 89–91; "Youth Council News," *Crisis*, April 1937, 121–22.

44. "Miss Jackson on Tour," *Crisis*, April 1937, 121.

45. Patricia L. Adams, "Fighting For Democracy in St. Louis: Civil Rights During World War II," *Missouri Historical Review* 80:1 (October 1985): 59; "Youth Day to be Held Soon," news clipping, ca. June 1936; S. R. Redmond, "St. Louis Branch NAACP Bulletin," October 30, 1936; Juanita Jackson to C. M. Powell, February 20, 1937; S. R. Redmond to Juanita Jackson, February 23, 1937; S. R. Redmond to Juanita Jackson, March 9, 1937, *NAACP Papers*, 12:C:17.

46. Roscoe Dunjee to Oklahoma Branches of the NAACP, ca. January 1937; Roscoe Dunjee to Juanita Jackson, February 4, 1937, *NAACP Papers*, 12:D:7; Kenneth M. Hamilton, "The Origin and Early Developments of Langston, Oklahoma," *Journal of Negro History* 62, no. 3 (July 1977): 270–82; "Youth Council News," *Crisis*, May 1937, 154; Charles H. Martin, "Oklahoma's 'Scottsboro' Affair: The Jess Hollins Rape Case, 1931–1936," *South Atlantic Quarterly* 79, no. 2 (Spring 1980): 175–88; Juanita Jackson to Walter White, March 9, 1937; Juanita Jackson to Walter White, March 10, 1937; Roscoe Dunjee to Charles Houston, March 18, 1937; Roscoe Dunjee to Walter White, March 19, 1937, *NAACP Papers*, 12:D:7.

47. Juanita Jackson to John M. Adkins, February 24, 1937; Juanita Jackson to Walter White, April 22, 1937; J. H. Harmon, Jr., to Walter White, April 7, 1937; Nadine Roberts to Juanita Jackson, June 17, 1937, *NAACP Papers*, 12:A:19; Michael L. Gillette, "The Rise of the NAACP in Texas," *Southwest Historical Quarterly* 81 (April 1978): 393–416; Juanita Jackson to James E. Gayle, February 23, 1937; Daisy Lampkin to James E. Gayle, February 24, 1937, *NAACP Papers*, 12:A:15; Adam Fairclough, *Race and Democracy: The Civil Rights Struggle in Louisiana, 1915–1972* (Athens: University of Georgia Press, 1995); Eugene Martin to Walter White, April 24, 1937, *NAACP Papers*, 12:A:10.

48. Juanita Jackson to Julian D. Steele, January 14, 1937; Minutes, December 9, 1936; Minutes, March 10, 1937, box 20, folder 6, Steele Papers; "Youth Council News," *Crisis*, May 1937, 154; "Branch News," *Crisis*, June 1937, 184; "Youth Council News," *Crisis*, July 1937, 218; Juanita Jackson to Roy Wilkins, April 17, 1937, *NAACP Papers*, 1:A:17.

49. Juanita Jackson to Walter White, April 28, 1937; Juanita Jackson to Walter White, April 30, 1937; Walter White to Juanita Jackson, May 3, 1937; Juanita Jackson to Walter White, May 4, 1937, *NAACP Papers*, 1:A:17; Juanita Jackson to Marjorie Penney, January 19, 1937; Juanita Jackson to Anne E. Butler, May 5, 1937, *NAACP Papers*, 12:B:8; "Youth Council News," *Crisis*, May 1937, 154–55; Juanita Jackson to Annie McDougald, May 22, 1937;

Juanita Jackson to Roberta Lewis Smith, May 27, 1937, *NAACP Papers*, 12:B:8; Philadelphia Youth Council News, June 28, 1937, *NAACP Papers*, 19:A:2; "Youth Council News," *Crisis*, July 1937, 218–19; "Youth Movement in the NAACP," ca. June 1937, *NAACP Papers*, 19:A:1.

50. "Youth Council News," *Crisis*, June 1937, 184; Gloster Current to Juanita Jackson, October 5, 1936; Gloster Current to Juanita Jackson, October 13, 1936; Gloster Current to Juanita Jackson, November 21, 1936; Louise Blackman, "An Invitation from Detroit Councils," *Crisis*, June 1937, 185; Hurewitz, "Civil Rights Warrior"; August Meier and Elliott Rudwick, *Black Detroit and the Rise of the UAW* (New York: Oxford University Press, 1979).

51. "Labor Leading Topic at Detroit Conference," *Crisis*, July 1937, 212–14; "Youth Council News," *Crisis*, July 1937, 217; Moran Weston, interview, July 22, 2000; "NAACP Youth Council Members Get Together," *Baltimore Afro-American*, July 10, 1937, 8; Juanita Jackson to Moran Weston, July 7, 1937; Juanita Jackson to Gloster Current, July 9, 1937, *NAACP Papers*, 19:A:2; "Second Annual Youth Conference of the Twenty-Eighth Annual Convention of the NAACP, June 29, 1937," *NAACP Papers*, 1:A:9.

52. "Second Annual Youth Conference of the Twenty-Eighth Annual Convention of the NAACP, June 30, 1937," *NAACP Papers*, 1:A:9.

53. Louis E. Martin, "CIO Issue Disrupts Peace of NAACP Meet," *Chicago Defender*, July 3, 1937, 1; Russ J. Cowans, "CIO Tilt Rocks NAACP," *Baltimore Afro-American*, July 10, 1937, 1, 2; Meier and Rudwick, *Black Detroit*, 38.

54. "Youth Day, July 1, 1937"; Joel Spingarn, "What the NAACP Expects of Its Youth," July 1, 1937, *NAACP Papers*, 1:A:9.

55. "7/2/37"; "7/3/37," *NAACP Papers*, 1:A:9; Juanita Jackson to Julian D. Steele, July 15, 1937, box 5, folder 4, Steele Papers; "Detroit Conference Largest in History," *Crisis*, August 1937, 242, 244–48; "Youth Council News," *Crisis*, August 1937, 249–51.

56. "They're Protesting," *New York Amsterdam News*, August 7, 1937, 2; "Youth Council News," *Crisis*, September 1937, 282; Height, *Open Wide*, 61; Steve Oney, *And the Dead Shall Rise: The Murder of Mary Phagan and the Lynching of Leo Frank* (New York: Random House, 2003). On the neglected origins of Decoration Day, see David Blight, "Decoration Days: The Origins of Memorial Day in North and South," in *The Memory of the Civil War in American Culture*, ed. Alice Fahs and Joan Waugh (Chapel Hill: University of North Carolina Press, 2004), 94–129.

57. Juanita Jackson to Lillie Mae Jackson, August 2, 1937; Juanita Jackson to Carl Murphy, September 8, 1937; Walter White to Lillie Mae Jackson, September 10, 1937, *NAACP Papers*, 12:A:17; "They Raised $287 For NAACP," *Baltimore Afro-American*, October 16, 1937, 22; "NAACP Drive Breaks Mark With $3,183," *Baltimore Afro-American*, October 30, 1937, 3; "Youth Council News," *Crisis*, July 1937; "Youth Council News," *Crisis*, September 1937, 283; "Youth Council News," *Crisis*, November 1937, 346.

58. "Youth Council News," *Crisis*, September 1937, 283; "Youth Council News," *Crisis*, October 1937, 314; "Report of Youth Councils and College Chapters, September, 1937, to date" ca. July 1938, *NAACP Papers*, 1:A:17; "Youth Council News," *Crisis*, November 1937, 346; "Youth Council News," *Crisis*, December 1937, 375; "Youth Council News," *Crisis*, January 1938, 25.

59. Robert Zangrando, *The NAACP Crusade Against Lynching, 1909–1950* (Philadelphia: Temple University Press, 1980), 149–52; "Youth Council News," *Crisis*, February 1938, 59; "Report of Youth Councils and College Chapters, September, 1937, to date" ca. July 1938, *NAACP Papers*, 1:A:17; "Youth Council News," *Crisis*, January 1938, 23; Juanita Jackson to Walter White, January 20, 1938, *NAACP Papers*, 1:A:17; "National Affairs," *Time*, January 24, 1938, 8–10; Juanita Jackson to Walter White, February 1, 1938; Juanita Jackson to Walter White, February 7, 1938, *NAACP Papers*, 1:A:17; "NAACP Council Plans Meeting," *New York Amsterdam News*, February 12, 1938, 19; "NAACP Schedules Demonstration Here," *New York Age*, February 12, 1938, 10.

60. "Program," *NAACP Papers*, 19:A:1; "23 Cities to Stage Lynch Protest Parade," *New York Amsterdam News*, February 12, 1938, 2; "Parade Against Lynching," *New York Amsterdam News*, February 19, 1938, 4; "Youth Council News," *Crisis*, March 1938, 87.

61. "Youth Council News," *Crisis*, February 1938, 58–60; "Youth Council News," *Crisis*, March 1938, 87–88; Janken, *White*, 229–30; Zangrando, *NAACP Crusade Against Lynching*, 155–56.

62. Minutes, March 9, 1938; Juanita Jackson to "Dear Friend in the Cause," March 23, 1938, box 20, folder 6, Steele Papers; "Boston Hears Lynch Fight in Meetings," *Boston Chronicle*, April 2, 1938; "NAACP Drive is Extended," *Boston Chronicle*, April 9, 1938, 1; "NAACP Drive Is a Success," *Boston Chronicle*, April 16, 1938, 1; Zangrando, *NAACP Crusade Against Lynching*, 155; Myrtle Cambell to Donovan E. Smucker, April 29, 1938; Juanita Jackson to Walter White, May 12, 1938, *NAACP Papers*, 1:A:17; "Youth Council News," *Crisis*, April 1938, 121; "Youth Council News," *Crisis*, May 1938, 153; "Youth Council News," *Crisis*, June 1938, 183.

63. Board minutes, June 30, 1938, *NAACP Papers*, 1:A:2; "She Quit to Marry," *Pittsburgh Courier*, July 9, 1938, 9; "Resigns To Wed," *Baltimore Afro-American*, July 9, 1938, 13; "Many Problems on Program at Columbus," *Crisis*, June 1938, 180; "17 Textbooks, Used in 12,000 Schools Tell Lies on Negro," *Pittsburgh Courier*, July 9, 1938, 7; "Tentative Youth Conference Program, 1938," *NAACP Papers*, 1:A:10; "Youth Section, 1938," *NAACP Papers*, 19:A:2; "A Fine Conference Held in Columbus," *Crisis*, August 1938, 270, 272; "Youth Council News," *Crisis*, August 1938, 273.

64. Juanita Jackson, "Young Colored America Awakes," *Crisis*, September 1938, 289, 307–8; "Report of Youth Councils and College Chapters, September, 1937, to date" ca. July 1938, *NAACP Papers*, 1:A:17. For competing interpretations of Jackson's decision to marry, see Cumberbatch, "What 'the Cause' Needs," 60; Ransby, *Ella Baker*, 128.

65. Lula Jones Garrett, "1500 Guests, Notables, See Jackson-Mitchell Nuptials," *Baltimore Afro-American*, September 10, 1938, 15; Lula Jones Garrett, "Mitchell Party Takes Station," *Baltimore Afro-American*, September 17, 1938, 17; Juanita Jackson Mitchell to Walter White, October 26, 1938, *NAACP Papers*, 1:A:17; Juanita Jackson Mitchell to Walter White, December 18, 1940, *NAACP Papers*, 17:A:10; "Ready for NAACP Drive," *Baltimore Afro-American*, September 28, 1940, 15; "All Set for NAACP Drive," *Baltimore Afro-American*, October 5, 1940, 11; "NAACP Drive Nets $4,027.50," *Baltimore Afro-American*, October 19, 1940, 8; "Branch News," *Crisis*, November 1940, 359–60; Walter White to Juanita Jackson Mitchell, April 2, 1941; Juanita Jackson to Roy Wilkins, May 9, 1941; Juanita Jackson to Roy Wilkins, June 10, 1941, *NAACP Papers*, 26:A:13; Thompson, "The Civil Rights Vanguard," 358–60.

66. "U.S. Urged to Strike Down Cops Who Draw Gun on Soldiers," *Baltimore Afro-American*, May 2, 1942, 9; "Die Fighting," *Baltimore Afro-American*, May 2, 1942, 10; "We Won't Stand Abuse Any Longer, Powell Tells 1,200," *Baltimore Afro-American*, May 2, 1942, 10; Will Haygood, *King of the Cats: The Life and Times of Adam Clayton Powell, Jr.* (Boston: Houghton Mifflin, 1993); Harvard Sitkoff, *A New Deal for Blacks: The Emergence of Civil Rights as a National Issue* (New York: Oxford University Press, 1978), 314–22.

67. B. M. Phillips, "2,000 Join in March on Md. Capitol," *Baltimore Afro-American*, May 2, 1942, 1, 2; "Let Freedom Ring!" *Baltimore Afro-American*, May 2, 1942, 4; "2,000 Baltimore Citizens in Impressive March on Annapolis," *Baltimore Afro-American*, May 2, 1942, 12; "Police Brutality," *Crisis*, June 1942, 197–98.

Chapter 6

1. "100 Groups to Attend Negro Parley Today," *Daily Worker*, June 27, 1942, 1; "Negro Victory Conference," *Daily Worker*, June 29, 1942, 1; C. Alvin Hughes, "Let Us Do Our Part: The New York City Based Negro Labor Victory Committee, 1941–1945," *Afro-Americans in New York Life and History* 10, no. 1 (January 1986): 19–29.

2. Franklin Roosevelt, "Annual Message to Congress," January 6, 1941, in *State of the Union: Presidential Rhetoric from Woodrow Wilson to George W. Bush*, ed. Deborah Kalb, Gerhard Peters, and John T. Woolley (Washington, DC: CQ, 2007), 298–304; Eleanor Roosevelt, "Race, Religion and Prejudice," *New Republic*, May 1942, 630.

3. On the Wilmington race riot and Its aftermath, see Raymond Gavins, "Fear, Hope, and Struggle: Recasting Black North Carolina in the Age of Jim Crow," in *Democracy Betrayed: The Wilmington Race Riot of 1898 and its Legacy*, ed. David Cecelski and Timothy Tyson (Chapel Hill: University of North Carolina Press, 1998), 185–206; Benjamin Justesen, *George Henry White: An Even Chance in the Race of Life* (Baton Rouge: Louisiana State University Press, 2001), 433.

4. Moran Weston, interview, July 22, 2000; Milton Weston, "The Value of Vision," Barber-Prize Speaking Contest (1926), box 3, folder 19; George Libaire to Milton M. Weston, June 26, 1928; George Libaire to Milton M. Weston, July 7, 1928; Bernard I. Bell to Milton M. Weston, August 14, 1928, box 3, folder 21; Milton Weston to Milton M. Weston II, September 27, 1928, box 3, folder 22, M. Moran Weston Papers, Rare Book and Manuscript Library, Columbia University in the City of New York.

5. Moran Weston, interview, July 22, 2000; Robert E. Fitch to Moran Weston, November 23, 1929; Robert E. Fitch to Moran Weston, March 12, 1930, box 3, folder 24, Weston Papers; "Students Answer the Professor," *Crisis*, October 1930, 336–37, 356.

6. Richard Wightman Fox, *Reinhold Niebuhr: A Biography* (New York: Pantheon, 1985), 82, 105–6, 111–12, 124–25, 128, 147; Moran Weston, interview, July 22, 2000; Transcripts, box 4, folder 29, Weston Papers.

7. "Students Meet at Columbia," *Baltimore Afro-American*, April 15, 1933, 21; Moran Weston to E. Franklin Frazier, ca. 1933, box 131–16, folder 26, E. Franklin Frazier Papers, Moorland-Spingarn Research Center, Howard University. For activity of faculty members of the Columbia Socialist Club that spring, see "Columbia Teachers Issue Peace Program," *New York Times*, May 23, 1933. Moran Weston, interview, July 22, 2000; Moran Weston to Joel Spingarn, ca. September 1933, box 95–11, folder 480, Joel Spingarn Papers, Moorland-Spingarn Collection, Howard University; Moran Weston to W. E. B. Du Bois, ca. August 1933; Moran Weston to W. E. B. Du Bois, September 9, 1933, reel 40, *The Papers of W. E. B. Du Bois*, microfilm (Sanford, NC: Microfilming Corp. of America, 1980–1981); Ralph Bunche to Moran Weston, November 10, 1933, Ralph Bunche Papers, Special Collections, Young Research Library, University of California at Los Angeles.

8. Moran Weston, interview, July 22, 2000; Clement Wood, *The Woman Who Was Pope: A Biography of Pope Joan, 853–855 A.D.* (New York: Faro, 1931); M. Moran Weston II, "Fact or Fancy: An Examination of the Historicity of Pope Joan," manuscript, 1934, box 4, folder 32, Weston Papers; *The Columbia Encyclopedia*, 6th ed., s.v. "Manning, William Thomas"; Fox, *Reinhold Niebuhr*, 159; "Union Seminary to Curb Radicals," *New York Times*, May 23, 1934; Hubert Herring, "Union Seminary Rousts Its Reds," *Christian Century*, June 13, 1934, 799–801.

9. Moran Weston, interview, July 22, 2000; Resume, ca. mid-1940s, box 3, folder 14, Weston Papers; James H. Baker, Jr. to Moran Weston, April 20, 1938, *Papers of the National Negro Congress*, microfilm (Frederick, MD: University Publications of America, 1988), part 1, reel 12; "Kern is Accused of Approving Red," *New York Times*, February 18, 1941; Harry Raymond, "Anti-Negro Attack Latest Move of Smith Committee," *Daily Worker*, February 18, 1941, 2; "Milton Weston, Former Welfare Office Supervisor, Denies Being Red," *New York Amsterdam News*, February 22, 1941, 3; Mark D. Naison, *Communists in Harlem during the Depression* (Urbana: University of Illinois Press, 1983), 305, 309. For one of Weston's contemporary's similar experiences in Harlem during these years, see Dorothy Height, *Open Wide the Freedom Gates* (New York: PublicAffairs, 2003), 61–64. Like Height, Weston mingled comfortably with members of the radical left, but he was not inclined to abandon his spirituality.

10. Thomas Sugrue, *Sweet Land of Liberty: The Forgotten Struggle for Civil Rights in the North* (New York: Random House, 2008), 46–47; August Meier and Elliott Rudwick, *Black Detroit and the Rise of the UAW* (New York: Oxford University Press, 1979), 188; Dominic J. Capeci, Jr., "Wartime Fair Employment Practice Committees: The Governor's Committee and the First FEPC in New York City, 1941–1943," *Afro-Americans in New York Life and History* 9, no. 2 (July 1985): 45; Naison, *Communists in Harlem*, 306; August Meier and Elliott Rudwick, "Communist Unions and the Black Community: The Case of the Transport Workers Union, 1934–1944," *Labor History* 23, no. 2 (Spring 1982): 165–97.

11. "Minutes of Organization Committee," February 3, 1941, box 16, folder 17, International Workers Order Papers, Labor-Management Documentation & Archives, Catherwood Library, Kheel Center, School of Industrial and Labor Relations, Cornell University; Arthur J. Sabin, *Red Scare in Court: New York versus the International Workers Order* (Philadelphia: University of Pennsylvania Press, 1993), 12–13, 20; Roger Keeran, "The IWO and the Origins of the CIO," *Labor History* 30, no. 3 (Summer 1989): 385–408; Keeran, "National Groups and the Popular Front: The Case of the International Workers Order," *Journal of American Ethnic History* 14, no. 3 (Spring 1995): 23–51; Ellen Schrecker, *Many Are the Crimes: McCarthyism in America* (New York: Little, Brown, 1998), 38–40; Martin Bauml Duberman, *Paul Robeson* (New York: Knopf, 1989), 250; "Paul Robeson, Musical Pageant at IWO Affair," *Daily Worker*, February 18, 1941, 7; "Brotherhood in Action," *Daily Worker*, February 27, 1941, 7; "Paul Robeson to Sing at Harlem Concert," *Daily Worker*, March 21, 1941, 4; Eugene Gordon, "Taking Negro Culture to the Negro People," *Daily Worker*, March 29, 1941, 5. Michael Denning, *The Cultural Front: The Laboring of American Culture in the Twentieth Century* (New York: Verso, 1996); Bill Mullen, *Popular Fronts: Chicago and African-American Cultural Politics, 1935–1946* (Urbana: University of Illinois Press, 1999); Lauren Rebecca Sklaroff, *Black Culture and the New Deal: The Quest for Civil Rights in the Roosevelt Era* (Chapel Hill: University of North Carolina Press, 2009). On the Golden Gate as a "staging ground" for Harlem protests, see Roi Ottley, *New World A-Coming* (New York: Houghton Mifflin, 1943), 230; Benjamin Davis, *Communist Councilman from Harlem: Autobiographical Notes Written in a Federal Penitentiary* (New York: International Publishers, 1969), 110.

12. "Minutes of the National Commission on Negro Work," April 30, 1941; "Supplementary Note to Minutes," May 6, 1941; "Minutes National Organization Committee," May 11, 1941; M. Moran Weston, "Report to the Organization Committee and Plan of Concentration for Negro Work," May 15, 1941, box 16, folder 17, IWO Papers.

13. Richard Sherman, *The Case of Odell Waller and Virginia Justice, 1940–1942* (Knoxville: University of Tennessee Press, 1992); Glenda Gilmore, *Defying Dixie: The Radical Roots of Civil Rights, 1919–1950* (New York: Norton, 2008), 329–45.

14. Moran Weston, interview, July 22, 2000; Moran Weston to John P. Davis, June 16, 1941; Moran Weston to John P. Davis, July 14, 1941; George B. Murphy, Jr. to Moran Weston, July 17, 1941, *NNC Papers*, 1:25; John Baxter Streator, Jr., "The National Negro Congress, 1936–1947" (Ph.D. diss., University of Cincinnati, 1981), 300–301; H. L. Mencken, "Designations for Colored Folk," *American Speech* 19 (October 1944): 168; Moran Weston to George Murphy, November 10, 1941, *NNC Papers*, 1:27; John P. Davis to Moran Weston, February 4, 1942; Moran Weston to John P. Davis, February 5, 1942; John P. Davis to Moran Weston, February 9, 1942, *NNC Papers*, 1:25; Hughes, "Let Us Do Our Part," 22; Evelyn Sherrer, "Labor Victory Committee Shows Signs of Growth," *Pittsburgh Courier*, ca. February 5, 1944, clipping, *NNC Papers*, 4:6; "Program, Negro Labor Victory Committee of Greater New York," April 29, 1942, *Negro Labor Committee Record Group, 1925–1969*, microfilm (New York: Schomburg Center for Research in Black Culture), reel 14; "City CIO, AFL Leaders Open Campaign to Kayo Jim Crow," *Daily Worker*, May 1, 1942, 5; Ewart Guinier to Michael Quill and Douglas MacMahon, May 27, 1942, *NNC Papers*, 4:9. On the National Maritime Union, see Gerald Horne, *Red Seas: Ferdinand Smith and Radical Black Sailors in the United States and Jamaica* (New York: New York University Press, 2005); Donald T. Critchlow, "Communist Unions and Racism," *Labor History* 17, no. 2 (Spring 1976): 230–44.

15. Naomi Kornacker to Moran Weston, April 25, 1942, *NNC Papers*, 1:29; Moran Weston to Ewart Guinier, May 26, 1942, *NNC Papers*, 4:9; M. Moran Weston to Max Bedacht, June 9, 1942, box 3, folder 12, IWO Papers; Unity for Victory Rally poster, ca. June 1942, *Negro Labor Committee Record Group*, reel 14.

16. "Wake Up, Negro America!" poster, *The Papers of A. Philip Randolph*, microfilm (Bethesda, MD: University Publications of America, 1990), reel 22; "2,000 Join March on Maryland Governor," *New York Amsterdam News*, May 2, 1942, 23; "March on Washington Committee Meeting at Garden," *New York Age*, April 18, 1942; Eugene Gordon, "Big Defense Firms Accused of War Job Discrimination," *Daily Worker*, February 17, 1942, 1, 4; J. Robert Smith, "FEPC's Labor Chiefs Clash over Policies," *New York Amsterdam News*, February 21, 1942, 1; "Pres. Roosevelt's FEPC Holds Hearings Here," *New York Age*, February 21, 1942, 1; Merl E. Reed, *Seedtime for the Modern Civil Rights Movement: The President's Committee on Fair Employment Practices, 1941–1946* (Baton Rouge: Louisiana State University Press, 1991), 41; Capeci, "Wartime Fair Employment Practice," 45–63; A. Philip Randolph to "Dear Friend," May 15, 1942, *A. Philip Randolph Papers*, reel 22; "Calling 50,000 Negroes to Storm Madison Square Garden," *New York Amsterdam News*, June 13, 1942, 3; J. Robert Smith, "Labor's Front," *New York Amsterdam News*, June 13, 1942, 7.

17. J. Robert Smith, "20,000 Storm Madison Square Garden to Help Bury Race's 'Uncle Toms,'" *New York Amsterdam News*, June 20, 1942, 1, 3; Julius J. Adams, "Sidelights on Garden's Big Rally," *New York Amsterdam News*, June 20, 1942, 2; Ellen Tarry, "Women Active in Big Garden Demonstration," *New York Amsterdam News*, June 20, 1942, 24; "Randolph Tells Why He Didn't Make His Talk," *New York Amsterdam News*, June 20, 1942, 1, 24; Will Haygood, *King of the Cats: The Life and Times of Adam Clayton Powell, Jr.* (Boston: Houghton Mifflin, 1993), 93; Adam Clayton Powell, Jr., *Marching Blacks: An Interpretive History of the Rise of the Black Common Man* (New York: Dial, 1945).

18. "20,000 Cheer 'For Freedom Now' at Stadium in Chicago," *Baltimore Afro-American*, July 4, 1942, 1, 2; "8-Point Program Adopted by March-on-Washington Group," *New York Amsterdam News*, June 20, 1942, 1; "'Uncle Tom's' Funeral," *New York Amsterdam News*, June 27, 1942, 6; "We Hope, We Hope!" *New York Amsterdam News*, June 27, 1942, 6; J. Robert Smith, "Labor's Front," *New York Amsterdam News*, June 27, 1942, 7.

19. "'Uncle Tom's Funeral," *New York Amsterdam News*, June 27, 1942, 6; Ben Davis, Jr., "Negro Rally Hits Jim Crow in War Effort," *Daily Worker*, June 18, 1942, 4, 6.

20. Unity for Victory Rally poster, ca. June 1942, *Negro Labor Committee Record Group*, reel 14. For such coverage, see "McNutt to Speak at Negro Victory Conference," *Daily Worker*, June 17, 1942, 5; "Negro Labor Parley to Hear Curran Message," *Daily Worker*, June 18, 1942, 3; "Negro Victory Group Raps World-Telegram," *Daily Worker*, June 19, 1942, 5; Art Shields, "Harlem Victory Rally Sunday," *Daily Worker*, June 24, 1942, 5; "Negro Victory Rally Sunday to Hear Marcantonio, McNutt," *Daily Worker*, June 25, 1942, 3; "World Telegram Most Rabid Enemy of Negro People—It Must Be Stopped," *Daily Worker*, June 25, 1942, 6; "CIO, AFL Unionists to be at Negro Parley," *Daily Worker*, June 26, 1942, 4; "100 Groups to Attend Negro Parley Today," *Daily Worker*, June 27, 1942, 1, 4.

21. Ferdinand C. Smith, "Labor and Negro People Unite for Victory," June 27, 1942, *NNC Papers*, 4:1; "FEPC Gets Results in Dixie," *Pittsburgh Courier*, June 27, 1942, 1; "FEPC Forces 8 War Plants to Hire Men," *Baltimore Afro-American*, June 27, 1942, 1; "Social Work Agencies Here Are Gratified that FEPC Is Cracking Down on War Plants," *New York Age*, June 27, 1942, 3.

22. Ferdinand C. Smith, "Labor and Negro People Unite for Victory," June 27, 1942, *NNC Papers*, 4:1; "100 Groups to Attend Negro Parley Today," *Daily Worker*, June 27, 1942, 1, 4; John A. Davis, June 27, 1942; Sam Kramberg, June 27, 1942; Edward Lawson, "Trade Unions and the Negro War Worker," June 27, 1942; Vito Marcantonio, June 27, 1942; Elmer Carter, June 27, 1942, *NNC Papers*, 4:1; "McNutt to Speak at Negro Victory Conference," *Daily Worker*, June 17, 1942, 5.

23. "Fact Sheet," no date, *NNC Papers*, 4:1.

24. Moran Weston to Ferdinand Smith, June 27, 1942, *NNC Papers*, 4:9. Photographs of the meeting appear in "Negro Victory Conference," *Daily Worker*, June 29, 1942, 1.

25. Scott DeVeaux, *The Birth of Bebop* (Berkeley: University of California Press, 1997), 138–39; Hazel Rowley, *Richard Wright: The Life and Times* (Chicago: University of Chicago Press, 2008), 227; "2,500 at Dance," *Crisis*, March 1940, 86; James Gavin, *Stormy Weather: The Life of Lena Horne* (New York: Simon & Schuster, 2009), 77; Dominic J. Capeci, Jr., "From Different Liberal Perspectives: Fiorello H. La Guardia, Adam Clayton Powell, Jr., and Civil Rights in New York City, 1941–1943," *Journal of Negro History* 62, no. 2 (April 1977): 164–65.

26. William L. O'Neill, *A Democracy at War: America's Fight at Home and Abroad in World War II* (Cambridge, MA: Harvard University Press, 1995), 207; Andrew Kersten, *Race, Jobs, and the War: The FEPC in the Midwest, 1941–1946* (Urbana: University of Illinois Press, 2000), 38–40.

27. "McNutt Talk at Negro Rally Here to be Broadcast," *Daily Worker*, June 22, 1942, 5; Louise Mitchell, "Kill Jim Crow to Aid War, McNutt Tells Negro Rally," *Daily Worker*, June 29, 1942, 1; Ted Bassett, "Negro Rally Urges Equal Rights as War Necessity," *Daily Worker*, June 30, 1942, 5; "Negro America Spoke for Victory, Equal Rights in Great Harlem Rally," *Daily Worker*, June 30, 1942, 4; "Negro Labor Parley to Hear Curran Message," *Daily Worker*, June 18, 1942, 3; "Negro Victory Rally Sunday to Hear Marcantonio, McNutt," *Daily Worker*, June 25, 1942, 3; J. Robert Smith, "'Discrimination Must Go,' McNutt Tells 6,000," *New York Amsterdam News*, July 4, 1942, 1–2; "Paul V. McNutt, Chairman of War Manpower Commission, Shares the Spotlight with Mother of Dorie Miller at Victory Rally Here," *New York Age*, July 4, 1942, 1, 12.

28. "Highlights of Mass Meeting," *New York Amsterdam News*, July 4, 1942, 2; Louise Mitchell, "Kill Jim Crow to Aid War, McNutt Tells Negro Rally," *Daily Worker*, June 29, 1942, 1, 5; Ted Bassett, "Negro Rally Urges Equal Rights as War Necessity," *Daily Worker*, June 30, 1942, 1, 5; "Negro America Spoke for Victory, Equal Rights in Great Harlem Rally," *Daily Worker*, June 30, 1942, 4; "Smash Jim Crowism—It Hampers Our War to Smash Hitler," *Daily Worker*, June 30, 1942, 6; J. Robert Smith, "Labor's Front," *New York Amsterdam News*, July 18, 1942, 7.

29. Frank Crosswaith, "Around and Beyond," *New York Amsterdam News*, July 4, 1942, 7; Frank Crosswaith to Morris Feinstone, June 11, 1942, *Negro Labor Committee Record Group*, reel 14. On Crosswaith, see John C. Walter, "Frank R. Crosswaith and the Negro Labor Committee in Harlem, 1925–1939," *Afro-Americans in New York Life and History* 3, no. 2 (July 1979): 35–49; John C. Walter, "Frank R. Crosswaith and Labor Unionization in Harlem, 1939–1945," *Afro-Americans in New York Life and History* 7, no. 2 (July 1983): 47–58. Robert Hill, ed., *The FBI's RACON: Racial Conditions in America during World War II* (Boston: Northeastern University Press, 1995), 58, 77, 186–87, 178–80, 615.

30. Hill, *The FBI's RACON*, 179, 615–18, 247–48.

31. Hill, *The FBI's RACON*, 618; Reed, *Seedtime*, 74–78, 90–92; NLVC Press Release, January 16, 1943; NLVC "Call to Action," February 23, 1943, *NNC Papers*, 4:2. Ferdinand Smith to Sam Burt, March 20, 1943, *NNC Papers*, 4:7.

32. Barbara Savage, *Broadcasting Freedom: Radio, War, and the Politics of Race, 1938–1948* (Chapel Hill: University of North Carolina Press, 1999).

33. Hill, *The FBI's RACON*, 607–8; Beth Bates, "'Double V for Victory' Mobilizes Black Detroit, 1941–1946," in *Freedom North: Black Freedom Struggles Outside the South, 1940–1980*, ed. Jeanne Theoharis and Komozoi Woodard (New York: Palgrave Macmillan, 2003), 17–39; M. Moran Weston, "National Roundup," *New York Age*, March 20, 1943, 6; M. Moran Weston, "National Roundup," *New York Age*, March 27, 1943, 6–7; M. Moran Weston, "National Roundup," *New York Age*, April 3, 1943, 6, 8; "Freedom Now," April 8, 1943, box 7, folder 51, Weston Papers; Moran Weston, interview, July 22, 2000; Moran Weston to Theodore Poston, April 8, 1943, box 7, folder 48, Weston Papers; M. Moran Weston, "Labor Forum," *New York Amsterdam News*, April 17, 1943; M. Moran Weston,

"National Roundup," *New York Age*, April 17, 1943, 6, 8; M. Moran Weston, "National Roundup," *New York Age*, April 24, 1943, 6, 8; Frank Griffin, Press Release, April 5, 1943, *NNC Papers*, 4:8; Ferdinand Smith to Julius Emspeak, April 16, 1943; Dorothy Funn to Michael Orfind, April 27, 1943, *NNC Papers*, 4:7; "Notes," ca. April 1943, box 300, folder 4926; "Notes," ca. May 1943, box 300, folder 4927, Langston Hughes Papers, James Weldon Johnson Collection in the Yale Collection of American Literature, Beinecke Rare Book and Manuscript Library, Yale University.

34. M. Moran Weston, "Labor Forum," *New York Amsterdam News*, April 24, 1943; M. Moran Weston, "National Roundup," *New York Age*, May 1, 1943, 6, 8; M. Moran Weston, "Labor Forum," *New York Amsterdam News*, May 1, 1943; M. Moran Weston, "Labor Forum," *New York Amsterdam News*, May 8, 1943; M. Moran Weston, "National Roundup," *New York Age*, May 8, 1943, 6, 8; M. Moran Weston, "Labor Forum," *New York Amsterdam News*, May 15, 1943; M. Moran Weston, "National Roundup," *New York Age*, May 15, 1943, 6, 8; M. Moran Weston, "Labor Forum," *New York Amsterdam News*, May 22, 1943; M. Moran Weston, "National Roundup," *New York Age*, May 22, 1943, 6, 8.

35. M. Moran Weston, "National Roundup," *New York Age*, May 29, 1943, 6; M. Moran Weston, "Labor Forum," *New York Amsterdam News*, May 29, 1943.

36. For instance, see the page 3 advertisements appearing in *New York Age*, May 1, 8, 15, and 22, 1943. Charles Collins to Murray Kudish, May 15, 1943, *NNC Papers*, 4:7; Reed, *Seedtime*, 112.

37. Frank Griffin to "Dear Friend," May 30, 1943, *NNC Papers*, 4:7; Negro Freedom Rally poster, June 1943, *NNC Papers*, 4:1; "War Wives, Mothers Start Campaign for All-Out Support of Freedom Rally at Garden, June 7," *People's Voice*, May 29, 1943, clipping; Adam Clayton Powell, Jr., "It's Either Uncle Tom or Fite!" *People's Voice*, June 5, 1943, clipping, *FBI File on Adam Clayton Powell, Jr.*, microfilm (Wilmington, DE: Scholarly Resources, 1995), reel 1; "Draft," June 1943, box 300, folder 4931; "Notes," ca. June 1943, box 300, folder 4925, Hughes Papers; *New York Amsterdam News*, June 5, 1943, 5; Paul Ashley Kent, "National Roundup," *New York Age*, June 12, 1943, 6, 8.

38. "Garden Packed for Negro Freedom Rally; Negro, White Leaders Unite in Demanding Discrimination End," *New York Age*, June 12, 1943, 3; Evelyn Sherrer, "Labor Victory Committee Shows Signs of Growth," *Pittsburgh Courier*, ca. February 5, 1944, clipping, *NNC Papers*, 4:6; "Excerpts of Address by Ferdinand Smith at Rally," *Daily Worker*, June 10, 1943, 4; Llewellyn Ransom, "20,000 Blast Fascism Here and Abroad," *People's Voice*, June 19, 1943, *FBI File on Adam Clayton Powell, Jr.*, reel 1; "Quill's Speech at Negro Freedom Rally at Garden," *Daily Worker*, June 11, 1943, 4; John Meldon, "The Great Negro Offensive Opens to 'Let My People Go,'" *Daily Worker*, June 9, 1943, 3; Ralph Warner, "Negro Role in American Life Brilliantly Told in Pageant," *Daily Worker*, June 10, 1943, 7; photograph, *New York Amsterdam News*, June 12, 1943, 12; Robert Minor, "The Negro Freedom Meeting, A Discovery of Strength," *Daily Worker*, June 9, 1943, 8; "A Few Highlights from Freedom Rally," *New York Amsterdam News*, June 12, 1943, 12; "Wendell Wilkie's Wire to Negro Freedom Rally," *Daily Worker*, June 11, 1942, 4; "Wilkie Salutes 'Freedom Rally,'" *New York Amsterdam News*, June 12, 1943, 12; "Highlights of Powell's Speech at Garden Monday," *Daily Worker*, June 10, 1943, 4.

39. *For This We Fight*, in *The Collected Works of Langston Hughes*, ed. Leslie Catherine Sanders, vol. 6, *Gospel Plays, Operas, and Later Dramatic Works* (Columbia: University of Missouri Press, 2004), 438–62; "'Freedom Rally' Set for June 7," *New York Amsterdam News*, June 5, 1943, 1, 12; "'For This We Fight' Drama Records Age-Old Battle," *New York Amsterdam News*, June 12, 1943, 12; Duberman, *Paul Robeson*, 248–49, 267; Ralph Warner, "Negro Role in American Life Brilliantly Told in Pageant," *Daily Worker*, June 10, 1943, 7; Arnold Rampersad, *The Life of Langston Hughes*, vol. 2, *I Dream A World* (New York: Oxford University Press, 1988), 71; Joseph McLaren, *Langston Hughes: Folk Dramatist in the Protest Tradition, 1921–1943* (Westport, CT: Greenwood, 1997), 156–58.

40. M. Moran Weston, "Labor Forum," *New York Amsterdam News*, June 19, 1943.

41. M. Moran Weston, "Labor Forum," *New York Amsterdam News*, June 3, 1944; M. Moran Weston, "Labor Forum," *New York Amsterdam News*, June 10, 1944; M. Moran Weston, "Labor Forum," *New York Amsterdam News*, June 17, 1944; Ferdinand Smith and Adam Clayton Powell to William Morris, May 8, 1944, *NNC Papers*, 4:8; Ferdinand Smith and Adam Clayton Powell to Owen Dodson, May 11, 1944, box 1, folder 21, Owen Dodson Papers, James Weldon Johnson Collection in the Yale Collection of American Literature, Beinecke Rare Book and Manuscript Library, Yale University; Ferdinand Smith and Adam Clayton Powell, Jr., to "Dear Friend," May 13, 1944, *NNC Papers*, 4:7; "Second Draft," May 13–14, 1944, box 4, folder 68; "Second Draft, Corrected," May 19, 1944, box 4, folder 69, Dodson Papers; Moran Weston to David Leeds, May 19, 1944; Moran Weston to Joseph Roberts, May 31, 1944, *NNC Papers*, 4:1; "Whipping 'New World A-Coming' into Shape," *New York Amsterdam News*, June 17, 1944, 5A; Robert Minor, "The Coming End of Jim Crow," *Daily Worker*, June 23, 1944, 6; "New World A-Coming in Preparatory Stages," *New York Age*, June 17, 1944, 11; Adam Clayton Powell, Jr., "Rally for Freedom and a New World," in *People's Voice*, ca. June 1944, *FBI File on Adam Clayton Powell, Jr.*, reel 2; Adam Clayton Powell, Jr., *Adam by Adam: The Autobiography of Adam Clayton Powell, Jr.* (New York: Dial, 1972), 67.

42. M. Moran Weston, "Labor Forum," *New York Amsterdam News*, July 24, 1943; M. Moran Weston, "Labor Forum," *Amsterdam News*, July 31, 1943; "Memo—Decisions and Motions Made at Executive Board Meeting," July 21, 1943, *NNC Papers*, 4:3; "Meeting—Budget Committee," July 27, 1943; "Minutes, Executive Board Meeting," August 13, 1943, *NNC Papers*, 4:3; "Memorandum, Moran Weston to Executive Board—Negro Labor Victory Committee," August 13, 1943, *NNC Papers*, 4:9; Francis Hass to Charles Collins, August 15, 1943, *NNC Papers*, 4:4.

43. Dominic J. Capeci, Jr., *The Harlem Riot of 1943* (Philadelphia: Temple University Press, 1977), 100–103; "NLVC Press Release," August 3, 1943, *NNC Papers*, 4:4; Ferdinand Smith and Charles Collins to Franklin Roosevelt, August 13, 1943, *NNC Papers*, 4:1; M. Moran Weston, "Labor Forum," *New York Amsterdam News*, August 14, 1943.

44. "Memorandum, Moran Weston to Executive Board—Negro Labor Victory Committee," August 13, 1943, *NNC Papers*, 4:9; Charles Collins to Thomas Harten, August 18, 1943, *NNC Papers*, 4:2; Moran Weston to Louis Weinstock, August 27, 1943; William Hastie to Moran Weston, August 9, 1943; Charles Collins to Francis Hass, August 11, 1943, *NNC Papers*, 4:4; Moran Weston to A.A. Lewis, August 30, 1943; Moran Weston to William Hopkins, September 10, 1943, *NNC Papers*, 4:5.

45. M. Moran Weston, "Labor Forum," *New York Amsterdam News*, August 21, 1943; M. Moran Weston, "Labor Forum," *New York Amsterdam News*, August 28, 1943; "Summary of Minutes of General Assembly," September 14, 1943, *NNC Papers*, 4:3; M. Moran Weston, "Labor Forum," *New York Amsterdam News*, September 4, 1943; M. Moran Weston, "Labor Forum," *New York Amsterdam News*, September 11, 1943; M. Moran Weston, "Labor Forum," *New York Amsterdam News*, September 18, 1943; Moran Weston to Ishmael Flory, September 23, 1943, *NNC Papers*, 4:5; Charles Collins to "Dear Committee Member," October 6, 1943, *NNC Papers*, 4:3; Gwendolyn Bennett to Ferdinand Smith and Charles Collins, *NNC Papers*, 4:9; Moran Weston to Richard Morford, October 27, 1943, *NNC Papers*, 4:1; Charles Collins to Frank Hogan, October 7, 1943, *NNC Papers*, 4:1; Moran Weston to Ishmael Flory, October 20, 1943, *NNC Papers*, 4:5.

46. M. Moran Weston, "Labor Forum," *New York Amsterdam News*, September 25, 1943; Gerald Meyer, *Vito Marcantonio: Radical Politician, 1902–1954* (Albany: State University of New York Press, 1989), 25–27; Martha Biondi, *To Stand and Fight: The Struggle for Civil Rights in Postwar New York City* (Cambridge, MA: Harvard University Press, 2003), 49–54; Robert D. Parmet, *Master of Seventh Avenue: David Dubinsky and the American Labor Movement* (New York: New York University Press, 2005), 194–95; Omar H. Ali, *In the Balance of Power: Independent Black Politics and Third-Party Movements in the United States* (Athens, OH: Ohio University Press, 2008), 121; S. W. Garlington, "Labor Committees Squabble over 'What's in a Name?'" *New York Amsterdam News*, October 2, 1943.

47. "Conference of Trade Union and ALP Leaders," ca. September 14, 1943; Charles Collins to "Dear Friend," September 21, 1945, *NNC Papers*, 4:1; Moran Weston to "Dear Committee Member," September 29, 1943, *NNC Papers*, 4:3; Memorandum, Moran Weston to Ferdinand Smith, October 18, 1943; Moran Weston to "Dear Captain," September 30; October 6; October 14; October 25, 1943; "Mass Outdoor Rally," broadside, October 1943, *NNC Papers*, 4:1; M. Moran Weston, "Labor Forum," *New York Amsterdam News*, October 2, 1943; M. Moran Weston, "Labor Forum," *New York Amsterdam News*, October 9, 1943; M. Moran Weston, "Labor Forum," *New York Amsterdam News*, October 16, 1943.

48. Davis, *Communist Councilman*, 109–12; Gerald Horne, *Black Liberation/Red Scare: Ben Davis and the Communist Party* (Newark: University of Delaware Press, 1993), 106; Moran Weston to "Dear Captain," October 25, 1943; Charles Collins to "Dear Reverend," October 29, 1943, *NNC Papers*, 4:1; M. Moran Weston, "Labor Forum," *New York Amsterdam News*, October 23, 1943; M. Moran Weston, "Labor Forum," *New York Amsterdam News*, October 30, 1943; "Guest Ticket," October 31, 1943, *NNC Papers*, 4:1.

49. Davis, *Communist Councilman*, 110–15; Ottley, *New World A-Coming*, 219; M. Moran Weston, "Labor Forum," *New York Amsterdam News*, November 20, 1943.

50. Moran Weston to "Dear Friend," September 24, 1943; "Don't Miss Victory Celebration," poster, ca. November 1943, *NNC Papers*, 4:2; M. Moran Weston, "Labor Forum," *New York Amsterdam News*, November 20, 1943; NLVC Press Release, November 29, 1943, *NNC Papers*, 4:1; Edith Lively and Jake Porter to "Dear Friend," November 4, 1943, *NNC Papers*, 4:5; Maude White to Moran Weston, November 9, 1943, *NNC Papers*, 4:1; M. Moran Weston, "Labor Forum," *New York Amsterdam News*, November 13, 1943; Arthur Fauset and John Lymas to "Dear Friend," November 23, 1943, *NNC Papers*, 4:5; M. Moran Weston, "Labor Forum," *New York Amsterdam News*, November 20, 1943; M. Moran Weston, "Labor Forum," *New York Amsterdam News*, November 27, 1943.

51. For instance, Moran Weston to Charles Berkley, December 15, 1943; Moran Weston to Albert Goldman, December 15, 1943, *NNC Papers*, 4:1; M. Moran Weston, "Labor Forum," *New York Amsterdam News*, December 4, 1943; M. Moran Weston, "Labor Forum," *New York Amsterdam News*, December 11, 1943.

52. "Negro Labor Victory Committee Launches Program for 50,000 Members by February 14th," *New York Age*, January 22, 1944; Evelyn Sherrer, "Labor Victory Committee Shows Signs of Growth," *Pittsburgh Courier*, ca. February 5, 1944, clipping, *NNC Papers*, 4:6.

53. Davis, *Communist Councilman*, 123–31; M. Moran Weston, "Labor Forum," *New York Amsterdam News*, January 8, 1944; M. Moran Weston, "Labor Forum," *New York Amsterdam News*, January 15, 1944; M. Moran Weston, "Labor Forum," *New York Amsterdam News*, January 22, 1944; NLVC, "Action," January 26, 1944, *NNC Papers*, 4:3; Moran Weston to Ben Davis, February 3, 1944, *NNC Papers*, 4:3; Moran Weston to John J. Cochran, January 25, 1944, *NNC Papers*, 4:3; Charles Collins to "Dear Friend," January 29, 1944, *NNC Papers*, 4:1; M. Moran Weston, "Labor Forum," *New York Amsterdam News*, February 5, 1944; Moran Weston to Fred Lark, January 17, 1944, *NNC Papers*, 4:1; Moran Weston to Michael Obermeier, February 21, 1944, *NNC Papers*, 4:9.

54. Memorandum, Moran Weston to Ferdinand Smith, January 7, 1944, *NNC Papers*, 4:3; "Executive Board Meeting," January 25, 1944, *NNC Papers*, 4:3; "Annual Membership Drive," ca. January 1944, *NNC Papers*, 4:2; Moran Weston to "Dear Friend," February 10, 1944, *NNC Papers*, 4:5; L. F. Coles to Moran Weston, February 14, 1944; Charles Collins to Fiorello La Guardia, February 7, 1944; Robert Wagner to Charles Collins, January 15, 1944; Charles Collins to James Mead, February 21, 1944, *NNC Papers*, 4:1; M. Moran Weston, "Labor Forum," *New York Amsterdam News*, December 4, 1943; M. Moran Weston, "Labor Forum," *New York Amsterdam News*, February 5, 1944; Moran Weston to Ishmael Flory, February 7, 1944; "Membership Meeting," March 1, 1944, *NNC Papers*, 4:5; M. Moran Weston, "Labor Forum," *New York Amsterdam News*, March 4, 1944; M. Moran Weston, "Labor Forum," *New York Amsterdam News*, March 18, 1944.

55. Moran Weston to "Dear Club Member," April 1, 1944, *NNC Papers*, 4:2; M. Moran Weston, "Labor Forum," *New York Amsterdam News*, April 1, 1944; M. Moran Weston, "Labor Forum," *New York Amsterdam News*, 8, 1944; Program, Anti-Poll Tax Meeting, April 15, 1944; Charles Collins to "Dear Friend," April 17, 1944, *NNC Papers*, 4:1; M. Moran Weston, "Labor Forum," *New York Amsterdam News*, April 15, 1944; M. Moran Weston, "Labor Forum," *New York Amsterdam News*, April 22, 1944; Charles Collins to Robert Wagner, May 9, 1944, *NNC Papers*, 4:1.

56. Moran Weston to Hope R. Stevens, May 6, 1944, *NNC Papers*, 4:7; Moran Weston to Adam Clayton Powell, May 20, 1944, *NNC Papers*, 4:1; Ferdinand Smith and Adam Clayton Powell, Jr., to Hardwick Moseley, April 27, 1944; Ferdinand Smith and Adam Clayton Powell, Jr., to Roi Ottley, May 6, 1944, *NNC Papers*, 4:7. The *New York Amsterdam News* began its twelve-part series digesting Roi Ottley's *New World A-Coming* on April 1, 1944. Columnist S. W. Garlington condensed Ottley's prose. Savage, *Broadcasting Freedom*, 247–56. Frank Griffin to Owen Dodson, April 12, 1944, box 1, folder 21; Howard Fast, Peter Lyon, Frank Griffin to Owen Dodson, April 17, 1944, box 1, folder 1; "First Draft," April 30–May 1, 1944, box 4, folder 67, Dodson Papers; "Writes Play for 'Freedom Rally,'" *New York Amsterdam News*, May 13, 1944, 2A.

57. M. Moran Weston, "Labor Forum," *New York Amsterdam News*, June 3, 1944; M. Moran Weston, "Labor Forum," *New York Amsterdam News*, June 10, 1944; M. Moran Weston, "Labor Forum," *New York Amsterdam News*, June 17, 1944; Ferdinand Smith and Adam Clayton Powell to William Morris, May 8, 1944, *NNC Papers*, 4:8; Ferdinand Smith and Adam Clayton Powell to Owen Dodson, May 11, 1944, box 1, folder 21, Dodson Papers; Ferdinand Smith and Adam Clayton Powell, Jr., to "Dear Friend," May 13, 1944, *NNC Papers*, 4:7; "Second Draft," May 13–14, 1944, box 4, folder 68; "Second Draft, Corrected," May 19, 1944, box 4, folder 69, Dodson Papers; Moran Weston to David Leeds, May 19, 1944; Moran Weston to Joseph Roberts, May 31, 1944, *NNC Papers*, 4:1; "Whipping 'New World A-Coming' into Shape," *New York Amsterdam News*, June 17, 1944, 5A; Robert Minor, "The Coming End of Jim Crow," *Daily Worker*, June 23, 1944, 6; "New World A-Coming in Preparatory Stages," *New York Age*, June 17, 1944, 11; Adam Clayton Powell, Jr., "Rally for Freedom and a New World," in *People's Voice*, ca. June 1944, clipping, *FBI File on Adam Clayton Powell, Jr.*, reel 2; Powell, *Adam by Adam*, 67.

58. 1944 Negro Freedom Rally poster, *NNC Papers*, 4:7; Savage, *Broadcasting Freedom*, 252; "Negro Freedom Sunday Scheduled for June 18," *New York Age*, June 17, 1944, 11; Moran Weston to Gordon Smith, June 12, 1944, *NNC Papers*, 4:6; "Rehearsals," June 1944, box 4, folder 66, Dodson Papers; "They Won 'Victory' Awards," *Daily Worker*, June 19, 1944, 4; "Negro Freedom Rally," *Daily Worker*, June 19, 1944, 11; "Negro Freedom Rally," *Daily Worker*, June 24, 1944, 8; "Negro Rally Attended by Thousands," *Daily Worker*, June 27, 1944, 2; "The Negro Freedom Rally," *Daily Worker*, June 28, 1944, 6.

59. Llewellyn Ransom, "Freedom Rally Gives Direction to the Negro," *People's Voice*, July 1, 1944, clipping; Adam Clayton Powell, Jr., "Soapbox," *People's Voice*, July 1, 1944, clipping, *FBI File on Adam Clayton Powell, Jr.*, reel 2; "Freedom Meet Asks End of Jim Crowism," *New York Amsterdam News*, July 1, 1944, 1, 5; "Rally Pageant Attacks Bias, Segregation," *New York Amsterdam News*, July 1, 1944, 5; Lola Paine, "25,000 Hail New World a-Coming, Pledge Unity Behind Roosevelt," *Daily Worker*, June 28, 1944, 4; "LaGuardia Speaks at Negro Freedom Rally," *New York Age*, July 1, 1944, 1; "A Program for Negro-White War Unity," *Daily Worker*, June 28, 1944, 4; "Negro Freedom Rally, Program," 1944, *NNC Papers*, 4:7; James Vernon Hatch, *Sorrow Is the Only Faithful One: The Life of Owen Dodson* (Urbana: University of Illinois Press, 1993), 102–3, 112–15; James Edward Smethurst, *The New Red Negro: The Literary Left and African American Poetry, 1930–1946* (New York: Oxford University Press, 1999), 225; John Louis Clarke, "Freedom Rally Crowd Packs Madison Square Garden," typescript, June 1944, *NNC Papers*, 4:7.

60. M. Moran Weston, "Labor Forum," *New York Amsterdam News*, July 8, 1944, 7; A. Sommers to Jehn H. Hyer, June 19, 1944, *NNC Papers*, 4:8; "Executive Board Meeting," July 15,

1944; "Executive Secretary's Notes," September 6, 1944, *NNC Papers*, 4:3; M. Moran Weston, "Labor Forum," *New York Amsterdam News*, July 15, 1944, 7; M. Moran Weston, "Labor Forum," *New York Amsterdam News*, July 29, 1944, 11; M. Moran Weston, "Labor Forum," *New York Amsterdam News*, August 5, 1944, 7.

61. Allan M. Winkler, "The Philadelphia Transit Strike of 1944," *Journal of American History* 59, no. 1 (June 1972): 73–89; M. Moran Weston, "Labor Forum," *New York Amsterdam News*, October 14, 1944, 12; M. Moran Weston, "Labor Forum," *New York Amsterdam News*, August 12, 1944, 6; Moran Weston to Franklin Delano Roosevelt, August 2, 1944; Ferdinand Smith and Charles Collins to Dorothy Funn, August 5, 1944, *NNC Papers*, 4:6.

62. M. Moran Weston, "Labor Forum," *New York Amsterdam News*, August 26, 1944, 6; Charles Collins to Franklin Roosevelt, September 21, 1944; Charles Collins to James Forrestal, September 22, 1944, *NNC Papers*, 4:1; "Executive Secretary's Notes," September 6, 1944, *NNC Papers*, 4:3; M. Moran Weston, "Labor Forum," *New York Amsterdam News*, September 16, 1944, 10; M. Moran Weston, "Labor Forum," *New York Amsterdam News*, September 23, 1944, 12; M. Moran Weston, "Labor Forum," *New York Amsterdam News*, September 30, 1944, 11.

63. M. Moran Weston, "Labor Forum," *New York Amsterdam News*, October 14, 1944, 12; M. Moran Weston, "Labor Forum," *New York Amsterdam News*, October 28, 1944, 14; Josh Lawrence, "Harlem for FDR; Task to Get Out the Vote," *Daily Worker*, November 4, 1944, 1; "Wallace Leads a Harlem 'Parade,'" *Daily Worker*, November 3, 1944, 4; "Harlem to Hear Wagner, Marcantonio Sunday," *Daily Worker*, November 3, 1944, 6.

64. M. Moran Weston, "Labor Forum," *New York Amsterdam News*, November 18, 1944, 12 M. Moran Weston, "Labor Forum," *New York Amsterdam News*, November 25, 1944, 12; Moran Weston to Ishmael Flory, November 18, 1944; November 30, 1944; Moran Weston to Ishmael Flory, November 18, 1944, *NNC Papers*, 4:5; Moran Weston to Hulan Jack, November 16, 1944; Moran Weston to Frances Williams, November 16, 1944; Moran Weston to Bernard Gittleson, November 16, 1944, *NNC Papers*, 4:3; NLVC Press Release, December 5, 1944, *NNC Papers*, 4:1; M. Moran Weston, "Labor Forum," *New York Amsterdam News*, December 2, 1944, 14; M. Moran Weston, "Labor Forum," *New York Amsterdam News*, December 16, 1944, 14; M. Moran Weston, "Labor Forum," *New York Amsterdam News*, December 23, 1944, 14; M. Moran Weston, "Labor Forum," *New York Amsterdam News*, December 30, 1944, 12.

65. Moran Weston to J. Raymond Jones, December 13, 1944, *NNC Papers*, 4:2; M. Moran Weston, "Labor Forum," *New York Amsterdam News*, February 10, 1945, 12; S. W. Garlington, "Carver School Non-Partisan Says Director," *New York Amsterdam News*, January 1, 1944, 1, 2, 3; "Weston Rejects Bid to Run against Davis," *Daily Worker*, February 10, 1945, 4; Charles Collins to "Dear Sir and Brother," December 12, 1944; "NLVC Press Release," January 1945, *NNC Papers*, 4:4; J. Raymond Jones to Moran Weston, February 5, 1945, *NNC Papers*, 4:2; M. Moran Weston, "Labor Forum," *New York Amsterdam News*, February 17, 1945, 12.

66. M. Moran Weston, "Labor Forum," *New York Amsterdam News*, March 10, 1945, 10; M. Moran Weston, "Labor Forum," *New York Amsterdam News*, March 17, 1945, 14; John Lyons to Moran Weston, March 18; March 21; April 2, 1945, *NNC Papers*, 4:1; "Summary Minutes of Executive Board Meeting," March 21, 1945, *NNC Papers*, 4:3; "Reconversion Topic of Labor 2-Day Confab," *New York Amsterdam News*, March 17, 1945, 7A; "NLVC Official Report, March 24–25, 1945," typescript, *NNC Papers*, 4:1; "Negro Parley Here Hails Army's Mixed Combat Policy," *Daily Worker*, March 26, 1945, 12; M. Moran Weston, "Labor Forum," *New York Amsterdam News*, April 7, 1945, 12; M. Moran Weston, "Labor Forum," *New York Amsterdam News*, April 14, 1945, 14; M. Moran Weston, "Labor Forum," *New York Amsterdam News*, May 26, 1945, 12.

67. M. Moran Weston, "Labor Forum," *New York Amsterdam News*, May 5, 1945, 10; Reed, *Seedtime*, 170; M. Moran Weston, "Labor Forum," *New York Amsterdam News*, May 12, 1945, 10; M. Moran Weston, "Labor Forum," *New York Amsterdam News*, April 21, 1945,

14; "'Carry-On America' Theme of Third Annual Negro Freedom Rally, June 25," *New York Age*, June 9, 1945, 2; Poster reprinted in *New York Amsterdam News*, June 23, 1945, 7B.

68. Adam Clayton Powell, Jr., and Ferdinand Smith to "Dear Friend," May 1, 1945; Ferdinand Smith and Adam Clayton Powell, Jr., to "Dear Friend," May 8, 1945; Charles Collins and Moran Weston to "Dear Friend," May 15, 1945, *NNC Papers*, 4:7; Adam Clayton Powell, Jr., and Ferdinand Smith, letter to the editor, *New York Amsterdam News*, May 12, 1945, 10; Rev. Edler G. Hawkins to "Dear Friend," May 21, 1945, *NNC Papers*, 4:7; M. Moran Weston, "Labor Forum," *New York Amsterdam News*, June 16, 1945, 12; Rev. Edler Hawkins to "Dear Friend," June 13, 1945, *NNC Papers*, 4:7; Press Release, "Save FEPC Outdoor Rallies," June 9, 1945, *NNC Papers*, 4:8; "Industry to Receive FEPC Merit Award at Negro Freedom Rally," *New York Age*, June 9, 1945, 2; NLVC Press Release, June 8, 1945, *NNC Papers*, 4:8; "Washingtonians Plan FEPC Mass Meeting June 22," *New York Amsterdam News*, June 23, 1945, 12; M. Moran Weston, "Labor Forum," *New York Amsterdam News*, June 23, 1945, 12.

69. "Robeson Draws Loud Applause at Freedom Meet," *New York Amsterdam News*, June 30, 1945, 12B; "Powell Exhorts Negroes to 'Take' to Picket Lines if Congress Kills FEPC," *New York Amsterdam News*, June 30, 1945, 1A, 11B; "Fight on Bias Cannot Wait, Powell Tells Freedom Rally," *Daily Worker*, June 26, 1945, 3; "Negro Freedom Rally to Have Head of FEPC," *Daily Worker*, June 23, 1945, 4; "To the Garden Tonight," *Daily Worker*, June 25, 1945, 6; "Negro Freedom Rally, Program," 1945, *NNC Papers*, 4:8; Gwynne Durham, "Speakers Urge Support of FEPC and Ives-Quinn Bill at Negro Freedom Rally; 20,000 Persons Present," *New York Age*, June 30, 1945, 1.

70. Reed, *Seedtime*, 171; M. Moran Weston, "Labor Forum," *New York Amsterdam News*, July 7, 1945, 10; M. Moran Weston, "Labor Forum," *New York Amsterdam News*, July 14, 1945, 12; M. Moran Weston, "Labor Forum," *New York Amsterdam News*, July 21, 1945, 12.

71. M. Moran Weston, "Labor Forum," *New York Amsterdam News*, August 25, 1945, 12; M. Moran Weston, "Labor Forum," *New York Amsterdam News*, September 1, 1945, 12; Ferdinand Smith and Charles Collins to Benjamin Davis, March 28, 1945; NLVC Press Release, July 27, 1945; August 1, 1945, *NNC Papers*, 4:2; Audley Moore to Moran Weston, September 27, 1945, *NNC Papers*, 4:2; Biondi, *To Stand and Fight*, 21–22.

72. M. Moran Weston, "Labor Forum," *New York Amsterdam News*, October 6, 1945, 10; Memorandum, Moran Weston to Ferdinand Smith, September 24, 1945; Moran Weston to Charles Collins, ca. October 1945; Memorandum, "Electoral Campaign," ca. 1945; Program, "Small's Paradise," October 21, 1945, *NNC Papers*, 4:2.

73. FBI File 100–949, October 31, 1945; FBI File 100–949, January 30, 1946, *FBI File on the National Negro Congress*, microfilm (Wilmington, DE: Scholarly Resources, 1987), reel 2; "Proposals for the merger of the Negro Labor Victory Committee with the National Negro Congress," February 16, 1946, box 7, folder 52, Weston Papers; Ellen Schrecker, *The Age of McCarthyism* (Boston: Bedford/St. Martin's, 1994), 191; Eric Bentley, ed., *Thirty Years of Treason: Excerpts from Hearings before the House Committee on Un-American Activities, 1938–1968* (New York: Viking, 1971), 416.

74. "Picked for Job," *New York Amsterdam News*, January 12, 1946, 24; Julius J. Adams, "Political Roundup," *New York Amsterdam News*, January 12, 1946, 24; M. Moran Weston, "Labor Forum," *New York Amsterdam News*, December 22, 1945, 12.

Chapter 7

1. Sterling Brown to Ralph Bunche, May 29, 1954, box 11, folder 1, Brian Urquhart Papers, Special Collections, Young Research Library, University of California, Los Angeles. Sterling the Dutchman was the poet Sterling Brown, Frank F. was the sociologist E. Franklin Frazier, and Sam Dorsey was political scientist Emmett Dorsey, each of whom had taught together at Howard since the 1930s. I am not certain about the identities of Mau Mau or Rabbit.

2. "Dr. Bunche Receives a Loyalty Hearing," *New York Times*, May 26, 1954; "Bunche Inquiry Called a 'Farce,'" *New York Times*, May 27, 1954.

3. Brian Urquhart, *Ralph Bunche: An American Life* (New York: Norton, 1993); Charles Henry, *Ralph Bunche: Model Negro or American Other?* (New York: New York University Press, 2000); John B. Kirby, "Ralph J. Bunche and Black Radical Thought in the 1930s," *Phylon* 35, no. 2 (Summer 1974): 129–41; Benjamin Rivlin, ed., *Ralph Bunche: The Man and his Times* (New York: Holmes & Meier, 1990); Ben Keppel, *The Work of Democracy: Ralph Bunche, Kenneth Clarke, Lorraine Hansberry, and the Cultural Politics of Race* (Cambridge, MA: Harvard University Press, 1995); Jonathan Scott Holloway, *Confronting the Veil: Abram Harris, Jr., E. Franklin Frazier, and Ralph Bunche, 1919–1941* (Chapel Hill: University of North Carolina Press, 2002).

4. Diary entry, "Monday 5/17/54," box 177, Ralph Bunche Papers, Special Collections, Young Research Library, University of California at Los Angeles. The most detailed account of the loyalty hearings is in Urquhart, *Ralph Bunche*, 243–46. See also Charles P. Henry, "Civil Rights and National Security: The Case of Ralph Bunche," in Rivlin, *Ralph Bunche*, 50–66.

5. Ellen Schrecker, *No Ivory Tower: McCarthyism and the Universities* (New York: Oxford University Press, 1986).

6. Robert Zieger, *The CIO, 1935–1955* (Chapel Hill: University of North Carolina Press, 1995); Gerald Horne, *Black Liberation/Red Scare: Ben Davis and the Communsit Party* (Newark: University of Delaware Press, 1993); Gerald Horne, *Black and Red: W. E. B. Du Bois and the Afro-American Response to the Cold War* (Albany: State University of New York Press, 1986); Martha Biondi, *To Stand and Fight: The Struggle for Civil Rights in Postwar New York City* (Cambridge, MA: Harvard University Press, 2003), 137–210; Kenneth Janken, *White: The Biography of Walter White, Mr. NAACP* (New York: Free Press, 2003) 307–8; Manfred Berg, "Black Civil Rights and Liberal Anticommunism," *Journal of American History* 94, no. 1 (June 2007): 75–96; Glenda Gilmore, *Defying Dixie: The Radical Roots of Civil Rights, 1919–1950* (New York: Norton, 2008), 414–44.

7. "Chronology of the Loyalty Saga," 1–2, box 178, Bunche Papers, UCLA.

8. "Fourth U.S. Civil Service Region Investigation Division, Report of Special Hearing," May 5, 1943; Ralph Bunche to William Jenner, March 16, 1953, reel 1, Ralph Bunche Papers, microfilm, Lamont Library, Harvard University; "Chronology of the Loyalty Saga," 1, box 178; diary entries, Tuesday, 3/10/53; Thursday, 3/12/53, box 177, Bunche Papers, UCLA.

9. "Chronicle of the Loyalty Saga," 2–3, box 178, Bunche Papers, UCLA.

10. "Chronicle of the Loyalty Saga," 3–4, box 178, Bunche Papers, UCLA; Wilson Record, *The Negro and the Communist Party* (Chapel Hill: University of North Carolina Press, 1951), 156. The Carnegie-Myrdal study was published as Gunnar Myrdal, *An American Dilemma: The Negro Problem and Modern Democracy* (New York: Harper & Brothers, 1944). For Bunche's role in the project, see Walter A. Jackson, *Gunnar Myrdal and America's Conscience: Social Engineering and Racial Liberation, 1938–1987* (Chapel Hill: University of North Carolina Press, 1990).

11. "Chronology of the Loyalty Saga," 4, box 178, Bunche Papers, UCLA; "Interrogatory," reel 1, Bunche Papers, Harvard University.

12. "Chronology of the Loyalty Saga," 5, box 178, Bunche Papers, UCLA.

13. "Chronology of the Loyalty Saga," 5–6, box 178, Bunche Papers, UCLA.

14. "Chronology of the Loyalty Saga," 5–6, box 178, Bunche Papers, UCLA; "Exhibits List," reel 1, Bunche Papers, Harvard University.

15. "Chronology of the Loyalty Saga," 6–7, box 178, Bunche Papers, UCLA.

16. "Annotated Reply to the Interrogatory," 1, reel 1, Bunche Papers, Harvard University.

17. "Annotated Reply to the Interrogatory," 9–10, reel 1, Bunche Papers, Harvard University.

18. On Douglass Hall, see Rayford Logan, *Howard University: The First Hundred Years, 1867–1967* (Washington, DC: Howard University Press, 1968), 174; "Program for National Conference," reel 1, Bunche Papers, Harvard University. On Davis, see Hilmar Jensen, "The

Rise of an African American Left: John P. Davis and the National Negro Congress" (Ph.D. diss., Cornell University, 1997)." Representative articles are John P. Davis, "What Price National Recovery?" *Crisis*, December 1933, 271–72; Davis, "Blue Eagles and Black Workers," *New Republic*, November 14, 1934, 7–9; Davis, "A Black Inventory of the New Deal," *Crisis*, May 1935, 141–42, 154–55.

19. Bunche, "Negro Political Laboratories," *Opportunity*, December 1928, 370–73; Bunche, "The Thompson-Negro Alliance," *Opportunity*, March 1929, 78–80; Bunche, "French Educational Policy in Togoland and Dahomey," *Journal of Negro Education* 3, no. 1 (January 1934): 69–97; Ralph J. Bunche, "French Administration in Togoland and Dahomey" (Ph.D. diss., Harvard University, 1934); Delmar Leighton to Ralph Bunche, June 19, 1934, box 126, Bunche Papers, UCLA; "Our Aims," *Race* 1, Winter 1935–1936, 3; Folder— NAACP Crime Conference Picketing 1934–1935, box 114, Bunche Papers, UCLA; Walter White to Ralph Bunche, December 20, 1934, reel 1, Bunche Papers, Harvard University; Michele F. Pacifico, "'Don't Buy Where You Can't Work': The New Negro Alliance of Washington," *Washington History* 6, no. 1 (Spring/Summer 1994): 66–88; Henry, *Ralph Bunche*, 40.

20. "Annotated Reply to the Interrogatory," 11; "Memorandum, Division of the Social Sciences," May 28, 1935, reel 1, Bunche Papers, Harvard University.

21. "The Negroes in Washington," *Fortune*, December 1934, 132, 137. For Davis's knowledge of the "Harris Report," see Abram Harris to Walter White, September 12, 1934; Walter White to Abram Harris, October 3, 1934; Walter White to Abram Harris, October 10, 1934, *Papers of the National Association for the Advancement of Colored People*, microfilm (Frederick, MD: University Publications of America, 1982–), part 16, series A, reel 8.

22. Mimeographed notice, Ralph Bunche and John P. Davis, March 1935, *Papers of the National Negro Congress*, microfilm (Frederick, MD: University Publications of America, 1988), part1, reel 1.

23. Davis, "Black Inventory of the New Deal," 141–42, 154–55. Hilmar Jensen describes an even deeper genealogy for the idea of a National Negro Congress than is generally appreciated. See Jensen, "African American Left," 479–500.

24. John P. Davis, "A Survey of the Problems of the Negro Under the New Deal," *Journal of Negro Education* 5, no. 1 (January 1936): 3; Ralph J. Bunche, "Critique of New Deal Social Planning as It Affects Negroes," *Journal of Negro Education* 5, no. 1 (January 1936): 65; "Program for National Conference," reel 1, Bunche Papers, Harvard University; "Workers Blame Race's Plight on Oppression at Economic Conference," *Washington Tribune*, May 25, 1935, 1, 2.

25. "Annotated Reply to the Interrogatory," 12; John P. Davis to "Dear Friend," May 19, 1935, reel 1, Bunche Papers, Harvard University.

26. "Annotated Reply to the Interrogatory," 13–14, 16, reel 1, Bunche Papers, Harvard University.

27. "Alumni Ired over Talks at Meeting," *Washington Tribune*, May 25, 1935, 2; Kelly Miller, "Kelly Miller Discusses," *Washington Tribune*, June 1, 1935, 4; "Showdown in H.U. Fight," *Washington Tribune*, June 1, 1935, 1, 2; Kelly Miller, "Experiments with Academic Freedom Are Called Risky," *Baltimore Afro-American*, June 15, 1935, 4; "Alleged Communistic Activities at Howard University, Washington, D.C., Senate Document No. 217, 74th Cong., 2nd sess. (Washington, DC: Government Printing Office, 1936); Kelly Miller, Open Letter, May 25, 1935; Minutes of Meeting of Social Sciences Division of Howard University, reel 2, Bunche Papers, Harvard University; Ralph Bunche, "A Critical Analysis of Tactics and Programs of Minority Groups," *Journal of Negro Education* 5, no. 3 (July 1936): 308–10, 320.

28. Clarence Pickett to Ralph Bunche, January 20, 1954, reel 3, Bunche Papers, Harvard University; Alain Locke to Ralph Bunche, February 1, 1935, box 1, folder 9; Ralph Bunche to George Streator, January 8, 1936, box 1, folder 10, Bunche Papers, UCLA; "Annotated Reply to the Interrogatory," 17; Ralph Bunche to E. P. Davis, February 27, 1936, reel 1, Bunche Papers, Harvard University.

29. Bunche, "Triumph?—or Fiasco?," *Race* 2, Summer 1936, 95, 96; Urquhart, *Ralph Bunche*, 62; "Institute of Race Relations, Swarthmore 1936," box 112, Bunche Papers, UCLA.

30. Ralph Bunche, *A World View of Race* (Washington, DC: Associates in Negro Folk Education, 1936), 3, 75, 84, 85, 90, 92. Seven years earlier, Herskovits had tempted Abram Harris with funding and the prediction that black anthropologists would soon produce the most significant work in the social sciences. As he was just months from completing his doctorate in economics, Harris had declined the offer. But, clearly, Bunche perceived the opportunity. Melville Herskovits to Abram Harris, November 18, 1929, box 9, folder 12, Melville Herskovits Papers, University Archives, Northwestern University.

31. "Annotated Reply to the Interrogatory," 18, reel 1, Bunche Papers, Harvard University.

32. "Annotated Reply to the Interrogatory," 19, 25, 26, 27, reel 1, Bunche Papers, Harvard University.

33. "Annotated Reply to the Interrogatory," 27, reel 1, Bunche Papers, Harvard University.

34. "Annotated Reply to the Interrogatory," 19, reel 1, Bunche Papers, Harvard University.

35. Gilbert Ware, *William Hastie: Grace under Pressure* (New York: Oxford University Press, 1984); "Chronology of the Loyalty Saga," 7–9, box 178; "Pocket Size Diary Notes, 1954," box 177, Bunche Papers, UCLA.

36. "Chronology of the Loyalty Saga," 9–10, box 178, Bunche Papers, UCLA.

37. "Chronology of the Loyalty Saga," 11–12, box 178; diary entry, Friday, 5/14/54, box 177, Bunche Papers, UCLA; Eslanda Good Robeson, "Loyalty, the Democratic Process, and Dr. Ralph J. Bunche," May 28, 1954, reel 3, Bunche Papers, Harvard University; "Manning Johnson," handwritten notes, reel 1, Bunche Papers, Harvard University; Biondi, *To Stand and Fight*, 173.

38. "Leonard Patterson," handwritten notes, reel 1, Bunche Papers, Harvard University.

39. "Leonard Patterson," handwritten notes; untitled handwritten notes, reel 1, Bunche Papers, Harvard University.

40. Untitled handwritten notes, reel 1, Bunche Papers, Harvard University.

41. Untitled handwritten notes, reel 1, Bunche Papers, Harvard University.

42. "John Davis," handwritten notes, reel 1, Bunche Papers, Harvard University. For Bunche's concern for Davis, see Joseph and Stewart Alsop, "Why Dr. Bunche Was Cleared," *Boston Globe*, July 2, 1954, newspaper clipping, Ralph Bunche biographical file, University Archives, Harvard University; "Inside Story on Bunche!" *Pittsburgh Courier*, July 10, 1954, 1. The press release was quoted in "Bunche Inquiry Called a 'Farce,'" *New York Times*, May 27, 1954. For the entire statement, see "Meeting of the Board of the NAACP, May 1954," reel 2, *NAACP Papers*, Supplement to part 1, 1951–1955.

43. "Walter White," handwritten notes, reel 1, Bunche Papers, Harvard University.

44. "John P. Davis," handwritten notes, reel 1, Bunche Papers, Harvard University; "Handwritten Notes—Loyalty Board Hearing, Final Day, 27 May 1954," box 178, Bunche Papers, UCLA.

45. Diary entry, Friday, 5/28/54, box 177, Bunche Papers, UCLA.

46. Redding interview, July 26, 1990.

47. James Booker, "Vindication of Bunche Is Approved," *New York Amsterdam News*, June 5, 1954, 1, 30; "Loyalty Board Gives Bunche Clearance," *Baltimore Afro-American*, June 5, 1954, 1; "Loyalty Board Clears Bunche," *Pittsburgh Courier*, June 5, 1954, 1, 4; *Chicago Defender*, June 12, 1954; "Editorial Excerpts from the Nation's Press on Segregation Ruling," *New York Times*, May 18, 1954; Darrell Garwood, "Supreme Court Strikes Again," *Pittsburgh Courier*, June 5, 1954, 1, 4.

Epilogue

1. Langston Hughes, *Fight for Freedom: The Story of the NAACP* (New York: Norton, 1962), 11.

2. Hughes, *Fight for Freedom*, 135.

3. Hughes, *Fight for Freedom*, viii; "The Reign of Terror," *Crisis*, October 1911, 236–39; "Along the Color Line," *Crisis*, August 1911, 143–44.

4. E. Franklin Frazier to Langston Hughes, ca. February 1962, box 64, folder 1234; Ira Reid to Langston Hughes, February 20, 1962, box 136, folder 2526, Langston Hughes Papers, James Weldon Johnson Collection in the Yale Collection of American Literature, Beinecke Rare Book and Manuscript Library, Yale University.

5. Sterling A. Brown, "Ralph Bunche at Howard University," *Crisis*, January 1972, 34.

INDEX